# The American Psychiatric Press Textbook of Substance Abuse Treatment

# The American Psychiatric Press Textbook of Substance Abuse Treatment

*Edited by*
*Marc Galanter, M.D., and*
*Herbert D. Kleber, M.D.*

American Psychiatric Press, Inc.

Washington, DC
London, England

**Note:** The authors have worked to ensure that all information in this book concerning drug dosages, schedules, and routes of administration is accurate as of the time of publication and consistent with standards set by the U.S. Food and Drug Administration and the general medical community. As medical research and practice advance, however, therapeutic standards may change. For this reason and because human and mechanical errors sometimes occur, we recommend that readers follow the advice of a physician who is directly involved in their care or the care of a member of their family.

Books published by the American Psychiatric Press, Inc., represent the views and opinions of the individual authors and do not necessarily represent the policies and opinions of the Press or the American Psychiatric Association.

Copyright © 1994 American Psychiatric Press, Inc.
ALL RIGHTS RESERVED
Manufactured in the United States of America on acid-free paper
97  96  95  94     4  3  2  1
First Edition

American Psychiatric Press, Inc.
1400 K Street, N.W., Washington, DC   20005

**Library of Congress Cataloging-in-Publication Data**
The American psychiatric press textbook of substance abuse treatment /
    edited by Marc Galanter and Herbert D. Kleber. — 1st ed.
        p.  cm.
    Includes bibliographical references and index.
    ISBN 0-88048-532-9 (alk. paper)
    1. Substance abuse—Treatment.  I. Galanter, Marc.  II. Kleber,
Herbert D.   III. Title: Textbook of substance abuse treatment.
    [DNLM:  1. Substance Abuse—therapy.  WM 270 A5107 1994]
RC564.A525   1994
616.86′06—dc20
DNLM/DLC
for Library of Congress                                                      93-26826
                                                                                    CIP

**British Library Cataloguing in Publication Data**
A CIP record is available from the British Library.

# $\mathbf{C}$ontents

Marc Galanter, M.D.
Herbert D. Kleber, M.D.

## S E C T I O N    1

## Overview of Treatment

Marc A. Schuckit, M.D.

Michael J. Bohn, M.D.
Roger E. Meyer, M.D.

Richard Steven Schottenfeld, M.D.

Reid K. Hester, Ph.D.

Dean R. Gerstein, Ph.D.

## S E C T I O N    2

## Treatment of Patients for Specific Drugs of Abuse

Don Gallant, M.D.

Robert B. Millman, M.D.
Ann Bordwine Beeder, M.D.

# S E C T I O N  3

## Treatment Modalities

*Subsection 3A: Individual Treatment*

# Contributors

**Kimberly Barrett, Ed.D.**
Department of Psychology, University of
Washington, Seattle, Washington

**Ann Bordwine Beeder, M.D.**
Department of Public Health, Cornell
University Medical College, New York,
New York

**Terry C. Blum, Ph.D.**
School of Management, Georgia Institute of
Technology, Atlanta, Georgia

**Michael J. Bohn, M.D.**
Department of Psychiatry, University of
Wisconsin Medical School,
Madison, Wisconsin

**Lisa Borg, M.D.**
Department of Psychiatry, New Jersey Medical
College, Newark, New Jersey

**Amin N. Daghestani, M.D.**
Department of Psychiatry, Loyola University
Medical Center, Maywood, Illinois

**George De Leon, Ph.D.**
Center for Therapeutic Community Research,
New York, New York

**Everett Ellinwood, Jr., M.D., Ph.D.**
Department of Psychiatry, Duke University
School of Medicine, Durham, North Carolina

**Chad D. Emrick, Ph.D.**
Department of Psychiatry, University of
Colorado Health Sciences Center,
Denver, Colorado

**Richard Frances, M.D.**
Department of Psychiatry, Hackensack Medical
Center, Hackensack, New Jersey

**John Franklin, M.D.**
Department of Psychiatry, Northwestern
Medical School, Chicago, Illinois

**Marc Galanter, M.D.**
Department of Psychiatry, Division of
Alcoholism and Drug Abuse, New York
University Medical School,
New York, New York

**Don Gallant, M.D.**
Department of Psychiatry and Neurology,
Tulane Medical School, New Orleans,
Louisiana

**Frank H. Gawin, M.D.**
Laboratory for the Study of Addictions, Drug
Abuse Research Center, University of
California at Los Angeles VA Hospital, Los
Angeles, California

**Dean R. Gerstein, Ph.D.**
Division of Drug and Alcohol Studies, National
Opinion Research Center at the University of
Chicago, Washington Office, Washington, DC

**Sarah J. Golden, Ph.D.**
Cambridge Hospital, Harvard Medical School,
Cambridge, Massachusetts

**Reid K. Hester, Ph.D.**
Behavior Therapy Associates, Albuquerque,
New Mexico

**Yifrah Kaminer, M.D.**
Department of Psychiatry and Alcohol
Research Center, School of Medicine,
University of Connecticut Health Center,
Farmington, Connecticut

**Edward Kaufman, M.D.**
Department of Psychiatry and Human
Behavior, University of California, Irvine
Medical Center, Orange, California

**M. Elena Khalsa, M.D., Ph.D.**
Drug Abuse Research Center, Neuropsychiatric
Institute, University of California at Los
Angeles, Los Angeles, California

**Edward J. Khantzian, M.D.**
Department of Psychiatry, Harvard Medical School, Cambridge, Massachusetts

**Herbert D. Kleber, M.D.**
Department of Psychiatry, Columbia University School of Medicine, New York, New York

**Jean L. Kristeller, Ph.D.**
Department of Psychology, Indiana State University, Terre Haute, Indiana

**Lester Luborsky, Ph.D.**
Department of Psychiatry, University of Pennsylvania, Philadelphia, Pennsylvania

**G. Alan Marlatt, Ph.D.**
Addictive Behaviors Research Center, Department of Psychology, University of Washington, Seattle, Washington

**William E. McAuliffe, Ph.D.**
Department of Psychiatry, Cambridge Hospital, Harvard Medical School, Cambridge, Massachusetts

**Delinda Mercer, M.S.**
Treatment Research Center, University of Pennsylvania, Philadelphia, Pennsylvania

**Roger E. Meyer, M.D.**
Department of Psychiatry, George Washington University School of Medicine, Washington, D.C.

**Robert B. Millman, M.D.**
Departments of Psychiatry and Public Health, Cornell University Medical College, New York, New York

**Charles P. O'Brien, M.D., Ph.D.**
Department of Psychiatry/VA Medical Center, University of Pennsylvania, Philadelphia, Pennsylvania

**Judith K. Ockene, Ph.D.**
Division of Preventive and Behavioral Medicine, Department of Medicine, University of Massachusetts Medical School, Worcester, Massachusetts

**Robert N. Pechnick, Ph.D.**
Department of Pharmacology, Lousiana State University Medical Center, New Orleans, Louisiana

**Paul M. Roman, Ph.D.**
Center for Research on Deviance and Behavioral Health, Institute for Behavioral Research, and Department of Sociology, University of Georgia, Athens, Georgia

**Sidney H. Schnoll, M.D., Ph.D.**
Division of Substance Abuse Medicine, Virginia Commonwealth University, Medical College of Virginia Hospitals, Richmond, Virginia

**Richard Steven Schottenfeld, M.D.**
Department of Psychiatry, Substance Abuse Treatment Unit, Yale University School of Medicine, New Haven, Connecticut

**Marc A. Schuckit, M.D.**
Alcohol Research Center, San Diego VA Medical Center, and Department of Psychiatry, University of California at San Diego School of Medicine, San Diego, California

**Edward C. Senay, M.D.**
Department of Psychiatry, University of Chicago School of Medicine, Chicago, Illinois

**James H. Shore, M.D.**
Department of Psychiatry, School of Medicine, University of Colorado Health Sciences Center, Denver, Colorado

**David E. Smith, M.D.**
Haight Ashbury Free Clinic, San Francisco, California

**Peter Steinglass, M.D.**
Ackerman Institute for Family Therapy, New York, New York

**J. Thomas Ungerleider, M.D.**
Department of Psychiatry and Biobehavioral Sciences, University of California at Los Angeles School of Medicine, Los Angeles, California

**Roger D. Weiss, M.D.**
Department of Psychiatry, Harvard Medical School, McLean Hospital, Belmont, Massachusetts

**Donald R. Wesson, M.D.**
Merritt Peralta Institute, Chemical Dependency Recovery Hospital, Oakland, California

**George E. Woody, M.D.**
Substance Abuse Treatment Unit, Philadelphia Veterans Affairs Medical Center, Philadelphia, Pennsylvania

**Sheldon Zimberg, M.D.**
Department of Psychiatry, St. Luke's/Roosevelt Hospital Center, New York, New York

# Preface

Substance abuse is one of the major public health issues confronting our country today and is a worldwide problem of major dimension. In the United States, 18% of the population experience a substance use disorder at some point in their lives. The cost of addictive illness to Americans is currently $144 billion per year in health care and job loss. Furthermore, an average of 20% of patients in general medical facilities and 35% in general psychiatric units present with substance use disorders—in some settings, many more. When the sequelae of addiction, such as cirrhosis, psychopathology, trauma, and infection, are present, they generally receive proper medical attention; patients' primary addictive problems, however, often go untreated.

We now stand on the threshold of important opportunities in the addiction field, however, with many advances in receptor mechanisms, membrane chemistry, and patterns of genetic transmission emerging in recent years. Public awareness of the need for greater research and treatment resources has been aroused as well, and substance-abusing individuals now seek help earlier, at a point where treatment can be administered more effectively. Furthermore, the health community has been alerted to the need for early diagnosis and provision of comprehensive care. New treatment concepts, both pharmacologic and psychosocial, have made recovery a possibility for the majority of alcohol and drug-abusing patients.

The origins of this volume can be seen in the emerging commitment of psychiatry to addressing the problem of substance abuse. In 1982, the American Psychiatric Association (APA) established a Task Force on Treatment of Psychiatric Disorders, consisting of 26 panels. We served as chairpersons of the panels on psychoactive substance use disorders, alcohol, and other drugs, respectively. In response to this APA initiative, we brought together a group of experts who could provide a carefully drawn perspective on addiction treatment, perhaps the most comprehensive one to date. After several years' work, our panels developed reports for the Task Force that were published by the APA in 1989 in the four-volume set, *The Treatment of Psychiatric Disorders.*

Soon after the appearance of these volumes, we decided that it was important to update and amplify the substance abuse treatment information in it. In addition, we wanted to focus on the most recent developments in biologic and psychosocial therapies, and the problems of specific populations. Over the last 2 years, we have brought together the original authors of the report, along with additional experts, to produce this current volume. We hope that it will offer the field a well-organized review on the best and most effective modalities currently available for managing the substance-abusing patient. We acknowledge as well the variety of approaches and the extensive innovations that are so essential in our emerging field.

Most important to the development of this volume is the maturation of the substance abuse field itself. As recently as the mid-1980s, American departments of psychiatry, as well as academic programs for other health professions, paid little heed to the importance of training for substance use treatment. Although the medical addiction community had been vocal in expressing the need for better care over the previous two decades, it was relatively small and had only a limited association with academic teaching centers. This situation has changed dramatically in recent years. Substance abuse training is now an integral part of undergraduate curriculum in most medical schools and a component of most psychiatry residency training programs. Courses also are taught in graduate psychology and social work programs. Postresidency fellowships in addiction, which are now numbering over 40, are demonstrating great vitality and are playing an influential role in ensuring quality treatment for the future. The federal institutes on drug and alcohol abuse are demonstrating a growing awareness of the need for research training and are working closely with organizations in the addiction field to promote growth in clinical teaching as well.

With this in mind, we designed this volume to serve clinicians in practice as well as trainees in psychiatry and related health professions. Although it focuses primarily on established treatment techniques, this volume also offers an understanding of basic biologic and social mechanisms that impinge on etiology and rehabilitation. This volume offers the latest in treatment research findings and includes the text of the section on substance use disorders of the APA's *Diagnostic and Statistical Manual of Mental Disorders, Fourth Edition.* We therefore hope that this book can serve as a definitive, valuable treatment resource for all clinicians who encounter the substance-abusing patient.

Marc Galanter, M.D.
Herbert D. Kleber, M.D.

# Overview
# of
# Treatment

# Goals of Treatment

*Marc A. Schuckit, M.D.*

At first glance, the appropriate goals of treatment for substance use disorders appear obvious. We all strive to help our patients and clients achieve their optimal levels of functioning for as long as possible (Schuckit 1989a).

However, we function in a complex world where health care providers must share scarce resources while reaching out to a pool of impaired individuals who, at least theoretically, have many more needs than we can possibly meet. Thus in addition to the obvious, we have to make decisions about which treatment tools we should use, which patients are most appropriate for care, and which is the most relevant treatment setting.

This chapter focuses on how clinicians in the field of substance use disorders need to make important decisions about specific treatment goals to be applied in the day-to-day situations in which we, the clinicians, function. The first section examines the components incorporated in our desire to help our patients function at an optimal level. The next section discusses the administrative and programmatic objectives that must be considered in our efforts to meet our patients' needs. This is then followed by an overview of some of the goals that may be less appropriate (and at times quite inappropriate) in substance disorders treatment programs. Finally, these thoughts are pulled together into a clinically oriented summary.

## ▼ PATIENT– AND CLIENT–ORIENTED GOALS

Life used to be so simple. Several decades ago, treatment programs focused mostly on the achievement and maintenance of abstinence. However, increasing levels of sophistication have helped us to realize that being substance free, while an essential step in the right direction, does not by itself guarantee optimal life functioning (Committee 1990). Thus we can, somewhat arbitrarily, divide patient-oriented goals into those aimed at the achievement of a substance-free life, those aimed at maximizing multiple aspects of life functioning, and those aimed at relapse prevention. In the 1990s, it is difficult to envision a successful treatment program that ignores any of these domains.

This work was supported by the Veterans Affairs Research Service and National Institute on Alcohol Abuse and Alcoholism Grants 05226, 08401, and 08403.

### Achieving a Substance-Free Life-Style

There are at least two components to achieving a substance-free life-style (Schuckit 1989a). The first involves enhancing motivation for abstinence, and the second relates to teaching our patients how to rebuild their lives after redirecting the focus of their activities away from substance use.

**Maximizing motivation for abstinence.** Substance dependence is, essentially, a condition in which the use of alcohol or other drugs has become such a central part of an individual's life that he or she is willing to give up important activities in order to continue to use the substance or resume substance intake (Babor, in press). Prior to our treatment efforts, the usual clinical course of substance-related problems often involves temporary periods of controlled substance intake established through rules regarding particular situations, times of day, or other conditions in which substances will be taken but "kept under control" (Schuckit 1989a; Vaillant 1983). Unfortunately, men and women with a history of severe substance-related life impairment are very likely to discover that rules can be bent, intake escalates, and a crisis develops. This is followed by a new intense level of resolve to stop taking the drug, "at least for a period of time," after which use begins again, efforts of control are instituted, and new crises develop yet again (Ludwig 1972, 1985).

In recognition of this pattern of repeated efforts at "controlled substance use," with the high likelihood (some would say almost certainty) of progression to the point of problems once use resumes, most programs dealing with substance-dependent individuals have chosen to make abstinence a clear goal. However, some men and women with substance dependence at least initially refuse a goal of abstinence. In the alcohol field, some clinicians and researchers have thus attempted to develop experimental programs aimed at teaching *controlled use* to those who refuse to give up their substance (Sobell and Sobell 1984). Unfortunately these programs generally have been relatively small in scope, follow-ups have tended to be incomplete (Pendery et al. 1982), and results have been inconsistent. Thus at least for alcohol-dependent individuals, most clinicians and scientists view efforts at teaching controlled use as worth investigation but not appropriate for inclusion in the usual treatment program. At the same time, however, some researchers have reported promising results regarding teaching control of alcohol use to individuals who have not met criteria for dependence but who have expressed concerns over their occasional heavy intake of alcohol while refusing to totally abstain.

For substance-dependent men and women, various maneuvers are appropriate for attempting to maximize the motivation for abstinence (Schuckit 1989a), including lectures, counseling sessions, self-help groups, and videotapes. The goal is to educate the individual and his or her family about the dangers involved with substance use, the usual clinical course of substance use disorders, and the fact that each individual is responsible for his or her own actions. Thus any return to substance use is likely to set off a series of events that lead to a fairly predictable group of severe life problems. On the other hand, the individual should be taught that abstinence is achievable, life patterns can change, and there is a high level of hope for success.

In summary, abstinence is accepted as the only clinically relevant goal for treatment programs that focus on those who meet criteria for dependence on any substance. Total abstinence is also the goal for tobacco use and for the intake of illegal drugs.

**Rebuilding a substance-free life-style.** Most programs admit to their patients that giving up all substance use is not easy. Patients are likely to have experienced years of heavy substance intake and to have developed a life pattern where a good deal of their time and the majority of their friends are involved with heavy, repeated substance intake. Even substance-free relatives and friends are likely to have developed expectations about the individual's behaviors and subtly, or sometimes more blatantly, communicated these probabilities to the individual, sometimes producing an almost "scripted" style of interaction. Thus important elements in developing a substance-free life-style include helping the individual to discover ways of dealing with free time, develop relationships with substance-free friends, adjust to the "mundane" aspects of day-to-day living in the absence of the crisis-upon-crisis life-style associated with substance use, and reestablish rewarding relationships with family members.

### Helping to Maximize Multiple Aspects of Life Functioning

As briefly discussed previously, becoming substance free is an essential first step in rebuilding one's life.

However, this achievement alone is rarely sufficient to optimize functioning. Thus most treatment programs attempt to address essential elements of day-to-day living. Although not all programs incorporate efforts directly aimed at each area of functioning, almost all recognize the need to deal with the majority of these domains.

**Optimizing medical functioning.**  The heavy use of alcohol and other drugs is likely to damage body systems, increase the risk for physical trauma through accidents, and (for depressants, stimulants, and opioids) produce clinically relevant levels of physical dependence (Schuckit 1990a). Therefore, it is hard to conceive of an effective program that would ignore the importance of a careful physical examination, neglect emergent physical difficulties, fail to deal with the appropriate treatment of withdrawal when needed, and make no effort to prevent future medical difficulties. These steps are not only essential parts of the responsibility assumed by a treatment program but are also important for optimizing the patient's ability to participate fully in rehabilitation.

**Identifying and treating psychiatric symptoms and disorders.**  During intoxication and withdrawal from substances, as many as 80% of substance-dependent individuals will demonstrate psychiatric symptoms (Regier et al. 1990). For example, perhaps as many as two-thirds of alcohol-dependent individuals will experience social phobic-like symptoms or panic attacks during withdrawal, whereas a similar proportion of actively drinking alcoholic individuals and individuals undergoing withdrawal from stimulants such as cocaine or amphetamines will demonstrate serious depressive symptoms that can last from 2 to 4 or more weeks (Brown and Schuckit 1988; Brown et al. 1991; Gawin and Ellinwood 1988; Schuckit 1990b). Treatment programs must be aware of these temporary conditions, carefully evaluate their patients for the possibility of independent psychiatric disorders, and take appropriate steps to address the clinical symptoms, even when they are only temporary and part of the substance-use pattern. In this latter instance, education, reassurance, evaluations for the potential temporary need for suicide precautions, along with cognitive, supportive, or behavioral counseling techniques, should be instituted temporarily when appropriate. The intense depression and anxiety related to intoxication or withdrawal improve fairly quickly, although some low-grade symptoms can linger for several months as part of a protracted abstinence syndrome (Satel et al. 1993).

In addition to these fairly common substance-related temporary conditions, individuals with substance use disorders have at least as high a risk for independent psychiatric disorders as the general population. Therefore, at least 5% of men and 10% of women might have major depressive disorders, and as many as 10% of both sexes could be expected to have one of the anxiety disorders by chance alone (Regier et al. 1988). However, men and women with manic-depressive disease, schizophrenia, or antisocial personality disorder have higher risks for subsequent substance-related problems than the general population (Hesselbrock et al. 1986; Salloum et al. 1991). Therefore, most treatment programs incorporate a careful history-gathering procedure that obtains information from both the patient and at least one knowledgeable friend or relative. This procedure helps determine whether psychiatric syndromes that meet criteria for severe disorders were apparent either before the onset of severe life problems from substances or during a period of perhaps several months or more when the individual was totally abstinent (Schuckit 1989a). Programs also are likely to incorporate procedures for observing the persistence of intense psychiatric symptomatology remaining approximately 6 weeks after abstinence, which is documented as indicative of potentially important independent disorders.

After an independent psychiatric syndrome has been established, through a careful history taking or observation of individuals over time following abstinence, appropriate treatments must be instituted. Thus the relatively small proportion of men and women who have both substance dependence and independent major depressive disorders are candidates for intense cognitive therapy and/or antidepressant medications, the 1%–2% of substance-dependent men and women who actually have manic-depressive disease may well require lithium, and the 1%–2% of patients who have both substance dependence and schizophrenia are almost certain to require antipsychotic medications (Schuckit 1989a). Recognizing and appropriately treating these independent psychiatric disorders in the minority of our patients is as important a part of our goals for substance-related treatment as carrying out steps to optimize medical functioning.

**Dealing with marital and other family issues.** Re-establishing and maintaining close relationships with their spouses, their children, and other family members is a demanding task for our patients. As difficult as these issues are to deal with for anyone, the nature of the behaviors likely to be observed in the course of substance use problems is likely to jeopardize these relationships even further. Thus most treatment programs in the substance use field have incorporated efforts that reach out to family members by establishing couples and family counseling sessions and incorporating as many family members and friends as appropriate into relevant aspects of rehabilitation efforts. These steps not only make good sense but also increase the probability of long-term abstinence in our patients (McCrady et al. 1991; Steinglass 1989).

**Enriching job functioning and financial management.** Most men and women who come to alcohol- and other substance-related programs have multiple financial problems. They are likely to have difficulty holding a job, spend far too much money on substance use, and have developed a pattern of responding to financial crises, rather than planning ahead. Obviously, an important part of helping individuals to optimize their life functioning involves vocational rehabilitation, helping them to find jobs that are not as closely intertwined in their minds with substance use and helping to develop patterns of financial planning that will keep food on the table. Thus financial management along with vocational education efforts are important parts of therapeutic interventions (Spittle 1991).

**Addressing relevant spiritual issues.** Many treatment programs have grown out of the Alcoholics Anonymous tradition and feel that an important part of reconstituting one's life is to recognize the importance of a "supreme being," or at least the need to address the care and nurturing of one's soul (Galanter et al. 1990). Although there is debate over whether spirituality is an *essential* aspect of treatment (Ellis and Schoenfeld 1990), most clinicians in the field agree that issues of religiosity or spirituality are worth exploring with patients who are attempting to rebuild their lives free of substance-related problems.

**Dealing with homelessness.** Homelessness used to be a topic that only applied to central-city, "skid-row"

programs. It is an unfortunate sign of our times that nowadays most treatment programs attempting to optimize functioning of their patients have to take the time to determine the stability of their current living situation (Segal 1991). An important part of treatment is determining appropriate placement. Thus it is worth the time and effort to scan not only present living situations but the likelihood of the need for help in the near future.

### Relapse Prevention

Many of the programmatic goals discussed later in this chapter emphasize the necessity of recognizing the limitation of financial resources. Because of this reality, in part, the period of time allowed for the intensive intervention phase in either an inpatient or outpatient mode has been considerably shortened in recent years. This limitation underscores the importance of efforts aimed at helping to prevent relapses.

An integral part of helping individuals to function is to raise their awareness of the need to develop high levels of vigilance against potential relapses and to help them produce a plan of action if they find themselves in a situation where relapse is highly likely or even if a temporary resumption of substance use (a "slip") has occurred (Marlatt 1985). Most treatment programs use the intensive phase of care to teach about relapse prevention, a subject that is even more fully emphasized through aftercare groups. Ways to minimize the risk of returning to substance use are taught through lectures, group discussions, and individual counseling sessions. Topics likely to be covered include the recognition of situations in which craving is likely to increase, the individual's responsibility for avoiding "accidental" exposure to stressful situations in which substances are freely available, developing a scenario of what to do and whom to contact if problems begin, and how to avoid allowing the occurrence of a temporary resumption of substance use to be used as an excuse for escalating intake even further.

## ▼ PROGRAMMATIC GOALS

Because resources are needed to develop a treatment program, clinicians should recognize that the goals for patients outlined previously are not enough to develop and maintain a program. The "institution" formed by individuals attempting to reach out to men and women with substance-related problems must itself function in relationship to a number of goals. These goals can be summarized as the steps required to develop an atmosphere that is optimally conducive to helping patients with substance-related problems. The following institutional-goals have been reviewed (Schuckit 1989b).

## Goal 1: To Consider Fiscal and Political Realities

The amount of monies available compared with the number of patients seeking care establishes some realities of day-to-day life. This ratio helps to determine the type of facility that will be used (e.g., inpatient versus outpatient, freestanding versus affiliated with a medical institution), the therapeutic regime (e.g., more versus less emphasis on physician care), the number of staff, the length of contact with patients, the number of hours that the facility will be open, and so on. The source of funding also dictates some political realities that impact on treatment goals. For instance, for a city-funded skid-row facility, the probable low 1-year rate of absolute abstinence for homeless drug- and alcohol-dependent individuals entering rehabilitation makes it unwise to judge the program solely on the number of patients who abstained over long periods of time (Powell et al. 1985; Schuckit 1989a). The funding agencies (including insurers) might consider that a more appropriate immediate goal is dealing with severe medical problems that require active treatment because efforts here can be lifesaving and outcomes more easily documented. This can, of course, occur in the context of efforts to help patients and clients achieve and maintain abstinence.

## Goal 2: To Carefully Use Financial and Staff Resources

In general, to achieve this goal requires that treatment approaches be kept as simple as possible, avoiding potentially expensive or potentially dangerous additions to a standard regimen until controlled studies have demonstrated that these more costly approaches are justified.

## Goal 3: To Clearly State the Philosophy of the Staff

In the substance use disorders field, it is not clear that one theoretical approach is likely to be more effective than another. Thus after considering the realities of financial and staff resources, different programs are likely to demonstrate different theoretical biases, without any one being apparently superior. The specific theoretical bent chosen by a program probably rests as much with chance and the training of the director as it does with any solid literature review. In any event, staff who hope to function optimally while reaching out to patients must develop a level of comfort with one another. This, in turn, often requires that the philosophy of the program (be it eclectic or committed to any specific model) be clearly stated and understood.

## Goal 4: To Remember That No Treatment Is Totally Safe

Patients can have adverse reactions to medications, develop complications of diagnostic procedures, might act on bad advice, and run the risk of exhausting their scarce resources of time and money. Therefore, all programs should attempt to conform with the goal of doing the most good possible while exposing their patients to the least possible risks (Goodwin and Guze 1989). This cost-benefit ratio depends on knowledge of the usual course of alcohol- and drug-related problems in order to be certain that the intervention poses less risk to the patient than the clinical course likely to be observed in the subsequent months. Thus isolated alcohol and drug problems, although certainly cause for concern, do not necessarily justify full-scale intervention.

One way to predict the probable course of problems likely to be observed over time with or without treatment is to carefully establish the diagnosis of abuse or dependence (Goodwin and Guze 1989; Schuckit 1989a). Once it is certain that actual dependence has developed, the risks and costs of most of the usual substance-related rehabilitation efforts are likely to be outweighed by the benefits of such treatments. At the same time, documenting isolated problems or showing that an individual fulfills criteria for abuse (in the absence of dependence) indicates that a confrontation is likely to be beneficial and that some form of intervention is justified (Schuckit

1989a). However, the lower level of intensity of the future course (assuming dependence does not subsequently develop) might not be sufficient to justify a 3-week inpatient rehabilitation program or assigning a patient to a long-term halfway or recovery home.

### Goal 5: To Determine That the Treatment Approaches Being Considered Are More Effective Than Chance Alone

Substance abuse problems fluctuate in intensity (Ludwig 1972; Vaillant 1983). Patients and clients are likely to come to a treatment program for care at the time of most intense problems. Therefore, it should not be surprising that with the passage of time alone and in the absence of aggressive treatment, individuals are likely to continue to experience a waxing and waning of symptom intensity. The result of these considerations is that using intervention $x$ and then following up an individual 6 months later simply does not prove that it was the intervention that was responsible for any improved level of functioning following care. Only through careful studies can we be sure that any intervention is useful.

Ideally, this requirement for careful studies to determine that an intervention is superior to the passage of time alone should be applied to all treatment efforts in medicine and in the behavioral sciences. Because of the costs involved in such studies, however, most clinicians in most programs have a basic treatment approach that they accept as potentially beneficial and that is rarely tested. This often includes the efforts described previously for increasing motivation for abstinence and helping people to rebuild their lives without the substance. On the other hand, the addition of any intervention beyond the basic program should require documentation, through carefully controlled research, that the additional approach adds significantly to the outcome. Therefore, it is not wise to add a medication or additional therapy time or to change the length of treatment without carefully considering whether our patients benefit adequately from the altered approach.

## ▼ POTENTIALLY INAPPROPRIATE GOALS

As is true of most things in life, it is sometimes the things that we do not do that are as important as the things that we do. Once a treatment program accepts the caveat of "do no harm," it is important to recognize goals that are potentially inappropriate in dealing with substance-related problems.

For example, while attempting to help a patient achieve and maintain abstinence as well as to develop a life-style free of substance use, it is unwise to use medications to treat insomnia, anxiety, or depression observed during intoxication or withdrawal (Litten and Allen 1991; Schuckit 1989a). For the physically addicting drugs (i.e., depressants, stimulants, and opioids), withdrawal-related psychological symptoms can be expected to be most intense during the first several weeks, with a great deal of improvement over the subsequent weeks (Brown and Schuckit 1988; Schuckit 1989a). However, it is likely that the body does not reach its optimal level of functioning in a substance-free environment for perhaps 3–6 months following abstinence (Satel et al. 1993). For these men and women, counseling, cognitive therapy, and behavioral approaches can help them deal with their temporary but troubling problems (e.g., insomnia, mood swings, nervousness) that are so likely to plague their existence in an off-again, on-again fashion during the early months of recovery. Of course, there are two exceptions to this general prohibition against medications for substance-related anxiety or depression. The first exception is the use of medications to deal with acute withdrawal, especially for depressant- and opioid-type drugs (Schuckit 1989a). The second exception relates to those individuals who have been documented to have an independent major psychiatric disorder and who, thus, require lithium for their manic-depressive disease, antidepressant medication for their severe major depressive disorder, or antipsychotic drugs for schizophrenia.

A related warning is the need to distinguish between treatments that might *possibly enhance* recovery rates and those that have been demonstrated through careful study to be worth the risks involved. By use of this approach, there are few medications that are justified for use on a routine basis among individuals with substance use problems. The exceptions include methadone for severely impaired opioid-dependent individuals (Ball and Ross 1991) and possibly disulfiram (Antabuse) for alcohol-dependent individuals (Fuller et al. 1986). Although many other potential drugs currently are being evaluated for the treatment of substance use disorders, few, if any, of these drugs have been subject to enough carefully controlled studies to justify their routine use.

Another potentially inappropriate goal is any attempt to change long-standing personality characteristics as a routine part of substance-dependence rehabilitation. There are few convincing data that a specific personality profile, other than antisocial personality disorder, is an important cause for substance dependence (Hesselbrock et al. 1986; Irwin et al. 1990). Even if such data existed, it is likely to be far beyond the financial and staff resources of the usual treatment program to offer intensive efforts at altering personality styles as an integral part of treatment.

## ▼ CONCLUSIONS

At first glance, the goals of treatment for substance use disorders appear so obvious. Few would argue with the appropriateness of stating that abstinence and the development of a substance-free life-style over an extended period of time are the central goals in almost all treatment efforts with substance-dependent individuals.

This chapter was written to demonstrate that the implementation of these general goals requires the recognition of many realities regarding our patients and the political and fiscal environments in which we work. Thus it is the manner in which we go about attempting to achieve our more global objectives that is likely to have a marked influence on the survival of both our patients and our programs.

The general goals of treatment, however, should be placed into proper perspective. Because they are general in nature, some individual goals will not apply to specific programs. Nonetheless, it is hoped that the thoughts offered above will help the interested clinicians reading this text to develop a framework through which many of the subsequent chapters will be viewed. Perhaps some of these thoughts might also be of use in developing new programs and in optimizing existing ones.

## ▼ REFERENCES

Babor TL: Nosological consideration in the diagnosis of substance use disorders, in Vulnerability to Drug Abuse. Edited by Glantz M, Pickens R. Washington, DC, American Psychological Association (in press)

Ball J, Ross A: The Effectiveness of Methadone Maintenance Treatments. New York, Springer-Verlag New York, 1991

Brown SA, Schuckit MA: Changes in depression among abstinent alcoholics. J Stud Alcohol 49: 412–417, 1988

Brown SA, Irwin M, Schuckit MA: Changes in anxiety among abstinent male alcoholics. J Stud Alcohol 52:55–61, 1991

Committee for the Study of Treatment and Rehabilitation Services for Alcoholism and Alcohol Abuse: Broadening the Base of Treatment for Alcohol Problems. Washington, DC, National Academy Press, 1990, pp 23–183

Ellis A, Schoenfeld E: Divine intervention and the treatment of chemical dependency (editorial). J Subst Abuse Treat 2:459–468, 1990

Fuller RK, Branchey L, Brightwell DR, et al: Disulfiram treatment of alcoholism. JAMA 256:1449–1455, 1986

Galanter M, Talbott D, Gallegos K, et al: Combined Alcoholics Anonymous and professional care for addicted physicians. Am J Psychiatry 147:64–68, 1990

Gawin FH, Ellinwood EH: Cocaine and other stimulants. New Engl J Med 318:1173–1182, 1988

Goodwin DW, Guze SB: Psychiatric Diagnosis, 4th Edition. New York, Oxford University Press, 1989

Hesselbrock VM, Hesselbrock MN, Workman-Daniels KL: Effects of major depression and antisocial personality on alcoholism: course and motivational patterns. J Stud Alcohol 47:207–212, 1986

Irwin M, Schuckit MA, Smith TL: Clinical importance of age at onset in Type 1 and Type 2 primary alcoholics. Arch Gen Psychiatry 47:320–324, 1990

Litten RZ, Allen JP: Pharmacotherapies for alcoholism: promising agents and clinical issues. Alcohol Clin Exp Res 15:620–633, 1991

Ludwig AM: On and off the wagon. J Stud Alcohol 33:91–96, 1972

Ludwig AM: Cognitive processes associated with "spontaneous" recovery from alcoholism. J Stud Alcohol 46:53–58, 1985

Marlatt GA: Relapse prevention, in Relapse Prevention: Maintenance Strategies in Treatment of Addictive Behaviors. Edited by Marlatt GA, Gordon J. New York, Guilford, 1985, pp 3–70

McCrady BS, Stout R, Noel N, et al: Effectiveness of three types of spouse-involved behavioral alcoholism treatment. British Journal of Addiction 86: 1415–1424, 1991

Pendery ML, Maltzman IM, West LJ: Controlled drinking by alcoholics? New findings and a reevaluation of a major affirmative study. Science 217: 169–175, 1982

Powell BJ, Penick EC, Read MR, et al: Comparison of three outpatient treatment interventions: a twelve-month follow-up of men alcoholics. J Stud Alcohol 46:309–312, 1985

Regier DA, Boyd JH, Burke JD, et al: One-month prevalence of mental disorders in the United States. Arch Gen Psychiatry 45:977–986, 1988

Regier DA, Farmer ME, Rae DS, et al: Comorbidity of mental disorders with alcohol and other drug abuse. JAMA 264:2511–2518, 1990

Salloum IM, Moss HB, Daley DC: Substance abuse and schizophrenia: impediments to optimal care. Am J Drug Alcohol Abuse 17:321–336, 1991

Satel SL, Kosten TR, Schuckit MA, et al: Should protracted withdrawal from drugs be included in DSM-IV? Am J Psychiatry 150:695–704, 1993

Schuckit MA: Drug and Alcohol Abuse: A Clinical Guide to Diagnosis and Treatment, 3rd Edition. New York, Plenum, 1989a

Schuckit MA: Goals of treatment, in Treatments of Psychiatric Disorders: A Task Force Report of the American Psychiatric Association, Vol 2. Washington, DC, American Psychiatric Association, 1989b, pp 1072–1076

Schuckit MA: Alcohol and alcoholism, in Harrison's Principles of Internal Medicine, 12th Edition. Edited by Wilson J, Braunwald E, Isselbacher KJ, et al. New York, McGraw-Hill, 1990a, pp 2146–2151

Schuckit MA: Treatment of anxiety in patients who abuse alcohol and drugs, in Handbook of Anxiety, Vol 4: The Treatment of Anxiety. Edited by Noyes R, Roth M, Burrows GD. New York, Elsevier, 1990b, pp 461–481

Segal B: Homelessness and drinking. Drugs and Society 5:1–150, 1991

Sobell MB, Sobell LC: The aftermath of heresy: a response to Pendery et al.'s (1982) critique of "individualized behavior therapy for alcoholics." Behav Res Ther 22:413–440, 1984

Spittle B: The effect of financial management of alcohol-related hospitalization. Am J Psychiatry 148: 221–223, 1991

Steinglass P: Family systems approach to the alcoholic family, in Alcoholism and the Family. Edited by Ishu T. Tokyo, Psychiatric Research Institute of Tokyo, 1989, pp 103–113

Vaillant G: The Natural History of Alcoholism. Cambridge, MA, Harvard University Press, 1983, pp 120–133

# Typologies of Addiction

Michael J. Bohn, M.D.
Roger E. Meyer, M.D.

Although substance use *disorders* have been defined categorically in the DSM-III, DSM-III-R, DSM-IV, and ICD-10 systems (American Psychiatric Association 1980, 1987, 1994; World Health Organization 1992), there is abundant evidence that *individuals* with substance use disorders present with many heterogeneous clinical and theoretical characteristics. Considerable data indicate that this heterogeneity is not random, suggesting distinct subtypes of individuals with substance use disorders. These subtypes, to be meaningful and valid, should discriminate distinct etiologic (e.g., heritable) and prognostic categories of substance-abusing individuals.

Although typologies in the alcoholism field are at least 100 years old, more recently clinicians and researchers have proposed several typologies of substance-abusing individuals using empiric rules, clinical wisdom, and theories about the etiology of substance abuse. Subgroups have been proposed on the basis of psychological, biological, and social characteristics of the individual. The vast majority of typologies of substance-abusing individuals have focused on those with alcoholism. In this chapter we will attempt to summarize recent work on alcoholism typologies, including work on patient-treatment matching strategies (Finney and Moos 1986; Institute of Medi-

cine 1990), supplementing our discussion with a review of typologies of drug-abusing individuals. We will discuss the potential utility of typologic assessment in choosing an effective treatment for particular patients with substance use disorders.

## ▼ HISTORIC OVERVIEW

Attempts to meaningfully classify subtypes of alcoholic individuals date from the Ebers Papyrus and include several schemes developed in the nineteenth century (Babor and Lauerman 1986). When the psychiatrist Karl Bowman and the biometrician E. M. Jellinek reviewed and synthesized alcoholic typologies in 1941, they identified 39 classifications of abnormal drinkers (Bowman and Jellinek 1941). Jellinek (1960) later described differences in drinking patterns and the pathologic consequences of drinking reported by Alcoholics Anonymous members. He proposed a fivefold alcoholism typology employing etiological elements; alcoholism process elements such as dependence; and physical, mental, and socioeconomic damage elements. Two of Jellinek's types, gamma alcoholics and delta alcoholics, have gained historic prominence. Gamma alcoholics are described as having high psychological vulnerability to develop dependence and inability to control their alcohol consumption following initiation of drinking. Although often able to abstain for long periods between drinking bouts, gamma alcoholics eventually develop problems in physical health and in socioeconomic function. Delta alcoholics, in contrast, develop alcoholism under strong influence of sociocultural and economic factors, such as societal encouragement to drink and an affordable supply of alcoholic beverages. Although able to limit the amounts of alcohol they consume per drinking occasion, delta alcoholics are primarily physically dependent on alcohol and unable to abstain for even short periods. Socioeconomic and, more variably, physical and mental damage eventually develop in delta alcoholics. Despite the heuristic and clinical appeal of Jellinek's multidimensional typology, little empiric research has been conducted to assess its ability to predict the longitudinal course or posttreatment outcomes of alcoholic subjects (Babor and Dolinsky 1988). Walton et al. (1966) found no significant differences in outcome status between groups of gamma and delta alcoholics.

## ▼ UNIDIMENSIONAL TYPOLOGIES

A priori procedures have been employed since the 1960s to systematically classify alcoholic and drug abuse subtypes. In a priori comparisons, substance-abusing subjects have been assigned to groups based on differences in theoretic criteria. Most of these typologies have divided subjects according to a *single* dimension or characteristic. For alcoholic individuals, the unidimensional typologic criteria proposed have included the individual's drinking history (Cahalan et al. 1969), drinking pattern (Tarter et al. 1977), severity of dependence (Skinner 1980), family history of alcoholism (Penick et al. 1978; V. M. Hesselbrock et al. 1982), sex (Schuckit 1969; Rimmer et al. 1971), personality style (Conley 1981; Nerviano and Gross 1983), primary or secondary psychopathology (Winokur et al. 1971), cognitive impairment (Eckhardt 1981; Shelly and Goldstein 1976), and sociopathy (Cadoret et al. 1985; M. N. Hesselbrock et al. 1984). Similar criteria have been applied in the small number of reported typologic studies of drug-abusing individuals. Following the as-

signment of substance-abusing subjects to groups based on these categories or dimensions, researchers have assessed the validity of the typology by comparing group differences on a variety of other relevant criteria such as drinking consequences or posttreatment functioning. These unidimensional typologies have suggested differences in clinical course (e.g., age at onset, treatment history, substance use problems) and prognosis among groups of substance-abusing individuals (Meyer 1989).

Beginning in the 1970s, combined abuse of alcohol and a variety of drugs became increasingly common in industrialized countries, particularly in urban settings. This trend, coupled with the increasing availability of various forms of licit and illicit drugs, has led to consideration of typologies based on the patterns of comorbid substance abuse. Carlin and Stauss (1978) proposed two groups of polydrug-abusing individuals based on their motivational patterns: *recreational users* and *self-medicators*. Self-medicators used drugs on a relatively regular basis, had more somatic preoccupation, and reported more depressive symptoms than did recreational users. Other typologies have distinguished between illicit and prescription polydrug-abusing individuals (Malow et al. 1988). In general, the reliability and predictive validity of these and other polydrug typologies have not been assessed.

An alternative typologic approach, which has also been applied in patient-treatment matching strategies, employs a dimensional view of the severity of substance dependence disorders. To some extent this is implicit in the diagnostic criteria employed in DSM-III-R, but not in DSM-III. The DSM-III-R criteria are based on the behaviorally defined alcohol dependence syndrome described by Edwards and Gross (1976). These authors proposed that alcohol dependence and disabilities be viewed along separate continua of severity. As applied to all substance dependence disorders in DSM-III-R, the dependence syndrome refers to a set of symptoms characterized by diminished capacity for control over psychoactive substance intake, salience of substance use, tolerance, withdrawal syndrome, and use of the substance to relieve withdrawal symptoms. Several reports have provided empirical evidence in support of the concept of a unitary dependence syndrome for alcohol (Babor et al. 1987; Hodgson et al. 1979; Skinner 1980, 1981a; Skinner and Allen 1982) and other drugs (Kosten et al. 1987). For alcohol, several research instruments have been developed to quantify the severity of dependence (Chick 1980; M. N. Hesselbrock et al. 1985; Skinner and Allen 1982; Stockwell et al. 1979). Most patients with alcohol use disorders who enter inpatient treatment are in fact alcohol dependent (M. N. Hesselbrock et al. 1985).

The severity of alcohol dependence predicts attendance at a treatment clinic (Skinner and Allen 1982), craving for alcohol after a drink (Hodgson et al. 1979), responsivity to alcohol and placebo alcohol cues (Kaplan et al. 1983), relapse to problem drinking (Polich et al. 1980), and *reinstatement of dependence* after a period of abstinence (Babor et al. 1987). Alcohol-related psychosocial disabilities are associated with a lifetime prevalence of psychopathology (including antisocial personality disorder [ASPD], major depression, and obsessive-compulsive disorder) and cultural factors, whereas severity of alcohol dependence is positively related to the quantity and frequency of alcohol consumption but not to psychopathology (M. N. Hesselbrock et al. 1985).

As described above, the presence or absence of coexisting psychopathology has been used to distinguish subgroups of substance-abusing individuals. Several groups have reported high rates of coexisting personality disorders and other major psychiatric disorders in samples of substance-abusing patients (M. N. Hesselbrock et al. 1985; Ross et al. 1988; Rounsaville et al. 1982; Rounsaville et al. 1991; Weiss et al. 1986). Penick et al. (1978) studied the prevalence of psychiatric syndromes and age at onset in 565 alcoholic men in five Veterans Administration (VA) treatment programs. Only 37% of the subjects met criteria for alcoholism alone; 63% had at least two syndromes, and the mean number of psychiatric syndromes was 2.4. Depression (42%), mania (22%), and ASPD (20%) were the most frequent disorders, followed by drug abuse, panic attacks, phobia, and obsessive-compulsive disorder (10%–15% each). Other conditions occurred in less than 5% of the subjects. Alcoholic subjects without other DSM disorders reported a significantly later onset of problem drinking than those patients who had at least one other disorder in addition to alcoholism.

The traditional clinical literature on psychopathology and substance abuse has tended to presume that the presence of addictive behavior was a consequence of preexisting psychopathology. Except for sociopathy, this is generally not the case, at least for men. For example, data from long-term longitudinal studies of men who became alcoholic (Vaillant 1983)

as well as from clinical laboratory studies of chronic alcohol intoxication (Mendelson and Mello 1966; Nathan et al. 1970) indicate that chronic heavy consumption of alcohol itself produces depression, anxiety, and other psychopathologic symptoms. Thus Winokur et al. (1971) divided alcoholic individuals into a group whose psychiatric syndrome antedated the onset of alcoholism (i.e., *secondary alcoholics*) and those whose psychiatric syndrome began after the onset of alcoholism (i.e., *primary alcoholics*). Secondary alcoholic men with primary depression had more depressive symptoms, less drug misuse, and longer periods of abstinence than did primary alcoholic men (Schuckit 1985). Among alcoholic women, subtypes with primary alcoholism and with alcoholism secondary to a primary affective disorder were found (Schuckit 1969; Schuckit and Winokur 1972). For alcoholic women, coexisting major depression was found to have a positive effect on drinking outcomes after alcoholism treatment. The converse was true for alcoholic men; those with major depression had worse drinking outcomes than did those without major depression (Rounsaville et al. 1987).

One clinical implication of the primary/secondary distinction is that individuals with secondary alcoholism may be less likely to relapse to heavy drinking following treatment of their primary affective or anxiety disorder (Schuckit 1985). Recently reported placebo-controlled clinical trials support this hypothesis. For example, alcoholic subjects with primary major depression were less likely to relapse to heavy drinking following imipramine (McGrath et al. 1992) or desipramine (Mason and Kocsis 1991) treatment of their primary depressive disorder.

There is controversy about the relative merit of using categorical or dimensional measures of psychopathology to differentiate subtypes of substance-abusing individuals. McLellan et al. (1983a) developed the Addiction Severity Index (ASI), an instrument that assesses treatment needs of substance-abusing individuals in several domains. The ASI includes a measure of the global need for treatment of psychiatric problems based on reported symptoms of depression, anxiety, psychosis, and cognitive dysfunction. They found that this ASI dimension was a good predictor of alcohol and drug use in patients who had entered a variety of different substance abuse treatment programs. Matching patients to different treatment *programs* based on this ASI dimension led to improved patient outcomes (McLellan et al. 1983b). Within a program, matching patients to distinct treatment methods may also be improved by assessment of psychiatric symptom severity. For example, Kadden et al. (1989) found that alcoholic subjects with high ASI psychiatric problem scores had superior drinking outcomes following randomized assignment to a coping skills treatment group, compared with similar patients assigned to an interactional treatment group. Conversely, alcoholic subjects with milder degrees of psychopathology had superior outcomes when randomized to the interactional therapy group. Another dimensional measure of global psychopathology, the average-scaled Minnesota Multiphasic Personality Inventory (MMPI) score, was less powerful than the categoric diagnoses of major depression or ASPD in predicting posttreatment outcome among alcoholic subjects (Rounsaville et al. 1987). Thus the relative merits of categoric and dimensional psychopathology measures in predicting posttreatment functioning may depend on the particular measures chosen and the treatments employed.

Several shortcomings of unidimensional alcoholism typologies have been identified (Babor and Dolinsky 1988; Babor et al. 1992b). First, there is considerable overlap among the unidimensional classifications (M. N. Hesselbrock 1986). For example, primary sociopathy, familial alcoholism, and impulsive personality traits commonly occur together in alcoholic men. The unique contributions of each particular dimension in discriminating alcoholic subgroups have not often been determined by typologic researchers. Second, different typologies have not been compared using a common set of validation criteria, such as measures of the natural history or clinical course of alcoholism. In short, typologies that focus on single elements, whether based on elements of risk (e.g., family history of alcoholism) or on elements of recent functioning (e.g., drinking pattern), may be inadequate in uniquely predicting future drinking, psychologic functioning, medical status, and alcohol-associated problems. The validity of several alcoholism typologies was examined by Babor et al. (1992b). The typologies examined were sex, parental alcoholism, primary versus secondary alcoholism, the gamma-delta distinction, and personality subtypes derived from the MMPI using Conley's criteria (1981). Babor et al. drew the heterogeneous University of Connecticut sample of 321 alcoholic inpatients from a state facility, a VA hospital, and a university hospital and evaluated them at baseline and at

follow-up 1 year later. Because considerable overlap was observed among these typologic classifications, the statistical technique called *multiple classification analysis* was used to independently assess the validity of each typology. A common set of validation criteria were used to compare the typologies. None of the classification systems was clearly superior in globally discriminating alcoholic individuals on measures of alcoholism vulnerability and risk factors, natural history and chronicity, alcohol consumption and drinking problems, psychological consequences, and indicators of treatment response. All but the sex typology showed some ability to distinguish alcoholic groups differing on measures of vulnerability to alcoholism, presenting symptoms, and drinking patterns. However, significant discriminations were generally limited to areas closely related to the defining characteristics of the particular typology. None of these classification schemes predicted more than 16% of the drinking and other 1-year posttreatment outcome variables. Thus it appears that these simple typologic schemes, thoroughly discussed in the alcoholism literature and highly regarded by many clinicians, offer limited potential to differentiate alcoholic individuals according to etiology, global clinical status, and posttreatment outcomes. We know of no similar studies among pure populations of drug-abusing individuals or among mixed alcohol- and drug-abusing populations.

## ▼ MULTIDIMENSIONAL TYPOLOGIES

Given the multiple determinants of onset and outcome of substance use disorders, it is not surprising that unidimensional typologies fail to account for the complex heterogeneity of substance-abusing individuals. Advances in classification of psychiatric disorders and in psychiatric genetics and epidemiology have led to renewed interest in multidimensional subtyping of patients with these disorders (Cloninger et al. 1989). Using increasingly sophisticated methodologies, investigators have moved away from a priori alcoholism typologies defined by single dichotomous variables and toward more complex, multivariate schemes. Examples of such theories are Cloninger's (1987) neurogenetic learning model, L. von Knorring et al.'s (1985) early- and late-onset subtyping, and Zucker's (1987) developmental sequencing model. These newer typologies of alcoholism have attempted to account for the independent and interactive effects of genetic predisposition, personality characteristics, coexisting psychopathology, and drinking patterns in alcoholic populations.

Cloninger and colleagues (1987, 1988) have conducted a series of prospective adoption studies of alcoholic individuals and proposed two subtypes of alcoholism. *Type 1,* or *milieu-limited* alcoholism, affects both men and women, has onset after age 25, and is typified by an ability to abstain from drinking and a loss of control of alcohol use after initiating a drinking period. The severity of alcoholism among Type 1 alcoholic individuals depends upon their childhood environment. A family environment marked by heavy drinking can increase the severity of subsequent alcohol problems in children who are genetically at risk of alcoholism. *Type 1 alcoholics* rarely engage in fights or are arrested when drinking and tend not to have a history of paternal criminality. *Type 2,* or *male-limited* alcoholism, occurs only in men, begins before age 25, and is typified by an inability to abstain from alcohol and heavy consumption rates in a given drinking episode. *Type 2 alcoholics* develop severe, recurrent medical and social consequences of alcoholism. Type 2 alcoholism is highly heritable and not influenced by parental drinking patterns in the postnatal environment. Typically, both the Type 2 alcoholic individual and his father have histories of criminality, including fighting and arrests while intoxicated. In another study of alcoholic families, each of which had two alcoholic brothers, Hill (1992) replicated Cloninger et al.'s typology and also described a third type of heritable alcoholism. This type was similar to the Type 2 of Cloninger et al. but had no paternal sociopathy. Hill's subject sample was drawn from largely intact, higher socioeconomic status families that had, because of the requirement that two alcoholic brothers be present, very high genetic loading for alcoholism. Such sample characteristics may have favored the detection of this third group.

Personality traits have been hypothesized to account for the heritability of these two types of alcoholism (Cloninger 1987). Type 1 alcoholics are low in novelty seeking and high in harm avoidance and reward dependence.[1] Type 2 alcoholics have personality traits that include high degrees of novelty seeking and low degrees of harm avoidance and reward dependence. Cloninger (1987) also proposed that differences in brain neurotransmitter systems account for these alcoholism-associated personality traits. Dopaminergic stimulation is proposed to mediate novelty seeking. Enhanced dopaminergic stimulation was believed to occur following alcohol consumption by Type 2 alcoholics and is perceived as novel and highly pleasurable. Type 2 alcoholics spontaneously seek dopaminergic stimulants such as alcohol beginning at an early age and maintain this novelty-associated pleasure by drinking heavily when alcohol is accessible. Serotonergic (5-HT) stimulation is proposed to mediate harm avoidance. The high basal levels of 5-HT activity postulated in Type 1 alcoholics would inhibit them from drinking heavily during a given drinking period primarily because it increased their perceived risk of acute injury or violence following heavy drinking. High 5-HT activity would, however, permit Type 1 alcoholics to slowly develop psychologic dependence on alcohol because low doses of alcohol release 5-HT and exert an anxiolytic effect. Conversely, the very low levels of 5-HT activity postulated for Type 2 alcoholics would serve to lessen their perception of heavy drinking as a risky behavior, permitting them to consume large quantities of alcohol per drinking episode. Finally, noradrenergic stimulation is proposed to mediate reward dependence. Type 1 alcoholics are believed to have low basal rates of noradrenergic stimulation and may thus be strongly dependent on external rewards to maintain many appetitive behaviors. In the absence of external rewards, such alcoholic individuals may appear depressed. This type of alcoholic individual is, however, believed to display exaggerated noradrenergic responses to alcohol. This noradrenergic response would thereby lessen the ability of Type 1 alcoholics to attenuate their drinking despite the gradual devel-

---

[1] Cloninger (1987, pp. 413–414) defines novelty seeking as "a heritable tendency toward frequent exploratory activity and intense exhilaration in response to novel or appetitive stimuli." Harm avoidance is "a heritable tendency to respond intensely to aversive stimuli and their conditioned signals, thereby facilitating learning to inhibit behavior in order to avoid punishment, novelty, and frustrative omission of expected rewards." Reward dependence is believed to "involve variation in behavioral maintenance or resistance to extinction of previously rewarded behavior."

opment of adverse physical and psychologic consequences of their chronic alcohol consumption.

In support of these hypothesized neurochemical abnormalities, several groups have reported findings suggesting that there is a subgroup of alcoholic individuals who have altered central 5-HT function. Early-onset alcoholic individuals with histories of violence have been found to have a low plasma ratio of the serotonin precursor tryptophan to other neutral amino acids (Buydens-Branchey et al. 1989b). Impulsive, violent alcoholic individuals have been found to have low levels of the serotonin metabolite 5-hydroxyindole acetic acid in their cerebrospinal fluid (CSF; Linnoila et al. 1989). In a study by George et al. (1992), early-onset alcoholic individuals were more likely than late-onset alcoholic individuals to report feeling an alcohol-like "high" or have an urge to drink after administration of the 5-HT agonist *m*-chlorophenylpiperazine. Self-reported aggressiveness and impulsivity increased after administration of the indirect 5-HT agonist fenfluramine to a group of impulsively violent polysubstance-abusing subjects, many of whom were alcoholic (Fishbein et al. 1989). Taken together, these findings are consistent with (but do not prove) Cloninger's (1987) hypothesis that Type 2 alcoholics have low levels of central serotonergic activity. If true, this hypothesis implies that serotonergic medications may reduce drinking in at least some groups of alcoholic individuals. Indeed, in placebo-controlled studies that combined coping skills and pharmacotherapeutic treatments for abstinent alcoholic subjects, the serotonergic agents buspirone and fluoxetine reduced posttreatment alcohol consumption (Kranzler 1991a, 1991b).

The Cloninger et al. typology shows greatest promise in accounting for differences in the pattern of inheritance of alcoholism (Gilligan et al. 1988). It also predicts posttreatment outcome: treated alcoholic individuals classified as Type 2 have lower frequencies of abstinence and social drinking during two decades after an index treatment episode than did Type 1 alcoholics (Nordstrom and Berglund 1987).

Zucker's (1987) fourfold alcoholism typology, based primarily on a synthesis of the alcoholism natural history literature, is also consistent with Cloninger's typology. In Zucker's construct, antisocial alcoholism is characterized as having a genetic basis, with early onset of alcohol problems and antisocial activity. It occurs more frequently in men and carries a poor prognosis. Developmentally cumulative

alcoholism occurs in both men and women, evolving as a cumulative extension of adolescent problem drinking and delinquency. Environmental features are more prominent in modulating genetic predisposition here than in antisocial alcoholism, and familial aggression is less prominent. Developmentally limited alcoholism, typified by frequent heavy drinking at times of increased autonomy during early adulthood, infrequently results in treatment entry and tends to remit to social drinking following successful adjustment to adult family and career roles. Finally, negative-affect alcoholism occurs primarily in women with a family history of depression. They drink alcohol heavily to enhance relationships and modulate their affect.

A central observation in the Cloninger et al. classification is that Type 2 alcoholics have an early age at onset of alcohol problems. A growing body of research supports the conclusion that an early age at onset of heavy drinking or alcohol problems identifies a clinically important subgroup of alcoholic individuals. Swedish investigators (A.-L. von Knorring et al. 1985) found at least two modal ages at onset of subjective alcohol problems in a clinical population of treated alcoholic and ex-alcoholic men. They divided the subjects into a group with onset before age 25, whom they labeled *Type II alcoholics*, and a group with onset after age 25, whom they labeled *Type I alcoholics*. Type II alcoholics had greater rates of aggressiveness, criminality, drug abuse, and familial alcoholism than did Type I alcoholics. They were also more extroverted and scored higher on measures of impulsivity and thrill and adventure seeking. They had more severe anxiety and guilt and scored significantly lower on measures of platelet monoamine oxidase activity (A.-L. von Knorring et al. 1985; L. von Knorring et al. 1985, 1987). Similar groups were reported among alcoholic women (Glenn and Nixon 1991). Among a group of 171 alcoholic men, a history of alcohol problems prior to age 25 was superior to Cloninger et al.'s Type 1/Type 2 features in discriminating alcoholic individuals with early criminality, drug use and associated problems, and high alcohol problem severity (Irwin et al. 1990).

Using slightly different onset criteria (i.e., heavy drinking prior to or after age 20), Buydens-Branchey et al. (1989a) found that early-onset alcoholic men in treatment had greater rates of depression, suicide attempts, and violent crimes than did late-onset alcoholic men. These early-onset alcoholic subjects also reported greater rates of paternal alcoholism than did late-onset alcoholic subjects. Another group reported that early-onset alcoholic subjects had greater lifetime rates of ASPD, drug abuse, bipolar disorder, suicide attempts, and panic disorder, as well as greater rates of paternal alcoholism than did a group of late-onset alcoholic subjects (Roy et al. 1991). In addition, early-onset alcoholic men in this study had lower CSF levels of diazepam-binding inhibitor and somatostatin than did late-onset alcoholic men; however, neither group differed significantly in these measures from a group of normal control subjects. The significance of these CSF peptide findings is therefore unclear and awaits replication.

One element common to these various typologies associated with an early age at onset of alcoholism is the presence of sociopathic personality traits. Indeed, the psychiatric disorder most consistently identified as a risk factor for both alcoholism and drug abuse is ASPD. Although ASPD is not found in all addicted or alcoholic individuals, among men it is one of the most prevalent associated psychiatric disorders. Frequencies of ASPD reported in alcoholic samples have ranged from 16% to 49%, and somewhat higher rates have been detected among opioid and other drug abuse populations. The frequency of occurrence of ASPD varies depending on the type of sample and the diagnostic criteria used (M. N. Hesselbrock et al. 1985; Rounsaville et al. 1983). The DSM-III and DSM-III-R criteria for ASPD are fairly broad and may result in higher prevalence rates of this disorder in alcoholic patients than have been previously reported. In the DSM-III and DSM-III-R diagnostic systems, an ASPD diagnosis requires antisocial behaviors occurring prior to age 15 years. These ASPD criteria are based in large measure on the longitudinal data of Robins (1966), who found that antisocial behaviors among boys seen at a child guidance clinic tended to predict subsequent adult antisocial behavior as well as drug abuse and alcoholism. Jessor and Jessor (1975) noted that adolescents who later became problem drinkers tended to be more assertive, extroverted, rebellious, and impulsive in childhood. Epidemiologic data suggest that sociopathy is most clearly a risk factor for development of alcoholism and drug abuse in those societies and subcultures where substance use is not normative (Robins 1978). Helzer et al. (1990), for example, found that ASPD was 75 times more likely to occur in alcoholic than in nonalcoholic Taiwanese.

The combination of ASPD and alcoholism may

represent one subtype of addictive disorder with major implications for research, prevention, and treatment. M. N. Hesselbrock et al. (1984, 1985) found that the presence of ASPD in alcoholic subjects affected the age at onset, course, and symptoms of their alcoholism. Both men and women with ASPD began drinking at a much earlier age, progressed to regular drinking at a much earlier age, and progressed from regular drinking to alcoholism much faster than did subjects without ASPD. They also reported substantially greater psychosocial disability symptoms in the ASPD alcoholic subjects. More than any other psychiatric diagnosis, ASPD had a significant adverse effect on the pretreatment course of alcoholism. Penick et al. (1978) and Babor et al. (1974) found a similarly poor course of alcoholism in subjects with ASPD in the United States and France, respectively.

Sociopathic alcoholic individuals have disproportionately high rates of attrition from alcoholism treatment (Mandell 1981) and have been reported to have worse posttreatment outcomes than nonsociopathic alcoholic individuals (Caster and Parsons 1977; Rounsaville et al. 1987; Schuckit 1985). Similar results have been found among sociopathic opioid-addicted individuals (Rounsaville et al. 1986; Woody et al. 1985).

In substance abuse treatment programs, sociopathic substance-abusing individuals are typically impulsive, slow to anticipate the reactions of others, and slow to learn from experience. They are interpersonally insensitive and lack trust in others, particularly in matters requiring a substantial degree of intimacy. Clinical wisdom suggests that such patients would fare better in substance abuse treatments that are highly structured and not heavily dependent on the development of insight or group affiliation. Treatments that foster the development of social skills, particularly skills relevant to management of impulsive drinking urges, anger, and anxiety, should be particularly useful to sociopathic substance-abusing individuals. Sociopathic substance-abusing individuals who are less sociopathic, conversely, are expected to find greater success in treatments that foster group cohesiveness and shared insight. This type of individual may find treatments employing structured social skills training irrelevant to their needs and unduly limiting in scope. Recent studies of clinical alcoholism treatment support these predictions. Drinking outcomes following alcoholism treatment were superior among sociopathic alcoholic subjects randomized to receive group coping skills treatment, whereas alcoholic subjects low on measures of sociopathy had superior outcomes when randomized to receive group interactional therapy (Cooney et al. 1991; Kadden et al. 1989). Studies of psychologic treatment of drug-addicted subjects have also supported these predictions. Methadone-maintained opioid-addicted subjects with ASPD had a poor outcome after insight-oriented psychotherapy (Woody et al. 1985), although outcomes improved when both the patient and therapist perceived trust and a good working alliance (Gerstley et al. 1989). Among methadone-maintained opioid-addicted subjects with ASPD, those who also had a lifetime history of major depression had somewhat better outcomes following treatment with insight-oriented psychotherapy (Woody et al. 1984). Studies comparing insight-oriented or interpersonal therapies with cognitive-behavioral therapies among sociopathic and nonsociopathic drug-abusing individuals have not been reported.

Among substance-abusing individuals with ASPD, subtypes of ASPD have also been proposed (Alterman and Cacciola 1991). Hare and colleagues (Harpur et al. 1989) have suggested two types of ASPD, the first based on psychopathic personality factors (e.g., lack of remorse, aggression) and a second based on antisocial life-style or environmental factors (e.g., drug dealing). A history of aggressive behaviors, especially in childhood, may identify a subgroup of individuals with ASPD who are at higher risk for developing substance use disorders (V. M. Hesselbrock et al. 1992). Among alcoholic individuals, anger and aggression when drinking were accounted for by histories of childhood aggression but not by the presence of ASPD alone (Jaffe et al. 1988). Among ASPD alcoholic individuals, violent behavior in childhood was a strong predictor of violent adult behavior (Buydens-Branchey et al. 1989a). At present, however, the significance of aggression as a modulator of the effect of ASPD on substance-abusing individuals is not completely understood.

## ▼ STATISTICAL APPROACHES TO CLASSIFICATION OF SUBTYPES

Instead of using unidimensional a priori approaches or genetic/developmental approaches, some investi-gators have separated substance-abusing individuals into different groups on the basis of a posteriori statistical analysis of data obtained from patients in substance abuse treatment programs (Skinner 1982). Typically, a group of substance-abusing subjects are first administered a comprehensive assessment battery. Empiric groupings of substance-abusing subjects are then generated by applying multivariate procedures such as cluster analysis to the assessment scores. In such cluster analyses, subjects are initially divided based on their differences from (and similarities to) the subject group mean scores; the process continues by iteration until a minimum number of subject clusters is found. Individuals within each cluster are more similar to each other than they are to individuals in other clusters. Although clustering procedures do produce different and relatively homogeneous groups, they do not ensure that all subjects assigned to one cluster manifest similar scores on all of the assessed attributes.

Researchers employing a cluster analysis have most often grouped alcoholic subjects by measures of personality, typically using MMPI scores. Goldstein and Linden (1969), for example, divided 513 alcoholic men into neurotic (depressive/anxiety) and personality disorder (psychopathic) groups based on cluster analysis of MMPI data. O'Leary et al. (1979) and Morey and Blashfield (1981) reviewed various studies that used cluster analysis of MMPI data to categorize alcoholic patients. They found consistent support for the existence of one or more subtypes scoring high on psychopathic personality, a second and distinct passive-dependent personality type, and a third more depressed-anxious group. Because these study subjects were disproportionately middle-age men recruited from state hospital and VA hospital treatment settings, the results lack generalizability to other settings.

Morey et al. (1984) performed a cluster analysis on a heterogeneous population of 725 treatment-seeking urban drinkers who completed an assessment of their alcohol history, alcohol-associated problems, and other drug use– and drinking-related measures. Three clusters of subjects were identified, labeled *early-stage problem drinkers, affiliative dependent drinkers,* and *schizoid dependent drinkers.* Early-stage problem drinkers had the lowest levels of psychologic disturbance and aggression, the highest levels of social stability, and the most defensive response style. Affiliative dependent drinkers were more likely to drink on a daily basis, be socially oriented, and have moderate dependence severity. Schizoid dependent drinkers were socially isolated, drank in binges, had the highest levels of aggression and impulsivity, and had severe alcohol dependence. Roberts and Morey (1985) derived a similar three-cluster typology using similar assessment instruments in a population of 334 VA patients. Differences in the treatment response or posttreatment course of individuals in these three clusters have not been reported.

Cluster analysis was used to analyze multidimensional baseline data from the University of Connecticut sample of 321 alcoholic men and women described previously. Babor et al. (1992a) identified two types of alcoholic individuals who differed consistently on 17 defining characteristics. The first group, labeled *Type A alcoholics,* had fewer childhood risk factors for alcoholism, later onset of problem drinking, fewer alcohol-related problems, less sociopathy and other psychopathology, and less severe alcohol dependence. *Type B alcoholics,* in contrast, had more childhood risk factors, earlier onset, more sociopathy and other psychopathology, more alcohol-related problems, and more severe dependence. By use of outcomes measured prospectively at 12 and 36 months after treatment, Type A alcoholics experienced longer intervals prior to returning to heavy drinking, had less distress, and used illicit drugs less often than did Type B alcoholics.

A strength of this A/B typologic formulation is its potential to improve drinking outcomes by matching patient types with different treatment modalities. Litt et al. (1992) found that this typology could be applied to patients enrolled in a randomized trial comparing coping skills and interactional group treatments following inpatient alcoholism rehabilitation. Although *neither* the patient type nor the therapy type predicted the rate of abstinence, number of heavy drinking days, or presence of alcohol-related problems in an 18-month, posttreatment follow-up period, the *match* of patient type and therapy type did predict these three outcome measures. When these drinking outcomes were measured during the 2 years after treatment, Type A alcoholics fared better with interactional treatment and more poorly with coping skills treatment. An opposite effect was noted with Type B alcoholics, who had superior outcomes following coping skills treatment and inferior outcomes following interactional treatment. In this typology, sociopathy contributed strongly to subtype membership. Indeed,

sociopathy alone predicted drinking outcomes as well as the more complex A/B typology.

## ▼ CONCLUSIONS

How many different types of alcoholism or drug abuse are there? To answer this question, we need to consider two central aspects of typologic research: the sample studied and the characteristics employed in assessing the sample. Ideally, typologic studies include a large, representative sample. In samples drawn from patients in treatment, one would predict greater dependence severity, a history of prior treatment episodes, and greater prevalence of comorbid psychopathology than in community samples (Berkson 1946). Many of the treatment samples that have been studied were drawn from substance abuse treatment programs in VA hospitals. It is unclear whether substance-abusing women will fall into these typologies.

Despite these caveats, there is a remarkable similarity between the typologies developed from assessment of treatment-seeking alcoholic patients and the subtypes derived from family/genetic study assessments. This is particularly true for early-onset alcoholism. These individuals frequently have coexisting psychiatric problems, such as impulsivity, aggressive tendencies, criminality, and other antisocial behaviors. Jellinek's gamma, Cloninger et al.'s Type 2, von Knorring et al.'s Type II, Zucker's antisocial, and Babor et al.'s Type B alcoholic individuals display many of these characteristics. This alcoholism type has a severe course and is poorly responsive to many traditional alcoholism treatments but may be more responsive to structured cognitive-behavioral treatment, which emphasizes social skills and concrete strategies for coping with alcohol urges, negative affects, and boredom during abstinence. Preliminary evidence suggests a role for serotonergic medications in treating this group of alcoholic individuals.

A more heterogeneous group of alcoholic subjects is described by Jellinek's delta alcoholics, Morey et al.'s affiliative dependent drinkers, Cloninger et al.'s Type 1, von Knorring et al.'s Type I, Zucker's developmentally cumulative, and Babor et al.'s Type A alcoholic individuals. Affective and anxiety disorders are often comorbid conditions, and pharmacologic treatments of primary psychiatric disorders may reduce both psychiatric symptoms and drinking behavior. This alcoholic "type" appears to respond better to psychologic treatments that foster self-reflection and group cohesiveness.

Finally, there is a group of problem drinkers whose drinking problems are relatively mild and occur primarily during young adulthood. Such socially stable problem drinkers have minimal coexisting psychopathology but are often ambivalent and defensive about altering their drinking habits. These features are found in Morey et al.'s early-stage problem drinkers and Zucker's developmentally limited alcoholism type. For such drinkers, use of brief counseling techniques such as motivational interviewing (Miller and Rollnick 1991) appear particularly useful in mobilizing the patient's ambivalence, negotiating reduced levels of alcohol intake or abstinence, and providing feedback and encouragement to reduce drinking so as to achieve other more productive tasks. For motivated early-stage problem drinkers, prophylactic and targeted use of short-acting antidipsotropic medications, such as calcium carbimide prior to occasions when heavy drinking is anticipated, may facilitate a reduction in alcohol intake (Annis and Peachey 1992).

A significant advance in the development of modern medicine was the discovery by Robert Koch of a system for obtaining pure cultures of bacteria. Using this method, microbiologists gained valuable insight into the heritable factors and growth conditions that confer virulence. Effective strategies for primary prevention of infection, identification of host conditions favorable to infection and contagion, and treatment of infected individuals also flowed from this discovery. In characterizing individuals with substance use disorders, use of methods that identify relatively pure subtypes of individuals with alcohol and/or drug problems may provide a similar impetus to understanding the development and phenomenology of substance use disorders and to developing more effective prevention and treatment strategies, including potential pharmacotherapies.

## ▼ REFERENCES

Alterman AI, Cacciola JS: The antisocial personality disorder diagnosis in substance abusers: problems and issues. J Nerv Ment Dis 179:401–409, 1991

American Psychiatric Association: Diagnostic and Statistical Manual of Mental Disorders, 3rd Edition. Washington, DC, American Psychiatric Association, 1980

American Psychiatric Association: Diagnostic and Statistical Manual of Mental Disorders, 3rd Edition, Revised. Washington, DC, American Psychiatric Association, 1987

American Psychiatric Association: Diagnostic and Statistical Manual of Mental Disorders, 4th Edition. Washington, DC, American Psychiatric Association, 1994

Annis HM, Peachey JE: The use of calcium carbimide in relapse prevention counselling: results of a randomized controlled trial. British Journal of Addiction 87:63–72, 1992

Babor TF, Dolinsky ZS: Alcoholic typologies: historical evolution and empirical evaluation of some common classification schemes, in Alcoholism: Origins and Outcome. Edited by Rose RM, Barrett J. New York, Raven, 1988, pp 245–266

Babor TF, Lauerman R: Classification and forms of inebriety: historical antecedents of alcoholic typologies, in Recent Developments in Alcoholism, Vol 5. Edited by Galanter M. New York, Plenum, 1986, pp 113–114

Babor TF, McCabe T, Mansanes P, et al: Patterns of alcoholism in France and America: a comparative study, in Alcoholism: A Multilevel Problem. Edited by Chafetz ME. Washington, DC, National Institute on Alcohol Abuse and Alcoholism, 1974, pp 113–128

Babor TF, Cooney NL, Lauerman R: The dependence syndrome concept as a psychological theory of relapse behaviour: an empirical evaluation of alcoholic and opiate addicts. British Journal of Addiction 82:393–405, 1987

Babor TF, Hoffman M, DelBoca FK, et al: Types of alcoholics; I: evidence for an empirically derived typology based on indicators of vulnerability and severity. Arch Gen Psychiatry 49:599–608, 1992a

Babor TF, Dolinsky ZS, Meyer RE, et al: Types of alcoholics: concurrent and predictive validity of some common classification schemes. British Journal of Addiction 87:1415–1431, 1992b

Berkson J: Limitations of the application of four-fold tables to hospital data. Biometric Bulletin 2:47–53, 1946

Bowman KM, Jellinek EM: Alcohol addiction and its treatment. Quarterly Journal of Studies on Alcohol 2:98–176, 1941

Buydens-Branchey L, Branchey MJ, Noumair D: Age

of alcoholism onset; I: relationship to psychopathology. Arch Gen Psychiatry 46:225–230, 1989a

Buydens-Branchey L, Branchey MJ, Noumair D, et al: Age of alcoholism onset; II: relationship to susceptibility to serotonin precursor availability. Arch Gen Psychiatry 46:231–236, 1989b

Cadoret RJ, O'Gorman TW, Troughton E, et al: Alcoholism and antisocial personality: interrelationships, genetic and environmental factors. Arch Gen Psychiatry 42:161–167, 1985

Cahalan D, Cisin IH, Crossley H: American Drinking Practices. New Brunswick, NJ, Rutgers Center for Alcohol Studies, 1969

Carlin AS, Stauss FF: Two typologies of polydrug abusers, in Polydrug Abuse: The Results of a National Collaborative Study. Edited by Wesson DR, Carlin AS, Adams KM, et al. New York, Academic Press, 1978, pp 97–127

Caster DV, Parsons OA: Relationship of depression, sociopathy, and locus of control to treatment outcome in alcoholics. J Consult Clin Psychol 45:751–756, 1977

Chick J: Alcohol dependence: methodological issues in its measurement: reliability of the criteria. British Journal of Addiction 75:175–186, 1980

Cloninger CR: Neurogenetic adaptive mechanisms in alcoholism. Science 236:410–416, 1987

Cloninger CR, Sigvardsson S, Bohman M: Childhood personality predicts alcohol abuse in young adults. Alcohol Clin Exp Res 12:494–505, 1988

Cloninger CR, Dinwiddie SH, Reich T: Epidemiology and genetics of alcoholism, in American Psychiatric Press Review of Psychiatry, Vol 8. Edited by Tasman A, Hales RE, Frances AJ. Washington, DC, American Psychiatric Press, 1989, pp 293–308

Conley JJ: An MMPI typology of male alcoholics: admission, discharge, and outcome comparison. J Pers Assess 45:33–39, 1981

Cooney NL, Kadden RM, Litt MD, et al: Matching alcoholics to coping skills or interactional therapies: two-year follow-up results. J Consult Clin Psychol 59:598–601, 1991

Eckhardt M: Central nervous system impairment in the alcoholic: a research and clinical perspective, in Evaluation of the Alcoholic: Implications for Research, Theory, and Treatment (NIAAA Monogr No 5). Edited by Meyer RE, Babor TF, Glueck BC, et al. Rockville, MD, Alcohol, Drug Abuse, and Mental Health Administration, 1981, pp 349–368

Edwards G, Gross MM: Alcohol dependence: provisional description of a clinical syndrome. BMJ 1:1058–1061, 1976

Finney JW, Moos RH: Matching patient with treatments: conceptual and methodological issues. J Stud Alcohol 47:122–134, 1986

Fishbein DH, Lozovsky D, Jaffe JH: Impulsivity, aggression, and neuroendocrine responses to serotonergic stimulation in substance abusers. Biol Psychiatry 25:1049–1066, 1989

George DT, Wozniak K, Linnoila M: Basic and clinical studies on serotonin, alcohol, and alcoholism, in Novel Pharmacological Interventions for Alcoholism. Edited by Naranjo CA, Sellers EM. New York, Springer-Verlag New York, 1992, pp 92–104

Gerstley L, McLellan AT, Alterman AI, et al: Ability to form an alliance with the therapist: a possible marker of prognosis for patients with antisocial personality disorder. Am J Psychiatry 146:508–512, 1989

Gilligan SB, Reich T, Cloninger CR: Alcohol-related symptoms in heterogeneous families of hospitalized alcoholics. Alcohol Clin Exp Res 12:671–678, 1988

Glenn SW, Nixon SJ: Applications of Cloninger's subtypes in a female alcoholic sample. Alcohol Clin Exp Res 15:851–857, 1991

Goldstein SG, Linden JD: Multivariate classification of alcoholics by means of the MMPI. J Abnorm Psychol 74:661–669, 1969

Harpur TJ, Hare RD, Hakstian AR: Two-factor conceptualization of psychopathy: construct validity and assessment implications. Psychological Assessment 1:6–17, 1989

Helzer JE, Canino GJ, Yeh E-K, et al: Alcoholism—North America and Asia. Arch Gen Psychiatry 47:313–319, 1990

Hesselbrock MN: Alcoholic typologies: a review of empirical evaluations of common classification schemes, in Recent Developments in Alcoholism, Vol 5. Edited by Galanter M. New York, Plenum, 1986, pp 191–206

Hesselbrock VM, Stabenau JR, Hesselbrock MN, et al: The nature of alcoholism in patients with different family histories for alcoholism. Prog Neuropsychopharmacol Biol Psychiatry 6:607–614, 1982

Hesselbrock MN, Hesselbrock VM, Babor TF, et al: Antisocial behavior, psychopathology and problem drinking in the natural history of alcoholism, in Longitudinal Research in Alcoholism. Edited by Goodwin DW, VanDusen KT, Mednick SA. Boston,

Kluwer-Nijhoff, 1984, pp 197–214

Hesselbrock MN, Meyer RE, Keener JJ: Psychopathology in hospitalized alcoholics. Arch Gen Psychiatry 42:1050–1055, 1985

Hesselbrock VM, Meyer RE, Hesselbrock MN: Psychopathology and addictive disorders: the specific case of antisocial personality disorder, in Addictive States. Edited by O'Brien CP, Jaffe JH. New York, Raven, 1992, pp 179–191

Hill SY: Absence of paternal sociopathy in the etiology of severe alcoholism: is there a Type III alcoholism? J Stud Alcohol 53:161–169, 1992

Hodgson RJ, Rankin JJ, Stockwell TR: Alcohol dependence and the priming effect. Behav Res Ther 17:379–387, 1979

Institute of Medicine: Broadening the Base of Treatment for Alcohol Problems. Washington, DC, National Academy Press, 1990

Irwin M, Schuckit M, Smith TL: Clinical importance of age at onset in type 1 and type 2 primary alcoholics. Arch Gen Psychiatry 47:320–324, 1990

Jaffe JH, Babor TF, Fishbein DH: Alcoholics, aggression and antisocial personality. J Stud Alcohol 49:211–218, 1988

Jellinek EM: Alcoholism: a genus and some of its species. Can Med Assoc J 83:1341–1345, 1960

Jessor R, Jessor SL: Adolescent development and the onset of drinking: a longitudinal study. J Stud Alcohol 36:27–51, 1975

Kadden RM, Cooney NL, Getter H, et al: Matching alcoholics to coping skills or interactional therapies: posttreatment results. J Consult Clin Psychol 57:698–704, 1989

Kaplan RF, Meyer RE, Stroebel CF: Alcohol dependence and responsivity to an ethanol stimulus as predictors of alcohol consumption. British Journal of Addiction 78:259–267, 1983

Kosten TR, Rounsaville BJ, Babor TF, et al: Substance use disorders in DSM-III-R: evidence for the dependence syndrome across different psychoactive substances. Br J Psychiatry 151:834–843, 1987

Kranzler HR: A placebo-controlled of buspirone in anxious alcoholics. Paper presented at the annual meeting of the Research Society on Alcoholism, Marco Island, FL, June 9–13, 1991a

Kranzler HR: Fluoxetine as an adjunct to relapse prevention treatment in alcoholics. Paper presented at the annual meeting of the American College of Neuropsychopharmacology, San Juan, PR, December 12–14, 1991b

Linnoila M, DeJong J, Virkkunen M: Family history of alcoholism in violent offenders and impulsive fire setters. Arch Gen Psychiatry 46:613–616, 1989

Litt MD, Babor TF, DelBoca FK, et al: Types of alcoholics: application of an empirically derived typology to treatment matching. Arch Gen Psychiatry 49:609–614, 1992

Malow RB, Pintard PF, Sutker PB, et al: Psychopathology subtypes: drug use motives and patterns. Psychology of Addictive Behaviors 2:1–13, 1988

Mandell W: Sociopathic alcoholics: matching treatment and patients, in Matching Patient Needs and Treatment Methods in Alcoholism and Drug Abuse. Edited by Gottheil E, McLellan AT, Druley KA. Springfield, IL, Charles C Thomas, 1981, pp 325–369

Mason BJ, Kocsis JH: Desipramine treatment of alcoholism. Psychopharmacol Bull 27:155–161, 1991

McGrath PJ, Nunes E, Quitkin FM: Imipramine in alcoholics with primary depression. Paper presented at the annual meeting of the American Psychiatric Association, Washington, DC, May 2–7, 1992

McLellan AT, Luborsky L, Woody GE, et al: Predicting response to alcohol and drug abuse treatments: role of psychiatric severity. Arch Gen Psychiatry 40:620–625, 1983a

McLellan AT, Woody GE, Luborsky L, et al: Increased effectiveness of substance abuse treatment: a prospective study of patient-treatment "matching." J Nerv Ment Dis 171:597–605, 1983b

Mendelson JH, Mello NK: Experimental analysis of drinking behavior of chronic alcoholics. Ann N Y Acad Sci 133:828–845, 1966

Meyer R: Typologies, in Treatments of Psychiatric Disorders: A Task Force Report of the American Psychiatric Association, Vol 2. Washington, DC, American Psychiatric Association, 1989, pp 1065–1071

Miller WR, Rollnick S: Motivational Interviewing: Preparing People to Change Addictive Behavior. New York, Guilford, 1991

Morey LC, Blashfield RK: Empirical classifications of alcoholism. J Stud Alcohol 42:925–937, 1981

Morey LC, Skinner HA, Blashfield RK: A typology of alcohol abusers: correlates and implications. J Abnorm Psychol 93:408–417, 1984

Nathan PE, Titler NA, Lowenstein LM, et al: Behavioral analysis of chronic alcoholism: interaction of alcohol and human contact. Arch Gen Psychiatry 22:419–430, 1970

Nerviano VJ, Gross HW: Personality types of alcoholics on objective inventories. J Stud Alcohol 44:837–851, 1983

Nordstrom G, Berglund M: Type 1 and Type 2 alcoholics (Cloninger and Bohman) have different patterns of successful long-term adjustment. British Journal of Addiction 82:761–769, 1987

O'Leary M, Donovan DM, Chaney EF, et al: Cognitive impairment and treatment outcome with alcoholics: preliminary findings. J Clin Psychiatry 40:397–398, 1979

Penick E, Reed MR, Crawley PA, et al: Differentiation of alcoholics by family history. J Stud Alcohol 39:19–44, 1978

Polich JM, Armor DJ, Braiker HB: The Course of Alcoholism: Four Years After Treatment. Santa Monica, CA, Rand Corporation, 1980

Rimmer J, Pitts F, Reich T, et al: Alcoholism; II: sex, socioeconomic status and race in two hospitalized samples. Quarterly Journal of Studies on Alcohol 32:942–952, 1971

Roberts WR, Morey LC: Convergent validation of a typology of alcohol abusers. Bulletin of the Society of Psychologists in Addictive Behaviors 4:226–233, 1985

Robins LN: Deviant Children Grown Up: A Sociologic and Psychiatric Study of the Sociopathic Personality. Baltimore, MD, Williams & Wilkins, 1966

Robins LN: Sturdy childhood predictors of adult antisocial behavior: replication from longitudinal studies. Psychol Med 8:611–622, 1978

Ross HE, Glaser FB, Germanson T: The prevalence of psychiatric disorders in patients with alcohol and other drug problems. Arch Gen Psychiatry 45:1023–1031, 1988

Rounsaville BJ, Weissman MM, Kleber HD, et al: Heterogeneity of psychiatric diagnosis in treated opiate addicts. Arch Gen Psychiatry 39:161–166, 1982

Rounsaville BJ, Eyre SL, Weissman MM, et al: The antisocial opiate addict. Adv Alcohol Subst Abuse 2:29–42, 1983

Rounsaville BJ, Kosten TR, Weissman MM, et al: Prognostic significance of psychopathology in treated opiate addicts: a 2.5-year follow-up study. Arch Gen Psychiatry 43:739–745, 1986

Rounsaville BJ, Dolinsky ZS, Babor TF, et al: Psychopathology as a predictor of treatment outcome in alcoholics. Arch Gen Psychiatry 44:505–513, 1987

Rounsaville BJ, Anton SF, Carroll K, et al: Psychiatric diagnoses of treatment-seeking cocaine abusers. Arch Gen Psychiatry 48:43–51, 1991

Roy A, DeJong J, Lamparski D, et al: Mental disorders among alcoholics: relationship to age of onset and cerebrospinal fluid neuropeptides. Arch Gen Psychiatry 48:423–427, 1991

Schuckit MA: Alcoholism: two types of alcoholism in women. Arch Environ Health 20:301–306, 1969

Schuckit MA: The clinical implications of primary diagnostic groups among alcoholics. Arch Gen Psychiatry 42:1043–1049, 1985

Schuckit MA, Winokur G: A short-term follow-up of women alcoholics. Diseases of the Nervous System 33:672–678, 1972

Shelly CH, Goldstein G: An empirically derived typology of hospitalized alcoholics, in Empirical Studies of Alcoholism. Edited by Goldstein D, Heuringer CC. New York, Ballinger, 1976, pp 243–262

Skinner HA: Factor analysis and studies on alcohol: a methodological review. J Stud Alcohol 41:1091–1101, 1980

Skinner HA: Different strokes for different folks: differential treatment for alcohol abuse, in Evaluation of the Alcoholic: Implications for Research, Theory, and Treatment (NIAAA Monogr No 5). Edited by Meyer RE, Babor TF, Glueck BC, et al. Rockville, MD, Alcohol, Drug Abuse, and Mental Health Administration, 1981, pp 349–368

Skinner HA: Statistical approaches to the classification of alcohol and drug addiction. British Journal of Addiction 77:259–273, 1982

Skinner HA, Allen BA: Alcohol dependence syndrome: measurement and validation. J Abnorm Psychol 91:199–209, 1982

Stockwell T, Hodgson R, Edwards G, et al: The development of a questionnaire to measure severity of alcohol dependence. British Journal of Addiction 74:79–87, 1979

Tarter RE, McBride H, Buonpane N, et al: Differentiation of alcoholics: childhood history of minimal brain dysfunction, family history and drinking pattern. Arch Gen Psychiatry 34:761–768, 1977

Vaillant G: The Natural History of Alcoholism. Cambridge, MA, Harvard University Press, 1983

von Knorring A-L, Bohman M, von Knorring L: Platelet MAO-activity as a biological marker in subgroups of alcoholism. Acta Psychiatr Scand 72:51–58, 1985

von Knorring L, Palm V, Andersson HE: Relationship between treatment outcome and subtype of alcoholism in men. J Stud Alcohol 46:388–391, 1985 von Knorring L, von Knorring A-L, Smigan L, et al: Personality traits in subtypes of alcoholics. J Stud Alcohol 48:523–527, 1987

Walton HJ, Ritson EB, Kennedy RI: Response of alcoholics to clinic treatment. BMJ 2:1171–1174, 1966

Weiss RD, Mirin SM, Michael JL, et al: Psychopathology in chronic cocaine abusers. Am J Drug Alcohol Abuse 12:17–29, 1986

Winokur G, Rimmer J, Reich T: Alcoholism; IV: is there more than one type of alcoholism? Br J Psychiatry 118:525–531, 1971

Woody GE, McLellan AT, Luborsky L, et al: Severity of psychiatric symptoms as a predictor of benefits from psychotherapy: the VA-Penn study. Am J Psychiatry 141:1172–1177, 1984

Woody GE, McLellan AT, Luborsky L, et al: Sociopathy and psychotherapy outcome. Arch Gen Psychiatry 42:1081–1086, 1985

World Health Organization: Mental and behavioural disorders, in International Statistical Classification of Diseases and Related Health Problems, 10th Revision. World Health Organization, Geneva, 1992, pp 311–387

Zucker RA: The four alcoholisms: a developmental account of the etiologic process, in Alcohol and Addictive Behavior. Edited by Rivers PC. Lincoln, University of Nebraska Press, 1987, pp 27–83

# ssessment of the Patient

*Richard Steven Schottenfeld, M.D.*

The primary goal of the substance abuse clinical evaluation is to make an accurate diagnostic assessment of substance abuse or dependence and the relationship of substance use to other psychiatric and medical disorders. The diagnostic assessment is then used to plan and initiate effective interventions and treatment where indicated.

The clinical assessment of substance use, abuse, and dependence should be considered a routine part of all psychiatric or medical evaluations. The rates of substance use disorders vary depending on sociodemographic factors (i.e., age, social class, race or ethnicity, occupation, and sex), with, for example, higher rates more often found in men than women. However, limiting assessment only to patients whose sociodemographic status leads to an initial high level of suspicion for substance use will lead to failure to detect clinically significant substance use disorders in many patients (Cyr and Wartman 1988). Several studies have documented that overall rates of routine detection of substance use disorders in medical and psychiatric practice are quite low and that physicians are even less likely to detect substance abuse in patients who are employed, married, white, insured, or women (Clark 1981; Cleary et al. 1988; Moore et al. 1989; Wolf et al. 1965). Needless to say, the failure to diagnose substance abuse or dependence precludes

effective intervention or treatment and also contributes to continued and more severe problems.

Accurate diagnosis of a substance use disorder is often made more difficult by the characteristic defenses of patients with these disorders (e.g., minimization, denial, projection, grandiosity) and the reluctance of the patient's family, friends, or co-workers to confront the patient or disclose information to the patient's physician about these sensitive issues (Nace 1987). Covert and overt attitudes of physicians about drug and alcohol dependence, such as reluctance to recognize the harmful effects of a patient's substance use because of the physician's own pattern of alcohol or drug use, a tendency to view these disorders as moral shortcomings of the patients rather than valid psychiatric disorders, or concerns about "labeling" a patient and the patient's potential angry response, may also interfere with timely diagnosis and treatment (Clark 1981; Lisansky 1975). Far from stigmatizing the patient, however, accurately diagnosing a substance use disorder and clearly labeling the patient's problems as a result of alcohol or drug use are critical steps in motivating behavioral change and commitment to treatment.

In this chapter, I will review the concept of the dependence syndrome and the diagnostic features of substance use disorders and then discuss ways of eliciting an accurate history and observing signs of a substance use disorder during the interview process. The utility of commonly used screening questionnaires and structured interviews will be reviewed. In addition to the diagnostic interview with the patient and mental status examination, a complete evaluation should include a review of the patient's medical records and results of physical examination and laboratory studies; use of reports from family members, friends, co-workers, or supervisors; and monitoring of breath alcohol concentration and urine for toxicological evidence of drug use. Special attention will be paid to diagnostic issues regarding comorbid substance use and other psychiatric disorders.

On the basis of a thorough clinical assessment, the physician will be in a position to document the relationship between the patient's substance use and the patient's other psychiatric symptoms and experience of current or past life problems, including medical, family, occupational, social, and legal difficulties. A complete assessment will determine the need for specific treatments, such as hospitalization or a medically supervised withdrawal, and provide guidance about necessary components of the overall treatment plan and optimal patient-treatment matching.

## ▼ DEPENDENCE SYNDROME AND DIAGNOSIS OF SUBSTANCE USE DISORDERS

Revisions in the DSM-III criteria for substance use disorders incorporated in DSM-III-R (American Psychiatric Association 1987) resulted from a developing consensus that dependence is best conceptualized as a biobehavioral construct characterized by compulsive use of a substance rather than as a purely or primarily physical state (Rounsaville and Kranzler 1989). Viewed in this fashion, the concept of dependence can be applied to the pathological use of any of a variety of psychoactive substances, including some highly addicting drugs, such as cocaine, that do not produce signs of physical dependence. The revised nomenclature places decreased emphasis on the signal importance of physiological measures of dependence (tolerance and withdrawal) or on the social consequences of use per se. Instead, the nomenclature stresses impaired control of psychoactive substance use and increasing salience of contin-

ued use as the diagnostic hallmarks of dependence.

In the DSM-IV, 11 classes of substances are identified: 1) alcohol, 2) amphetamine or similarly acting sympathomimetics, 3) caffeine, 4) cannabis, 5) cocaine, 6) hallucinogens, 7) inhalants, 8) nicotine, 9) opioids, 10) phencyclidine (PCP) or similarly acting arylcyclohexylamines, and 11) sedative, hypnotic, or anxiolytic. Based on their shared physiologic and psychological effects, some of these substances can be grouped into two general categories: 1) central nervous system depressants, including alcohol and sedatives, anxiolytics, or hypnotics, and 2) stimulants, including cocaine and amphetamine and related substances. Caffeine is not considered to cause either abuse or dependence, and nicotine is considered to lead to dependence but not abuse.

In the DSM-IV, a diagnosis of substance dependence requires at least three symptoms from a list of seven, occurring at any time in the same 12-month period. The first two symptoms indicate tolerance or physiological dependence: 1) tolerance (need for increased amounts to obtain desired effects or diminished effects with continued use of the same amount), and 2) withdrawal symptoms after discontinuation of use or abstinence, or use of the substance to relieve or avoid withdrawal symptoms. The next two symptoms indicate impaired control of substance use: 3) taking the substance in larger amounts or over longer periods than originally intended, and 4) persistent desire or one or more efforts to cut down or control use. The next three symptoms indicate the salience of persistent or continued drug use to the person. Preoccupation with alcohol or other drugs is indicated by the following: 5) spending a great deal of time acquiring, using, or recovering from substance use. Continuing use despite adverse consequences, another measure of the salience of alcohol or other drug use, is indicated by 6) giving up or reducing social, occupational, or recreational activities because of substance use, and 7) continued use despite knowledge of having a persistent or recurrent social, psychological, or physical problem that is caused or exacerbated by use of the substance.

Severity or intensity of dependence occurs along a continuum (i.e., from mild to moderate to severe) that can be indicated by the number of symptoms and importance of impairment or behaviors elicited in relation to use. *Mild dependence* could be defined as having few, if any, symptoms in excess of those required to make the diagnosis, and the symptoms result in no more than mild impairment in occupational or social functioning. *Severe dependence* could be defined as having many symptoms in excess of those required to make the diagnosis and those symptoms greatly interfere with occupational or social functioning. *Moderate dependence* could be defined as being intermediate between mild and severe dependence.

Substance abuse is the diagnosis for noting maladaptive or problematic patterns of substance use that have never met criteria for substance dependence. A maladaptive pattern of use is indicated by one or more of the following occurring within a 12-month period: 1) recurrent use resulting in failure to fulfill major role obligations, 2) recurrent use in situations in which use is physically hazardous, 3) recurrent substance-related legal problems, and 4) continued substance use despite having persistent or recurrent social or interpersonal problems caused or exacerbated by the effects of the substance.

Diagnostic features of substance-induced disorders are also detailed in DSM-IV. Included among them are intoxication, withdrawal, intoxication delirium, withdrawal delirium, dementia, amnestic disorder, psychotic disorder, mood disorder, anxiety disorder, sexual dysfunction, and sleep disorder. In addition to a history of substance use, diagnosis of these syndromes depends on a careful physical inspection and mental status examination of the patient.

## ▼ ELICITING PATIENT HISTORY

Regardless of the care and sensitivity of the interviewer, patients with substance use disorders will not easily or invariably give a reliable report. One of the diagnostic hallmarks of a substance use disorder is that continued use of the substance becomes extraordinarily important to the patient, often even at the expense of the patient's health, safety, or social functioning. It should not be surprising, then, that patients will attempt to protect their ability to continue to use by minimizing, denying, or even lying about the extent of their use and the problems resulting from it. Rationalization and projection are also common. One woman, for example, attributed a broken leg (suffered while walking down the street intoxicated) to her usual clumsiness and thus completely forgot to mention this problem during the evaluation. Many other patients blame others for all of their relationship, vocational, or legal problems,

rather than recognizing these problems as resulting from their own drug use.

In eliciting the history, psychiatrists need to be alert to these characteristic defenses and to take note of what the patient is trying to hide. It is also necessary to make use of independent reports and objective measures in the assessment. It goes without saying that patients who are intoxicated or delirious at the time of assessment cannot give an accurate history.

With these caveats in mind, several specific strategies and approaches to history taking can be recommended. As in all aspects of the psychiatric interview, a straightforward, nonjudgmental approach is most likely to elicit accurate information. As noted by some authorities, history taking is facilitated by questions beginning with *how* (e.g., "How did that affect you?") rather than with *why* (e.g., "Why did you smoke crack then?"). Not surprisingly, the latter approach is often perceived as judgmental and tends to evoke defensiveness (Kaufman and Reoux 1988).

In eliciting the history, the patient's concerns about disclosure of information to family members, employers, legal authorities, or licensing boards also need to be addressed directly. Sometimes the patient's reluctance to disclose sensitive information is lessened by a frank discussion about why this information is important, how the information will be used, and what measures can and will be taken to safeguard the patient's confidentiality. Because confidentiality regulations are set by both state and federal authorities, and differ from one jurisdiction to another (and according to whether the patient is an adult or minor), physicians need to be informed about the specific reporting requirements and confidentiality statutes affecting their practice (Senay 1992).

One general strategy for eliciting the history is to avoid questions, at least initially, that are most likely to make patients with substance use disorders particularly defensive. Thus it is often useful first to review the patient's life history, including successes and problems experienced in work, school, family, and friendships, as well as medical, legal, and psychological and emotional problems, without necessarily linking any of these problems to the patient's use of alcohol or other drugs. Following this general overview, a parallel chronology of the patient's use of alcohol and drugs can be obtained, and finally specific inquiry can be directed to the relationship between alcohol or drug use and the patient's life problems. This strategy may reveal a correlation between substance use and the patient's life problems that have not previously been recognized by the patient.

Although sensitivity to the patient's defensiveness is necessary, it is essential to obtain a complete history of the patient's use of alcohol and of all other drugs. Thus specific questions need to be addressed to all categories of psychoactive substances. The major categories include alcohol (beer, wine, and distilled spirits such as whiskey, vodka, gin), cannabinoids (marijuana, hashish), stimulants (cocaine, amphetamines), opioids (heroin, morphine, dilaudid, methadone, oxycodone, etc.), sedative-hypnotics and anxiolytics (barbiturates, benzodiazepines), psychomimetics and hallucinogens (PCP, LSD, mescaline), inhalants (glue, paint thinners, solvents), as well as nicotine and caffeine. Inquiry should be directed to a history of lifetime (e.g., "Have you ever used . . . ?") and recent use of substances from each of the categories. For drugs that can be prescribed for medical purposes, it is also essential to determine whether these drugs were taken only for the prescribed purpose or whether their use ever exceeded the prescribed dose or duration. When inquiring about use of drugs in each of the categories, it is useful to ask about the general category and then name specific substances, using generic, brand, and street names as examples (e.g., "Have you ever used any opioid or opiate-like drugs, such as morphine, demerol, dilaudid, methadone, Percodan, etc.? What about heroin, P-dope, smack, or horse?").

As part of the evaluation, for each of the drug categories patients should be asked about their lifetime use, recent or current use, and periods of heaviest use. Age and circumstances of first use, how the patient reacted initially, who was there, and how soon they used it again, are often diagnostically and therapeutically important.

Specific questions should be addressed to the pattern of use during each period of use, how drug use was supported, and what circumstances or personal efforts help to curtail or control use. *Pattern of use* refers to quantity used per occasion (average and maximum), frequency (how often used), duration of episodes of use, route of administration, and expense. The investigator needs to be alert to early and subtle indications of problematic use. With regard to alcohol, for example, these may include relief drinking, surreptitious drinking, anticipatory drinking, and gulping drinks. Rationalizing drinking, protecting the supply, geographic escapes to facilitate

drinking, and regular morning drinking are later occurrences and indicate greater problem severity (Pokorny and Kanas 1980). Changes in the pattern of alcohol or other drug use, including narrowing of the patient's alcohol or drug-taking repertoire, may also be a clue to a diagnosis of dependence. Patients often provide evidence of impaired control when they attempt to demonstrate that substance use is not a problem for them. For example, patient reports of "I never drink before 5 o'clock," "I never drink alone," or "I never drink spirits, only beer" may indicate some difficulty and attempt at controlling use.

Finally, attention needs to be directed to any medical, psychological or emotional, and social complications of use. The evaluator's familiarity with the details of how substance use affects these areas and willingness to direct specific questions to them are likely to be factors in the extent of patient disclosure. This approach facilitates recognition of early and later signs of problematic alcohol or drug use. Early indicators may include occurrence of blackouts, accidental overdoses, behavior changes, driving or engaging in other dangerous or aggressive activities while intoxicated, or feeling guilty about behaviors engaged in while using. Later sequelae include loss of nonusing friends; loss of interest in non-drug-related activities; impaired relationships with family, friends, co-workers; disruptions of job or social functioning; and occurrence of medical or legal problems.

Pattison (1986) has identified 10 components of an alcohol history that serve as a useful summary of the areas that need to be addressed in the patient's substance use history. In addition to 1) quantity/frequency measures; 2) tolerance and withdrawal; and assessment of adverse 3) medical, 4) interpersonal, 5) vocational, 6) social, and 7) legal consequences, components include assessment of 8) the behaviors engaged in when the patient is drinking or using drugs; 9) personality changes associated with drinking or drug use; and 10) emotional consequences (e.g., shame, diminished self-esteem, paranoid ideation, anxiety, dissociative states).

## ▼ PHYSICAL AND MENTAL STATUS EXAMINATION

The physical and mental status examination provides critical information regarding diagnosis, management, and treatment of substance use disorders. Although psychiatrists and other mental health and substance abuse treatment professionals may prefer to refer patients to primary care or internal medicine physicians for a complete physical examination, the patient's vital signs and a brief physical assessment, in combination with the mental status examination, may reveal evidence of recent or current use, intoxication, withdrawal, or potentially life-threatening medical sequelae of substance use disorders. Because many excellent references about the mental status examination in psychiatry are available, I will focus discussion in this chapter on elements that are particularly important to substance use disorders.

A brief physical assessment should be performed to look for evidence of recent or past intravenous drug use (e.g., track marks, abscesses) or of chronic use of drugs by insufflation (e.g., nasal discharge, ulcers, perforated septum). Impending drug overdose may be signaled by depressed respiration and marked somnolence. Signs of sepsis (fever, pallor, hypotension) or of nutritional deficiency (wasted appearance, gingivitis, cheilosis, or ulceration of the skin at the corners of the mouth) associated with alcohol or other drug dependence can also be noted during a brief physical assessment.

The physical and mental status examination should also be directed at detecting signs of acute intoxication, withdrawal, or delirium. Signs of alcohol, sedative or anxiolytic intoxication, for example, include slurred speech, incoordination, unsteady gait, nystagmus, impaired attention or memory, or (for alcohol) a flushed face. Signs of stimulant intoxication (including caffeine intoxication) include pupillary dilation, diaphoresis, restlessness, nervousness, excitement, flushed face, muscle twitching, psychomotor agitation, and pressured or rambling speech. Signs of opioid intoxication include pupillary constriction, drowsiness, slurred speech, and impaired attention or memory.

Signs of opioid withdrawal on physical examination include fever, lacrimation, rhinorrhea, dilated pupils, diaphoresis, piloerection, and yawning. Signs of withdrawal from alcohol, sedatives, or anxiolytics include tachycardia, elevated blood pressure, and tremulousness. Signs of delirium, which may result from intoxication with stimulants, cannabis, and hallucinogens, or withdrawal from alcohol, sedatives, or anxiolytics, include reduced ability to attend to external stimuli, disorganized thinking, disorientation, perceptual disturbances, memory impairment, psychomotor agitation or retardation, and reduced level of consciousness.

A careful mental status examination, including assessment of cognitive functioning, is also essential for accurate diagnosis of substance dependence, comorbid psychiatric disorders, and cognitive dysfunction. Major sequelae of substance abuse disorders that can be documented in the mental status examination include transient or persistent hallucinatory phenomena; mood and affective disturbances (panic, anxiety, depression, guilt, shame, diminished self-esteem); and paranoid, suicidal, or violent ideation or behavior. Assessment of cognitive function should include evaluation of attention and concentration, recent and remote memory, abstract reasoning, and problem-solving ability. All of these functions may be impaired by recent alcohol, sedative, anxiolytic, stimulant, or polydrug use. At least in the case of alcohol and as documented more recently, cocaine, memory deficits and other cognitive impairments may be persistent or permanent (Grant 1987; O'Malley et al. 1992).

Both obvious manifestations and more subtle signs and symptoms of substance use disorders documented in a careful mental status examination may provide critical information with regard to diagnosis and treatment. Affective instability or lability, irritability, anxiety, or depressed mood can be signs of current substance abuse or dependence. Sleep and appetite disturbances are also caused by use of alcohol and many other drugs. Many alcohol-dependent patients, for example, will report using alcohol to self-medicate difficulty falling asleep and interrupted sleep. They may be completely unaware that these problems are actually a result of or exacerbated by their alcohol use. The presence of any of these abnormalities on mental status examination provides presumptive evidence of problematic substance use in patients who otherwise report "controlled" or nonproblematic use of alcohol or other drugs. Confronting patients with this evidence may help to overcome their denial and increase recognition of the need to abstain.

The mental status examination should also document evidence, when present, of comorbid psychiatric disorders, including schizophrenia, bipolar disorder, major depression, and anxiety disorders. These comorbid disorders occur frequently, affect prognosis, and have important treatment implications, as discussed in this volume.

## ▼ SCREENING INSTRUMENTS AND STRUCTURED INTERVIEWS

A number of short, self-report questionnaires are available to aid in the routine detection of alcohol abuse and dependence. The four-question CAGE— "Have you ever 1) attempted to **C**ut back on alcohol? 2) been **A**nnoyed by comments made about your drinking? 3) felt **G**uilty about drinking? 4) had an **E**ye-opener first thing in the morning to steady your nerves?"—has been found to improve routine detection rates in primary care and medical settings (Clark 1981; Mayfield et al. 1974). A modified version of the CAGE (T-ACE, which replaces the question regarding ever feeling guilty about drinking with a question addressing alcohol tolerance) has been used to identify problem levels of drinking in pregnant women (Sokol et al. 1989). Obviously, neither of these questionnaires can substitute for a complete history or thorough evaluation.

The complete (25 items) and shortened versions (10 or 13 items) of the Michigan Alcoholism Screening Test (MAST) assess a lifetime history of problems related to drinking (Pokorny et al. 1972; Selzer 1971; Selzer et al. 1975). These and similar instruments, such as the Alcohol Dependence Scale (Skinner and Horn 1984), may help to elicit information necessary to make a diagnosis of abuse or dependence. Several brief screening and more detailed assessment instruments have also been developed for adolescents (National Institute on Drug Abuse 1991). Brief, self-report questionnaires such as the Beck Depression Inventory (Beck et al. 1961) may also be useful to aid in the detection of comorbid depressive disorders.

Structured interviews provide a reliable way to elicit diagnostic information and decrease the chance of omitting questions about significant signs or symptoms. Two of these merit special attention. The Structured Clinical Interview for DSM-III-R (SCID-P) is a clinically based interview that facilitates definitive diagnosis of DSM-III-R substance use and other psychiatric disorders (Spitzer and Williams 1985). The Addiction Severity Index (ASI) facilitates a multidimensional assessment of patients with substance use disorders by evaluating alcohol and drug problem severity and the severity of medical, psychiatric, social, legal, and occupational problems experienced by the patient (McLellan et al. 1980, 1992). Initial ASI ratings of problem severity are highly correlated with treatment outcome and can be used to determine the need for specialized psychiatric interventions or hospital-based treatment (McLellan et al. 1983). The ASI can also be used to monitor the effects of treatment and changes in the patient's functioning.

## ▼ INTERVIEWS WITH SIGNIFICANT OTHERS

Whenever possible, evaluation should include an interview with family members or other people who know and have had contact with the patient in a variety of other settings. Ideally, these informants should not themselves have problems with alcohol or drugs. Use of multiple informants can substantially increase the validity of the evaluation. Often just knowing that others will be asked about the patient's alcohol or drug use increases the reliability of self-reports. Although family members may not be aware of all of the details of the patient's substance use (e.g., quantity, frequency, or variety of drugs used), they may be in a position to provide critical information on the patient's behavioral changes or problems experienced as a direct result of alcohol or other drug use. Involvement of family members in the initial stages of the evaluation will also facilitate family-based interventions, limit setting, and long-term family support of treatment goals.

## ▼ LABORATORY EXAMINATION

Urine toxicology testing for drugs of abuse is an essential component of the substance abuse evaluation. Toxicology testing is critical in cases of suspected or possible drug overdose and should be included in the routine evaluation of patients with acute changes in mental status or with any indication of suspected alcohol or drug problems. For the minority of patients with substance use disorders who persistently deny any alcohol or drug use, urine toxicology testing may provide the only way to document the problem and the only opportunity to confront the patient's drug use effectively. Even for patients who acknowledge drug problems, however, urine toxicology testing often reveals surprising results. Patients may openly admit to using one substance that has become a problem for them (e.g., heroin) while continuing to deny their current use of other substances (e.g., cocaine, benzodiazepines, alcohol, cannabis) that they do not recognize or acknowledge as causing them any problems.

The clinical utility of drug abuse testing is enhanced by a thorough understanding of the methodologies that are used in the testing procedures (i.e., immunoassay, thin-layer chromatography, and gas chromatography/mass spectrometry), the sensitivity and specificity of the assays used, and the substances that can be detected by the assays (Chiang and Hawks 1986; Hawks and Chiang 1986; Manno 1986). Knowledge of the maximum length of time following last use that the drug or its metabolite can still be detected is also essential to interpret negative results accurately. A patient with a significant crack cocaine problem, characterized by a pattern of weekend binges, may have a negative drug screen on a urine sample collected on Friday morning, for example, since cocaine metabolites can only be detected reliably for a few days following last use. Urine drug testing is an expensive and inefficient way to check for alcohol use because alcohol can be detected only for a very short time following last use. Use of Breathalizer is a convenient, reliable, and inexpensive method to determine current alcohol intoxication or recent use.

A variety of biochemical tests have been used as markers of harmful alcohol use, but their value is limited by problems with sensitivity and specificity. Sensitivity and specificity of these markers is increased by using combinations of measures. Increased liver enzyme activity, measured by serum gamma-glutamyltransferase or aspartate aminotransferase, especially in conjunction with measures of increased red blood cell size (mean corpuscular volume), have shown relatively high sensitivity and specificity for heavy drinking (National Institute on Alcohol Abuse and Alcoholism 1990).

Laboratory evaluation of patients with substance use disorders should also be used to detect adverse medical consequences of alcohol and other drug use. In addition to a complete physical examination, a thorough initial evaluation of a patient with a substance use disorder should include a urinalysis (to detect kidney damage), a complete blood count, blood chemistry, and liver enzymes, serology (venereal disease research laboratory test, hepatitis antibody, and antigen), and testing for tuberculosis (purified protein derivative). After appropriate counseling, testing for HIV infection is also indicated, given the high rates of infection not only in intravenous drug users but also among users of freebase or crack cocaine and among alcoholic subjects.

## ▼ ASSESSMENT OF COMORBID PSYCHIATRIC DISORDERS

Acute and chronic use of psychoactive substances can have profound effects on cognitive functioning, mood, thought processes, and personality functioning. In the absence of a history of substance use, many of these effects may be indistinguishable, on the basis of signs and symptoms alone, from major Axis I or Axis II psychiatric disorders. Although these substance-induced syndromes should be classified as organic mental disorders, accurate diagnosis is problematic because patients with substance use disorders also experience high rates of nonorganic psychiatric disorders. Common examples of the difficult diagnostic dilemmas faced by clinicians include 1) differentiation of alcohol- and alcohol withdrawal–related depression and affective lability from unipolar and bipolar depression and anxiety disorders, or 2) differentiation of cocaine-induced paranoid delusional states from schizophrenia.

Several different guidelines for distinguishing primary psychiatric disorders from substance abuse–related disorders have been proposed. With regard to comorbidity in alcohol-dependent patients, Schuckit has proposed that a diagnosis of an independent psychiatric disorder can only be made if onset of the disorder either preceded the initial onset of alcoholism, persisted during past periods of abstinence, or continues after 4 weeks of abstinence (Schuckit 1986). This approach avoids making a diagnosis of an affective disorder in the majority of patients whose mood will recover spontaneously during the first 4 weeks of abstinence. This approach, however, may make it difficult to diagnose major psychiatric disorders and institute treatment of them in patients who are unable to maintain abstinence for 4 weeks, and the failure to treat underlying psychiatric disorder may contribute to relapse (Rounsaville and Kranzler 1989). Shortening the period of abstinence required for diagnosis to 10 days to 2 weeks, as suggested by these experts, permits more rapid institution of treatment and may improve treatment retention but is clearly more risky with regard to the increased likelihood that patients will mix alcohol or other drugs with prescribed medications.

Regardless of the decision rules used to diagnose comorbid psychiatric disorders and the exact timing of implementation of treatment for underlying psychiatric disorders, a diagnosis of comorbid psychiatric disorders has important prognostic and clinical implications. With the exception of depression among alcoholic women, the occurrence of comorbid psychiatric disorders usually confers a poorer treatment prognosis (Rounsaville et al. 1986; Rounsaville et al. 1987). Psychiatric treatment of underlying psychiatric disorders, however, has been shown to improve treatment outcome for both opioid-dependent patients and alcoholic patients (Rounsaville et al. 1985). Patient-treatment matching, based on assessment of comorbid psychiatric disorders, may also improve treatment outcome (McLellan et al. 1983). Most recently, Kadden et al. (1989) and Litt et al. (1992) have documented that sociopathic alcoholic patients have improved treatment outcomes when treated in structured group settings providing coping skills training, whereas interactional group therapy was more effective for less sociopathic alcoholic patients.

## ▼ REFERENCES

American Psychiatric Association: Diagnostic and Statistical Manual of Mental Disorders, 3rd Edition, Revised. Washington, DC, American Psychiatric Association, 1987

American Psychiatric Association: Diagnostic and Statistical Manual of Mental Disorders, 4th Edition. Washington, DC, American Psychiatric Association, 1994

Beck A, Ward CH, Mendelson M, et al: An inventory for measuring depression. Arch Gen Psychiatry 4:561–571, 1961

Chiang NC, Hawks RL: Implications of Drug Levels in Body Fluids: Basic Concepts, Urine Testing for Drugs of Abuse, NIDA Res Monogr 73. Rockville, MD, National Institute on Drug Abuse, 1986, pp 62–83

Clark WD: Alcoholism: blocks to diagnosis and treatment. Am J Med 71:275–285, 1981

Cleary PD, Miller M, Bush BT, et al: Prevalence and recognition of alcohol abuse in a primary care population. Am J Med 85:466–471, 1988

Cyr MG, Wartman SA: The effectiveness of routine screening questions in the detection of alcoholism. JAMA 259:51–54, 1988

Grant I: Alcohol and the brain: neuropsychological correlates. J Consult Clin Psychol 55:310–324, 1987

Hawks RL, Chiang CN: Examples of Specific Drug Assays, Urine Testing for Drugs of Abuse, NIDA Res Monogr 73. Rockville, MD, National Institute on Drug Abuse, 1986, pp 84–112

Kadden RM, Getter H, Cooney NL, et al: Matching alcoholics to coping skills or interactional therapies: posttreatment results. J Consult Clin Psychol 57:698–704, 1989

Kaufman E, Reoux J: Guidelines for the successful psychotherapy of substance abusers. Am J Drug Alcohol Abuse 14:199–209, 1988

Lisansky ET: Why physicians avoid early diagnosis of alcoholism. N Y State J Med 75:1788–1792, 1975

Litt MD, Babor TF, KelBoca FK, et al: Types of alcoholics; II: application of an empirically derived typology to treatment matching. Arch Gen Psychiatry 49:609–614, 1992

Manno JE: Specimen Collection and Handling: Urine Testing for Drugs of Abuse. NIDA Res Monogr 73. Rockville, MD, National Institute on Drug Abuse, 1986, pp 24–29

Mayfield DG, McLeon G, Hall P, et al: The CAGE questionnaire: validation of a new alcoholism screening instrument. Am J Psychiatry 131:1121–1123, 1974

McLellan AT, Luborsky L, Woody GE, et al: An improved diagnostic evaluation instrument for substance abuse patients: the Addiction Severity Index. J Nerv Ment Dis 168:26–33, 1980

McLellan AT, Luborsky L, Woody GE, et al: Predicting response to alcohol and drug abuse treatments. Alcohol and Drug Abuse 40:620–625, 1983

McLellan AT, Kushner H, Metzger D, et al: The Fifth Edition of the Addiction Severity Index. J Subst Abuse Treat 9:199–213, 1992

Moore RD, Bone LR, Geller G, et al: Prevalence, detection, and treatment of alcoholism in hospitalized patients. JAMA 261:403–407, 1989

Nace EP: The Treatment of Alcoholism. New York, Brunner/Mazel, 1987, pp 237–251

National Institute on Alcohol and Alcoholism: Alcohol alert: screening for alcoholism. Rockville, MD, National Institute on Alcohol and Alcoholism 8:PH285, April 1990

National Institute on Drug Abuse: The Adolescent Assessment/Referral System Manual (ADAMHA Publ

No ADM-91-1735). Rockville, MD, Alcohol, Drug Abuse, and Mental Health Administration, 1991

O'Malley S, Adamse M, Heaton RK, et al: Neuropsychological impairment in chronic cocaine abusers. Am J Drug Alcohol Abuse 18:131–144, 1992

Pattison EM: Clinical approaches to the alcoholic patient. Psychomatics 27:762–770, 1986

Pokorny AD, Kasas TE: Stages in the development of alcoholism, in Phenomenology and Treatment of Alcoholism. Edited by Farr WE, Karacan I, Pokorny AD, et al. New York, SP Medical & Scientific Books, 1980

Pokorny AD, Miller BA, Kaplan HB: The brief MAST: a shortened version of the Michigan Alcoholism Screening Test. Am J Psychiatry 129:342–348, 1972

Rounsaville BJ, Kranzler HR: The DSM-III-R Diagnosis of Alcoholism, Psychiatric Update. Washington, DC, American Psychiatric Press, 1989, pp 323–340

Rounsaville BJ, Kosten TR, Weissman MM, et al: Evaluating and Treating Depressive Disorders in Opiate Addicts, NIDA Res Monogr (DHHS Publ No ADM-85-1406). Washington, DC, National Institute on Drug Abuse, 1985, pp 1–80

Rounsaville BJ, Kosten TR, Weissman MM, et al: Prognostic significance of psychiatric disorders in treated opiate addicts. Arch Gen Psychiatry 43:739–745, 1986

Rounsaville BJ, Dolinsky ZS, Babor TF, et al: Psychopathology as a predictor of treatment outcome in alcoholics. Arch Gen Psychiatry 44:505–513, 1987

Schuckit MA: Genetic and clinical implications of alcoholism and affective disorder. Am J Psychiatry 143:140–147, 1986

Selzer ML: The Michigan alcoholism screening test: the quest for a new diagnostic instrument. Am J Psychiatry 127:1653–1658, 1971

Selzer ML, Vinokur A, van Rooijen L: A self-administered Short Michigan Alcoholism Screening Test (SMAST). J Stud Alcohol 36:117–126, 1975

Senay EC: Diagnostic Interview and Mental Status Examination: Substance Abuse A Comprehensive Textbook. Baltimore, MD, Williams & Wilkins, 1992, pp 416–424

Skinner HA, Horn JL: Alcohol Dependence Scale (ADS) User's Guide. Toronto, Canada, Addiction Research Foundation, 1984

Sokol RJ, Martier SS, Ager JW, et al: The T-ACE questions: practical prenatal detection of risk-drinking. Am J Obst Gynecol 160:863–870, 1989

Spitzer RL, Williams JWB: Structured Clinical Interview for DSM-III—Patient Version (SCID-P). New York, New York State Psychiatric Institute, 1985

Wolf I, Chafetz ME, Blane HT, et al: Social factors in the diagnosis of alcoholism: attitudes of physicians. Quarterly Journal of Studies on Alcohol 26:72–79, 1965

# Outcome Research

## *Alcoholism*

*Reid K. Hester, Ph.D.*

This chapter provides the clinician with an overview of research on the effectiveness of treatment for alcohol problems. I have chosen the term *alcohol problems* for several reasons. First, using the term *alcoholic* or *alcoholism* tends to imply a black-and-white distinction between the presence or absence of a unitary condition. Drinking and alcohol-related problems lie on continua, and the range and diversity of these problems is great. Second, epidemiological data (Polich 1981) clearly demonstrate that there are many more individuals with significant alcohol-related problems than those who could be diagnosed as alcohol dependent on DSM-III-R criteria. Third, a recent Institute of Medicine (1990) report has urged providers of services to broaden their perspective to include this broader group of individuals with alcohol problems who are not alcohol dependent. For these reasons, I have included in this review interventions that have been targeted not only to individuals with alcohol dependence but also to those with less severe, but still significant, alcohol-related problems.

Before beginning, it is appropriate to discuss how the scope of this review has been defined. First, space

limitations and the purpose of this book preclude a comprehensive and historical review of all alcohol problem treatments that have evolved. Instead, this chapter will focus on those interventions that are currently used or are coming into use. Second, discussion will be limited to published findings of controlled or comparative trials. The reasons for this are presented later in this chapter. Third, I will use the classification system of Holder et al. (1991) to group treatments on the basis of their effectiveness. Fourth, space limitations will allow only a summary of the data on effectiveness and some discussion of those interventions that are supported by research. I will spend more time discussing the treatments with fair to good evidence of effectiveness than those with little or no evidence of effectiveness. (For more detailed reviews, see Holder et al. [1991] and Miller and Hester [1980, 1986a].) Clinicians interested in learning how to provide many of these interventions might wish to read Hester and Miller (1989). Finally, I will conclude with a brief discussion of the influences of therapist characteristics and treatment setting on outcome, and the promising field of matching patients to treatments.

A few words are in order here to explain my decision to limit this review to controlled and comparative studies. In 1979, William Miller, Ph.D., and I began a project to review the treatment outcome literature in alcohol abuse. In this initial review we included all of the case studies and uncontrolled and controlled clinical trials published in the languages we could read. That initial review (Miller and Hester 1980) included over 600 studies. One of the most important lessons we learned from this was the value of controlled clinical trials. Historically, a number of treatments have been introduced with glowing results from case studies and uncontrolled clinical trials only to have subsequent controlled studies find that the new treatment did not contribute in any significant way to outcome. An example will illustrate this point. Metronidazole was introduced in 1959 as a treatment for vaginal infections. One of its reported side effects was the development of an aversion to the taste of alcohol. Based on this apparent side effect, Taylor (1964) and Semer et al. (1966) conducted uncontrolled clinical trials. They reported abstinence rates in the 90% range at 2- to 5-month follow-up. These results were widely reported by the media, and demand for metronidazole increased significantly. Eleven controlled clinical trials followed, 8 of which found no significant differences between metronidazole and placebo. Of the 3 positive studies, 2 had serious methodological flaws that rendered their results difficult to interpret. Following these reports, the use of metronidazole declined rapidly, and I have not seen any reports of its use as a treatment for alcohol problems since 1972. Indeed, many clinicians may not know that metronidazole was once considered a highly effective treatment for alcohol problems. Because of these difficulties in drawing reliable conclusions from uncontrolled studies, this review will focus only on studies that have had control or comparison groups—still a field of over 250 studies.

In their examination of the cost-effectiveness of treatment, Holder et al. (1991) devised a weighted evidence index (WEIn). They then used the WEIn to develop five distinct categories of the effectiveness of treatment: no, insufficient, indeterminate, fair, and good evidence of effectiveness. Because these categories seem to qualitatively differentiate the level of support from research for various treatments, they will be used here. Holder et al.'s findings are also consistent with previous narrative reviews of the research literature (Miller and Hester 1980, 1986a).

## ▼ EVIDENCE OF EFFECTIVENESS: WHAT RESEARCH REVEALS

### No Evidence of Effectiveness

A wide variety of treatments have been tested extensively in controlled trials and have been found not to yield results that are superior to comparison groups. The treatments include the following:

▼ Antianxiety medications
▼ Cognitive therapy
▼ Confrontational interventions
▼ Educational lectures/films
▼ Electrical aversion therapies
▼ General counseling
▼ Group therapies
▼ Insight-oriented psychotherapy
▼ Nausea aversion therapies
▼ Residential milieu therapies

This list of treatments might come as a surprise to clinicians familiar with treatment services in the United States. Indeed, informal discussions with colleagues in substance abuse programs reveal that some of these interventions are quite common and are thought to have great impact by the clinicians providing them. This discrepancy between clinicians' beliefs and the results of controlled clinical research illustrates the pitfalls of relying solely on personal experience to draw conclusions about the effectiveness of particular treatments.

### Insufficient Evidence of Effectiveness

Included in this category are treatments with only one or two controlled studies. Because of this limitation, it is difficult to draw firm conclusions about the impact of these treatments in relation to others. The treatments include the following:

▼ Alcoholics Anonymous (AA)
▼ Minnesota model of residential treatment
▼ Halfway houses
▼ Acupuncture
▼ Calcium carbimide (an antidipsotropic medication not available in the United States)

Many readers may be amazed that AA and the Minnesota model of residential treatment fall into this category. Unfortunately, there have only been two controlled studies of AA (Brandsma et al. 1980, Ditman and Crawford 1966). Both were with patients mandated to treatment by the criminal justice system. Neither study found that AA improved outcomes. It might be concluded from these studies that judges should not mandate individuals convicted of alcohol-related crimes to attend AA as an alternative to legal sanctions; however, these data do not address the issue of AA's effectiveness with individuals who attend AA voluntarily or do so as aftercare following treatment for alcohol abuse. Finally, it is noteworthy that AA considers itself a "fellowship" and not treatment. Although anecdotal evidence indicates that AA has been helpful to many people, evidence from controlled clinical trials is lacking. This in turn calls into question the wisdom of emphasizing the 12-step approach to the exclusion of others when treating individuals with drinking problems.

Although many treatment programs in the United States describe themselves as based on the Minnesota model of residential treatment, there has, to date, only been one study that has directly compared this model of treatment with another model of treatment (Keso and Salaspuro 1990). In this study, Keso and Salaspuro randomly assigned patients to receive either treatment based on the Minnesota model or treatment based on the Finnish model. At follow-up, they found that patients in the Minnesota model treatment fared slightly better than those receiving traditional Finnish treatment. Although somewhat encouraging, the control condition contained many elements of what Holder et al. (1991) classified as having no evidence of effectiveness. Unfortunately, there also has been only one controlled comparison each of the effectiveness of halfway houses (Annis and Liban 1979), acupuncture (Bullock et al. 1987), and calcium carbimide (Levy et al. 1967).

## Indeterminate Evidence of Effectiveness

Treatments in this category have had three or more controlled trials, but overall the mixed results make it difficult to conclude with any confidence that these treatments are effective. The treatments include the following:

▼ Nonbehavioral marital therapy
▼ Hypnosis
▼ Lithium

*Nonbehavioral marital therapies* include structural and strategic approaches, of which there have only been three controlled trials. Although they tend to use terms quite different from those used to describe behavioral marital therapy, in practice the two treatments seem similar. Conversely, the difficulties in operationally defining terms and strategies in nonbehavioral marital therapy may have hindered research on these approaches.

There are similar difficulties in studies of hypnosis. Clinicians and researchers alike have different ideas on how to define *hypnosis*. In reading descriptions of the hypnotic techniques used in the different studies, it seems that the two studies with positive results used techniques similar to covert sensitization, a form of aversion therapy discussed below.

Lithium has mixed results, with three positive and four negative studies. This treatment is thought to have some impact on drinking above and beyond its antidepressant effect and is a good example of an intervention that has been tested in well-designed, randomized double-blind, placebo-controlled trials, with quite inconsistent results. On the one hand, Fawcett et al. (1987) found that the abstinence rate for compliant patients was significantly better than for noncompliant patients on lithium. Among the compliant patients, those with therapeutic levels of lithium had higher rates of abstinence than those with subtherapeutic levels, suggesting a pharmacological effect beyond that of behavioral compliance. On the other hand, Dorus et al. (1989) found no significant differences between lithium and placebo groups and no differences between treatment compliers and noncompliers on four drinking-related measures and one measure of severity of depression. Both studies were well designed and controlled yet yielded quite different results. This discrepancy suggests that there might be significant patient-treatment interactions.

## Fair Evidence of Effectiveness

Treatments in this category have had four or more controlled trials and overall are reasonably well supported. The treatments include the following:

▼ Antidepressant medications
▼ Behavior contracting
▼ Covert sensitization (a form of aversion therapy)
▼ Oral and implant disulfiram

The effectiveness of antidepressants on drinking behaviors and depression was the focus of research from the mid-1960s to the early 1970s. The evidence of antidepressants' impact on drinking behaviors per se is modest. On the other hand, there is more evidence of its impact on mood. A clinical caveat is appropriate here. Although there is a relatively high incidence of affective disorders present on admission to alcohol treatment programs, there is also a high rate of spontaneous remission of these disorders during the first few weeks of sobriety. This situation suggests that clinicians should not begin medication treatment regimens unless there is either a clear history of affective disorders predating the development of alcohol problems or a persistence of depression into sobriety.

In *behavior contracting*, the therapist, patient, and often significant others set up clear contingencies for behaviors related to drinking and sobriety. A written contract is usually developed that specifies what kinds of reinforcers will be provided to the patient provided that he or she remains sober. Drinking behaviors, on the other hand, result in a loss of those reinforcers. Although this form of contingency management seems to be more widespread in the treatment of drug abuse, controlled trials have demonstrated its potential for use with alcohol problems (Miller 1975).

*Covert sensitization* is a form of aversion therapy that uses the patient's own imagination to develop aversive consequences. The goal of this treatment is to help the patient develop a conditioned avoidance of alcohol. Working with the patient, the therapist develops an individualized series of images and sensations of drinking alcohol and pairs them with unpleasant experiences such as nausea or negative consequences. Overall, the studies on covert sensitization indicate that it is a promising approach. Unfortunately, there has been a lack of standardization of procedures until recently. Rimmele et al. (1989) have proposed a protocol and developed a therapist manual useful for both clinicians and researchers.

Taken together, there have been 15 controlled trials of oral and implanted disulfiram. Disulfiram (Antabuse) is an antidipsotropic drug. Its effect is to create in the patient an aversive physical reaction to the consumption of alcohol. This reaction is accomplished by blocking the breakdown of acetaldehyde, a metabolic product of ethanol related to formaldehyde. In sufficient doses, acetaldehyde produces rapid heartbeat and breathing, nausea, headache, dizziness, and facial flushing.

Studies of oral disulfiram date back to 1953. Early studies were often flawed methodologically. Some (e.g., Hoff and McKeown 1953) compared subjects willing to take the medication with subjects unwilling or unable to take disulfiram. Others were plagued by high dropout rates. More recent studies have avoided these flaws, however, and have been able to parcel out some of the specific versus nonspecific pharmacological effects of the drug on outcome. Fuller and Roth (1979) randomly assigned alcoholic patients to receive either no medication, an inactive dose (1 mg), or a therapeutic dose of disulfiram. At follow-up they found no significant differences between the groups on outcome measures. They did note, however, a higher rate of abstinence in groups receiving the drug (including the inactive dose group) compared with the no-medication group. Subsequent analyses using life-table methods revealed a significant difference in favor of those receiving disulfiram. It should be noted, however, that the group with the highest abstinence rate at 12 months had received the inactive dose. This suggests a placebo therapeutic effect not attributable to the pharmacological actions of the drug.

Although there seems to be a fair level of evidence for the overall effectiveness of disulfiram, compliance has often been difficult to achieve, and high dropout rates are not unusual. The typical protocol for administering disulfiram is to give the patient a prescription and instructions on how to take it, what will happen if the individual drinks, and its side effects. The prescribing doctor or his or her nurse may then follow up periodically to assess compliance. High rates of noncompliance are common with this protocol. Fortunately, Azrin et al. (1982) have developed and evaluated a disulfiram behavioral compliance program that significantly increases compliance and outcomes at follow-up.

A number of studies have assessed the utility of subcutaneously implanting disulfiram. Because the potential for a placebo response to surgery itself is large, Wilson and colleagues (Wilson 1979, Wilson et al. 1976, Wilson et al. 1978) compared the impact of disulfiram implant with sham surgery. Both groups had substantial improvements in rates of abstinence relative to pretreatment that persisted up to 2-year follow-up. Whereas the disulfiram implant group had significantly greater rates of abstinence than the sham surgery group (367 and 307 days respectively), the greatest difference in abstinence was between the sham surgery group and an unoperated comparison group (27 days abstinence) during the follow-up period. In other words, the placebo effect (sham surgery versus no surgery) was substantially greater than the drug effect (disulfiram implant versus sham surgery).

## Good Evidence of Effectiveness

There is good evidence of effectiveness for the following treatments:

▼ Behavioral marital therapy
▼ Brief interventions
▼ Community reinforcement approach (CRA)
▼ Self-control training
▼ Social skills training
▼ Stress management

Treatments in this category have received consistent support from controlled research. Indeed, behavioral marital therapy, the CRA, and social skills training all have perfect track records.

*Behavioral marital therapy* emphasizes the improvement of communication skills and problem solving between partners. It also strives to increase the frequency of positive reinforcement each spouse gives to the other. Treatment has usually been provided conjointly, with one couple meeting with a therapist, but groups have also been used. Seven studies have found positive results. There are a number of therapist manuals available for interested clinicians. O'Farrell and Cowles (1989) have published a good primer. More advanced manuals and clinical case studies can be found in McCrady (1982), O'Farrell (1986), and O'Farrell and Cutter (1984).

*Brief interventions* hold great promise for impacting the drinking behaviors of individuals with alcohol-related problems. Such interventions, however, need not be conducted only by alcohol treatment programs. Indeed, in a recent report the Institute of Medicine (1990) concluded that brief interventions are the appropriate domain of health care providers outside of the specialized treatment sector (e.g., internists or psychiatrists in general practice).

Although there have been a variety of different interventions developed by clinical researchers over the years, there are commonalities in the components. The typical elements of a brief intervention can be represented by the acronym FRAMES: **F**eedback regarding a patient's drinking that is individual-

ized and objective; **R**esponsibility is placed on the patient for deciding what to do regarding drinking; clear **A**dvice to change; a *M*enu of interventions and options for change, including a willingness to negotiate the goals of change; an **E**mpathic style of counseling; and **S**elf-efficacy is emphasized (Miller and Rollnick 1991).

The time involved in conducting a comprehensive assessment and providing the patient with one or two brief feedback sessions is minimal, especially relative to comprehensive inpatient and outpatient programs. Outcome studies, however, that have compared brief versus more extensive interventions, have not found significant differences (e.g., Edwards et al. 1977). Clinicians interested in learning more about brief interventions might wish to consult Heather (1989) and Miller and Rollnick (1991).

The CRA focuses on altering contingencies in the patient's environment to reinforce sobriety and make drinking result in a time-out from those reinforcers. Working collaboratively, the therapist and patient rank order the patient's alcohol-related problems and pick strategies from a menu of alternatives designed to address these problems. The menu includes 1) a behavioral compliance program to take disulfiram (the program is abstinence oriented), 2) job-search training (if the patient is unemployed), 3) behaviorally oriented marital counseling, 4) problem-solving skills training, and 5) involvement in sober leisure-time activities. The CRA was originally developed and tested in the early 1970s. These early studies reported significant and positive outcomes when compared with control groups. Its impact on the field of alcohol treatment had been relatively minor until about the last 5 years. Since then, it has received more attention and is becoming more popular in both the United States and Europe. Sisson and Azrin (1989) have published guidelines for clinicians interested in this approach.

*Self-control training* involves teaching patients a set of self-management skills that can be used either to moderate consumption to nonproblematic levels or to become and remain abstinent. The most common elements of self-control training are goal setting, self-monitoring, rate control and reduction, self-reinforcement of progress and goal attainment, functional analysis, and learning alternative coping skills. Training has been conducted in groups, on an individual basis, and via self-help books. Controlled comparisons indicate that self-control training can be provided effectively in either therapist-directed or self-help formats (e.g., Harris and Miller 1990). Several therapist manuals are available for clinicians interested in learning how to provide this intervention (Hester and Miller 1989, Sanchez-Craig 1984).

*Social skills training* involves teaching patients how to form and maintain interpersonal relationships. It often includes communication skills, listening skills, problem solving, and assertiveness. It has been considered an adjunct to treatment and not a stand-alone treatment. Also, it has usually been conducted in groups. Studies that have evaluated the effectiveness of social skills training have typically selected patients for inclusion based on a patient's deficiency in some aspect of social skills. Taking this into consideration, controlled clinical trials have been consistently supportive. To date, 10 studies have evaluated its effectiveness, and all have found that adding this intervention improves outcomes. Chaney (1989) has published a therapist manual for clinicians interested in learning how to provide this type of training.

*Stress management* teaches individuals how to reduce tension and manage stress. A broad-based approach will usually include relaxation strategies, systematic desensitization, and cognitive strategies. The patient learns not only how to manage his or her responses to stressful situations but also how to make changes in the external environment. Stress management training is typically considered an adjunctive treatment rather than a stand-alone treatment. To date, six studies have reported positive results, whereas four have not found that adding it improved outcome. Stockwell and Towne (1989) have published a primer for clinicians interested in learning more about how to provide these interventions.

## ▼ ADDITIONAL FACTORS AFFECTING TREATMENT OUTCOME

### Therapist Characteristics

Recent research in the areas of models of change, motivation, brief interventions, and self-control training have highlighted the importance of therapist characteristics in the outcomes of treatment. Both retrospective analyses and prospective studies have found that the level of empathy of the therapist

contributes positively to favorable outcomes. Conversely, evidence is mounting that patient outcomes suffer when therapists confront patients in an aggressive manner. I will briefly discuss the results of two studies to illustrate this point.

In one study on the effectiveness of a brief intervention, Miller et al. (in press) randomly assigned patients to receive feedback during a brief intervention either from a empathic therapist or a confrontive therapist. They found that the number of times the therapist confronted the patient predicted increased levels of patient drinking at 12-month follow-up.

In 1980, Miller et al. (1980) reported the results of a study of self-control training that found no differences in outcome between therapist-directed and self-directed modes of treatment. Analysis of the levels of empathy of the clinician providing training, however, revealed a relationship between therapist empathy and outcome. When Miller et al. rank ordered clinicians on levels of empathy, they found that clinicians with relatively low levels of empathy had outcomes worse than the group that was given the self-help manual and worked on it by themselves with minimal therapist contact. On the other hand, therapists with high levels of empathy had outcomes better than the self-help group. Apparently if a therapist has low levels of empathy, the patient is better off going home with a good book.

Being empathic does not mean that the therapist is nondirective or nonconfrontive. An effective therapist can be directive, confrontive, and empathic all at the same time. An approach that incorporates these elements has come to be known as *motivational interviewing* (Miller and Rollnick 1991). Emerging data on the impact of this style of therapy suggest that it is a promising alternative to a hostile, aggressive style of confrontation as a way to motivate individuals to change.

### Impact of Setting on Treatment Outcome

In 1986, William Miller and I published a review of 24 controlled or comparative studies of the relative impact of providing treatment of different durations, intensities, and in different settings (Miller and Hester 1986b). Overall, the evidence was compelling and somewhat disturbing. We found that in studies in which patients were randomly assigned to receive longer or shorter inpatient treatment, more intense versus less intense treatment, and treatment in inpatient versus outpatient settings, there were no significant differences between groups on outcome measures at follow-up. Even nonsignificant trends favored less intensive treatments and outpatient settings. Only the results on the relative effectiveness of shorter versus longer outpatient treatment presented a somewhat mixed picture. Some studies found that longer outpatient treatment yielded better outcomes, whereas other studies did not. Also, there were indications that patients with more severe alcohol-related problems and greater social instability benefited differentially from longer or more intensive treatment. These results were unexpected, both for the researchers who conducted the trials as well as for many clinicians who read the review. Controversy followed, and interested readers might wish to review the published letters on the topic (Mazza 1988, Miller and Hester 1989, Templer and Kauffman 1988). Studies published since that review have likewise failed to document an advantage of inpatient settings over outpatient settings of treatment.

## Matching Patients to Treatments

The matching hypothesis states that when patients are appropriately matched to treatments, they will have better outcomes than patients who are unmatched or mismatched. Figure 4–1 shows how patient characteristics might interact with two different treatments. Let us assume for the moment that the patient characteristic is the level of alcohol dependence. In this interaction, patients with low levels of dependence would have better outcomes with treatment B than with treatment A. On the other hand, for patients with high levels of dependence the opposite is true. If a study comparing two such treatments had a sample with low levels of dependence, it would find treatment A to be superior to treatment B. The opposite would be true in a study with patients who have high levels of dependence, whereas a study with patients with moderate levels of dependence might find no significant differences between treatments A and B. Finally, if a study had a broad range of dependence levels in its sample, no significant differences might be found, even though there were significant patient-treatment interactions.

Overall, the literature on matching patients to treatments is in its infancy. Most studies have examined a single treatment and identified the patient characteristics that are predictive of success. There are some matching data available on the following interventions: AA, psychotropic medications, disulfiram, psychotherapy, aversion therapies, relaxation training, social skills, the CRA, marital/family therapy, and self-control training. Some studies have used a differential strategy that looks at the usefulness of particular patient characteristics in predicting the relative probability of success in two or more treatments. To date, the following patient characteristics have been examined: problem severity, cognitive style, neuropsychological status, self-esteem, social stability, patient choice, and other life problems. Clinicians interested in the specific matching data might wish to read Miller and Hester (1986c).

Currently the data for making optimal matches between patients and treatments are far from clear. However, an overview of the available data leads to the following initial conclusions:

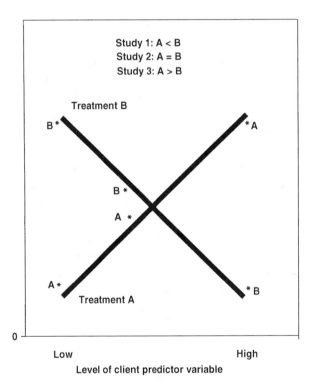

**Figure 4–1. A hypothetical patient-by-treatment interaction.**

*Source.* Reprinted with permission from Miller WR, Hester RK: "Matching Problem Drinkers With Optimal Treatments," in *Treating Addictive Behaviors: Process of Change.* Edited by Miller WR, Heather N. New York, Plenum, 1986, p. 177.

1. Having a patient participate in a various interventions in a broad-spectrum approach is useful to the extent that a patient has a particular problem for which the various interventions are effective treatments.

2. When patients receive a treatment that is consistent with their cognitive style, outcomes are improved relative to patients who are unmatched or mismatched to treatments.

3. Patients with more significant alcohol-related problems benefit differentially from more intensive treatment. The converse is true for patients with less significant alcohol-related problems. They benefit at least as much, if not more, from brief interventions.

4. Patients who participate in choosing their treatment approach from among alternatives show more motivation, compliance, and better outcomes than patients only offered a single approach.

## ▼ SUMMARY

At this point several conclusions can be drawn from the research literature on treatments for alcohol problems. First, the data indicate that there is no *one* treatment that is most effective. Rather, there are a number of interventions that have fair to good evidence of effectiveness. Given this, it would make sense for a program to offer a variety of different approaches rather than just one treatment for everyone. Second, in general, the content of treatment has a greater impact than does the setting in which the treatment occurs. Third, therapist characteristics, particularly empathy, appear to have a substantial influence on outcomes. Fourth, matching patients to treatments holds promise for improving outcomes. Because criteria for optimal matching are far from clear, however, it makes sense to choose interventions based on the patient's needs and desires as well as the therapist's perceptions but to realize that additional interventions might be needed if the initial choice is not robust enough in its effectiveness.

## ▼ REFERENCES

Annis HM, Liban CB: A follow-up study of male halfway-house residents and matched nonresident controls. J Stud Alcohol 40:63–69, 1979

Azrin NH, Sisson RW, Meyers R, et al: Alcoholism treatment by disulfiram and community reinforcement therapy. J Behav Ther Exp Psychiatry 13:105–112, 1982

Brandsma JM, Maultsby MC, Welsh RJ: The Outpatient Treatment of Alcoholism: A Review and Comparative Study. Baltimore, MD, University Park Press, 1980

Bullock ML, Umen AJ, Culliton PD, et al: Acupuncture treatment of alcoholic recidivism: a pilot study. Alcohol Clin Exp Res 11:292–295, 1987

Chaney EF: Social skills training, in Handbook of Alcoholism Treatment. Edited by Hester RK, Miller WR. Elmsford, NY, Pergamon, 1989, pp 206–221

Ditman KS, Crawford GG: The use of court probation in the management of the alcohol addict. Am J Psychiatry 122:757–762, 1966

Dorus W, Ostrow DG, Anton R, et al: Lithium carbonate treatment of depressed and nondepressed alcoholics in a double blind, placebo controlled study. JAMA 262:1646–1652, 1989

Edwards G, Orford J, Egert S, et al: Alcoholism: a controlled trial of "treatment" and "advice." J Stud Alcohol 38:1004–1031, 1977

Fawcett J, Clark DC, Aagesen CA, et al: A double-blind, placebo-controlled trial of lithium carbonate therapy for alcoholism. Arch Gen Psychiatry 44:248–256, 1987

Fuller RK, Roth HP: Disulfiram for the treatment of alcoholism: an evaluation in 128 men. Ann Intern Med 90:901–904, 1979

Harris KB, Miller WR: Behavioral self-control training for problem drinkers: components of efficacy. Psychology of Addictive Behaviors 4:82–90, 1990

Heather N: Psychology and brief interventions. British Journal of Addiction 84:357–370, 1989

Hester RK, Miller WR: Self-control training, in Handbook of Alcoholism Treatment Approaches: Effective Alternatives. Edited by Hester RK, Miller WR. Elmsford, NY, Pergamon, 1989, pp 141–150

Hoff EC, McKeown CE: An evaluation of the use of tetraethylthiuram disulfide in the treatment of 560 cases of alcohol addiction. Am J Psychiatry 109:670–673, 1953

Holder HD, Longabaugh R, Miller WR, et al: The cost effectiveness of treatment for alcoholism: a first approximation. J Stud Alcohol 52:517–540, 1991

Institute of Medicine: Prevention and Treatment of Alcohol Problems: Research Opportunities. Washington, DC, National Academy Press, 1990

Keso L, Salaspuro M: Inpatient treatment of employed alcoholics: a randomized clinical trial on Hazeldon-type and traditional treatment. Alcohol Clin Exp Res 14:584–589, 1990

Levy MS, Livingstone BL, Collins DM: A clinical comparison of disulfiram and calcium carbimide. Am J Psychiatry 123:1018–1022, 1967

Mazza D: Comment on Miller and Hester's "Inpatient alcoholism treatment: who benefits?" Am Psychol 43:199–200, 1988

McCrady BS: Conjoint behavioral treatment of an alcoholic and his spouse, in Clinical Case Studies in the Behavioral Treatment of Alcoholism. Edited by Hay WM, Nathan PE. New York, Plenum, 1982, pp 127–156

Miller PM: A behavioral intervention program for chronic public drunkenness offenders. Arch Gen Psychiatry 32:915–918, 1975

Miller WR, Hester RK: Treating the problem drinker: modern approaches, in The Addictive Behaviors: Treatment of Alcoholism, Drug Abuse, Smoking, and Obesity. Edited by Miller WR. London, Pergamon, 1980, pp 11–141

Miller WR, Hester RK: The effectiveness of alcoholism treatment: what research reveals, in Treating Addictive Behaviors: Processes of Change. Edited by Miller WR, Heather NH. New York, Plenum, 1986a, pp 121–174

Miller WR, Hester RK: Inpatient alcoholism treatment: who benefits? Am Psychol 41:794–805, 1986b

Miller WR, Hester RK: Matching problem drinkers with optimal treatments, in Treating Addictive Behaviors: Processes of Change. Edited by Miller WR, Heather NH. New York, Plenum, 1986c, pp 175–203

Miller WR, Hester RK: Rules of evidence and burden of proof: response to Mazza (letter). Am Psychol 44:1245–1246, 1989

Miller WR, Rollnick S: Motivational Interviewing. New York, Guilford, 1991

Miller WR, Taylor CA, West JC: Focused versus broad-spectrum behavior therapy for problem drinkers. J Consult Clin Psychol 48:590–601, 1980

Miller WR, Sovereign RG, Tonigan JS: Enhancing motivation for change in problem drinking: a controlled comparison of two therapist styles. J Consult Clin Psychol (in press)

O'Farrell TJ: Marital therapy in the treatment of alcoholism, in Clinical Handbook of Marital Therapy. Edited by Jacobson NS, Gurman AS. New York, Guilford, 1986, pp 513–535

O'Farrell TJ, Cowles KS: Behavioral marital therapy, in Handbook of Alcoholism Treatment. Edited by Hester RK, Miller WR. Elmsford, NY, Pergamon, 1989, pp 183–205

O'Farrell TJ, Cutter HSG: Behavioral marital therapy couples groups for male alcoholics and their wives. J Subst Abuse Treat 1:191–204, 1984

Polich JM: Epidemiology of alcohol abuse in military and civilian populations. Am J Public Health 71:1125–1152, 1981

Rimmele CT, Miller WR, Dougher MJ: Aversion therapies, in Handbook of Alcoholism Treatment. Edited by Hester RK, Miller WR. Elmsford, NY, Pergamon, 1989, pp 128–140

Sanchez-Craig M: Therapist's Manual for Secondary Prevention of Alcohol Problems: Procedures for Teaching Moderate Drinking and Abstinence. Toronto, Canada, Addiction Research Foundation, 1984

Semer JM, Friedland P, Vaisberg M, et al: The use of metronidazole in the treatment of alcoholism: a pilot study. Am J Psychiatry 123:722–724, 1966

Sisson RW, Azrin NH: The community reinforcement approach, in Handbook of Alcoholism Treatment. Edited by Hester RK, Miller WR. Elmsford, NY, Pergamon, 1989, pp 242–258

Stockwell T, Towne C: Anxiety and stress management, in Handbook of Alcoholism Treatment. Edited by Hester RK, Miller WR. Elmsford, NY, Pergamon, 1989, pp 222–230

Taylor JAT: A new agent for combined somatic and psychic therapy of alcoholism: a case study and preliminary report. Bulletin of the Los Angeles Neurological Society 29:158–162, 1964

Templer DI, Kauffman I: Exploitation or neglect. Am Psychol 43:200–201, 1988

Wilson A: Patient management in disulfiram implant therapy. Can J Psychiatry 24:537–541, 1979

Wilson A, Davidson WJ, White J: Disulfiram implantation: placebo, psychological deterrent, and pharmacological deterrent effects. Br J Psychiatry 129:277–280, 1976

Wilson A, Davidson WJ, Blanchard R, et al: Disulfiram implantation: a placebo-controlled trial with two-year follow-up. J Stud Alcohol 39:809–819, 1978

# Outcome Research

## *Drug Abuse*

*Dean R. Gerstein, Ph.D.*

P atient outcomes of treatment for drug dependence have been studied in light of the chronic, relapsing nature of the disorders, that is, not in terms of cure versus failure to cure during the course of treatment, but the extent of remission and degrees of improvement over time. Because the mechanisms of drug dependence remain veiled in complexity and treatment approaches vary widely, an iterative presentation is needed to convey the results of outcome studies. This chapter summarizes current knowledge about treatment outcomes within a threefold paradigm, repeated for each treatment modality:

▼ *What are the concepts behind the treatment?* That is, what is the theoretical rationale for each mode of treatment, what specific types of drug problems or population groups are being addressed, and what is the expected and observed efficacy at follow-up under trial conditions?

▼ *How well does each modality work in practice?* How adequate is the methodology to evaluate nonexperimental programs, and what do the best of these evaluations reveal?

▼ *Why do nonexperimental outcomes fall short of trial results?* To what extent is the problem poor implementation, unsuitable diagnosis (patient selection), high prevalence of complications, noncompliance, or adverse environmental effects?

The major modalities of drug treatment considered here are outpatient methadone maintenance, residential therapeutic communities, outpatient nonmethadone treatment, and inpatient/outpatient chemical dependency treatment. Some methods of treatment diverge from these general types. In particular, two well-known types of treatment are not covered here, for different reasons. First, there are virtually no data to answer the critical questions for

This chapter is a shortened and revised version of a previous article (Gerstein 1992). It draws extensively on work carried out under the auspices of the Institute of Medicine's Substance Abuse Coverage Study (Gerstein and Harwood 1990, 1992), supported by National Institute on Drug Abuse Contract 283-88-0009-SA. The author thanks M. Douglas Anglin, John C. Ball, David T. Courtwright, David A. Deitch, Robert L. Hubbard, Lawrence S. Lewin, Herbert D. Kleber, and Henrick J. Harwood, above all, for their insights and comments on the earlier versions.

**Outcome Research: Drug Abuse**

▼ 45 ▼

independent self-help fellowship groups such as Narcotics Anonymous (NA), Cocaine Anonymous (CA), or the Oxford Houses. Although the ideas underlying the Anonymous fellowships were incorporated at the outset into the clinical approaches of therapeutic communities and chemical dependency programs (in fact, the 12 steps of the Anonymous creed are so fundamental to the chemical dependency modality, that the latter has been referred to as the "professionalization of Alcoholics Anonymous [AA]"), the fellowships have shied away from formal evaluation.

The second exclusion is detoxification, or management of acute withdrawal symptoms. Detoxification *without subsequent treatment* has consistently been found to have no effects (in terms of reducing subsequent drug use behavior and especially relapse to dependence) that are discernibly superior to those achieved by untreated withdrawal (Cole et al. 1981; Newman 1983; Moffet et al. 1973; Resnick 1983; Sheffet et al. 1976). There has been significant success in the management of cocaine withdrawal symptoms and craving in ambulatory clinical trials (Dackis et al. 1987; Gawin et al. 1989a, 1989b; Mello et al. 1989; Tennant and Sagherian 1987), but dropout rates in the programs in which trials have been conducted range from 30% to 70%.

A special topic concluding the main section of the chapter is treatment in correctional institutions. A specialized literature on correctional treatment has arisen, and the vast growth in imprisoned populations makes this topic especially important.

## ▼ METHADONE MAINTENANCE

### What Is Methadone Maintenance?

Methadone maintenance (MM) is a treatment specifically designed for dependence on narcotic analgesics, particularly the narcotic of greatest concern in the United States, heroin. The controversy surrounding MM has made it the subject of hundreds of studies, including a number of clinical trials, from which good evidence has accumulated about the safety and efficacy of methadone.

At the base of MM is the empirical observation, made before the biological reasons for it were well understood, that all narcotic analgesics may be substituted for one another with sufficient adjustments in dose and route of administration. Methadone, however, has several unusual pharmacological properties that make it especially suited to a maintenance approach. It is effective orally, and because of its particular pattern of absorption and metabolism, a single dose within a train of level doses, in the typical maintenance range of 30–100 mg/day, has a gradual onset and yields a fairly even effect across a 24-hour period or longer. Methadone is thus conducive to a regime of single daily maintenance doses, eliminating dramatic subjective or behavioral changes and making it easy for the clinician and patient to fit into a routine clinic schedule. This pattern is very different from the shorter action and more dramatic highs and lows of heroin, morphine, and most other opioids.

The long-term toxic side effects of methadone, as of other opioids if taken in hygienic conditions in controlled doses, are notably benign. Since the mid-1960s, about 1.5 million person-years of MM have accumulated in the United States. The accumulated clinical experience, confirmed by thousands of carefully documented research cases, yields a well-supported conclusion that is epitomized by the following:

> [P]hysiological and biochemical alterations occur, but there are minimal side effects that are clinically detectable in patients during chronic MM treatment. Toxicity related to methadone during chronic treatment is extraordinarily rare. The most important medical consequence of methadone during chronic treatment, in fact, is the marked improvement in general health and nutritional status observed in patients compared with their status at the time of admission to treatment. (Kreek 1983, p. 474)

MM may be administered only within especially licensed programs. These programs are largely ambulatory, with daily visits to swallow doses under clinical observation. After several months of "clean" drug testing and compliance with other program requirements such as counseling appointments, patients may regularly take home 1 or more days' doses between every-other-day, twice-weekly, or even weekly visits—a revocable privilege. Some MM patients voluntarily taper their doses to abstinence and conclude treatment, others remain on MM indefinitely, and others are tapered and discharged because of poor response or compliance.

MM programs include numerous monitoring

and adjustment features that stress the need for patients to wean themselves away from street-drug seeking. Program clinics have specific hours for dispensing, counseling, and medical appointments. There are codes of proscribed behavior (e.g., no violence or threats of violence), and monitored drug tests are conducted at random intervals—at least monthly and as often as weekly—although the cost of the tests has led financially strained programs to cut them back to the minimum. Counseling includes the assessment of patient attitudes and appearance (important in themselves and as clues to drug behavior) and the gathering of information about employment, family, and criminal activities; counselors offer psychotherapy and individualized social assistance and recognition, depending on their case loads and their training for such tasks.

There was extensive research from the late 1960s to the late 1970s on a longer-acting methadone congener, L-α-acetylmethadol (LAAM), that requires less frequent doses (i.e., every 2–3 days instead of daily). LAAM has been studied in a series of phased clinical trials but has not yet been approved for nonexperimental use, although its safety and freedom from toxic side effects appear similar to those of methadone (Blaine et al. 1981; Ling et al. 1978; Savage et al. 1976). Overall, during the trials methadone was more successful than LAAM in retaining patients in treatment (by 20%) largely because more LAAM recipients felt that the medication was not "holding," that is, not keeping opioid withdrawal symptoms from beginning to emerge between doses. This lack of holding was a result that Goldstein and Judson (1974), after a double-blind study, judged to be more psychological than physiological in origin. LAAM recipients who stayed in treatment used less heroin and performed better on other clinical measures than methadone patients, particularly those on lower methadone doses. Some clinicians reported a substantially improved therapeutic climate in LAAM clinics owing to the more relaxed visiting schedule of 3 days per week (Goldstein 1976). It is probable that there are patients who would do better on LAAM than on methadone, and vice versa, with results for both likely to improve with better dose optimization and counseling about differences between the two drugs. A revival of interest in LAAM and an attempt to restore the initiative toward approval by the Food and Drug Administration for nonexperimental use are under way.

## How Well Does Methadone Maintenance Work?

Early trials of MM in New York (Dole and Nyswander 1965, 1967; Dole et al. 1966; Dole et al. 1968; Dole et al. 1969) noted two striking findings: 1) the majority of patients would remain in treatment for as long as it was available to them, in substantial contrast to the usual experience in outpatient psychotherapy; and 2) MM significantly improved the condition of patients as revealed by studies that considered behavior in the community for periods of several months to several years. Although there was some use of other drugs, including heroin, especially in the first few weeks after admission, such use generally fell off over time, contrasting sharply with the increasing return over time to heroin dependence that was the norm after detoxification or other typical medical or psychiatric treatments. The steadiness of employment increased somewhat, but a much more dramatic change was the sustained reduction in criminal behavior, especially drug trafficking crimes.

The most convincing results about the capacity of MM to induce patient changes, independent of initial selection or motivational effects, come from a handful of widely separated randomized clinical trials by Dole et al. (1969) in New York, Newman and Whitehill (1978) in Hong Kong, and Gunne and Gronbladh (1984) in Sweden. The latter may be taken as representative (Figure 5–1). Thirty-four heroin-dependent individuals applied for admission to the only methadone clinic in a Swedish community; 17 were randomly assigned to MM, and 17 were assigned to outpatient nonmethadone treatment (these individuals could not apply for admission to the methadone clinic again for 24 months). After 2 years, 71% of methadone patients were doing well, compared with 6% of control patients. After 5 years, 13 of the methadone patients remained in treatment and were still not using heroin, and 4 had been excluded from treatment because of unremitting drug problems. Among the control patients, 9 had applied for and entered MM; of these, 8 patients were not using drugs and were socially productive. Of the 8 control patients who did not apply for methadone when eligible it was reported that "five are dead (allegedly from overdose), two in prison, and one is still drug free" (p. 211).

Similar results have been reported in a number of California cities that abruptly closed publicly sup-

## Before

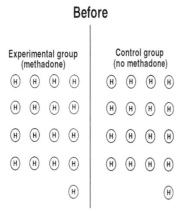

## After 2 years

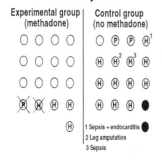

1 Sepsis + endocarditis
2 Leg amputation
3 Sepsis

## After 5 years

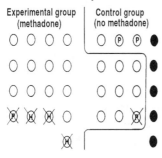

**Figure 5–1. Clinical trial of methadone maintenance (MM) versus outpatient nonmethadone treatment for heroin addiction conducted through the Swedish MM Program.** The left half represents the group assigned to MM; the right half represents control group. *Before admission*: Each circle represents a subject 20–24 years old. *H* indicates regular intravenous heroin abuse. *Two years after admission*: *White circles* = no drug abuse; *H* = abuse of heroin or (in experimental group) hypnotics; *P* = subject in prison; *black circle* = subject deceased; *crossed circle* = patient expelled from treatment. *Five years after admission*: Nine persons from the original control group have been accepted into MM.
*Source.* Gunne L, Gronbladh L: "The Swedish Methadone Maintenance Program," in *The Social and Medical Aspects of Drug Abuse.* Edited by Serban G. Jamaica, NY, Spectrum Publications, 1984, pp 205–213.

ported MM for fiscal and political reasons. In cities where MM became much less accessible as a result of such closures, former patients as a whole did appreciably less well at 2-year follow-up (in terms of heroin use, other criminal behavior, and, to a lesser degree, employment) than comparison groups in locations where there was continued access to treatment. In cities where public programs closed but private ones opened, those who transferred to the alternative MM programs did much better (in terms of staying free of drugs and out of crime) than those who did not or could not continue treatment (Anglin et al. 1989; McGlothlin and Anglin 1981; McGlothlin et al. 1977).

In all the studies cited and in later multisite studies (Hubbard et al. 1989; Simpson et al. 1979), longer retention in methadone as opposed to early attrition from the program was associated with much better results as measured by reduced heroin use and other criminal activity, even net of baseline conditions and covariates.

## Why Do the Results of Methadone Maintenance Vary?

A significant proportion of MM patients do not respond well to treatment for a variety of reasons relating to the patients themselves and to the programs. This proportion averages about one in four, although there is wide variation from program to program (Ball et al. 1988; Hubbard et al. 1989). Some patients enter MM for purposes other than to pursue recovery; such patients are not compliant or responsive and are most likely to leave treatment after short periods. It is much easier to identify these patients after the fact than at intake.

The largest group of patients perform at least moderately well in response to MM and would do poorly without it, even when other kinds of treatment are available. There is compelling evidence that program factors such as methadone-dosing policies and counselor characteristics affect their behavior beyond any initial differences in motivation or severity of problems. Program performance (in terms of patient retention and continued use of drugs) varies greatly across programs. The multisite Treatment Outcome Prospective Study (TOPS), for example, showed a large degree of variation in clinically important patient outcomes across nine MM programs (Hubbard et al. 1989). Twelve-month retention rates averaged 34% of admissions; five programs had rates of 7%–

25%, and two programs had rates greater than 50%. Regular heroin use by patients at follow-up (approximately 3 years later) was reported by 21% of the entire follow-up sample; two programs had rates greater than 30%, and three had rates of 11%–14%.

Variation in performance has been linked most strongly to variations in methadone dosage policies. Programs that are committed to maintaining low average doses (30–50 mg/day) as a virtual goal of treatment—because of therapeutic philosophy or because state regulators strongly discourage higher doses—are less tolerant of occasional patient drug use, missed counseling appointments, and other such treatment lapses, and have markedly lower patient retention rates than more tolerant, higher dosage programs. This lower tolerance does not, however, act as a stimulant to better patient behavior or as a conveyor to move poorly responding patients out and bring in or keep better ones. There is solid, experimentally grounded evidence, reviewed by Hargreaves and concluded by an expert consensus conference (Hargreaves 1983) that higher dose levels are fundamentally more successful than lower ones in controlling a patient's illicit drug consumption during treatment. MM programs that prescribe average doses of 60–100 mg/day yield consistently better results than those averaging less. Doses in excess of 120 mg/day are seldom needed.

However, many programs and regulatory officials are committed to low-dose regimes. Ball and colleagues (Ball and Ross 1991; Ball et al. 1988; Dole 1989) confirmed dramatic differences in opioid use among six methadone clinics in three eastern cities studied in 1985–1986, all of which had been selected as well-reputed programs. In the best clinic, urinalysis revealed that 10% of enrolled patients in the sample had used intravenous drugs in the month prior to 1-year follow-up. In the two worst clinics, more than 55% of patients had used intravenous drugs in the previous month.

Discriminant function analysis found that the most important factor in predicting intravenous drug use was dose level (see Table 5–1). However, programs with the highest illicit drug consumption not only had low methadone doses but also high rates of staff turnover and poor relationships between staff and patients. Knowledge of and sensitivity to the clinical significance of appropriate dose levels is probably one sizable element in a constellation of clinical competencies and strategies that contribute to the greater

or lesser effectiveness of MM programs. There are only rudimentary standards of training, credentialing, continuing education, evaluation, and clinical performance of counselors and other treatment program staff. Remarkably few research efforts have focused on the area of competence, appropriate training, and different service arrangements in the clinical management of MM patients. A serendipitous random-assignment opportunity for study by McLellan et al. (1988), which demonstrated striking differences in counselor effectiveness (among four counselors) within the framework of a large, stable, well-regarded MM program, is a lonely beacon in the literature.

## ▼ THERAPEUTIC COMMUNITIES

### What Is a Therapeutic Community?

Therapeutic communities (TCs) were originally developed to treat the same problem as MM programs: the "hard-core" heroin-dependent criminal. The residential TC has a broader perspective, however; it treats individuals who are severely dependent on any illicitly obtained drug or combination of drugs and whose social adjustment to conventional family and occupational responsibilities is severely compromised as a result of drug seeking—but most were compromised before drug seeking entered the picture. As of the 1980s, cocaine dependence has overtaken heroin dependence in the TC population. The profile of TC patients is also more demographically diverse than that of the heroin-dependent population. Generally, on average, TC patients in the early 1970s, when there was a national counting system, were several years younger and predominantly white by a modest margin: 57% of TC patients were white, 34% were black, and 9% were Hispanic; 16% of methadone patients were white, 58% were black, and 26% were Hispanic (Sells 1974b). This pattern has continued in later program samples (Hubbard et al. 1989).

The TCs' group-centered methods encompass the following, all of which are grounded in an interdependent social environment with a direct link to a specific historical foundation:

▼ Firm behavioral norms across a wide range of proscriptions and specifications

▼ Reality-oriented group and individual psychotherapy that extends to lengthy encounter sessions focusing on current living issues or more deepseated emotional problems

▼ A system of clearly specified rewards and punishments within a communal economy of housework and other roles

▼ A series of hierarchical responsibilities, privileges, and esteem achieved by working up a "ladder" of tasks from admission to graduation

▼ A degree of mobility from patient to staff statuses

To a significant extent the TC simulates and enforces a model family environment that the patient lacked during developmentally critical preadolescent and adolescent years. The TC tries to make up for lost years in an intensive, relatively short period of time: approximately 6–12 months of residential envelopment and an additional 6–12 months of gradual reentry to the outside community prior to "graduation." Continued alumni involvement is encouraged, as it provides role models for new residents, recognition and reinforcement for the graduate, and psychological and financial support for the program.

## How Well Do Therapeutic Communities Work?

Conclusions about the effectiveness of TCs are limited by the difficulties in maintaining randomized clinical trial protocols in a highly interactive treatment milieu and a population resistant to following instructions. The most notable attempt to evaluate the effectiveness of TCs compared with untreated or differently treated control subjects was conducted in California by Bale et al. (1980). The subjects were 585 heroin-addicted veteran men who sought and gained entry to the Veterans Administration (VA) Medical Center in Palo Alto, California, for a 5-day opioid detoxification program during an 18-month intake period in the mid-1970s. The subjects also met the study's requirements of no pending felony charges or major psychiatric complications. About one-fifth of the subjects denied any interest in transferring to a VA drug treatment program after detoxification (some later changed their minds). Those interested were randomly assigned to one of two MM clinics or one of three TCs.

The clinical staff invested significant time in trying to enlist every subject in his assigned program, and the overall rate of transfers from detoxification to VA programs doubled as a result. Nevertheless, the random-assignment design was thoroughly compromised (see Table 5–2). Less than half of the randomly assigned subjects entered and spent as long as 1 week in any of the VA treatment programs, and only half of those entered the specific programs they had been assigned to (the others waited out at least a 30-day exclusion period to enter their own preferred program). Altogether, 42% of the total study cohort did not enter any kind of treatment during the follow-up year, approximately 28% entered one of the VA TCs, 12% entered a VA methadone clinic, and 19% entered a non-VA program.

The lack of compliance affected the study so profoundly that research analysts (who were independent of the clinical staff) were obliged to use multivariate statistical procedures to control for initial differences in age, ethnicity, prior treatment, drug use patterns, and criminal history among treat-

**Table 5–1.** Heroin or cocaine consumption in the last 30 days by methadone dose of 338 clients in treatment for 6 months to 4.5 years

| Dose (mg/day) | (n) | % | Percentage who used drug within past 30 days | | | |
| | | | No heroin used | No heroin or cocaine used | Any heroin used | Any cocaine used |
| --- | --- | --- | --- | --- | --- | --- |
| 0–39 | 105 | 100 | 69 | 57 | 31 | 29 |
| 40–59 | 99 | 100 | 86 | 68 | 14 | 28 |
| 60–79 | 89 | 100 | 94 | 80 | 6 | 18 |
| 80–100 | 45 | 100 | 98 | 89 | 2 | 9 |
| Total | 338 | | | | | |

*Source.* Ball 1989.

ment and nontreatment groups. About 13% of the patients stayed less than 1 week (these were considered to be *no treatment* subjects), 57% dropped out within 7 weeks, and 85% left treatment before 6 months. In contrast, approximately 65% of patients entering MM were continuously in treatment for the follow-up year. The TC group was therefore divided at the median length of stay (for all admissions who had remained longer than a week), which was 50 days. On average, the short-term group stayed in treatment approximately 3 weeks, the long-term group stayed approximately 20 weeks, and the methadone group stayed approximately 40 weeks.

At 1-year follow-up, those who had been successfully recontacted (all but 7%) were divided among the no-treatment (41%), non-VA (21%), short-term TC (14%), long-term TC (14%), and methadone (11%) categories. Controlling for pretreatment characteristics, the combined long-term TC and methadone patient groups, compared with the combined no-treatment, non-VA treatment, and short-term TC groups, were

▼ One-third less likely to have used heroin in the past month (41% versus 64%)
▼ Two-fifths less likely to have been convicted during the year (22% versus 37%)
▼ Two-thirds less likely to be incarcerated at year's end (7% versus 19%)
▼ One-and-one-half times more likely to be at work or in school at year's end (59% versus 40%)

The long-term TC group ranked somewhat better than the total methadone group on each measure, but the differences were not large enough to be statistically significant in a sample of this size.

Beyond the efforts of Bale et al. (1980), there is a significant controlled observational literature on TCs. The bulk of these studies have focused on patients admitted to particular programs such as Phoenix House and Daytop Village in New York; in addition, TOPS and the Drug Abuse Reporting Program (DARP) separately examined patients who were admitted to about 10 TCs.

The most extensive outcome evaluations from a single program come from Phoenix House in New York. De Leon et al. (1982) studied a sample of 230 graduates and dropouts and found that before admission the two groups were very similar with respect to criminal activity and drug use but that dropouts had somewhat greater employment. After treatment, the status of both groups was much better than before, but graduates had dramatically superior posttreatment outcomes compared with dropouts (see Table 5–3).

One smaller study that is notable for its careful execution followed a random sample of graduates and dropouts from a Connecticut TC (Romond et al. 1975) with an 18- to 24-month treatment plan. The authors found few pretreatment differences between the graduate and dropout groups except that women were much less likely than men to graduate. All 20 graduates in the sample were successfully contacted,

**Table 5–2.** Subject compliance (percentage) with assignment to treatment programs

| Program entered | Program assigned | | | Methadone maintenance | Detox (self-selected) | Total |
|---|---|---|---|---|---|---|
| | TC I | TC II | TC III | | | |
| | (79)[a] | (147) | (137) | (94) | (128) | (585) |
| None | 44 | 40 | 36 | 28 | 59 | 42 |
| Non-VA | 9 | 16 | 20 | 20 | 28 | 19 |
| TC I | 18[b] | 1 | 2 | 5 | 0 | 4 |
| TC II | 13 | 24[b] | 9 | 9 | 6 | 13 |
| TC III | 13 | 10 | 22[b] | 8 | 2 | 11 |
| Methadone mainentance | 4 | 10 | 12 | 31[b] | 4 | 12 |
| Total[c] | 100 | 100 | 100 | 100 | 100 | 100 |

[a]Numbers in parentheses are subjects assigned to program.
[b]Percentage entering program to which assigned.
[c]Totals may not add to 100% due to rounding.
*Source.* Adapted from Bale RN, Van Stone WW, Kuldau JM, et al: "Therapeutic Communities vs. Methadone Maintenance: A Prospective Controlled Study of Narcotic Addiction Treatment: Design and One-Year Follow-Up." *Arch Gen Psychiatry* 37:179–193, 1980. Copyright 1980 American Medical Association.

10 of 31 dropouts in the sample were not located, and 1 refused an interview, yielding 20 successful contacts. Graduates had spent on average 21 months in treatment, compared with 5.7 months for dropouts (range = 10 days to 16 months). Interview data were corroborated through formal and informal community networks.

Graduates had consistently better outcomes. Only 1 of 20 graduates relapsed to dependence for some part of the follow-up period, another 5 sometimes used nonopioid drugs, and 14 remained drug free throughout the interval. Altogether, graduates spent 0.5% of the follow-up period dependent. Of the 20 dropouts interviewed, 14 relapsed to dependence for some of the follow-up period, 2 used nonopioids occasionally, 1 was incarcerated for the entire period, and 3 had used no drugs; 35% of the dropouts' posttreatment time was spent as drug dependent. Ninety-four percent of the graduates' posttreatment time had been in school or employed versus 40% of the dropouts' posttreatment time.

DARP provided further important controlled observational findings about the effectiveness of TCs (Sells 1974a, 1974b; Simpson et al. 1979). The mean and median lengths of stay in the traditional TCs involved in the DARP were close to 7 months, which was well below the average 16-month treatment plan. At 12 months after admission, 71% of those admitted had left the TC voluntarily or by expulsion, although only 5% had completed their treatment plan by then; the ultimate graduation rate was 23%.

Most of the DARP's outcome measures (i.e., daily opioids, daily nonopioids, arrests, incarceration) at 1 year after discharge were significantly better for TC patients compared with the outcomes of detoxification-only and intake-only cases. As in the Bale et al. study, the multivariate-adjusted outcomes for TCs and MM patients (matched for time since admission) on daily opioid use, nonopioid use, employment, and a composite index were quite similar. The length of stay in treatment was a positive, robust, significant predictor of posttreatment outcomes (i.e., drugs, jobs, and crime). Among patients staying more than 90 days in treatment, there was a positive and linear relationship between outcome and retention. The outcomes among patients staying less than 90 days were indistinguishable from detox-only and intake-only cases, and there was no discernible relation of outcome and length of stay.

The final results of the TOPS, which were derived using multivariate logistical regression to control for pretreatment demographics, drug use, and criminality, yielded the familiar positive relationship between length of stay and outcome but with no clear thresh-

**Table 5–3.** Follow-up results of treatment at Phoenix House (New York), measured on crime, drug use, and employment indices (percentage)

| Index | n | Pretreatment | Posttreatment | P |
|---|---|---|---|---|
| Crime | | | | |
| Total | 226 | 96.5 | 29.2 | < .001 |
| Dropouts | 154 | 97.4 | 40.9 | < .01 |
| Graduates | 72 | 94.4 | 4.2 | < .001 |
| Dropout/graduate differences (P) | | NS | < .001 | |
| Drug use | | | | |
| Total | 229 | 94.3 | 32.3 | < .001 |
| Dropouts | 156 | 96.8 | 43.6 | < .05 |
| Graduates | 73 | 89.0 | 9.2 | < .001 |
| Dropout/graduate differences (P) | | NS | < .001 | |
| Employed > 50% of the time | | | | |
| Total | 230 | 32.6 | 75.7 | < .001 |
| Dropouts | 156 | 36.5 | 66.0 | < .001 |
| Graduates | 74 | 24.3 | 95.9 | < .001 |
| Dropout/graduate differences (P) | | < .10 | < .001 | |

*Note.* NS = not significant.
*Source.* Reprinted from De Leon G, Wexler HK, Jainchill N: "The Therapeutic Community: Success and Improvement Rates 5 Years After Treatment." *Int J Addict* 17:703–747, 1982 by courtesy of Marcel Dekker, Inc.

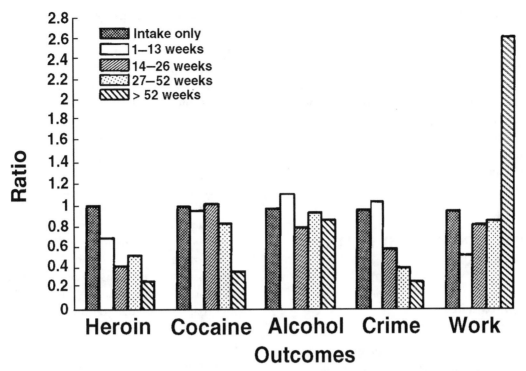

**Figure 5–2. Outcomes and retention in therapeutic communities included in the Treatment Outcome Prospective Study.** Outcomes are shown as odds ratios derived from multivariate analyses. The odds that members of the intake-only group will report a successful outcome at follow-up are compared with the odds for those who were in treatment for 1–13 weeks, 14–26 weeks, 27–52 weeks, and 53 weeks or more. The intake-only odds are standardized or set equal to 1 for each criterion; the other group odds are expressed as ratios of 1.
*Source.* Hubbard RL, Marsden ME, Rachal JV, et al: *Drug Abuse Treatment: A National Study of Effectiveness.* Chapel Hill, NC, The University of North Carolina Press, 1989.

old (Hubbard et al. 1989; see Figure 5–2). One year or more in a TC was significantly related to reduced heroin use, lower crime involvement, and increased employment at a 12-month follow-up. The odds of having problems with heroin or crime were about two-fifths as great for the long-term residential patients as for early dropouts, and their odds of having a job were nearly 1.7 times higher. Cocaine use followed a similar pattern, but the effect was not statistically significant. Alcohol problems were not related to treatment retention.

In summary, even in the absence of true clinical trials, it is difficult to credit any explanation of the multisite and single-site results other than the following: TCs can strongly affect the behavior of many of the drug-dependent individuals who enter them, and retention in treatment after some minimum number of months (how many months seems to vary with the program) is positively and significantly related to improved outcomes as measured by illicit drug con-

sumption, other criminal activity, and economically productive behavior.

## Why Do the Results of TCs Vary?

There are wide variations in outcome indicators across programs. In 1980, the last full year that national treatment patient information systems data were available, outcome data demonstrated graphically that effectiveness varied significantly from area to area and even more so from program to program. The year 1980 was one of relative program stability, yet very large variations were seen in the treatment "completion" rates reported for that year by residential programs in 54 cities (see Figure 5–3), most of which were TCs; inconsistent definitions of completion could not account for the breadth of these variations.

There has been virtually no systematic research about the determinants of patient success and failure in TCs. It is plausible that the results of TC treatment depend on three primary elements: patient motivations, quality (and quantity) of staffing, and the psychosocial organization and therapeutic design of the program. TC staffing has been particularly problematic during the 1980s because of constant budget pressures and rising competition for credentialed, experienced staff with for-profit outpatient and chemical dependency treatment providers. Yet there are no studies that specifically investigate how TC staffing relates to the effectiveness of treatment.

## ▼ OUTPATIENT NONMETHADONE TREATMENT

### What Is Outpatient Nonmethadone Treatment?

Outpatient nonmethadone (OPNM) programs range in designed duration from one session of assessment/referral to virtual outpatient TCs with daily psychotherapy and counseling for 1 year or longer (Kleber and Slobetz 1979). In between are the vast majority of programs, which practice 1–2 weekly visits for 3–6 months and use a panoply of therapeutic approaches from psychiatry, counseling psychology, social work, TCs, and the 12-step paradigm. Some OPNM programs contract extensively with probation departments, offering limited therapeutic services but monitoring compliance with probation conditions, particularly through administration of drug tests.

In some OPNM programs, medications are prescribed by staff psychiatrists or other physicians. These include ameliorants for acute withdrawal symptoms, maintenance antagonists to prevent intoxication (e.g., naltrexone), medications to control drug cravings after withdrawal, or treatments for psychiatric comorbidities (e.g., depression, mood disorders, schizophrenia). Programs with the requisite resources may deliver or link their patients to formal education, vocational training, health care (e.g., AIDS testing or treatment), housing assistance (especially for homeless patients), support for battered spouses and children, and other social services.

The diversity of OPNM treatment defies easy summary and is matched by the heterogeneity of its patient populations. These populations generally are not abusing opioids, usually are not involved in the criminal justice system (at least were not so during the DARP and TOPS periods), and include significant proportions of abusing rather than dependent individuals—differing in all these respects from typical methadone and TC patients.

### How Well Does Outpatient Nonmethadone Treatment Work?

The major conclusion that can be offered about OPNM is familiar: the longer patients remain in treatment, the better the outcomes at follow-up. These conclusions are based entirely on multivariate results (statistically controlled for baseline covariates of outcome) of the two major multisite evaluations, DARP and TOPS (Hubbard et al. 1989; Sells 1974a, 1974b; Simpson et al. 1979). OPNM patients in DARP exhibited statistically significant follow-up improvements relative to pretreatment in terms of employment and consumption of opioids and nonopioids, but not in terms of arrest rates, which were much lower before treatment than they were in TC or MM patients. The DARP comparison groups (those in detoxification programs or who made no contact after intake) reported no significant pre- to posttreatment changes except in opioid consumption (Simpson et al. 1979).

Analyses of retention (Simpson 1981) produced

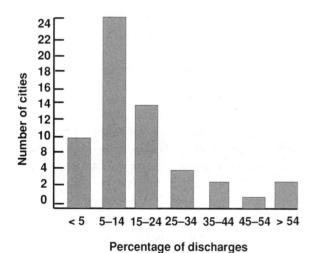

**Figure 5–3.** Variations in "completion" rates of opioid patients in residential programs in 54 U.S. cities. *Source.* National Institute on Drug Abuse 1981.

results identical to those for TC patients: patients staying in treatment less than 90 days showed no improvement relative to the detox-/intake-only patients, whereas those staying longer had improved outcomes on a composite score that incorporated drug use, criminality, and productivity scales. For the 90-days-plus group, outcome scores were strongly and significantly correlated with total length of stay.

The TOPS study (Hubbard et al. 1989) collected data on 1,600 OPNM patients admitted to 10 programs. Patients reported better performance during and after treatment than before admission, and multivariate analyses strongly related posttreatment outcomes to length of stay, using multivariate logistical regression to adjust for patient drug use histories and sociodemographic characteristics at admission (see Figure 5–4). The analysis suggested that the critical retention threshold may be 6 months, but only 17% of TOPS OPNM patients were retained this long. OPNM dropout rates were significantly higher than for methadone or TCs. At 4 weeks the programs retained only 59% of patients; 18% eventually completed the course of treatment.

### Why Do the Results of Outpatient Nonmethadone Treatment Vary?

There is no answer to this question for OPNM programs. Although there is evidence of variation in program retention rates, there is very little information about what the "active ingredients" in this treatment modality are that might lead to these variations. One can only speculate that the same factors that emerge from methadone and TC research, in

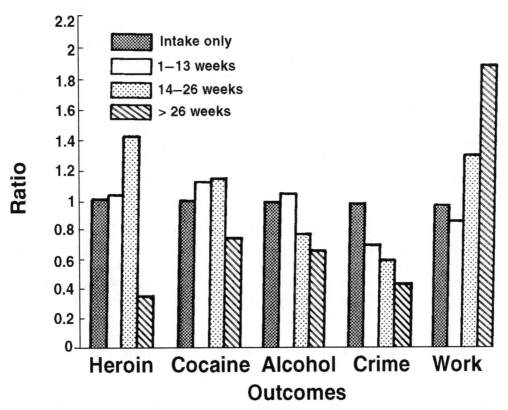

**Figure 5–4. Outcomes and retention in outpatient nonmethadone programs based on data from the Treatment Outcome Prospective Study.** Outcomes are shown as odds ratios derived from multivariate analyses. The odds that members of the intake-only group will report a successful outcome at follow-up are compared with the odds for those who were in treatment for 1–13 weeks, 14–26 weeks, and 26 weeks or more. The intake-only odds are standardized or set equal to 1 for each criterion; the other group odds are expressed as ratios of 1.
*Source.* Hubbard RL, Marsden ME, Rachal JV, et al: *Drug Abuse Treatment: A National Study of Effectiveness.* Chapel Hill, NC, The University of North Carolina Press, 1989.

particular staff quality and program design, may be equally important here.

## ▼ CHEMICAL DEPENDENCY TREATMENT

### What Is Chemical Dependency Treatment?

Chemical dependency (CD) treatment is also called Minnesota Model, 28-day, 12-step, or Hazelden-type treatment. It is the predominant therapeutic approach in inpatient and residential programs that are oriented heavily toward insured populations. Virtually all of these programs were originally oriented toward alcohol problems but have increasingly served patients who use illicit drugs. Cook (1988a, 1988b) has provided a concise historical review of the development of the Minnesota Model. He notes the similarities between the underlying theories that shape CD and TC treatment but observes that they developed almost completely independently of each other.

CD treatment is usually an intensive, highly structured 3- to 6-week inpatient regimen. Patients begin with an in-depth psychiatric and psychosocial evaluation and are actively engaged in developing and implementing a recovery plan, which is patterned on the *step work* (working through the 12 steps of recovery) of AA. Self-help is a large part of therapy; patients work with each other and are generally required to attend AA/CA/NA meetings. Virtually all CD programs incorporate daily classroom-type lectures plus two to three meetings per week in small task-oriented groups to teach patients about the disease concept of dependence, focusing on the harmful medical and psychosocial effects of illicit drugs and excessive alcohol consumption. There is also an individual track for each patient, meetings twice a week with a *focal counselor*, and appointments with other professionals if medical, psychiatric, or family services are needed. Recently, there has been increasing emphasis on family or codependent therapy.

Aftercare is considered quite important in CD treatment, but relatively few program resources are devoted to it. Patients are urged to continue an intensive schedule of AA/CA/NA attendance through the follow-up period of 3 months to 2 years, with continued contacts thereafter at a lower rate. Some programs follow up with monthly telephone calls, weekly group therapy, or individual counselling as needed.

CD treatment has some elements in common with the TC approach, but there are noteworthy differences. The inpatient or residential phase of the CD treatment plan is much shorter, and the aftercare phase is seldom a strongly integrated program element. CD programs do not require patients to perform housekeeping duties, so there is more time available for psychotherapy and educational tasks; in the TC process, however, performance of housekeeping and other program maintenance responsibilities are an integral component of treatment. CD program staff, like TC staff, are a mixture of stable, recovering (from alcohol or drug dependence) individuals and treatment professionals. CD programs are especially attractive to patients with greater initial functional and social resources, who can afford the better facilities and amenities; indeed, the prototypical CD patient used to be approximately 40 years old, middle class, employed, white, and dependent on alcohol, whereas TC patients have almost always had massive functional and social deficits. Today, although the CD population is more diversified (programs are now seeing more patients with combined cocaine/alcohol problems, as well as a segment of adolescents with both psychiatric and drug diagnoses), these origins continue to shape the CD approach.

### How Well Does CD Treatment Work?

Research data on CD treatment for illicit drug problems are weaker than for the other modalities. There are no relevant random-assignment trials or quasi-experimental studies. No CD programs were in the DARP or TOPS samples. Only one observational study of a CD program employs an untreated comparison group (Rawson et al. 1986), and none have included in analysis patients with short lengths of stay. There is practically no use of multivariate statistical methods.

The extent of reasonably certain knowledge about CD treatment is that patients who present with drug problems at admission have poorer outcomes at the posttreatment follow-up than patients with alcohol problems (with no illicit drug consumption) in the same programs. This finding is consistent across studies by the CareUnit system, the Chemical Abuse/ Addiction Treatment Outcome Registry follow-up service, and the Hazelden center in Minnesota.

The CareUnit study (Comprehensive Care Corporation 1988) drew a sample of 1,002 adult patients who stayed at least 5 days in any one of 50 CareUnit programs in 1987, during which year CareUnits treated 46,000 adults and adolescents in more than 200 locations. About 53% of the sample had used multiple substances before admission, 29% on a daily basis. Clinical staff interviewed 723 patients at least 1 year after discharge. Sixty-one percent were classified as recovering at follow-up (fewer than four instances of use since discharge). Abstinence was about 10 percentage points lower for heavy consumers of illicit drugs (at admission) than for consumers primarily of alcohol. The strongest indicator of outcome was attendance at self-help groups after discharge: only 48% of nonattenders were recovering, compared with 79% of those attending the groups more than 29 times.

The Rawson et al. (1986) study reported on 83 individuals who responded to advertisements offering referral to cocaine treatment and who then self-selected a CD program, an outpatient program, or no treatment following an education/information session. The study found no statistically significant differences between the CD and no-treatment groups 8 months later. Studies of Hazelden drug patients (Gilmore 1985; Laudergan 1982) are too limited methodologically to merit detailing, which is unfortunate, given the prominence of this program. The findings are consistent with other results in indicating lower abstinence rates at follow-up for drug patients than for alcohol-only patients.

### Why Do CD Treatment Results Vary?

No studies distinguish the reasons why some patients in CD programs do well and others do not. As with other treatments, patient motivation and program staff quality are suspected factors. But there is no readily available information on variations in drug patient outcomes across CD programs or any attempts to relate such differences to systematic variations among patients or in the therapeutic approach.

## ▼ CORRECTIONAL TREATMENT PROGRAMS

The context for research on prison-based drug treatment programs is the largely null-difference results of most therapeutic treatment prisoners in hopes of reducing their recidivism (Besteman 1992; Chaiken 1989; Vaillant 1988). Yet Falkin et al. (1992) sound an optimistic note:

> Given the current array of treatment programs (many offering only occasional counselling, drug education or other limited services), the finding of evaluation research that many programs are ineffective is not surprising. To adjudge that drug treatment is unable to control recidivism because many programs do not is to miss the crucial point that some programs have been quite successful. With the proper program elements in place, treatment programs could achieve a significantly greater reduction in recidivism than by continuing a policy of imprisonment without adequate treatment.

Falkin et al.'s list of the elements necessary for a successful prison drug treatment program is succinct:

▼ A competent and committed staff
▼ Adequate administrative and material support by correctional authorities
▼ Separation from the general prison population
▼ Incorporation of self-help principles and ex-offender aid
▼ Comprehensive, intensive therapy aimed at the entire life-style of a patient and not just the substance abuse aspects
▼ An absolute essential—continuity of care into the parole period

Three moderately well-designed evaluations of prison-based programs that incorporate these criteria are available. The most recent and currently most influential study (Falkin et al. 1992; Frohling 1989) is of Stay'n Out, a prison program in New York. Stay'n Out is based on the social organization of Phoenix House, a TC, which has been adapted to the prison setting, with community-based TCs extending treatment contact after release. Stay'n Out patients from 1977 to 1984 ($N = 682$) were compared with prisoner groups receiving either regular drug abuse counseling ($N = 576$), milieu therapy, or who were waiting for Stay'n Out admission but paroled without treatment for lack of an opening during the 6–12 month "window" prior to their release date ($N = 197$). All groups were followed 2–9 years (average over 4 years) after release from prison.

As indicated in Table 5–4, the TC group was arrested significantly less often than the control subjects, with differences of 8–14 percentage points (which represent 22%–35% reductions in rearrest rates) for men and 6–12 percentage points (25%–40% reductions) for women. For every arrest, such individuals have generally committed hundreds of crimes (Ball et al. 1981; Johnson et al. 1985; Speckart and Anglin 1986). The authors indicate, however, that intergroup differences at follow-up in rates of reincarceration, rapidity of rearrest, and parole revocation were statistically or substantively negligible, except that significantly more Stay'n Out–treated women than untreated women successfully completed parole.

A controlled observational study has been reported (Field 1984, 1989; see Table 5–5) on Cornerstone, a modified TC program (a mixture of milieu therapy and TC principles) located in Oregon State Hospital in Salem. It is designed for state prisoners in their last year before parole eligibility; after release, parolees move to a halfway house. In the 3 years following release, Cornerstone participants were convicted significantly less often than comparable parolees, and graduates were much better at follow-up than early dropouts from the program. In the Stay'n Out study, and in several other well-regarded, well-studied voluntary correctional programs (Falkin et al. 1992), length of stay in treatment correlated strongly with nonrecidivism, the same result seen in community-based programs. The fact that early dropouts from prison programs are even more likely to recidivate, by every measure, than are untreated control subjects suggests that prison-based TCs may be more efficient than community-based programs at sorting out and excluding (or encouraging self-exclusion by) the poorest responders.

California's Civil Addict Program (CAP), which began in 1961 (Anglin 1988; Anglin and McGlothlin 1984; McGlothlin et al. 1977), was the most comprehensive and well-studied example of a correctional treatment program combining treatment in a penal institution (OPNM-like therapy) with specialized parole supervision, including access to a variety of community-based treatments. CAP effort operated as designed for only 8 years, after which much of its original character was lost due to changing correctional policies and systemic overcrowding. Two similar civil commitment programs, one federal and one operated by the state of New York, fell far short of their design goals, ended fairly quickly, and were roundly regarded as failures (Besteman 1978, 1992; Inciardi 1988).

CAP permitted adjudication of heroin-dependent felons through a civil commitment procedure (rather than regular criminal sentencing) to a 7-year term of supervision, three-fourths of which, on average, was spent on parole. The first (repeatable) stop for CAP patients was a term in a medium-security prison with a large staff of psychotherapists. Community supervision was carried out by a specially trained cadre of parole officers with unusually small case loads (30 parolees) and weekly drug testing (Anglin 1988).

The civil commitment law was complex enough that legal-procedural errors were made in commit-

Table 5–4.    Evaluation of Stay'n Out program

| Group (no. of men/women) | Percentage rearrested | | Average months before rearrest | | Percentage reincarcerated | | Percentage not completing parole | |
|---|---|---|---|---|---|---|---|---|
| | Men[a] | Women | Men | Women | Men | Women | Men | Women |
| Stay'n Out (435/236) | 27 | 18 | 13 | 12 | 44 | [c] | 42 | 23 |
| Milieu[b] (576/0) | 35 | — | 11 | — | 45 | — | 47 | — |
| Counseling (261/113) | 40 | 30 | 12 | 15 | 41 | [c] | 47 | 32 |
| No treatment (159/38) | 41 | 24 | 15 | 9 | [c] | [c] | 39 | 47 |

[a]The differences in results in this column only are statistically significant beyond the .05 level ($\chi^2 = 172$, $P < .001$).
[b]Milieu therapy was not available to women prisoners.
[c]Reincarceration data were not collected for these groups.
*Source.*    Reprinted with permission from Falkin GP, Wexler HK, Lipton DS: "Drug Treatment in State Prisons," in *Treating Drug Abuse*, Vol 2. Edited by Gerstein DR, Harwood HJ. Washington, DC, National Academy Press, 1992. Copyright 1992 by the National Academy of Sciences. Courtesy of the National Academy Press, Washington, DC.

ting at least half of the early CAP patients. In such cases the commitments were challenged by writs of habeas corpus, and the individuals were released from CAP and returned to regular adjudication. The released group differed from those who continued in that many releasees had less serious offenses for which the 7-year CAP commitment was longer than the sentence they would probably otherwise have served; virtually all of the CAP group would probably have had longer sentences without CAP. The researchers therefore used matching procedures to select from within the writ-released group a comparison sample that was as similar as possible to the continuing group on 15 criteria, including criminal and drug histories and demographic characteristics.

Under CAP, heroin use (see Figure 5–5) and total criminality while not incarcerated fell to levels that were half or less than half that reported by the comparison group. These reductions became apparent immediately after their release into the community, and they were sustained. The difference between CAP parolees and control subjects narrowed over the next several years as more control subjects reduced their heroin use and other criminal behavior. By the time the continuing CAP group's parole ended, the control group was at a more nearly similar level, especially considering pretreatment (baseline) differences. The subsequent recovery paths of the two groups re-

mained parallel. The residential and community supervision components of CAP were evidently effective in accelerating the recovery of a significant fraction (at least half) of those treated.

## Boot Camps

A final type of prison-based treatment that has received much attention recently is the *boot camp* or *shock incarceration* (SI) concept. This comprises a 3- to 6-month sentence for young offenders to a facility employing rigorous physical exercise and a small-group organizational structure similar to Outward Bound or military training camps. A number of states have opened such facilities, largely as a way to reduce prison costs and improve resource management. SI segregates young offenders who would otherwise be mixed with either the general penitentiary population (in this case, SI reduces penitentiary overcrowding) or with the general probation population (in this case, SI worsens overcrowding).

Boot camps vary in nature. Some are militarized environments with few if any therapeutic staff or procedures; others incorporate many treatment elements but lack continuity of care when the individual returns to the community. Parent (1989), in a report to the National Institute of Justice, summarizes the current knowledge:

> Preliminary case tracking data raise questions about SI's capacity to reduce recidivism. The Oklahoma Department of Corrections used survival analysis to compare return rates of SI graduates with similar non-violent offenders sentenced to the DOC. After 29 months almost half the SI graduates, but only 28% of the other group, had returned to prison.
>
> In a 3-year follow-up, the Georgia DOC found that 38.5% of their SI graduates returned to prison. For Georgia SI graduates who were in their teens when admitted to SI, 46.8% returned to prison within 3 years of release. In an earlier study, Georgia researchers found little difference in 1-year return to prison rates for SI graduates, and similar offenders sentenced to prison and to a youthful offender institution. It should be emphasized that neither of these studies involved carefully constructed comparison groups.
>
> Until evaluation results become available, policy makers should view claims of incredible success with skepticism, and should be cau-

| Table 5–5. | Results of a 3-year follow-up at Cornerstone. | | |
|---|---|---|---|

| Group | N | Percentage newly convicted | Percentage reincarcerated |
|---|---|---|---|
| Graduates of Cornerstone | 144 | 46 | 29 |
| Cornerstone dropouts (> 1 month) | 27 | 75 | 74 |
| Combined Cornerstone groups | 171 | 54 | 36 |
| Untreated Oregon parolees with substance abuse histories | 179 | 74 | 37 |

*Source.* Field G: "The Cornerstone Program: A Client Outcome Study." *Federal Probation* 48:50–55, 1984.

tious about proceeding with SI development on the basis of high hopes, preliminary data, or press clippings.

## ▼ CONCLUSIONS ABOUT TREATMENT EFFECTIVENESS

Research on methadone has demonstrated the following:

▼ There is strong evidence from clinical trials and similar study designs that, on average, heroin-dependent (or other opioid-dependent) individuals have much better outcomes in terms of illicit drug consumption and other criminal behavior when they are maintained on methadone than when they are not treated at all, when they are simply detoxified and released, or when methadone is tapered down and terminated arbitrarily.

▼ Methadone clinics have significantly higher retention rates among opioid-dependent populations than do other treatment modalities for similar patients.

▼ When assessed following discharge from methadone treatment, patients who stayed in treatment longer have better outcomes than patients who left earlier.

▼ Methadone dosages need to be clinically monitored and individually optimized. Patients do much better, generally, when they are stabilized on higher rather than lower doses within the typical ranges that are currently prescribed (30–100 mg/day). Program characteristics such as inadequate methadone dosage levels and differences between counselors (which are not yet fully defined) are significantly related to differences in patient performance while in treatment.

The results of research on the effects of TC treatment are as follows:

▼ TC patients end virtually all illicit drug taking and other criminal behavior while in residence and perform better (in terms of reduced drug taking and other criminal activity and increased social productivity) after discharge than before admission. They also have better outcomes at follow-up than individuals who simply undergo detoxification or who contact but do not enter a TC pro-

gram. The length of stay is the strongest predictor of outcomes at follow-up, with graduates having the best outcomes at that point.

▼ Attrition from TCs is typically high—above the rates for MM but below the rates for OPNM treatment. Typically, about 15% of admissions will graduate after a continuous stay; the figure is higher (20%–25%) once later readmissions are considered.

▼ The minimum retention necessary to yield improvement in long-term outcomes seems to be several months, which covers one-third to one-half of a typical program's admissions. Improvements continue to be manifested for full-time treatment of up to 1 year.

Despite the heterogeneity of OPNM programs and patients, the limited number of outcome evaluations of OPNM programs has generated conclusions qualitatively similar to those from studies of TCs:

▼ OPNM patients during and following treatment exhibit better behavior than before treatment.

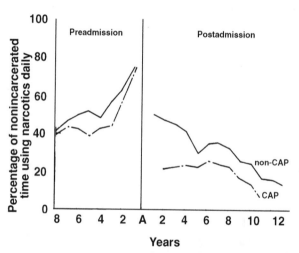

**Figure 5–5. Effects of the Civil Addict Program (CAP) on daily narcotics use.** The percentage of non-incarcerated time during which subjects reported using narcotics daily is shown for 8 preadmission and 13 postadmission years. The vertical line at *A* denotes admission. The CAP group (*N* = 289) was committed to the program for 7 years; the non-CAP group (*N* = 292) was discharged from the program by writ shortly after admission owing to procedural error. Data for CAP year 1 are missing because this group was incarcerated nearly the whole year in the CAP facility.
*Source.* McGlothlin et al. 1977.

Those patients who are actually admitted to programs have better outcomes than patients who contact but do not enter programs (and patients who only undergo detoxification). Outcome at follow-up is positively related to length of stay in treatment, and those who complete treatment have better outcomes than those who drop out.

▼ Retention in OPNM programs is poorer than for MM and TCs.

CD programs treat mainly primary alcoholism and have not been adequately evaluated for treatment of drug problems. A few follow-up studies of individuals who have completed CD treatment indicate that primary drug patients have poorer outcomes than primary alcohol patients.

Most of the prison drug treatment programs that have been studied, including specialized boot camp or SI facilities, have not been shown to reduce the typically very high postrelease rates of recidivism to drug seeking and other criminal behavior that occur among untreated prisoners. Nevertheless, a small number of well-designed controlled studies, involving prison TCs and residential programs that have strong linkages to community-based supervision and/or treatment programs, indicate that prison-initiated treatment can reduce the treated group's rate of *rearrest* by one-fourth to one-half; clear correlations are observed between positive outcome rates and length of time in treatment, just as in studies of entirely community-based modalities. The results have some anomalies, and there have been difficulties in sustaining the integrity of prison-based treatment programs, but the results argue that these programs should be carefully encouraged.

No single treatment "works" for a majority of the people who seek treatment. Each of the treatment modalities for which there is a baseline of adequate studies can fairly be said to work for many of the people who seek that treatment; enough of them do find the right treatment and stay with it long enough to make the current aggregate of treatment programs worthwhile.

## ▼ REFERENCES

Anglin MD: The efficacy of civil commitment in treating narcotic addiction, in Compulsory Treatment of Drug Abuse: Research and Clinical Practice, NIDA Res Monogr 86. Edited by Leukefeld CG, Tims FM. Rockville, MD, National Institute on Drug Abuse, 1988, pp 8–34

Anglin MD, McGlothlin WH: Outcome of narcotic addict treatment in California, in Drug Abuse Treatment Evaluation: Strategies, Progress, and Prospects, NIDA Res Monogr 5. Edited by Tims FM, Ludford JP. Rockville, MD, National Institute on Drug Abuse, 1984, pp 106–128

Anglin MD, Speckart GS, Booth MW, et al: Consequences and costs of shutting off methadone. Addict Behav 14:307–326, 1989

Bale RN, Van Stone WW, Kuldau JM, et al: Therapeutic communities vs. methadone maintenance: a prospective controlled study of narcotic addiction treatment: design and one-year follow-up. Arch Gen Psychiatry 37:179–193, 1980

Ball JC: Data Tables From the Eastern Cities Methadone Studies (mimeograph). Baltimore, MD, Addiction Research Center, National Institute on Drug Abuse, 1989

Ball JC, Ross A: The Effectiveness of Methadone Maintenance. New York, Springer-Verlag New York, 1991

Ball JC, Rosen L, Flueck JA, et al: The criminality of heroin addicts when addicted and when off opiates, in The Drugs-Crime Connection. Edited by Inciardi JA. Beverly Hills, CA, Sage Publications, 1981, pp 39–65

Ball JC, Lange WR, Meyers CP, et al: Reducing the risk of AIDS through methadone maintenance treatment. J Health Soc Behav 29:214–226, 1988

Besteman KJ: The NARA program, in Drug Addiction and the U.S. Public Health Service. Edited by Martin WR, Isbell H. Proceedings of Symposium Commemorating the 40th Anniversary of the Addiction Research Center at Lexington, KY. Rockville, MD, National Institute on Drug Abuse, 1978, 274–280

Besteman KJ: Federal leadership in building the national drug treatment system, in Treating Drug Abuse, Vol 2. Edited by Gerstein DR, Harwood, HJ. Washington, DC, National Academy Press, 1992

Blaine JD, Thomas DB, Barnett G, et al: Levo-alpha acetylmethadol (LAAM): clinical utility and pharmaceutical development, in Substance Abuse: Clinical Problems and Perspectives. Edited by Lowinson JH, Ruiz P. Baltimore, MD, Williams & Wilkins, 1981, pp 360–388

Chaiken MR: Prison Programs for Drug-Involved Offenders: Department of Justice Research in Action,

NCJ 118316. Washington, DC, U.S. Department of Justice, 1989

Cole SG, Lehman WE, Cole EA, et al: Inpatient vs outpatient treatment of alcohol and drug abusers. Am J Drug Alcohol Abuse 8:329–345, 1981

Comprehensive Care Corporation: Evaluation of Treatment Outcome. Irvine, CA, Comprehensive Care Corporation, 1988

Cook CCH: The Minnesota Model in the management of drug and alcohol dependency: miracle, method or myth? Part I: the philosophy and the programme. British Journal of Addiction 83:625–634, 1988a

Cook CCH: The Minnesota Model in the management of drug and alcohol dependency: miracle, method or myth? Part II: evidence and conclusions. British Journal of Addiction 83:735–748, 1988b

Dackis C, Gold MS, Sweeney D, et al: Single dose bromocriptine reverses cocaine craving. Psychiatry Res 20:261–264, 1987

De Leon G, Wexler HK, Jainchill N: The therapeutic community: success and improvement rates 5 years after treatment. Int J Addict 17:703–747, 1982

Dole VP: Methadone treatment and the acquired immunodeficiency syndrome epidemic. JAMA 262:1681–1682, 1989

Dole VP, Nyswander M: A medical treatment for diacetylmorphine (heroin) addiction: a clinical trial with methadone hydrochloride. JAMA 193:80–84, 1965

Dole VP, Nyswander M: Rehabilitation of the street addict. Arch Environ Health 14:477–480, 1967

Dole VP, Nyswander M, Kreek MJ: Narcotic blockade. Arch Intern Med 118:304–309, 1966

Dole VP, Nyswander M, Warner A: Successful treatment of 750 criminal addicts. JAMA 206:2708–2711, 1968

Dole VP, Robinson JW, Orraga J, et al: Methadone treatment of randomly selected criminal addicts. N Engl J Med 280:1372–1375, 1969

Falkin GP, Wexler HK, Lipton DS: Drug treatment in state prisons, in Treating Drug Abuse, Vol 2. Edited by Gerstein DR, Harwood HJ. Washington, DC, National Academy Press, 1992

Field G: The Cornerstone program: a client outcome study. Federal Probation 48:50–55, 1984

Field G: The effects of intensive treatment on reducing the criminal recidivism of addicted offenders. Federal Probation 53:51–72, 1989

Frohling R: Promising Approaches to Drug Treatment in Correctional Settings. Washington, DC, National Conference of State Legislatures, 1989

Gawin FH, Allen D, Humblestone B: Outpatient treatment of "crack" cocaine smoking with flupenthixol decanoate: a preliminary report. Arch Gen Psychiatry 46:322–325, 1989a

Gawin FH, Kleber HD, Byck R, et al: Desipramine facilitation of initial cocaine abstinence. Arch Gen Psychiatry 46:117–121, 1989b

Gerstein DR: The effectiveness of drug treatment, in Addictive States. Edited by O'Brien CP, Jaffe JH. New York, Raven, 1992, pp 253–282

Gerstein DR, Harwood HJ (eds): Treating Drug Problems, Vol 1. Washington, DC, National Academy Press, 1990

Gerstein DR, Harwood HJ (eds): Treating Drug Problems, Vol 2. Washington, DC, National Academy Press, 1992

Gilmore KM: Hazelden Primary Residential Treatment Program: Profile and Patient Outcome. Center City, MN, Hazelden, 1985

Goldstein A: A clinical experience with LAAM, in Rx LAAM: 3×/Week: LAAM Alternative to Methadone, NIDA Res Monogr 8. Edited by Blaine JD, Renault PF. Rockville, MD, National Institute on Drug Abuse, 1976, pp 115–117

Goldstein A, Judson B: Three critical issues in the management of methadone programs; critical issue 3: can the community be protected against the hazards of take-home methadone? in Addiction. Edited by Bourne G. New York, Academic Press, 1974, pp 140–148

Gunne L, Gronbladh L: The Swedish methadone maintenance program, in The Social and Medical Aspects of Drug Abuse. Edited by Serban G. Jamaica, NY, Spectrum Publications, 1984, pp 205–213

Hargreaves WA: Methadone dose and duration for methadone treatment, in Research on the Treatment of Narcotic Addiction: State of the Art, NIDA Treatment Res Monogr Series (DHHS Publ No ADM-83-1281). Edited by Cooper JR, Altman F, Brown BS, et al. Rockville, MD, National Institute on Drug Abuse, 1983, pp 19–79

Hubbard RL, Marsden ME, Rachal JV, et al: Drug Abuse Treatment: A National Study of Effectiveness. Chapel Hill, NC, The University of North Carolina Press, 1989

Inciardi JA: Some considerations on the clinical efficacy of compulsory treatment: reviewing the New York experience, in Compulsory Treatment of Drug Abuse: Research and Clinical Practice, NIDA Res Monogr 86. Edited by Leukefeld CG, Tims FM. Rockville, MD, National Institute on Drug Abuse, 1988, pp 126–138

Johnson BD, Goldstein PJ, Preble E, et al: Taking Care of Business: The Economics of Crime by Heroin Abusers. Lexington, MA, Lexington Books, 1985.

Kleber HD, Slobetz F: Outpatient drug-free treatment, in Handbook on Drug Abuse. Edited by Dupont RL, Goldstein A, O'Donnell J. Rockville, MD, National Institute on Drug Abuse, 1979, pp 31–38

Kreek MJ: Health consequences associated with the use of methadone, in Research on the Treatment of Narcotic Addiction: State of the Art, NIDA Treatment Res Monogr Series (DHHS Publ No ADM-83-1281). Edited by Cooper JR, Altman F, Brown BS, et al. Rockville, MD, National Institute on Drug Abuse, 1983, pp 456–482

Laundergan JC: Easy Does It! Alcoholism Treatment Outcomes, Hazelden and the Minnesota Model. Center City, MN, Hazelden, 1982

Ling W, Klett CJ, Gillis RD: A cooperative clinical study of methadyl acetate. Arch Gen Psychiatry 35:345–353, 1978

McGlothlin WH, Anglin MD: Shutting off methadone: costs and benefits. Arch Gen Psychiatry 38:885–892, 1981

McGlothlin WH, Anglin MD, Wilson BD: An Evaluation of the California Civil Addict Program, Services Research Monograph Series. Rockville, MD, National Institute on Drug Abuse, 1977

McLellan AT, Luborsky L, Woody G, et al: Counselor differences in methadone treatment, in Problems of Drug Dependence, 1987, NIDA Res Monogr 81. Edited by Harris LS. Rockville, MD, National Institute on Drug Abuse, 1988, pp 243–250

Mello NK, Mendelson JH, Bree MP, et al: Buprenorphine suppresses cocaine self-administration by Rhesus monkeys. Science 245:859–862, 1989

Moffet AD, Soloway IH, Glick MX: Post-treatment behavior following ambulatory detoxification, in Methadone: Experience and Issues. Edited by Chambers CD, Brill L. New York, Behavioral Publications, 1973, pp 215–227

National Institute on Drug Abuse: Effectiveness of Drug Abuse Treatment Programs (DHHS Publ No ADM-81-1143). Rockville, MD, National Institute on Drug Abuse, 1981

Newman RG: Critique, in Research on the Treatment of Narcotic Addiction: State of the Art, NIDA Treatment Res Monogr Series (DHHS Publ No ADM-83-1281). Edited by Cooper JR, Altman F, Brown BS, et al. Rockville, MD, National Institute on Drug Abuse, 1983, pp 168–171

Newman RG, Whitehill WB: Double-blind comparison of methadone and placebo maintenance treatment of narcotic addicts in Hong Kong. Lancet 2:485–488, 1979

Parent DG: Shock Incarceration: An Overview of Existing Programs. Department of Justice. Washington, DC, U.S. Department of Justice, 1989

Rawson RA, Obert JL, McCann MJ, et al: Cocaine treatment outcome: cocaine use following inpatient, outpatient, and no treatment, in Problems of Drug Dependence, 1985, NIDA Res Monogr 67. Edited by Harris LS. Rockville, MD, 1986, pp 271–277

Resnick R: Methadone detoxification from illicit opiates and methadone maintenance, in Research on the Treatment of Narcotic Addiction: State of the Art, NIDA Treatment Res Monogr Series (DHHS Publ No ADM-83-1281). Edited by Cooper RJ, Altman F, Brown BS, et al. Rockville, MD, National Institute on Drug Abuse, 1983, pp 160–178

Romond AM, Forrest CK, Kleber HD: Follow-up of participants in a drug dependence therapeutic community. Arch Gen Psychiatry 32:369–374, 1975

Savage C, Karp EG, Curran SF, et al: Methadone/LAAM maintenance: a comparison study. Compr Psychiatry 17:415–424, 1976

Sells SB (ed): Studies of the Effectiveness of Treatments for Drug Abuse; Vol 1: Evaluation of Treatments. Cambridge, MA, Ballinger Publishing Company, 1974a

Sells SB (ed): Studies of the Effectiveness of Treatments for Drug Abuse; Vol 2: Research on Patients, Treatments and Outcomes. Cambridge, MA, Ballinger Publishing Company, 1974b

Sheffet A, Quinones M, Lavenhar MA, et al: An evaluation of detoxification as an initial step in the treatment of heroin addiction. Am J Psychiatry 133:337–340, 1976

Simpson DD: Treatment for drug abuse: follow-up outcomes and length of time spent. Arch Gen Psychiatry 38:875–880, 1981

Simpson DD, Savage LJ, Lloyd MR: Follow-up evaluation of treatment of drug abuse during 1969 to 1972. Arch Gen Psychiatry 36:772–780, 1979

Speckart GR, Anglin MD: Narcotics and crime: a causal modeling approach. Journal of Quantitative Criminology 2:3–28, 1986

Tennant FS, Sagherian AA: Double-blind comparison of amantadine and bromocriptine for ambulatory withdrawal for cocaine dependence. Arch Intern Med 147:109–112, 1987

Vaillant GE: What can long-term follow-up teach us about relapse and prevention of relapse in addiction? British Journal of Addiction 83:1147–1157, 1988

# Treatment of Patients for Specific Drugs of Abuse

# A lcohol

*Don Gallant, M.D.*

T here has been an explosion in new research data from the multiple disciplines involved in the treatment of alcohol abuse and dependence. New findings abound on the treatment of the alcohol withdrawal syndromes, pharmacotherapy, and special psychosocial interventions, as well as in the disciplines of basic biochemistry and genetics. These findings are already beginning to affect the ways we treat alcoholic individuals at each stage of the illness. The number of outstanding researchers in the field of alcohol research has increased significantly during the past two decades. Excellent controlled research is now common, and important new treatment methods are available.

## ▼ DETOXIFICATION

Before considering treatment modalities for the alcohol withdrawal syndromes, it should be stressed that quantitative criteria measures are a necessary part of clinical management. The revised Clinical Institute Withdrawal Assessment for Alcohol Scale

(CIWA-Ar), a 10-item scale, and the 6-item Alcohol Withdrawal Scale (AWS) contain both objective and subjective criteria that enable the clinician to make a decision about the use of pharmacologic medication (Cushman et al. 1985; Sullivan et al. 1989). One of these short-form scales should be administered routinely to all patients admitted to detoxification units. The CIWA-Ar is a practical clinical instrument derived from the 15-item CIWA-A with no loss of clinical validity or reliability while it offers an increase in acceptance by ward personnel. The 10 items include sweating, anxiety, tremor, auditory disturbances, visual disturbances, agitation, nausea, tactile disturbances, headache, and orientation, with all of the items except orientation (0–4) weighted equally on a scale of 0–7. If the patient scores less than 10 on the scale, then pharmacological treatment is usually not indicated; the patient may be managed with supportive care alone (Sullivan et al. 1989). In one study (Sullivan et al. 1991), using the guideline of instituting psychopharmacologic medication only if the score was greater than 10, the results showed that patients scoring high on the scale with a greater de-

The author thanks W. W. Norton and Co. for permission to publish several excerpts from his book, *Alcoholism: A Guide to Diagnosis, Intervention and Treatment*, and Williams & Wilkins for permission to publish excerpts from several review articles that he wrote for their journal, *Alcoholism: Clinical and Experimental Research*, © by the Research Society on Alcoholism.

gree of physical dependence appropriately received higher doses of benzodiazepines, whereas those scoring in the lower part of the scale appropriately received lower doses of benzodiazepines. Thus use of the CIWA-Ar minimized both inadequate dosing of benzodiazepines (BZs) for patients in moderate to severe withdrawal and decreased overmedicating with BZs in those alcoholic patients who were in only mild withdrawal. However, it should be emphasized that the clinician has to be extremely careful not to undertreat those patients who have experienced repeated withdrawal because some investigators (Ballenger and Post 1978) believe that repeated inadequately treated withdrawal episodes could produce future withdrawal syndromes of increased severity with possible permanent central nervous system (CNS) changes.

The treatment of alcohol withdrawal syndromes has two primary goals: 1) to help a patient achieve detoxification in as safe and as comfortable a way as possible, and 2) to foster the patient's motivation to enter rehabilitation therapy. Recent advances in the treatment of alcohol withdrawal syndromes promise improvements in our ability to realize both goals.

## Mild to Moderate Alcohol Withdrawal

Outpatient treatment may be sufficient for a significant number of patients displaying the syndrome of alcohol withdrawal. In addition to using the CIWA-Ar or AWS, the blood alcohol level (BAL) can be used as another guideline for making a decision to place the patient in a social detoxification unit, to refer him or her to a medical ward for more intensive treatment of severe withdrawal symptoms, or to follow the patient at home with proper supervision. For example, if the alcohol level is 250–300 mg% and the patient appears to be alert and not dysarthric, then the physician should be on guard for possible moderate to severe withdrawal symptoms as the BAL decreases. In this situation, the tolerance for alcohol is too high, and the patient may have a predisposition to develop marked withdrawal symptoms upon cessation of drinking alcohol.

Successful outpatient treatment of patients with mild to moderate alcohol withdrawal symptoms has been described in a number of studies (Hyashida et al. 1989; Pattison 1977; Whitfield 1980). However, the patients in these studies are not representative of all alcoholic individuals who develop withdrawal symp-

tomatology because individuals displaying symptoms of delirium or convulsions could not be included in these investigations. In addition, some of the studies reporting successful outpatient treatment of these patient populations did not use specific criteria that delineated the subgroup of individuals who were selected for outpatient therapy. However, the clinician may feel relatively safe in treating an outpatient with alcohol withdrawal symptoms if the CIWA-Ar score is less than 10 and if the patient has no previous history of alcohol-related convulsions or delirium. These patients may be helped to decrease the intake of alcohol with family support and the use of a short-acting hypnotic for sleep in association with moderate dosages of BZs for day-time anxiety. The use of short-acting BZs such as oxazepam (30 mg qid) or lorazepam (1 mg tid or qid) in association with a short-acting hypnotic (e.g., chloral hydrate) will enable the patient to withdraw from alcohol comfortably over a period of 5–7 days. In this manner, the clinician avoids oversedating the patient with long-acting compounds, which can interfere with the patient's compliance and can cause accidents secondary to interference with cognition or manual dexterity. Of course, the patient must have a family member or friend available to accompany him or her to the clinic on a daily basis. In addition, it may be advisable to use thiamine (50–100 mg per day) to avoid potential future CNS damage such as Wernicke's Encephalopathy. Multivitamins can be given at the clinician's discretion since these patients are usually depleted of most vitamins and minerals. However, with adequate nutrition and abstinence, the alcoholic patient usually does not require extraordinary doses of minerals or vitamins, and hydration is best accomplished by oral fluids, which will significantly decrease the possibility of iatrogenic illnesses such as overhydration or electrolyte imbalance.

Introduction of the β-blockers, propranolol and atenolol, and of an $\alpha_2$-adrenergic receptor agonist, clonidine, have improved treatment of mild to moderate alcohol withdrawal syndromes by replacing more sedating medications (Kraus et al. 1985; Manhem et al. 1985; Sellers et al. 1977).

In one randomized, double-blind clinical trial of patients with alcohol withdrawal symptoms (Kraus et al. 1985), atenolol was compared with placebo. The atenolol patients had a significant reduction in the mean length of hospital stay and required significantly less concomitant BZs than the placebo group.

The β-blockers present a possible problem: they may potentiate hypoglycemia in the first 36 hours after ingestion of large amounts of alcohol by malnourished alcoholic subjects (Gallant 1982). Because alcoholic individuals seem to have an increased incidence of chronic obstructive pulmonary disease as well as alcoholic cardiomyopathy, precautions about the use of β-blockers should be further emphasized. Clonidine as well as guanabenz, both β-adrenergic agonists, have also been found to be effective in suppressing the symptoms and signs of alcohol withdrawal (Baumgartner and Rowen 1988; Manhem et al. 1985). In one study (Baumgartner and Rowen 1988) of the effects of clonidine (in doses as high as 0.2 mg tid) versus chlordiazepoxide (in doses as high as 50 mg tid), the results showed clonidine to be more effective in lowering the AWS scores, especially in the first 24 hours. In addition, there was less nausea and vomiting as well as a greater reduction of the systolic blood pressure and heart rate in the clonidine group. The use of β-blockers and α-adrenergic agonists has resulted in relatively nonsedative treatment approaches that enable the patient to participate in rehabilitation therapy within several days after admission to a detoxification unit or treatment as an outpatient. Unfortunately, the β-blockers and the α-adrenergic agonists do not have anticonvulsant and antihallucinogenic effects in human subjects (Liskow and Goodwin 1987). Thus the combination of clonidine and a BZ may be safer for patients with a previous history of alcohol-induced or postalcohol withdrawal seizures (Ng et al. 1988). Encouraging results in the treatment of the alcohol withdrawal syndrome have also been reported in clinical trials of other structural compounds, which will be discussed in the next section.

If a patient continues to drink sporadically during outpatient treatment of the mild to moderate alcohol withdrawal syndrome, inpatient detoxification may be required even though severe withdrawal symptoms are not present. From a therapeutic viewpoint, it may be necessary to interrupt the self-destructive cycle of heavy drinking followed by withdrawal symptoms that are then relieved through resumption of alcohol intake. In addition, if the patient has other serious medical problems accompanying the alcohol withdrawal syndrome, such as uncontrolled diabetes or a blood pressure that is considered to be dangerously high, then hospitalization is indicated. Other medical illnesses not only can complicate the symptomatology of the withdrawal syndrome but also may worsen if not carefully monitored in an inpatient setting.

## Severe Alcohol Withdrawal (Alcohol Withdrawal Delirium)

Criteria for alcohol withdrawal delirium include a clouding of consciousness, difficulty in sustaining attention, disorientation to present circumstances, autonomic hyperactivity associated with tachycardia, excessive sweating, and elevated blood pressure. On the CIWA-Ar, the patient usually scores more than 20. These symptoms occur within the first week after cessation or reduction of heavy alcohol ingestion. With adequate treatment, these symptoms should disappear by the end of the first week and surely by no later than the beginning of the second week (Gallant 1987a, pp. 111–117, 222, 240–241). This diagnosis warrants immediate hospitalization because it infers that the patient is unable to care for him- or herself and is seriously ill. The use of BZs may be of considerable help in alcoholic patients who have experienced recent alcohol withdrawal convulsions because these compounds possess anticonvulsant activity. If the patient is suspected of having a moderate amount of liver damage, the most appropriate BZs may be oxazepam or lorazepam because these drugs do not require metabolism by the liver and, therefore, do not accumulate. The dosage range for BZs should vary with the quantity of the alcohol consumption prior to withdrawal, the weight of the patient, and the severity of the presenting symptomatology such as a very high score on the CIWA-Ar. Although patients who present with high BALs usually experience more severe withdrawal symptoms than patients with relatively low BALs, these observations are not consistent. Exceptions may include patients who have experienced severe withdrawal symptoms following previous drinking episodes or those who have developed intercurrent illnesses during the present withdrawal stage. In severe cases of alcohol-withdrawal syndrome with delirium, a dosage of oxazepam as high as 60 mg qid may be needed, a dosage of lorazepam as high as 1–2 mg qid may be needed, and a dosage of diazepam as high as 20 mg qid may be needed. Diazepam-loading regimens (e.g., dosages of 40 mg hs) have also been successfully used (Romach and Sellers 1991).

Concerning the intramuscular use of BZs, the clinician should be aware that compounds such as chlordiazepoxide and diazepam are poorly absorbed. For example, within 2 hours after ingestion, 50 mg of oral chlordiazepoxide results in plasma levels that are significantly higher than those following a 50 mg im dose (Perry et al. 1978). If the patient is vomiting profusely and unable to tolerate oral medication, then the use of intramuscular lorazepam would be indicated because this compound absorbs quite readily after intramuscular administration. Prochlorperazine, 25 mg, as a suppository, can be used temporarily to inhibit the emesis. It should be stressed that intramuscular infusions should be used only in patients who are definitely dehydrated from excessive vomiting or diarrhea. Even in these cases, the clinician must be cautious with glycogen-depleted patients who may be thiamine deficient because the patient may develop Wernicke's encephalopathy if a glucose infusion is administered without additional thiamine. These patients should be weighed daily to evaluate their hydration state.

During the past several years, encouraging results in the treatment of severe alcohol withdrawal syndromes have been reported. One published double-blind controlled evaluation of carbamazepine (CBZ) versus oxazepam (OXZ) for the treatment of alcohol withdrawal confirmed the results of previous evaluations of the efficacy of CBZ (Malcolm et al. 1989). To be included in this trial, patients had to fit DSM-III criteria for alcohol dependence and had to score 20 or higher on the CIWA-A. Eighty-six subjects were randomly assigned to either the CBZ (200 mg qid) group or the OXZ (30 mg qid) group. The CIWA-A, physiologic measures, and neurologic examinations were administered twice daily, 1 hour after the administration of medication. A self-report psychologic-emotional visual analogue on a 100-mm scale was administered once daily, and the revised version of the Symptom Checklist—90 (SCL-90-R), standard psychologic testing and routine laboratory tests, including CBZ levels, were administered at baseline and on days 3 and 7 of the study. The mean CBZ level on day 3 was $9.8 \pm 2.9$ ng/ml and on day 7 was $8.5 \pm 2.5$ ng/ml. The clinical measures in both treatment groups showed that maximal reduction of symptoms was achieved between days 4 and 5. There were no significant differences between groups on the CIWA-A or on the other measures except that the global distress score of the SLC-90-R at the end of the study indicated significantly less psychological distress in the CBZ group than in the OXZ group.

Alcoholic patients who have made multiple attempts at alcohol withdrawal may be more likely to experience seizures and to develop long-term neurologic and psychiatric disabilities. If these sequelae are associated with *kindling-like* changes in the limbic areas, then the *antikindling* effects of CBZ may offer future protection against this type of CNS damage as well as ameliorate the acute phase of the withdrawal syndrome. The finding that CBZ was significantly more effective than OXZ in improving psychiatric symptoms and the relatively minimal sedative side effects of this compound are important features of CBZ withdrawal methodology. The findings suggest a potential use for a compound such as CBZ in the long-term pharmacologic management of the alcoholic patients. However, these findings require additional controlled research investigations with larger numbers of patients. It should be noted that thrombocytopenia is a rare occurrence secondary to CBZ treatment and usually occurs within the first 3 weeks of treatment (Tohen et al. 1991). Apparently, the hematologic abnormalities are rapidly corrected by discontinuing medication. A review of the literature on CBZ use found no reports of irreversible hematologic side effects occurring during the 1-week administration of CBZ for the alcohol withdrawal syndrome.

The anticonvulsant agent, sodium valproate, associated with more gastric distress but less CNS side-effects than CBZ, and the calcium channel blockers such as verapamil show some promise of therapeutic efficacy for the severe alcohol withdrawal states, but they have not yet been adequately evaluated in double-blind trials in the United States (Roy-Byrne et al. 1989). Data on the use of these compounds have been summarized in a symposium by the National Institute of Alcohol Abuse and Alcoholism (NIAAA) and in a review article by investigators from the same institute (Adinoff et al. 1988; Linnoila et al. 1987).

For patients with a recent history of alcohol withdrawal seizures, the use of phenytoin or magnesium has not been well established. In one double-blind controlled study of 100 alcoholic subjects displaying withdrawal symptomatology (Wilson and Vulcano 1984), the addition of magnesium to the chlordiazepoxide regimen did not result in additional therapeutic efficacy when compared with placebo, even in those patients with low magnesium levels. Intramuscular magnesium administration does cause discomfort to the patient and is not indicated for the management of alcohol withdrawal unless the patient develops low magnesium levels in association with cardiac arrhythmias or neurological symptoms. In experimental studies of phenytoin in animals, it has been reported that this compound is less effective than diazepam in the treatment of alcohol withdrawal convulsions (Gessner 1979). In fact, many authors recommend the elimination of the use of phenytoin for the prophylactic treatment of withdrawal seizures (Adinoff et al. 1988; Alldredge et al. 1989). In animal and human research related to alcohol withdrawal seizures, diazepam has been shown to be a very effective anticonvulsant (Guerrero-Figueroa et al. 1970). If seizures are present on admission to the hospital, diazepam may be given at a dosage of 10 mg iv for 1–2 minutes and then repeated until seizures stop, but no more than a total of 30 mg should be administered over 15–20 minutes. Diazepam should be administered slowly to avoid laryngospasm.

Recent publications in the European journals report other compounds that show promise for the treatment of moderate to severe alcohol withdrawal symptomatology. In one double-blind study of γ-hydroxybutyric acid (GHB; Gallimberti et al. 1989), a constituent of the mammalian brain that may act as a neuromodulator of γ-aminobutyric acid (GABA), GHB administration produced a prompt reduction of withdrawal symptoms, including tremors, sweating, nausea, anxiety, and restlessness. The only side effect noted in the administration of this compound was dizziness. It is interesting to note that, in rats, GHB not only suppresses ethanol withdrawal symptoms but also inhibits voluntary alcohol consumption. Other European journal publications have reported that chlormethiazole, a compound structurally related to thiamine, is quite effective for the treatment of withdrawal symptoms (Schuckit 1990). Not only does chlormethiazole appear to be comparable to the BZs in alleviating the withdrawal symptoms, but administration of this medication also appears to be associated with less severe gastrointestinal side effects.

In discussing the treatment of alcohol withdrawal, it is important to consider the increasing numbers of primary alcoholism patients who abuse habituating drugs in association with their intake of alcohol. The combined alcohol-BZ or alcohol-barbiturate patient presents an additional medical problem in the treatment of withdrawal because he or she is more likely to have seizures (Gallant 1987a, pp. 111–117, 222, 240–241). If the patient is dually addicted and does not have severe liver damage, there is a relatively safe procedure that can be applied to the combined alcohol-BZ habituation (Robinson et al. 1981). By use of the following technique, more than 50 barbiturate-addicted subjects were successfully detoxified without any seizures. Phenobarbital is administered at a dose of 120 mg, every hour, until the patient develops three of the five following symptoms: drowsiness, emotional lability, and the three cerebellar signs of dysarthria, ataxia, and nystagmus. The urine is maintained at a pH of less than 6.5, which slows the excretion of phenobarbital, allowing the patient to follow a "smooth" withdrawal from the combination of alcohol-BZ or alcohol-barbiturate addiction. Before beginning this regimen, the clinician should administer a dose of 200 mg of pentobarbital to determine the extent of physical dependence. The appearance of ataxia with slurred speech at this dose would suggest that the patient is not physically dependent and should not require a very large dosage of the long-acting barbiturate for withdrawal.

The combined alcohol-BZ withdrawal syndrome appears to be different from the classical alcohol withdrawal syndrome. These withdrawal symptoms can start anywhere from 2 to 10 days after abrupt discontinuation of drugs and are characterized by more psychomotor and autonomic nervous system signs than are usually seen in alcohol withdrawal (Benzer and Cushman 1980). The clinician may use the previously described barbiturate withdrawal regimen or feel free to use CBZ, which should be effective for the combined alcohol-BZ addictions, particularly since CBZ has been shown to be effective for both alcohol and BZ withdrawal (Ries et al. 1989). The same treatment regimen for CBZ, as used for the severe alcohol withdrawal syndrome, 800 mg daily for 1–2 days, followed by slow reduction over 5–7 days, can be used for the combined ethanol-BZ addiction. However, if alcohol-BZ addiction is associated with a compound that has a relatively long half-life, such as diazepam, it may be necessary to continue the CBZ regimen for approximately 2 weeks to avoid a delayed withdrawal seizure.

## ▼ PHARMACOTHERAPY DURING THE ABSTINENCE PHASE

### Disulfiram

The efficacy of disulfiram has been demonstrated in a number of studies by different authors (Fuller and

Williford 1980; Gerrein et al. 1973; Sereny et al. 1986). In one well-designed controlled evaluation of disulfiram in a Veterans Administration (VA) Hospital, a life-table analysis showed that the use of this compound significantly increased the number of abstinent months compared with a placebo group despite the fact that both groups of patients had requested disulfiram at the outset of the study, thus negating the variable of motivation for taking the medication. Although the 12-month endpoint of the study showed no significant differences in total abstinence rates between the groups, the evaluation of the effect of disulfiram on abstinence over time provided information about the number of additional months of abstinence before the 12-month endpoint. These additional months of abstinence may delay or possibly prevent the occurrence of alcohol-induced tissue damage to various organs (Fuller and Williford 1980). In other studies (Gerrein et al. 1973; Sereny et al. 1986), supervised disulfiram maintenance has been shown to be significantly superior to voluntary disulfiram therapy in keeping patients in treatment. In fact, administration of disulfiram to patients by spouses or cohabitants, who had received positive reinforcement therapy with social skills training for administering the disulfiram, resulted in even more therapeutic gains compared with patients receiving disulfiram on a routine basis from the cohabitant without positive reinforcement (Azrin et al. 1982). All of these studies have shown that disulfiram as an addition to other treatment modalities helps to increase the abstinence rate while it is only rarely associated with serious side effects (Gallant 1991b). Disulfiram can be used not only as an aversive agent for alcohol ingestion but also as a symbol of the patient's commitment to treatment. If the patient agrees to take disulfiram and then discontinues the medication either overtly or covertly without notifying his or her cohabitant or the physician, this action points out the patient's strong denial and/or lack of motivation for abstinence. Disulfiram compliance can be determined by testing the urine for diethylamine, a metabolite of disulfiram (Fuller and Neiderheiser 1980).

Because disulfiram inhibits dopamine-β-hydroxylase activity, it should be used only in small doses (e.g., 125 mg), with caution in alcoholic patients who have a comorbidity diagnosis of schizophrenia. In such patients, it may be advisable to prescribe an adequate dopamine-blocking agent such as a high-potency neuroleptic while the patient is being administered the disulfiram. (Calcium carbamide, a "disulfiram-like" compound, does cause an increase in acetaldehyde after alcohol administration while it lacks dopamine-β-hydroxylase activity [Gallant 1991b]. However, this compound is available only in Europe and Canada.) Other side effects of disulfiram such as peripheral nerve damage, including optic neuritis, have been described but are quite rare and are usually observed in association with daily disulfiram doses of more than 250 mg daily (Gallant 1987a, pp. 111–117, 222, 240–241). There are published reports (Berlin 1989) that indicate definite problems with disulfiram-induced hepatotoxicity. Despite the fact that there are only about 25 cases of disulfiram-induced liver damage reported in the world medical literature, the physician is obligated to monitor hepatic transaminases with a warning to the patient that if any clinical symptoms of hepatitis occur, the patient should immediately contact a physician and discontinue the disulfiram. At times, it may be difficult for the clinician to evaluate the side-effect complaints by the patient. In one placebo-disulfiram double-blind controlled study in alcoholic patients (Christensen et al. 1984), the evaluation of side effects in 158 patients completing the study showed no statistically significant differences between the two groups except for a greater number of complaints of sexual problems in the placebo group. Skin reactions, itching, fatigue or lethargy, and unpleasant taste were no more common in the disulfiram group than in the placebo group. There was a tendency for a more frequent number of complaints of "bad breath" in the disulfiram group. The dosage of disulfiram in this study was 250 mg daily, dissolved in plain soda water, administered daily for 6 weeks under staff supervision.

It appears that the threat of developing a disulfiram-ethanol reaction may be more therapeutic than the action of the drug. In a double-blind study of patients receiving disulfiram implants of 1,000 mg versus a placebo group receiving an implant (1 mg of disulfiram), no significant differences were found between the two groups in reduction of alcohol consumption or level of psychosocial functioning, although the 1,000 mg disulfiram implant group developed a significantly greater incidence of wound complications (Johnsen and Morland 1991). The authors concluded that the reduction of alcohol intake was probably due to the psychological deterrent effect because there were no significant differences between the two study groups.

## Lithium

The value of lithium in treating alcoholic individuals has been difficult to confirm (Gallant 1985). In one review of 61 published studies of lithium in alcoholic subjects (McMillan 1981), it was reported that the inadequacies of these studies range from lack of control subjects to problems with definitions of the illness. Very few attempts were made to separate patients with primary affective disorders who were using alcohol to decrease the dysphoria from primary alcoholic individuals who had developed a depression secondary to chronic excessive alcohol use and its consequences (Gallant 1987a, pp. 170–185).

High dropout rates, problems with compliance, and difficulties in measuring improvements interfere with the interpretation of long-term evaluations of pharmacologic and nonpharmacologic investigations in alcoholic patients. The most impressive published study of lithium carbonate in the treatment of alcoholism is a perspective double-blind placebo-controlled trial conducted for a 6-month period (de la Fuente et al. 1989). Of the 53 patients admitted to this research trial, the dropout rate was 50% for the lithium group and 48% for the placebo group, with 81% of the dropouts drinking before discontinuing their clinic visits. As observed in an earlier study that reported a trend in favor of lithium, a high dropout rate with a resultant small number of patients for evaluation at the end of the study did impose some limitations in interpreting the results (Fawcett et al. 1984). In addition, as the authors noted in their discussion of the results, reliance on the use of *total* abstinence as the only criteria for successful outcome may be unrealistic. However, reporting the *number of abstinent days is an extremely important indicator of outcome.*

Future studies of lithium in the treatment of alcoholism should take into consideration such factors as subgrouping of alcoholic patients into depressed and nondepressed subjects prior to initiation of the study; definition of outcome measures such as number of abstinent days, quantity of ethanol consumed, and quality of social and economic life-style; documentation of genetic variables and other relevant biographical data that could influence subsequent drinking episodes as well as response to psychopharmacologic medications; adequate control subjects; and compliance measures such as corroboration of patients' response to treatment by cohabitants and laboratory measures that tag the compounds that are administered to the patient. Until more adequate data are available, it would be a mistake to initiate widespread use of lithium in alcoholic individuals. It may be possible that certain subtypes of alcoholic individuals (e.g., individuals who may have an underlying bipolar II disorder not otherwise specified associated with depression, some episodes of hypomania, and personality disorders), may show more significant therapeutic responses to lithium or lithium plus an antidepressant than other subtypes of alcoholic individuals.

## Other Pharmacologic Approaches for Reducing Alcohol Intake

The effects of serotonin-enhancing compounds on alcohol consumption have been evaluated in a number of studies. They will be discussed in the following section on the use of antidepressant compounds for some comorbid disorders associated with alcoholism (Gatto et al. 1990; Naranjo et al. 1986; Pietraszek et al. 1991). Another interesting and potentially valuable pharmacologic approach by the outstanding Philadelphia VA Medical Center research team has incorporated the use of a long-acting oral narcotic antagonist, naltrexone (Volpicelli et al. 1992).

In a 12-week double-blind, placebo-controlled evaluation of naltrexone, 50 mg daily, in 70 alcoholic patients involved in outpatient group therapy, the naltrexone group had a significantly lower relapse rate and showed a decrease in subsequent drinking in subjects who had at least one drink. In the evaluation of those patients who had "sampled" alcohol, 95% of the placebo patients and only 40% of the naltrexone patients lost control of their drinking and met the criteria for relapse. The authors suggested that the initial drink stimulates alcohol craving in some subjects by increasing the activity of the opioid system, and blocking of this system by naltrexone dampens the alcohol craving. In another 12-week controlled study of naltrexone (O'Malley et al. 1992), 50 mg daily, and psychotherapy with specific guidelines, 97 alcoholic patients were divided into four treatment groups: naltrexone with coping skills, naltrexone with supportive therapy, placebo with coping skills, and placebo with supportive therapy. The naltrexone group was superior to the placebo subjects in abstention rate, severity of alcohol-related problems, number of drinking days, and relapse. Although the overall rate of abstinence was highest in the patient group receiving naltrexone with supportive therapy, the authors observed that those patients who received naltrexone and coping skills therapy were the least likely to relapse to heavy drinking after an initial lapse or drinking episode. Naltrexone appears to be a relatively safe compound without serious long-term side effects.

## Medications for Comorbidity Disorders Associated With Alcoholism

Before considering the various uses of psychopharmacologic agents in the treatment of alcoholic patients with coexisting psychiatric disorders, it is necessary to discuss the protracted withdrawal symptoms experienced by alcoholic individuals following cessation of alcohol intake. Some of the symptoms of protracted withdrawal syndrome (PWS) have been listed under other clinical terms such as *protracted abstinence syndrome* or *alcoholism-induced subacute organic mental disorders* (Grant et al. 1979, 1984; Schuckit 1991). Between the resolution of the acute alcohol withdrawal symptomatology and the plateau of improvement that may continue for 1 year or more following the cessation of alcohol, a slowly resolving, alcohol-related PWS was described in a number of articles during the late 1970s (Grant et al. 1979; Kissin 1979). Symptoms attributable to PWS include physiological variations such as changes in sleep latency; frequency of awakening; increases in respiratory rate, body temperature, blood pressure, and pulse; decrease in cold-stress response; persistence of tolerance to sedative effects; and tremor (Gallant 1982; Kissin 1979; Schuckit 1991). These patients may show frustration and irritability resulting from deficits in problem-solving, symptoms of spontaneous anxiety, and depressive episodes for no apparent reason (Gallant 1982; Grant et al. 1979, 1984). Some patients may become easily discouraged due to the development of these symptoms and resort to alcohol use in an attempt to alleviate such discomfort.

Inappropriate use of psychopharmacologic agents during these periods may cause additional discomfort due to anticholinergic or sedative side effects, further confusing the patient. A sensible therapeutic approach to this problem is a fully detailed explanation to the patient and the family, which will enable them to accept these symptoms as a normal part of the withdrawal phase of alcohol. This approach may help the patient to accommodate to the discomfort and maintain abstinence. The patient should realize that these symptoms are not a sign of relapse or psychological illness and that they will gradually resolve. At this time, the literature does not contain any well-controlled evaluations of psychopharmacologic medications that can alleviate the symptoms of PWS. Before diagnosing this syndrome, the clinician should be sure the patient does not have a combination of such symptoms prior to alcohol abstinence and should rule out all other possible metabolic, physiological, and psychological causes for these behavioral and emotional abnormalities before making the diagnosis of PWS.

**Reports of comorbidity with alcohol.** In the Epidemiologic Catchment Area survey conducted by the National Institutes of Mental Health, patients with an alcohol disorder had seven times the chance of having another addictive disorder compared with the rest of the population, and 37% of these patients had a comorbid mental disorder (Regier et al. 1990). Of the mental disorders in individuals with alcohol diagnoses, anxiety disorders were most frequent (19.4%), followed by antisocial personality disorders (14.3%) and affective disorders (13.4%), with some overlapping of more than one comorbid diagnosis for certain patients. Among patients with a primary mental disorder, the lifetime prevalence of an alcohol disorder was approximately 22%. In another study of 100 patients consecutively admitted to an inpatient psychiatry unit (Brady et al. 1991), 64% reported current or past problems with substance abuse, and 29%, evaluated by DSM-III-R criteria, had substance abuse disorder diagnoses in the 30 days prior to admission, with alcohol as the *most common drug* of choice. These data are extremely important because psychiatric diagnoses generally predict poor treatment outcome for alcoholic patients (Rounsaville et al. 1987). By assessing the high incidence of major psychiatric diagnoses in alcoholic patients, which has important therapeutic and prognostic implications, it becomes apparent that skilled interviewing or screening techniques associated with diagnostic abilities and appropriate use of psychopharmacologic compounds are essential for any individual treating alcoholic patients.

The suicide risk in known alcoholic individuals is indeed startling. In a 30-year prospective study of 1,312 alcoholic subjects, 88 (16%) of the 537 deaths were found to be definite suicides (Berglund 1984). The highest frequency of suicide was found during the years immediately following discharge from the hospital, additional data that emphasize the importance of evaluating the possibility of a comorbid psychiatric diagnosis when an alcoholic patient is first admitted to a treatment program.

**Use of antidepressant agents.**   Before discussing the specific antidepressant or anxiolytic pharmacotherapies for alcoholic patients during their abstinence phase, it should be stressed that any compound that requires oxidation by the liver may have different pharmacokinetics when administered to an alcoholic patient during the early phase of the illness, when there may be an induction of the microsomal enzyme oxidation system, than when it is administered during the later phase of alcoholism, which may be associated with cirrhosis of the liver, causing a subsequent reduction of available metabolic enzymes. As of this time, no commercially available antidepressant has been found to be more effective than other antidepressants for use in alcoholic patients presenting major depressive episodes. The most common mistakes in the use of antidepressants are prescribing too low a dosage for too short a period of time and premature discontinuation of the medication once an adequate therapeutic response has occurred.

The delineation of primary versus secondary affective disorder in patients presenting the syndrome of alcoholism may be one of the most difficult diagnostic problems in psychiatry. A number of patients present a history of alcoholism and affective disorder starting at approximately the same age, and it is often quite difficult to decide if the excessive use of alcohol resulted in depression or if the patient was self-medicating the depression with alcohol. Certain biographical and clinical data are helpful to the clinician in making the diagnosis of a primary major depression disorder (or bipolar disorder): 1) affective disorder preceding the onset of alcoholism or a history of an affective disorder occurring during sustained periods of abstinence; 2) early childhood history of separation anxiety, phobic behavior, or neurasthenia; 3) occurrence of a hypomanic or manic reaction to antidepressant medication; 4) family history of bipolar illness; 5) family history of affective illness in two or more consecutive generations; and 6) a positive dexamethasone suppression test after the patient has been abstinent for 4 or more weeks (Gallant 1987a,

pp. 170–185). However, inadequate histories presented by some alcoholic patients create difficulties in dating the initial onset of loss of control of alcohol and the development of the affective disorder. If the affective symptomatology is secondary to excessive alcohol intake and the accompanying life failures, then the affective disorder should resolve within a period of several weeks as abstinence continues. These patients usually do not require specific psychopharmacologic intervention for their affective symptomatology. However, if the affective illness persists for more than 1–2 months despite psychotherapeutic attempts to alleviate the discomfort, it then may be worthwhile to initiate psychopharmacologic therapy to avoid an alcoholic relapse or suicide attempt secondary to painful affective symptomatology.

In a preliminary report of a 6-month double-blind, placebo-controlled trial of desipramine in abstinent alcoholic patients who were stratified for the presence or absence of an associated depression (Mason and Kocsis 1991), there was a trend for the desipramine subjects to maintain sobriety for a longer duration during the study; only 33.3% of the depressed placebo patients and 9.1% of the nondepressed placebo patients had their longest period of sobriety during the study, compared with 60% of the depressed desipramine patients and 41.7% of the nondepressed desipramine patients. However, the dropout rate of this small-numbered group was significant, and these percentages may be misleading (Gallant 1992b). If these data can be replicated with larger numbers of patients, the findings would suggest that not only is desipramine useful for alcoholic patients with secondary depression but it may also be of help to nondepressed alcoholic patients in maintaining their sobriety. Until more data are available, routine use of desipramine in a general population of alcoholic patients should not be recommended.

The serotonin system has been implicated in a number of studies, not only in relation to the onset of depression but also to the decrease of alcohol intake in both animals and humans (Gatto et al. 1990; Naranjo et al. 1986; Pietraszek et al. 1991). In one study of male volunteers (Pietraszek et al. 1991), blood serotonin concentration was significantly reduced after drinking alcohol, whereas no changes were observed in the tryptophan level. The diurnal rhythm of serotonin in subjects who had drunk alcohol the day before was quite different from the control group but very similar to that of patients with depression. The authors suggest that the mechanism of depression after alcohol drinking may be related to serotonin function.

In another study (Gatto et al. 1990) evaluating the effects of fluoxetine and desipramine on alcohol consumption, which was induced in alcohol-non-preferring rats by making the solution more palatable, fluoxetine was found to decrease alcohol consumption in these alcohol-nonpreferring rats; this compound has also produced similar results in alcohol-preferring rats. The authors suggested that "fluoxetine is increasing the physiologically active pool of 5-HT in neuronal circuits mediating the aversive properties of ethanol" (Gatto et al. 1990). Relative to the results of these animal studies, investigations of inhibitors of serotonin uptake have been conducted in humans. In one controlled double-blind study in alcoholic patients (Naranjo et al. 1986), citalopram, a selective serotonin uptake inhibitor, produced a significant increase in the number of abstinent days and a decrease in the number of drinks consumed compared with control patients. However, the active drug was administered for only 4 weeks in this crossover study. Another criticism of this investigation was that not all of the patients were diagnosed by standard criteria such as the DSM-III-R (Moore and Libert 1991). Viqualine, another inhibitor of serotonin uptake, has been reported to produce similar results (Naranjo et al. 1989). Thus the inhibitors of serotonin uptake, such as the commercially available compound fluoxetine, do look interesting, but additional studies are needed with larger numbers of patients, for longer periods of time, and with definitive diagnoses of alcohol dependence as defined by the ICD-10 or the DSM-IV.

Some of the antidepressant agents that are capable of producing sedative side effects, such as doxepin, amitriptyline, and trazodone, can be used for hypnotic purposes in alcoholic patients without fear of habituation. The sedative side effects of these antidepressants, used at relatively low dosages between 25 to 100 mg hs, can be quite helpful in some alcoholic patients who have a history of chronic insomnia. A recent controlled trial of trazodone (Nirenberg et al. 1991), 50–100 mg hs versus placebo, was conducted in 10 inpatients who were receiving nonsedating antidepressants and complaining of persistent insomnia. In a 4-day crossover study of this group, all of the trazodone patients showed significant improvement on the sleep measures compared with the placebo group. They were able to distinguish the active drug from the placebo and wanted to continue treatment with trazodone. These medications, which are not habit-forming, are easily discontinued after the patient has developed adequate sleep habits.

**Use of anxiolytics.** In the treatment of alcoholism patients with generalized anxiety disorder, panic disorder, or other anxiety-related disorders, the ideal anxiolytic agent should not interfere with the patient's cognitive processes or manual dexterity or interfere with the recovery of the patient who may be likely to abuse a habit-forming drug. The compound should be suitable, if necessary, for prolonged use without any undue risks and therefore should produce neither high-dose tolerance nor normal-dose dependence withdrawal symptoms. Unfortunately, as in other areas of alcohol research, there are only a relatively small number of well-conducted clinical trials of anxiolytic drug treatment in patients with the problem of alcoholism. As previously mentioned, outpatient studies usually suffer from a high dropout rate as well as deficiencies in markers of alcohol intake and abstinence. When these studies are conducted on inpatient treatment units that emphasize psychotherapy and 12-step programs, the placebo and control group therapeutic gains may be so significant that they obscure the anxiolytic efficacy of the active drug (McFarlain et al. 1976). Anxiety reduction resulting from the extensive therapy available to alcoholic patients in a carefully planned ward milieu could mask additional therapeutic gains from pharmacotherapy. In this particular environment, it may be impossible to draw any conclusions from an anxiolytic investigation unless the study includes a very large number of patients.

The use of BZs for anxiety reduction in alcoholic patients during their maintenance phase of abstinence is somewhat controversial. In controlled placebo studies, BZs such as diazepam and alprazolam have been shown not only to cause a significant increase in symptoms of euphoria in alcoholic men but also in the adult male offspring of alcoholic men; these offspring had not yet developed alcoholism (Ciraulo et al. 1989). If the clinician finds it necessary to use a BZ in an alcoholic patient, a good rule of thumb is to plan the duration of therapy for no more than 4–6 weeks, using that period of time to instruct the patient on the use of cognitive and behavioral therapies to reduce the anxiety. If the alcoholic patient has a history of abusing other drugs, the use of mild to moderate dosages of some antidepressant medications may be of help (Gallant et al. 1969). In one controlled evaluation of doxepin versus diazepam in 100 abstinent chronic alcoholic inpatients displaying the target symptomatology of anxiety and tension (Gallant et al. 1969), an average dosage of doxepin (100–150 mg daily) appeared to be just as effective as 15–30 mg of diazepam. In addition to the potential habituation problems that BZs pose for the alcoholic patient, the side effects of decrease in performance of cognitive tasks and manual dexterity as well as the appearance of anterograde amnesia may interfere with the alcoholic patient's recovery phase.

Buspirone does not appear to be addicting or cause significant impairment of the cognitive processes. In one randomized, double-blind placebo-controlled trial of buspirone in alcoholic patients with the comorbid symptomatology of a generalized anxiety disorder associated with depressive features, buspirone was significantly superior to placebo in reducing anxiety and depressive symptoms on the Hamilton Anxiety and Depression Rating scales (Tollefson et al. 1991). Unfortunately, the anxiety reduction on the Hamilton Anxiety Scale did not significantly favor buspirone until the 12th week of the study; the same results were noted on the Depression Rating Scale. Since the early dropout rate of alcoholic outpatients in treatment is usually quite high, the practical utility of buspirone is still in question. In this clinical investigation of buspirone, only 14 of 51 patients completed the study (Tollefson et al. 1991). However, the dropout rate due to the patient's condition being rated worse or not improved did favor buspirone; 12 placebo patients and only 3 buspirone subjects were withdrawn for this reason ($P < .05$). The patients were able to tolerate dosage increases; the maximum dosage of buspirone in this study was 60 mg daily.

Patients with panic disorder, especially those with agoraphobia, show relatively good therapeutic responses to monoamine oxidase inhibitors (MAOIs), particularly when administered in conjunction with behavioral modification techniques. In studies of social phobias, a frequent comorbid diagnosis in alcoholic patients, phenelzine has been shown to be significantly superior to both atenolol and placebo (Liebowitz et al. 1990). Hepatotoxicity has been associated with MAOIs, but the incidence appears to be relatively low in alcoholic individuals without previous severe liver pathology (Gallant 1987a, pp. 170–185).

The β-adrenergic blockers also have been used to reduce the symptomatology of anxiety and tension as well as to treat mild to moderate withdrawal symptoms in alcoholic patients. In one double-blind study (Gallant et al. 1973) of inpatient alcoholic patients with the target symptoms of "anxiety and tension," propranolol, 120 mg daily, was compared with placebo during a 4-week period. Despite the significant placebo response in this inpatient alcoholic population, there was a statistically significant improvement in the global ratings of the propranolol group compared with the placebo group ($P < .05$.) The side effects in this study were unusually mild and infrequent, but the clinician should be aware that this type of compound can precipitate asthmatic attacks in patients who have a history of bronchial asthma and obstruction and can interfere with myocardial contractility in patients who have already developed an alcohol cardiomyopathy. Additional controlled studies of β-blockers should be conducted in severely anxious alcoholic patients who have completed detoxification and are beginning the maintenance phase of sobriety.

In France, an interesting compound named acamprosate, an agonist of GABA (affecting the GABA complex as do BZs, ethanol, and barbiturates), has been shown to decrease voluntary alcohol intake in rats and humans (Moore and Libert 1991). In a large-scale multicenter investigation of "severely dependent alcoholics," patients were evaluated for relapse 3 months after abstinence was initiated (Moore and Libert 1991). Although the evaluations for abstinence significantly favored the acamprosate group compared with the placebo group, a shortcoming of this study was that monitoring of daily alcohol intake was not considered to be feasible.

It is not unusual for a patient with adult attention-deficit hyperactivity disorder to develop a problem with alcohol or drug abuse. This syndrome can be diagnosed only in patients who 1) had a childhood history of definite hyperactivity and attention problems and 2) have present symptoms of adult hyperactivity and difficulty with attention in addition to "two of the following five characteristics: 1) affective lability, 2) disorganization and inability to complete tasks, 3) hot temper, 4) impulsivity, and 5) stress intolerance" (Wender and Reimherr 1990). Concern about alcoholic individuals abusing drugs such as methylphenidate or amphetamines has made many clinicians hesitant to use these compounds, which have definite efficacy in reducing the hyperactivity of this syndrome. However, there are no valid data to indicate that patients with this comorbid diagnosis do abuse these drugs. This ambivalence may be partially resolved by a recent report of bupropion treatment (an effective antidepressant) of attention-deficit hyperactivity disorder in adults (Wender and Reimherr 1990). In this open trial of bupropion, the patients had previously received maintenance medication or MAOIs for an average of 3.7 years. The mean dose of bupropion in this study was $359 \pm 118$ mg daily, with a range of 150–450 mg daily. Of the 19 patients in this study, 14 experienced moderate to marked benefit from bupropion; 10 of these patients chose to continue the medication rather than resume their former medication. This preference for bupropion speaks well for the use of this drug in alcoholic patients who show symptoms of the adult attention-deficit hyperactivity disorder because bupropion is not an abusable drug. A word of caution should be noted with the use of bupropion in alcoholic patients who have had a past history of withdrawal seizures. Bupropion, as noted with other antidepressant drugs, tends to lower seizure threshold as the dosage is increased; at a daily dose of 600 mg the incidence of seizures was 2.3% in one survey (Johnston et al. 1991). However, in an 8-week open trial of 3,341 depressed patients in 102 sites, using a maximum dosage of 450 mg daily, the observed seizure rate for the entire study was 0.40% (Johnson and Morland 1991).

**Use of neuroleptic medications.** It was noted in the beginning of this section that the degree of psychopathology appears to be a predictor of treatment outcome in alcoholic patients (Rounsaville et al. 1987). Therefore, appropriate pharmacologic treatment with neuroleptic drugs is absolutely necessary for alcoholic patients with a comorbid diagnosis of schizophrenia. However, the clinician must exercise caution in the dosage regimen for these patients. It may well be that some of the schizophrenic patients who are abusing alcohol may actually be self-medicating one of their neuroleptic-induced side effects such as akathisia. Therefore, one has to seek the minimal optimal dosage of the neuroleptic that alleviates the psychotic symptomatology but is associated with minimal to absent extrapyramidal side effects, particularly akathisia. Even though high-potency neuroleptics are usually preferable for schizophrenic patients with alcoholism because they are less likely to cause uncom-

fortable sedation and orthostatic hypotension, it may be necessary to change the medication to a low-potency neuroleptic if the akathisia cannot be controlled by a β-blocker such as propranolol or one of the standard antiparkinson drugs. If the patient gives a previous history of self-medication with alcohol secondary to neuroleptic-induced akathisia, then prophylactic use of propranolol would be indicated when reinstituting a high-potency neuroleptic drug.

If disulfiram is added to the regimen after a neuroleptic has been initiated, the patient then should be seen more frequently for close observation of possible exacerbation of psychotic symptoms (secondary to inhibition of dopamine-β-hydroxylase) that would necessitate immediate increase of the neuroleptic dosage.

Because schizophrenic patients who abuse alcohol tend to be more noncompliant than patients experiencing schizophrenia without substance abuse disorders, the use of a long-acting intramuscular depot form of a neuroleptic may be indicated. This compliance problem should be addressed in group therapy with other patients presenting similar comorbid diagnoses. Because the schizophrenic patient may be less prone to stop drinking, as alcohol may provide one of his or her few social outlets, group therapy with this patient provides more than one advantage. In addition to enabling the patient to see how alcohol intoxication can result in noncompliance or forgetting to take the neuroleptic medication, it also offers the patient an opportunity for social interactions without the use of alcohol. In these patients who present with comorbid schizophrenia and alcoholism, adequate use of a neuroleptic plus group therapy may enable the patient not only to remain abstinent but to enhance the quality of his or her life.

The clinician should be aware that the problem of neuroleptic-induced tardive dyskinesia may be more frequent in neuroleptic-treated psychiatric patients with alcoholism. In one sample of 284 psychiatric patients who chronically abused street drugs and received neuroleptic treatment for an average of $10.5 \pm 5.8$ years, the overall incidence of tardive dyskinesia was 15.9% (Olivera et al. 1990). In those groups of psychiatric patients who abused alcohol alone or in combination with cannabis, the incidence of tardive dyskinesia was *highest*, 25.4% and 26.7%, respectively. The possibility exists that chronic alcohol intake may be associated with structural or chemical changes that provide a substrate for development of tardive dyskinesia when neuroleptic drugs are administered over a relatively long period of time. Because there has been an increase in the use of alcohol and other drugs of abuse by psychiatric patients, it is essential that future psychopharmacologic investigations evaluate the effects of these psychoactive substances upon the development of tardive dyskinesia in patients receiving neuroleptic therapy. In the meantime, most psychiatric patients receiving neuroleptic drugs should be informed of the present data concerning the possible enhancement of neuroleptic-induced side effects by alcohol.

A comment should be made about alcoholic patients who have a comorbid drug dependence problem of methadone maintenance. These alcoholic, ex-heroin-addicted individuals should usually be treated for alcoholism without withdrawing them from methadone (Gordis 1988). Although the prevalence of alcoholism among patients on methadone maintenance is as high as 50%, rates of relapse back to heroin may be as high as 70%–80% if they discontinue methadone maintenance (Gordis 1988). These comorbid patients are difficult to treat, and the clinician is more likely to treat this type of individual successfully if the patient is maintained on methadone throughout the alcoholism rehabilitation program. Consequences of maintaining a rigid guideline against continuing methadone in these patients prior to alcoholism rehabilitation will not only result in an increase in hepatitis and possible HIV infections but will also subsequently cause a spread of these infections to the patients' sexual partners. The NIAAA *Alcohol Alert* concludes that "requiring individuals to terminate methadone maintenance as a condition of acceptance into alcoholism treatment should be rejected as a standard practice by alcohol treatment service providers" (Gordis 1988).

**Use of vitamins.** It is not unusual for many alcoholic patients to have one or more nutritional deficiencies such as magnesium, zinc, and various vitamins. It is generally agreed that supplemental thiamine should be administered to all patients who have a history of chronic alcoholism. Thiamine administration is the recommended treatment for Wernicke's encephalopathy, a rapidly deteriorating organic mental syndrome that may be difficult to diagnose (Gallant 1987a, pp. 170–185). Another disease that may benefit from supplemental thiamine therapy is alcoholic amblyopia, characterized by blurring of vision due to

central scotomas, which can develop into optic atrophy if untreated (Edmondson 1980). Improvement of alcoholic amblyopia has been reported in association with vitamin B supplements, but there are no controlled studies in this area. Controlled data are similarly lacking in most of the other areas involving vitamin therapy of alcohol-related diseases. A significant percentage of alcoholic individuals have peripheral neuropathies; it may be that chronic thiamine deficiency, as well as pantothenic acid and pyridoxine deficiency, are responsible for development of this syndrome (Gallant 1987a, pp. 170–185). However, it is not known whether one or several of these vitamin deficiencies are specific causes of the development of this syndrome; it is also uncertain as to what part direct alcohol toxicity plays in producing this pathology. Multiple mega-B therapy is recommended for these patients. Thiamine therapy, vitamin A, and zinc supplements have been recommended by some clinicians for alcoholic patients who complain about night blindness. If the patient does not show any significant neurologic or hematologic problems secondary to chronic excessive alcohol intake, routine orders should include only thiamine, 100 mg daily, and a multivitamin supplement.

**Pharmacotherapy of organ damage secondary to chronic excessive intake of ethanol.** There is an encouraging report of fluvoxamine administration (inhibitor of serotonin uptake) resulting in improvement of Alcoholic Amnestic Disorder (AAD) symptoms (Martin et al. 1989). Despite the small number of patients in this study, the results were impressive because many clinicians previously believed that AAD was an irreversible phenomenon. In a 4-week double-blind crossover evaluation of six patients with AAD, three patients with global dementia associated with alcoholism, and one patient with compensated alcoholic liver disease, fluvoxamine dosages of 100–200 mg daily were found to improve episodic memory in only the patients with AAD. The investigators chose to use fluvoxamine because its serotonin-uptake blocking properties appear to be highly selective. The preliminary conclusion was that enhancement of serotonergic neurotransmission improves episodic memory failure in patients with AAD. As they infer in their conclusion, additional controlled studies with a larger number of patients are now clearly warranted.

Diverse treatment outcomes on the efficacy of β-blocker treatment and prophylactic sclerotherapy for the prevention of first-episode and recurrent bleeding and subsequent improved survival time in patients with esophageal varices have been reported (Gallant 1992a). A large-numbered multisite evaluation of prophylactic sclerotherapy versus sham therapy in patients with esophageal varices and alcoholic liver disease without a history of variceal bleeding has apparently settled the controversy (Veterans Affairs Cooperative Variceal Sclerotherapy Group 1991). The study had to be terminated after 22.5 months because the 32% mortality rate in the sclerotherapy group was significantly higher ($P < .004$) than the sham group (17%) at that point in the study. Statistical analyses showed that only the Child's score on severity of cirrhosis and the assigned treatment were independent predictors of mortality. It is noteworthy that during the 37-month follow-up after termination of sclerotherapy, the mortality rate in both groups was almost identical. Concerning the available data on prophylactic therapy for large esophageal varices and recurrent bleeding from severe portal hypertensive gastropathy in men with chronic liver disease, propranolol administration appears to be the safest and most effective treatment at this time (Gallant 1992). In fact, a meta-analysis of all of the controlled clinical trials of β-adrenoreceptor blocking drugs has shown that these β-blockers have significantly reduced the occurrence of variceal bleeding deaths and overall fatality (Hayes et al. 1990). These results indicate the value of β-adrenergic blocking drugs for prevention of hemorrhage from large esophageal varices.

Other encouraging results in patients with chronic alcoholic liver disease have been reported with the use of propylthiouracil (Orrego et al. 1987). In a long-term, double-blind randomized clinical trial of 310 alcoholic patients with mild to severe liver disease, the group receiving propylthiouracil (300 mg daily) had a mortality rate at the end of the 2-year study that was half that of the entire group receiving placebo ($P < .05$) and less than half of the placebo subgroup of severely ill patients. The criteria for admission to the study included clinical or laboratory evidence of liver disease; the severity of each case was determined with the use of a clinical and laboratory index. The report contains a table that itemizes the graded score for severity of liver disease, using the clinical and laboratory abnormalities (Orrego et al. 1987). It should be emphasized that protection by propylthiouracil was not observed in patients who continued to drink during the study. Despite the fact

that propylthiouracil can cause hepatitis in rare instances, the administration of this drug is definitely recommended to reduce the mortality secondary to alcoholic liver disease (Orrego et al. 1987, 1988).

There have been attempts by neuropsychopharmacologic researchers to reverse the supposedly terminal syndrome of hepatic encephalopathy (HE; Basile et al. 1991; Grimm et al. 1988; Mullen et al. 1988; Olasmaa et al. 1989). Facilitation of GABA synaptic transmission associated with an increase in BZ receptor binding in cerebrospinal fluid has been postulated as an important factor in the development of HE in a subgroup of patients with this syndrome (Basile et al. 1991; Mullen et al. 1988; Olasmaa et al. 1989). Trials of flumazenil, a selective BZ-receptor antagonist, in patients with HE have reported improvement in the level of consciousness. (Ferenci et al. 1989; Grimm et al. 1988). Such results offer patients some hope of recovery from an illness that was once thought to be irreversible. In one case report from Austria, oral flumazenil administration (25 mg bid) resulted in a sustained alleviation of HE symptoms in a patient with a history of "intractable" HE coma (Ferenci et al. 1989).

In summary, we now see serious efforts devoted not only to the treatment of alcoholism before permanent liver and CNS damage develop but also to the maintenance of patients who have already developed permanent organ damage that is serious enough to shorten their lives unless pharmacologic steps are taken in association with their sobriety. However, clinicians should remember that not all of the answers to the treatment of alcoholic patients depend solely upon psychopharmacologic agents. In one very interesting controlled trial of acupuncture in severely alcoholic patients, with control patients treated at ear points ≤ 5 mm from the specific points of treatment, 21 of 40 patients in the treatment group completed the program compared with only 1 of 40 control patients (Bullock et al. 1989). Not only was there a significant difference between the groups in completion of the treatment program, but more of the control patients expressed a moderate to strong need for alcohol and had more than twice the number of drinking episodes and admissions to a detoxification center as the active treatment group. These significant treatment effects persisted at the end of a 6-month follow-up. One important shortcoming of this study was that a breath analyzer was not used to monitor drinking episodes; also, there was no systematic attempt to obtain confirmatory reports of the alcoholic patients' abstinence periods by cohabitants. Nonetheless, these initial data are impressive enough to warrant further research to evaluate the efficacy of the specific type of acupuncture used in this study.

# ▼ SPECIFIC PSYCHOSOCIAL INTERVENTIONS

## Psychologic and Behavioral Interventions

**Psychologic interventions.** The classical interpersonal intervention technique was originally described in 1973 (Johnson 1973). A number of modifications of this technique have been published since that time (Gallant 1987a, pp. 66–68, 82–84; Gallant 1987b). Early intervention with the alcoholic (or drug-abusing) individual compresses past crises caused by the misuse of alcohol into one dramatic confrontation. This confrontation helps to brush aside the denial mechanism so that the patient will agree to get help. This therapeutic maneuver is designed to help the patient immediately. The alternative is to wait interminably for the alcoholic patient to "hit bottom" and/or lose or destroy his or her family, health, or job. If the family, friends, or employer wait until the patient hits bottom, it may be far too late. Early intervention, when used with adequate preparation and sensitivity, may save the patient and the family many years of suffering and, in some cases, prevent total loss of the patient's human support systems. Adequate preparation, interpersonal sensitivity, and experience are required for this therapeutic intervention.

The following steps describe the approach I use to treat patients with these disorders. Usually, it is the alcoholic patient's spouse who calls saying that he or she is upset and feels hopeless because the patient refuses to see the problem or the need for help. An initial interview should be arranged with the spouse to obtain a history of the problem and to identify the key people in the environment who have the most influence on the patient. The therapist explains to the spouse that he or she is the patient; thus the confidentiality of the patient is not involved. The spouse's name is on the primary medical chart. Of course, the patient has affected the emotional state of the spouse, and the spouse's chart includes the history of the

patient's drinking behavior and its effects upon the family and friends. The next meeting should include the teenage or adult children, if available, and possibly one or two close friends whose attendance is requested to validate the spouse's history. At the same time, they are also educated about the disease of alcoholism. If considered to be suitable for the task at hand, all of these people become members of the intervention team. They are asked to make a list of three to five painful or embarrassing events, avoiding labels and name-calling, associated with the behavior demonstrated by the patient while intoxicated. The individuals involved have to always be nonjudgmental as well as honest and have genuine concern for the patient. If any one of these three qualities is lacking, then the participant may not be suitable to include in the final confrontation.

The spouse is told to inform the patient about each meeting and to invite the patient to attend because the specific goal of the intervention is to have the chemically dependent person visit the therapist at least once. It is then the therapist's job to convince the patient to begin treatment. In this way, the patient's anger does not become too intense during the final confrontation or intervention meeting because he or she has been informed about the previous meetings with the spouse and other important people in the patient's environment. (This is one way in which the modification of this present method differs from the original description of the intervention technique; Johnson 1973). The spouse also should explain to the patient that the children and friends were included at the request of the therapist, not the spouse, so that some of the anger would be directed toward the therapist and any additional anger in the household would be avoided. The sense of a conspiracy is thus lessened. This method is considered to be safer than the classical approach; it is less likely to precipitate such unexpected tragic events as a sincere or manipulative suicide attempt.

The intervention team is requested to prepare a list of significant events relating to the patient's drinking behavior such as those incidents that frightened or intimidated them by an explosion of anger, or embarrassed them. Having prepared these lists of significant events, the members of the newly composed intervention team should rehearse part of the confrontation with the physician during the fourth or fifth meeting in order to avoid disagreements and to eliminate any individuals who may tend to overprotect the patient. This rehearsal is helpful in several ways: 1) it increases the confidence of the intervention team; 2) it enhances the ability of the team to be concise and work together; 3) it explores resistance; and 4) it identifies unexpected problems. The time of the final confrontation with the patient is planned so that the he or she will be alcohol free. It should be stressed that there must be a commitment by the entire intervention team, with the understanding that there is a great deal at stake if the patient refuses the treatment options of the intervention. The intervention team should be prepared for the worst. It should be agreed that, if the patient absolutely refuses to come in to see the clinician for even one meeting, they will discontinue all communications with the patient until he or she makes that commitment. It is unlikely for the patient to refuse this commitment because he or she is facing a choice between separation versus one visit to the clinician. In this manner, the patient has not been pushed into a corner without any options. For further details of this technique and case histories that are applicable for intervention, the following references are recommended: Gallant 1987a, pp. 66–68, 82–84; Gallant 1987b; Johnson 1973.

There are certain crises in an alcoholic individual's life when intervention may have more impact than at other times. For example, research shows that the recidivism rate among women following arrest for driving under the influence of alcohol (DUI) is considerably lower than those recidivism rates found for men (Maisto et al. 1979). Perhaps the legal procedures that follow the arrest of a woman for DUI serve as a more powerful deterrent for them than for men. At that particular time, intervention by the alcoholic woman's family and/or employer may be more effective because the embarrassment may provide a higher degree of cooperation and motivation for help.

For intervention with alcoholic adolescents, modification of the previously described technique is necessary. It should be noted that alcohol is one of the *gateway* drugs leading to involvement with other drugs such as marijuana and subsequently even the so-called "more illegal" drugs, such as LSD (lysergic acid diethylamide), PCP (phencyclidine), or cocaine (Gallant 1987b). Much of this progression of drug use is peer related. Therefore, when attempting to treat the alcoholic or alcohol-abusing adolescent, the clinician is more likely to see a polydrug abuse problem. Several factors are involved in the excessive use of alcohol and/or other drugs in this population, such as poor parental role models who use legal drugs to excess or even illegal drugs; severe impulsivity, which is not unusual for adolescents; nonconforming or rebellious behavior, which is another rather typical adolescent problem; and associating with peers who are using alcohol or drugs and consider it "square" to be totally abstinent. The effect of peer impact on this age group is tremendous, frequently far stronger than the influence of the school, family physician, or even, at times, the home environment. Therefore, it is recommended that the intervention team should include at least one or two relatively "straight" peers of the substance-abusing adolescent. Inclusion of one or two healthy young adult models with whom the substance-abusing adolescent has a positive identification may also be of considerable help as these individuals can have a great influence over the alcoholic adolescent. One of the initial steps during the intervention is contracting with the young substance-abusing patient about staying away from any individuals in the environment who continue to drink excessively or take drugs in front of them; it is practically impossible for any adolescent to remain abstinent while their intimate peers are engaging in overt substance abuse.

Other psychologic-behavioral intervention techniques involve the use of scales that measure the degree of alcoholism and are administered to special populations. In one study of schizophrenic inpatients, the Michigan Alcohol Screening Test (MAST) significantly differentiated the alcoholic and nonalcoholic schizophrenic patients (Searles et al. 1990). The overall accuracy of the MAST was found to be 80%, and a logistic regression analysis revealed that use of the following four MAST items yields a classification rate of 83%: 1) Do relatives complain about your drinking? 2) Do you feel guilty about your drinking? 3) Has drinking created family problems? and 4) Have there been any alcohol-related inpatient psychiatric admissions (Searles et al. 1990)? The use of scales such as the MAST in certain patient populations not only can identify the individual with the alcoholism problem but also can prepare the way for an intervention by staff and/or family members.

**Behavioral interventions with biofeedback measures.** Other psychologic-behavioral techniques include a variety of laboratory and clinical measures undertaken to interrupt the course of alcohol abuse or dependence before inpatient hospitalization becomes necessary. In addition to the use of clinical instruments such as MAST or CAGE, some laboratory measures can be of help with the intervention of the alcoholic patient. In one 5-year study of 8,859 men, patients in the top 10% of the γ-glutamyltransferase (GGT) distribution were requested to return for repeat analyses within 3 weeks to validate their elevated GGT values (Kristenson et al. 1983). Heavy drinking (more than 40 grams of alcohol daily) was determined in 54% of the high GGT group. Patients were randomly assigned to either the intervention group or a control group. The intervention group had follow-up consultations with the same physician every third month and monthly GGT tests with positive reinforcing contacts with the same nurse, with the goal of reducing these GGT levels. Instead of using a rigid goal of total abstinence, counseling with the nurse focused mainly on living habits, with the goal of reducing ethanol intake to decrease GGT values. Moderate drinking was tolerated as long as GGT values continued to decrease as the study progressed. The control subjects were informed by letter that their liver tests had revealed some damage and were told to restrict their alcohol beverages. They were also informed that they would be invited for follow-up liver tests every year. The intervention group showed significantly greater improvement than the control group in the following areas: 50% lower mortality rate, 60% fewer hospitalization days, and 80% fewer days sick or absent from work.

In an investigation of 300 consecutively admitted adult health-center outpatients with a mean cell volume of 100 fl or greater, 80.2% of the men and 34.1% of the women were abusing alcohol (Seppä et al. 1991). No underlying cause except excessive alcohol intake was found for the macrocytosis in 6.8% of the men and 35.8% of the women. Thus a relative macrocytosis, even in the absence of anemia, should never be ignored even though the vitamin $B_{12}$ and serum folate levels are normal. Macrocytosis may be the only indicator of alcoholism and is another laboratory marker that indicates the possible need for therapeutic intervention.

Serum carbohydrate-deficient transferrin (CDT) may be the most reliable and sensitive laboratory marker for heavy drinking (Stibler and Borg 1986; Stibler et al. 1979; Storey et al. 1987). In one study (Storey et al. 1987), the mean value of CDT was significantly higher in 20 alcoholic patients ($P < .01$) than the mean for all other comparison groups, in-

cluding 7 patients with nonalcoholic stereohepatitis, 10 patients with diabetes, 7 patients with genetic hemochromatosis, 2 subjects with cholestatic jaundice, and 13 healthy control subjects. No false positives were found in the control groups, which is quite impressive because nonalcoholic stereohepatitis is morphologically indistinguishable from alcoholic hepatitis. In a very important recent publication (Xin et al. 1991), CDT values were evaluated by a new technique: isoelectric focusing combined with Western blotting. In an evaluation of this technique for CDT levels, the severity of liver disease among the recently drinking alcoholic patients and liver disease in nondrinking patients did not influence the CDT levels. The authors concluded that this laboratory modification for determination of serum CDT levels is practical for routine implementation by clinical laboratories. This highly reliable marker of recent heavy alcohol consumption, with a half-life of 16–17 days, provides the clinician with an excellent tool to intervene in the course of a patient's alcoholic illness (Xin et al. 1991).

Even routine laboratory measures such as obtaining BALs on all emergency room patients may provide data for early intervention. Studies of positive BALs among emergency room patients have shown that up to 25% have BALs and 16% have readings above 0.10%, which is the legal intoxication limit in most states (Teplin et al. 1989). This simple laboratory measure provides the emergency room physician or nurse with an opportunity to institute an early intervention or least an early referral for evaluation, possibly avoiding a return to the emergency room with a fatal outcome.

These types of biochemical interventions can be accomplished with complete confidentiality and without invasion of privacy. When such biochemical biofeedback fail, therapeutic psychologic interventions, as described earlier in this section, can be attempted.

## Social Interventions

It is my opinion that all physicians should be aware of the primary and secondary prevention measures that involve legal as well as laboratory procedures to intervene early in the course of this widespread illness and that they have a moral responsibility to play an active role in their community for preventing alcohol-related deaths.

**Legal approaches.** One legal approach for detecting early cases of alcohol and/or drug abuse is screening the driving records of individuals convicted of DUI. The DUI records have shown that the average time interval between DUI convictions decreases with each subsequent arrest and conviction (Maisto et al. 1979). After an initial DUI conviction, recommendation by the court for treatment and/or education on alcoholism can provide an opportunity for a therapeutic intervention with family and friends as well as by the court. Compulsory treatment of such traffic violators may be helpful if the duration of the sentence is long enough to work out the subject's initial anger when the sentence provides harsh penalties for noncompliance (Gallant et al. 1968). In addition, the practice of using a Breathalyzer on the day of pretrial evaluation of DUI subjects has identified a number of offenders whose drinking behaviors definitely required alcoholism treatment (Scoles et al. 1986). Positive BALs were found in 26.4% of 500 DUI offenders on the day of their scheduled presentencing evaluations. These DUI offenders were most likely to be diagnosed with alcoholism, had a history of higher alcohol intake, and had higher BALs at the time of their arrests than those subjects who did not have positive BALs on the day of presentence evaluation.

Another type of legal intervention approach involves compulsory treatment of paroled *criminal alcoholics*. In one study (Gallant et al. 1968) of 19 criminal alcoholic paroled men who had recently served a sentence of 1 year of more in the state penitentiary for a major offense (e.g., auto theft, grand larceny, burglary, homicide) directly or indirectly associated with alcoholism, each man was randomly assigned to either a compulsory or voluntary outpatient treatment group. The compulsory treatment group was required, in addition to the usual conditions of parole, to visit an outpatient alcoholism clinic for a minimum period of 6 months. Individual psychotherapy and job counseling sessions were scheduled weekly for 3 months and then biweekly for 3 months. Failure to keep one clinic appointment without satisfactory health reasons was a violation of parole with subsequent return to prison to complete the sentence. After the initial compulsory treatment period of 6 months, the patients were then encouraged to continue their therapy on a voluntary basis, if indicated. Abstinence from alcohol was not included as a condition of parole. The voluntary treatment group was required to keep the first appointment at the clinic, at which time they were encouraged to continue treatment on a voluntary basis; further treatment was not considered to be a condition of parole. Seven of the 10 compulsory patients were abstinent after 1 year compared with none of the 9 voluntary patients. Seven of the compulsory patients were employed after 1 year, compared with none of the voluntary patients. At the 1-year follow-up, 5 of the voluntary patients were back in prison (only one compulsory patient was back in prison) and 2 were at large after violating parole (only one compulsory patient). The differences between the groups were statistically significant ($P < .02$). The number of cases in the study was relatively small, and the results could be less dramatic if this procedure was replicated with a larger sample. Nonetheless, these findings strongly suggest that enforced clinic treatment may be a valuable technique for follow-up treatment of the criminal alcoholic patient after release from prison, and future studies of compulsory treatment of the criminal alcoholic offender (or drug-addicted offender) at the time of release from prison would be worthwhile. In association with compulsory clinic therapy of the alcoholic offender, court procedures to direct the alcoholic offender to Alcoholic Anonymous (AA) offer another important social intervention that is available in every community. It has been shown that AA membership is associated not only with the reduction in per capita consumption of alcohol but also interacts with a reduction in drinking-driving problems (Smart et al. 1989).

Taxing alcoholic beverages to reduce per capita consumption, a form of public health intervention, is a politically sensitive subject (Cook 1982; Gallant 1983; Popham et al. 1978). Many researchers in the field of alcoholism believe that a significant increase in alcohol taxes may have a much greater impact than expensive national education efforts and treatment services to reduce alcohol-related morbidity and mortality (Gallant 1983). In an excellent review, Cook (1982), using cirrhosis mortality rates (a good indicator of heavy drinking during the previous one to two decades), was able to demonstrate that 30 states that raised their liquor tax during the years 1960–1974 had a significantly greater reduction in cirrhosis mortality than other states during the same years. In this study, the states' cirrhosis mortality rates were reduced by 1.97% for each 1-dollar tax increase for each proof gallon of liquor. Using a parametric statistical method for these data, it was predicted that doubling the U.S. federal alcohol tax would reduce the nation's cirrhotic mortality rate by a minimum of 20%. A beneficial side effect would be reduction of the U.S. budget deficit.

The minimum drinking age laws provide another type of legal intervention. A recent comprehensive study (O'Malley and Wagenaar 1991) designed to assess the effect of the minimum drinking age on individual behaviors conclusively established the lifesaving value of raising the minimum drinking age to 21 years. The data for years 1976–1977 were obtained from 17,000 respondents in a high school senior alcohol and drug use survey. During that period of time, 26 states had raised their minimum drinking age to 21 years. Analysis of the high school data showed that the effect of raising the minimum drinking age resulted in a 2.8% decrease in the 2-week prevalence of heavy drinking (5 or more drinks in a row in the prior 2-week period) and a 13.3% decrease in drinking during the previous 30 days. During this same time, there was a significant decline in self-reported alcohol use with a decrease in high school seniors frequenting bars and taverns. Self-report and crash data for 3 years before and after a change in the minimum drinking age laws, with single-vehicle nighttime fatal crashes used as an indicator for alcohol-related accidents, showed a decrease in alcohol-involved, single-vehicle nighttime fatal crashes of 26.3% in drivers under the age of 21. This decrease occurred in states whose minimum drinking age was increased from 18 to 21 years, whereas the decline in single-vehicle nighttime fatal crashes in drivers 21 years or older was only 17.7%. These impressive data make it morally binding for all states to uniformly enforce rigid application of the minimum drinking age laws to decrease the number of deaths among today's youth.

**Educational approaches.** Recent studies suggest that incorporation of a cognitive-behavioral intervention within the school curricula may have some impact on dissuading adolescents from using alcohol and other drugs (Botvin et al. 1990; Gallant 1991a). A recent publication presented 1-year follow-up data from a research design that evaluated the efficacy of a cognitive-behavioral substance abuse prevention program (Botvin et al. 1990). The five treatment conditions included 1) a prevention program without teaching life-skills led by older students, 2) a prevention program with life-skills and *booster* sessions taught by older students, 3) a teacher-led prevention pro-

gram without life-skills, 4) a teacher-led program with life-skills and booster sessions, and 5) a test-retest control group. In this study of 1,185 eighth grade students, the booster prevention program implemented by older student leaders and teachers included intervention strategy activities such as basic life-skills to improve personal competence and coping mechanisms to resist substance abuse in association with booster sessions of these intervention strategies. Analyses of the data revealed that the *peer booster condition* (older student leaders) produced significantly fewer users of alcohol, tobacco, and marijuana. Surprisingly, the teacher-led program produced results that were no better and in some instances, even worse, than control conditions. Some of the shortcomings of the study included the use of a select student population with an absence of urban or central city schools and the disappointing failure of the majority of the teachers to implement the intervention according to the research protocol. The results of this study are still extremely promising, and the cognitive-behavioral approaches described in this investigation should be evaluated in other school populations, particularly because this effective technique is less expensive in personnel time. The most obviously difficult and serious challenge is the alcohol and drug abuse problem among school dropouts in poverty areas, a problem that will probably not significantly decrease without accompanying immense social and economic changes in addition to treatment intervention strategies (Gallant 1991a).

In another study (Ringwalt and Palmer 1990) comparing the differences in white and black youths who drink heavily, analysis of the data revealed that the black youths were significantly more likely than the white youths to believe that getting drunk would lead to health problems and that alcohol was addicting. The black youths were also more concerned about their parents' disapproval of their drinking, whereas the white youths were more concerned about their friends' disapproval. One of the authors' conclusions was that alcohol intervention programs for black youths who are heavy drinkers should focus more on involving parents and/or other significant adults in their environment and to have these adults clearly state their negative attitudes toward the use of alcohol. Considering these cultural differences, the intervention cognitive-behavioral approaches that are effective for one subgroup of the young population may have to be modified for other subgroups.

It should also be noted that in families with histories of child abuse, spouse battery, or other types of extreme violence such as rape or assault, it is not uncommon to find the problem of alcoholism (Gallant 1987a, pp. 111–117, 222, 240–241). The tragic consequences of alcohol abuse and alcoholism do provide opportunities for specific social interventions in these cycles of abuse. Identification of the alcoholic offender and assurance that this individual receives follow-up treatment to avoid future violence are the moral responsibility of all medical personnel.

The specific psychosocial intervention measures described in this section of the chapter should be considered as only several of many potential intervention measures that are available and as only the initial steps to reduce the morbidity and mortality rates caused by the devastating illness of alcoholism, which affects all segments of the American communities.

## ▼ REFERENCES

Adinoff B, Bone GHA, Linnoila M: Acute ethanol poisoning and the ethanol withdrawal syndrome. Medical Toxicology 3:172–196, 1988

Alldredge BK, Lowenstein DH, Simon RP: Placebo-controlled trial of intravenous dyphenylhydantoin for short-term treatment of alcohol withdrawal seizures. Am J Med 87:645–648, 1989

Azrin WH, Sisson RW, Meyers R, et al: Alcoholism treatment by disulfiram and community reinforcement therapy. J Behav Ther Exp Psychiatry 13:105–112, 1982

Ballenger JC, Post RM: Kindling as a model for alcohol withdrawal syndromes. Br J Psychiatry 133:1–14, 1978

Basile AS, Hughes RD, Harrison PM et al: Elevated brain concentrations of 1,4-benzodiazepines in fulminant hepatic failure. N Eng J Med 325:473–478, 1991

Baumgartner GR, Rowen RC: Follow-up cross-over comparison of clonidine with chlordiazepoxide in alcohol withdrawal management. Journal of Psychiatry and Neurology 1:5–6, 1988

Benzer D, Cushman P Jr: Alcohol and benzodiazepines: withdrawal syndromes. Alcohol Clin Exp Res 4:243–247, 1980

Berglund M: Suicide in alcoholism. Arch Gen Psychiatry 41:888–891, 1984

Berlin RG: Disulfiram toxicity: a consideration of biochemical mechanism and clinical spectrum. Alcohol Alcohol 24:241–246, 1989

Botvin GJ, Baker E, Filazzola AD, et al: A cognitive-behavioral approach to substance abuse prevention: one year follow-up. Addict Behav 15:47–63, 1990

Brady K, Casto S, Lydiard RB, et al: Substance abuse in an inpatient psychiatric sample. Am J Drug Alcohol Abuse 17:389–397, 1991

Bullock ML, Culliton PD, Olander RT: Controlled trial of acupuncture for severe recidivist alcoholism. Lancet 1:1435–1438, 1989

Christensen JK, Ronstead P, Vaag UH: Side effects after disulfiram. Acta Psychiatr Scand 69:265–273, 1984

Ciraulo DA, Barnhill JG, Ciraulo AM, et al: Parental alcoholism as a risk factor in benzodiazepine abuse: a pilot study. Am J Psychiatry 146:1333–1335, 1989

Cook PJ: Alcohol taxes as a public health measure. British Journal of Addiction 77:244–250, 1982

Cushman P, Forbes R, Lerner W, et al: Alcohol withdrawal syndromes: clinical management with lofexidine. Alcohol Clin Exp Res 9:103–108, 1985

de la Fuente J-R, Morse R, Niven RG, et al: A controlled study of lithium carbonate in the treatment of alcoholism. Mayo Clin Proc 64:177–180, 1989

Edmondson HA: Pathology of alcoholism. Am J Clin Pathol 74:725–742, 1980

Fawcett J, Clark DC, Gibbons RD, et al: Evaluation of lithium therapy for alcoholism. J Clin Psychiatry 45:494–499, 1984

Ferenci P, Grimm G, Meryn S, et al: Successful long-term treatment of portal-systemic encephalopathy by the benzodiazepine antagonist flumazenil. Gastroenterology 96:240–243, 1989

Fuller RK, Neiderheiser DH: Evaluation and application of urinary diethylamine method to measure compliance with disulfiram therapy. J Stud Alcohol 42:202–207, 1980

Fuller RK, Williford WO: Life-table analysis of abstinence in a study evaluating the efficacy of disulfiram. Alcohol Clin Exp Res 4:298–301, 1980

Gallant DM: Psychiatric aspects of alcohol intoxication, withdrawal, and organic brain syndromes, in Alcoholism and Clinical Psychiatry. Edited by Solomon J. New York, Plenum, 1982, pp 73–93

Gallant DM: Taxation of alcohol as a public health measure. Alcohol Clin Exp Res 7:343–344, 1983

Gallant DM: Does lithium have value in the treatment of alcoholism? Alcohol Clin Exp Res 9:297–298,

1985

Gallant DM: Alcoholism: A Guide to Diagnosis, Intervention, and Treatment. New York, WW Norton, 1987a

Gallant DM: Successful treatment of substance abuse: early diagnoses and intervention. Medical Times 115:131–140, 1987b

Gallant DM: Alcohol and drug abuse prevention in adolescents. Alcohol Clin Exp Res 15:308–309, 1991a

Gallant DM: Recent advances in research and treatment of alcoholism and drug abuse, in ASAM Review Course Manual. Edited by Geller A. New York, 1991b, pp 589–618

Gallant DM: Prophylactic therapy of first-episode bleeding in esophageal varices. Alcohol Clin Exp Res 16:139–140, 1992a

Gallant DM: Reduction of ethanol intake by pharmacologic agents—investigational problems. Alcohol Clin Exp Res 16:472–473, 1992b

Gallant DM, Faulkner M, Stoy B, et al: Enforced clinic treatment of paroled criminal alcoholics. Quarterly Journal of Studies on Alcohol 29:77–83, 1968

Gallant DM, Bishop MP, Guerrero-Figueroa R: Doxepin versus diazepam: a controlled evaluation in 100 chronic alcoholic patients. J Clin Pharmacol 9:57–61, 1969

Gallant DM, Swanson WC, Guerrero-Figueroa R: A controlled evaluation of propranolol in chronic alcoholic patients presenting the symptomatology of anxiety and tension. J Clin Pharmacol 13:41–43, 1973

Gallimberti L, Gentile N, Canton G, et al: Gamma-hydroxybutyric acid for treatment of alcohol withdrawal syndrome. Lancet 2:787–789, 1989

Gatto GJ, Murphy JM, McBride WJ, et al: Effects of fluoxetine and desipramine on palatability-induced ethanol consumption in the alcohol-nonpreferring (NP) line of rats. Alcohol 7:531–536, 1990

Gerrein JR, Rosenberg C, Manohar V: Disulfiram maintenance in outpatient treatment of alcoholism. Arch Gen Psychiatry 28:798–802, 1973

Gessner PK: Treatment of the alcohol withdrawal syndrome. Substance Abuse 1:2–5, 1979

Gordis E: Methadone maintenance and patients in alcoholism treatment. Alcohol Alert, August 1988, pp 1–3

Grant I, Adams KM, Reed R: Neuropsychological abilities of alcoholic men in their late thirties. Am J Psychiatry 136:1263–1268, 1979

Grant I, Adams KM, Reed R: Aging, abstinence, and medical risk factors in the prediction of neuropsychologic deficit among long-term alcoholics. Arch Gen Psychiatry 41:710–718, 1984

Grimm G, Ferenci P, Katzenschlager R, et al: Improvement of hepatic encephalopathy treated with flumazenil. Lancet 2:1392–1394, 1988

Guerrero-Figueroa R, Rye MM, Gallant DM, et al: Electrographic and behavioral effects of diazepam during alcohol withdrawal in cats. Neuropsychopharmacology 9:143–150, 1970

Hayes PC, Davis JM, Lewis JA, et al: Meta-analysis of propranolol in prevention of variceal hemorrhage. Lancet 2:153–156, 1990

Hyashida M, Alterman AI, McClellan AT, et al: Comparative effectiveness and costs of inpatient and outpatient detoxification of patients with mild to moderate withdrawal syndrome. N Eng J Med 320:358–365, 1989

Johnsen J, Mørland J: Disulfiram implant: a double-blind placebo controlled follow-up on treatment outcome. Alcohol Clin Exp Res 15:532–536, 1991

Johnson V: I'll Quit Tomorrow. New York, Harper & Row, 1973

Johnston JA, Lineberry CG, Ascher JA, et al: A 102-center prospective study of seizure in association with bupropion. J Clin Psychiatry 52:450–456, 1991

Kissin B: Biological investigations in alcohol research. J Stud Alcohol 8:146–181, 1979

Kraus ML, Gottlieb LD, Horwitz RI, et al: Randomized clinical trial of atenolol in patients with alcohol withdrawal. N Eng J Med 313:905–909, 1985

Kristenson H, Ohlin H, Hulten-Nosslin M-J, et al: Identification and intervention of heavy drinking in middle-aged men: results and follow-up of 24–60 months of long-term study with randomized controls. Alcohol Clin Exp Res 7:203–209, 1983

Liebowitz MR, Schneir F, Campeas R, et al: Phenelzine and atenolol in Social Phobia. Psychopharmacol Bull 26:123–125, 1990

Linnoila M, Mefford I, Nutt D, et al: NIH conference: alcohol withdrawal and noradrenergic function. Ann Intern Med 107:875–889, 1987

Liskow BI, Goodwin DW: Pharmacological treatment of alcohol intoxication, withdrawal, and dependence: a critical review. J Stud Alcohol 48:356–370, 1987

Maisto SA, Sobell LC, Zelhart PF, et al: Driving records of persons convicted of driving under the influence of alcohol. J Stud Alcohol 40:70–77, 1979

Malcolm R, Ballenger JC, Sturgis ET, et al: Double-blind controlled trial comparing carbamazepine to oxazepam treatment of alcohol withdrawal. Am J Psychiatry 146:617–621, 1989

Manhem P, Nilsson LH, Moberg AL, et al: Alcohol withdrawal: effects of clonidine treatment on sympathetic activity, the renin-aldosterone system, and clinical symptoms. Alcohol Clin Exp Res 9:238–243, 1985

Martin PR, Adinoff B, Eckardt MJ, et al: Effective pharmacotherapy of alcoholic amnestic disorder with fluvoxamine. Arch Gen Psychiatry 46:617–621, 1989

Mason BJ, Kocsis JH: Desipramine treatment of alcoholism. Psychopharmacol Bull 27:155–159, 1991

McFarlain RA, Mielke DH, Gallant DM: Comparison of muscle relaxation with placebo medication for anxiety reduction in alcoholic inpatients. Current Therapeutic Research 20:173–176, 1976

McMillan TN: Lithium and the treatment of alcoholism: a critical review. British Journal of Addiction 76:245–258, 1981

Moore N, Libert C: Acamprosate, citalopram, and alcoholism (letter). Lancet 1:1228, 1991

Mullen KD, Mendelson WB, Martin JV, et al: Could an endogenous benzodiazepine ligand contribute to hepatic encephalopathy? Lancet 2:457–459, 1988

Naranjo CA, Sellers EM, Lawrin MO: Modulation of ethanol intake by serotonin uptake inhibitors. J Clin Psychiatry 47:16–22, 1986

Naranjo CA, Sullivan J, Kadlee K, et al: Differential effects of viqualine on alcohol intake and other consummatory behaviors. Clin Pharmacol Ther 46:301–309, 1989

Ng SKC, Hauser WA, Brust JCM, et al: Alcohol consumption and withdrawal in new-onset seizures. N Engl J Med 319:666–673, 1988

Nirenberg AA, Adler LA, Peselow E, et al: A controlled trial of trazodone in antidepressant-associated insomnia. Abstract presented at the American College of Neuropsychopharmacology Annual Meeting, San Juan, PR, December 11–15, 1991

Olasmaa M, Guidotti A, Costa E, et al: Endogenous benzodiazpeines in hepatic encephalopathy. Lancet 1:491–492, 1989

Olivera AA, Kiefer MW, Manley NK: Tardive dyskinesia in psychiatric patients with substance use disorders. Am J Drug Alcohol Abuse 16:57–66, 1990

O'Malley PM, Wagenaar AC: Effects of drinking age laws on alcohol use, related behaviors and traffic crash involvement among American youth. J Stud Alcohol 52:478–491, 1991

O'Malley SS, Jaffe A, Chang G, et al: Naltrexone and coping skills therapy for alcohol dependence: a controlled study. Arch Gen Psychiatry 49:881–887, 1992

Orrego H, Blake JE, Blendis LM, et al: Long-term treatment of alcoholic liver disease with propylthiouracil. N Eng J Med 317:1421–1427, 1987

Orrego H, Blake KE, Blendis LM, et al: To the editor. Lancet 1:1471–1472, 1988

Pattison ME: Management of alcoholism in medical practice. Med Clin North Am 61:797–809, 1977

Perry PP, Wilding DC, Fowler RC, et al: Absorption of oral intramuscular chlordiazepoxide by alcoholics. Clin Pharmacol Ther 23:535–541, 1978

Pietraszek MH, Urano T, Sumioshi K, et al: Alcohol-induced depression: involvement of serotonin. Alcohol Alcohol 26:155–159, 1991

Popham R, Schmidt W, DeLint J: Government control measures to prevent hazardous drinking, in Drinking: Alcohol in American Society—Issues and Current Research. Edited by Ewing JA, Rouse BA. Chicago, IL, Nelson-Hall, 1978, pp 239–266

Regier DA, Farmer ME, Rae DS, et al: Comorbidity of mental disorders with alcohol and other drug abuse. JAMA 264:2511–2518, 1990

Ries RK, Roy-Byrne PP, Ward NG, et al: Carbamazepine treatment for benzodiazepine withdrawal. Am J Psychiatry 146:536–537, 1989

Ringwalt CL, Palmer JH: Differences between white and black youth who drink heavily. Addict Behav 15:455–460, 1990

Robinson GN, Sellers EM, Janacek E: Barbiturate and hypnosedative withdrawal by multiple oral phenobarbital loading dose techniques. Clin Pharmacol Ther 30:71–76, 1981

Romach MK, Sellers EM: Management of the alcohol withdrawal syndrome, in Annual Review of Medicine. Edited by Creger WP, Coggins CH, Hancock EW. Palo Alto, CA, Annual Reviews Inc, 1991, pp 323–339

Rounsaville BJ, Dolinsky ZS, Babor TF, et al: Psychopathology as a predictor of treatment outcome in alcoholics. Arch Gen Psychiatry 44:505–513, 1987

Roy-Byrne PP, Ward NG, Donnell PJ: Valproate in anxiety and withdrawal syndromes. J Clin Psychiatry 50:44–48, 1989

Schuckit MA: Chlormethiazole (Heminevrin): a drug

for alcohol withdrawal? Drug Abuse Alcohol News 19:1–3, 1990

Schuckit MA: Is there a protracted abstinence syndrome with drugs? Drug Abuse Alcohol News 20:1–3, 1991

Scoles PE, Fine EW, Steer RA: DUI offenders presenting with positive blood alcohol levels at presentencing evaluation. J Stud Alcohol 47:500–502, 1986

Searles JS, Alterman AI, Purtill JJ: The detection of alcoholism in hospitalized schizophrenics: a comparison of the MAST and the MAC. Alcohol Clin Exp Res 14:557–560, 1990

Sellers EM, Zilm DH, Degani NC: Comparative efficacy of propranolol and chlordiazepoxide in alcohol withdrawal. J Stud Alcohol 38:2096–2108, 1977

Seppä K, Laippala P, Saarni M: Macrocytosis as a consequence of alcohol abuse among patients in general practice. Alcohol Clin Exp Res 15:871–876, 1991

Sereny G, Sharma V, Holt J, et al: Mandatory supervised Antabuse therapy in an outpatient alcoholism program: a pilot study. Alcohol Clin Exp Res 10:290–292, 1986

Smart RG, Mann RE, Anglin L: Decrease in alcohol problems and increased Alcoholics Anonymous membership. British Journal of Addiction 84:507–513, 1989

Stibler H, Borg S: Carbohydrate composition of serum transferrin in alcoholic patients. Alcohol Clin Exp Res 10:61–64, 1986

Stibler H, Borg S, Allgulander C: Clinical significance of abnormal heterogeneity of tranferrin in relation to alcohol consumption. Acta Medica Scandinavica 206:275–281, 1979

Storey EL, Anderson GJ, Mack U, et al: Desialylated transferrin as a serological marker of chronic excessive alcohol ingestion. Lancet 1:1292–1294, 1987

Sullivan JT, Sykora K, Schneiderman J, et al: Assessment of alcohol withdrawal: the revised clinical institute withdrawal assessment for alcohol scale (CIWA-Ar). British Journal of Addiction 84:1353–1357, 1989

Sullivan JT, Swift RM, Lewis DC: Benzodiazepine requirements during alcohol withdrawal syndrome: clinical implications of using a standardized withdrawal scale. J Clin Psychopharmacol 11:291–295, 1991

Teplin LA, Ebram KM, Michaels SK: Blood alcohol level among emergency room patients: a multivariate analysis. J Stud Alcohol 50:441–447, 1989

Tohen M, Castillo J, Cole JO: Thrombocytopenia associated with carbamazepine: a case series. J Clin Psychiatry 52:496–498, 1991

Tollefson GD, Lancaster SP, Montague-Clouse J: The association of buspirone and its metabolite 1-pyrimidinyl piperazine in the remission of comorbid anxiety with depressive features and alcohol dependency. Psychopharmacol Bull 27:163–170, 1991

Veterans Affairs Cooperative Variceal Sclerotherapy Group: Prophylactic sclerotherapy for esophageal varices in men with alcoholic liver disease. N Engl J Med 324:1779–1784, 1991

Volpicelli JR, Alterman AI, Hyashida M, et al: Naltrexone in the treatment of alcohol dependence. Arch Gen Psychiatry 49:876–880, 1992

Wender PH, Reimher FW: Bupropioin treatment of attention-deficit hyperactivity disorder in adults. Am J Psychiatry 147:1018–1020, 1990

Whitfield CL: Nondrug detoxification in Phenomenology and Treatment of Alcoholism. Edited by Whitfield C. New York, Spectrum Press, 1980

Wilson A, Vulcano B: A double-blind, placebo-controlled trial of magnesium sulfate in the ethanol withdrawal syndrome. Alcohol Clin Exp Res 8:542–545, 1984

Xin Y, Lasker J, Rosman AS, et al: Isoelectric focusing/Western blotting: a novel and practical method for quantification of carbohydrate-deficient transferring in alcoholics. Alcohol Clin Exp Res 15:814–821, 1991

# Cannabis

*Robert B. Millman, M.D.*
*Ann Bordwine Beeder, M.D.*

**M**arijuana is the most frequently abused illicit psychoactive drug in our society. Use of the drug may be associated with significant psychopathology. It is often difficult to determine the role in which marijuana use plays in the psychopathology on individual patients. In some individuals, psychopathology can be a result of or can precede marijuana use or dependence, and is a determinant of the drug-use pattern. In others, the intermittent or occasional use of the drug may not be associated with adverse sequelae. It is the task of the clinician to do the following: 1) provide a comprehensive evaluation of each patient to assess the patterns of abuse of cannabis and other drugs; 2) characterize current and past psychopathology and behavioral patterns and problematic behaviors; 3) attempt to define the relationship of the drug-taking patterns to the psychopathology; and 4) provide treatment or effect a referral. As with other substance abuse disorders, the provision of appropriate treatments and referrals depends on an appreciation of the various determinants of the drug-taking patterns as well as their consequences.

## ▼ EPIDEMIOLOGY

The prevalence of marijuana use increased dramatically during the mid to late 1960s, peaked in the period 1978–1980, and since then has steadily decreased. According to the High School Senior Survey (Johnston et al. 1991), lifetime prevalence of marijuana use increased from 20% in the class of 1969 to 60.4% in the class of 1979 and fell to 50.2% and 40.7% in the classes of 1987 and 1990, respectively. Respondents' use in the last 30 days declined from a high of 37.1% in the class of 1978 to 14% in the class of 1990. Daily users, the group presumably most at risk, declined most significantly, from a high of 10.7% in the class of 1978 to 2.2% in 1990. The annual prevalence among college students declined from a peak of 51% in 1980 to 29% in 1990; among all young adults who were 1–10 years past high school, use declined to 26%. It should be noted that annual prevalence and daily use are similar in high school seniors and young adults. Males are more likely than females to use most illicit drugs including marijuana; daily marijuana use is reported by 3.2% of male high school seniors compared with 1.0% of female high school seniors and by 3.7% of young adult males compared with 1.6% of young adult females.

Emergencies involving marijuana according to the Drug Abuse Warning Network have declined significantly in recent years. Most marijuana emergency room episodes involved at least one other drug, usually alcohol, cocaine, or both. Treatment program admissions with marijuana as the primary drug of abuse are declining nationwide. In New York City there were 2,408 admissions in 1985 and 1,662 in 1990 (Frank et al. 1991).

The reasons for the general decline in marijuana use in recent years are complex but may be attributed in part to changing perceptions of the drug and to cultural trends. According to the High School Senior Survey (Johnston et al. 1991), the proportion of students perceiving regular marijuana use as involving significant risk increased from 35% in 1978 to 77.8% in 1990. Those who disapproved of regular use increased from a low of approximately 65% in the class of 1977 to 91% in the class of 1990. In the class of 1988, 63% of the respondents believed that their friends would disapprove of even experimental use, and 86% would disapprove if they smoked marijuana regularly; this trend has continued to the present. Undoubtedly there are many factors that contribute to adolescent initiation of drug use. A study (Bailey and Hubbard 1990) examined variables predicting initiation of marijuana use across three grade levels and found evidence to suggest that the primary influence on sixth and seventh grade students was the intensity of parental attachment. Seventh and eighth graders were found to be influenced by both parental and peer attachments. Eighth and ninth graders relied solely on peer attachment but also considered the perceived risk of use significant.

It is possible that the increasing perception of the drug as dangerous and unattractive and the decreased use are based in part on the adverse effects and disbelief many individuals have noted in their peers who use the drug frequently, on the strongly antidrug parents' movement, and on national and local media campaigns. Even though the epidemiologic surveys suggest that availability is perceived as largely unchanged, the price of marijuana has increased markedly. It is likely that this has driven use downward as well.

These well-documented changes in attitudes and beliefs also may be based on broad cultural trends. The protean style of the 1960s and 1970s, with its loss of or disregard for the traditional symbols of religion, government, family, and authority that was associated with marijuana, may have given way to a more conventional style. A view of reality that depended on set and setting, that allowed marked shifts in personal involvement and beliefs, and that encouraged multiple images of how one is to live may have been congruent with the use of marijuana and other drugs. The more conservative and more controlled style of the late 1970s and 1980s, in which people recognized that they must survive in a relatively unchanging world, may render the altered consciousness sought from marijuana less attractive. However, Johnston and co-workers (1991) found no evidence to support the view that the decline in marijuana use reflected an increase in conservative views and life-styles among high school seniors. They suggest that increased perception of risks and consequences solely accounted for the changes. In addition to the decreased prevalence of marijuana use reported, there has been a considerable decrease in use per individual over time that has not been well appreciated. Surveys that rely on large samples of relatively superficially collected data do not recognize decreased use patterns within broad classifications, such as use in the past 30 days or even daily use. Previously, many people associated their identity and group membership in large part based on their cannabis use. The drug has now become one of many drugs taken for a variety of purposes, and the behavior has lost much of its symbolic value (Millman and Sbriglio 1986).

## ▼ PATTERNS OF ABUSE

There is a continuum of cannabis use from occasional or experimental use of the drug to compulsive use patterns. Marijuana is generally the first illicit drug used by young people, although experiences with beer, wine, and cigarettes generally precede its use. Social, cultural, and geographic considerations determine whether a person will use cannabis; personality characteristics and psychopathology, interacting with the psychoactive effects of the drug, are important in determining the patterns and frequency of subsequent use (Jessor et al. 1980).

Occasional users generally smoke in groups in

which the ritual of preparation and smoking of the "joint" is an integral part of social interaction. The drug may be peripheral to the life of occasional users, and there may be no other drug use except intermittent alcohol. Persistent adverse effects are rare in this group.

More frequent users may use the drug on a weekly or daily basis after school or work to relax or listen to music. Other people, particularly some adolescents, engage in compulsive use patterns in which the drug is used every day, and the goal is to remain intoxicated ("stoned") all day long. Acquisition, evaluation, discussion, and use of the drug come to dominate the activities of daily living. The drug use becomes a defining characteristic and even a source of pride in some individuals ("pothead"). Marijuana is often used to modify the effects of other drugs. It is used to reduce the anxiety or "wired" feelings induced by cocaine and other stimulants and to amplify the intoxication associated with alcohol use. Most individuals who use the drug frequently take a variety of other drugs, when they are available, although a few are purists who pride themselves on their exclusive use of cannabis preparations.

## ▼ MARIJUANA AND STRONGER DRUGS

Controversy persists as to whether marijuana use leads to the use of stronger drugs, the so-called stepping stone hypothesis (O'Donnell and Clayton 1979). It has been well demonstrated that there is a hierarchy of drug use and that marijuana is generally used before depressants, hallucinogens, cocaine, or heroin (Jessor 1975). Moreover, the frequency of use of cannabis correlates with the use of stronger drugs. It has been shown in one nationwide study (O'Donnell et al. 1976) that of those young men who had never used marijuana, less than 1% subsequently used heroin or cocaine. Of those who had used marijuana 1,000 times or more, 73% used cocaine, and 33% used heroin. In another study (Clayton and Voss 1981) of young men in Manhattan, no non-marijuana-using subjects had used psychedelics, whereas 37% of marijuana-using subjects had used psychedelics. Similarly, whereas only 1%–5% of non-marijuana-using subjects had used prescription stimulants, sedatives, or opioids, 34%–36% of the marijuana-using subjects had used these drugs. More recently, national survey data confirmed this association (O'Malley et al. 1985). Of the survey subjects who had ever tried cocaine, 98% had used marijuana and 93% used marijuana first. Of those survey subjects who have used cannabis at least 100 times, 75% had used cocaine. Of most high school students who used cocaine in 1985, 84% also used marijuana (O'Malley et al. 1985). Marijuana use usually precedes other illicit drug use and individuals who smoke cannabis more frequently are more likely to use other illicit drugs.

Causality is not necessarily proven by demonstrating previous use because most of these individuals had used cigarettes, wine, beer, coffee, tea, and even milk prior to their cannabis use. It is likely, however, that the use of marijuana, often called a *gateway drug*, is a major determinant of whether someone will go on to use the stronger drugs. Positive experiences with one psychoactive drug or the recognition that the drug experience was not as dangerous as one had been led to believe by the media or parents may certainly encourage experimentation with other mind-altering chemicals. Because marijuana use is illegal, deviant behavior, the barriers to use of the harder drugs, which are even more frowned upon by conventional authority, may be lowered. The acquisition and use of marijuana also may facilitate association with individuals who use or have access to other drugs. The recent increase in the use of heroin by middle- and upper-class people, mostly young adults, who had presumably been using marijuana and cocaine for the past 5–10 years may reflect this phenomenon. Interestingly and unfortunately, the cost of more potent cocaine and heroin preparations have decreased significantly in recent years, whereas the cost of marijuana continues to increase sharply. This trend contributes to the use of cocaine and heroin rather than marijuana, although they are also much more associated with dependency and compulsive use patterns.

It should be appreciated, however, that experimental or intermittent use of marijuana or even cocaine is very different from compulsive use and dependence. Dependence is determined by psychosocial factors in addition to pharmacologic ones. Cannabis use then does lead to experimentation with other drugs, and these drugs may in fact be more difficult to control. This is significant in that users are often unable to predict that their "controlled" use of cannabis will not translate into a similar pattern with other drugs.

Increasingly potent cannabis preparations have become available during the past 15 years because of more sophisticated cultivation techniques. During the past 4–5 years, the average content of Δ-9-tetrahydrocannabinol (THC), the most important psychoactive compound in marijuana, has been in the range of 3%–4%, more than double the 1.5% average found in 1977. Even higher Δ-9-THC concentrations (up to 9%) have been found in sinsemilla and other specially culturated cannabis preparations (Deahl 1991). In New York City, a new and more potent form of marijuana called "chocolate thai" has recently become available. As noted previously, the drug has become expensive; an ounce of potent marijuana may cost between $200 and $400, and the so-called "nickel bags" formerly available on the street for $5 may now cost between $10 and $20 and contain a relatively small amount of marijuana (Frank et al. 1991).

## ▼ NATURAL HISTORY OF CANNABIS USE

Given the vast number of people who began smoking heavily in the mid 1960s to the 1970s, it is surprising that more people have not sought treatment for problems related to continued daily use of the drug. According to the High School Senior Survey, daily use of marijuana generally occurs before the 10th grade, and 86% of those who were to become daily users had begun this use pattern before the end of the 10th grade and confirmed to abuse the drug through early adulthood. Whereas the use patterns in older age groups have not been well studied, clinical experience suggests that the frequency and intensity of use in formerly heavy users declines significantly with advancing age.

A significant determinant of the decline in prevalence of daily use with advancing age is likely to be the downward trend of marijuana use in all age groups as noted previously. In addition, a natural history of marijuana use may exist in which formerly heavy users decrease their use as they enter their 30s and 40s because they find the drug increasingly less attractive and fraught with dysphoric psychoactive effects (Millman and Sbriglio 1986).

In a 5-year follow-up of regular marijuana-using subjects, Weller and Halikas (1982) reported that continued use of the drug was associated with a diminution of the earlier reported positive feelings of peacefulness, relaxation, enhanced sensitivity, self-confidence, and subjective impressions of heightened mental powers. A descriptive study of a group of reasonably successful white middle-class men and women who had been habitual and daily marijuana smokers during the decade between the late 1960s and the late 1970s may shed additional light on this phenomenon. Whereas previously they enjoyed being stoned on high-potency marijuana and described themselves with some pride as potheads, in clinical interviews they related with some embarrassment and chagrin that they now become uncomfortable, anxious, or paranoid when smoking the drug and that their use gradually diminished during their 30s and 40s. They reported increased use of alcohol and less often use of cocaine, although they recognized that these were much more dangerous; several developed severe dependencies. They claimed that they still like marijuana and would like to use it more often rather than the other drugs, but they find that they cannot tolerate the psychoactive effects (Millman and Sbriglio 1986).

Marijuana intoxication is marked by an altered time sense, during which time seems to pass slowly, concentration is altered, and little may be accomplished. We postulate that this experience may be appreciated when individuals are young and do not understand the limits of their time or when they feel powerless to alter their situations or their society. The passivity and lassitude induced by the drug may become anxiety provoking for individuals who are more profoundly experiencing the aging process and have come to value productivity and ambition (Millman and Sbriglio 1986). The impairment of short-term memory and related performance problems associated with cannabis may contribute to these dysphoric feelings as well (Deahl 1991; Relman 1982). It is interesting that drugs that promote the illusion of power, energy, or productivity (e.g., cocaine, alcohol) are preferred by these people. The actual level of productivity is not the issue; it is possible that these people get less done after drinking alcohol than after using marijuana. The issue is the perception of power and control. Moreover, although marijuana smoking is most often done in groups, individuals remain somewhat solitary, reminiscent of the parallel play of young children. Conversation is disjointed and often aimless. Palpable achievement, power, and satisfaction associated with involvement in the real world or the desire for these may render this behavior less attractive for many people.

It is also possible that the anxiety and other dysphoric feelings that increase after long-term, intensive marijuana use might be related to the processes of *kindling* and sensitization hypothesized to occur in cocaine-associated seizures and the development of panic attacks associated with anxiety and depressive disorders (Post and Kopanda 1976). Clinical evidence also suggests that the chronic use of cocaine, with its frequently associated anxiety symptoms, is associated with decreased cannabis use.

## ▼ DIAGNOSIS

### Evaluation Procedures

Evaluation of all patients with behavioral disorders, particularly those patients in whom the use of psychoactive drugs is suspected, requires a comprehensive history, physical examination, and psychiatric assessment. Physical examination of the chronic cannabis-using individual is often unremarkable. Conjunctival vascular injection, a swollen uvula, and chronic bronchitis are physical signs that are sometimes present. A complete history of all psychoactive drug taking, including alcohol, should be obtained, detailing the chronology of use, the psychoactive effects sought and obtained, the circumstances under which the drugs were used, the combinations of the drugs used, and the routes of administration. The relationship of the drugs to mood states and psychiatric symptomatology should be determined, including if possible the time course of the psychopathology relative to the drug use. A supportive, interested stance should be maintained, recognizing that many drug-abusing patients will deny or minimize the extent or impact of the drugs, consciously or otherwise. Patients with severe drug problems often believe that their drug use is similar to that of their friends and has not caused any problems. When the accuracy of the data is in question, it is important to attempt to gently clarify the issues. It is generally not effective to confront a patient too strongly in initial interviews; data of questionable veracity can be followed up in subsequent contacts (Beeder and Millman 1992).

Marijuana is generally used in association with other drugs. The relationship of the various substances should be elucidated. For example, a cocaine-abusing individual may use marijuana to alleviate some of the anxiety or wired feelings from the cocaine; a heroin-abusing individual may be seeking to extend the high. Marijuana is also used in association with alcohol to potentiate the feelings of intoxication.

Chronic cannabis-abusing individuals, particularly adolescents, often affect styles of dress and carriage that may be quite characteristic and are reminiscent of the styles of the 1960s. They may appear sullen and uninterested in the evaluation process or even openly hostile. To facilitate the assessment process, initially it may be necessary to find areas of common interest and then move to the health-related issues. For example, discussing popular music with a teenager may produce useful data. Discussing how patients integrate cannabis into their lives and how the various drugs work will often lead to productive conversation. Unlike most other disorders, patients often know more about aspects of substance abuse and dependence than do their therapists. Many of these patients pride themselves on their knowledge of the pharmacology, adverse effects, and sociology of the drugs of abuse. If they believe that the therapist is reasonably knowledgeable and interested in these areas as well, they are often quite forthcoming about their abiding interest.

With younger patients, it is often useful to ask the parents to accompany the patient to the initial interviews. The therapist should have the parents sit in for the first few minutes of the interview to describe why they are concerned and what they think is the problem. Subsequently, they should be asked to wait outside, with the remainder of the session being devoted to conversation with the patient. It is often helpful for a therapist to explain to the patient that he or she will not disclose confidential information to the patient's parents. The therapist and patient will attempt to come up with a workable plan of action that can be presented to the parents. If the therapist should determine that the patient is in imminent danger, and the patient is unwilling or unable to follow appropriate recommendations, after the therapist explains what he or she is going to do, he or she must apprise the patient's parents of the situation. Toward the end of the evaluative session, the therapist should ask the parents to return and either arrange for a subsequent meeting or make the appropriate treatment plans.

## Diagnosis of Cannabis Abuse and Dependence

According to the DSM-IV (American Psychiatric Association 1994), individuals with cannabis dependence display compulsive use and do not generally develop physiological dependence, although tolerance to most of the substance's effects has been reported by individuals who engage in chronic use. Cannabis dependence is characterized by use of very potent cannabis throughout the day over a period of months or years. The individual may spend several hours a day acquiring and using the substance which can interfere with school, work, or recreational activities. Persistence is use despite knowledge of physical or psychological problems is another indicator of cannabis dependence. The DSM-IV diagnosis of abuse is made when the disorder does not meet the tolerance, or physical/psychological problem criteria for dependence yet the use of the substance is maladaptive. It has been suggested that because cases that were once considered abuse (using DSM-III [American Psychiatric Association 1980] criteria) are now being diagnosed as dependence by using either DSM-III-R (American Psychiatric Association 1987) or the new DSM-IV, early detection and treatment will be encouraged before the drug has caused significant life problems.

## Laboratory Diagnosis

As part of the initial evaluation procedures with a reluctant patient, it is generally useful to obtain an observed urine for toxicologic analysis. This obviates the need to rely on self-report data. It may be difficult for many psychiatrists to accomplish this because of logistics or because of an unwillingness to be so intrusive. Some psychiatrists may believe that testing may hinder the development of a therapeutic alliance. However, many experienced therapists who were initially unwilling to seek these data have ruefully come to the conclusion that it significantly facilitates the evaluation process.

Analysis of urine, and rarely of blood, for marijuana and the other major drugs of abuse should be performed under a variety of other circumstances as well. Certainly the tests should be performed on patients where there is evidence suggesting marijuana or other drug use. During the treatment process, it is often useful to obtain drug screens at intervals. Testing should also be performed to clarify the diagnosis of any acute intoxications; to evaluate a sudden change in mental status, mood, or behavior; and to perform "under-the-influence" evaluations for use at the scene of accidents. Given the widespread use of marijuana and its relationship to psychiatric disorders, testing for marijuana and the other drugs of abuse should be performed on all psychiatric admissions and probably at intervals on inpatients who have had unsupervised contact with society (Verebey et al. 1986).

There is much controversy over whether testing should be performed as part of preemployment screens and at random intervals while individuals are on the job. The intrusiveness of the tests and the abrogation of privacy rights must be balanced against the dangers of drug use. Performance and behavior are more carefully monitored with less reliance on toxicological screens. There has been a move to increased use of drug screening tests on individuals who have jobs that put others or themselves at risk. It has also been suggested that drug testing be done in schools (Schwartz and Hawks 1985). Critics of widespread drug testing at the work site believe that a voluntary program using an employee assistance model is more appropriate.

It should be noted that there is a poor correlation between drug concentrations in body fluids and the level of intoxication or performance impairment, and it is quite difficult to estimate the time when cannabis was last smoked. Although the intoxication with cannabis lasts only a few hours, urine metabolites can be detected for weeks. Residual effects such as changes in mood (Halikas et al. 1974; Moskowitz et al. 1981), fine motor control (Yesavage et al. 1985), and impairment of short-term memory (Schwartz et al. 1989) may be measured for substantially longer periods, although the correlation with the magnitude of urinary metabolites is tenuous. The size of the dose, the method of administration, and the extent of the behavioral or metabolic tolerance all influence the level of drug or metabolite in the urine. Undue reliance on these tests to explain behavior is not warranted.

Approximately 17% of the THC, the major psychoactive component in a marijuana cigarette, becomes bioavailable after smoking. Blood levels are therefore quite low. Peak plasma levels of 3–50 ng/ml THC are seen in occasional smokers for up to 20 minutes; these levels drop to 1–2 ng/ml 24 hours after smoking. Therefore, analytic techniques to determine the immediacy of marijuana smoking must be quite sensitive.

THC and its metabolites are cleared more slowly from the body than most other psychoactive drugs, probably related to high lipid solubility and storage for long periods of time in lipid tissue. The major urinary metabolite of THC is 11-nor-$\Delta$-9-THC-9-carboxylic acid (THCA). The average time of detection in the urine of THCA is 4–6 days in acute users and 20–30 days in chronic users. When a 100-ng/ml cutoff is used, positives might be expected from 1 to 72 hours after smoking. Therefore, a positive urine test for marijuana confirms use of the drug at any time between hours and weeks. Salivary analysis, an experimental procedure, may determine whether marijuana use has occurred in the previous 4–8 hours (Schwartz and Hawks 1985).

Although there is a proliferation of legal cases questioning the reliability of procedures, current testing technology is quite accurate. When the tests are performed correctly, the incidence of false negatives according to various studies is 2%–3%, whereas the incidence of false positives, which is more critical from the legal standpoint, is considered negligible particularly when confirmation testes are performed (Verebey et al. 1985). In practice, by virtue of the markedly variable quality of commercial laboratories, the incidence of inaccurate results may be considerable.

# ▼ THE TREATMENT OF ACUTE PSYCHIATRIC REACTION TO CANNABIS

## Intoxication

*Intoxication* is defined by the DSM-IV as a syndrome that occurs after recent use of marijuana and is marked by tachycardia, the development of particular psychological symptoms within 2 hours of use, and at least one of the following physical symptoms within 2 hours of use: conjunctival injection, increased appetite, or dry mouth. There also may be maladaptive behavioral effects (discussion follows). Psychological symptoms are remarkably variable and depend on the dose, the route of administration, the personality of the individual, previous experience with the drug, personal expectations, and the environmental and social setting in which the drug is used.

During intoxication, perceptions of sounds, colors, tastes, textures, and patterns are commonly altered. Ideas may flow rapidly in a disconnected manner and be altered in emphasis and importance. Individuals may become withdrawn or more talkative. Mood changes vary profoundly; a mild euphoria may be experienced, although anxiety and depression also may occur. Problems may be experienced as either more or less pressing. Drowsiness or hyperactivity and hilarity may be noted. Time is experienced as passing slowly, with little activity needed and no sense of boredom. People often spend long periods of time listening to music or reading. As with the hallucinogens, cannabis-intoxicated subjects describe the unique ability to be able to observe their own intoxication, including dysphoric effects (Grinspoon 1983). Individuals who use cannabis intermittently or occasionally are often attempting to facilitate concentration at a concert or movie or to enhance sensitivity in sensual situations.

## Adverse Reactions

The most frequently reported adverse reactions to cannabis include anxiety reactions and panic attacks. Depressive episodes of varying intensity have also been reported. These generally occur during the period of intoxication and abate within minutes to hours, rarely persisting for more than 24 hours (Knight 1976).

These reactions are more likely to occur in naive users who are unfamiliar with the drug's effects and who take it in an unfamiliar or threatening setting (Khantzian and McKenna 1979). They are quite variable in intensity and characteristics and range from mild discomfort to frank hysteria, sometimes associated with the sensation of being unable to move or breathe or of an impending heart attack. It is likely that psychologically predisposed people are more susceptible to these reactions and may be vulnerable to the persistence of symptoms, the development of a cannabis-induced psychotic disorder, or even the development of a psychotic reaction.

Treatment consists of calm and gentle reassurance in a warm and supportive atmosphere (*talking down*). These people are often brought to emergency rooms, and the attempt should be made to find an appropriate, quiet place out of the mainstream of traffic. It is useful to remind the patient continually that the symptoms being experienced are related to the drug, are quite common, and will wane rapidly. When necessary, an anxiolytic should be administered, preferably one with a rapid onset of effects and long duration of action such as diazepam 10–30 mg or lorazepam 1–3 mg.

## Cannabis-Induced Psychotic Disorder

According to the DSM-IV, cannabis-induced psychotic disorder may develop shortly after cannabis use and usually involves persecutory delusions or delusions marked by jealousy. This disorder is apparently rare. When this disorder does occur it usually remits within a day, although in some cases it has lasted a few days. Anxiety, emotional lability, depersonalization, and subsequent amnesia for the episode are associated with this disorder. Hallucinations are rare except when very high blood levels are reached.

This disorder is difficult to distinguish from the panic and anxiety states that often occur with cannabis intoxication and may in large part be precipitated by these affective events. As with the adverse sequelae of marijuana intoxication, the psychotic disorder appears to be influenced by the dose of the drug, the premorbid psychopathology of the individual, and the environment. In predisposed individuals, the cannabis-induced psychotic disorder may be a prelude to a persistent psychotic reaction.

Treatment includes close observation in a warm and supportive environment with gentle and continual reassurance provided to the effect that these thoughts and feelings are due to the drug and will abate. When necessary, an anxiolytic should be administered (diazepam 10–30 mg). In patients with persistent and severe symptoms, it may be necessary to administer neuroleptic medication (haloperidol 2–4 mg).

## Delirium

A *toxic delirium* occurs most often from the oral ingestion of a large amount of cannabis in one of its many forms. It is marked by clouding of consciousness, confusion, depersonalization, impaired and sluggish thinking, and motor imbalance. There may be memory impairment, visual and auditory hallucinations, paranoia, and violent or bizarre behavior. Speech is disconnected; nystagmus is often present. Four cases of mutism in addition to symptoms of delirium have been reported (Marlotte 1972). The syndrome lasts from a few hours to a few days and is indistinguishable from other acute reactions that have been described variously as *acute toxic psychoses*, *ganja psychoses*, or *acute organic brain symptoms* (Keup 1970; Talbott and Teague 1969). The relationship of this syndrome to a schizophreniform psychosis remains unclear. Treatment is symptomatic. Both anxiolytics and neuroleptics have been used with varying success.

## Flashback Syndrome

A *flashback* is the transitory recurrence of feelings and perceptions originally experienced while under the influence of a psychedelic drug, although they do occur after cannabis use as well. Marijuana smoking some time after the use of a psychedelic drug is the most common cause of flashbacks, although flashbacks may occur in the context of emotional stress, fatigue, or altered ego functioning. Flashbacks are quite variable in character, intensity, and duration and may last from seconds to hours and may be pleasant or horrifying. Most flashbacks are episodes of visual distortion, reexperienced intense emotion, depersonalization, or physical symptoms. They generally decrease in number and intensity over time; in rare cases they have become more frequent repetitions of frightening images or thoughts (Grinspoon and Bakalar 1986).

Frequent cannabis or psychedelic drug use may increase the incidence of flashbacks. Although the etiology is unclear, flashback experiences have been variously explained as similar to traumatic neuroses, as based on persisting neurochemical change, and as a type of visual seizure.

The treatment for flashbacks consists of reassurance. Occasionally, anxiolytic medication is useful if the flashback is severe. Individuals should be cautioned against the continued use of marijuana or psychedelic drugs. Psychotherapy might be indicated to relieve the anxiety or to resolve the conflicts that may precipitate these episodes, although there is little evidence to confirm this. Rarely, chronic neuroleptic medication might be indicated in severe cases.

## ▼ TREATMENT OF CHRONIC PSYCHIATRIC DISORDERS ASSOCIATED WITH CANNABIS

Chronic psychopathology noted in chronic marijuana users as with all other drug abusers is determined by the interaction of the psychobiology of the user with the pharmacology and psychoactive effects of the drug. It remains difficult in individual patients to differentiate what came before the drug use from what is seen after, to distinguish the correlates of abuse and dependence from the consequences. Chronic marijuana use may reflect impaired premorbid social or occupational functioning and psychopathology as well as be a cause of psychiatric symptomatology and behavioral disability (Beeder and Millman 1992).

### Psychosocial Correlates

According to surveys performed during the early 1970s to the early 1980s, the psychosocial correlates of marijuana use include placing less value on academic achievement, higher value on independence relative to achievement values, greater social criticism and tolerance of deviant behavior, and less religiosity. Social measures that relate to marijuana use include psychosocial unconventionality, less perceived control from friends, lower compatibility between the expectations of friends and of parents, greater influence of friends relative to parents, and greater involvement in other problem behaviors such as excessive drinking, delinquency, and precocious sexual behavior. These findings demonstrate that marijuana use and other drug use are associated with a larger network of personal, social, and behavioral attributes (Jessor et al. 1986).

Drug use in many young people may represent purposeful, goal-directed behavior; they may feel older, more mature, or more in control when using drugs. The drug is used to cope with dysphoric feelings of boredom, anxiety, frustration, and inadequacy in relation to the demands or expectations of peers, parents, and school authorities. Marijuana may serve to alter perceptions sufficiently such that these feelings are less intense, and the situations attendant to these feelings may be perceived as less important (Jessor et al. 1980). Compulsive marijuana use may facilitate a regressive avoidance of stress. Persistence

and cessation of cannabis use has been related to the ability to assume an adult role such as maintaining a long-term relationship, having children, and maintaining employment (Hammer and Vaglum 1990).

### Cannabis as Self-Medication

Cannabis abuse and dependency is often associated with significant premorbid psychopathology ranging from personality and affective disorders to psychotic disorders. In some of these disorders, the drug is used as self-medication. It is necessary to define the meaning of the drug use for each patient (Milkman and Frosch 1973). The anxiolytic and sedative properties of the drug may serve to reduce painful affects of depression, rage, shame, and loneliness in people who are postulated to have major defects in affect defense (McLellan et al. 1979; Millman and Sbriglio 1986). The drug may alleviate the symptomatology associated with these personality disorders.

A variety of workers have reported on patients with schizophrenic and manic or hypomanic disorders who self-medicated their psychotic symptoms with marijuana, with a consequent deterioration of the clinical picture (Andreasson et al. 1989). A study (Mathers et al. 1991) of 908 psychiatric inpatients in the United Kingdom found a significant correlation between urines positive for cannabis and an initial diagnosis of psychosis. Because cannabis weakens perceptual cues and is itself psychotomimetic, it has been difficult to understand why cannabis would be used as self-medication by psychotic individuals. Certainly alcohol, depressants, and particularly the opioids would be more effective as self-medication for these disorders. Schizophrenic patients often report that the antipsychotic medication they may take produce feelings of emptiness; they felt uninspired, passive, and subdued. With cannabis, patients reported a two-phased experience, with initial feelings of relaxation, increased energy, and improved mood followed by a deterioration marked by increased severity of auditory hallucinations and disorganization. This suggests that schizophrenic patients might be willing to accept predictably worsening symptomaticology to be able to experience fleeting moments of escape and euphoria. It has also been postulated that the anticholinergic effects of cannabis may diminish the therapeutic efficacy of neuroleptic agents (Bernhardson and Gunne 1972; Knudsen and Vilmar 1984). The manic and hypomanic patients described may have been attempting to control their symptomatology and experienced a worsening of symptoms leading to a transient marijuana-induced schizophreniform phase of their manic illness (Harding and Knight 1973; Knight 1976). Some of these patients seem to have been trying to distance themselves from threatening symptomatology in any way possible. It has been shown that a major determinant of schizophrenic patients returning to psychiatric hospitals is cannabis use and failure to take neuroleptic medication. For these patients, the issue often seems to be whether they should take the prescribed medication and feel empty and sad, although their function improves, or take illicit drugs that offer them moments of joy and pleasure, although the symptoms are likely to worsen. Interestingly, there are also anecdotal reports of psychosis occurring from cessation of cannabis use.

A related phenomenon may be the attempt by some individuals, particularly adolescents, to rationalize their psychopathology, abnormal or bizarre behavior, and inability to relate to their peers. They would prefer to attribute their strange thoughts and feelings to the drug and not to their own psychopathology. The deviant subculture of potheads and "druggies" is certainly more tolerant of the strange ways of psychologically impaired people than conventional society. Some of these people become expert in acquiring, selling, and using drugs such that they have an honored role in their group, albeit an antisocial role in a bizarre society.

The type of treatment for patients with premorbid psychopathology depends on the characterization of their disorder when they have ceased marijuana use. It is often necessary to institute treatment presumptively based on the clinical picture. Psychotic symptoms associated with cannabis use should be treated in the same manner as functional psychotic symptoms. Patients should be carefully educated with respect to issues such as their attempt at self-medication and at rationalization of their psychopathology. Patients on neuroleptics must be specifically cautioned against the use of cannabis and may require group support in this effort.

## Cannabis as a Cause of Psychotic Disorders

Reports from all over the world suggest that prolonged or chronic psychotic disorders have been precipitated by high-dose and prolonged cannabis use (Bernhardson and Gunne 1972; Chopra and Smith 1974). Whereas many researchers have attempted to distinguish the disorders associated with marijuana use from schizophrenic disorders, present evidence suggests that the syndrome is indistinguishable from classic schizophrenia. It is likely that premorbid psychopathology or vulnerability is necessary for the development of this disorder. In most cases, the psychotic symptoms abate after days or weeks; in other situations the disorders have proven to be chronic (Keup 1970). It is unclear whether this symptom picture can be precipitated de novo in normal individuals, although anecdotal reports suggest that prolonged psychotic disorders can occur in nonpredisposed subjects who are given high enough doses of the drug through ingestion. It is possible that the disorder may be shorter lived than that induced in a predisposed patient. Although not well-documented, our clinical impression is that after patients recover from a cannabis-precipitated psychotic episode, there occasionally is residual psychopathology, including paranoid thoughts and low-level auditory hallucinations that persist for long periods. These may be a function of anxiety, a form of flashback, or evidence of a persisting neurochemical deficit. Perhaps a kindling phenomenon is occurring in some of these people. It has been suggested that some of these people may represent a new group of chronic psychiatric patients; typically, they are young males who are highly transient, often homeless, and prone to depression, anger, and aggressive, self-destructive acts (Schwartz and Goldfinger 1982). The chronic drug use in association with psychopathology may produce this clinical picture.

Psychotic episodes precipitated by marijuana should be treated as functional psychotic disorders if symptoms persist. In our center, if anxiety is prominent early on and seems to be a determinant of the clinical picture, anxiolytic therapy is used to attempt to allay the anxiety and abort the psychotic episode rapidly (diazepam 40–60 mg per day in divided doses). Subsequently, if necessary, neuroleptic agents without prominent anticholinergic effects (e.g., haloperidol) should be administered in appropriate doses to reduce symptoms. These patients require a great deal of support and reassurance during this period. When symptoms are brought under control and if patients can tolerate involvement, the cannabis or other drug dependence should be addressed in a focused drug treatment program with provision for these patients. Programs to treat these patients are difficult to find.

## Chronic Cannabis Syndrome

An amotivational syndrome has been described in individuals who chronically use high doses of marijuana in various parts of the world, which is marked by apathy, diminished goal-directed activity, and an inability to master new problems. Personal habits deteriorate; the subjects are described as withdrawn, passive, and easily distracted, with poor judgment and impaired communication skills (Stefanis et al. 1976). The syndrome has been invoked to explain poor school performance and personality deterioration particularly in adolescents. These reports are compromised by the absence of control subjects and the inability to distinguish the pharmacologic effects of the drug from antecedent psychological and social conditions. Other reports of chronic users have subsequently failed to demonstrate the existence of this syndrome (Carter 1980; Rubin and Comitas 1975). These reports are also flawed in that they focused on low-level workers doing relatively minimal tasks. The syndrome has not been demonstrated in controlled laboratory studies (Brady et al. 1986).

Given the pharmacologic actions of cannabis, which include sedation, disruption of concentration, impairment of short-term memory, even alleviation of performance-related anxiety, the drug does seem to stifle ambition and drive and impair school performance in some individuals who are perhaps in some way vulnerable. In other young individuals, chronic heavy cannabis use has been associated with profound changes in perspective, dress, and behavior, although they have demonstrated laudable energy and ambition in the pursuit of their particular goals, such as intense involvement with popular music and the pursuit of musical groups such as the Grateful Dead or identification with drug-using cults such as Rastafarians. The term *aberrant motivational syndrome* has been suggested as a more precise description of the phenomenon (Millman and Sbriglio 1986).

The pharmacologic effects of cannabis, interacting with psychological and social factors, may be responsible for the clinical picture seen. In other highly motivated, productive people, the drug is reported to facilitate performance and productivity, perhaps as self-medication of incapacitating anxiety and to enhance relaxation. The dose and frequency of the drug used is generally lower than that used by most compulsive users.

The chronic cannabis syndrome may be considered to be a variant of the cannabis dependence disorder that has been described previously. Cessation of cannabis use in the absence of severe psychopathology and committed involvement to a treatment program frequently results in a marked and rapid improvement in mental clarity and energy levels. In addition to being a result of the waning of drug effects, the often remarkable behavioral changes seen may be a function of decreased feelings of isolation and demoralization that many previously chemically dependent individuals experience on rejoining the ranks of consensual society, however shunned it previously was.

## ▼ TREATMENT OF CANNABIS ABUSE AND DEPENDENCE

As with all other drug-taking syndromes, the treatment of cannabis-related disorders requires an appreciation of the psychosocial characteristics of the patient as well as the pharmacology and patterns of abuse of marijuana. Treatment should be conceptualized as including initial and extended phases. During the initial phases, acute medical or psychological reactions must be dealt with and withdrawal from the drug effected. The extended phase must include provisions to maintain the abstinent state, relapse prevention techniques, and the treatment of associated psychosocial pathology. As in the treatment of other drug-dependent patients, much attention is directed toward what they should not do. It is critical to remember that patients also need help to determine what they *should* do. A major element in any treatment program must be the attempt to provide realistic and rewarding alternatives to the drugs and the associated life-style (Millman and Botvin 1983).

As noted earlier, although some people abuse marijuana exclusively, most others use the drug in association with the various other drugs of abuse. The treatment of cannabis dependence should therefore be considered in the context of treating patients who are more eclectic in their tastes and behaviors.

### Cessation of Cannabis Use

Patients must be helped to recognize that their drug use is significantly interfering with aspects of their lives. All drug use must cease, and patients should be encouraged to make a commitment to abstinence. There is often significant denial and sometimes open hostility present during this stage, and considerable skill and tact may be necessary to "break through" the denial and motivate the patient to comply with the program. Many programs adhere to a disease model of chemical dependency, in which much emphasis is placed on the patient's recognizing that he or she has the disease of chemical dependency, is addicted, and must have help to control, never cure, the cannabis or other drug dependency. Some programs use written contracts to concretize the treatment requirements. Patients should be seen on a frequent basis, perhaps even daily if possible, and both group and individual therapies should be provided.

During this phase, a comprehensive drug education component should be provided for the patient and the patient's family. Regular family sessions and attendance at 12-step or other self-help program meetings should be strongly encouraged if appropriate. Patients must be helped to terminate drug-related associations and activities and to develop a productive support network comprised of a carefully selected group of family and friends. It has proven useful to formalize this support network through regular meetings.

Regular urine drug testing for the major drugs of abuse should be a routine element in the treatment process. Despite the development of a good relationship with the patient, toxicologic data provide an objective measure of treatment progress, enhance the patient's own control over drug-seeking behavior, and may prevent the reemergence of denial that is common to the drug treatment process (Swatek 1984). Patients often do not reveal the presence of a relapse because they do not want to disappoint the therapist. At the same time, by virtue of guilt or anger, if the drug use remains undetected they may lose faith in the therapist or the program and leave treatment. The most experienced clinicians have sometimes been unable to recognize a relapse to drug use in the absence of these data.

Most patients are referred for treatment of drug problems other than cannabis. At the same time, most of them used marijuana before they progressed to other drug use and most continue to use the drug in addition to their primary drug(s) of abuse. They often do not consider it a problem. Different treatment programs approach this issue in different ways. Use of any drug, including alcohol and marijuana, often provides the conditioned associations or disinhibition necessary to resume use of the more destructive substances. Current practice suggests that viewing all drugs as chemical dependency and requiring across-the-board abstinence from all psychoactive drugs promises the best results. In some cases, people with a primary cocaine or heroin dependence have been able to use cannabis or alcohol, intermittently or rarely, and do not relapse to more destructive drug use patterns.

## Abstinence Syndrome

Controversy persists as to whether cessation of regular use of cannabis produces a stereotyped withdrawal syndrome of clinical significance. A syndrome marked by nausea, myalgia, irritability, restlessness, nervousness, depression, and insomnia has been reported to occur in animals and humans after abrupt cessation of chronic use of high doses, although it is not well defined and may not occur for days to a week after the drug was discontinued (Jones 1983). Animal studies have variously suggested that the endogenous opioid, the catecholamine, and the serotonergic systems may be implicated in this withdrawal syndrome (Kumar et al. 1984). Most individuals have few withdrawal symptoms; some will experience signs and symptoms that are quite variable in nature and severity. As with other drugs but perhaps more importantly with cannabis, withdrawal symptoms seem to be importantly dependent on the premorbid personality of the user and the associations that have been conditioned by environmental cues or expectations.

In general, reassurance, firm support, and an attempt to reduce the availability of the drug are sufficient to facilitate the withdrawal process. Medication is not generally indicated. Experiments in animals and humans suggest that because the drug reduces noradrenergic activity and endogenous opioids, desipramine, a potent blocker of the reuptake of norepinephrine, and tyrosine, a norepinephrine precursor, may be indicated as withdrawal agents (Tennant 1986), although this work has not been confirmed. Anecdotal reports suggest that certain patients dropped out of treatment if they did not receive medication. It is also possible that nonspecific alteration of internal feeling states with medication may allay withdrawal symptoms by altering the reinforcement properties of dysphoric symptoms, and this promotes abstinence. If extreme anxiety occurs, a long-acting benzodiazepine may be indicated for a brief period. Psychopathology that is present, precipitated, or unmasked by the withdrawal process should be appropriately treated.

### Early Recovery

This phase of treatment may require 2–12 months and focuses on relapse prevention and the development of new modes of living. Many relapse prevention strategies were developed using a social learning theory model; these techniques also may be adapted to treatments adhering to the disease model (Marlatt 1980). It has proven useful to structure the relapse prevention techniques in group and individual encounters. Some of the critical elements that should be covered include helping the patient to recognize the earliest warning signs of relapse; combating *euphoric recall*, the tendency to remember only the positive aspects of the drug experience, often from early on in the drug user's career; overcoming the inevitable desire to attempt to regain control over the drug use; reinforcement of the negative aspects of the drugs *(thinking through the drug);* avoiding situations that have become powerful conditioned stimuli for the resumption of drug-taking behavior; insulating "slips" so that they do not become full-blown relapses; learning new methods to cope with dysphoric symptoms, including identifying internal feeling states that had become the conditioned stimuli for drug craving; and developing pleasurable and rewarding alternatives to drugs (Galanter 1983; Schnoll and Daghestani 1986; Washton 1986).

Some young people in particular do not have the skills to develop healthy relationships or productive life-styles. They often do not know how to have fun without drugs. Structured activities and exercises are often valuable in this regard.

Relapses are common during this phase and often occur in well-understood situations. Initially patients feel proud and happy at how well they are doing and may decide that treatment is no longer needed. They may then experiment with cannabis or another drug to demonstrate that they have become stronger and can now control the drug use. Intermittent, careful use then occurs, then escalates, until the control is lost and a relapse occurs.

### Long-Term Treatment

During this phase, treatment contacts may be reduced to weekly group sessions to maintain the commitment to abstinence, to enhance interpersonal skills, to combat renewed denial and overconfidence, and to work toward goals and aspirations. Continued participation in self-help groups should be encouraged. In programs based on 12-step principles, participants are encouraged to continue to think of themselves as addicted, albeit in a recovering stage. This has proven to be quite useful for adults who are drug dependent. With respect to marijuana-abusing youth, it may not be necessary to maintain this identification so powerfully. After a year or more of abstinence and appropriate social adjustment, young people might be encouraged to think of themselves as similar to their peers though with the recognition that they continue to be at increased risk. Treatment of psychopathology should be continued as needed.

During this phase, evaluative procedures should continue to characterize more precisely the psychopathology that may have antedated the drug use or may be a result of it. Psychotherapy and pharmacotherapy should be provided as needed.

## ▼ TREATMENT FACILITIES AND PROCEDURES

There are few programs that focus primarily on marijuana-abusing individuals. Most of the inpatient and outpatient treatment programs are primarily focused on the individuals who abuse the so-called harder drugs. Recently, in part in response to the increased prevalence of cocaine use in young populations, a large number of programs have developed adolescent divisions that are often appropriate for cannabis-abusing adolescents. Whenever possible, these patients should be treated as outpatients and encouraged to remain at work or in school.

### Inpatient Programs

It will sometimes be necessary to treat some cannabis-using patients as inpatients. This is an important clinical decision. The criteria for institutionalization include the following: 1) the inability to cease drug use despite appropriate outpatient maneuvers; 2) psychologic or (rarely) medical conditions that require close observation and treatment such as severe depressive symptoms, psychotic states, or extreme debilitation; 3) the absence of adequate psychosocial supports that might be mobilized to facilitate the cessation of drug use; 4) the necessity to interrupt a living situation that reinforces continued drug taking; and 5) the need to enhance motivation or break through denial.

Because institutions vary considerably in their organizing principles and methods, an appropriate referral attempts to match the program to the needs of the patient. There are three primary referral options. The first is the psychiatric hospital. This modality is generally indicated when severe psychopathology is present, although these facilities often lack an organized drug treatment program and may be insensitive to the needs of drug abuse patients, particularly those who are young and demonstrably rebellious. Too often adversarial relationships are set up between patient and staff over stylistic differences. There may be insufficient structure, and patients often break the rules. Cannabis-dependent adolescents may be less obviously symptomatic than other patients and may feel uncomfortable in this milieu. The second option, rehabilitation programs, are based on the disease model of chemical dependency and generally have a strong 12-step program component. These programs are often effective, particularly if they have well-defined adolescent units that encourage the patient to identify strongly with the program. In other cases, cannabis-abusing individuals with severe adjustment problems may find little in common with other drug patients (e.g., alcoholic patients) and may "go through the motions," with little real change effected. These programs often have inadequate psychiatric backup to treat some of the severely disturbed cannabis-abusing patients; others are too confrontational. The third option, therapeutic communities, was originally developed to treat heroin-addicted patients. In recent years, these facilities have developed programs geared for polydrug-abusing patients, particularly adolescents. These vary considerably with respect to the characteristics of positive and negative reinforcements offered and with respect to the availability of psychiatric evaluation and the treatments available. Severely disturbed patients often find these programs intensely confrontational and may panic or leave prematurely.

It should be appreciated that there are little data available on which programs are effective for which patients. Referrals often must be made on relatively tenuous grounds. For example, there is anecdotal evidence to suggest that some cannabis or polydrug abusers with severe personality disorders do better in rehabilitation programs or therapeutic communities than in psychiatric hospitals; they seem to thrive in a milieu that is tightly structured, relies predominantly on group techniques, and encourages strong identification and pride in the program. Difficult transferential issues that occur in individual therapy situations are diffused and diminished by the group identification.

Innovative programs have been developed that provide a variety of experiences and meet particular needs. For example, halfway houses have proven to be useful for some young cannabis-abusing patients, in which they may sleep and eat in the facility but also resume or maintain contacts with school or work.

## Outpatient Programs

Outpatient programs are generally organized according to the perspectives of the three major inpatient modalities described above and have many of the same strengths and weaknesses. These provide a range of services from day-long programs to group or individual sessions on a weekly basis.

Optimally, during the early phases of treatment, provision is made for intensive group; individual contacts and the program should be a major focus of the patient's life. With continued progress, the degree of involvement is reduced and the program becomes more peripheral to the life of the patient.

## Psychotherapy

Psychotherapeutic intervention may be a crucial treatment option for patients with psychopathology who have cannabis-related problems. In later treatment stages, in particular, treatment of symptoms and resolution of the conflicts that may have led to or are associated with the drug use may be an effective tool to prevent relapse. It should be understood, however, that the primary goal of treatment should be abstinence; resolution of psychological conflicts is not a necessary condition for the achievement or maintenance of abstinence (Blume 1984).

It is often quite difficult to develop a therapeutic alliance with marijuana-abusing patients, particularly those who are young and who have assumed a rebellious, antisocial stance. These patient may deny the presence or the extent of the problem, they may have had repeated treatment failures, and they have lost control of the drug use. They are often controlling and provocative; their behavior may be perceived as self-indulgent, primitive, or uncivilized by the therapist (Imhoff et al. 1984). It is generally agreed on by most workers that during the early treatment stages, the therapist must be quite active in fostering the relationship and should adopt an attitude of empathy and acceptance (Blane 1977). It obviously cannot be unquestioning acceptance; a good deal of tact and discipline should be used as well.

Positive transference should be encouraged, particularly in the early stages of treatment. It is probably only necessary to interpret negative transference if it threatens the therapeutic relationship (Blane 1977). Patients will often develop powerful dependencies on the therapist. This should be accepted, although it may require some fortitude. As with most patients, it is critical that the patient believes that the therapist is perceiving him or her accurately.

It is also critical that the therapist have a good understanding of the pharmacology and psychoactive effects of marijuana and the other drugs of abuse. Patients are instantly aware of the sophistication of the therapist and often find it difficult to place trust in this admittedly well-meaning person who does not know whether you buy an ounce or gram of the substance (Millman 1986).

There are no data suggesting that specific psychotherapeutic techniques for patients with cannabis-related disorders are better than others or that marijuana-dependent patients should be treated differently from other drug-dependent patients in this regard. Clinical experience and some controlled studies do suggest that certain psychotherapeutic methods may be most useful. With patients dependent on narcotics and cocaine, there is evidence that cognitive-behavioral, supportive-expressive, and interpersonal psychotherapeutic techniques may be effective (Rounsaville et al. 1985). Perhaps these experiences can be extrapolated to apply to cannabis dependence as well.

At the outset, the focus of treatment should be on the drug use and difficulties in interpersonal functioning. As with other substance-abuse patients, an emphasis on consistency of focus, problem solving, and brevity has proven useful.

During the initial stages, the therapist should as-sume an active, educative, empathetic sometimes confrontational role. As treatment progresses, and as the drug use becomes less of an imminent danger, the therapist should attempt to assume a stance of more neutrality and make efforts slowly to wean the patient off the powerful dependency created. Involvement of the patient with peer support groups or 12-step programs may facilitate the process.

Patients who are receiving psychotherapy as an element of a treatment program for dependency on drugs other than marijuana may wish to continue to use marijuana. They may not have had a problem with its control, and they may ascribe increased insight into the world or their personal problems to the drug experience. Rather than challenge their contention, it may be useful to suggest to them that chronic alterations in consciousness with any drug is likely to reduce or negate the value of psychotherapeutic intervention. Growth or learning through psychotherapy requires the experienced recognition of anxiety, other symptomatology, or maladaptive behaviors, and acceptance of the need to change these (Millman 1986).

## Family Therapy

Because many individuals with problems relating to marijuana use still reside in family groups and are dependent on parental resources, family therapy may be a critical adjunct to other treatment modalities. It is important to deal with issues such as improved communication patterns, parental expectations, and parental or sibling drug use. At times, the marijuana-using subject may be using the drug to cope with intolerable family conflicts that might be resolved through skilled family therapy. Increasingly, inpatient and outpatient drug treatment programs are mandating family involvement in the treatment process (Kaufman and Kaufman 1979). The concept of family involvement has been expanded by some therapists to include selected friends and business associates. The therapist and the patient attempt to develop a unit that will function as a source of support during the early stages of treatment.

## Group Therapy

Group therapy has become the most frequently used modality for all classes of drug abusers, including those who primarily abuse cannabis. In distinction to more analytically oriented group techniques for psychiatric patients, drug treatment groups generally encourage strong identification with the group and use behavioral techniques and coercion to reinforce abstinence. Education in regard to the determinants and consequences of drug use is often included, and some programs include audio-visual aids and reading materials to supplement the group process. Groups are useful in teaching socialization and problem-solving skills and may reduce the sense of isolation that drug-abusing patients often feel. Groups may be more or less confrontational in their approach. Many groups encourage members to maintain contact with each other outside of the group.

Patients sometimes appear to be intoxicated at group meetings or may regale the group with stories of their continued drug taking. If the group is unable to take the initiative, group leaders must be prepared to ask a group member to leave a session if his or her behavior is inappropriate. In other cases, group members may be asked to drop out of the group until their drug-taking ceases or their behavior is more conducive to the group process. It is the group leaders' responsibility to make other arrangements for these patients.

## 12-Step Programs

Whereas 12-step programs modeled after Alcoholics Anonymous have proven useful for many drug-abusing individuals, to date individuals who are primarily dependent on cannabis have not participated extensively in these groups. In the past this has been due in large part to cultural and stylistic differences between programs and the individuals. Many of these predominately young individuals believed that the groups were to conventional ("straight") and were not sensitive to their concerns, or appreciative of their tastes (e.g., in music, clothing, and language). In fact, many of the groups are made up of older people as well as those who have "hit bottom." Recently, many meetings of Drugs Anonymous and other self-help groups have become more sensitive to the styles and value systems of these people, and the programs are likely to become a more prominent part of the rehabilitation process in the future.

Many patients will resist attending self-help group meetings; they may feel they have nothing in common with the people who attend, or they may not be in the habit of publicly discussing themselves and their problems. At the same time, patients should be strongly encouraged to participate in the appropriate meetings. Psychiatrist and other mental health professionals often find themselves at odds with their patients over these programs. Members of the groups accept dependence on a "higher power" and are encouraged to adhere to steps, traditions, and value systems based primarily on sobriety. It has been suggested that these groups may strengthen the fixation of patients at symbiotic levels of development; they do not encourage analytic self-examination, they may be infantilizing, and they may reduce complex psychological issues to the issue of chemical dependence. These characteristics may appear to be antithetical to professional therapeutic objectives and procedures (Zinberg 1977).

At the same time, it should be appreciated that dependence on these groups is often essential if patients are to abandon primitive methods of coping and drug use. These groups often reduce the sense of isolation most compulsive drug-abusing individuals feel; these groups enhance self-esteem and provide a powerful structure within which many of these demoralized, dispirited individuals can find solace. Patients often become disenchanted with professionals and their programs, and many drop out of treatment, sometimes with the encouragement of their sponsors or other members of the self-help fellowship. Therapists may feel threatened by the groups and sometimes assume an adversarial stance with respect to them. Great caution must be exercised by the treatment team; it should be recognized that it is difficult for a patient to transfer the powerful dependence on the group to a therapist. The therapeutic issues involved relate to separation and individuation, and splitting, classic issues dealing with character pathology. When the patient loses the group, there is a tendency to feel extreme anxiety and to experience a powerful recurrence of the need to resume cannabis and other drug use. Then too, the difficult transference problems that a patient with character pathology might have relating to an individual therapist may be diffused by the relationship to the groups.

A frequent although quite effective progression often entails initial evaluation and early intensive treatment by a psychiatrist and treatment team. The therapist effects the referral to the self-help fellowship, which may result in decreased intensity or even cessation of professional therapeutic contacts during the early stages of sobriety and until stability is achieved. Some patients then come to believe that there are issues and symptoms that should be worked on with the psychiatrist or mental health professional and seek to reestablish or intensify the therapeutic relationship. They may recognize that their psychopathology or their difficulties with realizing aspirations need to be considered according to psychiatric perspectives. Many others will not.

## Behavioral Therapy

Although there are no good studies demonstrating efficacy, many of the techniques currently used by drug treatment programs are informed by behavioral therapeutic perspectives. These include skill-building techniques (e.g., relaxation exercises, assertiveness training) and positive reinforcement for the attainment and maintenance of sobriety or other approved behaviors. Contingency contracting has proven useful with individuals who abuse other classes of drugs and is used in the treatment of marijuana-using patients as well. Aversive conditioning has produced modest results in promoting abstinence in controlled situations with other drugs, although the value of these primarily experimental techniques usually fails to generalize to settings outside the research center, and positive effects appear to erode over time.

## The Need for No Treatment

It should be well recognized that for many individuals, particularly adolescents, intermittent or experimental marijuana use is normative for their peer group, has had no impact on their psychosocial adjustment, and may have little impact on their health. Coercing them into treatment, particularly inpatient treatment, may serve to disrupt their lives and school careers, reinforce the insecurity that many young people feel about their abilities or even their sanity, and stigmatize them. The problem may be complicated by well-meaning although understandably anxious parents or relatives who have learned through the media or from friends that the presumed patient should be forced into one program or another. On the other hand, it should be recognized that most drug abusers minimize their involvement with drugs and deny any impact the drugs might be having.

Then too, marijuana use, even that which is intermittent or experimental, may presage more dangerous drug abuse at a later date.

This is often a difficult clinical problem, and intense pressure may be brought to bear on the practitioner. Clinicians must provide a careful evaluation to determine that the marijuana use is peripheral to the identity to the individual, is appropriate to that of the individual's peers, is intermittent or rare, and has not had any impact on the social, occupational, or medical status or the individual. In these cases, the attempt should be made to educate the individual as to the possible adverse effects of the drug use, and provisions should be made to follow these individuals at intervals. Whenever possible and appropriate, parents and relatives should be helped to feel that they are part of the evaluative process.

## ▼ REFERENCES

American Psychiatric Association: Diagnostic and Statistical Manual of Mental Disorders, 3rd Edition. Washington, DC, American Psychiatric Association, 1980

American Psychiatric Association: Diagnostic and Statistical Manual of Mental Disorders, 3rd Edition, Revision. Washington, DC, American Psychiatric Association, 1987

American Psychiatric Association: Diagnostic and Statistical Manual of Mental Disorders, 4th Edition. Washington, DC, American Psychiatric Association, 1994

Andreasson S, Allebeck P, Rydberg U: Schizophrenia in users and nonusers of cannabis: a longitudinal study in Stockholm county. Acta Psychiatr Scand 79:505–510, 1989

Bailey SL, Hubbard RL: Developmental variation in the context of marijuana initiation among adolescents. J Health Soc Behav 31:58–70, 1990

Beeder AB, Millman RB: Treatment of patients with psychopathology and substance abuse, in Substance Abuse: A Comprehensive Textbook, 2nd Edition. Edited by Lowinson JH, Ruiz P, Millman RB, et al. Baltimore, MD, Williams & Wilkins, 1992, pp 675–690

Bernhardson G, Gunne LM: Forty-six cases of psychosis in cannabis abusers. Int J Addict 7:9–16, 1972

Blane HT: Psychotherapeutic approach, in The Biology of Alcoholism, Vol 5. Edited by Kissin B, Begleiter H. New York, Plenum, 1977

Blume SB: Psychotherapy in the treatment of alcoholism, in Psychiatry Update: The American Psychiatric Association Annual Review, Vol 3. Edited by Grinspoon L. Washington, DC, American Psychiatric Press, 1984, 338–346

Brady JV, Fotin RW, Fischman MW, et al: Behavioral interactions and the effects of marijuana. Alcohol, Drugs, and Driving 2:93–103, 1986

Carter WE: Cannabis in Costa Rica: a study of chronic marijuana use. Philadelphia, PA, Institute for the Study of Human Issues, 1980

Chopra GS, Smith JW: Psychotic reactions following cannabis use in East Indians. Arch Gen Psychiatry 30:24–27, 1974

Clayton RR, Voss HL: Young Men and Drugs in Manhattan: A Casual Analysis, NIDA Res Monogr No 39. Washington, DC, U.S. Government Printing Office, 1981

Deahl M: Cannabis and memory loss. British Journal of Addiction 86:249–252, 1991

Frank B, Golea J, Simeone R: Drug Use Trends in New York City. New York, New York State Division of Substance Abuse Services, 1991, pp 5–61

Galanter M: Psychotherapy for alcohol and drug abuse: an approach based on learning theory. Journal of Psychiatric Treatment and Evaluation 5:551–556, 1983

Grinspoon L: Effects of marijuana. Hosp Community Psychiatry 34:307, 1983

Grinspoon L, Bakalar JB: Psychedelics and arylcyclohexylamines, in Psychiatry Update: American Psychiatric Association Annual Review, Vol. 5. Edited by Frances AJ, Hales RE. Washingon, DC, American Psychiatric Press, 1986, pp 212–225

Halikas J: Marijuana use in psychiatric illness, in Marijuana: Effects On Human Behavior. Edited by Miller L. New York, Academic Press, 1974, pp 265–302

Hammer T, Per Vaglum: Initiation, continuation, or discontinuation of cannabis use in the general population. British Journal of Addiction 85:899–909, 1990

Harding T, Knight F: Marijuana-modified mania. Arch Gen Psychiatry 29:635–637, 1973

Imhoff J, Hirsch R, Terenzi RE: Countertransferential and attitudinal considerations in the treatment of drug abuse and addiction. J Subst Abuse Treat 1:21–30, 1984

Jessor R: Predicting time of marijuana use: a developmental study of high school youths, in Predicting Adolescent Drug Abuse: A Review of Issues, Methods, and Correlates; Research Issues, II. Edited by Lettieri DJ. Rockville, MD, National Institute on Drug Abuse, 1975

Jessor R, Chase JA, Donovan JE: Psychosocial correlates of marijuana use and problem drinking in a national sample of adolescents. Am J Public Health 70:604–613, 1980

Jessor R, Donovan J, Costa F: Psychoactive correlates of marijuana in adolescent and young adulthood: the past as prologue, in Marijuana, Cocaine, and Traffic Society. Edited by Moskowitz H. Alcohol, Drugs and Driving 2:3–4, 1986

Johnston LD, O'Malley PM, Bachman JG: Drug Use Among American High School Seniors, College Students, and Young Adults 1975–1990. Rockville, MD, National Institute on Drug Abuse, U.S. Department of Health and Human Services, Alcohol, Drug Abuse and Mental Health Administration, 1991

Jones RT: Cannabis and health. Ann Rev Med 34:247–258, 1983

Kaufman E, Kaufman PW: Family Therapy of Drug and Alcohol Abuse. New York, Gardner Press, 1979

Keup W: Psychotic symptoms due to cannabis abuse. Diseases of the Nervous System 31:119–126, 1970

Khantzian EJ, McKenna GJ: Acute toxic and withdrawal reactions associated with drug use and abuse. Ann Intern Med 90:361–373, 1979

Knight F: Role of cannabis in psychiatric disturbance. Ann N Y Acad Sci 282:64–71, 1976

Knudsen P, Vilmar T: Cannabis and neuroleptic agents in schizophrenia. Acta Psychiatr Scand 69:162–174, 1984

Kumar MSA, Patel V, Millard WI: Effect of chronic administration of delta-9-tetrahydrocannabinol on the endogenous opioid peptide and catechotamine levels in diencephalon and plasma of the rat. Substance Alcohol Actions Misuse 5:201–210, 1984

Marlatt GA: Relapse prevention: a self-control program for the treatment of addictive behaviors, in Adherence, Compliance, and Generalization in Behavioral Medicine. Edited by Stuart RB. New York, Brunner/Mazel, 1980

Marlotte DB: Marijuana and mutism. Am J Psychiatry 129:475–477, 1972

Mathers DC, Ghodse AH, Caan AW, et al: Cannabis use in a large sample of acute psychiatric admissions. British Journal of Addiction 86:779–784,

1991

McLellan AT, Woody GE, O'Brien CP: Development of psychiatric illness in drug abusers: possible role of drug preference. N Engl J Med 301:1310–1314, 1979

Milkman H, Frosch WA: On the preferential abuse of heroin and amphetamine. J Nerv Ment Dis 156: 242–248, 1973

Millman RB: Considerations on the psychotherapy of the substance of the substance abuser. J Subst Abuse Treat 3:103–109, 1986

Millman RB, Botvin GJ: Substance use, abuse, and dependence, in Developmental Behavioral Pediatrics. Edited by Levine MD, Carey WB, Crocker AS, et al. Philadelphia, PA, WB Saunders, 1983

Millman RB, Sbriglio R: Patterns of use and psychopathology in chronic marijuana users. Psychiatr Clin North Am 9:533–545, 1986

Moskowitz H, Sharma S, Zieman K: Duration of skills performance impairment. Proceedings of the 25th Conference of the American Association of Automotive Medicine, San Francisco, CA, 87–96, 1981

O'Donnell JA, Clayton RR: The stepping stone hypothesis: a reapprasial, in Youth Drug Abuse: Problems, Issues, and Treatment. Edited by Beschner GM, Friedman AS. Lexington, MA, Lexington Books, 1979

O'Donnell JA, Voss HL, Clayton RR, et al: Young men and drugs: a nationwide survey, NIDA Res Monogr No 5 (DHEW Publ No ADM-76-311). Washington, DC, U.S. Government Printing Office, 1976

O'Malley PM, Johnston LD, Bachman JG: Cocaine use among American adolescents and young adults, in Cocaine Use in America: Epidemiologic and Clinical Perspectives. Edited by Kozel NJ, Adams EH. NIDA Res Monogr 61:50–75, 1985

Post RM, Kopanda RT: Cocaine, kindling and psychosis. Am J Psychiatry 133:627–634, 1976

Relman A (ed): Marijuana and Health. Washington, DC, Institute of Medicine, National Academy Press, 1982

Rounsaville BJ, Gawin FH, Kleber HD: Interpersonal Psychotherapy (IPT) adapted for ambulatory cocaine abusers. Am J Drug Alcohol Abuse 11:171–191, 1985

Rubin V, Comitas L: Ganja in Jamaica. The Hague, Mouton, 1975

Schnoll S, Daghestani A: Treatment of marijuana abuse: marijuana update. Psychiatric Annals 16: 249–254, 1986

Schwartz RH, Hawks RL: Laboratory detection of marijuana use. JAMA 254:788–792, 1985

Schwartz RH, Gruenewold PJ, Klitzner M, et al: Short-term memory impairment in cannabis-dependent adolescents. Am J Dis Child 43:1214–1219, 1989

Schwartz SR, Goldfinger SM: The new chronic patient: clinical characteristics of an emerging subgroup. Hosp Community Psychiatry 32:470–474, 1982

Stefanis C, Boulougouris I, Liakos A: Clinical and psychophysiological effects of cannabis in long-term users, in Pharmacology of Marijuana. Edited by Brause MC, Szara S. New York, Raven, 1976

Swatek R: Marijuana use: persistence and urinary elimination. J Subst Abuse Treat 1:265–270, 1984

Talbott JA, Teague JW: Marijuana psychosis. JAMA 210:299–302, 1969

Tennant FS: The clinical syndrome of marijuana dependence. Psychiatric Annals 16:225–234, 1986

Washton A: Nonpharmacologic treatments of cocaine abuse. Psychiatr Clin North Am 9:563–571, 1986

Weller RA, Halikas JA: Change in effects from marijuana: a 5- to 6-year study. J Clin Psychiatry 43:363–365, 1982

Verebey K, Jukofsky P, Mule SJ: Evaluation of a new TLC confirmation technique for positive EMIT cannabinoid samples. Research Communications in Substance Abuse 6:1–9, 1985

Verebey K, Gold MS, Mule SJ: Laboratory testing in the diagnosis of marijuana intoxication and withdrawal (letter). Psychiatric Annals 16:235, 1986

Yesavage JA, Leirer VO, Denari M, et al: Carry-over effects of marijuana intoxication on aircraft pilot performance: a preliminary report. Am J Psychiatry 142:1325–1329, 1985

Zinberg NE: Alcoholics Anonymous and the treatment and prevention of alcoholism. Alcohol Clin Exp Res 1:91–102, 1977

# CHAPTER 8

# Stimulants

Frank H. Gawin, M.D.
M. Elena Khalsa, M.D., Ph.D.
Everett Ellinwood, Jr., M.D., Ph.D.

Treating the stimulant-abusing patient requires broad understanding, including the understanding of recent cultural changes and older historical forces; the characteristics of acute stimulant euphoria and acute postuse dysphoria; the significance of administration route, neurochemical effects, and medical consequences; and the clinical characteristics of the transition to dependence, abstinence phases and symptoms, and interactions with psychiatric disorders. All of these factors must be understood before the clinical presentation of any stimulant-abusing individual can be adequately interpreted and before effective treatment for that individual can be implemented. Consequently, the initial pages of this chapter provide brief reviews of recent history and epidemiology, acute stimulant effects, medical morbidity, clinical descriptions of phases in dependence, and clinical psychiatric presentations in order to provide a foundation for the discussion of stimulant abuse treatment.

## ▼ HISTORY AND EPIDEMIOLOGY

The cocaine abuse "epidemic," now a decade old, has become endemic. Individuals who use cocaine number almost half as many as those who use marijuana. Cocaine "addiction," although different from opioid dependence, exists in 1–5 million individuals, compared with half a million heroin-addicted individuals. After a decade of decreased use, more recent reports indicate methamphetamine abuse is again increasing, perhaps becoming the "poor man's cocaine." For the first time, smokable ("freebase" or "crack") cocaine, in ready-to-smoke form, is freely available on the streets of all major cities. Smoking cocaine has the abuse liability of intravenous injection without the stigma of injection and may be the most dangerous change in substance abuse to have appeared in the 1980s.

Surprisingly, much of the public and the medical community considered cocaine a safe, nonaddictive euphoriant, different from amphetamine or methamphetamine, until approximately 10 years ago. Psychiatric texts stated "cocaine creates no serious problems" (Grinspoon and Bakalar 1980). Two national drug abuse commissions determined that cocaine created minimal morbidity or societal costs (National Commission on Marihuana and Drug Abuse 1973; Strategy Council on Drug Abuse 1973). Clinical reports of adverse cocaine effects from the beginning of the century were considered exaggerations, similar to exaggerated marijuana reports from the same era. Societal acceptance of all drug use had reached unprecedented levels. No systematic clinical cocaine abuse research existed. The absence of objective systematically derived data in humans was misinterpreted as meaning that cocaine use had no adverse consequences. Paradoxically, animal research demonstrated very close similarity between cocaine and amphetamine, and pharmacologists warned that historical reports might not be exaggerated.

By 1985, cocaine abuse exploded in the middle and upper classes, and by 1988, crack extended this explosion to the poor. Increased social acceptance of drug use, the illusion of safety, increased availability, and a new, powerful route of administration (cocaine smoking) all combined to produce an explosion of cocaine use and abuse, which in turn led to obvious harm from cocaine and the beginning of medical and public awareness of cocaine's dangers. Sadly, this re-enacted cyclical "discovery" of old knowledge. In the 1890s and 1920s, cocaine use surged and was temporarily considered safe. In the 1930s, a potent, allegedly safe stimulant was synthesized: amphetamine. But in the early 1950s and late 1960s, amphetamine abuse epidemics proved amphetamine was as dangerous as cocaine (Byck 1986).

Stimulant epidemics run consistent, predictable courses (Ellinwood 1974). After an epidemic re-emerges, adverse consequences first slowly change the way the drug-using individuals are perceived, decreasing the glamour associated with stimulant abuse. (For example, "speed kills" became a common slogan in the drug subculture after widespread methamphetamine or "speed" abuse appeared.) The incidence of new users then diminishes, and the clinical consequences for those already exposed run their course, producing a simultaneous increase in treatment demands and emergency room contacts. Decreasing the stimulant supply also sometimes limits epidemics; decreased production and prescription of amphetamines a decade ago contributed to the waning of that epidemic. After an epidemic wanes, stimulant use quiesces for 5–15 years, then a misperception of stimulant safety again appears. Initial clinical statements that are recorded in each stimulant epidemic uniformly describe illusory safety, perhaps because, except for smoking and injection, the period between an individual's first stimulant use and abuse can be up to 4 years (Schnoll et al. 1985; Siegel 1985b) and because we forget or ignore history.

By 1984, more than 10% of the U.S. population had tried cocaine, with almost 50% experimenting in some age groups (Abelson and Miller 1985). A seven-fold increase occurred between 1976 and 1983 in emergency room visits attributed to cocaine, in cocaine-related deaths (> 2 per 1,000 deaths), and in public treatment admissions for cocaine (Adams and Durell 1984). Sevenfold increases occurred through 1990, and the consequence curve for emergency room admissions may have peaked in 1991–1992. These data do not include private treatment contacts and thus underrepresent actual morbidity. Fortunately, public perception of cocaine's danger has now reversed, and onset of use has substantially declined except in impoverished crack-available areas.

In the Bahamas, smokable cocaine was introduced in 1983 and resulted in greater than sevenfold increases in hospital and outpatient admissions for cocaine abuse by the end of 1984. Moreover, in the United States, there is no indication of any decrease in cocaine importation. Because 18–48 months intervene between first intranasal use and appearance for treatment, adverse health effects and clinical treatment demands probably have just peaked. Finally, because total use and exposure to cocaine is now many times higher than ever before, the stimulant epidemic has left a legacy of high endemic use, continued human distress, and continued demands for treatment.

## ▼ ACUTE ACTIONS

The most extensively abused psychomotor stimulants, cocaine and amphetamine, are also the best understood, although major gaps in our knowledge do exist. All high-abuse stimulants share very similar neurochemical and clinical characteristics, but other centrally stimulating agents, such as caffeine or xanthines, have very different use patterns, less abuse potential, and different neurochemical actions (Goodman and Gilman 1985). These "mild" stimulants do not present major abuse or management problems. The different stimulants and their abuse liabilities are listed in Table 8–1. The remainder of this review describes high-abuse stimulants such as cocaine and amphetamine.

Stimulants create an activated euphoria. Cocaine, amphetamine, and many other similar stimulants are self-administered in pursuit of intensified pleasure. Acutely, stimulants produce profound subjective well-being with alertness. Normal pleasures are magnified and anxiety is decreased. Self-confidence and self-perceptions of mastery increase. Social inhibitions are reduced and interpersonal communication is facilitated. All aspects of the personal environment take on intensified qualities but without hallucinatory perceptual distortions. Emotionality and sexual feelings are enhanced (Freud 1884; Gawin 1978; Lasagna et al. 1955; Lewin 1924; Nathanson 1937; Van Dyke et al. 1982). Although intranasal or oral stimulant use is initially enjoyable and seemingly easily controlled, repeated use gradually produces obsessions over recapturing stimulant-induced euphoria and extreme, compulsive urges for more use. Injection or smoking of stimulants produces this transition much more rapidly, sometimes as quickly as a few weeks. Regardless of time to onset, compulsive use alters behavior and often causes severe psychological distress.

Stimulants with high abuse potential activate mesolimbic or mesocortical dopaminergic pathways to produce euphoria (Goeders and Smith 1982; Yokel and Wise 1983). In animals, electrical self-stimulation of these pathways mirrors stimulant self-administration. Increases in behavioral and physiologic reward indices are produced by either electrical stimulation of these dopaminergic reward regions or by stimulants. Such increases in reward are decreased by pharmacologic dopamine receptor blockade or lesions in dopaminergic reward pathways. Substantial preclinical research generated over the past two decades supports the central role of dopamine in stimulant reward (reviewed in Gawin 1991), and there is minimal contradictory evidence (Gawin 1986b; Reith et al.

1983; Spyraki et al. 1982). The neurochemical and neuroanatomic localization of stimulant euphorigenic effects in dopaminergic reward regions is extremely important because it provides new avenues toward understanding and researching both stimulant withdrawal and potential treatments (Gawin 1991). In contrast to other abused substances such as heroin, activation of opioid receptors or endorphinergic-enkephalinergic pathways are not necessary to support stimulant reward or euphoria (Ettenburg et al. 1981).

Cocaine, the amphetamines, methylphenidate, and other stimulants are structurally dissimilar but neuropharmacologically alike. On acute, blind laboratory administration in humans, abused stimulants are indistinguishable (Brown et al. 1978; Fischman et al. 1976). In animals, stimulants produce cross-tolerance and stimulus generalization to each other as well as very rapid learning of self-administration (Colpaert et al. 1979; Leith and Barrett 1976, 1981). Table 8–2 summarizes known neurochemical actions of stimulants. None of the single neurochemical actions is responsible for stimulant euphoria; each known action is also produced by other pharmacologic agents that have not been reported to produce euphoria, are not self-administered by animals, and are not abused by humans. Thus euphorigenic stimulant central nervous system activation clearly occurs in dopaminergic pathways. However, the neurochemical mechanisms responsible for this activation are unclear. In addition, the relative contribution of direct stimulant actions on dopaminergic neurons, as opposed to actions on dopaminergic systems by nondopaminergic collateral neuronal systems that are also affected by stimulants, cannot be easily differentiated at this time.

There are no proven distinctions, pertinent to abuse, between individual stimulants except for differences in half-life. Other differences in activity (e.g., varied local anesthetic properties) do not have known drug abuse consequences. Cocaine's half-life is less than 90 minutes, but tachyphylaxis reduces the half-life of single-dose euphoria to 30 minutes (Van Dyke et al. 1982). Amphetamine half-life is more than 4 hours, and euphoria from single doses can last several hours (Gunne and Angard 1973). This variation may produce different patterns of administration and influences the likelihood of adverse sequelae. Cocaine binges are characterized by up to 10 readministrations of the drug per hour. Rapid and frequent

**Table 8–1.** Stimulants

| High-abuse stimulants | Low-abuse stimulants |
| --- | --- |
| Cocaine | Caffeine |
| Amphetamine | Nicotine |
| Methamphetamine | Phenylpropanolamine |
| Methylenedioxy-amphetamine | Ephedrine |
| Phenmetrazine | Pseudoephedrine |
| Phendimetrazine | Theophylline |
| Dietylpropion | Fenfluramine |
| Methylphenidate | Strychnine |

changes in mood occur as a last dose wears off and a new dose is administered. Although cocaine binges can last as long as 7 consecutive days or more, it is more common for them to last less than 12 hours (Gawin and Kleber 1985a). Amphetamine binges are characterized by several hours between administrations, less variability of mood, generally more sustained and intense abuse, and longer total duration, often lasting more than 24 hours (Kramer et al. 1967). It is not certain that differences in morbidity occur, but it is our impression that amphetamines' less frequent readministrations and decreased total dosage required, combined with lower cost and the relatively larger personal amphetamine supplies available to the individual (amphetamine is about 10 times as potent as cocaine but is sold for equivalent prices in similar amounts), all make amphetamines more likely to produce prolonged high-intensity abuse. Fortunately, amphetamine and methamphetamine are far less available than crack. When the intensity and duration of cocaine abuse approximates high-dose amphetamine abuse, as can occur with cocaine smoking or with large cocaine supplies, then the two do not appear clinically distinguishable. Because of the basic similarity between these agents in all areas except those just noted, the term *stimulants* in the remainder of this chapter refers jointly to amphetamine and cocaine.

## ▼ CLINICAL CHARACTERISTICS AND TREATMENT OF STIMULANT–ABUSING PATIENTS

There are multiple, consistent clinical reports on the characteristics of stimulant-abusing patients appearing for treatment in the literature. Observations from the beginning of this century (Lewin 1924; Maier 1926), through the latest U.S. amphetamine

epidemic of 1967–1972 (Connell 1969; Ellinwood 1967; Kramer et al. 1967; Smith 1969), and the current surge in cocaine abuse (Gawin and Kleber 1986a; Gold and Estroff 1985; Siegel 1982) all indicate that 1) predictable psychiatric complications can occur acutely during or after individual episodes or binges of stimulant abuse, and 2) chronic abuse might be associated with separate chronic psychiatric sequelae, particularly mood dysfunctions. Clinical presentations often include a mixture of acute and chronic symptoms, with differing intensities of each. Separation of these dimensions requires ongoing longitudinal assessments. Descriptions of specific components of psychiatric presentations in stimulant-abusing patients follow, along with guidelines for clinical management.

## ▼ ACUTE STIMULANT USE SEQUELAE AND THEIR TREATMENT

### Stimulant Intoxication

Stimulant euphoria is phenomenologically distinct from opioid-, alcohol-, or other substance-induced euphorias. As noted earlier, qualities of acute intoxication in usual street dosages include euphoria, activation, decreased anxiety (initially), disinhibition, heightened curiosity and increased interest in the personal environment, feelings of increased competence and self-esteem, and a clear sensorium without hallucinations or cognitive confusion. Adverse consequences of stimulant intoxication reflect atypical reactions or exaggerations of these sought-after components of stimulant euphoria. Exaggerations include euphoric disinhibition, impaired judgment, grandiosity, impulsiveness, irresponsibility, atypical generosity, hypersexuality, hyperawareness, compul-

| Table 8–2. | Neurochemical actions of stimulants | | | | |
| --- | --- | --- | --- | --- | --- |
| Stimulant | Catecholamine reuptake blockade | Serotonin release or reuptake blockade | Local anesthesia | Dopamine release | Monoamine oxidase inhibition |
| Amphetamine | Marked | Moderate | Mild | Moderate | Mild |
| Cocaine | Marked | Moderate | Marked | Moderate | None |
| Methylphenidate | Marked | Unknown | Unknown | Moderate | None |

sive repetitive actions, and extreme psychomotor activation. Adverse sequelae include the psychosocial and economic consequences of actions undertaken while intoxicated—such as abrogation of responsibilities, loss of money, sexual indiscretions, or atypical illegal activities—but can also include physical injury that results from dangerous acts performed while judgment is impaired.

If intoxication is uncomplicated, no treatment is indicated other than observation through a return to baseline. Observation is also always indicated because complications such as acute psychiatric disorders or medical emergencies can occur. It should be noted that treatable medical emergencies are not common because of rapid stimulant actions; effective emergency intervention occurs only if administration of the drug is in close temporal proximity to medical attention, usually within one half-life, or if absorption is delayed (e.g., through oral cocaine or amphetamine use). Marked stimulant intoxication strongly resembles the mania or hypomania of bipolar psychiatric disorder and can sometimes trigger mania. If stimulant activation is not self-remitting within less than 24 hours in an observed, stimulant-free setting, then mania is probably present and treatment for mania may be required.

## Stimulant Delirium

Euphoric stimulation can become dysphoric as the dosage and duration of administration increase. In most stimulant intoxications, an admixture of anxiety and irritability soon accompany the desired euphoric effects. Anxiety ranges from mild dysphoric stimulation to extreme paranoia or to a panic-like delirium. In moderate form, a state of global sympathetic discharge occurs, which strongly resembles a panic anxiety attack and is often associated with a fear of impending death from the stimulant. Disorientation is not usually present but may develop. In more severe forms, an organic psychosis with disorientation occurs. When frank delirium exists, neuroleptics and restraints may be needed. However, extreme caution is indicated in treating stimulant delirium because such symptoms may indicate impending stimulant overdose. In this circumstance, emergency medical management and monitoring should absolutely take precedence over psychiatric management.

## Stimulant Delusions

Delusional psychoses occur after prolonged and intense stimulant binges. These have been experimentally induced by amphetamine in unselected normal subjects and appear related to the amount and duration of stimulant administration rather than to predisposition to psychosis (Bell 1970). Identical experiments have not been done with cocaine, but similar clinical reports exist for cocaine (Satel et al. 1991). The delusional content is usually paranoid, and, if mild, the stimulant-abusing individual may retain awareness that induced fears are a consequence of the immediately preceding stimulant intake (Ellinwood 1967). If severe, however, reality testing is completely impaired and caution is required. Case reports of homicides involving stimulant psychoses have been reported (Ellinwood 1970).

Cocaine delusions are usually transient and usually remit after sleep normalization. Amphetamine delusions are most often similarly brief, but clinicians more frequently report longer episodes that last several days. Even longer episodes, however, have been described after very prolonged stimulant binges or in individuals having preexistent schizophrenic or manic psychoses. Short-term neuroleptic treatment is routinely used to ameliorate delusional symptomatology. Observation is essential until the delusions remit. Flashback phenomena or delayed reemergence of symptoms have not been described for stimulant-induced psychoses.

## Poststimulant Dysphoria

If a stimulant use episode involves several serial readministrations or substantial doses, even in a naive, nondependent user, then mood does not return to baseline when use ceases but instead rapidly descends into dysphoria. This dysphoria, called the "crash" by abusers, is usually self-limited and resolves following sleep. Clinically, the crash fully mimics unipolar depression with melancholia, except for its comparatively brief duration. It is a regular accompaniment of the recurrent binges that occur in stimulant dependence and will be discussed more fully later. However, because emergency presentations of the crash are clinically common, require specific acute interventions, and can occur in nondependent individuals, treatment for the crash itself is discussed here.

The depression of the crash can be extremely intense and may include potentially lethal, but temporary, suicidal ideation that remits completely when the crash is over. This transient suicidal ideation can occur in individuals who have no prior history of depression or of suicidal ideation or suicide attempts. True unipolar depression (which is not self-remitting and requires antidepressant treatment) may also occur in a subpopulation, as discussed later in this chapter. Usual clinical management occurs in two stages. First, observation is indicated to prevent self-harm and to provide an opportunity for sleep and recovery of mood. Second, evaluation after sleep is needed to ensure that neurovegetative symptoms and suicidal ideation have remitted. In most cases, this can be done in an emergency room setting, and hospital admission is most often not necessary to manage the crash.

## ▼ STIMULANT MORBIDITY

The full extent of morbidity caused by chronic stimulant abuse is not known with certainty. Many different types of adverse consequences have been identified, ranging from medical complications, including overdose to pathology due to administration route, cardiotoxicity, neurotoxicity, interactions with major psychiatric disorders, and psychosocial disruption without clear physiologic or psychiatric insult. Preclinical and clinical assessment of stimulant abuse has been far from exhaustive. Surprisingly, there are no human data that rigorously define the extent of chronic medical or psychiatric consequences of long-term stimulant abuse, and few animal studies have been designed to reflect chronic human abuse. Most of what is known is based on survey data such as Drug Abuse Warning Network reports (or telephone surveys with inherent limitations based on sample self-selection) or on clinical observations of single cases or small sample, on emergency room populations with self-selection limitations, or on animal data with questionable generalizability. Such research helps define the range, or types, of confirmed or suspected adverse stimulant sequelae but does not specify the extent or quantity of the sequelae, nor their likelihood for a given subject. The research therefore provides a starting point for treatment design but not detailed guidelines.

## ▼ CHRONIC STIMULANT ABUSE: MEDICAL COMPLICATIONS

Death can result from stimulant-induced sympathomimetic storms that can cause hypertensive cerebrovascular accidents, hyperpyrexia, or myocardial infarction and cardiorespiratory collapse; over 100 reports now exist in the world literature (Cregler and Mark 1985; Kalant and Kalant 1979; Roberts et al. 1984). Plasma cholinesterases metabolize cocaine. Pseudocholinesterase deficiency should produce hypersensitivity (Jatlow et al. 1979), but this has not yet been clinically reported. Emergency medical treatment of cocaine and amphetamine largely involves providing routine countermeasures for toxic symptoms such as cardiac arrhythmias or seizures. It should be noted that acid loading facilitates amphetamine excretion and that propranolol, often used previously to reduce adrenergic tone with cocaine overdose, has been shown to cause some toxic interaction. Details of overdose management have been reviewed elsewhere (Gay 1982) and will not be covered here.

Nonlethal cardiovascular or cerebrovascular injury can also follow overdose. Gross cerebrovascular injury and diffuse microinfarctions have been reported (Rumbaugh et al. 1971, 1980). No systematic outcome data on treatment for such complications exist. Cocaine hepatotoxicity has been described in animals (Rauckman et al. 1982) but not as yet in humans. Colitis, pseudomediastinum, and bullous disease (Bush et al. 1984; Fishel et al. 1985) as well as neonatal complications in children of stimulant-addicted mothers have been reported (Chasnoff et al. 1985). Lack of other documented medical problems caused by stimulants may not reflect their absence but may instead indicate a lack of systematic clinical investigations. For example, we are not aware of any studies of physiologic functioning, excluding pulmonary function in subjects who smoke cocaine, in any population of chronic stimulant-abusing individuals.

Other medical complications are consequences of administration route. Complications of intravenous stimulant administration include thrombosis, hepatitis, AIDS, local sepsis, abscess, angiitis, endocarditis, and septicemia. Cocaine smoking causes pulmonary dysfunction (Itkonen et al. 1984; Weiss et al. 1981), and intranasal stimulant use can be associated with rhinitis and mucosal excoriation. Treatment for stimulant-related medical disease does not differ from routine management.

## ▼ CHRONIC STIMULANT ABUSE: PSYCHIATRIC COMPLICATIONS AND TREATMENT

### Knowledge About Stimulant Abuse Treatment

Current clinical understanding and management of chronic stimulant abuse are largely based on research and clinical experience gained treating those using other abused substances and on nonsystematic, descriptive reports of treatment for stimulant-abusing patients. Few large-scale clinical investigations of either the clinical psychiatric consequences of stimulant abuse or their treatment exist. We are only now witnessing the appearance of systematic observations of abuse and abstinence patterns, of well-designed treatment experiments, and of refined conceptualizations of stimulant abuse and dependence. Further, rigorous substantiation is needed in all areas. A substantial proportion of the following discussion is therefore based on clinical consensus, not on the precise, scientific observation or experimentation available for some other psychiatric and substance abuse disorders.

### The Spectrum of Stimulant Use and Abuse

*Early stimulant use*

Stimulant use occurs across a wide spectrum. In the early 1960s, millions of individuals were prescribed chronic amphetamines for depression or weight loss, and yet millions of amphetamine-abusing individuals clearly did not result. Most patients were successfully and relatively easily weaned from stimulants when restrictions were applied because use became uncontrolled in small subgroups. Similarly, before crack the National Institute on Drug Abuse once estimated that of 30 million individuals who had tried cocaine in the United States, 6 million were regular users, and one-fourth of those were in immediate need of treatment. These data indicate that most individuals use intranasal cocaine intermittently and

that controlled low-intensity regular use may occur, as with oral amphetamine in the preceding stimulant epidemic (National Institute on Drug Abuse 1986).

Stimulant dependence develops within a social-occupational matrix (Gawin and Ellinwood 1988). Initially, low doses enhance interactions with the environment, facilitating performance and confidence to enable productive increases in interpersonal or occupational industry and adventurousness (Connell 1969; Ellinwood and Petrie 1977; Gawin and Kleber 1985a; Siegel 1985a). Euphoria in early stimulant use is thus primarily due to increasingly positive external feedback to the individual instead of direct pharmacologic effects; it is often misperceived by the individual as originating in the environment rather than in the drug (Gawin and Ellinwood 1988). Combined with absent or scarcely apparent negative contingencies, such early stimulant experiences are seductive (Ellinwood and Petrie 1977; Kleber and Gawin 1984).

Perhaps the most fundamental and important treatment questions for stimulant abuse are 1) what distinguishes those who can easily cease stimulant use from those who cannot, and 2) how can the capacity to cease use be restored? With the exception of one study of recreational cocaine-using subjects by Siegel (1985a), no detailed data on controlled stimulant-using subjects exist. Telephone hot line surveys provide little information on controlled use because these lack clinical detail. Further, caller characteristics are similar to treatment samples, rather than to community survey populations. Detailed abuse reports are, however, available from patients in treatment, and retrospective data from abusers who develop dyscontrol and appear for treatment, combined with judicious application of animal data, provide a preliminary answer to the questions posed.

*The high-intensity transition*

Animals given free access to stimulants engage in continuous self-administration. Death from cardio-respiratory collapse or infection follows, usually within 14 days (reviewed in Johanson 1984). Stimulants are chosen over food, sex, opioids, alcohol, sedatives, hallucinogens, and phencyclidine. In limited stimulant-administration paradigms, animals can be kept alive, but they generally adjust self-administration to maintain maximum effects within the limits of the paradigm (Gay 1982). Humans appear to be similar. Individuals who are severely impaired from abuse report virtual exclusion of all nonstimulant-related thoughts during stimulant binges. Sex, nourishment, sleep, safety, survival, money, morality, loved ones, and responsibility all become immaterial when juxtaposed with the desire to reexperience stimulant euphoria (Ellinwood and Petrie 1977; Gawin and Kleber 1986a; Lasagna et al. 1955; Lewin 1924; Siegel 1982). Supplies of money or stimulants are drawn on until they are exhausted. Abuse is limited only by access, and human abusers appear to function like the nonhumans in preclinical studies. Only the extreme monetary cost of cocaine and legal limitations on distribution appear to limit this human street paradigm.

Paradoxically, heavy human abusers report being similar to the millions of noncompulsive users during their early stimulant use (Gawin and Kleber 1985a). No animal studies reported a similar low-intensity use. We believe a phenomenon, the *high-intensity transition* to compulsive use, underlies this paradox. Abusers describe that compulsive use begins when administration route changes, or availability and dosage increases markedly (e.g., increased resources, improved supply sources, engaging in cocaine commerce). Our experience suggests that stimulant use is controlled until episodes of extremely intense euphoria have occurred. Such episodes produce what become *persecutory* memories of intense euphoria. These memories are later contrasted to any immediate dysphoria to become the fount of stimulant craving. Early in stimulant use, high-intensity episodes are precluded by price, availability, and concerns over safety that limit the amounts used or that preclude experimenting with rapid administration routes.

Intravenous or smoking stimulant administration uniformly produces very intense euphoria. Consistent with this explanation, noncompulsive use has not been described for these administration routes (Kleber and Gawin 1984; Siegel 1982, 1985a). This "controlled" nondependent crack use has not been described. Intranasal or oral administration produces intense euphoria if initial doses are large enough, but they are less likely to produce the transition because of slower absorption.

Chronic animal studies on stimulants employ substantial boluses and usually intravenous administration. In effect, they begin after the high-intensity transition, explaining the lack of animal data on the transition itself or on low-intensity use. Systematic clinical studies to examine the high-intensity transition, or any other explanation of the apparent dichotomy of stimulant use and abuse, have not been done. Both animal and clinical studies are clearly needed.

Popular misconception has held that intranasal cocaine use does not lead to abuse and that severe abuse requires daily administration. Both of these conceptions appear to be wrong. Pre-crack treatment data from multiple sources show more than 50% of abusers seeking treatment are exclusively intranasal users, with no differences in impairment between administration routes (reviewed in Kleber and Gawin 1984). Preliminary reports indicate that as many as 90% of abusers appearing for treatment use cocaine in extended binges, which disrupt sleep (Gawin and Kleber 1985a), duplicating a pattern previously observed in amphetamine-abusing subjects (Connell 1969; Kramer et al. 1967). Several days of abstinence often separate binges, and abusers report that limited daily use patterns precede binge abuse (Connell 1969; Gawin and Kleber 1985a). Even in daily crack-abusing subjects, use generally occurs in binges that last several hours, rather than throughout the day. In contrast to nonstimulant substance abuse, daily stimulant use is not the maximal abuse pattern if normal sleep patterns are maintained, and severe abuse can exist without incessant daily administration. Some abusers with unlimited access do develop an unceasing binge lasting weeks or months with severely disrupted functioning (Siegel 1982), but such cases are rare.

No personality variables predisposing individuals to stimulant abuse have been demonstrated, but major psychiatric mood and attention disorders, in which stimulants are used as self-medication, appear to be overrepresented in treatment samples (review follows). Genetic predispositions to stimulant abuse may exist; alcohol abuse in family members has been extensively commented on by clinicians but not systematically studied. Studies of genetic factors similar to those reported in alcohol abuse have not been done in stimulant-abusing populations. Taken together, the animal and clinical data presently available clearly support only three clinically applicable predictors of abuse susceptibility or severity: use patterns, availability, and impairment of self-control. More circumscribed categorizations of stimulant abuse are being proposed and evaluated but are as yet arbitrary and inconclusive. These are discussed elsewhere (Gawin and Kleber 1986a; Gold and Estroff 1985; Kleber and Gawin 1984; Siegel 1982, 1985a).

## Abstinence Phases

The existence and characteristics of stimulant withdrawal are subjects of current controversy. This reflects dissimilarity between cocaine and opioids or alcohol. Classic pharmacologic drug abuse constructs—such as withdrawal, dependence, and tolerance—do not provide models that can be easily applied to cocaine or other stimulants. Dependence and withdrawal reflected by gross physiologic indices verge on being imperceptible in stimulant-abusing individuals. This accounts for the common perception that cocaine and amphetamine are only "psychologically" addictive. DSM-III (American Psychiatric Association 1980) reflected the belief that cocaine abuse does not lead to dependence or withdrawal; consequently, there was no diagnostic category for cocaine dependence. DSM-IV (American Psychiatric Association 1994) does contain this category for cocaine.

Chronic stimulant abuse regularly produces cyclical reoccurrences of use as well as time-dependent evolution of abstinence symptoms. We have recently described a triphasic cocaine abstinence pattern that dispels the recent perceptions that cocaine use produces no withdrawal. Stimulant abstinence is schematized in Figure 8–1 and is described below (see Gawin and Kleber 1986a).

In the discussion that follows, we first describe all the stages of abstinence, accompanied by pertinent data from the animal literature, to describe an emerging conception of neurophysiologically based stimulant dependence. We then review treatment for chronic dependence, which treaters should adapt according to the needs, progress, and phase of abstinence of each stimulant-abusing individual. Finally, special treatment implications of possible coexistence of DSM-III Axis I psychiatric disorders will be discussed.

### Crash: Acute Dysphoria (Phase 1)

As noted under acute sequelae, when euphoria decreases during a binge of stimulant use, anxiety, fatigue, irritability, and depression increase. This usually leads to stimulant readministration and prolongs binges. However, supplies are eventually exhausted, or a state of extreme acute tolerance occurs, in which further high-dose administration produces little euphoria and instead augments anxiety or paranoia, and self-administration ends. The crash is initially a descent into depressed mood with continued stimulation and anxiety. Then a desire for rest and escape from the hyperstimulated dysphoria often cause use of anxiolytics, sedatives, opioids, or alcohol to induce sleep. Whether or not sleep is pharmacologically induced, a later period of hypersomnolence and hyperphagia (during brief awakenings or after the hypersomnolence) eventually occurs. The duration of these periods is related to the duration and intensity of the preceding binge (Gawin and Kleber 1986a).

Following week-long stimulant binges, hypersomnolence may last several days (Kramer et al. 1967; Siegel 1982). Awakening from the hypersomnolence is usually associated with markedly improved mood, although some residual dysphoria may occur, particularly in high-intensity abusers. The exhaustion, depression, and hypersomnolence of the crash probably result from acute neurotransmitter depletion secondary to the preceding stimulant binge. Such depletion has been demonstrated directly in animal experiments (Taylor et al. 1979) and in experiments using indirect peripheral indices in humans (reviewed in Gawin and Ellinwood 1988). Clinical recovery from the crash probably depends on sleep, diet, and time for new dopamine and norepinephrine synthesis. One report (Gold et al. 1983) of precursor loading with tyrosine indicates that tyrosine decreases crash symptoms, but this report has not been replicated or extended to clinical treatment. Clinical management of the crash was discussed earlier. The crash has sometimes been equated with a withdrawal state (Gold et al. 1983; Siegel 1982; Smith 1969). Acute tolerance to stimulant effects, occurring within a binge, has been clearly described clinically and in laboratory experiments (reviewed in Gawin and Ellinwood 1988). Furthermore, changes in peripheral catecholamine indices and sleep electroencephalogram (EEG) immediately after stimulant administration have been used as support for the existence of a dependent state (Watson et al. 1972, 1992). However, unlike opioids and alcohol, stimulant abuse usually does not occur daily. Chronic tolerance has not been experimentally proven, and clinical consensus is that it is much less substantial; craving is usually absent immediately after the crash and is episodic only later on (Connell 1969; Gawin and Kleber 1986a; Kramer et al. 1967; Siegel 1982). In opioid or alcohol withdrawal, craving for the abused substance to alleviate withdrawal symptoms is rapid, marked, and continuous. Relapse follows such craving directly. With the exception of the beginning of the stimulant crash, however, craving occurs only for sleep or rest, and further stimulant use is often strongly rejected in the hope that sleep rest may be attained (Gawin and Kleber 1986a).

The crash appears in first-time users if the dose and duration of stimulant administration are large. It thus appears that the crash may be similar to immediate high-dose alcohol aftereffects rather than to alcohol or opioid withdrawal. The crash thus appears to be a self-limiting acute state that does not itself require active treatment. It apparently does not contribute to chronic relapse and abuse but only to prolonging stimulant binges (Gawin and Kleber 1986a).

### Withdrawal: Poststimulant Mood Dysfunction (Phase 2)

Assessing the stimulant withdrawal is a crucial focus of current treatment research. The nervous system's usual response to persistent, drug-induced neurochemical perturbation is compensatory adaptation in the perturbed systems. Dysregulation occurs when the drug is not present. Despite the recent perception that stimulants may only be psychologically addictive, it is illogical to assume neuroadaptation does not occur in stimulant abuse. This does not mean a classic drug abstinence syndrome uniformly occurs; instead, chronic high-dose stimulant use could generate sustained neurophysiologic changes in brain systems that regulated psychological processes only. Changes in these neurophysiologic systems produce a true physiologic addiction and withdrawal, but one whose clinical expression is psychological.

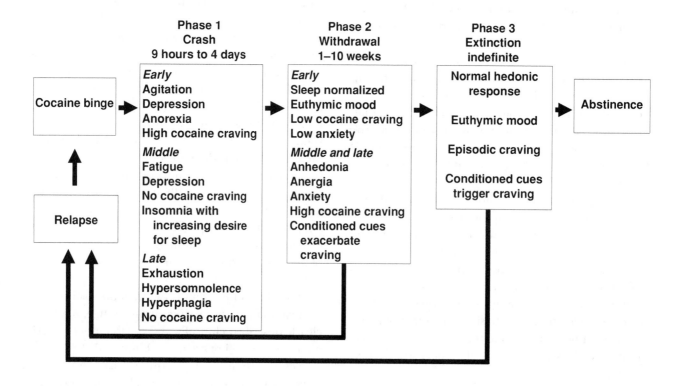

**Figure 8–1. Cocaine abstinence phases.** Duration and intensity of symptoms vary on the basis of binge characteristics and diagnosis. Binges range in duration from under 4 hours to 6 or more days. High cocaine craving in phase 1 usually lasts less than 6 hours and is followed by a period of noncraving with similar duration in the next subphase (middle phase 1). Substantial craving then returns only after a lag of 0.5–5 days, during phase 2.
*Source.* Reprinted with permission from Gawin FH, Kleber HD: "Abstinence Symptomatology and Psychiatric Diagnosis in Cocaine Abusers." *Arch Gen Psychiatry* 43:107–113, 1986. Copyright 1986, American Medical Association.

Both extensive experimental data in animals and clinical evidence, summarized in Table 8–3, support this view. Briefly, animal experiments using electrical stimulation at brain reward sites show a decrease in sensitivity after chronic stimulant use (Colpaert et al. 1979; Kokkinidis et al. 1980; Leith and Barrett 1976; Simpson and Arnau 1977; Markou and Koob 1991) that is reversible with antidepressant administration (Kokkinidis et al. 1980; Simpson and Arnau 1977). Human stimulant abusers display a symptom constellation (description follows) that is consistent with a decreased capacity to perceive reward or pleasure. Further, chronic stimulants produce long-term animal neurotransmitter and neuroreceptor changes (Banerjee et al. 1979; Borison et al. 1979; Fitzgerald and Reid 1991; Henry and White 1991; Karoum et al. 1990; Ricuarte et al. 1980; Robertson et al. 1991; Taylor et al. 1979), animal behavioral changes (Utena 1966; Yagi 1963), and human positron emission tomography (PET), computerized electroencephalography, neuroendocrine and sleep EEG changes (Alper et al. 1990; Gawin and Kleber 1985b; Hollander et al. 1990; Lee et al. 1990; Volkow et al. 1988; Watson et al. 1972, 1992). Combined, these data support the presence of a neuroadaptive process. The data are complex and are critically reviewed in more detail elsewhere (Gawin 1991; Gawin and Ellinwood 1988).

Protracted dysphoria, occurring long after the crash, has been clinically identified in stimulant-abusing subjects (Connell 1969; Gawin and Kleber 1986a). Protracted dysphoric symptoms are frequent antecedents of stimulant craving, often leading to unceasing cycles of recurrent binges. These chronic symptoms are not quickly self-remitting and therefore have great importance to treatment. They thus have greater clinical similarity to withdrawal in other substances of abuse than other abstinence symptoms, such as the crash.

In most individuals who abuse stimulants heavily, a regular symptom progression follows the resolution of intoxication and crash symptoms. On awakening from hypersomnolence, a euthymic interval with normal mood and little stimulant craving occurs. In individuals who are attempting to cease use, this interval is usually associated with vivid memories of the misery of the crash and acute awareness of the psychosocial costs of continued stimulant abuse. This lasts from several hours to several days (Gawin and Kleber 1986a). It is slowly supplanted by increasing anxiety, inactivation, irritability, amotivation, and restricted pleasurable responses to the environment. These symptoms have been variously labeled anergia, depression (Connell 1969; Kramer et al. 1967), anhedonia (Gawin and Kleber 1984, 1986a), or psychasthenia (Ellinwood and Petrie 1977) by different clinical observers.

The dysphoric symptoms wax and wane; they are often not constant or severe enough to meet psychiatric diagnostic criteria for major affective disorders. The abusers' limited hedonic reactions to existence, contrasted with memories of stimulant-induced euphoria, nonetheless makes resumption of use compellingly seductive. Furthermore, the symptom intensity is responsive to environmental cues: the same stimuli that trigger memories of stimulant euphoria and craving for stimulants also intensify awareness of an abuser's baseline dysphoria. During the experience of craving there is a remarkable lack of memory of the crash or the adverse psychosocial consequences of abuse. Such negative memories often reemerge only when the episode of craving, and possibly relapse, has passed.

Stimulant-abusing individuals often describe amelioration of anhedonic symptoms within days to weeks if they can sustain abstinence (Connell 1969; Ellinwood and Petrie 1977; Gawin and Kleber 1986a; Smith 1969). Animal studies administering sufficiently chronic and high-dose stimulants report behavioral depression on withdrawal for a similar time period (Utena 1966; Yagi 1963). Both the severity and duration of these symptoms depend partially on the intensity of the preceding chronic abuse. Predisposing mood disorders may also amplify these symptoms. Conversely, in intermittent controlled stimulant-using individuals without psychiatric disorders, an anhedonic-psychasthenic phase may not occur at all. We speculate that the high-intensity transition and the coinciding neuroadaptation may be required before psychasthenia and anhedonia emerge.

Cocaine withdrawal symptoms, initially based on clinical observations, have now been substantiated by systematic rating instruments and factor analytic studies in humans (Khalsa et al., in press, 1992). Further, as with nicotine and opioids, drug availability and the drug-taking environment may be essential for the appearance of full withdrawal because very modest symptom expression occurs in inpatients (Satel et al. 1991; Weddington et al. 1990).

*Extinction: Postwithdrawal*
*Conditioned Dysfunction*
*(Phase 3)*

Following successful initiation of abstinence and the resolution of early anhedonia and craving, intermittent stimulant craving continues to be reported (Ellinwood and Petrie 1977; Gawin and Kleber 1986a; Maier 1926). Such craving is not accompanied by the baseline dysphoria of the second phase, and there is no known neurophysiologic mechanism for these episodes. Cravings appear in the context of such divergent factors as particular mood states (positive as well as negative); specific persons, locations, events, or times of year; intoxications with other substances; interpersonal strife; or abuse objects (i.e., money, white powder, pipes, mirrors, syringes, single-edged razor blades). These factors vary; none are uniformly associated with craving. They appear to be conditioned cues, varying according to the abuse habits of the individual abuser. Stimulants are the most potent reinforcing agents known (Johanson 1984) and as such can be expected to produce classical and operant conditioning. Animal experiments have clearly established that strong conditioning to stimulants occurs. The craving is intense and can reemerge months or even years after last stimulant use (Gawin and Kleber 1986a). Conditioned craving is also reported during abstinence from other substances, although our impression is that conditioned cravings are more unpredictable and intense in former stimulant abusers than in those who abuse other drugs.

Systematic studies of the reemergence of conditioned craving are being carried out but are not yet complete. Clinical impressions indicate that the craving is episodic, lasting only hours with, in long abstinent abusers, very long periods free of craving. The magnitude and episodic nature of the craving, the variety of the cues, and their temporal contiguity to stimulant abuse episodes support the view that this craving is conditioned.

By far the most common clinical example of a conditioned cue is alcohol. Alcohol disinhibition can overcome early hesitancies toward trying stimulants based on their extreme expense or illegality. Mild alcohol intoxication often precedes initial stimulant use or early repetitions of use. If this association occurs regularly, alcohol intoxication then becomes a conditioned cue for stimulant craving. Such abusers report little craving except immediately after alcohol intake. Relapse in such patients often follows prolonged abstinence but occurs with regularity when social contacts are reestablished, following weeks of relative social isolation imposed to initiate abstinence, and occurs only after one or two drinks. In such cases, individuals with years of nonproblematic recreational alcohol use and a total weekly alcohol intake of less than half a dozen drinks may require total alcohol abstinence to become stimulant-free.

The conditioning hypothesis is testable and has important research and treatment implications. Psychodynamic, behavioral, interpersonal, and psychosocial explanations for craving and relapse have all also been offered (Anker and Crowley 1982; Rounsaville et al. 1985; Wurmser 1979a, 1979b). Contributions from each of these areas may exist but have less immediate treatment relevance and often have limited scientific testability.

## Chronic Stimulant-Induced Psychiatric Disorders

Do permanent neurotoxic changes occur as a consequence of stimulant abuse? Because most clinical reports indicate that anhedonic symptoms decrease weeks to months after stimulant use ceases, these changes appear reversible. However, permanent dopaminergic neuronal degeneration has been documented in animal studies (Seiden 1984) and is complemented by disturbing clinical observations. Reports from Scandinavia, Japan, and rare cases in the United States (Schuster and Fischman 1985; Utena 1966) describe chronic high-dose stimulant-using individuals, primarily intravenous amphetamine users, who have persistent anhedonia, energia, and craving that do not remit even after abstinence as long as 10 years. PET studies in chronic, very heavy cocaine users demonstrate withdrawal changes that *do not* normalize at 6 months (Volkow et al. 1988, 1990, 1991). More systematic long-term follow-up studies in abstinent former abusers are thus clearly needed.

Chronic stimulant-induced paranoid psychoses have also been intermittently reported; in the context of how widespread stimulant use has been over the last two decades, however, they occur infrequently. It is not clear whether reported cases had preexistent psychiatric disorder. Persistent schizophreniform psychoses, induced by chronic rather than acute stimulant administration, have been expected on theoretical grounds (Post et al. 1976). Data from one retrospective analysis (McLellan et al. 1979) indicate that long-term psychoses caused by chronic stimulant use may occur, but selection flaws in that study, lack of attempts at replication, and the absence of other supportive data preclude any general conclusions at this time.

## ▼ TREATMENT OF CHRONIC STIMULANT ABUSE

Current stimulant abuse treatment as practiced in the United States is usually alcohol or opioid abuse treatment, applied without adaptation for specific problems associated with stimulant abuse (Kleber and Gawin 1984). Specialized treatments are, however, being explored. Interventions employed have included adaptations of most major types of psychotherapy as well as pharmacotherapeutic trials (Anker and Crowley 1982; Connell 1969; Gawin and Kleber 1984, 1986a; Gold and Estroff 1985; Khantzian and Khantzian 1984; Kleber and Gawin 1984; Maier 1926; Rounsaville et al. 1985; Siegel 1982; Wurmser 1979b).

Treatment should be subdivided into three parts—engagement, abstinence initiation, and relapse prevention—that approximately correspond to the euthymic and anhedonic phases of withdrawal and extinction, respectively.

### Engagement and Abstinence Initiation

The paramount immediate treatment goal is breaking cycles of recurrent stimulant binges or of daily use. Immediate relapse is a strong possibility as long as anergic and anhedonic symptoms are present. Multiple outpatient approaches have been employed to initiate abstinence. Because stimulant dependence has until recently been considered psychological, established treatments have consisted of psychological strategies aimed at modifying addictive behaviors. Almost all psychotherapeutic treatment of stimulant-abusing patients can be organized around three dimensions: behavioral, supportive, and psychodynamic (Kleber and Gawin 1984).

### Behavioral therapy

Behavioral methods help the stimulant-abusing individual to recognize and experience the deleterious effects of stimulants and accept the need to stop use. For the vast majority of individuals who need treatment, stimulant use has become a central part of their lives. Some seek treatment, with a strong internal conviction that they have lost control of their drug use and pay too heavy a price for it, both financially and personally. Most have more ambivalent feelings. Although they recognize that stimulant use harms them, they still hope they can control their drug use and do not want to give up drug-induced euphoria. Often powerful external pressure from family members, employers, or the law pushes them to enter into treatment. If these individuals are to remain in treatment, psychotherapy must have an impact on this ambivalence early in the treatment process.

The most systematized behavioral method, contingency contracting, emphasizes this area by focus-

| Table 8–3. | Evidence for protracted stimulant adaptation and anhedonia |
|---|---|
| **Animal** | **Human** |
| • ICSS brain reward indices decreased after chronic stimulants | • Clinical observations of anhedonia |
| • ICSS normalization after chronic antidepressant treatment | • Decreased craving and abstinence after antidepressant treatment |
| • Experimentally induced behavioral depression lasting 2–8 weeks | • Similar time course for clinical observations |
| • Neuroreceptor and neurotransmitter alterations | • PET, CEEG, neuroendocrine and sleep EEG alterations |
| • Tolerance and cross-tolerance between abused stimulants | • Tolerance to euphoria |

*Note.* ICSS = intracranial self-stimulation; PET = positron emission tomography; CEEG = computerized electroencephalography; EEG = electroencephalogram.

ing and magnifying the particular harmful effects of drug use. This technique has a long history of use in amphetamine abuse (Boudin 1972) and has been applied to cocaine (Anker and Crowley 1982). According to Anker and Crowley (1982), contingency contracting has two basic elements; agreement to participate in a urine-monitoring program and attachment of an aversive contingency to either a positive sample or a failure to appear to deliver a urine sample. The aversive contingencies are derived from the patient's own statements of the adverse consequences expected to result from continued cocaine use. An adverse effect is then scheduled to occur at their very next use of cocaine. The patient may be requested to write a letter of irrevocable personal consequences, such as a letter admitting to cocaine abuse addressed to his or her employer or professional licensing board. This letter is then held by the therapist and mailed to the addressee in the event of positive or missed urinalysis. Such contracts, coupled with supportive psychotherapy, appear to be effective as long as patients are willing to take part in the treatment and the contract remains in effect.

Anker and Crowley (1982) reported 48% of an outpatient sample were willing to engage in this treatment; more than 80% were abstinent from cocaine during the duration of the contract, which averaged 3 months. However, more than one-half of these patients relapsed following completion of the contract. Patients refusing to enter into contracts (52%) were treated with supportive psychotherapy only; more than 90% of noncontract patients dropped out and/or resumed cocaine abuse within 2–4 weeks. Anker and Crowley presented no comparisons of severity of cocaine use and thus ignored the possibility that cocaine-abusing individuals with severe craving and problems of control recognize their inability to comply with such treatment and consequently avoid it. In addition to problems of long-term efficacy and possible inapplicability to more severe cocaine abuse, there are obvious ethical problems existing in those cases in which the procedure could have been based on positive reinforcement or on less aversive techniques.

The major lesson from this treatment approach is straightforward: contingency contracting focuses on and magnifies the actual harm to the self that can result from cocaine abuse. The clear emphasis this method gives to the deleterious effects of cocaine abuse can also be repeatedly reinforced in psycho-

therapy using individual, group, and family techniques in a less potentially harmful manner than the contingency contracts. Less severe contingencies can be used as well in a graduated fashion. The technique also requires that the patient has something to lose; when patients come to treatment only after they have lost everything, therapists may be hard-pressed to find appropriate contingencies.

Further, positive contingencies can be employed—for example, starting with a sum of money taken from a patient and returning part of that sum each week in exchange for clean urines. Most treatment programs suggest that control over funds should be abrogated to a responsible significant other to initiate abstinence. Gradual return of monetary control occurs, but it is often unrecognized that this is a positive contingency. In most treatment programs, positive and negative contingencies are numerous, but they are not clearly identified or prospectively planned. Contingency contracting demonstrates the therapeutic benefit of such identification and planning. It is our opinion that patients maximally benefit from an overt, individualized, planned combination of both positive and negative contingencies and reinforcements that are under continuous scrutiny throughout treatment. The relative efficacy of emphasizing negative contingencies without formal contracts, with formal contracts, with graduated contingencies, and with positive contingencies has not yet been subject to direct, systematic treatment studies.

More recently, Higgins et al. (1991) have described a systematized behavioral approach to cocaine smoking using contingency contracts including positive contingencies as well as group behavioral methods and support. They describe almost a twofold increase in abstinence initiation compared with a conventional 12-step program. However, sample size in this investigation was quite small.

### Supportive therapy

This approach initially separates the user from the use-fostering environment by way of external controls and then gradually facilitates internalization of controls through psychotherapy. Siegel (1982) described using frequent supportive psychotherapy sessions, self-control strategies, "exercise therapy," and liberal use of hospitalization during initial detoxification. One-half of his sample of 32 heavy cocaine smokers dropped out of treatment, but 80% of those remaining were cocaine free at 9-month follow-up.

Anker and Crowley (1982) described key points in their supportive therapy as encouraging increased contract with nonusing friends, eliminating paraphernalia and drug caches, terminating relationships with dealers or drug-using friends, changing telephone numbers or even residences if there is a need to stop drug-related telephone calls and visits, counseling and education of spouse and family, and examining related problem areas in the patient's life. Such common sense interventions, often overlooked, can be crucial and simple contributions to abstinence.

Because it is not uncommon for heavy users to become dealers to support their habits (and for dealers to become heavy users as a consequence of easy access to large, inexpensive quantities of stimulants), it is important to emphasize that all commerce in stimulants, as well as use of stimulants, must cease. Drastic changes in life-style and socioeconomic status are often required.

Supportive self-help groups such as Alcoholics Anonymous, Narcotics Anonymous, and Cocaine Anonymous are widely used in the United States. They provide structure and limits as well as group support, a helping network, and an important spiritual dimension (Ehrlich and McGeehan 1985). They employ behavioral as well as supportive techniques. Although patients and clinicians have described them as effective, and clinical consensus strongly supports the usefulness of self-help groups, they have not yet been the subject of outcome studies for stimulant abuse.

In general, such programs insist on the cessation of all mood-altering drugs on the reasonable grounds that the patient has already demonstrated addictive tendencies and thus is likely to become addicted to another drug or relapse if he or she continues any drug use. Often, however, patients have to learn this lesson firsthand by relapsing before they are willing to give up their use of other drugs.

Regular urinalysis is also a supportive mechanism. It is a deterrent to use as well as a means of detection of early relapses. Because cocaine can be detected consistently in the urine by way of its principal metabolite, benzoylecgonine, for only 1–3 days, random testing at least one to two times weekly is important. Regular urines are sufficient to detect amphetamine, but because most users will abuse either agent, random urinalysis for amphetamine-abusing patients is also necessary to detect cocaine abuse. Early in treatment, the knowledge that urinalysis will occur precludes any internal struggle over whether the patient can hide use and forms an external support to promote abstinence.

### Psychodynamic therapy

Psychodynamic treatment approaches aim at making the stimulant-abusing patient aware of the needs that stimulants have satisfied in the patient's life and to help the patient meet these needs without drugs (Wurmser 1979a). Stimulant use meets a variety of needs. Narcissistic needs are often met by the glamour associated with cocaine use. The need for a sense of identity is often met by becoming part of a stimulant-using subculture. Anaclitic needs can be met by way of stimulant-heightened intimate interactions. Stimulants may be used to compensate for interpersonal or professional failures as well as for inadequate rewards perceived from achieved success. Pursuit, acquisition, and sale of stimulants may help to deal with inadequate time-structuring and leisure skills. Stimulants may also be used to cope with an existential sense of inner emptiness and for self-medication of many other psychological symptoms. Perhaps most importantly, understanding these needs may provide an increased sense of control for the individual that often limits the need to turn to stimulant use for an illusory sense of power and control (Rounsaville et al. 1985).

A combination of all three orientations—behavioral, supportive, and psychodynamic—is probably the most common form of both early and long-term treatment in both inpatient and outpatient settings. The optimal combination of these orientations is best determined by a careful evaluation of the patient and the development of an individualized treatment plan, rather than by simple program structure. For example, severe cocaine-abusing patients attempting abstinence may not respond to psychodynamic interventions until abstinence is long substantiated, whereas moderate abusers seem readier to utilize them earlier. Also, the mild abuser may need little more than clarification of the consequences of abuse, perhaps using mild contingency methods, in order to stop cocaine use. Therefore, choice of primary therapeutic orientation might shift from behavioral to psychodynamic to supportive as abuse severity increases and in the opposite direction as length of abstinence increases (Kleber and Gawin 1984). These notions have not yet received any empirical testing.

If abstinence does not closely follow initiation of outpatient treatment, then escalating interventions become necessary. Two types of additional interventions are clinically employed to facilitate abstinence: hospitalization and pharmacotherapies.

*Outpatient versus inpatient treatment*

Hospitalization ensures removal from the stimulant-available environment. Some consider it appropriate as an initial treatment (reviewed in Kleber and Gawin 1984). When used routinely, regardless of abuse severity, this may be excessive. Many treaters strongly favor hospitalization for initial detoxification. However, in recent studies using pharmacologic agents (Gawin and Kleber 1984) as well as in nonpharmacologic studies by Anker and Crowley (1982), need for hospitalization was infrequent. The differing impressions may be the result of treatment variables. For examples, Siegel treated heavy cocaine smokers with minimal pharmacotherapy; pharmacotherapy in other studies may have controlled symptoms that would otherwise have required hospitalization.

Individual cases of severe abuse exist in which hospitalization is the only way to separate the patient from stimulants and to ensure safety. In severe crack dependence, for example, crack availability may be so extreme that abstinence initiation is impossible without removal from the crack-available environment. The only clearly accepted factors indicating need for inpatient cocaine abuse treatment are severe neurovegetative depression or psychotic symptoms lasting beyond 1–3 days of the postcocaine crash as well as repeated outpatient failures. Other factors remain controversial. The decision to hospitalize should be based on estimations of the patient's support network, stimulant availability, severity of abstinence symptoms, ego strength, motivation, concurrent medical problems, and prior responses to treatment. Length of hospitalization varies but should provide for ensured abstinence through the resolution of phase 2 symptoms.

The only outcome data comparing outpatient-alone with inpatient-alone treatment suggest it is less successful than outpatient-alone treatment (Rawson et al. 1986). This could be due to the absence of relapse prevention treatment techniques (detailed below) when hospitalization is not followed by outpatient therapy. Our clinical impressions, gained from work with both severe amphetamine- and cocaine-abusing subjects, lead us to favor outpatient treatment whenever possible. Because the stimulant-abusing patient must resume everyday life at some point, hospitalization merely defers this point. Studies of animal behavior as well as clinical work with humans (Maddox and Desmond 1982; Wikler 1973) concur with our opinion, highlighting the importance of environment in conditioning and drug-taking behavior. We have observed that a period of abstinence, akin to a period of *extinction* within the context of everyday life and stressors, is necessary before long-term reduction in craving can occur. This cannot occur purely in the hospital environment, which is devoid of cues and drugs that may simply delay this important task.

*Experimental pharmacotherapies*

The second type of intervention for patients who continue to abuse stimulants, pharmacotherapy, is currently controversial. Attempts at pharmacotherapeutic interventions were initially based on two observations. First, changes in animal intracranial self-stimulation indices and neuroreceptor sensitivity after chronic treatment with antidepressants are opposite to those demonstrated from chronic stimulants (Gawin 1991). Second, antidepressants facilitated abstinence in psychasthenic-anhedonic amphetamine-abusing patients, according to anecdotal reports (Ellinwood and Petrie 1977). If pharmacotherapies are to be used in patients undergoing stimulant withdrawal, the patients should be advised that this is not a use approved by the Food and Drug Administration, and their informed consent to this use should be recorded.

**Antidepressants.** Multiple open clinical trials and five multidimensional, well-controlled double-blind trials have appeared to support the efficacy of desipramine and other heterocyclic antidepressants for initiating abstinence in cocaine-abusing patients (Bakti et al. 1990, 1993; Brotman et al. 1988; Gawin and Kleber 1984; Gawin et al. 1989a; Giannini et al.

1986; Hall et al. 1992; Khalsa et al. 1993a; Margolin et al. 1991; Nunes et al. 1989; Pollack and Rosenbaum 1991; Tunis 1992). Effect sizes vary according to the population investigated, but have ranged from two to sevenfold increases in abstinence initiation and/or engagement (see Figure 8–2 for an example of changes in cocaine usage). Self-reported cocaine craving is decreased by such agents and has been demonstrated in double-blind human laboratory experiments (Gawin 1991; Kosten et al. 1992; see Figure 8–3). One small negative study and one case report (Weiss 1988) administered desipramine after abstinence initiation had been produced by 30-day or longer inpatient stays and so does not pertain to the abstinence initiation hypothesis at issue here, which is assessed in the other studies (cited above). The only negative double-blind trial had multiple confounds, as recognized by its authors (Weddington et al. 1990), including 1) a very high placebo response rate to heavy, daily doses of psychotherapy; 2) inadequate sample size relative to previously reported effect sizes and the high placebo response rate; and 3) absence of consistent plasma level assessments.

Further, the guidelines for desipramine dosage and the target plasma concentrations used in past cocaine abuse treatment studies were originally drawn from clinical experience with melancholia (Gawin and Kleber 1984) and may not be optimal for cocaine abuse. First, the goals of treatment differ for cocaine-abusing patients: reduced cocaine use and craving are the principal objectives rather than diminished melancholic symptoms. Second, cocaine abuse treatment populations differ from depressed populations. For example, cocaine-abusing individuals have a greater likelihood of pharmacodynamic and/or pharmacokinetic interactions with treatment medications. These interactions could be caused by one or more of the following: 1) chronic neurophysiological adaptations to cocaine, 2) accompanying chronic use of alcohol/anxiolytics/sedatives/opioids to improve the high or ease the crash, or 3) the acute effects of multiple current intoxicant use. There also may be differences between the two populations with regard to the neurochemical mechanisms responsible for desipramine's therapeutic effects because reward subsensitivity may or may not also be central to desipramine's action in affective disorder. Age and sex differences also exist between melancholic and cocaine-abusing populations. Finally, compliance is vastly more problematic in an actively cocaine-abus-

ing population. Early optimization of desipramine dosage is particularly important in the cocaine-abusing populations of the 90s, in which any delay in treatment efficacy results in premature abandonment of treatment to ubiquitous crack availability and relapse.

Retrospective analyses of plasma level data from three double-blind studies have unexpectedly demonstrated that a clear desipramine ceiling (200 ng/ml) is the most robust predictor of outcome observed (Khalsa et al. 1993a). That is, virtually no subjects with initial plasma desipramine concentrations attained initial (3–4 consecutive weeks) abstinence, compared with > 50% combined rates in subjects below the ceiling (or ~20% in placebo groups). Follow-up evaluations indicated that many subjects above the ceiling found that desipramine was countertherapeutic, producing a dysphoric stimulation at high levels, which acted as a cue for the euphoric stimulation of cocaine. Prospective fixed-dose studies are now needed to evaluate this potentially important guide to cocaine pharmacotherapy.

Overall, with the one exception mentioned above, the data on heterocyclics are almost entirely supportive of their efficacy, when combined with rou-

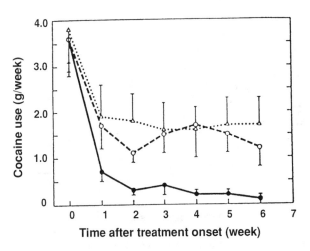

**Figure 8–2. Desipramine facilitation of initial cocaine abstinence.** End-point analysis of reported cocaine use (grams) during treatment of cocaine-abusing outpatients with desipramine hydrochloride (2.5 mg per kg or body weight per day, *n* = 24, *solid line*), lithium carbonate (17.5 mg per kg, *n* = 24, *dashed line*), or placebo (*n* = 24, *dotted line*).
*Source.* Reprinted with permission from Gawin FH, Kleber HD, Byck R, et al: "Desipramine Facilitation of Initial Cocaine Abstinence." *Arch Gen Psychiatry* 46:117–121, 1989. Copyright 1989, American Medical Association.

tine outpatient psychotherapy, for individuals dependent on cocaine.

However, this may not be the case for one specific subpopulation. For individuals who are opioid dependent and treated with methadone maintenance and who concurrently abuse cocaine, there is inadequate research on the efficacy of cyclic antidepressants in managing concurrent withdrawal from cocaine. In double-blind trials, none of these agents has demonstrated clinically robust efficacy in methadone maintenance samples. There exist two careful double-blind trials with reasonable sample sizes done in individuals on methadone that, at best, demonstrate minimal efficacy (Arndt et al. 1992; I. O. Arndt et al., unpublished data, 1993; Leal et al. 1993). However, Arndt et al. (I. O. Arndt et al., unpublished data, 1993) have demonstrated desipramine findings similar to those observed in nonmethadone samples when individuals with antisocial personality disorder (per DSM-IV criteria) are excluded. Such individuals

are apparently motivated to join such studies in order to avoid being terminated from methadone for cocaine use, not to cease cocaine use (I. O. Arndt et al., unpublished data, 1993). This has been replicated in a subanalysis of the data of Kosten et al. (1990b). The following are two further reasons that the authors suggest that these two studies alone offer insufficient evidence to determine whether desipramine is effective for treating cocaine use by methadone-maintained former opioid-addicted subjects.

Fully interpreting findings on the utility of desipramine for crack abuse in methadone-maintained subjects requires that both the desipramine ceiling and the pharmacodynamics of methadone and desipramine must also be seriously considered. Recent data suggest that desipramine has a plasma ceiling for efficacy in non-opioid-addicted cocaine-using subjects (Gawin et al. 1992). Further, methadone decreases the metabolism of desipramine, contributing to the likelihood of excessive dosages (Kosten et al. 1990a; O'Brien et al. 1990). It is possible that these two confounds combined to decrease the measured response rate (cocaine abstinence initiation) of desipramine in prior studies done in methadone-maintained populations. Without consistent desipramine levels it is impossible to be certain whether the subjects in these studies were in or out of the therapeutic range. When these prior studies were originally implemented, there was no suggestion that a desipramine ceiling existed that affected cocaine treatment results or that a ceiling existed for any other antidepressant in any indication excepting nortriptyline. Because an interaction could only increase desipramine concentration, the interaction would increase both the likelihood of being above threshold and of having desipramine side-effects. Because routine clinical dosage reduction would result from reports of side-effects, there was no apparent need in these studies for tight plasma level assessments. However, most individuals with desipramine concentrations of 200–300 ng/ml do not have intolerable side-effects. In light of a ceiling effect, plasma assessments become crucial. In fact, by using the limited extant data for estimators (given the dosages provided in these studies and the magnitude of the interaction between desipramine and methadone that has been thus far reported), a calculated approximation is that 40% of the subjects were above 200 ng. If so, this level of subjects surpassing a desipramine ceiling would be sufficient to explain the apparent inefficacy

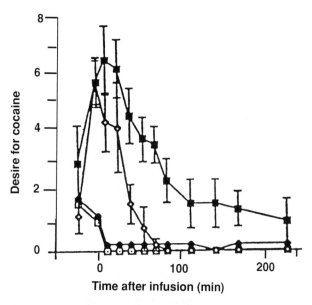

**Figure 8–3.** **Effect of chronic desipramine treatment on cocaine-induced cocaine craving.** Intravenous cocaine (0.5 mg per kg of body weight) or cocaine placebo infused in five subjects after long-term treatment with desipramine hydrochloride (150 mg per day for greater than 10 days) or placebo maintenance. □ = placebo/placebo, ♦ = placebo/desipramine, ■ = cocaine/placebo, and ◊ = cocaine/desipramine.

Source.   Reprinted with permission from Gawin FH: "Cocaine Addiction: Psychology and Neuropsysiology." *Science* 251:1580–1586, 1991. Copyright 1991 American Association for the Advancement of Science.

of desipramine in these two trials. In addition, this interaction produces increases in methadone levels, which were not measured in either study. It is plausible that increased methadone produces a mild opioid high that in turn provides a cue for the stimulant high and potential countertherapeusis. Hence, comparisons of methadone levels in placebo and medication cells, and possibly raising (placebo) or lowering (desipramine) doses for matching on this variable, becomes essential.

Another possibility explaining the lack of robust desipramine effects in prior methadone trials concerns pharmacodynamics. It remains possible that cyclic antidepressants do not produce an antianhedonic effect in cocaine-neuroadapted individuals who are on methadone. The rationale for cyclic antidepressant use for cocaine dependence is that chronic cocaine disrupts reward activity and that cyclic antidepressants, via a secondary or tertiary effect that requires a time lag, increase reward function. Opioid receptors have been clearly identified on the cell bodies of dopaminergic reward neurons, and it appears that opioid euphoria (and other substance-induced euphorias) occurs via activation of these same neurons. Neuroadaptations to chronic opioid use decrease dopamine efflux, explaining clinical reward disruption and increasing psychological symptoms of withdrawal dysphoria as well as decreases in electrophysiological indices of reward (such as response threshold increments and firing rate decreases) in chronic opioid administration to animals. In rodents, opioid administration has been used to reverse opioid neuroadaptations and reverse some symptoms of opioid dependence and protracted withdrawal by normalizing intrasynaptic dopamine concentrations. The increased tonic activation of the cell body by methadone increases reward cell firing and would make it appear, based on resultant dopamine efflux, that neuroadaptive desensitization does not exist, which might *eliminate the signal for cyclic antidepressants to act and produce receptor counter-adaptation.* Tricyclic antidepressants have no positive mood effects in normal individuals, presumably because intrasynaptic dopamine concentrations in reward regions of the brain are already normal, as they would be in someone with opioid dependence while compensated by methadone treatment. No data exist to exclude the possibility that methadone itself substantially interferes with desipramine resensitization of cocaine-induced neuroadaptation. If this possibility is shown to be a reality,

then new pharmacological strategies will need to be devised for this subpopulation. These considerations open new avenues to investigate other treatments.

One such strategy is buprenorphine treatment. Originally, buprenorphine was thought to attenuate cocaine self-administration in primates by attenuating cocaine euphoria (Mello et al. 1989), but more revealing place-preference studies in rodents (Brown et al. 1991) demonstrate self-administration decreases because buprenorphine amplifies cocaine euphoria. Preliminary clinical trials using buprenorphine have demonstrated partial efficacy in facilitating abstinence, but multiple, larger scale controlled trials are needed.

A newer treatment for depression and substance abuse, with a markedly different mechanism of action than cyclic antidepressants regarding brain reward effects, is the group of promising, selective antagonists, which work by interfering with self-regulatory dopaminergic receptor sites at presynaptic dopaminergic autoreceptors; dopamine, subtype 1 ($D_1$), receptors; and perhaps $D_5$ receptors, to regulate dopamine reward efflux. Flupenthixol is under substantial scrutiny as an aid to abstinence initiation and an anticraving agent in non-methadone-maintenance crack cocaine dependence. Flupenthixol is a thioxanthene derivative used for two decades throughout Europe, Canada, the Middle and Far East, and South America. Double-blind assessments, principally in Scandinavia, demonstrate that flupenthixol possesses unique properties, having both rapid antidepressant activity at low doses (Poldinger and Sieberns 1983) and neuroleptic activity at higher doses (Robertson and Trimble 1982). The mechanism for flupenthixol's dual, dose-dependent actions is not yet established with certainty, but the prevailing explanation is that flupenthixol's neuroleptic properties are produced like those of other neuroleptics, by conventional postsynaptic, $D_2$ receptor blocking activity, resulting in decreases in dopaminergic activation of postsynaptic elements. Neuroleptics and other dopamine blocking agents, including high-dose flupenthixol, attenuate stimulant effects in animals, presumably by diminishing postsynaptic receptor exposure to stimulant-induced increases in synaptic dopamine concentrations (Wise 1984). In humans, the dosages employed would be considered extreme. In humans, low, clinically acceptable concentrations of conventional phenothiazine or butyrophenone neuroleptics appear to be incapable of completely blocking stimulant effects

(Wise 1984; Sherer et al., in press) and also appear to exacerbate anhedonic stimulant withdrawal symptoms (Wise 1984; Gawin 1986b), resulting in an extreme patient resistance to neuroleptic treatment. Thus neuroleptic efficacy and dosing does not appear consistent with promoting cocaine abstinence initiation.

As an antidepressant, flupenthixol, in low doses, is thus far reported to be virtually devoid of side effects and to act more rapidly than conventional antidepressants in as few as 3 days (Poldinger and Sieberns 1983). At such dosages its high-affinity binding to block $D_1$ receptors presumably predominates. Its $D_1$ receptor affinity is far greater than its $D_2$ receptor affinity. This property does not exist in any other U.S. marketed agent. Flupenthixol's antidepressant activities were discovered during routine clinical use and confirmed by double-blind experiments comparing its efficacy in depressive disorders to the efficacy of tricyclics (reviewed in Gawin et al. 1989b). We have previously hypothesized that flupenthixol's low-dose antidepressant effects occur because, at lower concentrations, flupenthixol blocks negative feedback inhibition. We initially suggested flupenthixol may demonstrate greater affinity for dopamine autoreceptors than postsynaptic receptors and preferentially bind to these inhibitory sites. Increased dopaminergic activity and antianhedonic, antidepressant activity would thus follow administration of low doses of flupenthixol. At higher dosages and plasma concentrations, as effects on postsynaptic $D_2$ receptors predominate, cocaine-blocking, anhedonia-inducing, neuroleptic-like activity might occur. Significantly, low-dose flupenthixol has been demonstrated to lack the anhedonia-inducing effects of neuroleptics in animal models (Ettenburg et al. 1981) and to lack characteristic neuroleptic-like behavioral effects in humans (Mattila 1988). Recent data demonstrate that postsynaptic $D_1$ receptors can be inhibitory, with effects opposite to $D_2$ receptors on cyclic adenosine monophosphate (cAMP) and the second messenger system. Other data suggest $D_1$ receptors exist on interneurons that provide inhibitory feedback to mesolimbic dopaminergic neurons. Either of these, or a selective presynaptic autoreceptor effect, would explain flupenthixol's dual dose-dependent actions. Finally, assessments at the recently discovered $D_5$ receptor disclose flupenthixol properties that are identical to those of $D_1$ receptors. Again, all other neuroleptics in U.S. clinical use are devoid of similar $D_5$ activity. Hence, collectively or individually, these selective, highly potent actions explain how flupenthixol may display unique, decidedly nonneuroleptic, prohedonic properties when employed at low doses (Gawin et al. 1992; Khalsa et al. 1993b).

**Other pharmacological strategies for treatment.** Other pharmacologic treatment strategies are at stages of preliminary investigation (Gawin and Kleber 1984, 1986b; Jonsson et al. 1969; Nunes et al. 1989; Rowbotham et al. 1984). Possible stimulant blockade has been tried using lithium, carbamazepine, $\alpha$-methyl-para-tyrosine, trazodone, imipramine, fenfluramine, or neuroleptics as well as multiple specific agonists and antagonists of the known serotonin-receptor subtypes. Efforts are also under way to design a molecule that blocks cocaine's activity by binding to dopamine reuptake sites without blocking reuptake itself. These efforts have either not demonstrated greater than partial blockade or present side effects that preclude compliance. Preliminary attempts aimed at increasing dopaminergic neurotransmission either directly or via manipulation of serotonergic inputs using L-dopa/carbidopa, mazindol, pergolide, fenfluramine, ondansetron, $\alpha$-methyl-para-tyrosine, methysergide, tyrosine, amantadine, trihexyphenidyl, bromocriptine, carbamazepine, ritanserin, mianserin, and methylphenidate have generally reported short-term decreases in craving, but longer term, controlled, double-blind assessments are needed to ensure these effects generalize to outpatients and are not overly transient (Chadwick et al. 1990; Dackis and Gold 1985; Gawin et al. 1985; Gold et al. 1983; Halikas et al. 1991; Khantzian 1983; Tennant and Tarver 1986). Monoamine oxidase inhibitors (MAOIs) have also been reported to be useful in preventing relapse (Resnick and Resnick 1985). The dangers of using MAOIs while concurrent stimulant use might occur, however, are unclear. Potentially lethal interaction could occur. Almost half of the initial reports of death due to amphetamine involved MAOI interactions (Kalant and Kalant 1979); it is not clear if interactions with cocaine are less dangerous. Potential dangers have consequently limited trials with these agents. No systematic pharmacotherapy outcome trials were reported during the previous amphetamine epidemic.

It should be noted that experimental pharmacotherapies are included here under treatments for engagement and abstinence initiation. No long-term pharmacotherapy conferring enduring immunity to stimulant abuse is being tested in humans. Although some blocking agents have been tried clinically without evident blockade and preclinical trials of new blocking agents are under way, there does not yet appear to be a naltrexone-like agent to block relapse in stimulant-abusing patients.

## Relapse Prevention

Relapse prevention techniques are introduced gradually at treatment onset. They become central after abstinence has been initiated. Although the techniques described for abstinence initiation also promote long-term abstinence, other relapse prevention measures include specific, additional techniques, described in detail in reports by Marlatt and Gordon (1980) and Washton et al. (1985), to facilitate enduring abstinence.

All outpatient treatments provide prolonged support to help patients withstand craving without relapse. Most often, long-term group psychotherapy is used, modeled on self-help support groups like those of Alcoholics Anonymous. Groups are often combined with individualized peer support, family or couples therapy, behavioral contracts with aversive contingencies (Anker and Crowley 1982), or individual psychotherapies that actively focus on relapse issues such as "slips," cognitive factors, and the development of tools to manage future episodes of craving without relapse (Khantzian et al. 1984; Rounsaville et al. 1985; Washton et al. 1985).

The techniques used are largely the same as those used postwithdrawal in other substance abuse treatments (Marlatt and Gordon 1980). As noted, extinction of conditioned cues may be the most important relapse prevention measure for stimulant-abusing individuals (O'Brien et al. 1990). Stimulant-abusing individuals face a situation similar to one of those who smoke cigarettes or abuse alcohol, in which the drug must become *psychologically unavailable* because it cannot, with certainty, be made physically unavailable (Kleber and Gawin 1984). Abusers must eventually sustain abstinence within the setting where abuse developed. Under a conditioning model, abstinence in the context of everyday cues and stressors—an opportunity for extinction to occur with controlled cravings without relapse—is a prerequisite to consistent long-term amelioration of stimulant craving (Kleber and Gawin 1984).

Systematic studies that compare relapse prevention approaches to other therapies are in progress. Until they appear, all approaches claim success. It is our opinion that all are partially successful, producing sustained reductions in stimulant craving, despite divergent techniques, through the common mechanism of supporting abstinence while extinction of conditioned craving is allowed to proceed.

In these treatments, there are four stages for extinction of craving. First, during abstinence initiation, enforced abstinence from drug use is linked to strict avoidance of conditioned cues. Second, stimuli and cues are reintroduced psychologically in the context of developing strategies for managing stimulant temptation. Third, reentry into the cue-rich environment gradually occurs under controlled conditions. Fourth, successful abstinence is supplemented with maintenance therapies (e.g., continuous self-help and aftercare groups, resumptions of treatment) to counteract the long-term episodic reemergence of stimulant craving.

Current research is beginning to assess specific psychotherapeutic techniques in relapse prevention (O'Brien et al. 1990). Systematic desensitization, used originally to extinguish conditioned anxiety, is beginning to be researched in conditioned stimulant craving. This technique initially uses imaging and relaxation techniques to induce manageable craving and then proceeds to a graded series of actual craving-inducing situations. Research tools, such as manual-guided therapies, are now being used for the first time to determine what techniques are most useful, and in what subpopulations, among stimulant-abusing individuals.

## Stages in Recovery and Treatment

The stage of recovery on seeking treatment varies for each stimulant-abusing individual. Some break cycles of abuse themselves, appearing after numerous prolonged periods of abstinence could not be sustained. Such patients clearly require a treatment focus on relapse prevention. Because craving is intermittent after abstinence has been consolidated, there is often a tendency to leave treatment prematurely as episodes between cravings prolong. This must be countered in treatment. Some appear after multiple unsuccessful attempts to sustain any abstinence and have never attained more than a few days free of stimulants. The patient's recent history of abuse and past treatment history are thus crucial to determining appropriate treatments.

## Outcome Studies

Data from multiple programs using different psychotherapeutic approaches in pre-crack samples indicate outpatient treatment regularly initiates abstinence. Of the patients who remain in outpatient treatment programs, 10%–90% cease stimulant use (Anker and Crowley 1982; Higgins et al. 1991; Kang et al. 1991; Kleber and Gawin 1984; Rawson et al. 1986; Siegel 1982; Washton et al. 1985). Samples and methods are not comparable between these treatment programs, however, and there is no evidence to suggest any one treatment approach is superior. Further, those patients who remain in treatment probably make up the less-impaired portion of the abuse spectrum, and dropouts are ignored in most reports. Thus far, collective experience can be simply summarized: staying in treatment is the single most important determinant of successful outcome. Further, it is our impression that the recent generation of cocaine-abusing patients was more treatment responsive than prior amphetamine- or current crack-abusing patients. Treatment of crack-only populations, perhaps the most difficult of all, are only now beginning to be researched and published. Anecdotal reports indicate outpatient treatment engagement may be as low as 8%–15% in psychotherapy alone programs.

## Diagnostic Considerations

A presentation of stimulant use does not always indicate a diagnosis of stimulant abuse. The wide spectrum of stimulant use is reflected in the impression that a wider severity spectrum exists in stimulant-abusing individuals who are seeking treatment than in other substance-abusing populations (Kleber and Gawin 1984). Because of cocaine's now adverse reputation, its great expense, and the substantial amount of nonaddictive (or not-yet-addictive) use that exists, severe psychosocial disruption can lead to treatment seeking despite use in almost homeopathic amounts. When stimulant use is itself minor, it may serve as a symptom of other primary problems (e.g., family discord), and alternative or adjunctive treatment may be indicated.

Excluding coexistent psychiatric disorders is a clinical necessity in stimulant abuse treatment. Psychiatric patients with major affective disorders, atypical depressive disorders, adult attention-deficit hyperactivity disorder (ADHD), bipolar or cyclothymic disorder, or narcolepsy have all been reported to cease illicit stimulant use when appropriate medications are substituted (Gawin and Kleber 1984; Khantzian et al. 1984; Rounsaville et al. 1991; Weiss et al. 1983). Schizophrenic patients have also been known to abuse stimulants. In four systematic studies using DSM-III or DSM-IV criteria, lifetime psychiatric disorders were present in 25%–50% of stimulant abusers seeking treatment (Gawin 1986a; Gawin and Kleber 1985a; Rounsaville et al. 1991; Weiss et al. 1986). Because acute aftereffects of a stimulant binge can mimic delusional or depressive disorders, and acute intoxication can mimic mania, it is crucial to separate out effects of acute stimulant use in clinical presentations. In practice, this involves careful clinical interviewing—searching for family history of psychiatric disorder as well as searching personal histories for psychiatric symptoms during intervals free of substance abuse.

Because substance abuse and psychiatric disorder often both become evident in young adulthood, establishing a primary diagnosis in this way is often difficult. Tentative diagnoses, warranting appropriate pharmacotherapies, therefore usually must be made based on symptom presentation, provided that several nights of sleep normalization and ensured abstinence (hospitalization or urinalysis) have occurred, if depressive, manic, or psychotic symptoms have not remitted. If abstinence is maintained, whether the diagnosis is primary or secondary can then be determined based on the subsequent clinical course. In many cases, continued, sporadic, stimulant use makes it impossible to determine whether stimulant abuse or another Axis I disorder is primary or secondary.

These preliminary data, as well as collective clinical experience, indicate that important subpopulations with Axis I diagnoses exist that are responsive to specific pharmacotherapies. Recent reports indicate a great escalation in cocaine abuse among schizophrenic individuals has occurred with the advent of inexpensive crack cocaine, but no systematic treatment studies in this population have as yet been reported. However, larger samples and double-blind comparisons are needed to substantiate these preliminary findings before clinical conclusions can be drawn. Our current clinical approach is to adhere strictly to maximal diagnostic criteria for ADHD-residual type, requiring both a childhood diagnosis of ADHD and a treatment trial with stimulants during childhood, before employing stimulant treatment for cocaine abuse. We also require that DSM-IV criteria for cyclothymia be fully met before using lithium.

Finally, it should be noted that panic anxiety may protect against stimulant use, particularly if stimulant-induced anxiety attacks have occurred (Geracioti and Post 1991).

## ▼ RESEARCH CONSIDERATIONS

Compared with treatment of depression, both psychotherapy and pharmacotherapy data for stimulant abuse are at a primitive developmental stage. In this chapter, we have summarized current knowledge and treatment strategies. We would like to conclude with the hope that more scientific stimulant abuse treatment will evolve by summarizing important methodological points for future stimulant abuse research. These points will all require clarification and consensus. Then, more definitive research might create a coherent, scientifically acceptable body of outcome data on treatment for cocaine-abusing individuals. These methodological points include the following:

1. *Severity.* No treatment studies reported thus far have stratified samples according to any criteria of abuse severity, and no generally accepted indices of severity of abuse exist that would allow comparisons across samples to be made.

2. *Self-selection artifacts.* Most of the treatment studies described have a substantial proportion of early dropouts or patients eliminated at screening who have not been contrasted to those remaining in treatment. No systematic engagement assessments have been described. Data characterizing the populations that find particular treatments aversive or inadequate are needed.

3. *Recovery.* There is no consensus regarding how long abstinence must be maintained before recovery occurs or treatment can end. Outcome criteria are widely variable across the studies conducted thus far and, as of this writing, no studies have reported outcome in terms of changes in indices of psychosocial functioning.

4. *Heterogeneity.* Multiple sources of sample heterogeneity exist in cocaine treatment populations, including variations in sociodemographics, psychiatric symptomatology, psychosocial resources, patterns and duration of use, degree of impairment, treatment history, and other substances abused, among many others. Do such factors differ among treatment populations, and do they differentially affect outcome?

5. *Course and neuroadaptation.* There are few data available on the natural history of stimulant abuse and few data available regarding which patients are likely to deteriorate, which may be expected to maintain stable states of dysfunction, and which will improve. This issue is related to the relative importance of preexisting psychopathology versus neuroadaptation. Although improved characterizations of abstinence symptoms have emerged, more systematic assessments of clinical course are needed, and the contribution of neuroadaptation to continuation of human abuse requires further clarification.

On balance, several treatment approaches are in current use and are demonstrating encouraging but controversial results. Others are being investigated and promise even further improvements. It now appears no more likely that any single treatment will arise as a definitive treatment for all cocaine-abusing patients than it has for opioid- or alcohol-abusing patients. Today, treatment for cocaine-abusing patients should be based on a flexible integration of various approaches, based on the clinical assessment of the characteristics and needs of the individual patient.

## ▼ REFERENCES

Abelson HI, Miller JD: A decade of trends in cocaine use in the household population, in Cocaine Use in America: Epidemiologic and Clinical Perspectives, NIDA Res Monogr 61. Edited by Adams EH, Kozel NJ. Rockville, MD, Department of Health and Human Services, 1985

Adams EH, Durell J: Cocaine: a growing public health problem, in Cocaine: Pharmacology, Effects, and Treatment of Abuse, NIDA Res Monogr 50. Edited by Grabowski J. Rockville, MD, Department of Health and Human Services, 1984, pp 9–14

Alper KR, Chabot RJ, Kim AH, et al: Quantitative EEG

correlates of crack cocaine dependence. Psychiatry Res 35:95–105, 1990

American Psychiatric Association: Diagnostic and Statistical Manual of Mental Disorders, 3rd Edition. Washington, DC, American Psychiatric Association, 1980

American Psychiatric Association: Diagnostic and Statistical Manual of Mental Disorders, 4th Edition. Washington, DC, American Psychiatric Association, 1994

Anker AL, Crowley TJ: Use of contingency contracts in specialty clinics for cocaine abuse, in Problems of Drug Dependence, National Institute on Drug Abuse Research Monograph. Edited by Harris LS. National Institute on Drug Abuse, 1982, pp 452–459

Arndt IO, Dorozynsky L, Woody GE, et al: Desipramine treatment of cocaine dependence in methadone-maintained patients. Arch Gen Psychiatry 49:888–893, 1992

Bakti SL, Manfredi L, Sorenson JL, et al: Fluoxetine for cocaine abuse in methadone patients: preliminary findings. NIDA Res Monogr 105:516–517, 1990

Bakti SL, Manfredi L, Jacob P, et al: Double-blind fluoxetine treatment of cocaine dependence in methadone maintenance treatment patients: interim analysis (NIH Publ No 93-3505). National Institute on Drug Abuse Research Monograph, Problems of Drug Dependence 132:102, 1993

Banerjee SP, Sharman VK, Kung-Cheung LS, et al: Cocaine and D-amphetamine induce changes in central beta-adrenoceptor sensitivity: effects of acute and chronic drug treatment. Brain Res 175:119–130, 1979

Bell DS: The experimental reproduction of amphetamine psychosis. Arch Gen Psychiatry 127:1170–1175, 1970

Borison RL, Hitri A, Klawans HL, et al: A new animal model for schizophrenia: behavioral and receptor binding studies, in Catecholamines: Basic and Clinical Frontiers. Edited by Usdin E. New York, Pergamon, 1979

Boudin HM: Contingency contracting as a therapeutic tool in the deceleration of amphetamine use. Behav Res Ther 3:604–608, 1972

Brotman AW, Witkie SM, Gelenberg AJ, et al: An open trial of maprotiline for the treatment of cocaine abuse: a pilot study. J Clin Psychopharmacol 8:125–127, 1988

Brown EE, Finlay JM, Wong JT, et al: Behavioral and neurochemical interactions between cocaine and buprenorphine: implications for the pharmacotherapy of cocaine abuse. J Pharmacol Exp Ther 256:119–26, 1991

Brown WA, Corrivieau P, Egert MH: Acute psychologic and neuroendocrine effects of dextroamphetamine and methylphenidate. Psychopharmacology (Berl) 58:189–195, 1978

Bush MN, Rubenstein R, Hoffman I, et al: Spontaneous pneumomediastinum as a consequence of cocaine use. N Y State J Med 84:618–619, 1984

Byck R: Cocaine use and research: three histories, in Cocaine: Clinical and Biobehavioral Aspects. Edited by Fisher S, Raskin A, Uhlenhuth EH. New York, Oxford University Press, 1986

Chadwick MJ, Gregory DL, Wendling G: A double-blind amino acids, L-tryptophan and L-tyrosine, and placebo study with cocaine-dependent subjects in an inpatient chemical dependency treatment center. Am J Drug Alcohol Abuse 16:275–286, 1990

Chasnoff IJ, Burns WJ, Schnoll SH, et al: Cocaine use in pregnancy. N Engl J Med 313:666–669, 1985

Colpaert FC, Niemegeers CH, Janssen PA: Discriminative stimulus properties of cocaine: neuropharmacological characteristics as derived from stimulus generalization experiments. Pharmacol Biochem Behav 10:535–546, 1979

Connell PH: Some observations concerning amphetamine misuse: its diagnosis, management, and treatment with special reference to research needs, drugs and agement, and treatment with special reference to research needs, in Drugs and Youth. Edited by Wittenborn JR, Brill H, Smith JP, et al. Springfield, IL, Charles C Thomas, 1969, pp 125–134

Cregler LL, Mark H: Relation of acute myocardial infarction to cocaine abuse. Am J Cardiol 56:794, 1985

Dackis CA, Gold MS: Bromocriptine as a treatment of cocaine abuse. Lancet 1:1151–1152, 1985

Ehrlich P, McGeehan M: Cocaine recovery support groups and the language of recovery. J Psychoactive Drugs 17:11–17, 1985

Ellinwood EH Jr: Amphetamine psychosis; I: description of the individuals and process. J Nerv Ment Dis 144:273–283, 1967

Ellinwood EH: Assault and homicide associated with amphetamine abuse. Am J Psychiatry 127:1170–

1175, 1970

Ellinwood EH: The epidemiology of stimulant abuse, in Drug Use: Epidemiological and Sociological Approaches. Edited by Josephson F, Carroll E. Washington, DC, Hemisphere, 1974, pp 303–329

Ellinwood EH, Petrie WM: Dependence on amphetamine, cocaine and other stimulants, in Drug Abuse: Clinical and Basic Aspects. Edited by Pradhan SN. New York, Mosby, 1977, pp 248–262

Ettenburg A, Pettit H, Bloom F, et al: Heroin and cocaine intravenous self-administration in rats: mediation by separate neural systems. Psychopharmacology (Berl) 78:204–209, 1981

Fischman MW, Schuster CR, Resnekov I, et al: Cardiovascular and subjective effects of intravenous cocaine administration in humans. Arch Gen Psychiatry 10:535–546, 1976

Fishel R, Hamamoto G, Barbul A, et al: Cocaine colitis: is this a new syndrome? Dis Colon Rectum 28:264–266, 1985

Fitzgerald JL, Reid JJ: Chronic cocaine treatment does not alter rat striatal $D_2$ autoreceptor sensitivity to pergolide. Brain Res 541:327–333, 1991

Freud S: Uber Coca. Centralblat für Gesamulte Therape 2:289–314, 1884

Gawin FH: Drugs and eros: reflections on aphrodisiacs. J Psychoactive Drugs 10:227–235, 1978

Gawin FH: Cocaine: psychiatric update. Presented at the 139th Meeting of the American Psychiatric Association, Washington, DC, May 15, 1986a

Gawin FH: Neuroleptic reduction of cocaine-induced paranoia but not euphoria? Psychopharmacolgy (Berl) 90:142–143, 1986b

Gawin FH: Cocaine addiction: psychology and neurophysiology [published erratum appears in Science 253:494, 1991]. Science 251:1580–1586, 1991

Gawin FH, Ellinwood EH: Stimulants: actions, abuse, and treatment. N Engl J Med 318:1173–1183, 1988

Gawin FH, Kleber HD: Cocaine abuse treatment: open pilot trial with desipramine and lithium carbonate. Arch Gen Psychiatry 42:903–910, 1984

Gawin FH, Kleber HD: Cocaine abuse in a treatment population: patterns and diagnostic distractions, in Cocaine Use in America: Epidemiologic and Clinical Perspectives, NIDA Res Monogr 61. Edited by Adams EH, Kozel NJ. Rockville, MD, Department of Health and Human Services, 1985a, pp 182–192

Gawin FH, Kleber HD: Neuroendocrine findings in chronic cocaine abusers. Br J Psychiatry 147:569–573, 1985b

Gawin FH, Kleber HD: Abstinence symptomatology and psychiatric diagnosis in cocaine abusers. Arch Gen Psychiatry 43:107–113, 1986a

Gawin FH, Kleber HD: Pharmacological treatment of cocaine abuse. Psychiatr Clin North Am 9:573–583, 1986b

Gawin FH, Riordan C, Kleber HD: Methylphenidate use in non-ADD cocaine abusers: a negative study. Am J Drug Alcohol Abuse 11:193–197, 1985

Gawin FH, Kleber HD, Byck R, et al: Desipramine facilitation of initial cocaine abstinence. Arch Gen Psychiatry 46:117–121, 1989a

Gawin FH, Allen D, Humblestone B: Outpatient treatment of crack cocaine smoking with flupenthixol decanoate: a preliminary report. Arch Gen Psychiatry 46:322–325, 1989b

Gawin FH, Khalsa ME, Brown J, et al: Flupenthixol treatment of crack users: initial double-blind results (NIH Publ No 93-3505). NIDA Research Monograph Problems of Drug Dependence 132:319, 1992

Gay GR: Clinical management of acute and toxic cocaine poisoning. Ann Emerg Med 11:562–572, 1982

Geracioti TD Jr, Post RM: Onset of panic disorder associated with rare use of cocaine. Biol Psychiatry 29:403–406, 1991

Giannini AJ, Malone DA, Giannini MC, et al: Treatment of depression in chronic cocaine and phencyclidine abuse with desipramine. J Clin Pharmacol 26:211–214, 1986

Goeders NE, Smith JE: Cortical dopaminergic involvement in cocaine reinforcement. Science 253:195–203, 1982

Gold MS, Estroff TW: The comprehensive evaluation of cocaine and opiate abusers, in Handbook of Psychiatric Diagnostic Procedures, Vol 2. Edited by Hall RCW, Beresford TP. Jamaica, NY, Spectrum Publications, 1985, pp 213–230

Gold MS, Pottash ALC, Annitto WD, et al: Cocaine withdrawal: efficacy of tyrosine. Presented at the 13th Annual Meeting of the Society for Neuroscience, Boston, MA, November 7, 1983

Goodman LS, Gilman A: The Pharmacological Basis of Therapeutics, 6th Edition. New York, Macmillan, 1985

Grinspoon L, Bakalar JB: Drug dependence: nonnarcotic agents, in Comprehensive Textbook of Psychiatry, 3rd Edition. Edited by Kaplan HI,

Freedman AM, Sadock BJ. Baltimore, MD, Williams & Wilkins, 1980

Gunne LM, Anggard E: Pharmacokinetic studies with amphetamines: relationship to neuropsychiatric disorders. J Pharmacokinet Biopharm 1:481–495, 1973

Halikas JA, Crosby RD, Carlson GA, et al: Cocaine reduction in unmotivated crack users using carbamazepine versus placebo in a short-term, double-blind crossover design. Clin Pharmacol Ther 50:81–95, 1991

Hall S, Tanis S, Banys D: The interaction of enhanced continuity of care and desipramine in early cocaine treatment (NIH Publ No 93-3505). National Institute on Drug Abuse Research Monograph, Problems of Drug Dependence 132:207, 1992

Henry DJ, White FJ: Repeated cocaine administration causes persistent enhancement of $D_1$ dopamine receptor sensitivity within the rat nucleus accumbens. J Pharmacol Exp Ther 258:882–90, 1991

Higgins ST, Delaney D, Budney A, et al: A behavioral approach to achieving initial cocaine abstinence. Am J Psychiatry 148:1218–24, 1991

Hollander E, Nunes E, Decaria CM, et al: Dopaminergic sensitivity and cocaine abuse: response to apomorphine. Psychiatry Res 33:161–169, 1990

Itkonen J, Schnoll S, Glassroth J: Pulmonary dysfunction in "freebase" cocaine users. Arch Intern Med 144:219–257, 1984

Jatlow P, Barash PG, Van Dyke C, et al: Cocaine and succinylcholine sensitivity: a new caution. Anesthesia and Analgesia Current Research 58:235–238, 1979

Johanson CE: Assessment of the dependence potential of cocaine in animals, in Cocaine: Pharmacology, Effects and Treatment of Abuse, NIDA Res Monogr 50. Edited by Grabowski J. Rockville, MD, Department of Health and Human Services, 1984, pp 54–71

Jonsson LE, Gunne LM, Anggard E: Effects of alpha-methyltyrosine in amphetamine-dependent subjects. Pharmacologia Clinica 2:27–29, 1969

Kalant H, Kalant OJ: Death in amphetamine users: causes and rates, in Amphetamine Use, Misuse, and Abuse. Edited by Smith DE, Wesson DR, Buxton ME, et al. Boston, MA, GK Hall & Co, 1979

Kang SY, Kleiman PH, Woody GE, et al: Outcomes for cocaine abusers after once-a-week psychosocial therapy. Am J Psychiatry 148:630–5, 1991

Karoum F, Suddath RL, Wyatt RJ, et al: Chronic co-

caine and rat brain catecholamines: long-term reduction in hypothalamic and frontal cortex dopamine metabolism. Eur J Pharmacol 186:1–8, 1990

Khalsa ME, Anglin D, Paredes A: Cocaine abuse: outcomes of therapeutic interventions. Substance Abuse 13:165–179, 1992

Khalsa ME, Gawin FH, Rawson R, et al: A desipramine ceiling in cocaine abusers (NIH Publ No 93-3505). National Institute on Drug Abuse Research Monograph, Problems of Drug Dependence 132:318, 1993a

Khalsa ME, Jatlow P, Gawin FH: Flupenthixol and desipramine markedly increase engagement in crack abuse treatment. Paper presented at the 55th annual scientific meeting of the College on Problems of Drug Dependence, Inc., Toronto, Canada, June 1993b

Khalsa ME, Paredes A, Anglin D: Combinations of treatment modalities and therapeutic outcome for cocaine dependence, in NIDA Research Monograph: Assessing Neurotoxicity of Drugs of Abuse. Washington, DC, U.S. Government Printing Office (in press)

Khantzian EJ: Cocaine dependence, an extreme case and marked improvement with methylphenidate treatment. Am J Psychiatry 140:784–785, 1983

Khantzian EJ, Khantzian NH: Cocaine addiction: is there a psychological predisposition? Psychiatric Annals 14:753–759, 1984

Khantzian EJ, Gawin FH, Riordan C, et al: Methylphenidate treatment of cocaine dependence: a preliminary report. J Subst Abuse Treat 1:107–112, 1984

Kleber HD, Gawin FH: Cocaine abuse: a review of current and experimental treatments, in Cocaine: Pharmacology, Effects, and Treatment of Abuse, NIDA Res Monogr 50 (DHHS Publ No 84-1326). Edited by Grabowski J. Rockville, MD, Department of Health and Human Services, 1984

Kokkinidis L, Zacharko RM, Predy PA: Post-amphetamine depression of self-stimulation responding from the substantia nigra: reversal by tricyclic antidepressants. Pharmacol Biochem Behav 13:379–383, 1980

Kosten TR, Gawin FH, Morgan C, et al: Evidence for altered desipramine disposition in methadone-maintained patients treated for cocaine abuse. Am J Drug Alcohol Abuse 16:329–336, 1990a

Kosten TR, Morgan CM, Falcione J, et al: Pharmacotherapy for cocaine-abusing methadone-maintained patients using amantadine or desipramine. Arch Gen Psychiatry 49:894–898, 1990b

Kosten TR, Gawin FH, Silverman DG, et al: Intravenous cocaine challenges during desipramine maintenance. Neuropsychopharmacology 7:169–176, 1992

Kramer JC, Fischman VS, Littlefield DC: Amphetamine abuse patterns and effects of high doses taken intravenously. JAMA 201:305–309, 1967

Lasagna L, von Felsinger JM, Beecher HK: Drug induced mood changes in man; I: observations on healthy subjects, chronically ill patients, and postaddicts. JAMA 157:1066–1020, 1955

Leal J, Ziedonis D, Kosten T: Antisocial personality disorder as a prognostic factor for pharmacotherapy of cocaine dependence. Paper presented at the 55th annual scientific meeting of the College on Problems of Drug Dependence, Inc., Toronto, Canada, June 1993

Lee MA, Bowers MM, Nach JF, et al: Neuroendocrine measures of dopaminergic function in chronic cocaine users. Psychiatry Res 33:151–9, 1990

Leith NJ, Barrett RJ: Amphetamine and the reward system: evidence for tolerance and post-drug depression. Psychopharmacology (Berl) 46:19–25, 1976

Leith NH, Barrett RJ: Self-stimulation and amphetamine: tolerance to $d$ and $l$ isomers and cross tolerance to cocaine and methylphenidate. Psychopharmacology (Berl) 74:23–28, 1981

Lewin L: Phantastica. Berlin, Verlang von Georg Stilke, 1924

Maddox JF, Desmond DP: Residence relocation inhibits opioid dependence. Arch Gen Psychiatry 39:1313–1317, 1982

Maier HW: Der Kokainismus. Leipzig, Georg Thieme Verlag, 1926

Margolin A, Kosten T, Petrakis I, et al: An open pilot study of bupropion and psychotherapy for the treatment of cocaine abuse in methadone-maintained patients. NIDA Res Monogr 105:367–8, 1991

Markou A, Koob GF: Postcocaine anhedonia. An animal model of cocaine withdrawal. Neuropsychopharmacology 4:17–26, 1991

Marlatt GA, Gordon JR: Determinants of relapse: implications for the maintenance of behavior change, in Behavioral Medicine: Changing Health Lifestyles. Edited by Davidson PO, Davidson SM, New York, Brunner/Mazel, 1980, pp 410–452

Mattila MJ, Mattila M, Aranko K: Objective and subjective assessments of the effects of flupenthixol and benzodiazepines on human psychomotor performance. Psychopharmacology (Berl) 95:323–328, 1988

McLellan AT, Woody GE, O'Brien CP: Development of psychiatric illness in drug abusers: possible role of drug preference. N Engl J Med 301:1310–1314, 1979

Mello NK, Mendelson MP, Bree MP, et al: Science 245:859–862, 1989

Nathanson MH: The central action of beta-aminopropyl-benzene (Benzedrine). JAMA 108: 528–531, 1937

National Commission on Marihuana and Drug Abuse: Drug Use in America: Problems in Perspective. Second Report of the National Commission on Marihuana and Drug Abuse. Washington, DC, National Institute on Drug Abuse, 1973

National Institute on Drug Abuse: NIDA Capsules: 1985 National Household Survey on Drug Abuse. Rockville, MD, Press Office of the National Institute on Drug Abuse, 1986

Nunes E, Quitkin FM, Klein D: Imipramine treatment of ambulatory cocaine abusers. Paper presented at the Annual Meeting of the American Psychiatric Association. San Francisco, CA, May 12, 1989

O'Brien CP, Childress AR, McLellan T, et al: Integrating systemic cue exposure with standard treatment in recovering drug dependent patients. Addict Behav 15:355–65, 1990

Poldinger W, Sieberns S: Depression-inducing and antidepressant effects of neuroleptics: experiences with flupenthixol and flupenthixol decanoate. Neuropsychobiology 10:131–136, 1983

Pollack MH, Rosenbaum JF: Fluoxetine treatment of cocaine abuse in heroin addicts. J Clin Psychiatry 52:31–33, 1991

Post RM, Kopanda RT, Black KE: Progressive effects of cocaine on behavior and central amine metabolism in rhesus monkeys: relationship to kindling and psychosis. Biol Psychiatry 11:403–419, 1976

Rauckman EJ, Rosen GM, Cavagnaro J: Norcocaine nitroxide: a potential hepatotoxic metabolite of cocaine. Mol Pharmacol 21:458–462, 1982

Rawson R, Obert J, McCann M, et al: Cocaine Treatment Outcome: Cocaine Use Following Inpatient, Outpatient, and No Treatment, NIDA Res Monogr 67. Rockville, MD, National Institute on Drug

**Stimulants**

Abuse, 1986, 271–277

Reith M, Sershen H, Allen DL, et al: A portion of (3H) cocaine binding in brain is associated with serotonergic neurons. Mol Pharmacol 23:600–606, 1983

Resnick R, Resnick E: Psychological issues in the treatment of cocaine abusers. Paper presented at the Columbia University Symposium on Cocaine Abuse: New Treatment Approaches, New York, January 5, 1985

Ricuaurte GA, Schuster CR, Seiden LS: Long-term effects of repeated methylamphetamine administration on dopamine and serotonin neurons in rat brain: a regional study. Brain Res 193:153–163, 1980

Roberts JR, Quattrochi E, Howland MA: Severe hyperthermia secondary to intravenous drug abuse (letter). Am J Emerg Med 2:373, 1984

Robertson M, Trimble M: Major tranquilizers used as antidepressants. J Affect Disord 4:173–195, 1982

Robertson MW, Leslie CA, Bennett JP Jr, et al: Apparent synaptic dopamine deficiency induced by withdrawal from chronic cocaine treatment. Brain Res 538:337–339, 1991

Rounsaville BJ, Gawin FH, Kleber HD: Interpersonal psychotherapy (IPT) adapted for ambulatory cocaine abusers. Am J Drug Alcohol Abuse 11:171–191, 1985

Rounsaville BJ, Anton SF, Carroll K, et al: Psychiatric diagnoses of treatment-seeking cocaine abusers. Arch Gen Psychiatry 48:43–51, 1991

Rowbotham M, Jones RT, Benowitz N, et al: Trazadone-oral cocaine interactions. Arch Gen Psychiatry 41:895–899, 1984

Rumbaugh C, Bergeron R, Fang H, et al: Cerebral angiographic change in the drug abuse patient. Radiology 101:355–344, 1971

Rumbaugh CL, Fang HCH, Wilson GH, et al: Cerebral CT findings in drug abuse: clinical and experimental observations. J Comput Assist Tomogr 4:330–334, 1980

Satel SL, Southwick SM, Gawin FH, et al: Clinical features of cocaine-induced paranoia. Am J Psychiatry 148:495–8, 1991

Schnoll SH, Karrigan J, Kitchen SB, et al: Characteristics of cocaine abusers presenting for treatment, in Cocaine Use in America: Epidemiologic and Clinical Perspectives, NIDA Res Monogr 61. Edited by Adams EH, Kozel NJ. Rockville, MD, Department of Health and Human Services, 1985, pp 171–181

Schuster CR, Fischman MW: Characteristics of human volunteering for a cocaine research project, in Cocaine Use in America: Epidemiologic and Clinical Perspectives, NIDA Res Monogr 61. Edited by Adams EH, Kozel NH. Rockville, MD, Department of Health and Human Services, 1985, pp 158–170

Seiden L: Neurochemical toxic effects of psychomotor stimulants. Presented at the 23rd Annual Meeting of the American College of Neuropsychopharmacology, San Juan, PR, December 12, 1984

Sherer M, Kumor K, Jaffe J: Effects of intravenous cocaine are partially attentuated by haloperidol. Psychiatry Res (in press)

Siegel RK: Cocaine smoking. J Psychoative Drugs 14:321–337, 1982

Siegel RK: New patterns of cocaine use: changing doses and routes, in Cocaine Use in America: Epidemiologic and Clinical Perspectives, NIDA Res Monogr 61. Edited by Adams EH, Kozel NJ. Rockville, MD, Department of Health and Human Services, 1985a, pp 204–220

Siegel RK: Treatment of cocaine abuse: historical and contemporary perspectives. J Psychoative Drugs 17:1–9, 1985b

Simpson DM, Arnau Z: Behavioral withdrawal following several psychoactive drugs. Biochemistry and Behavior 7:59–64, 1977

Smith DE: The characteristics of dependence in high-dose methamphetamine abuse. Int J Addict 4:453–459, 1969

Spyraki C, Fibiger HC, Phillips AC: Cocaine-induced place preference conditioning: lack of effects of neuroleptics and 6 hydroxydopamine lesions. Brain Res 253:195–203, 1982

Strategy Council on Drug Abuse: Federal Strategy for Drug Abuse and Drug Traffic Prevention 1973. Washington, DC, U.S. Government Printing Office, 1973

Taylor DL, Ho BT, Fagan JD: Increased dopamine receptor binding in rat brain by repeated cocaine injection. Community Psychopharmacology 3:137–142, 1979

Tennant F, Tarver A: Double-blind comparison of desipramine and placebo in withdrawal from cocaine dependence, in Problems of Drug Dependence, NIDA Res Monogr 55. Edited by Harris LS. Rockville, MD, Department of Health and Human Services, 1986, pp 159–163

Tunis SL: Assessing thoughts about cocaine and the relationship to short term treatment outcome. Paper presented at the 54th Problems in Drug Dependence Conference, Keystone, CO, June 1992

Utena H: Behavioral aberrations in methamphetamine intoxicated animals and chemical correlates in the brain. Prog Brain Res 21:192–207, 1966

Van Dyke C, Ungerer J, Jatlow P, et al: Intranasal cocaine dose relationships of psychological effects and plasma levels. Int J Psychiatry Med 12:1–13, 1982

Volkow ND, Mullani N, Gould K, et al: Cerebral blood flow in chronic cocaine users: a study with positron emission tomography. Br J Psychiatry 152:641–648, 1988

Volkow ND, Fowler J, Wolf A, et al: Effects of chronic cocaine abuse on postsynaptic dopamine receptors. Am J Psychiatry 147:719, 1990

Volkow ND, Fowler JS, Wolf AP, et al: Changes in brain glucose metabolism in cocaine dependence and withdrawal. Am J Psychiatry 148:621–626, 1991

Washton AM, Gold MS, Pottash ALC: Cocaine abuse: techniques of assessment, diagnosis and treatment. Psychiatr Med 3:185–195, 1985

Watson R, Hartmann E, Schildkraut JJ: Amphetamine withdrawal: affective state, sleep patterns and MHPG excretion. Am J Psychiatry 129:263–269, 1972

Watson R, Bakos L, Compton P, et al: Cocaine use and withdrawal: the effect on sleep and mood. Am J Drug Alcohol Abuse 18:21–28, 1992

Weddington W, Brown B, Haertzen C, et al: Changes in mood, craving, and sleep during short-term abstinence reported by male cocaine addicts. Arch Gen Psychiatry 47:861–868, 1990

Weiss RD: Relapse to cocaine abuse after initiating desipramine treatment. JAMA 260:22545–2546, 1988

Weiss RD, Goldenheim PD, Mirin SM: Pulmonary dysfunction in cocaine smokers. Am J Psychiatry 138:1110–1112, 1981

Weiss RD, Mirin SM, Michael JL: Psychopathology in chronic cocaine abusers. Paper presented at the 136th Annual Meeting of the American Psychiatric Association. New York, May 4, 1983

Weiss WD, Mirin SM, Michael JL, et al: Psychopathology in chronic cocaine abusers. Am J Drug Alcohol Abuse 12:17–29, 1986

Wikler A: Dynamics of drug dependence: implications of a conditioning theory for research. Arch Gen Psychiatry 28:611–616, 1973

Wise R: Neural mechanisms of the reinforcing action of cocaine. NIDA Res Monogr 50:15–53, 1984

Wurmser L: Psychoanalytic considerations of the etiology of compulsive drug use. J Am Psychoanal Assoc 22:820–843, 1979a

Wurmser L: The Hidden Dimension: Psychopathology of Compulsive Drug Use. New York, Jason Aronson, 1979b

Yagi B: Studies in general activity; II: the effect of methamphetamine. Annals of Animal Psychology 13:37–47, 1963

Yokel RA, Wise RA: Increased lever pressing for amphetamine after pimozide in rats: implications for a dopamine theory of reward. Science 221:773–774, 1983

# CHAPTER 9

# Hallucinogens

*J. Thomas Ungerleider, M.D.*
*Robert N. Pechnick, Ph.D.*

Hallucinogens that are likely to be abused include the ergot hallucinogen lysergic acid diethylamide (LSD), which is the prototype of these drugs of abuse; other indolealkylamines such as psilocybin ("magic mushrooms") and dimethyltryptamine (DMT); the phenalkylamines, including mescaline, dimethoxymethylamphetamine (DOM or "STP"), methylenedioxyamphetamine (MDA), and methylenedioxymethamphetamine (MDMA, "Ecstasy," or "X"). The hallucinogen-like drugs, marijuana and phencyclidine (PCP), are covered elsewhere. These hallucinogens, called *psychotomimetics* or *psychedelics* (mind-manifesting), are a group of drugs that produce thought, mood, and perceptual disorders. Depending on dosage, expectation (set), and environment (setting), they also can induce euphoria and a state similar to a transcendental experience.

The term *hallucinogen* means "producer of hallucinations." Many drugs can cause auditory and/or visual hallucinations. These hallucinations may be present as part of a delirium, accompanied by disturbances in judgment, orientation, intellect, memory, and emotion (e.g., an organic brain syndrome). Such delirium also may result from drug withdrawal (e.g., sedative-hypnotic withdrawal or delirium tremens in alcohol withdrawal). When referring to substance abuse, however, the term *hallucinogens* generally refers to a group of compounds that alter consciousness without delirium, sedation, excessive stimulation, or impairment of intellect or memory. The label *hallucinogen* actually is inaccurate because true LSD-induced hallucinations are rare. What are commonly seen are illusory phenomena. An illusion is a perceptual distortion of an actual stimulus in the environment. To "see" someone's face melting is an illusion; to "see" a melting face when no one is present is a hallucination. Consequently, some have called these drugs *illusionogenic*. Those who use the terms *psychedelic* or *mind-manifesting* for hallucinogens (a term coined in 1957 by Osmond) have been criticized as being "pro-drug" much as those who use the term *hallucinogen* have been accused of being "anti-drug" (Osmond 1957). The term *psychotomimetic*, meaning a producer of psychosis, also has been widely used.

Peyote, containing mescaline, is the only halluci-

The authors would like to thank Casaundra Williams Franker for her editorial assistance. Robert N. Pechnick is supported by National Institute on Drug Abuse grants DA04112 and DA05448.

nogen that can be legally used in this country and even this practice has been challenged. Members of Native American religious communities have used it during certain ceremonies in a number of states and in Canada for many years.

In the last few years, there have been some interesting developments with the use of hallucinogens. On the one hand, the production and distribution of hallucinogens remains limited to clandestine laboratories and "street" dealers. The focus of illicit drug use in general has shifted away from those drugs that were once used in an attempt to enhance self-awareness. The new focus has been on drugs that users feel will elevate their mood and increase work output, such as cocaine. To be sure, some still use hallucinogens such as LSD, but cases requiring treatment for acute adverse reactions (e.g., acute panic states, psychoses, flashbacks) have become relatively rare even though its use may again be on the rise (discussion follows). There also have been fewer reports of those using other hallucinogens that were once popular, such as mescaline and psilocybin. However, the one group of hallucinogenic compounds that has been used increasingly over the last few years are the *stimulant-hallucinogens*, such as MDMA and similar substances, which are referred to as *designer drugs.*

The annual prevalence of use of hallucinogens declined throughout the 1980s. College students, followed 1–4 years beyond high school, showed an annual prevalence rate for LSD that steadily dropped from 6% in 1980 to 3.4% in 1989 (Johnston 1990). The estimated availability of LSD also decreased fairly steadily from 1975 to 1989 (Johnston 1990). During the early 1990s, however, there was some indication that LSD has been making a comeback. The Washington, DC, Board of the Drug Enforcement Administration confiscated 14 doses of LSD in 1990 and 5,600 doses in 1991. The annual survey of high school seniors found that in 1990 and 1991, for the first time since 1976, more seniors had used LSD than cocaine in the previous 12 months (Nagy 1992; Seligmann 1992).

LSD initially was used in the 1960s primarily by those interested in its ability to alter perceptual experiences (i.e., sight, sound, and taste). Much attention was paid to "set," the expectation of what the drug experience would be like, and "setting," the environment in which the drug was used. Thus the early drug missionaries promulgated the erroneous notion that only good LSD "trips" would result if the prospective user ensured a number of preconditions for his or her drug experience, including a guide. In more recent times, users have attended concerts, films (particularly psychedelic or brightly colored ones), or "rave" parties during the drug experience. Users rarely indulge more than once weekly because tolerance to LSD occurs so rapidly.

There is no abstinence syndrome after repeated use of hallucinogens. Thus there is no detoxification required for the chronic effects of the hallucinogens and little direct pharmacotherapy for toxic effects. We will therefore focus on the acute and chronic effects of these drugs and the psychosocial interventions necessary to treat the adverse reactions. Again, LSD will be discussed as the prototypical hallucinogen.

## ▼ PHYSIOLOGIC EFFECTS

The hallucinogens produce significant autonomic activity. They can dilate the pupils, increase the heart rate, and produce slight hypertension and hyperthermia. While under the influence, the face may flush, and the deep tendon reflexes quicken. On occasion, piloerection, salivation, nausea, a fine tremor, and lacrimation may be noted. In addition, a minor degree of incoordination, restlessness, and visual blurring can occur. A stress response with elevation of 17-hydroxycorticoids may be present.

Some of these autonomic effects of the hallucinogens are variable, and may be due, in part, to the anxiety state of the user. LSD also can cause nausea; nausea and sometimes vomiting are especially noteworthy after the ingestion of mescaline. MDA and MDMA may produce typical amphetamine-like autonomic effects.

## ▼ PSYCHOLOGIC EFFECTS

When the hallucinogens are taken orally, the psychic phenomena noted vary considerably, depending on the amount consumed and the set and the setting of both the subject and of the observer. The overall psychologic effects of the hallucinogens are quite similar; however, the rate of onset, duration of action, and absolute intensity of the effects can differ. Both Hofmann (1961) and Hollister (1978) have described the effects of LSD in great detail. The absorption of LSD from the gastrointestinal tract and other mucous membranes occurs rapidly, with drug diffusion to all tissues, including the brain and across the placenta to the fetus. The onset of psychologic and behavioral effects occurs approximately 30–60 minutes after oral administration and peaks at 2–4 hours after administration, with a gradual return to the predrug state in 8–12 hours. DMT produces similar effects but is inactive after oral administration and must be injected, sniffed, or smoked. It has a very rapid onset and short duration of action (60–120 minutes). Thus DMT previously was known as the "businessman's LSD" (i.e., one could have a psychedelic experience over the lunch hour and be back at work in the afternoon). In contrast, the effects of DOM have been reported to last for over 24 hours. The various hallucinogens also differ widely in potency and slope of the dose-response curve. Thus some of the apparent qualitative differences between hallucinogens may be due, in part, to the amount of drug ingested relative to its specific dose-response characteristics. LSD is one of the most potent hallucinogens known, with behavioral effects occurring in some individuals after doses as low as 20 μg. Typical street doses range from 70 to 300 μg. Because of its high potency, LSD can be applied to paper blotters or to the backs of postage stamps. There is some anecdotal evidence that today's street LSD is less potent than that available in the 1960s, 20–80 μg versus 150–250 μg. It should be pointed out that the reported street dose many times is highly inaccurate. The current cost of one street dose is about $5 versus $70 for ¼ ounce of marijuana and $50 for ½ gram of cocaine (Seligmann 1992). MDMA, currently advocated by some professionals for use in psychotherapy, is sold in powder, tablet, or capsule form for $5–$30 per dose (50–150 μg) on the street; its effects typically last 4–6 hours.

Perceptual alterations are notable with the hallucinogens; the initial subjective effect may be a colorful display of geometric patterns appearing before one's closed eyes. Distorted human, animal, or other forms may be projected onto the visual fields. With the eyes open, the color of perceived objects becomes more intense. Afterimages are remarkably prolonged; fixed objects may undulate and flow. Such illusions are common and may be given personal or idiosyncratic meaning. Auditory hallucinations are seldom described, but hyperacusis is commonly reported. Greater sensitivity to touch is regularly noticed, and sometimes taste and smell are altered.

Synesthesia is frequently described with an overflow from one sense modality into another; colors are "heard," and sounds are "seen." Subjective time is frequently affected; users often feel that time is standing still. Hypersuggestibility and distractibility are notable, perhaps because the critical functions of the ego become diminished or are absent.

The emotional responses to the hallucinogens can vary markedly. Initial apprehension or mild anxiety is common, but the most frequent response is one of euphoria. Elation and a "blissful calm" have also been described. Less frequently, tension and anxiety culminating in panic have occurred. The mood is labile, shifting easily from happiness to depression and back. Prolonged laughter or tears may seem inappropriate emotional responses to any situation. Complete withdrawal (catatonic states) and severe paranoid reactions have been encountered. An alternating intensification and fading out of the experience is present, with the subject going deeply in and out of the intoxicated state.

Performance on tests involving attention, concentration, and motivation is impaired. Thought processes are significantly altered under the influence of hallucinogenic drugs. A loosening of associations is regularly noted. Thoughts are nonlogical and fantasy laden. Thoughts flood consciousness; on the other hand, a complete absence of thought occurs on occasion. Intelligence test scores drop, but this may be due to a lack of motivation to perform or a preoccupation with the unusual experiences. Orientation is ordinarily not impaired, but judgments are not reliable. Paranoid grandiosity, and less frequently persecutory ideation, are common.

Changes in ego functioning may be imperceptible at the lower dosage ranges; however, the ego can be completely disrupted when large amounts of the hallucinogens have been ingested. At first one observes the ego's usual defense mechanisms operating to cope with these perceptions. Eventually, the ego may become overwhelmed to the point that depersonalization occurs. Current external events may not be differentiated from remote memories. The body image is frequently distorted, and the parts of the body may seem to become larger, smaller, or to disappear completely.

Chronic personality changes with a shift in attitudes and evidences of magical thinking also can occur after the use of hallucinogens. An atypical schizophrenic-like state may persist, but whether the use of hallucinogens causes or only unmasks a predisposition to this condition is unclear. There is always the associated risk that self-destructive behavior may occur during both the acute and the chronic reaction (e.g., thinking one can fly and jumping out of a window). In addition, the hallucinogenic drugs interact in a variety of nonspecific ways with the personality, which may particularly impair the developing adolescent (Miller 1973). Today, many chronic LSD users eventually come to use a variety of drugs (polydrug or multiple drug use), particularly the sedative-hypnotics and stimulants. This is a marked departure from the LSD users seen in the 1960s, whose entire life-style was organized around the use of hallucinogens and involvement in the psychedelic subculture, adopting the motto "turn on, tune in, drop out."

## ▼ DIAGNOSIS

The diagnosis of hallucinogen exposure is normally made from the patient's or an accompanying individual's report. The diagnosis can be made clinically when an individual is actively hallucinating, is delusional, and is describing illusions, changes in body size or shape, slowing of time, and a waxing and waning of these and related symptoms. Ordinarily, the individual is able to report having taken a substance prior to the acute onset of the symptoms. The presence of dilated pupils, tachycardia, and quickened deep tendon reflexes increases the possibility that a hallucinogen has been consumed.

The routine clinical drug screen does not include testing for the hallucinogens in body fluids. However, they can be detected in the research laboratory in blood, and for longer periods in urine, by thin-layer chromatography, gas chromatography, fluorometry, or gas chromatography-mass spectrometry (Basalt 1982). A radioimmunoassay for LSD is also available. Shifts in body metabolism from hallucinogen ingestion are insufficient to induce specific abnormalities in blood chemistries, blood counts, or urine analyses.

The differential diagnosis of the psychotomimetic state includes consumption of deliriant drugs such as the atropine-like agents or the atypical hallucinogens PCP and tetrahydrocannabinol (THC) in marijuana. Many drugs can produce a toxic psychosis, but this state can readily be differentiated from the psychotomimetic picture. In the former condition, confusion and loss of some aspects of orientation are present. With hallucinogens, the perceptual changes occur with a clear sensorium, intact orientation, and retention of recent and remote memory. In addition, the hallucinogens produce electroencephalographic (EEG) arousal, whereas drugs that cause delirium result in slowing of the EEG (Fink and Itil 1968). The THC psychosis frequently occurs with drowsiness rather than with the hyperalertness characteristic of the LSD state. PCP psychosis is accompanied by marked neurologic signs (e.g., vertical nystagmus, ataxia) and more pronounced autonomic effects than are seen with the psychotomimetics. Patients with amphetamine psychoses often fail to differentiate their perceptual distortions from reality, whereas LSD users are usually aware of the difference.

The differential diagnosis also must distinguish between an acute schizophrenic reaction and a hallucinogen-induced (or other drug-induced) psychosis. The differentiation is not always easily made. It should be recalled that initial research interest in LSD arose because of the possibility that it might provide an artificially induced model of schizophrenia. Although the notion that LSD induces a *model psychosis* similar to schizophrenia has several serious shortcomings, the use of the potent hallucinogens may have a variety of effects on the individual who is predisposed to schizophrenia: 1) they may cause the psychosis to become manifest at an earlier age, 2) they may produce a psychosis that would have remained dormant if drugs had not been used, or 3) they may cause relapse in an individual who has previously suffered a psychotic disorder (Bowers 1987).

It has also become more difficult to distinguish between LSD psychosis and paranoid schizophrenia, particularly because patients who in fact are paranoid often now complain of being poisoned with LSD, much as they once felt they were being talked about on radio or on television programs. Hallucinations in schizophrenic psychosis are usually auditory in contrast to the hallucinations from psychotomimetics, which are predominantly visual. A history of prior mental illness, a psychiatric examination that reveals the absence of an intact, observing ego, auditory (rather than visual) hallucinations, and the lack of development of drug tolerance all suggest schizophrenia. An organic brain syndrome in general speaks against LSD, especially if obtunded consciousness is also present. The brief reactive schizophrenic psychosis is of sudden onset but usually follows psychosocial stressors and is associated with emotional turmoil.

## ▼ INTERVENTION

### Intervention With the Acute Adverse Reactions

An individual's experience of the effects of the drug may be either pleasant or unpleasant; a perceptual distortion or illusion may provide intense anxiety in one individual and be a pleasant interlude for another. Social factors, media presentations, and public fear have all shaped perceptions of the drug's effects. Individuals who place a premium on self-control, advance planning, and impulse restriction may do particularly poorly on LSD. Prediction of who will have an adverse reaction is unreliable (Ungerleider et al. 1968). The occurrence of multiple previous good LSD experiences renders no immunity from an adverse reaction. Traumatic and stressful external events can precipitate an adverse reaction (i.e., being arrested and read one's rights in the middle of a pleasant experience may precipitate an anxiety reaction). Thus acute adverse behavioral reactions generally are not dose-related but are a function of personal predisposition, set, and setting. Adverse reactions have occurred after doses of LSD as low as 40 µg, and no effects have been reported from using 2,000 µg, although in general the hallucinogenic effects are proportional to dosage levels.

Acute dysphoric reactions are commonly known as "bummers" or "bad trips." These reactions are caused by loss of control, the inability to cope with ego dissolution, and/or marked environmental dissonance. The result is anxiety and, in some instances, panic. In terms of adverse physiological effects, LSD has a very high *therapeutic* index. The lethal dose in humans has not been determined, and fatalities that have been reported usually are secondary to perceptual distortions with resultant accidental death. Overdose with the psychotomimetic drugs is rare. Instances are known of people surviving 10,000 mg of LSD, 100 times the average dose. On the other hand, a few deaths have been reported from large amounts of the methoxylated amphetamine analogues. Hemiplegia has been reported after taking LSD, possibly due to the production of vasospasm (Sobel 1971).

These acute anxiety/panic reactions usually wear off before medical intervention is sought. Symptoms of these acute reactions are best managed by using the hypersuggestibility of the hallucinogenic state to calm and reassure the individual that he or she will be protected and that the condition will soon subside. Thus the use years ago of a "guide, sitter, or baby sitter" prevented marked anxiety from developing. Most LSD is metabolized and excreted within 24 hours, and most panic reactions are usually over within this time frame. Paranoid ideation, depression, hallucinations, and occasionally a confusional state (organic brain syndrome) are the other commonly reported acute adverse reactions (Ungerleider 1972). Some of the adverse reactions that occur after the ingestion of hallucinogens can be due to other contaminants in the product, such as strychnine, phencyclidine, and amphetamine.

MDMA users report nausea, jaw clenching, teeth grinding, increased muscle tension, and blurred vision as well as panic attacks. A type of "hangover" the day after taking this drug has been described; it is manifested by insomnia, fatigue, drowsiness, sore jaw muscles, loss of balance, and headache.

Because the anxiety and paranoid reactions from hallucinogens may last for an hour or for a few days, the patient may require unobtrusive protection for an extended period of time. Reassurance and support, or the *talkdown*, is done in a quiet, pleasant environment, usually in a home-like setting. Because closing the eyes intensifies the state, the patient should sit up or walk about. Reminding the patient that a drug has produced the extraordinary ideas and feelings and that they will soon disappear may be helpful. The time sense distortion that makes minutes seem like hours should also be explained. If drugs are needed for continuing panicky feelings, a benzodiazepine can be given. Phenothiazines are sometimes helpful in cases of extreme anxiety, but paradoxical reactions have been reported with an increase in anxiety after their administration (Schwartz 1968).

*Acute paranoid states* are adverse responses resulting from the hypervigilant state, overreading of external cues, and the unusual thoughts that occur in the course of the hallucinogenic experience. Although likely to be grandiose or megalomaniacal, they sometimes are manifested by suspiciousness and persecutory thoughts.

There is no generally accepted evidence of brain cell damage, chromosomal abnormalities or teratogenic effects after the use of the indole-type hallucinogens and mescaline. However, currently there is controversy surrounding the possible neurotoxic effects of MDA and MDMA. The controversy centers on the suitability of extrapolating results from studies using laboratory animals to human MDMA users, on how neurotoxicity is defined, and on the degree to which the neurochemical changes caused by exposure to MDMA diminish or disappear over time.

## Intervention With the Chronic Adverse Reactions

The effects of the chronic use of LSD must be differentiated from the clinical picture seen with personality disorders, particularly in those who use a variety of drugs in polydrug abuse-type patterns. Personality changes that result from LSD use may occur after a single experience, unlike that with other classes of drugs—PCP, perhaps, excepted (Fisher 1972). In some individuals with well-integrated personalities and with no previous psychiatric history, chronic personality changes also have resulted from repeated LSD use. The suggestibility that may come from many experiences with LSD may be reinforced by the social values of a particular subculture in which the drug is used. For instance, if some of these subcultures embrace withdrawal from society and a noncompetitive approach toward life, the person who withdraws after the LSD experience(s) may be suffering from a side effect that represents more of a change in social values than a physiologic drug effect. Use of hallucinogens can lead to a diminution of a variety of acceptable social behaviors.

Schizophreniform reactions lasting from weeks to years have followed the psychotomimetic experience. Closely following a dysphoric experience or developing shortly after a positive one, the manifestations of psychosis may emerge. These reactions are likely to be precipitated in characterologically predisposed individuals who have decompensated due to the upsurge of repressed material that overwhelms their ego defenses.

The management of these prolonged psychotic reactions does not differ from that of schizophrenia. Neuroleptics are used, sometimes in a residential setting when behavioral dysfunction makes it necessary. Efforts at self-medication are often made by these patients, and serious polydrug abuse patterns have been seen (Wesson and Smith 1978). The prognosis of these psychotic states is usually favorable; however, a few remain recalcitrant to treatment.

**Chronic anxiety and depressive states.** It is evident that to some individuals (perhaps to everyone under adverse circumstances) the LSD experience can be an unsettling one. In general, the psyche is capable of reconstituting itself surprisingly well within a reasonable period. A few individuals continue to experience anxiety and depression for unusually long periods of time, however, and they may attribute these feelings to whatever psychotomimetic they took. It is difficult to know how much of the state that sometimes occurs is due to a disruption of psychological homeostasis and how much was because a fragile personality was exposed to it. At any rate, the anxiety and depression may persist despite psychiatric therapy and anti-anxiety and/or antidepressant medication.

Nondrug anti-anxiety techniques such as relaxation exercises and behavioral therapy may be helpful. One should not accede to the magical thinking of the patient that maybe another psychedelic session (or doubling the dose) might reshuffle the psychological fragments back into their premorbid pattern.

**Flashbacks.** A phenomenon unique to the hallucinogens has emerged during the past 25 years. This is the *flashback*, the apparently spontaneous recrudescence of the same effects that were experienced during the psychotomimetic state. These are usually brief visual, temporal, or emotional recurrences, complete with perceptive (time) and reality distortion, that may first appear days or months after the last drug exposure. Because flashbacks appear suddenly, unexpectedly, and inappropriately, the emotional response to them may be one of dread. Even a previously pleasant drug experience may be accompanied by anxiety when the person realizes there no way to control its recurrence. Fear of insanity may arise because no external cause for the strange, often recurrent phenomena is apparent. Others seem to enjoy the experience, however.

The exact mechanism of action of the flashback remains obscure. Only a small proportion of LSD and other users of hallucinogens experience flashbacks (Shick 1970), and they can continue to reoccur spontaneously a number of weeks or months after the original drug experience. These flashbacks may or may not be precipitated by stressors, fatigue, or subsequent use of another psychedelic like psilocybin or marijuana. In time, these flashbacks decrease in intensity, frequency, and duration (although initially they often last only a few seconds) whether treated (with tranquilizers and reassurance) or not. Flashbacks can usually be handled with psychotherapy. It is possible that these recurrences represent a response learned during a state of hyperarousal (Cohen 1981).

*Treatment* of chronic hallucinogen abuse usually involves long-term psychotherapy to determine—*after* cessation of use—what needs are being fulfilled by the long-term use of the drug for this particular person. Support in the form of 12-step program meetings and family involvement also are crucial for reinforcement of the decision to remain abstinent. The most important aspect of treatment consists of reassurance that the condition will pass, that the brain is not damaged, and that the hallucinogen is not retained in the brain. If the patient is agitated because of repeated flashbacks, an anxiolytic drug is indicated. The patient's physical and mental status should be improved with the appropriate hygienic measures, and all hallucinogens, including marijuana, must be avoided. If no flashbacks have occurred during the 1–2 years since the last ingestion of the hallucinogen, it is unlikely that any more will occur.

## ▼ SUMMARY

We have discussed the psychotropic drugs called hallucinogens from several perspectives. These have included the acute and chronic adverse effects of these drugs, their patterns of abuse, and their relationship to mental illness. Diagnostic and treatment issues have been considered. We have emphasized the prototype hallucinogen LSD.

## ▼ REFERENCES

Basalt RC: Disposition of Toxic Drugs and Chemicals in Man. Davis, CA, Biomedical Publications, 1982

Bowers MB Jr: The role of drugs in the production of schizophreniform psychoses and related disorders, in Psychopharmacology: The Third Generation of Progress. Edited by Meltzer HY. New York, Raven, 1987, pp 819–828

Cohen S: The Substance Abuse Problems. New York, Haworth, 1981

Fink M, Itil TM: Neurophysiology of phantastica: EEG and behavioral relations in man, in Psychopharmacology: A Review of Progress, 1957–1967. Edited by

Efrom DH. Washington, DC, U.S. Department of Health, Education, and Welfare, 1968, pp 1231–1239

Fisher DD: The chronic side effects from LSD, in The Problems and Prospects of LSD. Edited by Ungerleider JT. Springfield, IL, Charles C Thomas, 1972, pp 69–80

Johnston L: Monitoring the Future: The National High School Senior Survey. Rockville, MD, National Institute on Drug Abuse, 1990

Hofmann A: Chemical, pharamacological, and medical aspects of psychotomimetics. Journal of Experimental Medical Sciences 5:31–51, 1961

Hollister LE: Psychotomimetic drugs in man, in Handbook of Psychopharmacology, Vol II. Edited by Iversen LL, Iversen SD, Snyder SH. New York, Plenum, 1978, pp 389–424

Miller D: The drug dependent adolescent, in Adolescent Psychiatry. Edited by Feinstein SC, Giovachini P. New York, Basic Books, 1973

Nagy J: A Comparison of Drug Use Among 8th, 10th, and 12th Graders From NIDA's High School Senior Survey. Rockville, MD, National Institute on Drug Abuse, 1992

Osmond H: A review of the clinical effects of psychotomimetic agents. Ann N Y Acad Sci 66:418–434, 1957

Schwartz CJ: The complications of LSD: a review of the literature. J Nerv Ment Dis 146:174–186, 1968

Seligmann J, Mason M, Annin P, et al: The New Age of Aquarius. Newsweek, pp 66–67, February 3, 1992

Shick JFE, Smith DE: An analysis of the LSD flashback. Journal of Psychedelic Drugs 3:13–19, 1970

Sobel J, Espinas O, Friedman S: Carotid artery obstruction following LSD capsule ingestion. Arch Intern Med 127:290–291, 1971

Ungerleider JT: The acute side effects from LSD, in The Problems and Prospects of LSD. Edited by Ungerleider JT. Springfield, IL, Charles C Thomas, 1972, pp 61–68

Ungerleider JT, Fisher DD, Fuller MC, et al: The bad trip: the etiology of the adverse LSD reaction. Am J Psychiatry 125:1483–1490, 1968

Wesson DR, Smith DE: Psychedelics in treatment aspects of drug dependence. West Palm Beach, FL, CRC Press, 1978

# Phencyclidine

*Amin N. Daghestani, M.D.*
*Sidney H. Schnoll, M.D., Ph.D.*

Phencyclidine (1-[1-phencyclohexyl] piperidine monohydrochloride; PCP) was synthesized in the late 1950s. It was the first of a new class of general anesthetics known as cataleptoid anesthetics or dissociative anesthetics. PCP can be manufactured easily in unsophisticated laboratories from simple materials. Other arylcyclohexylamines include *N*-ethyl-1-phencyclohexalamine (PCE), 1-(1-2-thienyl-cyclohexyl) piperidine (TCP), 1-(1-phencyclohexyl) pyrrolidine (PHP), 1-piperidinocyclohexane carbonitrile (PCC), and ketamine. These products have been found as contaminants in samples of PCP sold on the street (Schnoll 1980).

PCP was originally described as a drug of abuse in both New York and San Francisco in the mid-1960s but rapidly disappeared as a popular drug of abuse because of the unexpected reactions that often occurred following its use. In the late 1960s and early 1970s, PCP emerged as a frequent contaminant of other drugs sold on the illicit market, most often in samples of hallucinogens and tetrahydrocannabinol (THC). In the past few years, PCP has once again become a sought after drug of abuse as well as being a contaminant in other drugs of abuse. Recent data suggest that PCP abuse is not widespread in the United States but has become concentrated among post-high-school age, black males in a limited number of cities (Thombs 1989).

PCP can be taken through several routes of administration: oral, intravenous, smoking, or insufflation ("snorting"). As a frequent contaminant of street drugs, it is often used in conjunction with other drugs. Although the absorption with oral administration usually takes more than 1 hour, the effect is almost immediate after smoking. This crystalline, water-soluble, and lipophilic substance penetrates easily into fat stores and other cells, resulting in a long half-life. Metabolism takes place primarily in the liver by oxidation, hydroxylation, and conjugation with glucuronic acid. Only a small amount of the active drug is excreted directly in the urine.

For some time, it was unclear how PCP worked in the central nervous system (CNS). It had been proposed that PCP interacted with numerous CNS neurotransmitters including 5-hydroxytryptamine, norepinephrine, acetylcholine, dopamine, and glutamic acid. Recent evidence has demonstrated that PCP binds to the σ-opioid receptor and is a non-

This work was supported in part by the Commonwealth of Virginia Center on Drug Abuse Research

competitive antagonist at the *N*-methyl-D-aspartate (NMDA) receptor complex. It is believed that the binding at this later site may be responsible for PCP's behavioral effects, although drugs that bind to the σ-opioid site are known to produce dysphoria and hallucinations. Further elucidation of PCP's action on these binding sites may play an important role in our understanding of schizophrenia (Johnson and Jones 1990).

Clinically the CNS effects result in a rise in blood pressure, heart rate, and respiratory rate. These catecholamine-mediated actions may be related to panic reactions sometimes seen in users. Its effect on reflexes probably leads to muscle rigidity, and its cholinergic effects lead to increased CNS acetylcholine activity, with resulting, sweating, flushing, drooling, and pupillary constriction. Its serotonergic effects cause dizziness, incoordination, slurred speech, and nystagmus. PCP has been shown to bind to specific receptors in the liver, kidney, lung, heart, and brain (Weinstein et al. 1981).

PCP produces brief dissociative psychotic reactions similar to schizophrenic psychoses. These reactions are characterized by changes in body image, thought disorder, depersonalization, and autism. At higher doses, subjects have great difficulty differentiating between themselves and their surroundings. Other users will experience hostility, paranoia, violence, and preoccupation with death. The differences in the response to PCP may be dose related or based on the individual response of the user (National Institute on Drug Abuse 1979).

There has been an increasing interest in using PCP as a model to study schizophrenia. As opposed to amphetamines, PCP-induced psychosis incorporates both positive as well as the negative symptoms of schizophrenia (Javitt and Zukin 1991). Other researchers have investigated positron emission tomography of PCP-using patients as a possible drug model of schizophrenia (Wu et al. 1991).

Tolerance to the disruptive effects of PCP on operant behavior has been reported. PCP withdrawal has been observed in animals within 4–8 hours after the drug is discontinued. In humans, because of a longer half-life, the withdrawal may not be seen for several days, if at all. Increased neuromuscular activity and bruxism are common. Diarrhea and abdominal pain have also been described (Balster and Woolverton 1981).

PCP is used primarily by adolescents and young adults. First use is usually between the ages of 13 and 15 years. Three percent of young people in the 12-to 17-year age group have taken PCP. PCP users are usually polydrug abusers; more than 90% of PCP users report use of other substances, mainly marijuana and alcohol. In the past, PCP was often found as a contaminant in other street drugs. However, at the present time, samples of PCP are often contaminated by other drugs. The lack of knowledge of PCP's interactions with other drugs has led to problems in treating PCP reactions (Schnoll 1980).

On the street, PCP has been known by many names, including angel dust, Cadillac, dummy mist, dust, embalming fluid, green, hog, horse, jet, K, mist, peace pill, purple, rocket fuel, Sherman, THC, tic, tac, and whack. The abundance of street names for this substance is probably related to the initial lack of popularity of the oral route of PCP use. It has been suggested that a new drug with a bizarre name that is smoked or snorted can be assumed to be PCP until proven otherwise.

Infants exposed to PCP in utero, may have intrauterine growth retardation and prolonged hospitalizations. They are less likely than cocaine-exposed infants to be born prematurely (Tabor et al. 1990).

## ▼ PCP INTOXICATION

Diagnosis of PCP or similarly acting arylcyclohexylamine intoxication is based on behavioral changes that occur following ingestion of PCP (i.e., belligerence, assaultiveness, impulsiveness, unpredictability, psychomotor agitation, impaired judgment, and impaired social and occupational function). Physical findings may include horizontal and/or vertical nystagmus, hypertension, tachycardia, diminished pain sensation, ataxia, dysarthria, muscle rigidity, seizures, and hyperacusis. A diagnosis of PCP intoxication should be confirmed with toxicologic analysis of blood or urine. Without this confirmation, the diagnosis can only be presumptive at best.

Although not discrete from each other, three stages for PCP intoxication have been described depending on the dose taken: behavioral toxicity, stuporous state, and comatose stage. The behavioral toxicity presents with the symptoms described above. The stuporous stage is characterized by a stupor with open eyes and a wakeful appearance. The patient may fluctuate between the stuporous stage and the stage of behavioral toxicity in 1- to 2-hour periods. While in the stuporous condition, the patient will respond appropriately to deep pain and show purposeless movements, myoclonus, and exaggerated deep tendon reflexes. In the comatose stage, the patient is rigid and may show repetitive stereotyped movements and profuse sweating. The gag and corneal reflexes may be absent. This stage may last 1–4 days, depending on the dose of PCP taken and rate of excretion of the drug. The electroencephalogram shows delta wave activity followed by theta activity.

The differential diagnosis for PCP intoxication should include head trauma, schizophrenia or acute psychosis, organic brain syndrome, mania, cerebrovascular accident, and stupor and/or coma (of metabolic origin, from drug overdose, or from other unexplained etiology).

The clinical picture that should lead the physician to consider the possibility of PCP abuse in patients presenting with an unusual behavior includes cerebellar symptoms (nystagmus, "Groucho eyes," ataxia, and dysarthria), elevation of pulse and blood pressure, reduced sensitivity to pain, increased deep tendon reflexes, excessive salivation, and nausea. These signs and symptoms should be used with urine and blood toxicology to differentiate PCP intoxication from acute psychosis or schizophrenia.

Emergency rooms should have available laboratory techniques to detect the presence of PCP in body fluids to assist in making an accurate diagnosis. PCP should also be tested for in the body fluids in arrests associated with impulsive bizarre behavior or unexplained assaultive acts. As in all instances of toxicologic analysis, a positive urine for PCP should be verified by using a second analytical technique.

The presence of ataxia and nystagmus and the absence of dilated pupils are useful in ruling out the CNS stimulants and lysergic acid diethylamide (LSD) when evaluating acutely agitated and confused patients. The presence of hyperreflexia and hypertension differentiate PCP intoxication from sedative-hypnotic intoxication (National Institute on Drug Abuse 1979), although these signs may be present in acute withdrawal from sedative-hypnotic medications or ethanol.

## Management of PCP Intoxication

Because of poor judgment, the patient usually will require protective supervision in a nonstimulating environment that should include protection from self-injury. When possible, a careful history should be taken, including drugs taken, duration of use, time of last dose, adverse reactions to drugs and psychiatric history. Obtaining history from companions or family members may be useful. Belongings should be carefully searched for the presence of drugs or paraphernalia that should be analyzed to assist in making the diagnosis.

A thorough physical and neurologic examination should be performed. Vital signs need to be monitored for laryngeal stridor or respiratory depression, and a respirator may be required. Restraints should be avoided; Lahmeyer and Stock (1983) reported that the use of restraints may cause rhabdomyolysis and acute renal failure, and Mercy et al. (1990) identified PCP as a major factor associated with the death of prisoners who were restrained by police.

Although the *talking-down* technique has been used to treat acute hallucinogen reactions, this approach should be avoided in PCP-intoxicated patients because it may intensify agitation.

To establish the diagnosis, other types of obtundation should be ruled out. Naloxone may be given to rule out opioid intoxication. Toxicology screen on blood (10 ml) and urine (50 ml) samples is important, although reliance on blood levels is hazardous because the active substance may be repeatedly released from fat stores. The serum concentration of PCP is a less accurate indicator of a patient's level of intoxication than a fat biopsy.

There is no specific antagonist for PCP. If PCP is taken orally, a gastric lavage performed with a liter or more of half normal saline could be done. Following this, the patient could be placed on continuous gastric suction using a nasogastric tube. An alternative to gastric lavage is the administration of activated charcoal to adsorb the PCP that is secreted back into the acid environment of the stomach.

The concentration of PCP in the body fluids and tissues is profoundly influenced by pH. Some PCP is retained in fatty tissues and in the brain, where it escapes hepatic metabolism. Acidification of urine increases the excretion rate of PCP roughly 100-fold because the drug is a weak base. If acidification is done prior to toxicologic screens of urine and blood for the presence of other drugs, excretion and analysis for other drugs (e.g., barbiturates or salicylates) may be adversely affected.

In cases of coma secondary to acute PCP intoxication, residual drug should be removed from the stomach and sent off for analysis. Before the nasogastric tube is removed, ammonium chloride 2.75 mEq/kg dissolved in 60 ml of saline could be given through the nasogastric tube every 6 hours until the urine pH is 5.5 or less. Another approach to urine acidification is to administer vitamin C (ascorbic acid) with intravenous fluids at the rate of 2 g in 500 ml every 6 hours. Urine pH needs to be checked two to four times each day. When the pH is 5.5, diuresis could be forced by using furosemide (Lasix) 20–40 mg iv. After consciousness returns, urine acidification should continue for a week, giving cranberry juice along with ammonium chloride 500 mg po qid, or ascorbic acid 1 g po tid. Throughout the initial treatment, electrolytes should be maintained, and blood gases should be monitored periodically. Acidification is contraindicated in severe liver disease and in the presence of renal insufficiency. Other than the use of acidifying agents, medication should be avoided in the patient who is comatose from PCP intoxication. The exception to this rule is a patient who is hypertensive secondary to PCP. In this case, antihypertensive medications should be administered to reduce the blood pressure. If the patient is severely agitated and poses a potential threat to self or others, haloperidol has been demonstrated to be effective in controlling the agitation. When there is doubt about the drug the individual has taken or when a combination of drugs may be present, diazepam 5 to 20 mg iv slowly or orally could be used. Recent studies indicate that barbiturates may be more efficacious in treating the psychotomimetic effects of PCP-like drugs (Olney et al. 1991).

### Complications of PCP Intoxication

1. *Undetected PCP overdose.* This usually follows oral ingestion of the compound or a compound in which PCP was a contaminant. Adding to the confusion is the late onset of action of the orally ingested form. This should be suspected in children as well as in patients who fail to improve after 3 hours of observation or in those whose level of confusion seems to increase rather than decrease with time. In any case in which there is suspicion of PCP ingestion, urine, blood, or gastric contents should be collected and sent for toxicologic analysis to confirm or rule out the diagnosis.

2. *Seizure and status epilepticus.* The association of seizure with PCP use has been well documented in the literature (Alldredge et al. 1989). No medication is necessary to treat a single seizure; however, if there are repeated seizures or if the patient is in an epileptic state, use diazepam 10–20 mg iv.

3. *Hypertension.* Use hydralazine (Apresoline) or phentolamine iv drip (2–5 mg over 5–10 minutes).

4. *Hyperthermia.* Use hypothermic blankets or ice.

5. *Opisthotonos and acute dystonia.* This usually clears as blood levels of the drug decrease. If the problem persists, diazepam iv to relax the musculature is often effective.

6. *Cardiac arrhythmia.* In the case of a severe arrhythmia that does not clear, a cardiology consultation should be called.

7. *Rhabdomyolysis, myoglobinuria, and acute renal failure.* When acute renal failure is present, a nephrology consultation should be called.

8. *PCP psychosis.* See the following on PCP delirium.

9. *Stroke.* Ischemic and hemorrhagic stroke have been reported in association with PCP (Sloan et al. 1991; Gorelick 1990).

### ▼ PCP DELIRIUM

PCP is considered one of the most common causes of emergency room admissions for drug-induced psychoses (Yago et al. 1981). Intravenous PCP has produced schizophrenic-like symptoms in subjects with no previous history of psychotic behavior (Gallant 1981). Initially, alterations of body image occur, with a loss of body boundaries and a sense of unreality. Feelings of estrangement and loneliness follow, sometimes associated with an intensification of dependency needs. Progressive disorganization of thought, negativism, and hostility can also develop. Some subjects become catatonic with dream-like experiences. Distortion of body image and depersonalization are universal reactions, and attention and cognitive deficits are often present.

The psychosis may persist in some individuals anywhere from 24 hours to several months or even years after the cessation of active PCP use. Whether this is a direct effect of PCP or the drug exacerbating an underlying psychotic disorder is not clear; administration of PCP to schizophrenic patients has been reported to exacerbate schizophrenic-psychotic symptoms acutely.

A PCP psychosis in the presence of a clear sensorium is rare. It is important to examine the patient for the presence of horizontal or vertical nystagmus, ataxia, or slurred speech. These signs indicate PCP intoxication rather than PCP psychosis. Preexisting psychiatric disorders should be ruled out. Daghestani (1987) emphasized the importance of a thorough diagnostic workup with all patients who present with acute psychotic decompensation. Anticholinergic drug intoxication must be ruled out before initiating treatment with an antipsychotic agent.

The clinical picture is dominated by insomnia, restlessness, and behavior that is purposeless, hyperactive, bizarre, aggressive, or agitated. The mental state may fluctuate to include paranoia, mania, grandiosity, rapid thought, and speech with emotional lability. The degree of psychosis is usually related to the amount of drug used.

Three phases for PCP psychosis have been described, each lasting approximately 5 days: 1) agitated phase, 2) mixed phase, and 3) resolution phase. Factors reported to reduce the duration of each phase are individual susceptibility, degree of exposure to the drug, dosage of antipsychotic, and urine acidification.

Luisada and Brown (1976) observed that "about one-fourth of the patients originally treated for PCP psychosis return about 1 year later with schizophrenia in the absence of drug use. These later episodes have lacked the characteristic violence of the phencyclidine-induced psychosis, and they respond quickly to antipsychotic drugs."

## Management of PCP Delirium

The guidelines for treatment approaches discussed in the management of PCP intoxication apply here to a large extent. The goals of treatment should include prevention of injury, facilitation of the excretion of PCP from urine, and the amelioration of psychosis. The patient should be hospitalized in a closed psychiatric unit and assigned to a quiet room. If agitated, the patient could be restrained by trained personnel. All efforts should be made to avoid physical restraints. Because of the intense physical exertion often associated with the agitation seen in PCP delirium, the patient should be

given adequate hydration.

The principles of urine acidification discussed above are the same, although the acidifying agents should be given orally: cranberry juice (8–16 oz qid), ascorbic acid (1 g qid), or ammonium chloride (liquid solution 500 mg/5 ml, with an initial loading dose of 15–20 ml of ammonium chloride followed by 10 ml qid).

Once the urine pH is 5.5 or less, diuresis may be encouraged by the administration of furosemide 40 mg bid. Oral potassium supplement will be necessary to avoid potassium depletion, and serum electrolytes should be monitored daily. Improvement could be expected 6–8 hours after diuresis. Urine acidification should continue for at least 3 days after all evidence of psychosis has disappeared, and most patients will require a 3- to 10-day course of acidification.

The use of antacids, which act as alkalinizing agents, should be avoided while attempts are being made to enhance excretion of PCP by acidifying the urine. The antacids significantly reduce the ability of ammonium chloride and other acidifying drugs to lower the urine pH, resulting in retention of PCP in the serum.

The use of psychotherapeutic drugs should be undertaken carefully and judiciously. Both benzodiazepines and haloperidol have been described as being useful in the treatment of delirium caused by PCP. Pitts (1984) suggested that a standard dose of a benzodiazepine, a neuroleptic, and a β-blocker given together will resolve the delirious psychotic state within minutes. This approach is based on the premise of the multiple receptor effects of PCP. It was thought that blockers or competitors would blunt the responses seen in these patients. According to Pitts, few patients who maintain confusional symptoms will require long-term therapy. There have been no subsequent reports verifying the effectiveness of this approach.

Rosen et al. (1984) described four patients who had a history of PCP abuse, prolonged psychosis, and poor neuroleptic response. Three of these patients were given electroconvulsive therapy (ECT); all showed a dramatic response after the third or fourth treatment. The authors recommended that ECT be tried in psychotic patients who have used PCP if they fail to respond to antipsychotic medications after 1 week of inpatient treatment. Further reports on the improvement of PCP-associated psychosis with ECT were made by Grover et al. (1986).

Following the resolution of the acute confusional psychotic state, a referral to long-term therapy would be important.

# ▼ PCP ORGANIC MENTAL DISORDER

This chronic mental impairment is believed to result from chronic PCP use. This condition is characterized by memory deficits and a state of confusion or decreased intellectual functioning with associated assaultiveness. There are also visual disturbances and speech difficulty, such as a blocking or an inability to retrieve the proper words. A differential diagnosis should rule out other possible causes of organicity. The course of the disorder may be quite variable. The reasons for this variability are not clear but may be related to residual drug being released from adipose tissues of the chronic user. The confusional state may last 4–6 weeks. The condition may improve with time if PCP exposure does not recur and if residual PCP is excreted by acidifying the patient's urine as described above.

## Management of PCP Organic Mental Disorder

The basic management plan is that of protecting the patient from injury and helping the patient deal with disorientation by using a simple, structured, and supportive approach. Sensory input and stimuli have to be kept to a minimum. Nonthreatening environment and nonjudgmental staff are of paramount importance. Excessive stimulation can result in agitation and violent and aggressive behavior.

# ▼ PCP ABUSE AND PCP DEPENDENCE

The diagnostic criteria for PCP or similarly acting arylcyclohexylamine abuse include the following:

1. Pattern of pathologic use: intoxication throughout the day; episodes of PCP or similarly acting arylcyclohexylamine delirium or mixed organic mental disorder
2. Impairment in social or occupational functioning due to substance use, for example, fights, loss of friends, absence from work, loss of job, or legal difficulties (other than due to a single arrest for possession, purchase, or sale of the substance)
3. Duration of disturbance of at least 1 month.

The criteria stated above should be supported by the presence of PCP or other arylcyclohexylamines in the blood or urine.

In addition to the listed criteria, Smith et al. (1978) reported that a significant number of individuals experience profound depression from chronic use of PCP.

## Management of PCP Abuse and Dependence

Therapists should be cognizant of the fact that PCP users display a wide range of behaviors, including flattened affect, belligerence, depression, and anxiety. They are often unable to cope with the demands and expectations of a structured intensive confrontive environment of the type often found in some residential treatment programs. Bolter (1980) suggested that the following management strategies may be effective at the beginning of treatment: 1) establish clear ground rules that are enforced; 2) keep decision making to a minimum; 3) accept some absentmindedness initially—directions may have to be repeated; 4) develop a short list of tasks with a regular routine; 5) avoid stressful situations; and 6) set realistic consequences for both positive and negative behavior and be consistent in the application of these consequences.

Because of the cognitive impairments associated with PCP abuse, the therapeutic environment should provide a supportive structure. All staff members must be aware of the treatment plan to prevent the patient from playing one staff member against another (splitting). The treatment staff should be well trained in the effects of PCP so they can work effectively with the types of problems presented.

Caracci et al. (1983) described three patients with PCP-induced depression. Many of the patients had poor compliance with regular clinic attendance, making it difficult to engage them in a meaningful therapeutic alliance. Individual and group therapies appear to have a weak impact. Because of these problems and the high suicide risk, Caracci et al. recommended hospitalization for treatment of PCP-induced depression and suicidal potential.

For the treatment of PCP withdrawal, Tennant et al. (1981) suggested the use of desipramine 50–150 mg in the first day to be decreased over the following 2 weeks. The use of this technique has not been verified in additional studies.

There are some differences between long-term narcotic-dependent individuals and chronic PCP-abusing individuals, making the therapeutic community approach inappropriate for those individuals needing long-term treatment for chronic PCP abuse. PCP-abusing individuals tend to be younger, more immature, and do not tolerate the usual confrontation techniques employed in therapeutic communities (De Angelis and Goldstein 1978).

Chronic PCP-abusing individuals exhibit characteristics similar to a child with learning disabilities. They generally show emotional lability, social incompetence, overt impulsiveness, poor social judgment, poor attention span and concentration, poor interpersonal relationships, and social maladjustment. These characteristics may be reversible if PCP use stops and appropriate treatment is provided.

During the course of outpatient therapy, educational and nutritional awareness will enhance the level of self-care of the patient. Vocational counseling and training may prove to be beneficial in enhancing the self-esteem of the patient.

Using self-help groups has become an established and essential part of any successful treatment of PCP and other drug dependence. Narcotics Anonymous (NA) groups have begun to gain increasing acceptance of PCP users, and many patients have been able to use NA as part of a recovery program.

Outpatient follow-up treatment is aimed at keeping the patient away from resuming drug use. It is important to assist staff in being realistic about their expectations for treatment.

PCP-abusing patients may not be expected initially to join extensively in group therapy, individual therapy, or school or recreation programs. They may be belligerent toward treatment, especially on program entry.

The following are important considerations when structuring a program responsive to PCP-abusing patients. First, there should be minimal confrontation or hostility-provoking behavior by staff. Second, patients should be provided with a non-threatening, supportive environment in which they can begin to feel comfortable. Third, minimal patient involvement in specific therapeutic intervention should be anticipated initially.

De Angelis and Goldstein (1978) found that chronic PCP-abusing patients stay in treatment longer than individuals who use PCP occasionally. Individual, family, couples, and group therapies have been used with some success. Body awareness therapy, yoga, and progressive relaxation techniques help patients to focus and help to improve attention span and concentration. Many PCP-abusing individuals have a sense of loss of contact with their bodies. These exercises can be helpful in restoring a healthy body image. Consistent with this, patients should be encouraged to seek out athletic activities.

Treatment of PCP abuse and dependence, like all other chemical dependence problems, requires long-term treatment. Persistence and patience on the part of staff are necessary to achieve a satisfactory outcome.

## ▼ REFERENCES

Alldredge BK, Lowenstein DH, Simon RP: Seizures associated with recreational drug abuse. Neurology 39:1037–1039, 1989

Balster RH, Woolverton WH: Tolerance and dependence to phencyclidine, in PCP (Phencyclidine): Historical and Current Perspectives. Edited by Domino EF. Ann Arbor, MI, NPP Books, 1981, pp 293–306

Bolter A: Issues for inpatient treatment of chronic PCP abuse. Journal of Psychedelic Drugs 12:287–288, 1980

Caracci G, Migoni P, Mukherjee S: Phencyclidine abuse and depression. Psychosomatics 24:932–933, 1983

Daghestani AN: Phencyclidine–associated psychosis (letter). J Clin Psychiatry 48:386, 1987

De Angelis GG, Goldstein E: Treatment of adolescent phencyclidine (PCP) abusers. Am J Drug Alcohol Abuse 5:399–414, 1978

Gallant D: PCP: clinical and laboratory diagnostic problems, in PCP (Phencyclidine): Historical and Current Perspectives. Edited by Domino EF. Ann Arbor, MI, NPP Books, 1981, pp 437–447

Gorelick PB: Stroke from alcohol and drug abuse: a current social peril. Postgrad Med 88:171–174, 177–178, 1990

Grover D, Yeragani VK, Keshanan MS: Improvement of phencyclidine: associated psychosis with ECT. J Clin Psychiatry 47:477–478, 1986

Javitt DC, Zukin SR: Recent advances in the phencyclidine model of schizophrenia. Am J Psychiatry 148:1301–1308, 1991

Johnson KM, Jones SM: Neuropharmacology of phencyclidine: Basic mechanisms and therapeutic potential. Annu Rev Pharmacol Toxicol 30:707–750, 1990

Lahmeyer HW, Stock PG: Phencyclidine intoxication, physical restraints, and acute renal failure: case report. J Clin Psychiatry 44:184–185, 1983

Luisada P, Brown B: Clinical management of phencyclidine psychosis. Clinical Toxicology 9:539–545, 1976

Mercy JA, Heath CW Jr, Rosenberg ML: Mortality associated with the use of upper-body control holds by police. Violence Vict 5:215–222, 1990

National Institute on Drug Abuse: Diagnosis and Treatment of Phencyclidine (PCP) Toxicity. Rockville, MD, National Institute on Drug Abuse, 1979

Olney JW, Labruyere J, Wang G, et al: NMDA antagonist neurotoxicity: mechanism and prevention. Science 254:1515–1518, 1991

Pitts FN Jr: Pharmacological therapies for PCP abuse called fairly effective. Clinical Psychiatry News 12:17, 1984

Rosen AM, Mukherjee S, Shinbach K: The efficacy of ECT in phencyclidine-induced psychosis. J Clin Psychiatry 45:220–222, 1984

Schnoll SH: Street PCP scene: issues on synthesis and contamination. Journal of Psychedelic Drugs 12:229–233, 1980

Sloan MA, Kittner SJ, Rigamonti D, et al: Occurrence of stroke associated with use/abuse of drugs. Neurology 41:1358–1364, 1991

Smith DE, Wesson DR: Barbiturate and other sedative hypnotics, in Treatment Aspects of Drug Dependence. New York, CRC Press, 1978, pp 117–130

Tabor BL, Smith-Wallace T, Yonekura ML: Perinatal outcome associated with PCP versus cocaine use. Am J Drug Alcohol Abuse 16:337–348, 1990

Tennant FS, Rawson RA, McCann M: Withdrawal from chronic phencyclidine (PCP) dependence with desipramine. Am J Psychiatry 138:845–847, 1981

Thombs DL: A review of PCP abuse trends and perceptions. Public Health Reports, University of Maryland 104:325–328, 1989

Weinstein H, Maayuni S, Glick S, et al: Integrated studies on the biochemical, behavioral and molecular pharmacology of phencyclidine: a progress report, in PCP (Phencyclidine): Historical and Current Perspectives. Edited by Domino EF. Ann Arbor, MI, NPP Books, 1981, pp 131–175

Wu JC, Buchsbaum MS, Bunney WE: Positron emission tomography study of phencyclidine users as a possible drug model of schizophrenia. Irvine, CA, Department of Psychiatry, University of California 11:47–8, 1991

Yago KB, Pitts FN Jr, Burgoyne RW, et al: The urban epidemic of phencyclidine (PCP) use: clinical and laboratory evidence from a public psychiatric hospital emergency service. J Clin Psychiatry 42:193–196, 1981

# CHAPTER 11

# Tobacco

Judith K. Ockene, Ph.D.
Jean L. Kristeller, Ph.D.

The mounting evidence linking cigarette smoking with serious illness and premature death has placed increasing demands on the medical and mental health community. Viewed as an addictive behavior, cigarette smoking can be treated from psychosocial, behavioral, and pharmacologic perspectives. A mental health professional in a clinical setting can play an important role in preventing and treating this psychological and/or physiologic addiction.

The DSM-IV (American Psychiatric Association 1994) and the World Health Organization (World Health Organization 1978) recognize tobacco dependence as an addiction. Tobacco dependence deserves attention as a serious problem not only because of the health risks involved but also because nicotine is a psychoactive substance that may control significant aspects of an individual's behavior. Tobacco shares a number of common factors with the other recognized euphoriants (i.e., cocaine, opioids, and alcohol): it produces centrally mediated effects on mood and feeling states, it is a reinforcer for animals, it leads to drug-seeking behavior with deprivation, and it shows similar patterns of social mediation and persistence in the face of evidence that it is damaging (Benowitz 1985; Fagerstrom 1991; Henningfield 1984). Within the neuropsychiatric patient population, there is growing evidence that nicotine can profoundly affect central nervous system processes (Newhouse and Hughes 1991). Individual variability in the intensity of the dependence is wide, and despite the large number of smokers who successfully quit on their own, many others can and do benefit from a variety of interventions. As with any behavior change process, patients will have individual needs requiring different approaches to achieve maximum effect during treatment.

In this chapter, we examine the current strategies available to the mental health professional and offer guidelines for initial and long-term intervention. We also discuss the smoking patient who presents special clinical problems: the alcoholic patient, the marijuana-smoking patient, and the patient with other serious psychiatric problems, in particular depression and anxiety disorders.

## ▼ IMPACT OF CIGARETTE SMOKING: WHY SHOULD PEOPLE STOP?

Unlike the other addictions considered in this section, heavy use of tobacco has not been widely recognized as producing significant psychological disturbance, other than craving and difficulty in stopping. Only recently has the powerful addictive nature of nicotine been more thoroughly investigated and better understood (U.S. Department of Health and Human Services 1988). Jaffe and Kranzler (1979) noted in a review of the psychiatric literature that prior to publication of the DSM-III in 1980, virtually no attention had been paid to excessive tobacco use as a psychological problem worthy of treatment. Only in the last few years have social disapproval and even legal sanctions become factors in curbing tobacco use; these developments are becoming increasingly important reasons for individuals to seek treatment. The medical problems arising from cigarette smoking have led to the need to take smoking seriously as an addictive disorder; thus it is appropriate to review first the health risks of smoking. Since the first Surgeon General's report on smoking and health (U.S. Department of Health, Education, and Welfare 1964), smoking has been recognized as a serious medical problem and, in the last 15 years, has been linked irrefutably to many serious diseases, including cancer, heart disease, lung disease, complications of diabetes, and ulcers. Comprehensive discussions of health risks are available in the Surgeon General's reports (e.g., U.S. Department of Health and Human Services 1983; U.S. Department of Health and Human Services 1985; U.S. Department of Health Education and Welfare 1964; U.S. Department of Health Education and Welfare 1979) and most recently in the 1989 Surgeon General's report (U.S. Department of Health and Human Services 1989) celebrating the 25 years of progress since the 1964 report. A much briefer summary is presented by Fielding (1985).

## Physiologic Effects of Cigarette Smoke

### Carbon monoxide and other gases

The health consequences and symptoms of smoking have been attributed to the many noxious substances found in cigarette smoke, including carbon monoxide and other toxic gases. Carbon monoxide develops a strong bond with hemoglobin, causing smokers to lose as much as 15% of the oxygen-carrying capacity of their red blood cells. The loss of this

oxygen can have a deleterious effect on the heart and circulatory system and may be a significant causal factor for the increased risk of cigarette smokers for coronary heart disease (CHD). Although levels of tar and nicotine have declined in cigarettes manufactured in recent years, the level of carbon monoxide has not decreased.

Inhaled along with carbon monoxide in cigarette smoke are other toxic gases such as hydrogen cyanide, ammonia, hydrogen oxide, and nitrogen oxide, all of which have been shown to produce toxic effects. These gases are most immediately responsible for coughing and narrowing of the bronchial tubes and, over time, paralysis of the cilia, thickening of the mucus-secreting membranes, and eventually chronic obstructive pulmonary disease (COPD).

### Tar

Tar is a toxic particulate of cigarette smoke and is considered a *complete carcinogen*, not only causing but promoting malignant changes. In cigarettes manufactured in the United States over the last three decades, tar yield has decreased from an average of 37 mg per cigarette to 12 mg. Among the many toxic organic compounds found in the tar phase are nonvolatile *N*-nitrosamines and aromatic amines, both known human carcinogens. The smoke from the burning end of the cigarette, *sidestream* smoke, contains considerably higher amounts of the carcinogenic aromatic amines than does *mainstream* smoke and has been demonstrated to have an effect on the health of individuals who do not smoke themselves but are in the smoker's environment (passive smoking or involuntary smoking; Glantz and Parmley 1991; U.S. Environmental Protection Agency 1992).

### Nicotine

Nicotine causes the release of catecholamines, epinephrine, and norepinephrine, causing an increase in the following: heart rate, blood pressure, cardiac output, oxygen consumption, coronary blood flow, arrhythmias, peripheral vasoconstriction, and mobilization and utilization of free fatty acids. Nicotine is thought to contribute to heart disease through the acute strain placed on the cardiovascular system while smoking and, over time, as an irritant in the blood vessels, increasing the buildup of plaque and promoting arteriosclerosis. Thus nicotine and carbon monoxide appear to produce the major adverse effects leading to CHD. In the diabetic patient, nicotine is a factor in both acute and chronic reduction of blood flow to the limbs, contributing to death of tissue and amputation. Nicotine as the primary psychoactive substance in tobacco will be discussed later in this chapter (U.S. Department of Health and Human Services 1988).

### Medical impact

The impact of cigarette smoking on morbidity and mortality from chronic disease is great. The development of lung cancer is 10 times more likely for smokers than nonsmokers and 15–25 times greater for heavy smokers (2 or more packs per day). Smokers have two to four times greater risk of dying from CHD than nonsmokers, depending on their rate of smoking (U.S. Department of Health and Human Services 1983). Of as much concern is smoking's effect on major respiratory ailments; it accounts for 90% of the development of chronic bronchitis and emphysema (Fielding 1985). Babies of smoking mothers weigh less at birth compared with those of nonsmoking mothers and are at higher risk for still-birth and neonatal death, possibly through absorption of lead, cadmium, and cyanide from cigarette smoke (Kleinman et al. 1988; Kuhnert and Kuhnert 1985; Sexton and Hebel 1984). Of more immediate concern to many smokers are troublesome symptoms such as morning cough; shortness of breath; fatigue; sputum production; hoarseness; increased pulse; skin and teeth stains; and increased incidence, severity, and duration of colds. Increased attention is being paid to the particular issues of smoking in hospitalized medical patients, particularly given the Joint Commission on Accreditation of Healthcare Organizations, which required all medical centers to implement smoke-free policies by January 1, 1992. The effects of passive smoking on respiratory and cardiac patients have received the most attention; however, recognition of the particular issues for other medical patients, such as those with cancer and diabetes, is also growing. Consequently, the role of the psychiatrist in addressing smoking within a consultation-liaison service is also increasing (Kristeller and Ockene 1987).

Assessment of a smoking patient also necessitates a consideration of other risk factors that act synergistically to cause CHD, COPD, and cancer. The risk for individuals with hypercholesterolemia and hypertension is greater than just the additive effect of each risk factor. Similarly, smoking, when coupled with exposure to asbestos and other occupationally encountered substances, greatly increases the smoker's risk of cancer of the lung when compared with smokers who are not so exposed. Recently more attention has also been given to the synergistic effect of smoking and alcohol use on mortality (Hughes, in press). The importance of intervening with alcoholic smokers will be discussed later in this chapter.

Smokers sometimes believe that the damage caused by smoking has already been done and there is little value in quitting. It is important to inform patients that for many diseases this is not so. Of note is that the 1990 Surgeon General's report, *The Health Benefits of Smoking Cessation* (U.S. Department of Health and Human Services 1990) addresses the benefits of stopping, rather than the risks of continuing to smoke. From an interventional perspective, such an approach is very valuable. A major conclusion of this report was that "smoking cessation has major and immediate health benefits for men and women of all ages. Benefits apply to persons with and without smoking-related disease." For example, life expectancy is longer among patients who stop smoking after the diagnosis of CHD than in those who continue to smoke. The risk of heart disease attributable to smoking drops 50% in the first year of abstinence and with the next year returns to that of someone who has never smoked (Rosenberg et al. 1985). Similarly, with certain lung diseases and circulation problems, cessation of smoking greatly improves the prognosis; symptoms may reverse quickly following cessation (Fielding 1985), although risk of mortality does not drop as quickly as for heart disease.

In summary, the constituents of cigarette smoke in both the gas and particulate phases affect almost every organ of the body and cause excess mortality and morbidity for all of the major diseases. The symptoms of smoking are often obvious, and the more mental health professionals and other health care providers are able to relate these "personally relevant" effects to smoking, the greater the likelihood that the smoker will be motivated with personal reasons to attempt cessation. The provider also must be able to convey the benefits of cessation to the patient. The provider's knowledge of these health risks and benefits of cessation is important and must be used skillfully to educate patients without giving them unrealistic expectations and without frightening them unnecessarily, which is counterproductive if it leads to increased denial or resistance.

## ▼ FACTORS SUPPORTING SMOKING BEHAVIOR

### Etiology and Stages of Smoking

Cigarette smoking is a complex behavior pattern that, like most behavior patterns, is affected by many psychosocial factors and goes through a sequence of stages. During the initiation phase, individuals start experimenting with cigarettes, generally before age 20 years and then move into the transition phase, in which environmental and psychological factors influence their becoming smokers or nonsmokers. Smokers then develop and maintain their smoking habit or attempt cessation. Stopping smoking proceeds in stages, precontemplation is followed by contemplation, followed by readiness for action, taking action or steps toward quitting, followed often by several relapses before long-term cessation is maintained (DiClemente et al. 1991).

Initiation of smoking is strongly associated with social forces or forces extrinsic to the individual (e.g., peer pressure) and with psychological variables (e.g., self-esteem, status needs, other personal needs). The sociological variables that are so important during the formation of the habit seem to play a minor role in the maintenance stage once smoking has become part of the life-style of the individual. As the habit continues, it becomes more and more tied to psychological and physiologic needs and becomes an intrinsic part of the person's life, having many functions. Cessation and maintenance of cessation are affected by a combination of social, psychological, and physiologic variables acting on and within the individual (Leventhal and Cleary 1980). One study (Salber et al. 1968) suggested that 85%–90% of those who smoke four cigarettes become regular smokers, making smoking as highly addictive in this respect as other substances such as heroin or cocaine. However, even teenage smokers may express a desire to quit (Stone and Kristeller 1992). By use of DSM-III-R criteria, 50% of self-quitters fulfill criteria for nicotine withdrawal (Breslau et al. 1992; Hughes et al. 1990), mak-

ing it likely that this group is physiologically addicted. In comparison, 78%–86% of the smokers who enter treatment for cessation experience withdrawal symptoms that are sufficient to fulfill DSM-III-R criteria (Hughes et al. 1991). Thus most smokers, unlike users of alcohol, can be considered biochemically addicted.

### Physiologic Factors

As evidence currently stands, it is likely that cigarette smoking is maintained by at least three physiologic processes: avoidance of nicotine withdrawal effects, desire for the immediate peripheral and central effects of nicotine, and the anticipation of the conditioned reinforcement consequences associated with smoking (Pomerleau and Pomerleau 1984; U.S. Department of Health and Human Services 1988). The first process largely interferes with immediate attempts to withdraw from cigarettes. The second process involves active effects of nicotine, such as the anorexic impact, arousal from norepinephrine activity, increased improvement in concentration, and euphoriant effects possibly mediated by β-endorphin release. The third process, the conditioning of these effects, is probably responsible for relapse under stress during the maintenance phase of cessation. The presence of this last process is still somewhat hypothetical but has been implicated in relapse processes in other drug abuse patterns (Pomerleau 1981). The extent of the physiologic addiction is most easily indirectly quantified in a clinical setting using the Fagerstrom Tolerance Questionnaire (FTQ; Fagerstrom 1978), which will be discussed more fully later. The FTQ is sensitive to amount of nicotine intake and to smoking to avoid immediate withdrawal effects (e.g., smoking immediately on awakening); lower scores tend to predict greater ability to stop smoking (Fagerstrom and Schneider 1989).

Although pharmacologic and physiologic factors play a role in smoking behavior change, they fail to explain the great variability observed in individual responses. There is a greater likelihood that lighter smokers will be more successful at cessation, but there are light smokers who cannot stop just as there are heavy smokers who quit easily. Most of the effects of nicotine are short-term, and therefore it is difficult to understand how they can explain relapse after a somewhat extended period of cessation except as a

## Psychological Factors

Tomkins's (1966) model of smoking and affect, one of the earliest accepted theories of smoking maintenance, proposed that smoking, like other behaviors, is maintained because it provides a way of minimizing negative affects (e.g., distress, anger, fear, shame, contempt) and evokes the positive affects of excitement, enjoyment, and surprise.

Similarly, other researchers noted that a smoker's primary use of cigarettes is to regulate emotional states. Laboratory studies have supported this conclusion that smoking significantly reduces fluctuations or changes in mood or affect during stress (Pomerleau and Pomerleau 1987; Schachter 1978). However, the specific mechanisms for such modulation of anxiety by smoking are still not clear but may relate to nicotine's effects on the hypophysealadrenal axis (Pomerleau and Pomerleau 1991). For many individuals it also becomes a habitual pattern with little conscious forethought. The cigarette serves as an artificial aid that reinforces smoking behavior.

Smokers who experience more stress in their lives or who have few resources for handling the stress have greater difficulty in the process of smoking cessation and in the maintenance of recently initiated nonsmoking behavior than those who have less stress or more effective resources. Aside from the physiologic effects, many smokers use cigarettes functionally as a way to provide a sanctioned "break" in their routine. The more addictive smoking patterns—which embrace a craving or compulsion, a need to control or prevent high levels of negative affect, or a belief that the cigarette can help control or stabilize troublesome situations—seem well outside the realm of conscious control. Thus some smokers' behavior fits the description of addiction as obsessive behavior centered around obtaining and using a substance. Heavier smokers generally have been found to experience more feelings of negative affect and more withdrawal symptoms than lighter smokers. The more excessive the habit, the less dependent it is on external cues and the more it shows a relationship to internal experiences and negative affect (Ockene et al. 1981).

Individuals who have had positive past experience with regard to behavior change have been able to develop good resources for dealing with stress; have an expectation that they can stop smoking or, as Bandura (1977) called it, a positive self-efficacy; and have a greater likelihood of successful cessation than those individuals with negative experiences (Condiotte and Lichtenstein 1981; Yates and Thain 1985). This will be discussed more fully later.

## Social Demographic and Medical Factors

The social and cultural environments of smokers also have been shown to affect their ability to stop smoking. Individuals who experience more social support for cessation and have fewer smokers in their environment are more successful at cessation attempts (Ockene et al. 1982). Likewise, smokers who are older and better educated and are at a higher occupational level are more likely to be able to stop smoking than the younger, less educated smoker who is at the lower end of the occupational scale (Ockene et al. 1982; Ockene and Camic 1985). Although approximately 40% of blue collar workers presently smoke, only about 27% of white collar individuals do so (U.S. Department of Health and Human Services 1988). Because of the demonstrated effect of the cultural and social environment on smokers, an area now under more intensive investigation is the use of work-site and hospital-based smoking intervention programs. These programs offer the promise of creating a more favorable environment and support for nonsmokers while at the same time providing the smoker with skills and resources necessary to become and remain a nonsmoker.

Individuals who present with more severe disease, at least with regard to CHD, have demonstrated a greater likelihood of cessation (Ockene et al. 1992). Ockene and colleagues found that the impact of an intervention program for patients after coronary arteriography was strongly affected by the reason for admission to the hospital and the extent of underlying coronary disease. At 6-month follow-up, smokers whose coronary arteriography took place after a myocardial infarction (MI) on the same admission were much more likely to be abstinent at 6 months (74% abstinent) than were either patients whose diagnosis was angina without a history of MI (49% abstinent) or patients who had had an MI in the recent past and were being admitted for further diagnostic evaluation (52% abstinent). That the intervention was most effective with sicker patients leads us to continue to need to investigate the development of effective and deliverable interventions directed at patients with demonstrated but milder levels of disease. In summary, individuals who have been found to be most successful in cigarette smoking cessation are those who are older, more educated, have good personal resources to help them mediate and implement change, receive support for the change from individuals in their environment; among diseased individuals, more severely diseased individuals are likely to stop smoking.

## ▼ GENERAL ISSUES IN TREATING SMOKING IN A MENTAL HEALTH FACILITY

Treatment for smoking cessation is available from many sources. Mental health professionals who offer such treatment have a responsibility to recognize that other psychiatric problems may exist along with the presenting problems and that the addiction to smoking, both physiologic and psychological, may require additional professional attention. Mental health practitioners may also be functioning as part of a health care team, in which knowledgeable attention to broader health issues is important. These responsibilities may be summarized as,

1. Assess psychiatric issues that may be present (e.g., current status; history; use of other addictive substances, especially alcohol, marijuana, and prescription medications) and recognize the potential role of smoking in the management of mental illness.
2. Evaluate the impact of these other problems on the patient's ability to stop smoking. Other problems may seriously complicate the course of the patient's ability to stop smoking or to maintain abstinence, resulting in a decision to treat such problems either prior to or concurrently with smoking. On the other hand, the best professional recommendation may be that, despite other problems, the patient can pursue a smoking cessation program because the smoking appears disassociated from the other difficulties.
3. Offer treatment or make appropriate referrals for other problems that may become apparent. If

a mental health facility or hospital offers a smoking cessation program, patients may use their smoking as a safer and more acceptable route through which to gain help for other problems.
4. Be familiar with the physiologic processes to which smoking is related, the physiologic aspects of nicotine addiction, and the appropriate use of nicotine replacement therapy (NRT).
5. Provide treatment sensitive to patient needs, which may mean a range of treatment from offering self-help materials to brief counseling plus follow-up to formal smoking intervention programs.

## ▼ DIAGNOSIS AND ASSESSMENT

Most of the evaluation of a smoker is assessment-rather than diagnosis-oriented. Two important diagnostic questions, however, are the extent to which nicotine addiction is present and the coexistence of other addictive or psychiatric problems. Frequently, a medical diagnosis has led to the urgency of treatment. In such an instance, the practitioner would benefit by communicating with the treating physician, with the patient's permission; if the patient is complaining of physical symptoms (e.g., shortness of breath, chest pain) that have not been evaluated, arranging a medical referral is necessary.

The assessment covers the three areas outlined earlier: physiologic components of addiction, psychological components, and social factors. Within these areas, the evaluation of psychological components is the broadest, including behavioral patterns, cognitive or attitudinal aspects, and the emotional significance of smoking for the patient.

How extensive the evaluation is depends on the setting, the apparent needs of the patient, and the types of treatment available. In some settings, patients may be asked to complete a standardized assessment battery prior to the initial interview, including material related to smoking patterns; screening for psychiatric difficulties using a self-report questionnaire, such as the revised version of the Symptom Check List-90 (SCL-90-R; Derogatis 1977); and any other special requirements, such as the evaluation of the patient as a subject for hypnosis. Any areas of special concern can be followed up in that interview or in a subsequent one. A standardized assessment might be appropriate when large numbers of individuals are being screened for a standard group treatment in a clinical setting or at a work-site treatment program. If the treatment offered is individual sessions, then the assessment process can be incorporated more appropriately into the initial session.

The distinction between assessment and intervention is usually blurred within a cognitive-behavioral framework; gathering information about the external contingencies supporting smoking or about cognitions related to motivation increases self-aware-ness in a way that facilitates behavior change. Figure 11–1 is a flowchart of the major assessment issues in the following discussion in relation to possible treatment choices.

## Assessment of Physiologic Addiction

There are three primary ways to evaluate the extent of nicotine addiction and the likelihood that the in-

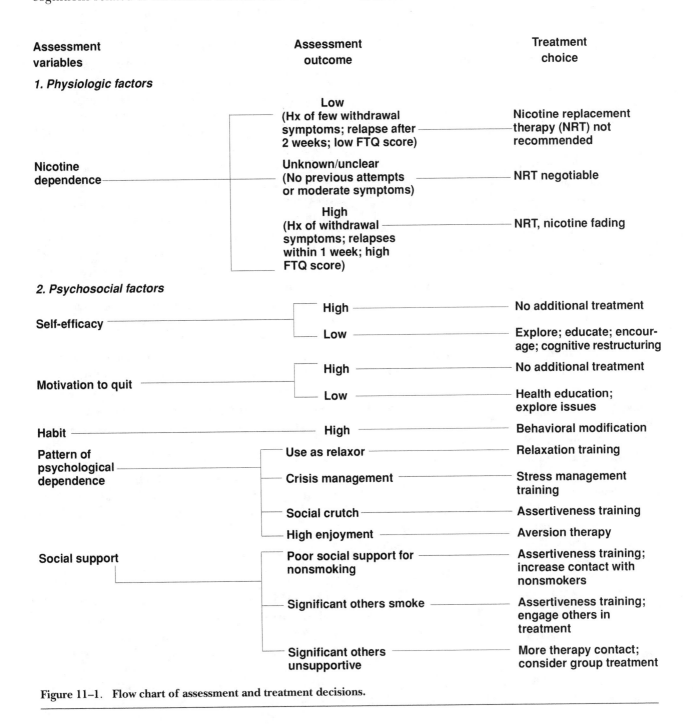

Figure 11–1. Flow chart of assessment and treatment decisions.

dividual will need special assistance during the withdrawal phase. One of the best indications is the reported difficulty of previous cessation attempts and the experience of withdrawal symptoms. The second is the score on the aforementioned FTQ (Fagerstrom 1978; Fagerstrom and Schneider 1989) or on the recent revision, which is psychometrically more reliable and predictive of the value of NRTs (i.e., gum containing nicotine or transdermal nicotine patches) during treatment (Heatherton et al. 1991). Recently, recommendations for minor revisions have been made to improve the sensitivity of scoring, validity, and internal reliability (Heatherton et al. 1991). The third way is to ask if the smoker thinks that he or she is addicted to nicotine.

If the smoker reports having had intense withdrawal symptoms in the past, has a pattern of relapsing within a few hours or days, and scores high on the addiction scale, then nicotine addiction probably plays an important role in maintaining the behavior. Not all heavy smokers (more than 1 pack per day) report intense withdrawal symptoms, and some relatively light smokers appear more susceptible.

If nicotine addiction is a significant problem, a number of treatment options are available that will be discussed in more detail later. Some individuals simply require more reassurance and support. Others may benefit from nicotine fading; the data are fairly clear that prescription of a NRT will benefit the addicted smoker more than the nonaddicted smoker. The degree of addiction, given identical nicotine intake, appears to be highly variable. Many ex-smokers or relapsed smokers report that withdrawal symptoms lasted longer than might be predicted from what is known of the pharmacology of nicotine, in which, for some individuals, psychological stimuli cue physiologic reactions that mimic withdrawal symptoms (Pomerleau and Pomerleau 1984).

Finally, while evaluating nicotine addiction patterns, it is important to assess the use of other substances, in particular alcohol, caffeine, marijuana, and anxiolytics.

## Psychological Assessment

### Behavioral assessment

Much can be learned from a simple smoking history questionnaire. In addition to basic descriptive infor-

mation, the smoker also should be asked about past attempts at quitting, resources that helped, factors that hindered, experience with other behavioral changes, factors that may have led to relapse, and highest- and lowest-"need" cigarettes.

In addition to the collection of this information, the smoker can be introduced to behavioral self-monitoring, which requires the smoker to record the time, place, mood, need, and thoughts associated with each cigarette smoked. This is best accomplished by the smoker carrying around a sheet of paper wrapped around a cigarette pack (a "wrap sheet") that the smoker is instructed to fill out before smoking each cigarette because delayed recall is very unreliable. After 1 week, it is possible to graph the pattern of cigarettes smoked during the course of the week. These records give the patient and provider an understanding of what behaviors, cognitions, and environmental factors are related to smoking. Following self-monitoring, the smoker is asked to identify any patterns observed; the clinician can then examine the sheets further with the smoker. Some patients are uncomfortable or resistant to keeping behavioral records and should not be unduly pressured to do so. An attempt at a 24-hour recall of cigarettes smoked can be a reasonable replacement for this, accompanied by focused questions such as "Which cigarettes tend to be 'automatic' ones you really wouldn't miss?", or "In what situations do you tend to smoke?"

If a patient is seen only once for an initial evaluation before referral to a treatment group, then self-monitoring can be incorporated into the early group sessions. Otherwise, self-monitoring between the first and second individual session is an effective way to gather more information, engage the patient immediately in the treatment process, and assess level of motivation. Most patients will also find that monitoring in this way assists them in cutting back, particularly on cigarettes smoked automatically.

### Assessment of attitudes and cognitions

The individual's reasons for smoking can be assessed with the Why Do You Smoke? self-test, consisting of 18 questions that assess the aspects of the smoking habit that predominate for that individual: stimulation, handling, accentuation of pleasure-relaxation, reduction of negative feelings, psychological addiction, and habit. These dimensions are similar to those provided by Tomkins (1966) and are identified in factor-analytic studies (Kozlowski 1979). Although not evaluating attitudes per se, this scale provides a convenient way to assess a patient's perception of his or her smoking. The responses can be used quite effectively to introduce the need for a multicomponent approach to treatment. For example, suggestions for behavioral substitution can be tied specifically to those dimensions ranked highest.

More central to assessment of attitude is an evaluation of the patient's commitment to cessation and sense of self-efficacy in reaching a goal of abstinence. A 14-item self-efficacy questionnaire developed by Yates and Thain (1985) and derived from research by Condiotte and Lichtenstein (1981) was able to predict with a high degree of accuracy which patients would relapse by 6 months. A cognitive approach to behavior change emphasizes two types of self-efficacy expectations that mediate the decision to change and the eventual behavior change (Bandura 1977). The first type is a response-outcome expectancy that a given course of action will lead to a particular outcome. For example, how firmly does the patient expect that stopping will improve health? These cognitions must be favorable if the decision to change is to occur; understanding the health impact of smoking has been shown to be a critical factor in maintenance of cessation by post-MI patients. If beliefs are not favorable, then intervention and education must begin at this level. High levels of both positive expectancy and self-efficacy tend to predict success (Strecher et al. 1986).

The second type of self-efficacy has to do with an individual's belief in his or her ability to make the desired change—an expectation of success. A positive belief that one has the necessary tools and resources to live comfortably and effectively without cigarettes leads to a greater commitment to change and to a persistence of efforts. Research in smoking cessation strongly supports the idea that expectation of success is an important factor in changing this behavior. For smokers with little expectation of their ability to quit due either to perceived or actual deficits in personal skills or environmental supports, treatment will begin with enhancing mastery expectations or skills. Once treatment is initiated, expectation enhancement can occur with the use of self-monitoring, successful performance accomplishments, cognitive restructuring, physiologic feedback, and mastery of physiologic or emotional arousal leads.

*Emotional meaning of cigarettes*

In some cases, it may become apparent that for certain patients strong symbolic issues are related to smoking. This should be pursued, particularly if there are many unsuccessful attempts at quitting, if the smoker has serious health problems related to smoking, if the cigarettes appear closely tied to self-image, or if a family member has had severe health problems as a smoker. The use of cigarettes probably always had some special meaning to the individual. This meaning need not always be explored in an initial evaluation. Even in a group setting, imagery work or hypnosis may facilitate the uncovering of this meaning in a powerful way. In other cases, the smoker may be aware of the connection but needs encouragement to explore it fully. The clinician can also consider the impact of other issues in the smoker's life on his or her ability to stop smoking. In what way do other psychiatric issues appear to affect the ability to stop smoking? Are there any unusual life stressors occurring so that treatment for smoking might be more successful at another time? Stopping smoking during periods of moderate stress may help the patient realize that alternative coping strategies can be available and may protect against relapse at a future period of higher stress.

**Social Assessment**

Three aspects of social support are important: 1) the number of smokers among the patient's friends, family, and co-workers; 2) the quality of support for cessation that can be expected by the smoker; and 3) the extent to which the smoker is able to be assertive in resisting social pressures to smoke. These can be assessed either in a questionnaire or in the assessment interview. The latter is preferable if time is available.

## ▼ INTERVENTION

A wide variety of interventions have been shown to be effective in helping people stop smoking, and many interventions show long-term outcome at 6–12 months to be better than in an untreated comparison group. Investigations evaluating smoking cessation interventions have indicated that treatments that incorporate behavioral and cognitive-behavioral approaches have been the most effective (Lichtenstein 1982). NRT, including both gum and patches, pharmacologic interventions for smoking cessation, has recently become available and has been successfully integrated with these cognitive-behavioral approaches (Tonnesen et al. 1991; Transdermal Nicotine Study Group 1992). The methods and treatment program proposed here are based on a cognitive-behavioral model of smoking behavior with incorporation of the physiologic factors (see Figure 11–1 for selected treatment options and their relationship to assessment outcomes).

Smoking cessation has three stages, which various researchers have identified as the following: 1) contemplation and commitment to change, 2) an action phase for actual change, and 3) maintenance of change (Marlatt and Gordon 1985; Prochaska and DiClemente 1983). The second stage or period of initial change has tended to be the major focus of smoking treatment programs, although of late it has become increasingly evident that it is as important to understand the process of developing a commitment to change and how to prevent relapse once change occurs. Prevention of relapse has gained most of its attention in the alcoholism field. In a natural history study of almost 1,000 smokers, Prochaska and DiClemente (1983) found that most individuals cycle through these three stages several times before being abstinent for 1 year. The clinician may feel less frustrated in attempts to promote change by recognizing that many smokers quit several times before successful cessation occurs. Strategies corresponding to the stages of change will be presented in the following sections, although these strategies and stages are in fact not clearly separated and blend into each other during treatment.

## ▼ STAGE 1: COMMITMENT TO CHANGE AND GOAL SETTING

The ambivalent patient is the norm. The patient may be attempting to quit for the first time, or may have a history of numerous frustrating attempts and relapses. The patient may be expecting the clinician to perform some magic to remove all ambivalence. Without offering such a promise, the clinician must help the patient become aware of, understand, and accept these mixed feelings. Before entering this

cycle, there is a *pre-contemplation* period in which the smoker is actively resistant to new input that encourages change. The need to work with patients who are actively resistant may increase as social and medical pressures to stop smoking increase, and smokers who are resistant to stopping feel coerced into doing so. Four steps that use the information gathered during the assessment process are suggested to help the provider work with the smoker in the process of developing a commitment to change:

1. Examine the risks of smoking and benefits of quitting in relation to the patient's medical, psychological, and social status. Results from the physical examination can be used effectively here. Smokers who have already experienced the onset of disease have a greater likelihood of quitting (Ockene et al. 1991; Pederson 1982). As noted in the discussion of assessment of motivation, a positive response-outcome efficacy is necessary before the patient will be willing to initiate change. If this is lacking, then it may be that the smoker has a distorted or erroneous view of the effects of smoking and of cessation on his or her health or may be denying the seriousness of the disease. A pamphlet or other written material about the relationship between smoking and disease can reinforce the verbal message to the patient. The National Cancer Institute pamphlet "Clearing the Air" (National Cancer Institute 1989) has a list of useful suggestions. The clinician may have to help the smoker explore other reasons for cessation that may be more important or personally relevant. For example, an individual may be more concerned about the effects of smoking on his or her children than on his or her own health.

2. Review past efforts at behavior change and current smoking patterns. It should be made clear to the patient that the pattern of repeated attempts leading to eventual success at smoking cessation is a common one. Focusing on a past history of even short successes or of successful change in other behaviors can be used to help facilitate self-confidence. Relabeling of past cessation periods (no matter how short) as successes rather than failures is important.

3. Determine the patient's strengths and weaknesses that can help facilitate change or interfere with change. As previously noted, factors that

contribute to successful smoking cessation and maintained abstinence are the following:

▼ A belief in the value of the change
▼ A belief in one's ability to change
▼ A strong sense of personal security
▼ A low level of stress or life changes
▼ Good social support
▼ Low levels of negative affect (e.g., depression, anger, anxiety)

The first two factors were noted to develop during the initial stages of intervention. If there are deficits in the other factors (e.g., a low sense of personal security, high levels of stress, poor social supports, or high levels of negative affect), interventions will be needed to decrease these deficits. Some of these changes may need to occur before an attempt at complete cessation is realistic.

4. Establish specific goals that are important to the patient and within the patient's current abilities. The three main alternatives for the patient are to make no immediate change in smoking, to reduce the amount smoked, or to quit. Some patients will need time to think over the information they have been given; others prefer to taper, going through a gradual retraining process in order to believe they are capable of making the desired change; and others may be ready to set a quit date at this point.

The aforementioned series of steps can be generally accomplished during the first visit with a smoker who does not have other psychological or substance abuse problems.

## ▼ STAGE 2: INITIAL CHANGE

Once the patient has made the commitment to stop smoking, a number of treatment options are available in the physiologic, psychological, and social domains. These options may be more limited in any given setting, but the full range will be reviewed here. In addition to the treatment modalities, other structural considerations must be made. These include number of sessions, individual versus group treatment, setting the quit date, cost of treatment, use of a written contract, and plans for follow-up.

Each of the above domains and structural consid-

erations will be discussed briefly here. The group protocol described here incorporates group support, nicotine fading or NRT, behavioral management techniques, physiologic feedback, contracting, relaxation training, and relapse prevention, with follow-up arranged on an individual basis. This program is illustrative rather than prescriptive, as many different types of treatment have been shown to be effective for both initial change and maintenance of change. Nicotine fading can be replaced with nicotine replacement for those smokers who are suitable candidates for gum or the patch. Much briefer versions of these intervention components provided in self-help manuals and by audiotape, and supplemented with telephone follow-up, also have demonstrated effectiveness for many smokers.

With few exceptions, adequate evidence does not exist to recommend which approaches might be more effective for given patients. One exception is the better response of more highly addicted patients to treatment directly addressing nicotine addiction (i.e., nicotine fading, use of nicotine-containing gum, or transdermal nicotine patches). Adequate hypnotizability for hypnosis programs is another individual characteristic of significance.

## Techniques to Decrease Physiologic Addiction

### *Nicotine fading*

*Nicotine fading* (Foxx and Brown 1979) has two components: brand switching to a lower nicotine level cigarette and gradual reduction of number of cigarettes (tapering). Despite laboratory evidence that smokers will compensate for decreased nicotine content by puffing more heavily or more often (Benowitz 1985), brand switching in the context of a treatment program can be effective if patients are instructed to guard against such behavioral compensation. Encouraging patients to switch to a less preferred brand also helps to weaken pleasant associations attached to smoking. Tapering the number of cigarettes before quitting not only reduces the probability of severe withdrawal but allows more dependent smokers to learn how to suppress smoking urges as well as to develop other skills that are helpful in quitting. A nicotine fading or dosage-reduction program is also helpful for smokers who may have a difficult time with immediate cessation. A complete list of brands and their tar and nicotine contents can be readily obtained from the Federal Trade Commission. Smokers should not plan to taper to nothing but should plan to set a quit date after a level of 5–10 cigarettes per day has been reached. As numbers of cigarettes smoked decrease, carbon monoxide levels in expired air can be measured to provide feedback on dosage reduction.

## NRT

Over-the-counter drugs purporting to aid in smoking cessation have been available for some time but have generally been found to be no more effective than placebo. In 1984 the Food and Drug Administration approved the use of nicotine-containing chewing gum as a prescription treatment for tobacco dependency to be used in combination with behavioral treatment. Nicotine-containing gum has been shown to be effective in aiding cessation, in combination with behavioral treatment (Lam et al. 1987; Schneider et al. 1983), but certain side effects and its often improper use has limited compliance and the value of the gum. When prescribing and discussing use of the gum, correct instruction for its use is a must. Some patients reject the gum because of the purposefully unappealing flavor, dislike for chewing, lack of a nicotine "high," or concern for replacing one drug of addiction with another. The inadequate instruction offered by providers in the use of the gum in many instances also limits the efficacy of this approach. Common errors in its use include chewing too fast, using too few pieces, not "parking" it (i.e., letting it sit between the cheek and teeth for proper absorption), and using it for too short a period of time.

The nicotine transdermal patch, marketed by several pharmaceutical companies in slightly different formulations and delivery systems, has also been shown to be effective (Rose et al. 1990; Tonnesen et al. 1991; Transdermal Nicotine Study Group 1992). It provides a more passive delivery system, thereby improving compliance; allows for a more continuous administration, avoiding *peaks* and *troughs* in nicotine delivery; and avoids the gastrointestinal and oral side effects associated with the gum. In one major trial (Transdermal Nicotine Study Group 1992), 6-month abstinence rates, when used in combination with be-

havioral treatment, were 26% compared with 12% for the placebo group. Withdrawal symptoms were decreased, including craving. The patch, therefore, may be a particularly useful adjunct for treatment of nicotine withdrawal. The instructions can be found on the drug inserts.

There have been no studies to indicate which NRT, gum or patch, is more efficacious with certain smokers. The gum is a more active administration permitting the smoker to regulate nicotine intake, and the patch permits a more steady state of nicotine. The needs of the smoker must be assessed to determine which should be used. Contraindications for using NRTs include recent heart attack, increasing angina, severe arrhythmia, pregnancy, or lactation.

Although NRTs may be safer than continued use of cigarettes, individuals in the above categories should explore other means to stop smoking. The α-adrenergic agonists (e.g., clonidine) have been found to decrease both nicotine withdrawal symptoms and craving, but more recent research (Covey and Glassman 1991; Glassman et al. 1988; Glassman et al. 1990) suggests that the positive effect on cessation may primarily be present for women. Use of such medication is still considered experimental. Jarvik and Henningfield (1988) have written an excellent review of the theoretical and clinical issues in the pharmacologic treatment of tobacco dependence.

## Psychological Dependency: Treatment Modalities

### Cognitive-behavioral treatment

Cognitive-behavioral treatment of smoking has been developed from treatment techniques used to intervene with a wide range of behavioral and addictive disorders. Rather than review these interventions extensively here, only illustrative examples are offered. The reader is directed to primary treatment texts such as Bandura (1969) and Goldfried and Davison (1976); the discussions of behavioral treatment of smoking in Marlatt and Gordon (1985), Lichtenstein and Brown (1985), or Ockene and Ockene (1992); or to treatment manuals such as *Taking Charge of Your Smoking* (Nash 1981).

**Behavior change strategies.** Patients can be helped to develop specific strategies to employ to stop smoking. These strategies can be grouped under the following categories of behavioral methods:

▼ Avoiding specific situations or events that bring on a desire or urge to smoke
▼ Substituting alternative behaviors incompatible with smoking cigarettes when urges arise (e.g., use of deep muscle or mental relaxation, exercise, low-calorie snacking)
▼ Cognitive restructuring to help reduce positive associations with cigarettes; to develop alternative thought responses to stressful situations; or to develop the belief that other methods can help reduce anxiety, depression, or other uncomfortable affects
▼ Activating social support of friends, family, and/or co-workers

These strategies can be introduced in conjunction with review of the patient's self-monitoring form, which provides a means to identify higher- and lower-need cigarettes. The patient then begins to use behavior change strategies to eliminate first low-need cigarettes and then higher-need cigarettes.

**Rewards.** Planning rewards throughout the change process will help sustain patient motivation over what may be a long road toward permanent cessation. Advise patients to plan periodic rewards not associated with smoking for successes in meeting goals for a week, a month, and so on (e.g., make a special purchase or a special phone call, treat yourself to an evening out, set time aside for a hobby). As a provider, you can reward signs of progress and reinforce the belief in the patient's ability to change.

**Contracts.** A behavioral contract can serve as an aid to the provider and patient in establishing realistic goals and steps by which to accomplish them. The contract should include specific information about whether the patient will taper or stop smoking, a quit date, reasons for stopping, steps to follow in response to situational factors that could interfere with efforts to stop smoking, and a plan for follow-up. The contract's purpose is to make explicit the specific ways in which the patient will attempt to change the smoking behavior. The methods listed should be as specific as possible. For example, the patient who chooses exercise as a substitution activity for smoking should identify the type of activity, when it will be done,

where it will be done, how it will be done, and with whom. It is also advisable to have alternative strategies written down in case the first choice of coping methods cannot be accomplished (e.g., carrying sugarless candy in your pocket while at a business meeting where it would be inappropriate to start physical activity). The provider and patient can design an appropriate contract, either verbal or written. Written contracts seem to be more effective in sealing the commitment of both parties and are very effectively used in brief interventions to underscore the concern of the caregiver.

Another aspect of contracting is to set weekly goals for specific changes, an exercise that can be particularly valuable in a group setting. Members can gain feedback on whether their goals are appropriate and support for achieving them. Group members who are on the periphery may be encouraged to focus more attention on specific tasks.

*Aversive techniques*

The use of aversive stimuli to promote desired behavior change has a strong theoretical foundation in behavioral interventions (within both operant and classical conditioning models). These techniques have included electric shock, covert sensitization (aversive imagery), and aversive manipulation of smoke intake (i.e., rapid smoking, satiation smoking, and smoke holding). In addition, maintenance plans may include forfeiture of money (perhaps to a charity) if relapse occurs.

Most of these techniques appear to be relatively weak when used alone. Electric shock, in particular, appears to fail in generalizing to outside therapy (Pechacek 1979) and is not often used. Covert sensitization, the use of vivid imagery of unpleasant sensations (e.g., nausea) paired with the behavior of smoking, is one variation on imagery techniques. Use of cigarette smoke as the aversive stimulus is intuitively appealing. Aversion to the smoke itself characterizes many ex-smokers. Rapid smoking (inhaling every 6 seconds) and satiation (doubling or tripling daily consumption) may help a smoker weaken a positive attachment to cigarettes. Smoke holding (holding smoke in the mouth while continuing to breathe) is also promising because it contains aversive aspects without the medical risks of rapid smoking. It has been shown to be an effective adjunct in combination with other components (Lando and McGovern 1985), seems to have minimal side effects, but has generally been underused.

### Hypnosis

Broadly defined, there are two basic approaches to the use of hypnosis in the treatment of smoking. In the first, hypnosis is the focus of a single-session treatment, instructions are often standardized, and the therapy may be offered in a group format (Barabasz et al. 1986; Neufeld and Lynn 1988; Williams and Hall 1988). The best-known version of this approach, developed by Spiegel (1970), focuses on health-promoting suggestions (e.g., "For your body, smoking is a poison . . . you need your body to live . . . you owe your body respect") and includes the use of self-hypnosis. With a well-motivated patient group, this approach has been shown to produce 6-month abstinence rates in the range of 20%–40%, with higher success rates associated with individualized induction, greater clinical experience, and greater patient hypnotizability (Barabasz et al. 1986; Holroyd 1980; Nuland and Field 1970; Spiegel 1970). The second approach uses hypnosis to explore individual motives more fully and to overcome resistance and usually incorporates other adjunctive techniques as indicated. An excellent discussion of the use of hypnobehavioral and hypnoprojective techniques in treatment of smoking is found in Brown and Fromm (1987). When a multimodal approach is taken that may include multiple sessions, self-hypnosis, hypnoprojective techniques, and follow-up, 6-month abstinence rates have been reported in the range of 50%–68% (Holroyd 1980; Nuland and Field 1970).

Degree of hypnotizability, whether measured directly with the Stanford Hypnotic Clinical Scale (Morgan and Hilgard 1975) or indirectly with the Tellegan Absorption Scale (Tellegan and Atkinson 1974), helps to predict 6-month abstinence from smoking after treatment with hypnosis (Baer et al. 1986; Barabasz et al. 1986).

### Relaxation techniques

Relaxation training can be a valuable adjunct to smoking cessation treatment. One of the most common reasons that patients give for relapse is an in-

ability to handle stressful situations (Shiffman 1982). Habitual smokers may report having few, if any, alternative ways to manage stress (other than avoidance of it).

Certain types of relaxation training (e.g., deep breathing, brief meditation, visualization exercises) can serve as effective functional equivalents to smoking. Once well learned, they can be used for a few moments at a time, under almost any circumstances, and may provide two of the benefits associated with smoking: a brief break from ongoing activity and a physiologically active relaxation effect. Training in diaphragmatic breathing, use of a personal positive relaxing image, or a simple focused mantra meditation technique can be done relatively quickly and then strengthened with home practice and a few minutes of use in treatment sessions.

*Restricted environmental stimulation therapy* (REST) is an intervention related to both relaxation and hypnosis techniques and has been shown to be a promising treatment for smoking, with high maintenance rates when used in combination with self-management techniques (Best and Suedfeld 1982). A clinical follow-up of several hundred smoking patients found that a combination of hypnosis and REST produced high long-term abstinence rates (Barabasz et al. 1986). A more extensive review of the use of REST in behavioral medicine is found elsewhere (Suedfeld and Kristeller 1982).

## Social Support and Number of Contacts

Some programs recommend patient contact be of very high frequency during the initial withdrawal period. The American Lung Association program uses 1 week of daily contact. Although this frequency of contact has been effective, it is usually not realistic for the patient or provider. Brief counseling, particularly in medical settings, provided by the physician (Ockene et al. 1988) or another health care professional, has also demonstrated effectiveness. For more intensive individual treatment, we have found weekly contact for approximately 4 weeks and then biweekly contact for another 4 weeks to be a reasonable frequency and one that provides the tapering of contact necessary for the patient to internalize control. This frequency allows the provider to give reinforcement directly and to alter the plan as needed. For the more dependent smoker or one who has other problems, a longer program may be indicated. A follow-up plan is important for helping the patient to maintain the changed behavior and allows the provider to detect the possibility of relapse. Minimal intervention protocols generally include weekly and then monthly telephone contact, for which there is high patient acceptance, with the opportunity for an additional visit if desired or if relapse occurs (Ockene et al. 1992). The group protocol outlined here has eight weekly sessions, with a 2-week interval before the final eighth session to wean the participants from dependence on the group. One or more follow-up sessions are scheduled individually. Most relapse occurs within 3 months, although it continues at a slower rate thereafter (Ockene 1983). The smoking relapse curve appears to be similar to that of other addictive disorders (Hunt et al. 1971).

Patients can be instructed to call a help line any time they have a problem in maintaining the smoking behavior change, but use of such lines is generally very low. Smokers can be helped and encouraged to build up social support systems of individuals in their natural environment. Some individuals have a difficult time asking others for help; the provider can aid in the development of this ability. Significant others may also be invited to participate in the intervention sessions if this seems appropriate. A patient who has a natural support system that is weak and cannot be strengthened may need more frequent contacts.

## Other Structural Considerations

### Individual versus group treatment

Group treatment has the advantage of social support and sharing of strategies and problems by group members. Group programs usually are cognitive-behavioral in orientation and should incorporate tapering, nicotine fading, or use of NRT for the more dependent smoker. The American Cancer Society and American Lung Association sponsor such treatment programs, and they are often offered through clinics or worksites. Hypnosis can also be effectively offered in a group format, either as a single session (Holroyd 1980) or as part of a multimodal treatment program (Brown and Fromm 1987).

Individual treatment is more appropriate when a provider has few smokers in his or her practice, for patients who have other problems that complicate treatment, and for patients who refuse to participate in a group. Some techniques, such as acupuncture or hypnosis, are more commonly offered individually. All of the noted cognitive-behavioral techniques may be used either individually or in a group. Some clinicians who consider the use of NRT for selected patients have found it useful to insist that these patients attend a cognitive-behavioral group such as the one offered by the American Lung Association before prescribing the gum or patch. Individualized sessions can then be devoted to specialized problems. Brief individual treatment is also more appropriate when there is a desire or need to reach all smokers within a given population, such as on an inpatient cardiac service, in an outpatient medical clinic, in a prenatal care clinic, or on a psychiatric service.

### Setting the quit date

In group treatment, all patients are advised to use the same quit date. In the 8-week program we outline here, the quit date is set at the fifth session, providing a tapering phase before and a relapse prevention phase following. Other group programs may set it earlier or later. In any case, the patient should prepare for the quit date, removing environmental signals to smoke (e.g., cigarettes or ashtrays), and take social pressures into mind (the initial 3 days of withdrawal are the most difficult). In individual treatment, more flexibility is possible. Some patients appear for a first session planning to quit at that point and should not be discouraged from doing so if their decision is judged to be appropriate. The first session must then include a brief review of withdrawal symptoms and an initial development of strategies to be used in lieu of smoking. For the patient who plans to use the patch or nicotine-containing gum, the quit date may need to be week 1 instead of week 5. Quitting immediately may need to be reconsidered, however, if an initial assessment indicates that the patient has an unrealistic view of what can be accomplished or appears to have few resources available. As mentioned above, other patients may hope to taper gradually to nothing, but such a plan is usually unrealistic and further exploration of feelings of loss related to giving up cigarettes may be necessary.

## ▼ STAGE 3: MAINTENANCE OF NONSMOKING—MONITORING AND EVALUATING PATIENT PROGRESS

A major difficulty in smoking cessation, as with other substance abuse behaviors, is maintenance of the changed behavior. As many as 70% of those who stop smoking relapse within a year. Up to 65% of self-quitters relapse within the first week after cessation (Hughes and Hatsukami 1992). Changing smoking patterns takes time, and a focus on relapse prevention is necessary during the behavior change phase and the maintenance phase. Preparation for coping with withdrawal symptoms may begin with the initial interview and then become more focused and personalized after the actual quit date (Shiffman 1986). Most quitters who relapse have at least one symptom of nicotine withdrawal (Gritz et al. 1991). The following strategies facilitating maintenance of nonsmoking behavior can be used in the last two sessions of a smoking intervention program as well as during follow-up.

### Coping With Withdrawal Effects

Almost all smokers who use a "cold turkey" approach to quitting cigarettes will experience some withdrawal distress (Gunn 1986). Informing patients and preparing them to cope with some of the possible symptoms and side effects of cessation, as described in the DSM-IV tobacco withdrawal syndrome, can add to the success of the smoking intervention. The symptoms will begin within 24 hours and decrease quickly and most will disappear within 1 month (Hughes et al. 1990). Craving, decreased heart rate, hunger, and weight gain may persist over a longer period of time. All withdrawal symptoms except decreased heart rate may be partly eased by exercise or relaxation or the use of nicotine-containing gum or transdermal nicotine patches. An additional symptom of nicotine withdrawal may include excess sputum production as the bronchial tubes regain their ability to clean out the lungs. Abstinence has also been shown to affect performance on attention tasks (Hughes et al. 1990). This may be present for at least 1–10 days and is reversed by NRT (U.S. Department of Health and Human Services 1990).

### Relapse Prevention

Relapse prevention as a treatment technique was originally developed by Marlatt and Gordon (1980) to deal with preventing the relapse of alcohol abuse and has been extrapolated to use with smokers (Lichtenstein and Brown 1985). It has been demonstrated that smokers and ex-smokers who learn relapse prevention skills maintain cessation longer and smoke fewer cigarettes if they relapse than their counterparts who do not receive such training (Davis and Glaros 1986). An excellent discussion of relapse prevention from a self-management approach is presented by Shiffman et al. (1985) in a text on relapse prevention edited by Marlatt and Gordon. The four key elements summarized below can provide preparation for maintaining nonsmoking behavior. The use of NRT can also decrease the withdrawal symptoms and aide in the maintenance of cessation while the ex-smoker is continuing to work on the behavioral aspects of smoking cessation.

### 1. Identifying high-risk situations

Identification of high-risk situations is the first step to relapse prevention. A high-risk situation is any situation in which a "slip" or lapse is very likely to occur. It is important for the patient to anticipate high-risk situations as it is difficult to deal with a potential slip at the last moment. Situations formerly associated with smoking can trigger urges to smoke and intense craving even though initial cessation and nicotine withdrawal have occurred. Research studies have revealed three types of situations in which ex-smokers are most likely to slip (Shiffman 1982): 1) situations involving negative emotional states (e.g., anger, frustration, stress); 2) situations involving positive emotional states (being relaxed, in a good mood), often involving the consumption of alcohol; and 3) situations in which others are observed to be smoking cigarettes. Using this information as a guide, patients can be helped to try to predict specific situations that might cause difficulty and then anticipate various means to cope with them. The initial self-monitoring can be a guide to this process, and group support can be particularly valuable. An important reason to continue either group or individual sessions past the quit date and the nicotine withdrawal period is to allow time for such high-risk situations to occur.

## 2. Coping rehearsal

The outcome of exposure to a high-risk situation is determined by whether the ex-smoker produces a coping response (Shiffman et al. 1985). Once the patient has identified a situation in which the risk of resuming smoking is high, the patient can do the following to help prepare for the actual situation when it arises:

▼ *Vividly imagining the high-risk situation.* Patients are asked to imagine themselves in an identified high-risk situation: where, when, with whom? Visualization creates details of the people, the place, and what the patient is feeling, thinking, and doing in the situation.

▼ *Developing and rehearsing specific coping strategies.* Once the high-risk situation has been visualized in sufficient detail, the ex-smoker specifies what could be done to cope with events surrounding this high-risk scene, other than smoking. Such strategies might include excusing yourself briefly from a party to take a walk, carrying gum as substitute, calling a friend if feeling tense, or identifying yourself as a nonsmoker when offered a cigarette. The goal is to develop and mentally to rehearse specific strategies to prevent a slip, which could lead to a full-blown relapse.

## 3. Identifying and combating undermining self-statements

The cognitive aspects of relapse prevention are equally important. The smoker can think about self-statements as thoughts that can undermine the goal to remain an ex-smoker. Certain self-statements can be a setup for possible slips, which could lead to relapse if one is not prepared. Such thoughts, or rationalizations to resume smoking, often develop without really being aware of them, and the smoker needs to learn how to respond to them. Examples of resumptive thinking include the following:

▼ *Nostalgia.* "I remember how nice it was when I smoked at parties."

▼ *Testing oneself.* "I'll bet I could smoke just one and then put it down!"

▼ *Crisis.* "I think I can handle this better with a cigarette."

▼ *Self-doubts.* "I'm one of those people who doesn't have any self-control."

**Combating resumptive thinking.** There are various ways that the patient can respond to these thoughts about smoking. The following four methods provides convenient strategies.

▼ *Challenging.* This involves a direct mental confrontation with the logic of the thoughts. Training and rehearsal of positive responses can help the patient feel that there are choices available and that they need not inevitably lead back to smoking. Such responses would include, "Taking just one cigarette may be an excuse for returning to smoking. I do not need to test myself."

▼ *Visualization of benefits of nonsmoking.* It is useful at this point to remind the ex-smoker to think about emerging personal benefits. Thoughts about these benefits can help against rationalizations to resume smoking.

▼ *Visualization of unpleasant smoking experiences.* Another strategy is specific recollection of smoking's unpleasant aspects. For example, have the patient think back to how he or she felt the morning after smoking heavily.

▼ *Distractions.* Rather than confronting thoughts directly, the ex-smoker can simply divert attention from smoking to pleasant, enjoyable subjects (e.g., vacation spot, relaxation) that help the patient take his or her mind off smoking.

## 4. Avoiding the abstinence violation effect

If a slip or lapse occurs while a person is committed to abstinence, many people will have a highly emotional reaction known as the *abstinence violation effect* (AVE; Marlatt and Gordon 1980), which includes guilt and feelings of low self-esteem or depression. The individual often feels weak and lacking in willpower, leading to such thoughts as "I blew it" and "I might as well keep on smoking." Patients need to be reminded to remember the following points:

▼ *Just knowing about the AVE will help considerably.* Help the patient realize that the AVE is a common reaction to a slip, and it is natural to feel guilty and lacking in willpower if one slips. The important point is that the feeling will pass. The challenge is to let the AVE reaction subside without smoking another cigarette to cope with the associated stress.

▼ *A slip is different from a relapse.* A slip is nothing

more than an error or mistake—everyone makes mistakes—and smoking one cigarette need not imply personal weakness or lack of willpower. A relapse involves a complete resumption of smoking.

▼ *You can learn from your slips.* A slip can be a learning experience. Patients can retrace their steps to determine what might be done differently next time to avoid another slip.

▼ *How the individual chooses to interpret the slip is critical.* Emphasize that one slip does not make a smoker, unless the person chooses to make it so.

*If relapse occurs*

In the event of relapse, providers can emphasize the positive aspects of having stopped even briefly and be prepared to recommend another strategy to achieve cessation, rather than focusing on the image of failure. To decide on the future of the intervention process will call for a realistic appraisal of progress so far and willingness to rethink the cessation strategy, if necessary.

## ▼ SUMMARY OF TREATMENT RECOMMENDATIONS

To stop smoking, a smoker must perceive this change as being beneficial; a smoking cessation program needs to be seen by the smoker as efficacious. The smoker must thus be helped to develop self-confidence and a belief that he or she can become a nonsmoker. From the behavioral perspective, the smoker must learn new skills or enhance old skills that can be used in place of cigarettes to deal with problems as they arise. The individual needs also to be able to attribute changes in smoking behavior to personal abilities and skills rather than to will power or to the external aspects of treatment (Bandura 1977). From the pharmacologic perspective, a smoker who demonstrates a high physiologic dependency on nicotine would benefit from nicotine replacement therapy or tapering. This would allow him or her to work on the behavioral aspects without needing to also deal with the physiologic withdrawal at the same time. Finally, the patient will benefit from relapse prevention training, including anticipation of the abstinence violation effect, and ways to recognize and manage resumptive thinking. In re-

ferring back to Figure 11–1, it becomes clearer how assessment outcome may point the way toward different treatment choices, allowing the clinician to tailor a multicomponent treatment program to the needs of each patient.

## ▼ REFERENCES

American Psychiatric Association: Diagnostic and Statistical Manual of Mental Disorders, 3rd Edition, Revised. Washington, DC, American Psychiatric Association, 1987

American Psychiatric Association: Diagnostic and Statistical Manual of Mental Disorders, 4th Edition. Washington, DC, American Psychiatric Association, 1994

Baer L, Carey RJ, Meminger S: Hypnosis for smoking cessation: a clinical follow-up. Int J Psychosom 33: 13–16, 1986

Bandura A: Principles of Behavior Modification. New York, Holt, Rinehart, and Winston, 1969

Bandura A: Self-efficacy: toward a unifying theory of behavioral change. Psychol Rev 84:191–215, 1977

Barabasz A, Baer L, Sheehan D, et al: A three year clinical follow-up of hypnosis and REST for smoking: hypnotizability, absorption and depression. Int J Clin Exp Hypn 34:169–181, 1986

Benowitz N: The use of biologic fluid samples in assessing tobacco smoke consumption, in Measurement in the Analysis and Treatment of Smoking, NIDA Res Monogr 48. Edited by Grabowski J, Bell C. Rockville, MD, Department of Health and Human Services, 1985, pp 6–26

Best J, Suedfeld P: Restricted environmental stimulation therapy and behavioral self-management in smoking cessation. Journal of Applied Social Psychology 12:408–419, 1982

Breslau N, Kilbey M, Andreski M: Nicotine withdrawal symptoms and psychiatric disorders: findings from an epidemiologic study of young adults. Am J Psychiatry 149:464–469, 1992

Brown D, Fromm E: Hypnosis and Behavioral Medicine. Hillsdale, NJ, Lawrence Erlbaum Associates, 1987

Condiotte M, Lichtenstein E: Self-efficacy and relapse in smoking cessation programs. J Consult Clin Psychol 49: 648–658, 1981

Covey L, Glassman A: A meta-analysis of double-blind placebo-controlled trials of clonidine for smoking cessation. British Journal of Addiction 86:991–998, 1991

Davis J, Glaros A: Relapse prevention and smoking cessation. Addict Behav 11:105–114, 1986

Derogatis L: SCL-90-R: Administration Scoring and Procedures Manual I. Baltimore, MD, Clinical Psychometrics Research, 1977

DiClemente C, Prochaska J, Fairhurst S, et al: The process of smoking cessation: an analysis of precontemplation, contemplation, and preparation stages of change. J Consult Clin Pschol 59:295–304, 1991

Fagerstrom K: Measuring degree of physical dependency to tobacco smoking with reference to individualization of treatment. Addict Behav 3:235–241, 1978

Fagerstrom K: Towards better diagnoses and more individual treatment of tobacco dependence (Special Issue: Future Directions in Tobacco Research). British Journal of Addiction 86:543–547, 1991

Fagerstrom K, Schneider N: Measuring nicotine dependence: a review of the Fagerstrom Tolerance Questionnaire. J Behav Med 12:159–182, 1989

Fielding J: Smoking: health effects and control. N Engl J Med 313:491–498, 1985

Foxx R, Brown R: Nicotine fading and self-monitoring for cigarette abstinence or controlled smoking. J Appl Behav Anal 12:111–125, 1979

Glantz S, Parmley: Passive smoking and heart disease: epidemiology, physiology, and biochemistry. Circulation 83:1–12, 1991

Glassman A, Stetner F, Walsh B, et al: Heavy smokers, smoking cessation and clonidine: results of a double-blind, randomized trial. JAMA 259:2863–2866, 1988

Glassman A, Helzer J, Covey L, et al: Smoking, smoking cessation, and major depression. JAMA 264:1546–1549, 1990

Goldfried M, Davison G: Clinical Behavior Therapy. New York, Holt, Rinehart, and Winston, 1976

Gritz E, Carr C, Marcus A: The tobacco withdrawal syndrome in unaided quitters. British Journal of Addiction 86:57–69, 1991

Gunn R: Reactions to withdrawal symptoms and success in smoking cessation clinics. Addict Behav 11:49–53, 1986

Heatherton T, Kozlowski L, Frecker R: The Fagerstrom Test for Nicotine Dependence: a revision of the Fagerstrom Tolerance Questionnaire. British Journal of Addiction 86:1119–1127, 1991

Henningfield J: Pharmacologic basis and treatment of cigarette smoking. J Clin Psychiatry 45:24–34, 1984

Holroyd I: Hypnosis treatment for smoking: an evaluative review. Int J Clin Exp Hypn 23:341–357, 1980

Hughes J: Treatment of smoking cessation in smokers with past alcohol/drug problems. J Subst Abuse Treat (in press)

Hughes J, Hatsukami D: The nicotine withdrawal syndrome: a brief review and update. International Journal of Smoking Cessation 1:21–26, 1992

Hughes J, Higgins S, Hatsukami D: Effects of abstinence from tobacco: a critical review, in Research Advances in Alcohol and Drug Problems, Vol 10. Edited by Kozlowski L, Annis H, Cappell HD, et al. New York, Plenum, 1990, pp 317–398

Hughes J, Gust S, Skoog K, et al: Symptoms of tobacco withdrawal: a replication and extension. Arch Gen Psychiatry 48:52–59, 1991

Hunt W, Barnett L, Branch L: Relapse rates in addiction programs. J Clin Psychol 27:455–456, 1971

Jaffe JH, Kranzler M: Smoking as an addictive disorder, in Research on Smoking Behavior, NIDA Res Monogr 23. Edited by Krasnegor NA. Rockville, MD, U.S. Department of Health, Education, and Welfare, Public Health Service, 1979, pp 4–23

Jarvik M, Henningfield J: Pharmacological treatment of tobacco dependence. Pharmacol Biochem Behav 30:279–294, 1988

Kleinman J, Pierre M, Madans J, et al: The effects of maternal smoking on fetal and infant mortality. Am J Epidemiol 127:274–281, 1988

Kozlowski L: Psychosocial influences on cigarette smoking, in The Behavioral Aspects of Smoking, NIDA Res Monogr 26 (DHEW Publ No ADM-79-882). Edited by Krasnegor N. Rockville, MD, U.S. Department of Health, Education, and Welfare, Public Health Service, 1979, pp 97–125

Kristeller J, Ockene J: Assessment and treatment of smoking on a consultation service, in Consultation Liaison Psychiatry and Behavioral Medicine, Vol 2, Psychiatry. Edited by Cavenar O Jr. Philadelphia, PA, Lippincott, 1987, pp 1–13

Kuhnert B, Kuhnert P: Placental transfer of drugs, alcohol, and components of cigarette smoke and their effects on the human fetus, in Prenatal Drug Exposure: Kinetics and Dynamics, NIDA Res Monogr 60. Edited by Chiang CN, Lee CC. Rockville, MD, U.S. Department of Health and Human Services, 1985, pp 98–109

Lam W, Sxe P, Sacks H, et al: Meta-analysis of randomized controlled trials of nicotine chewing gum. Lancet 2:27–29, 1987

Lando H, McGovern P: Nicotine fading as a nonaversive alternative in a broad-spectrum treatment for eliminating smoking. Addict Behav 10:153–161, 1985

Leventhal H, Cleary P: The smoking problem: a review of the research and theory in behavioral risk modification. Psychol Bull 88:370–405, 1980

Lichtenstein E: The smoking problem: a behavioral perspective. J Consult Clin Psychol 50:804–819, 1982

Lichtenstein E, Brown A: Current trends in the modification of cigarette dependence, in International Handbook of Behavior Modification and Therapy. Edited by Bellack A, Hersen H, Kazdin A. New York, Plenum, 1985, pp 575–612

Marlatt GA, Gordon JR: Determinants of relapse: implications for the maintenance of behavior change, in Behavioral Medicine: Changing Health Lifestyles. Edited by Davidson PO, Davidson SM. New York, Brunner/Mazel, 1980, pp 410–452

Marlatt G, Gordon J (eds): Relapse Prevention. New York, Guilford, 1985

Morgan A, Hilgard J: Stanford Hypnotic Clinical Scale (SHCS), in Hypnosis in the Relief of Pain. Edited by Hilgard E, Hilgard J. Los Altos, CA, Kaufmann, 1975, pp 209–221

Nash J: Taking Charge of Your Smoking. Palo Alto, CA, Bull Publishing Co, 1981

National Cancer Institute: Clearing the Air (NIH Publ No 89-1647). Febraury 1989

Neufeld V, Lynn S: A single-session group self-hypnosis smoking cessation treatment: a brief communication. Int J Clin Exp Hypn 36:75–79, 1988

Newhouse P, Hughes J: The role of nicotine and nicotinic mechanisms in neuropsychiatric disease (Special Issue: Future Directions in Tobacco Research). British Journal of Addiction 86:521–525, 1991

Nuland W, Field P: Smoking and hypnosis: a systematic clinical approach. Int J Clin Exp Hypn 18:290–306, 1970

Ockene J: Changes in cigarette smoking behavior in clinical and community trials, in The Health Consequences of Smoking: Cardiovascular Disease: A Report of the Surgeon General. Washington, DC, U.S. Government Printing Office, 1983, pp 241–290

Ockene J, Camic P: Public health approaches to cigarette smoking cessation. Annals of Behavioral Medicine 7:14–18, 1985

Ockene J, Ockene I: Helping patients to reduce their risk for coronary heart disease: an overview, in Prevention of Coronary Heart Disease. Edited by Ockene I, Ockene J. Boston, MA, Little, Brown, 1992, pp 173–199

Ockene J, Nutall R, Benfari R, et al: A psychosocial model of smoking cessation and maintenance of cessation. Prev Med 10:623–638, 1981

Ockene J, Benfari R, Hurwitz I, et al: Relationship of psychosocial factors to smoking behavior change in an intervention program. Prev Med 11:13–28, 1982

Ockene J, Quirk M, Goldberg R, et al: A resident's training program for the development of smoking intervention skills. Arch Intern Med 148:1039–1045, 1988

Ockene J, Kristeller J, Goldberg R, et al: Increasing the efficacy of physician-delivered smoking intervention: a randomized clinical trial. J Gen Intern Med 6:1–8, 1991

Ockene J, Kristeller J, Goldberg R, et al: Smoking cessation and severity of disease: the Coronary Artery Smoking Intervention Study. Health Psychol 11:119–126, 1992

Pechacek T: Modification of smoking behavior, in Smoking and Health: A Report of the Surgeon General. Washington, DC, U.S. Government Printing Office, 1979, pp 5–63

Pederson L: Compliance with physician advice to quit smoking: a review of the literature. Prev Med 11:71–84, 1982

Pomerleau O: Underlying mechanisms in substance abuse: examples from research on smoking. Addict Behav 6:187–196, 1981

Pomerleau O, Pomerleau C: Neuroregulators and the reinforcement of smoking: towards a biobehavioral explanation. Neurosci Biobehav Rev 8:503–513, 1984

Pomerleau C, Pomerleau O: The effects of a psychosocial stressor on cigarette smoking and subsequent behavioral and physiological responses. Psychophysiology 24:278–285, 1987

Pomerleau O, Pomerleau C: Research on stress and smoking: progress and problems. British Journal of Addiction 86:599–603, 1991

Prochaska J, DiClemente C: Stages and processes of self–change of smoking: toward an integrative model of change. J Consult Clin Psychol 51:390–395, 1983

Rose J, Levin E, Behm F, et al: Transdermal nicotine facilitates smoking cessation. Clin Pharmacol Ther 47:323–330, 1990

Rosenberg L, Kaufman D, Helmrich S, et al: The risk of myocardial infarction after quitting smoking in men under 55 years of age. N Engl J Med 313: 1511–1514, 1985

Salber E, Freeman H, Abelin T: Needed research on smoking: lessons from the Newton study, in Smoking, Health and Behavior. Edited by Borgatta E, Evans R. Chicago, IL, Aldine, 1968, pp 128–139

Schachter S: Pharmacological and psychological determinants of smoking. Ann Intern Med 88:104–114, 1978

Schneider N, Jannik M, Forsythe A, et al: Nicotine gum in smoking cessation: a placebo-controlled, double-blind trial. Addict Behav 8:253–262, 1983

Sexton M, Hebel J: A clinical trial of change in maternal smoking and its effect on birth weight. JAMA 251:911–915, 1984

Shiffman S: Relapse following smoking cessation: a situational analysis. J Consult Clin Psychol 50:71–86, 1982

Shiffman S: A cluster-analytic classification of smoking relapse episodes. Addict Behav 11:295–307, 1986

Shiffman S, Read L, Maltese J, et al: Preventing relapse in ex-smokers: a self-management approach, in Relapse Prevention: Maintenance Strategies in Treatment of Addictive Behaviors. Edited by Marlatt G, Gordon J. New York, Guilford, 1985

Spiegel H: A single-treatment method to stop smoking using ancillary self-hypnosis. Int J Clin Exp Hypn 18:235–250, 1970

Stone S, Kristeller J: Attitudes of adolescents towards smoking cessation. Am J Prev Med 8:221–225, 1992

Strecher V, DeVellis B, Becker M, et al: The role of self-efficacy in achieving health behavior change. Health Educ Q 13:73–92, 1986

Suedfeld P, Kristeller J: Stimulus reduction as a technique in health psychology. Health Psychol 1:337–357, 1982

Tellegan A, Atkinson G: Openness to absorbing and self altering experiences ("absorption"), a trait related to hypnotic susceptibility. J Abnorm Psychol 83:268–277, 1974

Tomkins S: Psychological model for smoking behavior. Am J Public Health 56:17–20, 1966

Tonnesen P, Norregaard J, Simonsen K, et al: A double-blind trial of a 16-hour transdermal nicotine patch in smoking cessation. New Engl J Med 325: 311–315, 1991

Transdermal Nicotine Study Group: Transdermal nicotine for smoking cessation. JAMA 266:3133–3138, 1992

U.S. Department of Health and Human Services: The Health Consequences of Smoking: Cardiovascular Disease: A report of the Surgeon General. Washington, DC, U.S. Government Printing Office, 1983

U.S. Department of Health and Human Services: The Health Consequences of Smoking: Cancer and Chronic Lung Disease in the Workplace: A Report of the Surgeon General. Rockville, MD, Office on Smoking and Health, 1985

U.S. Department of Health and Human Services: The Surgeon General's Report on Nutrition and Health. Washington, DC, U.S. Government Printing Office, 1988

U.S. Department of Health and Human Services: Reducing the Health Consequences of Smoking: 25 Years of Progress. Washington, DC, U.S. Government Printing Office, 1989

U.S. Department of Health and Human Services: The Health Benefits of Smoking Cessation: A Report of the Surgeon General. Washington, DC, U.S. Government Printing Office, 1990

U.S. Department of Health, Education, and Welfare: Smoking and Health: Report of the Advisory Committee to the Surgeon General of the Public Health Service. Rockville, MD, Centers for Disease Control, 1964

U.S. Department of Health, Education, and Welfare: Smoking and Health: A Report of the Surgeon General. Washington, DC, U.S. Government Printing Office, 1979

U.S. Environmental Protection Agency: Respiratory Health Effects of Passive Smoking: Lung Cancer and Other Disorders (Review Draft). Washington, D.C, Office of Research and Development, 1992

Williams J, Hall D: Use of single session hypnosis for smoking cessation. Addict Behav 13:205–208, 1988

World Health Organization: Mental Disorders: Glossary and Guide to Their Classification, 9th Revision. Geneva, World Health Organization, 1978

Yates A, Thain J: Self-efficacy as a predictor of relapse following voluntary cessation of smoking. Addict Behav 10:291–298, 1985

# Benzodiazepines and Other Sedative-Hypnotics

*David E. Smith, M.D.*
*Donald R. Wesson, M.D.*

## ▼ INTRODUCTION

In medical therapeutics, benzodiazepines have largely replaced the short-acting barbiturates and other nonbarbiturate sedative-hypnotics that were available before 1960. For this reason, this chapter focuses on the treatment of physical dependence on benzodiazepines and discusses other prescription sedative-hypnotics in terms of their similarities or differences from benzodiazepines.

The term *sedative-hypnotic* is a pharmacological classification that draws attention to medications' therapeutic applications. Sedative-hypnotics, commonly prescribed to reduce anxiety and to treat insomnia, are a chemically diverse group of compounds, yet they have pharmacological similarities that makes the sedative-hypnotic classification useful. For example, an overdose of about 10 times the usual therapeutic dose can be lethal.

Although most benzodiazepines could also be classified as sedative-hypnotics, they are more commonly grouped, as we have done here, by their *chemical* class name. This convention calls attention to benzodiazepines' clinical differences from the older sedative-hypnotics. The chemical classification for benzodiazepines is clinically useful because all benzodiazepines that are currently available in the United States for prescription, except for the benzodiazepine antagonist, flumazenil (Mazicon), share many pharmacological effects. Although there are significant differences among benzodiazepines (e.g., therapeutic indications, metabolic profile, receptor affinity, side effects, abuse potential), all benzodiazepine agonists produce sedation and little respiratory depression even in doses much higher than those used to treat anxiety or insomnia. Even when a

This chapter was supported in part by National Institute on Drug Abuse Grant R18 DA6082 to Friends Medical Sciences Research Center, Inc., and R01 DA06038 to Merritt Peralta Institute in Oakland, CA. The authors wish to acknowledge the assistance of Susan Steffens, Sandy Dow, and Annie Pan in the preparation of the manuscript; Benjamin Wesson for preparation of the graphics; and Walter Ling, M.D., for critiquing successive drafts of the manuscript.

benzodiazepine is taken in an overdose of 50–100 times the usual therapeutic dose, fatality from respiratory depression is rare. The "safety" of benzodiazepines in the overdose situation is an important advantage of the benzodiazepines over the older sedative-hypnotics.

Benzodiazepines exert their physiological effects by attaching to a subunit of γ-aminobutyric acid (GABA) receptors. The GABA receptor is made up of an ion channel and several subunits that bind to different drugs: one subunit binds GABA, another benzodiazepines, and another barbiturates.

The subunit that binds benzodiazepines has been designated the *benzodiazepine receptor* (Braestrup et al. 1977; Möhler and Okada 1977; Squires and Braestrup 1977). Benzodiazepines that enhance the effect of GABA are called *agonists*. Although receptors are usually named for the endogenous ligand that is an agonist at the receptor, the natural ligand for the benzodiazepine receptor was unknown at the time of its discovery and has still not been identified. Several nonbenzodiazepine compounds have been identified that attach to the receptor, however, it has not been established that these compounds attach to the receptor during normal physiological function.

GABA is the major inhibitory neurotransmitter in the brain, and GABA synapses, distributed throughout the brain and spinal cord, comprise as many as 40% of all synapses. The physiological function of GABA synapses is to modulate the polarization of neurons. The GABA receptor does this by opening or closing chloride ion channels (ionphores). Opening chloride channels allows more chloride ions to enter neurons. The influx of negatively charged chloride ions increases the electrical gradient across the cell membrane and makes the neuron less excitable. Closing the channels decreases electrical polarization and makes the cell more excitable.

Attachment of an agonist at the benzodiazepine receptor facilitates the effect of GABA (i.e., opens the chloride channel). The clinical effects are anxiety reductions, sedation, and increased seizure threshold. Except for flumazenil, all benzodiazepines listed in Table 12–1 are agonists.

Substances that attach to the benzodiazepine receptor and close the channel produce an opposite effect: they are anxiogenic and lower seizure threshold. Compounds, such as betacarboline, which produce the opposite effects from benzodiazepine agonists are called *inverse agonists*.

Some compounds attach to the benzodiazepine receptor but neither increase nor decrease the effect of GABA. In the absence of benzodiazepine agonist or inverse agonist, they are neutral ligands (i.e., they attach to the receptor and block the effects of both agonist and inverse agonist). Consequently, neutral agonists are often called *antagonists*. If the receptor is already occupied by an agonist or inverse agonist, the neutral agonist will displace the agonist or inverse agonist. Displacement of benzodiazepine agonist has clinical utility. For example, the benzodiazepine antagonist flumazenil (Mazicon-Roche, previously designated ro 15-1788), was made available in the United States in 1992 to reverse the sedation produced by a benzodiazepine overdose.

The interaction of benzodiazepine receptors with their ligand is extremely complex. Attachment of the ligands can alter the pharmacology of the receptor (e.g., alter the number of receptors or change the affinity of the ligand for the receptor).

## Benzodiazepines Abuse and Dependence

Most individuals who are not anxious do not find the effects of benzodiazepines reinforcing or pleasurable; therefore, benzodiazepines are not commonly used as recreational drugs. Studies indicate that individuals who abuse sedative-hypnotics prefer pentobarbital to diazepam, even at high doses (Griffiths et al. 1980).

Investigations of benzodiazepine dependency differed in focus in the United States from that in the United Kingdom. In the United States, investigators focused on high-dose abuse; in the United Kingdom, they focused on therapeutic dose dependency (Lader 1991).

Patients who become physically dependent on benzodiazepines can generally be classified into one of three groups:

1. Street drug–abusing individuals who self-administer benzodiazepines
2. Alcoholic individuals and prescription drug–abusing individuals who are being medically prescribed benzodiazepines for treatment for chronic anxiety or insomnia
3. Patients with depression or panic disorders who are prescribed high-doses of benzodiazepines for long periods of time

Street drug–abusing individuals may take benzodiazepines to ameliorate the adverse effects of cocaine or methamphetamine, to self-medicate heroin or alcohol withdrawal, to enhance the effects of methadone, or to produce intoxication when other drugs are not available. Benzodiazepines are rarely their drug of choice. Even if their use of benzodiazepines would not qualify as "abuse" according to DSM-IV criteria (American Psychiatric Association 1994), most people would call the use of benzodiazepines by street drug–abusing individuals *abuse* because their self-administration of benzodiazepines falls outside the context of medical treatment and is part of a polydrug abuse pattern. Further, benzodiazepines are often obtained by purchase on the street, theft, or forged prescriptions. When benzodiazepine dependency occurs in such patients, they must be treated in a comprehensive drug treatment program.

Alcoholic and prescription drug–abusing individuals who are being treated for chronic anxiety or insomnia are prime candidates for developing benzodiazepine dependency. They may receive benzodiazepines for long periods of time and may be biologically predisposed to develop benzodiazepine

dependency. For them, the subjective effects of benzodiazepines may be different. A study of alprazolam (1 mg) in alcoholic and nonalcoholic men found that alprazolam produced positive mood effects in alcoholic men that were not reported by the nonalcoholic men (Ciraulo et al. 1988).

Patients with depression or panic disorders may be prescribed high doses of benzodiazepines for long periods of time. Some of these patients will develop benzodiazepine dependency that, in this context, does not necessarily equate with a substance abuse disorder or contraindicate benzodiazepine treatment. A history of sedative-hypnotic abuse, alcoholism, or a history of severe symptoms following benzodiazepine discontinuation, however, is a relative contraindication.

## Other Sedative-Hypnotics

The short-acting sedative-hypnotics (e.g., secobarbital, pentobarbital) are primary drugs of abuse. Addicted individuals take them alone by mouth or by injection to produce intoxication. Intoxication with sedative-hypnotics is qualitatively similar to intoxication with alcohol. The desired effect of intoxication

**Table 12–1.** Benzodiazepines and their phenobarbital withdrawal equivalents

| Generic name | Trade name | Common therapeutic indication(s) | Therapeutic dose range (mg/day) | Dose equal to 30 mg phenobarbital for withdrawal (mg)[a] |
|---|---|---|---|---|
| Alprazolam | Xanax | Sedative, antipanic | 0.75–6 | 1 |
| Chlordiazepoxide | Librium | Sedative | 15–100 | 25 |
| Clonazepam | Klonopin | Anticonvulsant | 0.5–4 | 2 |
| Clorazepate | Tranxene | Sedative | 15–60 | 7.5 |
| Diazepam | Valium | Sedative | 4–40 | 10 |
| Estazolam | ProSom | Hypnotic | 1–2 | 1 |
| Flumazenil | Mazicon | Benzodiazepine antagonist | n/a | n/a |
| Flurazepam | Dalmane | Hypnotic | 15–30[b] | 15 |
| Halazepam | Paxipam | Sedative | 60–160 | 40 |
| Lorazepam | Ativan | Sedative | 1–16 | 2 |
| Midazolam | Versed | Intravenous sedation | n/a | n/a |
| Oxazepam | Serax | Sedative | 10–120 | 10 |
| Prazepam | Centrax | Sedative | 20–60 | 10 |
| Quazepam | Doral | Hypnotic | 15[a] | 15 |
| Temazepam | Restoril | Hypnotic | 15–30[a] | 15 |
| Triazolam | Halcion | Hypnotic | 0.125–0.50[a] | 0.25 |

[a]Phenobarbital withdrawal conversion equivalence is not the same as therapeutic dose equivalency. Withdrawal equivalence is the amount of the drug that 30 mg of phenobarbital will substitute for and prevent serious high-dose withdrawal signs and symptoms.
[b]Usual hypnotic dose.

is a state of *disinhibition*, in which mood is elevated; self criticism, anxiety, and guilt are reduced; and energy and self-confidence are increased. During intoxication, the mood is often labile and may rapidly shift from euphoria to dysphoria. Users may also be irritable, hypochondriacal, anxious, and agitated.

An individual who is intoxicated on sedative-hypnotics commonly has difficulty with recent memory, poor judgment, ataxia, slurred speech, and *sustained* vertical and horizontal nystagmus.

Buspirone (Buspar), a new class of anti-anxiety medication, appears to have minimal abuse potential and does not produce physical dependence. Its anti-anxiety effects take from days to weeks to develop. Buspirone will not prevent sedative-hypnotic withdrawal (i.e., it is not cross-tolerant with benzodiazepines) nor will it effectively treat the low-dose benzodiazepine withdrawal syndrome.

## ▼ BENZODIAZEPINE WITHDRAWAL SYNDROMES

The chronic use of either benzodiazepines or sedative-hypnotics at doses above the therapeutic range produces physical dependence, and both have similar withdrawal syndromes that may be severe and life-threatening. Therapeutic doses of benzodiazepines taken chronically also will produce physical dependence.

### High-Dose Benzodiazepine Withdrawal Syndrome

Studies in humans have established that large doses of chlordiazepoxide (Hollister et al. 1961) and diazepam (Hollister et al. 1963), taken for a month or more, produces a withdrawal syndrome that is clinically similar to the withdrawal syndrome produced by high doses of barbiturates (Isbell 1950). Other benzodiazepines have not been studied under such precise conditions, but numerous case reports leave no doubt that they too produce a similar withdrawal syndrome.

Signs and symptoms of sedative-hypnotic withdrawal include anxiety, tremors, nightmares, insomnia, anorexia, nausea, vomiting, postural hypotension, seizures, delirium, and hyperpyrexia. The syndrome is qualitatively similar for all sedative-hypnotics; however, the time course of symptoms de-

pends on the particular drug. With short-acting sedative-hypnotics (e.g., pentobarbital, secobarbital, meprobamate, and methaqualone) and short-acting benzodiazepines (e.g., oxazepam, alprazolam, and triazolam), withdrawal symptoms typically begin 12–24 hours after the last dose and peak in intensity between 24 and 72 hours. (Symptoms may develop more slowly in patients with liver disease or in the elderly because of decreased drug metabolism.) With long-acting drugs (e.g., phenobarbital, diazepam, and chlordiazepoxide), withdrawal symptoms peak on the fifth to eighth day.

During untreated sedative-hypnotic withdrawal, the electroencephalogram may show paroxysmal bursts of high-voltage, slow-frequency activity that precedes the development of seizures. The withdrawal delirium may include confusion and visual and auditory hallucinations. The delirium generally follows a period of insomnia. Some patients may have only delirium, others only seizures, and some may have both delirium and convulsions.

### Low-Dose Benzodiazepine Withdrawal Syndrome

In addiction medicine literature, the low-dose benzodiazepine withdrawal syndrome is also referred to as *therapeutic-dose withdrawal*, *normal-dose withdrawal*, or *benzodiazepine discontinuation syndrome*.

Through the 1960s and early 1970s, most physicians in the United States believed that benzodiazepines taken within the usual recommended therapeutic dosage range did not produce physical dependence. The knowledge that some patients had a withdrawal syndrome emerged from clinical observations and case studies.

For example, in 1978, investigators at the Addiction Research Center in Lexington, Kentucky, published a detailed case study of an incarcerated 37-year-old man who had been prescribed 30–45 mg of diazepam daily for 20 months (Pevnick et al. 1978). Five days after the subject was crossed over to placebo, he reported muscle twitches, muscle cramps, facial numbness, and abdominal cramping. The patient lost weight and had an increased pulse rate. Symptoms occurred primarily between days 5 and 9 and had abated by day 16.

Winokur et al. (1980) reported a similar placebo crossover study of a 32-year old-man who had been taking 15–25 mg of diazepam for 6 years. Two days following crossover to placebo, the patient began complaining of anxiety, dizziness, blurred vision, constipation, and palpitations. During the next 2 days, he became increasingly anxious and irritable, diaphoretic, grossly tremulous, and had difficulty expressing his thoughts coherently. His auditory and olfactory senses were "at times so hypersensitive that normally unobtrusive sounds (a watch ticking) or odors (an orange peel) were acutely uncomfortable to him." He was also hypersensitive to tactile stimuli, to the point that he could not stand to have clothes on his body. His symptoms subsided over the next 30 days.

Standard medical texts prior to 1980 generally concurred that therapeutic doses of benzodiazepines produced minimal withdrawal. The 1980 edition of Goodman and Gilman stated the following:

> High doses of benzodiazepines must be given for long periods of time and then abruptly withdrawn before marked withdrawal symptoms, including seizures, appear . . . . In most instances after usual doses, there is no withdrawal syndrome.

In 1979, lay attention about benzodiazepine dependence was heightened by the publication of Barbara Gordon's book, *I'm Dancing as Fast as I Can* (Gordon 1979), which chronicled her difficulty in quitting Valium.

During the 1980s, clinical studies and case reports established that therapeutic doses of benzodiazepines could produce physical dependency. Many patients experienced a transient increase in symptoms for 1–2 weeks after withdrawal. A few patients experienced a severe, protracted withdrawal syndrome that included symptoms (e.g., paresthesias and psychosis) that were not present before. It is this latter withdrawal syndrome that has generated much of the concern about the long-term "safety" of the benzodiazepines.

Because of psychiatrists' concerns about benzodiazepines' serious side effects and dependency, the American Psychiatric Association (APA) formed a task force that reviewed the issues and published its report in book form (American Psychiatric Association 1990). The task force's conclusions were unambiguous about therapeutic dose dependency:

> Physiological dependence on benzodiazepines, as indicated by the appearance of dis-

continuance symptoms, can develop with therapeutic doses. Duration of treatment determines the onset of dependence when typical therapeutic anxiolytic doses are used: clinically significant dependence indicated by the appearance of discontinuance symptoms usually does not appear before four months of such daily dosing. Dependence may develop sooner when higher antipanic doses are taken daily. (p. 56)

The chronology of therapeutic dose dependency is important for medical-legal reasons. During the 1980s, some patients who developed therapeutic dose dependency sued their physicians for malpractice, claiming that their physicians were negligent in not warning them about the possibility of therapeutic dose dependence and in treating them with benzodiazepines for extended periods of time, often many years. Some of these patients were treated, however, during the 1960s and 1970s. During those decades, therapeutic dose dependency was not part of mainstream medical knowledge.

Indeed, many people who have taken benzodiazepines in therapeutic doses for months to years can abruptly discontinue the drug without developing symptoms. But others, taking similar amounts of a benzodiazepine, develop symptoms ranging from mild to severe when the benzodiazepine is stopped or the dosage is substantially reduced. Characteristically, patients tolerate a gradual tapering of the benzodiazepine until they are at 10%–20% of their peak dose. Further reduction in benzodiazepine dose causes patients to become increasingly symptomatic.

There are at least three explanations of symptoms that emerge following benzodiazepine cessation. Two of these, *symptom rebound* and the *protracted withdrawal syndrome*, are the result of dependence; the other, *symptom reemergence*, is not.

**Symptom rebound.** *Symptom rebound* is an intensified return of the symptoms for which the benzodiazepine was prescribed (e.g., insomnia or anxiety). The term comes from sleep research in which rebound insomnia is commonly observed following sedative-hypnotic use. Symptom rebound lasts a few days to weeks following discontinuation (American Psychiatric Association 1990, p. 16). Symptom rebound is the most common consequence of prolonged benzodiazepine use.

**Protracted withdrawal from benzodiazepines.** This syndrome should be distinguished from the protracted withdrawal syndrome that has been described for most drugs, including alcohol (Geller 1991). The symptoms generally attributed to protracted withdrawal syndromes consist of relatively mild symptoms such as irritability, anxiety, insomnia, and mood instability. The protracted withdrawal syndrome from benzodiazepines can be severe and disabling and lasts many months.

Many symptoms are nonspecific, and they often mimic an obsessive-compulsive disorder with psychotic features. Some symptoms—increased sensitivity to sound, light, and touch, and paresthesias—are particularly suggestive of low-dose withdrawal.

The waxing and waning symptom intensity illustrated in waviness of the line in the phase IV section of Figure 12–1 is characteristic of the low-dose protracted benzodiazepine withdrawal syndrome. Patients are sometimes asymptomatic for several days, then, without apparent reason, they become acutely anxious. Often there are concomitant physiological signs (e.g., dilated pupils, increased resting heart rate and blood pressure). The intense waxing and waning of symptoms is important in distinguishing low-dose withdrawal symptoms from symptom reemergence.

The protracted benzodiazepine withdrawal has no pathognomonic signs or symptoms, and the broad range of nonspecific symptoms produced by the protracted benzodiazepine withdrawal syndrome also could be the result of agitated depression, generalized anxiety disorder, panic disorder, partial complex seizures, and schizophrenia. The time course of symptom resolution is the primary differentiating feature between the symptoms generated by withdrawal and symptom reemergence. The symptoms from withdrawal gradually subside with continued abstinence, whereas symptom reemergence and symptom sensitization do not.

**Symptom reemergence (recrudescence).** Patients' symptoms of anxiety, insomnia, or muscle tension abate during benzodiazepine treatment. When the benzodiazepine is stopped, symptoms return to the

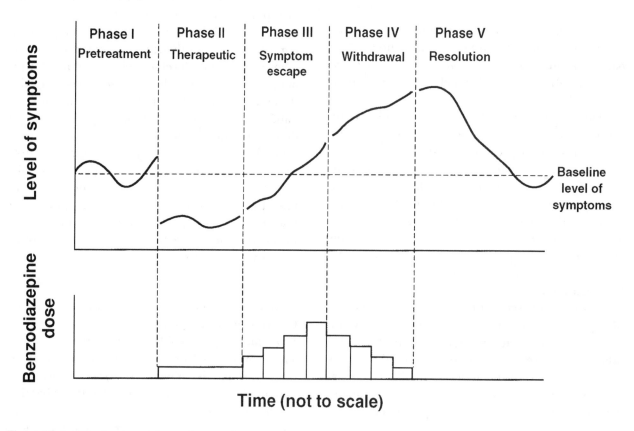

**Figure 12–1.** The treatment-dependence cycle.

same level as before benzodiazepine therapy. The reason for making a distinction between symptom rebound and symptom recurrence is that symptom recurrence suggests that the original symptoms have not been adequately treated, whereas symptom rebound suggests a form of withdrawal syndrome (American Psychiatric Association 1990, p. 17).

## Benzodiazepine Receptor Hypothesis of Low-Dose Withdrawal

From a clinical perspective, we postulate that the low-dose benzodiazepine withdrawal syndrome is caused by alteration in GABA receptor function (Smith and Wesson 1983, 1985). A receptor-site mediated withdrawal syndrome would explain why benzodiazepine withdrawal symptoms develop at low doses and why symptoms develop when tapering patients from the last few milligrams of the benzodiazepine. This is consistent with other receptor-mediated withdrawals. For example, when tapering a patient from methadone following methadone maintenance, patients generally tolerate slow taper with few symptoms until the daily dose of methadone is reduced below 20 mg.

## Risk Factors for Low-Dose Withdrawal

Some drugs or medications may facilitate neuradaptation by increasing the affinity of benzodiazepines for their receptors. Phenobarbital, for example, increases the affinity of diazepam to benzodiazepine receptors (Skolnick et al. 1981; Olsen and Loeb-Lundberg 1981), and prior treatment with phenobarbital has been found to increase the intensity of chlordiazepoxide (45 mg per day) withdrawal symptoms (Covi et al. 1973). Patients at increased risk for development of the low-dose withdrawal syndrome are those with a family or personal history of alcoholism, those who use alcohol daily, or those who concomitantly use other sedatives. Case control studies suggest that patients with a history of addiction, particularly to other sedative-hypnotics, are at high risk for low-dose benzodiazepine dependence. The short-acting, high-milligram potency benzodiazepines appear to produce a more intense low-dose withdrawal syndrome (Rickels et al. 1990).

## The Dependence/Withdrawal Cycle

When dependence arises during therapeutic treatment, there is often a sequence of phases, illustrated in Figure 12–1. The clinical course described here most often occurs during long-term treatment of a generalized anxiety disorder, panic disorder, or severe insomnia.

**Pretreatment phase.**   The first panel on Figure 12–1 represents the time before the patient was treated with benzodiazepines. Patients' symptoms generally vary in intensity from day to day depending on life stresses and the waxing and waning of their underlying disorder. For purposes of the illustration, the average symptom, shown by the horizontal dotted line, illustrates the patient's baseline level of symptoms.

**Therapeutic response phase.**   When treatment with a benzodiazepine is started, patients often have initial side effects, such as drowsiness, psychomotor impairment, or memory impairment. Tolerance to such side effects usually develops within a few days, and afterwards the patient's overall level of symptoms decreases. The therapeutic phase, illustrated in phase II of Figure 12–1, may last months to years.

**Symptom escape/dosage escalation phase.**   During long-term treatment, benzodiazepines may suddenly lose their effectiveness in controlling symptoms. For some patients, the *symptom escape* coincides with a period of increased life stress; for others, no unusual psychological stressor is apparent. Patients are often aware that the medication "no longer works" or that its effect is qualitatively different. The increasing symptoms are illustrated by the ascending wavy line in phase III of Figure 12–1.

As the usual doses of benzodiazepines lose effectiveness, patients may increase their benzodiazepine consumption in the hope that symptoms will again be controlled. As the daily dosage of benzodiazepine increases, they may develop subtle benzodiazepine toxicity that is difficult to diagnose without psychometric assessment. This may be a common clinical problem that generally goes unrecognized. It has not received sufficient research attention, and evidence at this time is scanty and indirect. Although many studies have demonstrated that acute doses of benzodiazepines impair cognitive function, there has been little study of the effects of benzodiazepines with prolonged use. One psychometric study, which compared long-term benzodiazepine-using subjects with subjects who were benzodiazepine abstinent, found that the long-term benzodiazepine-using subjects performed poorly on tasks involving visual-spatial ability and sustained attention (Golombok et al. 1988). Clinically, patients may not be aware that their impairment is benzodiazepine induced. Coping skills that were previously bolstered by the benzodiazepine become compromised. Some patients attempt suicide or participate in self-defeating behavior that is out of character for them.

The symptom escape phase is not an invariable consequence of long-term benzodiazepine treatment. Patients who have experienced symptom escape and dosage escalation may also be the most likely to have a protracted withdrawal syndrome.

**Withdrawal phase.** When patients stop taking the benzodiazepine or the daily dose falls below 25% of the peak maintenance dose, patients become increasingly symptomatic. The symptoms, represented by the wavy ascending line in phase IV of Figure 12–1, may be the result of symptom rebound, symptom reemergence, or the beginning of a protracted withdrawal syndrome. The symptoms that occur during this phase may be a mixture of symptoms that were present during the pretreatment phase and *new* symptoms. During the first few weeks, it is not possible to know exactly what is producing the symptoms or to estimate their duration. Symptoms of the same type that occurred during the pretreatment phase suggest symptom rebound or symptom reemergence. New symptoms, particularly alterations in sensory perception, suggest the beginning of a protracted withdrawal syndrome. Increasing the benzodiazepine dose will reduce symptoms because benzodiazepines have not completely lost effectiveness and because the withdrawal syndrome is reversed; however, symptom reduction will not be as complete as during the initial therapeutic phase.

**Resolution phase.** The duration of the resolution phase is highly variable. Most patients will have only symptom rebound lasting a few weeks; others will have a severe, protracted abstinence syndrome lasting months to over a year. During early abstinence, the patient's symptoms will generally vary in intensity from day to day. If abstinence from benzodiazepines is maintained, symptoms will gradually return to their baseline level. An encouraging finding of one discontinuation study was that "patients who were able to remain free of benzodiazepines for at least 5 weeks obtained lower levels of anxiety than before benzodiazepine discontinuation" (Rickels et al. 1990).

## ▼ PHARMACOLOGICAL TREATMENT OF BENZODIAZEPINE WITHDRAWAL

Physicians' response during the withdrawal phase is critical to achieving a resolution. Some physicians interpret patients' escalating symptoms as evidence of patients' "need" for benzodiazepine treatment and reinstitute higher doses of benzodiazepines or switch to another benzodiazepine. Reinstitution of any benzodiazepine agonist usually does not achieve satisfactory symptom control and may prolong the recovery process. Benzodiazepine withdrawal, using one of the strategies described below, generally achieves the best long-term outcome.

Another common response is to declare patients "addicted to benzodiazepines" and refer them to primary chemical dependency treatment. Referral to a chemical dependency program is not appropriate unless the patient has a substance abuse disorder.

The salient features of the various benzodiazepine withdrawal syndromes are summarized in Table 12–2. Benzodiazepine withdrawal strategies must be tailored to suit three possible dependence situations:

1. A high-dose withdrawal (i.e., doses greater than the recommended therapeutic doses for more than one month)
2. A low-dose withdrawal (i.e., doses below those in the upper range of Table 12–1)
3. A combined high-dose and low-dose withdrawal (i.e., following daily high doses for more than 6 months, both a high-dose sedative-hypnotic withdrawal syndrome and a low-dose benzodiazepine withdrawal syndrome may occur)

### High-Dose Benzodiazepine Withdrawal

Abrupt discontinuation of a sedative-hypnotic in patients who are severely physically dependent on it can result in serious medical complications and even death. There are three general strategies for withdrawing patients from sedative-hypnotics, including benzodiazepines. The first is to use decreasing doses of the agent of dependence. The second is to substitute phenobarbital or some other long-acting barbiturate for the addicting agent and gradually withdraw the substitute medication (Smith and Wesson 1970, 1971, 1983, 1985). The third, used for patients with a dependence on both alcohol and a benzodiazepine, is to substitute a long-acting benzodiazepine, such as chlordiazepoxide, and taper it over 1–2 weeks.

The pharmacologic rationale for phenobarbital substitution is that phenobarbital is long-acting, and little change in blood levels of phenobarbital occurs between doses. This allows the safe use of a progressively smaller daily dose. Phenobarbital is safer than the shorter-acting barbiturates; lethal doses of phenobarbital are many times higher than toxic doses, and the signs of toxicity (i.e., sustained nystagmus, slurred speech, and ataxia) are easy to observe. Finally, phenobarbital intoxication usually does not produce disinhibition, so most patients view it as a medication, not as a drug of abuse.

The method selected will depend on the particular benzodiazepine, the involvement of other drugs of dependence, and the clinical setting in which the detoxification program takes place.

The gradual reduction of the benzodiazepine of dependence is used primarily in medical settings for dependence arising from treatment of an underlying condition. The patient must be cooperative, able to adhere to dosing regimens, and not abusing alcohol or other drugs.

Substitution of phenobarbital can also be used to withdraw patients who have lost control of their benzodiazepine use or who are polydrug dependent. The phenobarbital substitution has the broadest use for all sedative-hypnotic drug dependencies and is widely used in drug treatment programs.

**Stabilization phase.**   The patient's history of drug use during the month before treatment is used to compute the stabilization dose of phenobarbital. Although many addicted patients exaggerate the number of pills they are taking, patient history is the best guide to initiating pharmacotherapy for withdrawal. Patients who have overstated the amount of drug they

**Table 12–2.**   Characteristics of syndromes related to benzodiazepine withdrawal

| Syndrome | Signs/symptoms | Time course | Response to reinstitution of benzodiazepine |
|---|---|---|---|
| High-dose withdrawal | Anxiety, insomnia, nightmares, major motor seizures, psychosis, hyperpyrexia, death | Begins 1–2 days after a short-acting benzodiazepine is stopped; 3–8 days after a long-acting benzodiazepine is stopped | Signs and symptoms reverse 2–6 hours following a hypnotic dose of a benzodiazepine |
| Symptom rebound | Same symptoms that were present before treatment | Begins 1–2 days after a short-acting benzodiazepine is stopped 3–8 days after a long-acting benzodiazepine is stopped; lasts 7–14 days | Signs and symptoms reverse 2–6 hours following a hypnotic dose of a benzodiazepine |
| Protracted, low-dose withdrawal | Anxiety, agitation, tachycardia, palpitations, anorexia, blurred vision, muscle cramps, insomnia, nightmares, confusion, muscle spasms, psychosis, increased sensitivity to sounds and light, and paresthesias | Signs and symptoms emerge 1–7 days after discontinuation of the benzodiazepine or after reduction of the benzodiazepine to below the usual therapeutic dose | Signs and symptoms reverse 2–6 hours following a sedative dose of high-potency benzodiazepine |
| Symptom reemergence | Recurrence of the same symptoms that were present before taking a benzodiazepine (e.g., anxiety, insomnia) | Symptoms emerge when benzodiazepine is stopped and continue unabated with time | Signs and symptoms reverse 2–6 hours following usual therapeutic dose of a benzodiazepine |

**Benzodiazepines and Other Sedative-Hypnotics**

are taking will become intoxicated during the first day or two of treatment. Intoxication is easily managed by omitting one or more doses of phenobarbital and recalculating the daily dose.

The patient's average daily sedative-hypnotic dose is converted to phenobarbital equivalents, and the daily amount divided into three doses. (The conversion equivalents for various benzodiazepines are listed in Table 12–1 and for other sedative-hypnotics in Table 12–3.)

The computed phenobarbital equivalence, dosage is given in three or four doses daily. If the patient is using significant amounts of other sedative-hypnotics (including alcohol) the amounts of all the drugs are converted to phenobarbital equivalents and added together (30 cc of 100-proof alcohol is equated to 30 mg of phenobarbital for withdrawal purposes). The maximum starting phenobarbital dosage is 500 mg per day.

Before receiving each dose of phenobarbital, the patient is checked for signs of phenobarbital toxicity: sustained nystagmus, slurred speech, or ataxia. Of these, sustained nystagmus is the most reliable. If nystagmus is present, the scheduled dose of phenobarbital is withheld. If all three signs are present, the next two doses of phenobarbital are withheld, and the daily dosage of phenobarbital for the following day is halved.

If the patient is in acute withdrawal and has had or is in danger of having withdrawal seizures, the initial dose of phenobarbital is administered by intramuscular injection. If nystagmus and other signs of intoxication develop 1–2 hours following the intramuscular dosage, the patient is in no immediate danger from barbiturate withdrawal. Patients are maintained on the initial dosing schedule of phenobarbital for 2 days. If the patient has neither signs of withdrawal nor phenobarbital toxicity, then phenobarbital withdrawal is begun.

**Withdrawal phase.** Unless the patient develops signs and symptoms of phenobarbital toxicity or sedative-hypnotic withdrawal, phenobarbital is decreased by 30 mg per day. Should signs of pheno-

**Table 12–3.** Sedative-hypnotics and their phenobarbital withdrawal equivalents

| Generic name | Trade name | Common therapeutic indication(s) | Therapeutic dose range (mg per day) | Dose equal to 30 mg phenobarbital for withdrawal (mg)[a] |
|---|---|---|---|---|
| Barbiturates | | | | |
| Amobarbital | Amytal | Sedative | 50–150 | 100 |
| Butabarbital | Butisol | Sedative | 45–120 | 100 |
| Butalbital | Fiorinal, Sedapap | Sedative/ analgesic[b] | 100–300 | 100 |
| Pentobarbital | Nembutal | Hypnotic | 50–100[b] | 100 |
| Secobarbital | Seconal | Hypnotic | 50–100[b] | 100 |
| Other sedative-hypnotics | | | | |
| Buspirone | BuSpar | Sedative | 15–60 | NC |
| Chloral hydrate | Noctec, Somnos | Hypnotic | 250–1,000 | 500 |
| Ethchlorvynol | Placidyl | Hypnotic | 500–1,000 | 500 |
| Glutethimide | Doriden | Hypnotic | 250–500 | 250 |
| Meprobamate | Miltown, Equanil, Equagesic | Sedative | 1,200–1,600 | 400 |
| Methylprylon | Noludar | Hypnotic | 200–400 | 200 |

*Note.* NC = not cross-tolerant with barbiturates.
[a]Phenobarbital withdrawal conversion equivalence is not the same as therapeutic dose equivalency. Withdrawal equivalence is the amount of the drug that 30 mg of phenobarbital will substitute for and prevent serious high-dose withdrawal signs and symptoms.
[b]Butalbital is usually available in combination with opiate or nonopiate analgesics.

barbital toxicity develop during withdrawal, the daily phenobarbital dose is decreased by 50%, and the 30-mg-per-day withdrawal is continued from the reduced phenobarbital dose. Should the patient have objective signs of sedative-hypnotic withdrawal, the daily dose is increased by 50%, and the patient is restabilized before continuing the withdrawal.

### Low-Dose Benzodiazepine Withdrawal

Most patients experience only mild to moderate symptom rebound that disappears after a few days to weeks. No special treatment is needed. The patient may need much reassurance that rebound symptoms are common and that they will subside.

Some patients experience severe symptoms that may be quite unlike preexisting symptoms. The phenobarbital regimen described above will not be adequate to suppress symptoms to tolerable levels. There are several pharmacological options. One strategy is to increase the phenobarbital dose to 200 mg per day and then slowly taper the phenobarbital over several months. Another is to block somatic symptoms, such as tachycardia, with propranolol. A dose of 20 mg every 6 hours can be used, alone or in combination with phenobarbital, to reduce low-dose benzodiazepine withdrawal symptom intensity (Tyrer et al. 1981). This schedule is continued for 2 weeks and then stopped. Even after phenobarbital withdrawal is complete, propranolol can be used episodically if needed to control tachycardia, increased blood pressure, and anxiety. Continuous propranolol therapy for more than 2 weeks is not recommended, as propranolol itself may result in symptom rebound when discontinued after prolonged therapy (Glaubiger and Lefkowitz 1977).

### Outpatient Treatment of Withdrawal

Withdrawal from high-doses of barbiturates and other sedative-hypnotics should generally be done in a hospital. Outpatient barbiturate withdrawal is not generally successful unless the patient is unusually motivated to stop using drugs. Patients must be evaluated daily and withdrawal medication dispensed daily.

With patients who are withdrawing from therapeutic doses of benzodiazepines, a slow outpatient taper is generally a reasonable strategy and should be continued as long as patient can tolerate withdrawal symptoms.

### Postwithdrawal Treatment

Withdrawal is usually successful when the patient cooperates, but many patients do not remain abstinent. Detoxification alone is not adequate treatment of sedative-hypnotic dependency but rather the first step in the recovery process. Patients must learn alternative methods of coping with anxiety (e.g., biofeedback, exercise).

Supportive individual psychotherapy or a self-help recovery group is virtually always needed. The goal of psychotherapy is to enable abstinence. Analytic psychotherapy mobilizes anxiety and for that reason is contraindicated during early recovery.

## ▼ CONCLUSIONS

Benzodiazepines have many therapeutic uses, and in treatment of some conditions, such as panic disorders, chronic treatment is an appropriate strategy. Dependency is not always an avoidable complication. Physicians should discuss with patients before initiating a course of prolonged therapy the possibility of their developing new or intensified symptoms when the benzodiazepines are discontinued.

Knowledge about low-dose dependency developed from clinical observations outside the usual drug development studies monitored by the Food and Drug Administration (FDA). The FDA has been remarkably silent about low-dose dependency, and the 1992 package inserts for benzodiazepines give physicians little practical guidance.

The APA could play a leadership role in reframing dependency that develops during pharmacotherapy. The DSM-III-R (American Psychiatric Association 1987) listed benzodiazepine dependency only in the context of a substance abuse disorder. For patients whose benzodiazepine dependency develops during pharmacotherapy, benzodiazepine dependency does not necessarily equate with a substance abuse disorder. To label it as a substance abuse disorder unnecessarily stigmatizes patients and their psychiatrists.

# ▼ REFERENCES

American Psychiatric Association: Diagnostic and Statistical Manual of Mental Disorders, 3rd Edition, Revised. Washington, DC, American Psychiatric Association, 1987

American Psychiatric Association: Diagnostic and Statistical Manual of Mental Disorders, 4th Edition. Washington, DC, American Psychiatric Association, 1994

American Psychiatric Association Task Force on Benzodiazepine Dependency: Benzodiazepine Dependence, Toxicity, and Abuse. Washington, DC, American Psychiatric Association, 1990

Braestrup C, Albrechtsen R, Squires RF: High densities of benzodiazepine receptors in human cortical areas. Nature 269:702–704, 1977

Ciraulo DA, Barnhill JG, Greenblatt DJ, et al: Abuse liability and clinical pharmacokinetics of alprazolam in alcoholic men. J Clin Psychiatry 49:333–337, 1988

Covi L, Lipman RS, Pattison JH, et al: Length of treatment with anxiolytic sedatives and response to their sudden withdrawal. Acta Psychiatr Scand 49:51–64, 1973

Geller A: Protracted abstinence, in Comprehensive Handbook of Drug and Alcohol Addiction. Edited by Miller NS. New York, Marcel Dekker, 1991, pp 905–913

Glaubiger G, Lefkowitz RJ: Elevated beta-adrenergic receptor number after chronic propranolol treatment. Biochem Biophys Res Commun 78:720–725, 1977

Golombok G, Moodley P, Lader M: Cognitive impairment in long-term benzodiazepine users. Psychol Med 18:365–374, 1988

Gordon B: I'm Dancing as Fast as I Can. New York, Harper & Row, 1979

Griffiths RR, Bigelow GE, Leibson I, et al: Drug preference in humans: double-blind choice comparison of pentobarbital, diazepam, and placebo. J Pharmacol Exp Ther 215:649–661, 1980

Hollister LE, Motzenbecker FP, Degan RO: Withdrawal reactions from chlordiazepoxide (Librium). Psychopharmacology (Berl) 2:63–68, 1961

Hollister LE, Bennett JL, Kimbell I, et al: Diazepam in newly admitted schizophrenics. Diseases of the Nervous System 24:746–750, 1963

Isbell H: Addiction to barbiturates and the barbiturate abstinence syndrome. Ann Intern Med 33:108–120, 1950

Lader M: History of benzodiazepine dependence. J Subst Abuse Treat 8:53–59, 1991

Möhler H, Okada T: Benzodiazepine receptors: demonstration in the central nervous system. Science 198:849–851, 1977

Olsen RW, Loeb-Lundberg F: Convulsant and anticonvulsant drug binding sites related to GABA-regulated chloride ion channels, in GABA and Benzodiazepine Receptors. Edited by Costa E, DiChiara G, Gessa GL. New York, Raven, 1981, pp 93–102

Pevnick JS, Jasinski DR, Haertzen CA: Abrupt withdrawal from therapeutically administered diazepam: report of a case. Arch Gen Psychiatry 35:995–998, 1978

Rickels K, Schweizer E, Case WG, et al: Long-term therapeutic use of benzodiazepines; I: effects of abrupt discontinuation. Arch Gen Psychiatry 47:899–907, 1990

Skolnick P, Concada V, Barker JL, et al: Pentobarbital: dual action to increase brain benzodiazepine receptor affinity. Science 211:1448–1450, 1981

Smith DE, Wesson DR: A new method for treatment of barbiturate dependence. JAMA 213:294–295, 1970

Smith DE, Wesson DR: Phenobarbital technique for treatment of barbiturate dependence. Arch Gen Psychiatry 24:56–60, 1971

Smith DE, Wesson DR: Benzodiazepine dependency syndromes. J Psychoactive Drugs 15:85–95, 1983

Smith DE, Wesson DR: Benzodiazepine dependency syndromes, in The Benzodiazepines: Current Standards for Medical Practice. Edited by Smith DE, Wesson DR. Hingham, MA, MTP Press, 1985, 235–248

Squires RF, Braestrup C: Benzodiazepine receptors in rat brain. Nature 266:732–734, 1977

Tyrer P, Rutherford D, Huggett T: Benzodiazepine withdrawal symptoms and propranolol. Lancet 1:520–522, 1981

Winokur A, Rickels K, Greenblatt DJ, et al: Withdrawal reaction from long-term, low-dosage administration of diazepam. Arch Gen Psychiatry 37:101–105, 1980

# Opioids

## *Detoxification*

*Herbert D. Kleber, M.D.*

*"Patients from whom morphine is taken get well in spite of the treatment."*

—Kolb and Himmelsbach 1938

The 1980s saw a dramatic rise in cocaine use among all social classes, culminating in the creation of the federal Office of National Drug Control Policy and the war on drugs. The 1990s appear to be the decade of heroin. Its availability and purity are higher than in decades, and the cost per pure milligram at this writing continues to drop. Many cocaine-addicted individuals are switching over to heroin and treatment programs are seeing more heroin-addicted patients. Physicians who may have been seeing relatively few heroin-addicted patients will once again need to pay attention to this problem and various treatment methods.

Prior to the advent of maintenance approaches to heroin addiction, such as methadone and more recently buprenorphine, detoxification with or without follow-up therapy was often the only treatment available for the heroin-addicted patient. It is still for many addicted individuals a pretreatment route before the residential therapeutic community, narcotic antagonist maintenance, or outpatient drug-free treatment. Although drug detoxification is often the route into treatment, it is also true that many who begin it do not complete it, and many who complete it do not go on to more definitive treatment. Some had planned this from the beginning and entered detoxification only to lower their level of dependence and thus have an easier time supporting their habit, but others fully be-

---

*Editor's note.* An *opiate* is any drug that is derived from opium. Although the term *opioid* was originally used for drugs with opiate-like activity but that are not derived from opium, *opioid* has gradually become the term for the entire family of natural, semisynthetic, and synthetic opiates. For the purposes of this textbook, the term *opioid* is used to refer to both the naturally occurring opiates and any drug that has opiate-like activity, unless there is need to distinguish between the two.

**Opioids: Detoxification**

lieve that detoxification is all that is necessary and that they will be able to then remain drug free. This is especially true with younger addicted individuals who have not yet frequently relapsed. Addicted individuals entering detoxification often describe themselves as tired of the drug life and indicate that the negative consequences—the legal problems, the need to raise large sums of money day in and day out, the health problems especially in this era of AIDS and tuberculosis, the family and social pressure, and the frequent withdrawal sickness—have begun to outweigh the pleasure from the drug-induced high.

## ▼ WHAT IS DETOXIFICATION?

*Detoxification* refers to the process whereby an individual who is physically dependent on a drug is taken off that drug either abruptly or gradually (Kleber 1981). There are several options in the use of medications to aid in detoxification: 1) the drug on which the individual is dependent, 2) other drugs that produce cross tolerance, 3) medications to provide symptomatic relief, or 4) drugs that affect the mechanisms by which withdrawal is expressed. Settings for detoxification can include inpatient, residential, or outpatient programs.

In our current state of knowledge, detoxification should be able to be carried out safely, relatively quickly, and with a minimum of discomfort. However, the method chosen is often dependent more on what is available than what would be ideal. This in turn relates to factors such as physician or patient preference or bias, the availability of physicians, federal and state regulations, insurance or other funding mechanisms, and the availability of a particular method in a particular setting in a particular geographic locale.

## ▼ GOALS OF DETOXIFICATION

1. Ridding the body of the acute physiological dependence associated with the chronic daily use of narcotics
2. Diminishing or eliminating the pain and discomfort that can occur during withdrawal
3. Providing a safe and humane treatment to help the individual over the initial hurdle of stopping narcotic use
4. Providing a situation conducive to a more long-

range commitment to treatment and making appropriate referrals to these other treatment modalities
5. Treating any medical problems discovered or making appropriate referrals
6. Beginning the process of educating the patient around issues related to health and relapse prevention, and exploring issues such as family, vocational, and legal problems that may need referral

## ▼ WHEN IS DETOXIFICATION SUCCESSFUL?

Because relatively few narcotic-addicted patients discontinue their drug habit immediately after detoxification, detoxification is usually viewed as pretreatment or at best the first stage of treatment. It is thus unrealistic to apply to it the more ambitious goals for long-term treatment that include not just abstinence but other outcome measures relating to employment, criminality, interpersonal relationships, and general physical and psychological well-being. Successful outcome criteria can include safety and minimal discomfort, the percentage of patients who complete the treatment, and, finally, the percentage going on to longer term treatment. This does not mean that the detoxification is necessarily a failure if the patient does not agree to go on to long-term treatment. Younger addicted patients who are often unrealistic about being able to remain drug free often believe that detoxification is all that is necessary to get rid of their habit and remain off drugs. They see no need for long-term treatment. When they return for a second or third detoxification, they are often more realistic about what is involved in staying drug free and at this point are usually more willing to consider going into long-term treatment. It is often said that substance abuse is a chronic relapsing disorder. To the extent that this is true, it would not be surprising if formal detoxification occurs at least several and often many times over the course of the disorder.

## ▼ CHOICE OF SETTING

Detoxification can take place in an inpatient, partial hospitalization, or outpatient setting. The advantages of each are fairly obvious. Outpatient detoxification is the least expensive of the three and enables the patient to remain at work, if employed, or otherwise to carry on his or her life. It forces patients to cope with the home and/or work settings where they will be after they have become drug free; often going from the protected inpatient setting to everyday reality is accompanied by rapid relapse. The disadvantages include patients being surrounded by temptations at a time when they are least able to handle it; more difficulty assessing and dealing with other medical conditions; and the possible need for detoxification to proceed more slowly so as not to subject the patient to undue stress in the unprotected environment. Inpatient detoxification has the advantages of being in a protective setting where access to drugs or even to craving-inducing stimuli are absent; the patient can be observed more closely for possible medical problems or complications of withdrawal, and the withdrawal can be done more rapidly. Also, more attention can be focused, if the program is a comprehensive one, on other aspects of the patient's life-family, vocational, medical, and psychiatric issues. The disadvantages are also obvious, primarily the cost, but also the disruption of the patient's life and the need to be away from work and home. Partial hospital programs are considerably less expensive than inpatient programs and yet have some of their advantages. Unfortunately, they are relatively uncommon, and the clinician is usually forced to choose between inpatient or outpatient, with the decision often being made by factors such as insurance coverage and availability of programs in the community.

## ▼ HISTORICAL OVERVIEW

In the past century, many treatments have been introduced for relieving the symptoms of opioid withdrawal. Many have proven either more addicting than the drug being withdrawn from or else more dangerous than untreated withdrawal. In a masterful review, Kolb and Himmelsbach (1938) looked back on 40 years of mostly futile attempts to treat narcotic withdrawal, on treatments ranging from autohemotherapy (injection of blood previously withdrawn from the patient) to water balance therapy and including in between numerous chemicals, alone or in combination. In 1982, I and a colleague (Kleber and Riordan 1982) reviewed the earlier work by these

writers and updated it with the techniques that had been used in the 40 years since Kolb and Himmelsbach's article. The interested reader is referred to these articles for a more detailed account and description of the various approaches. Of the techniques reviewed, the one that has stood the test of time and scientific study has been that of methadone substitution and gradual withdrawal. In addition, since the 1982 article, there have been a few other techniques that have gained varying degrees of acceptance. These will be discussed later in this chapter.

## ▼ CLINICAL CHARACTERISTICS OF THE OPIOID (μ–AGONIST) WITHDRAWAL SYNDROME

Natural occurring opioids such as opium, morphine, and codeine; derivatives such as heroin, dihydromorphine, and dihydrocodinone; and synthetics-such as methadone and meperidine, are all capable of creating physical dependency and may require detoxification if they have been taken in sufficient quantities over a period of time. Although some withdrawal can be shown to occur when a single dose of morphine is followed a few hours later by a narcotic antagonist, in general it is estimated that 3 weeks of more or less daily administration are required to produce a clinically relevant withdrawal syndrome.

### Factors Influencing Symptom Severity

The nature and severity of withdrawal symptoms when opioid-type drugs are halted relate to a variety of factors. These include the following:

1. *Specific drug used.* Rapidly metabolized drugs such as heroin are generally associated with more severe withdrawal phenomena, whereas ones that bind tightly to the receptor, such as buprenorphine, or are slowly excreted from the body, such as methadone, have a slower onset with a less intense but also more protracted withdrawal syndrome. The general rule is—the longer the duration of the drug, the less intense but longer lasting the withdrawal symptoms. Thus the short-

acting drug, heroin, has a more intense but shorter withdrawal period than the long-acting drug, methadone.

2. *Total daily amount used.* In general, the larger the daily amount, the more severe the withdrawal from that particular narcotic.

3. *Duration and regularity of use.* Clinically significant withdrawal usually requires daily use of an adequate amount for at least 3 weeks; at the other end, it appears that duration of use much beyond 2–3 months is not associated with any greater severity. The more intermittent the drug use, the less likely there will be severe withdrawal.

4. *Psychological factors.* In general, the greater the expectation of the patient that suffering will be relieved by medication becoming available, the more severe the withdrawal symptoms. Thus if an individual is in a setting where there is little hope of obtaining symptom relief, there seems to be a diminution in the intensity experienced. Individual sensitivity is also a factor. Some individuals experience abdominal cramps every time they kick an opioid habit, whereas other individuals experience primarily backaches or muscle aches. The patients' personality and state of mind can also influence withdrawal severity as can their general physical health and ability to handle stress.

## Signs and Symptoms of Opioid Withdrawal

In general, withdrawal phenomena are the opposite of the acute agonistic effects of the opioid (e.g., acute opioids cause constipation and pupillary constriction, whereas withdrawal is associated with diarrhea and pupillary dilatation). There are several ways of describing the clinical characteristics of opioid withdrawal. Some authors separate purposive from nonpurposive symptoms, others separate into objective signs and subjective symptoms, and still others separate signs and symptoms into grades on the basis of severity. None of these classifications are totally satisfactory. The division into objective versus subjective, especially where the latter is defined as not observable or possible to be feigned, implies that symptoms are less important or severe than observable signs. Experienced clinicians know that this may not be the case, and, in fact, subjective symptoms even under controlled conditions are often the worse part of the syndrome. Different treatment

agents affect different parts of the syndrome. It has also been shown experimentally that opioid-dependent patients may experience major withdrawal symptoms with minimal or no objective signs to confirm this discomfort. For the purposes of this chapter, the most common signs and symptoms are listed:

| Symptoms | Signs |
|---|---|
| Abdominal cramps | Diarrhea |
| Anorexia | Increased blood pressure |
| Anxiety | Increase pulse |
| Broken sleep | Lacrimation |
| Craving | Low-grade fever |
| Dysphoria | Muscle spasm |
| Fatigue | (hence the term *kicking* |
| Headache | *the habit)* |
| Hot or cold flashes | Mydriasis |
| Irritability | (with dilated fixed pupils |
| Muscle aches | at the peak) |
| Nausea | Piloerection (goose flesh) |
| Perspiration | Rhinorrhea |
| Restlessness | Vomiting |
| Yawning | |

When a short-acting opioid such as heroin has been taken chronically, the onset of withdrawal begins with anxiety and craving about 8–10 hours after the last dose. If the drug is not obtained, this progresses to dysphoria, yawning, lacrimation, rhinorrhea, perspiration, restlessness, and broken sleep. Later, there are waves of goose flash, hot and cold flashes, aching of bones and muscles, nausea, vomiting, diarrhea, abdominal cramps, weight loss, and low grade fever. An untreated addicted individual in withdrawal may be noted to lie in a fetal position (to ease the abdominal cramps) and to be covered with a blanket even on warm days (because of the hot and cold flashes). The skin may be exquisitely sensitive to the touch. The heroin withdrawal syndrome reaches its peak typically between 36 and 72 hours after the last dose, and the acute symptoms have substantially subsided by 5 days. With methadone withdrawal, on the other hand, the peak occurs between days 4 and 6, and symptoms do not substantially subside until 10–12 days (Table 13–1; Kleber 1981). With a shorter acting drug than heroin, such as meperidine, craving is intense but the autonomic signs such as pupillary dilatation are not particularly prominent. There is usually little nausea, vomiting, or diarrhea, but at peak intensity the muscle twitching, restlessness, and nervousness have been described as worse than during morphine withdrawal (Jaffe and Martin 1975). Regardless of which opioid used, even after the acute symptoms have subsided there is some evidence of a more protracted abstinence syndrome with subtle disturbances of mood and sleep that can persist for weeks or months (Martin and Jasinski 1969). Therefore, an addicted individual may not feel that he or she has returned to normal for months after the last ingestion of the drug. Fatigue, dysphoria, irritability, and insomnia may all lead to a state that increases the likelihood of relapse.

## ▼ EVALUATION AND DIAGNOSIS

When an individual is first seen, the evaluation done is to determine whether detoxification is needed. Once this is determined and the patient accepted for treatment, a more complete assessment is necessary to devise an individual treatment plan. Thus it will be necessary to gather information on a wider range of areas including psychological, psychosocial, and physical status (Kleber 1981).

### The Interview

**Drug history.** A review of current and past drug and alcohol use or abuse is necessary for adequate patient assessment. The following information should be obtained for each current substance or group of sub-

stances, with special emphasis on substance use during the past week:

▼ Name of drug used
▼ Length of time used
▼ Frequency of use
▼ Date or time of last use
▼ Route
▼ Amount
▼ Cost
▼ Purpose (e.g., to get high, relieve depression or boredom, sleep, for energy, relieve side-effects of other drugs)
▼ For drugs previously used: name, age started, length of time used, adverse effects
▼ Previous treatment experiences: where, what kind, outcome
▼ Prescription drugs currently used: name, reason for use, amount, frequency and duration of use, last dose

**Other medical history.** This history includes serious illnesses, accidents, and hospitalizations. In addition to the usual medical history, special attention should be given to the possible medical complications of drug abuse, noted below.

**Existence of current symptoms in the various body systems.** It is important to look for illnesses that may complicate withdrawal as well as ones ignored because of the chaotic life-style.

While gathering the above information, espe-

**Table 13–1.** Usual frequency of use in established habits and first appearance of withdrawal

| Drug | Usual frequency of use (hours) | Appearance of nonpurposive withdrawal symptoms (hours) | Peak (hours) |
|------|-------------------------------|--------------------------------------------------------|--------------|
| Meperidine | 2–3 | 4–6 | 8–12 |
| Dilaudid | 3 | 4–5 | |
| Heroin | 4 | 8–12 | 48–72 |
| Morphine | 5–6 | 14–20 | |
| Codeine | 3 | 24 | |
| Methadone | 8–12 | 36–72 | 72–96 |
| | | Majority of symptoms over | |
| Heroin | | 5–10 days | |
| Methadone | | 14–21 days | |

*Source.* Reprinted with permission from Kleber HD: "Detoxification From Narcotics," in *Substance Abuse: Clinical Issues and Perspectives.* Edited by Lowinson JH, Ruiz P. Baltimore, MD, Williams & Wilkins, 1981, pp 317–339.

cially the drug history, a nonjudgmental attitude is more likely to elicit the necessary data. Disdainful behavior is likely to create ongoing difficulties, produce false information, and even drive away the patient.

**Social functioning.** Material should be elicited on the following: 1) living arrangements (alone, with family, etc.); 2) marital status; 3) sexual orientation and functioning; 4) employment and/or educational status; 5) family members' (parents, siblings, spouse, other key members) occupation, education, psychological state, history of drug or alcohol problems; 6) friends (particularly, are there non-drug-using ones); 7) recreational and leisure time activities; and 8) current and past legal status. The Addiction Severity Index (McLellan et al. 1980) is a useful instrument to fill out for this.

The interviewer should try to get a feel of the emotional as well as factual aspects of the above areas (e.g., What is the patient's attitude toward his or her job and what type of job is it? What is the quality of his or her marital or family relations and what type is it? How does he or she cope with spare time nights and weekends when relapse is most likely to occur?). Such questioning can reveal the nature and degree of the patient's social supports and aid in planning for postdetoxification treatment. Prior attempts at withdrawal and what was associated with relapse should be especially explored.

**Psychological status.** Psychological evaluation has a number of purposes. When carried out by a non-psychiatrist, it may single out patients who need early psychiatric referral around the possibility of psychosis, organic brain syndrome, serious depression, suicide, or being violence prone. The psychiatrist, in addition to evaluating the above factors that could complicate withdrawal, can look for conditions for which special treatments exist (e.g., lithium for mania). It is helpful to try to ascertain whether detectable psychiatric conditions predate or postdate the drug abuse. Certain patients take drugs on a self-medicating basis to try to cope with dysphoric states of loneliness, depression, or anxiety or to control unacceptable aggressive or sexual drives. Conversely, continued use of certain drugs may lead to or exacerbate psychiatric states not evident before. Opioids seem to have an ameliorating effect on psychosis in some patients, and withdrawal can lead to exacerbation or sudden appearance of psychotic symptoms.

As part of evaluating the psychological state, a mental status review should be carried out and include orientation for place, person, and date; presence or absence of hallucinations, delusions, or suicidal ideation; memory; intelligence, mood, and affect; thought processes; preoccupations and behavior during interview; judgment; and insight.

## The Physical Examination

Although there is no special physical examination for narcotic-addicted individuals, it is useful to keep in mind certain conditions that can be either direct or indirect sequelae of drug abuse. Although many of these conditions can be found in nonaddicted individuals, and many addicted individuals may have few or none of them, their presence helps in the diagnostic process.

**Cutaneous signs.** These cutaneous signs may be directly or indirectly associated with drug abuse.

1. *Needle puncture marks.* Usually found over veins, especially in the antecubital area, dorsum of the hands, and forearms, but can be found anywhere on the body where a vein is reachable, including the neck, tongue, and dorsal vein of the penis.
2. *"Tracks."* One of the most common and readily recognizable signs of chronic injectable drug abuse. Tracks are scars located along veins and are usually hyperpigmented and linear. They result both from frequent unsterile injections and from the deposit of carbon black from attempts to sterilize the needle with a match. Tracks tend to lighten over time but may never totally disappear.
3. *Tattoos.* Because tracks are such a well-known indication of drug abuse, addicted individuals may try to hide them with tattoos over the area. Tattoos elsewhere also are not uncommon among certain groups of drug-abusing individuals.
4. *Hand edema.* When addicted individuals run out of antecubital and forearm veins, they often turn to finger and dorsum of the hand veins, which can then lead to hand edema. Such edema can persist for months.
5. *Thrombophlebitis* (blockage or inflammation of veins). Commonly found on the arms and legs of addicted individuals both because of the unsterile nature of the injections and the irritating

quality of some of the adulterants used with the active drug.

6. *Abscesses and ulcers.* Particularly common among individuals who inject barbiturates because of the irritating quality of these chemicals. These abscesses are often secondary to narcotic injection and are more likely to be septic and around veins.

7. *Ulceration or perforation of the nasal septum.* Frequent inhalation, or "snorting," of heroin can lead to ulceration of the septum, whereas similar chronic use of cocaine can cause perforation secondary to the vasoconstriction and loss of blood supply.

8. *Cigarette burns or scars from old burns.* Can occur due to drug-induced drowsiness. Fresh burns are usually seen between the fingers, and old scars are often seen on the chest as a result of the cigarette falling out of the user's mouth. It has been estimated that over 90% of drug-addicted and alcoholic individuals smoke.

9. *Piloerection.* An opioid withdrawal sign, usually found on the arms and trunk.

10. *Cheilosis* (cracking of skin at corners of mouth). Cheilosis is especially seen in chronic amphetamine-using individuals and in opioid-addicted individuals prior to or during detoxification.

11. *Contact dermatitis.* In solvent-abusing individuals, contact dermatitis is seen around the nose, mouth, and hands and sometimes called "glue-sniffer's rash." In other abusers, it may occur around areas of injection secondary to use of chemicals to cleanse the skin.

12. *Jaundice.* Jaundice may be seen in these individuals; this is due to hepatitis and is usually secondary to use of unsterilized shared needles and syringes.

13. *Monilial infection.* Monilial infection, or "thrush," of the mouth can be a sign of AIDS.

## Medical complications associated with drug abuse.

1. Cardiovascular-endocarditis, myocarditis, cardiac arrhythmias, thrombophlebitis, arteritis, necrotizing angiitis, hypertension, hypotension

2. Pulmonary-multiple microinfarcts, chronic pulmonary fibrosis, foreign body granulomas, pulmonary edema, bacterial pneumonia, aspiration pneumonia, tuberculosis, pneumonias related to HIV infection

3. Hepatic-serum hepatitis, cirrhosis

4. Reproductive system, menstrual irregularities

5. Neurological-seizures, usually grand mal but also can have focal seizures and status epilepticus; acute delerium; blindness; acute transverse myelitis; peripheral nerve lesions; acute rhabdomyolysis; chronic fibrosing myopathies; bacterial meningitis; central nervous system abscess; tetanus

6. Hematopoietic-bacteremia; bone marrow depression, rarely aplastic anemia; HIV status

7. Genitourinary-nephrotic syndrome

8. Skeletal-septic arthritisa, osteomyelitis

9. Gastrointestinal-chronic constipation or diarrhea, pancreatitis

## Laboratory tests.

1. Urine screen for drugs, including narcotics, barbiturates, amphetamines, cocaine, benzodiazepines, tricyclic antidepressants, and phencyclidine

2. Complete blood count and differential-leukocytosis is common, and white blood cell counts above 14,000 are not unusual

3. Urinalysis

4. Blood chemistry profile (e.g., sequential multiple analysis 20 with serum amylase and magnesium)

5. Veneral Disease Research Laboratory Test

6. HIV test (permission from the patient is necessary in many states)

7. Hepatitis antigen and antibody test

8. Chest X ray

9. Electrocardiogram in patients over age 40 years

10. Pregnancy test (hold chest X ray until this is done)

11. Tuberculin skin test (PPD) plus antigen testing because HIV-positive individuals may give false-negative PPD.

12. Any other test suggested by the history or physical examination, (e.g., failure to take in adequate food and fluids plus vomiting, sweating, and diarrhea can lead to weight loss, dehydration, ketosis, and disturbed acid-base balance)

## ▼ TECHNIQUE OF WITHDRAWAL

With the possible exception of some of the newer withdrawal approaches discussed later in the chapter, the best method of withdrawal currently is that of methadone substitution and withdrawal. Methadone is a long-acting, orally effective synthetic narcotic. Because of cross tolerance and cross dependence between the various synthetic and natural narcotics, one could in theory use any of them to prevent withdrawal and gradually detoxify any individual dependent on any of the others. The advantage of methadone over these other agents lies in the fact that it is orally effective (thus avoiding the risks associated with injection and avoiding continuing a needle habit); it is long acting (longer-acting opioids produce withdrawal syndromes that are milder although lasting longer. They also need to be given less often and thus produce a smoother withdrawal with fewer ups and downs); it is safe in that the long experience with and ease of using methadone make it a safe method of opioid detoxification as long as certain precautions are followed regarding initial dosing. In general, a more addictive drug should not be used to detoxify a patient from a less addicting one. In practice this means that while methadone can be used to withdraw from narcotics such as heroin, morphine, dilaudid, or meperidine, it should be avoided for drugs such as propoxyphene or pentazocine where the withdrawal should be handled by gradually decreasing the dose of the agent itself or by an agent such as clonidine. Codeine and oxycodone are in between these two groups, and clinicians differ as to whether to use methadone or the drugs themselves during their withdrawal.

Food and Drug Administration (FDA) guidelines for narcotic detoxification describe two types of detoxification: short term and long term. Short-term detoxification is for a period not more than 30 days; long-term detoxification is for a period not more than 180 days. Short-term detoxification is most likely to occur with individuals currently addicted to opioids other than methadone. Long-term detoxification is used either for individuals already on methadone and wishing to come off, or, in some programs, individuals are taken directly from heroin to long-term detoxification on methadone over a 6-month period. The theory behind this is that prolonged detoxification avoids having the individual go into long-term methadone maintenance, avoids some of the withdrawal symptoms that occur in more rapid detoxification, and provides a setting in which psychosocial rehabilitation can take place. However, long-term effectiveness of this option, as opposed to shorter-term detoxification or methadone maintenance, has not yet been demonstrated.

## Initiation of Detoxification

In a case where a patient has been taking narcotics for medical purposes and the physician is reasonably sure about the amount being used, Table 13–2 can be used to convert the dose into methadone. When a patient presents with illicit drug use, the picture is very different. Even if the patient could be trusted to give an honest portrayal of the amount of drug used, that knowledge is usually not available to him or her. The amount of narcotics in illegal "bags" can vary from dealer to dealer, week to week, city to city, and even from day to day. Under these circumstances, the physician must guess at the initial dose. Given that the quality of heroin on the street has increased in the past few years, in some cities from as little as 5% to as high as 45%–50% (but could just as easily turn down again), the choice of an initial dose is an important one. In general, the dose needs to be high enough to adequately suppress withdrawal symptoms so that the patient feels that he or she is being appropriately medicated and does not simply leave the program but, on the other hand, low enough that if the patient's habit was not as great as anticipated, it would not be health or life threatening. Because 40 mg of methadone has proven to be a fatal

**Table 13–2.** Drug relationships for withdrawal

| Methadone—1 mg is equivalent to | |
| --- | --- |
| Heroin | 1–2 mg |
| Morphine | 3–4 mg |
| Dilaudid | 0.5 mg |
| Codeine | 30 mg |
| Meperidine | 20 mg |
| Paregoric | 7–8 ml |
| Laudanum | 3 ml |
| Dromoran | 1 mg |
| Levo-dromoran | 0.5 mg |
| Pantopon | 4 mg |
| Leritine | 8 mg |

*Source.* Reprinted with permission from Kleber HD: "Detoxification From Narcotics," in *Substance Abuse: Clinical Issues and Perspectives.* Edited by Lowinson JH, Ruiz P. Baltimore, MD, Williams & Wilkins, 1981, pp 317–339.

dose in some individuals when given without adequate verification of prior habit, it is important that the *initial* dose be substantially below that. One way of doing this is to start with a dose of 10–20 mg, large enough to control many if not most illicit habits and yet small enough not to be particularly dangerous. The patient should be kept under observation so as to judge the effect of the dose. If withdrawal symptoms are present initially, the dose should suppress them within 30–60 minutes; if not, an additional 5–10 mg of methadone can be given. If withdrawal symptoms are not present, the patient should be observed for drowsiness or depressed respiration. When 10–20 mg is given as the initial dose, a similar amount may be given 12 hours later if deemed necessary. This is usually not practical in outpatient detoxification but is not uncommon in inpatient or residential settings. Unless there is documented evidence of narcotic use in excess of 40 mg of methadone equivalent a day, the initial dose should not exceed 30 mg and the total 24-hour dose should not exceed 40 mg in the first few days.

There is some disagreement as to whether to start the withdrawal regimen without the actual presence of withdrawal signs and symptoms. It is usually difficult to know with certainty that an individual is currently physically addicted. The information gathered during the interview, physical examination, and laboratory tests do not usually prove the diagnosis of narcotic dependence sufficient to need withdrawal treatment, unless one has found the actual signs and symptoms of opioid withdrawal. The history of drug taking, regardless of the description of its length, amount, and recent use, is not always reliable and can be altered, either by exaggeration to increase the amount of narcotic obtained or by minimizing to conceal a habit. This practice is not uncommon among addicted physicians and nurses. It may be wrong even when the patient is trying to be honest because of the variable nature of illicitly obtained drugs. Although this has been true for decades, the range of the quality has been especially great in the past few years. Physical signs such as tracks tell of past drug use, not necessarily current use. Fresh needle marks say nothing about the frequency, nature, or amount of what was injected. Urinalyses that are positive for drugs suggest recent use but are not evidence of a duration long enough to require detoxification. Heroin, detected as morphine in the urine, can be found up to approximately 48 hours after last use; quinine, a common diluent, can last to a week or more.

If definitive evidence of physical dependence is needed, there are only two methods by which to obtain it: 1) wait until the patient develops withdrawal signs and symptoms, or 2) do a naloxone provocative test. It has been shown in humans that parenteral naloxone can distinguish opioid-abusing from non-abusing individuals and that the severity of withdrawal is related to the dose of naloxone. One way of doing this test is to inject 0.2 mg of naloxone subcutaneously, to be followed by 0.4 mg in 30–60 minutes if the results are inconclusive from the smaller dose. Some physicians recommend an initial dose of 0.6–0.8 mg to speed up the process and rule out false negatives. Because of the possibility of fetal injury or induced abortion, the naloxone test should not be done if the patient is pregnant.

Whether the program is inpatient or outpatient and the availability of trained medical personnel will often determine whether programs will prefer to wait for withdrawal signs to develop, use a naloxone challenge, or use the combined evidence of the history, physical, and urine screen as interpreted by experienced personnel to form a presumptive diagnosis. If the latter method is chosen, probably most often the case, the program should still be prepared to use one of the first two approaches in borderline or doubtful situations. Once a decision has been made that there is sufficient narcotic use to require detoxification, decisions still have to be made regarding the setting, whether there is concurrent physical or emotional problems that may require separate treatment during withdrawal, and the choice of the method. When there are serious physical or emotional problems present, it is not uncommon to delay withdrawal by temporarily maintaining the individual on methadone, attending to the acute problem, and then beginning withdrawal once some stability has been achieved in the other areas. Even with gradual methadone withdrawal, detoxification produces some mental and physical stress that the patient at that time may not be able to handle.

### Length of Withdrawal

The total dose necessary to stabilize a patient for the first 24 hours should be repeated on day 2, either in one dose for outpatients or divided doses for inpatients. Corrections can then be made either up or down if the dose is either too sedating or fails to adequately suppress the abstinence syndrome. Revision to a higher dose should preferably be made on the basis of objective signs of opioid withdrawal rather than on subjective complaints alone. This is not always easily done because certain signs such as pupillary dilatation may be modified by the dosage of methadone, but the patient may still be undermedicated. After the patient is stabilized, the dose can then be gradually withdrawn. Two common approaches are either to decrease by 5 mg per day until zero dose is reached or to decrease by 5 mg per day until a dose of 10 mg is reached, and then decrease more slowly such as by 2–3 mg per day. In general, inpatient withdrawal takes place over 5–10 days, whereas outpatient withdrawal may be stretched out longer to minimize symptoms even more and decrease the likelihood of the patient leaving the program or reverting back to the use of opioids. Under FDA guidelines for narcotic detoxification, short-term detoxification consists of a period not in excess of 30 days, and long-term detoxification consists of a period not in excess of 180 days. Some inpatient programs complete the process in as little as 4 or 5 days, whereas some outpatient programs may stretch on for months. Even though methadone detoxification can be completed fairly rapidly with little in the way of objective withdrawal symptoms, there may be lingering symptoms for weeks or months, including insomnia, fatigue, and feelings of irritability or anxiety. In terms of discharge, however, from the detoxification program, if there are no objective signs of opioid withdrawal 48 hours after the last dose of methadone, the patient can be considered to be over the acute withdrawal phase.

## Withdrawal From Methadone Maintenance

For a patient withdrawing from a methadone maintenance program, the technique of withdrawal tends to relate to why the patient is being withdrawn. Patients who are in good standing on the program and desirous of trying to become drug free should in general be withdrawn slowly over a 3- to 6-month period. The most difficult period is when the dose gets below 25 mg per day because at that level methadone may not last the full 24 hours, and some withdrawal symptoms may occur before the next dose. Split doses may help with this but are not always possible or practical. Five to 10 mg per week can be with-

drawn from the established methadone dose until the patient gets to 25 mg, and at that point no more than 5 mg a week is often recommended. If the individual needs to be detoxified more rapidly because they are being discharged in bad standing, must leave the geographic locale, or may be going to prison, then withdrawal usually takes place somewhere between a 10- to 30-day period. For example, the patient dose may be decreased by 10 mg per day until a total dose of 40 mg per day is reached, then 5 mg per day until the dose of 5 mg is reached, at which point that dose is given for 2–3 days. If the patient is on an inpatient or residential basis, use of divided doses is helpful, especially when the total dose is below 25 mg.

## Other Drugs and Supportive Measures

Even with gradual withdrawal, all withdrawal symptoms may not be totally suppressed, and certain mild symptoms may persist sometimes for days after treatment has been completed. There is no consensus on use of other drugs during these periods. Tranquilizers or bedtime sedation can help allay the patient's anxiety and minimize the craving for morphine-like drugs, but nonnarcotic medications are generally ineffective in relieving the specific symptoms of opioid abstinence, with the exception of certain α-adrenergic agonists such as clonidine. If insomnia and other withdrawal symptoms are unusually severe, especially in older patients, relief can be provided by an increment in the next dose of methadone and therefore a slower withdrawal schedule.

Insomnia can be one of the more debilitating withdrawal symptoms. It is not only difficult to tolerate in and of itself, but it also weakens the addicted individual's ability to deal with other withdrawal problems. Barbiturates, because of their dependence potential, should not be used to treat insomnia. Drugs that have been advocated include flurazepam, oxazepam, diphenhydramine, and tricyclic antidepressants (e.g., amitriptyline, doxepin). All of these have been used in withdrawal, although objective comparisons are not available. Flurazepam appears to be preferred by most patients; because of flurazepam's cumulative nature, it should not be continued for longer than 2 weeks. Because many narcotic-addicted individuals also abuse benzodiazepine-type drugs, choice of such agents need to be made carefully; any history of benzodiazepine abuse should especially be taken into account.

Nonpharmaceutical supports can also play an important and useful role. A warm, kind, and reassuring attitude of the treatment staff is most helpful. Involvement of patients in their own detoxification schedule has been found to be of positive value and usually is not abused. It is therefore usually not necessary for an adversarial role to develop around the issue of medication dose. Visitors are a different story, and a firm stand is necessary on this point. It is not uncommon to have them attempt to smuggle in drugs. Therefore, visitors should be limited to only immediate family (parents or spouse) who are known not to abuse drugs. Even parents have been known to smuggle in drugs under the pressure of a patient's entreaties that the staff does not understand their needs and distress. A watchful presence is thus necessary for all visitors. Such attempts at deception are less likely to occur if there are family meetings and patient involvement.

Other measures that have been advocated include warm baths, exercise (when the patient feels up to it), and various diets. Except when there are specific nutritional deficiencies, there is no evidence of the usefulness of any one dietary regime. Because addicted patients are often malnourished, general vitamin and mineral supplements should be given.

## ▼ SPECIAL PROBLEMS

### Seizures

Opioid withdrawal or intoxication usually does not lead to seizures, except with intoxication from meperidine or propoxyphene when they may occasionally occur. A seizure therefore usually signifies undiagnosed sedative withdrawal, another medical condition (e.g., head injury or epilepsy), or a faked or hysterical seizure. Because most addicted individuals are polydrug users, abuse of sedative-type drugs (including alcohol, barbiturates, and benzodiazepines) should be kept in mind when treating them. If a patient is suspected of this abuse, 200 mg of pentobarbital can be given. A nontolerant individual administered this dose will either be asleep in an hour or show coarse nystagmus, gross ataxia, positive Romberg's sign, and dysarthria. If these are lacking, addiction to one or more of these drugs should be presumed and correspondingly treated.

### Mixed Addictions

Sedative dependence can lead to serious hazards, including not only seizures but toxic psychosis, hyperthermia, and even death. Withdrawal from stimulant-type drugs is much less of a physical hazard, although it can be associated with severe depression and even suicide unless the physician is experienced in withdrawal techniques. If sedative dependence is present, it is often useful to maintain the patient on methadone, withdraw the sedative gradually, and then withdraw the methadone.

### Vomiting

Although vomiting can be a symptom of withdrawal, it can occur with no relation to the degree of physical abstinence and in spite of all kinds of support measures, including reintoxication with opioids. It can usually be handled by intramuscular injections of a drug such as trimethobenzamide or perphenazine.

Patients sometimes vomit to get repeat medication or intramuscular doses. Observation for 15–30 minutes after a dose usually eliminates this.

### Intoxication

Intoxication is not necessary to prevent withdrawal and can complicate the safety and adequacy of care. If it occurs, a sufficient dose cut should be made to prevent it at the next medication period. Intoxicated smoking should not be permitted, and patients should be assisted when ambulatory to avoid injury.

### Repetitive Withdrawal

Addicted patients often have a characteristic withdrawal syndrome focused on a particular organ system. Withdrawal may involve for one patient the gastrointestinal system, with abdominal cramps the usual symptom; for another it may be the musculoskeletal system, in which aching in the bones is typical. A supportive, reassuring but firm approach is usually successful in helping patients with these symptoms. In the absence of psychosis, major or minor tranquilizing drugs are usually unnecessary.

### Other Medical Conditions

Opioid withdrawal is usually not accompanied by high fevers although low-grade temperature elevation can occur. Acute febrile illnesses may temporarily increase the severity of withdrawal symptoms, thus necessitating more methadone. When serious medical or surgical problems are present, withdrawal should be very gradual to minimize the degree of stress. The patient should be brought to the point of tolerance, kept there for several days, and then slowly withdrawn. With certain illnesses (e.g., acute myocardial infarction, renal colic), the patient should be maintained on methadone until stable enough to permit withdrawal. They should also be evaluated carefully to see whether longer term maintenance is indicated instead of withdrawal. When withdrawal does take place, giving methadone three or four times per day instead of once or twice can minimize discomfort and stress.

### Pregnancy

When pregnancy is complicated by heroin addiction, the patient and her physician are faced with the choice as to which of several undesirable alternatives is the least undesirable. The best circumstance would be for the woman to abstain totally from drugs, licit or illicit, during the pregnancy. This is often, unfortunately, not likely to occur. On an outpatient, drug-free regime, many patients go in and out of heroin use, subjecting the fetus to periods of intoxication and withdrawal and a risk of spontaneous abortion, stillbirth, prematurity, and anomalies. The drug effects are compounded by the life-style, poor prenatal care, inadequate diet, and drug adulterants. Residential placement to ensure the drug-free status is usually resisted, especially if there are other children at home or, if desired, is hard to find. Narcotic antagonists have not yet been approved for maintenance during pregnancy. Methadone maintenance at the lowest dose possible is left as the least undesirable available option for most such patients. The infant will be born addicted and will need to be withdrawn but should otherwise not have problems *if* there has been adequate obstetrical care during the pregnancy.

If withdrawal from methadone maintenance is necessary, it should be slow, no greater than 5 mg of reduction per week, and take place during the middle trimester. During the first trimester, withdrawal may be especially deleterious to fetal development; during the third trimester, withdrawal may trigger premature labor.

## ▼ OTHER DETOXIFICATION AGENTS AND METHODS

### Clonidine Hydrochloride

The $\alpha_2$-agonist drug, clonidine (Catapres), marketed as an antihypertensive, has been used to facilitate opioid withdrawal in both inpatient and outpatient settings (Charney et al. 1986; Gold et al. 1978; Kleber et al. 1985). Clonidine in doses of 0.6–2 mg per day reduces many of the autonomic components of the opioid withdrawal syndrome, although craving, lethargy, insomnia, restlessness, and muscle aches are not well suppressed (Charney et al. 1981; Jasinski et al. 1985). Clonidine is believed to exert its ameliorative actions by binding to $\alpha_2$-autoreceptors in the brain (e.g., locus coeruleus) and spinal cord. Both opioids and clonidine can suppress the activity of the locus coeruleus, which is hyperactive during opioid withdrawal.

Inpatients stabilized at 50 mg per day or less of methadone can be abruptly switched to clonidine. Doses reaching 2.5 mg per day have been used. Sedation and hypotension are the major side effects.

Clonidine has also been used for outpatient detoxification either from heroin or methadone maintenance. Patients maintained on 20 mg per day or less of methadone are about as successful after abrupt substitution of clonidine as after reduction of methadone by 1 mg per day (Kleber et al. 1985). With experienced personnel, street addicts can also be successfully withdrawn using clonidine. In a recent study (O'Connor et al. 1992) 43% of such patients completed withdrawal and entered the next phase of treatment. Other $\alpha_2$-adrenergic agonists such as lofexidine and guanabenz also appear to ameliorate aspects of opioid withdrawal syndrome (Washton and Resnick 1981). Although available as an antihypertensive agent, the use of clonidine as an agent for controlling withdrawal has not yet been given FDA approval, but has been used so widely now, both in the United States and abroad that it has become accepted as an alternative to gradual methadone reduction.

### Techniques of Withdrawal From Opioids With Clonidine Hydrochloride

On the day before clonidine detoxification is started, the usual dose of opioid is given. The following day (day 1) the opioid is withdrawn completely, and clonidine is given in divided doses as shown in Table 13–3. Clonidine is to be used with caution in patients with hypotension or patients receiving antihypertensive medications. Use of tricyclic antidepressants within 3 weeks precludes use of clonidine because these agents render the $\alpha_2$-receptors hyposensitive to the clonidine. Other exclusions include pregnancy, history of psychosis, cardiac arrhythmias, or other medical conditions in which use of clonidine might aggravate the associated medical problems. Because clonidine can cause sedation, patients should be cautioned about driving and operating equipment.

When used on an outpatient basis, it is usually advisable not to give more than 2 days' supply at a time. The patient should not drive during the first few days. Blood pressure should be checked when the patient is seen. If dizziness occurs, instruct the patient to cut back on the dose or to lie down.

Lower clonidine doses are used on day 1 because narcotic withdrawal is less severe at that point, and the patient usually needs time to adjust to the sedative effects of clonidine. It is useful to give 0.1 mg clonidine as the initial dose and observe the patient's reaction and blood pressure at least over the next hour. The total daily dose should be divided into three parts given at 6-hour intervals. Unless the patient is either very thin or very obese, standard doses are used rather than basing dose on patient's body weight. However, the doses from days 2–10 usually should not exceed 17 µg per kg per day.

During withdrawal from long-acting opioids such as methadone, clonidine doses can be increased over several days. In treating withdrawal from short-acting opioids, doses of clonidine are increased (titrated to symptoms) as rapidly as is consistent with concern for side effects because serious withdrawal symptoms ap-

**Table 13–3.** Clonidine-aided detoxification

| Type of patients | Total dose per day in three divided doses of clonidine (mg) |
| --- | --- |
| **Schedule for methadone maintained patients (20–30 mg per day methadone)** | |
| Outpatients | |
| Day 1 | 0.3 |
| 2 | 0.4–0.6 |
| 3 | 0.5–0.8 |
| 4 | 0.5–1.2 |
| 5–10 | Maintain on above dose |
| 11 to completion | Reduce by 0.2 mg per day; give in two or three divided doses; the nighttime dose should be reduced last. If the patient complains of side effects, the dose can be reduced by one-half each day, not to exceed 0.4 mg per day |
| Inpatients | |
| Day 1 | 0.4–0.6 |
| 2 | 0.6–0.8 |
| 3 | 0.6–1.2 |
| 4–10 | Maintain or increase if any withdrawal signs occur |
| 11 to completion | Reduce 0.2 mg per day or by one-half each day; not to exceed 0.4 mg per day |
| **Schedule for heroin, morphine, oxycodone HCl, meperidine HCl, and levorphanol patients** | |
| Outpatient/inpatient | |
| Day 1 | 0.1–0.2 mg orally every 4 hours up to 1 mg |
| 2–4 | 0.1–0.2 mg orally every 4 hours up to 1.2 mg |
| 5 to completion | Reduce 0.2 mg per day; given in divided doses; the nighttime dose should be reduced last, or reduce by one-half each day not to exceed 0.4 mg per day |

*Source.* Reprinted from Kleber HD: "Detoxification From Narcotics," in *Substance Abuse: Clinical Issues and Perspectives.* Edited by Lowinson JH, Ruiz P. Baltimore, MD, Williams & Wilkins, 1981, pp 317–339.

pear earlier. However, the duration of clonidine dosing is shorter.

Antiwithdrawal effects usually begin within 30 minutes and peak at 2–3 hours. For inpatients, blood pressure should be checked before each dose; if 85/55 mm Hg or lower, subsequent doses are withheld until the pressure stabilizes. Dizziness between doses is best handled by monitoring blood pressure and having the patient lie down. If the pressure is too low, dosage should be reduced. Sedation is commonly experienced, especially within the first few days, but usually remits by day 3 or 4. Dry mouth and facial pain are less common.

Insomnia is not usually a problem until day 3 or 4 of withdrawal from methadone but occurs by day 2 or 3 with short-acting opioids. Paradoxically, clonidine may worsen the insomnia associated with detoxification even while causing sedation during the day. Other withdrawal symptoms not relieved by clonidine are primarily muscle aching, nervousness, and irritability. Benzodiazepines may be used both for the muscle aching and the insomnia, but they should be given with caution because many addicted individuals abuse this class of drugs.

Clonidine is known to have mild analgesic effects. Thus in withdrawing "medical opioid addicts," there may be no need for analgesia during the withdrawal period, even though the original painful condition persists to some extent. Pain usually returns 24–48 hours after the last clonidine dose; if naltrexone is to be used, pain needs to be treated with nonnarcotic analgesics.

**Clonidine-naltrexone withdrawal.** Although clonidine can be an effective alternative to methadone for opioid withdrawal, it does not shorten substantially the time required for withdrawal. Further, the success rate in outpatient withdrawal leaves much to be desired. To solve these two problems, researchers first combined clonidine and naloxone and then subsequently clonidine and naltrexone to provide a safe, effective, and rapid withdrawal for patients detoxifying either from heroin or methadone. The method uses the known ability of naltrexone to produce immediate withdrawal from opioids as it displaces the opioid from the endogenous receptor. By itself this would produce an immediate and severe withdrawal syndrome that would be unacceptable to most patients. When clonidine is used as pretreatment and after the naltrexone, symptoms are substantially relieved. For those symptoms not adequately controlled, other medications such as oxazepam for muscle spasm and antiemetics are used. The method was described in detail in 1988 (Vining et al. 1988) and updated in an article aimed at the primary practitioner (O'Connor et al. 1992). The patient is premedicated with clonidine and oxazepam and then the naltrexone is begun. Although initially the naltrexone was given in divided doses, the more recent modification provides an easier technique in which only one dose per day is used, with the clonidine being given every 4 hours as needed. Table 13–4 describes the method in detail. Ninety-five percent of the patients in the O'Connor study were able to successfully complete detoxification and move on to the next phase of treatment. By 1 month later, however, there was no difference in treatment retention between the clonidine alone and the clonidine-naltrexone groups. The limitation of this method is the need to monitor patients for 8 hours on day 1 due to the potential severity of withdrawal that can incur after the first dose of naltrexone as well as the need for careful blood pressure monitoring during the detoxification procedure. Thus trained staff and space are necessary for using this procedure. An even more rapid version was developed (Brewer et al. 1988) for inpatient use. By use of higher doses of naltrexone and clonidine on day 1, the average withdrawal time was reduced from approximately 3½ days to a little over 2 days. It has been hypothesized that, because the dose of clonidine needed actually decreases after the first day, even though the dose of naltrexone is increasing, that naltrexone is rapidly normalizing the number and sensitivity of opioid receptors and reversing the opioid-induced central noradrenergic hypersensitivity (Kleber et al. 1987).

## Acupuncture

Although acupuncture has been used for thousands of years in Chinese medicine to relieve pain, its use in the treatment of narcotic withdrawal is much more recent. The first article on it (Wen and Cheung 1973) reported more or less favorable results in 40 patients using acupuncture with electrical stimulation. A review 5 years later (Whitehead 1978) concluded that there were inadequate controls in the studies to justify that the procedure was shown to work adequately.

It is difficult to interpret the literature without at

least clarifying the different types of acupuncture employed. Acupuncture itself refers to the use of thin needles inserted subcutaneously at points on the body believed related to the organs that need to be stimulated. For detoxification it is usually points on the external ear that are used. Electro-acupuncture involves applying small amounts of electricity to needles or staples, again applied to those acupuncture points believed to affect opioid withdrawal on the external ear. Cranial electrostimulation involves applying small amounts of electricity presumably to the central nervous system through electrodes applied to the skin surface over the cranium. There is evidence from animal studies that electro-acupuncture is mediated through the endorphin system, and its effects can be blocked by the use of naloxone. Although programs that use these methods tend to be enthusiastic about the results, published reviews tend to be more critical. There are a number of methodological problems including high dropout, different placement of electrodes, electrical parameters, and problems in blinding patient and staff. Thus we are not as far along as we should be since the review by Whitehead in 1978 concluded there was inadequate evidence. There have been studies asserting that acupuncture or the other variants work and others asserting they do not (e.g., Alling et al. 1990; Riet et al. 1990; National Council Against Health Fraud 1991; Lipton et al., in press; Ulett 1992).

However, there appears to be some effect that does occur, especially in reducing both the objective signs of withdrawal and subjective discomfort. Thus it may be useful for some patients. What remains to be clarified are the best techniques to be used; the most appropriate duration of the procedure, each time and overall; frequency; and the nature of the psychosocial adjuncts. In short, is acupuncture an adjunct to a psychosocial approach during withdrawal, enabling clinicians to hold patients in therapy and work with them better; or is psychosocial treatment the ancillary to acupuncture, helping to educate and encourage the patient to go on to the next step of treatment? It also remains to be determined how acupuncture relates to the other methods described above, especially methadone detoxification and clonidine. For those who prefer not to use medications, clearly there is something appealing about a technique which relieves discomfort without involving them.

Although to what extent the effects reported in the literature are due to placebo and to what extent the technique itself has not been adequately clarified, the realistic question at this point appears to be less, Does the method work? than, How well does it work, for whom, under what circumstances? Is it the most effective method for 5% or 50% of people seeking opioid detoxification? Who are these people, what are the best circumstances for them to receive this,

| Table 13–4. | Clonidine/naltrexone rapid detoxification | | |
|---|---|---|---|
| **Day 1** | 9:00 A.M. | Clonidine 0.2–0.4 mg orally, oxazepam 30–60 mg | |
| | 11:00 A.M. | Naltrexone 12.5 mg orally, then clonidine 0.1–0.2 mg every 4 hours up to 1.2 mg | |
| | | Oxazepam 15–30 mg every 6 hours as needed | |
| **Day 2** | Clonidine | 0.1–0.2 mg every 4 hours up to 1.2 mg | |
| | Naltrexone | 25 mg orally (not sooner than 1 hour after the clonidine dose) | |
| | Oxazepam | 15–30 mg every 6 hours as needed | |
| **Day 3–5** | Clonidine | 0.1–0.2 mg every 4 hours, tapering total dose by 0.2–0.4 mg per day | |
| | Naltrexone | 50 mg orally daily, not sooner than 1 hour after the clonidine dose | |
| | Oxazepam | 15–30 mg every 6 hours as needed | |
| | Adjuvant medications: Nonnarcotic analgesics (e.g., ibuprofen); antiemetics (e.g., prochlorperazine) | | |

*Note.* Patients remain in the clinic until 5:00 P.M. on the first day and are then seen daily.
*Source.* Reprinted from Kleber HD: "Detoxification From Narcotics," in *Substance Abuse: Clinical Issues and Perspectives.* Edited by Lowinson JH, Ruiz P. Baltimore, MD, Williams & Wilkins, 1981, pp 317–339.

**Opioids: Detoxification**

and which approach increases the likelihood of the patient going on to longer term treatment? What are the optimal circumstances under which the treatment is to be given?

### Buprenorphine

Buprenorphine is a partial opioid agonist. Although introduced originally as an analgesic, there have been recent explorations of its use in a variety of ways for treatment of narcotic addiction. These include the following: as a maintenance agent itself, as a transition from full agonists such as methadone or heroin to a full antagonist such as naltrexone, and as a detoxification agent from an agonist such as methadone or heroin. The first step in detoxification is to transfer the patient from either heroin or methadone maintenance to buprenorphine. Detoxification can then be accomplished by gradual tapering of the buprenorphine, abrupt discontinuation of buprenorphine, or discontinuing buprenorphine and precipitating withdrawal using naltrexone. In all these methods, the patient is usually first stabilized on buprenorphine, which may be for as a brief a period as 3 days on relatively low doses of 2 or 3 mg sublingual daily, or may involve longer term maintenance of 6 months or more, on doses of up to 16 mg daily.

If buprenorphine is abruptly stopped, the withdrawal syndrome is mild, although in some patients it may be protracted. The literature is not clear on the exact duration of this withdrawal. Various periods have been reported, ranging from no signs of abstinence after being maintained for 10 days on 8 mg (Mello and Mendelson 1980); to mild symptoms after 2–3 days, which peaked at approximately 2 weeks after the last dose (Jasinski et al. 1978); or another study in which there are mild symptoms peaking at 3–5 days, going away after another 5 days (Fudala et al. 1990). Gradual tapering of buprenorphine appears to be less successful than abrupt discontinuation and has not been recommended (Bickel et al. 1988). Buprenorphine stabilization doses may need to be adjusted in reference to the time course of the opioid being withdrawn. Because heroin's peak is 1.5–3 days and methadone's not till day 4–6, buprenorphine doses need to be increased on day 2 of heroin withdrawal and day 4 of methadone withdrawal (Johnson et al. 1989).

The most recent studies have involved rapid detoxification using naltrexone. In a study done by Kosten et al. (1991), 23 patients maintained on buprenorphine for one month at a dosage range of 3–6 mg were abruptly given naltrexone, 1 mg, 24 hours after the last buprenorphine dose, followed by 6, 12.5, 25 and 50 mg of naltrexone on successive days. Minimal withdrawal occurred, and 20 of the 23 patients took the initial 6 mg naltrexone dose. However, only 4 patients stayed on the naltrexone at 50 mg daily beyond the 2 weeks. Given the milder withdrawal from buprenorphine than from heroin or methadone, it would appear that ultimately a rapid detoxification method involving first transition to buprenorphine and then some variant of the clonidine-naltrexone approach will be ultimately least painful and produce the highest rate of success. The mildness of the buprenorphine withdrawal syndrome is not yet totally understood. One hypothesis is that being a partial $\alpha$-agonist, buprenorphine only induces partial tolerance and dependence. A second hypothesis is that buprenorphine's long duration of action and slow dissociation from receptors produces a self-tapering effect. A summary of the various detoxification studies using buprenorphine has been done recently (Rosen and Kosten, in press).

## ▼ CONCLUSION

Although some patients see detoxification as the only treatment to obtain stable abstinence, for the majority of patients detoxification from narcotics is only the first step in the long process of remaining off illicit drugs. Success, therefore, is a function not just of how painless the procedure, but of the number of patients retained and the likelihood that they will go on to longer term treatment. Whatever method is chosen, there must be appropriate psychosocial interventions and education to prepare the patient for this next step. The ideal detoxification method would be relatively short, cheap, and painless, able to be done in an outpatient setting, and leave the patient with a desire to seek longer term help. Although none of the techniques reviewed in this chapter are perfect in these regards, it appears we are closing in on methods to deal with all the pharmacologic ramifications and thus need to focus not just on better pharmacologic methods, but on what approaches combined with them will most likely keep the patient in treatment for both detoxification and the next stage. Compared to 50 years ago, the current methods are able to detoxify individuals with little discomfort and in a much shorter period of time.

## ▼ REFERENCES

Alling FA, Johnson BD, Elmoghazy E: Cranial electrostimulation (CES) use in the detoxification of opiate dependent patients. J Subst Abuse Treat 7:173–180, 1990

Bickel WD, Stizter ML, Bigelow GE, et al: A clinical trial of buprenorphine: comparison with methadone in the detoxification of heroin addicts. Clin Pharmacol Ther 43:72–78, 1988

Brewer C, Rezae H, Bailey C: Opioid withdrawal and naltrexone induction in 48–72 hours with minimal drop-out, using a modification of the naltrexone-clonidine technique. Br J Psychiatry 153:340–343, 1988

Charney DS, Sternberg DE, Kleber HD, et al: The clinical use of clonidine in abrupt withdrawal from methadone. Arch Gen Psychiatry 38:1273–1277, 1981

Charney DS, Heninger GR, Kleber HD: The combined use of clonidine and naltrexone as a rapid, safe, and effective treatment of abrupt withdrawal from methadone. Am J Psychiatry 143:831–837, 1986

Fudala PJ, Jaffe JH, Dax EM, Johnson RE: Use of buprenorphine in the treatment of opioid addiction; II: physiologic and behavioral effects: effects of daily and alternate day administration and abrupt withdrawal. Clin Pharmacol Ther 47:525–534, 1990

Gold MS, Redmond DE, Kleber HD: Clonidine blocks acute opiate withdrawal symptoms. Lancet 2:599–602, 1978

Jaffe JH, Martin WR: Narcotic analgesics and antagonists, in The Pharmacological Basis of Therapeutics, 5th Edition. Edited by Goodman LS, Gilman A. New York, Macmillan, 1975, pp 245–324

Jasinski DR, Pevnick JS, Griffith JD: Human pharmacology and abuse potential of the analgesic buprenorphine. Arch Gen Psychiatry 35:501–516, 1978

Jasinski DR, Johnson RE, Kocher TR: Clonidine in morphine withdrawal: differential effects on signs and symptoms. Arch Gen Psychiatry 42:1063–1066, 1985

Johnson RE, Cone EJ, Henningfield JE, et al: Use of buprenorphine in the treatment of opiate addiction; I: physiological and behavioral effects during a rapid dose induction. Clin Pharmacol Ther 46:335–343, 1989

Kleber HD: Detoxification from narcotics, in Substance Abuse: Clinical Issues and Perspectives. Edited by Lowinson JH, Ruiz P. Baltimore, MD, Williams & Wilkins, 1981, pp 317–339

Kleber HD, Riordan CE: The treatment of narcotic withdrawal: a historical review. J Clin Psychiatry 43 (section 2):30–34, 1982

Kleber HD, Riordan CE, Rounsaville B, et al: Clonidine in outpatient detoxification from methadone maintenance. Arch Gen Psychiatry 42:391–394, 1985

Kleber HD, Topazian M, Gaspari J, et al: Clonidine and naltrexone in the outpatient treatment of heroin withdrawal. Am J Drug Alcohol Abuse 13:1–17, 1987

Kolb L, Himmelsbach CK: Clinical studies of drug addiction; III: a critical review of the withdrawal treatments with method of evaluating abstinence. Am J Psychiatry 94:759–799, 1938

Kosten TR, Morgan C, Kleber HD: Treatment of heroin addicts using buprenorphine. Am J Drug Alcohol Abuse 17:119–128, 1991

Lipton DS, Brewington V, Smith M: Acupuncture as a substance abuse treatment: a review of the literature. J Subst Abuse Treat (in press)

Martin WR, Jasinski DR: Physiological parameters of morphine dependence in man: tolerance, early abstinence, protracted abstinence. J Psychiatr Res 7:9–17, 1969

McLellan AT, Luborsky L, Woody GE, et al: An improved diagnostic evaluation instrument for substance abuse patients: the Addiction Severity Index. J Nerv Ment Dis 168:26–33, 1980

Mello NK, Mendelson JH: Buprenorphine suppresses heroin use by heroin addicts. Science 207:657–659, 1980

National Council Against Health Fraud: Acupuncture: the position paper of the National Council Against Health Fraud. American Journal of Acupuncture 19:273–279, 1991

O'Connor PG, Waugh ME, Schottenfeld RS, et al: Ambulatory opiate detoxification and primary care: a role for the primary care physician. J Gen Intern Med 7:532–534, 1992

Riet GT, Kleijnen J, Knipschild P: A meta analysis of

studies into the effect of acupuncture on addiction. Br J Psychiatry 40:379–382, 1990

Rosen MI, Kosten TR: Detoxification studies, in Buprenorphine. Edited by Cowan A, Lewis JW, New York, Wiley Liss (in press)

Ulett GA: Beyond Yin and Yang: How Acupuncture Really Works. St. Louis, MO, Warren H. Green, 1992, pp 1–170

Vining E, Kosten TR, Kleber HD: Clinical utility of rapid clonidine-naltrexone detoxification for opioid abuse. British Journal of Addiction 83:567–575, 1988

Washton AM, Resnick RG: Clonidine in opiate withdrawal: review and appraisal of clinical findings. Pharmacotherapy 1:140–146, 1981

Wen HL, Cheung SYC: Treatment of drug addiction by acupuncture and electrical stimulation. American Journal of Acupuncture 1:71–75, 1973

Whitehead PC: Acupuncture in the treatment of addiction: a review and analysis. Int J Addict 13:1–16, 1978

# Opioids

## *Methadone Maintenance*

*Edward C. Senay, M.D.*

In almost all individuals who are dependent on opioids, properly prescribed methadone substantially reduces and frequently eliminates use of nonprescribed opioids (Dole and Nyswander 1965; Newman and Whitehill 1979). Because many addicted individuals must commit crimes to get the money for illegal opioids, an indirect effect of legal methadone is to reduce or frequently to eliminate associated crime (Ball et al. 1988a). Methadone has no direct effect on low self-esteem, posttraumatic stress disorder, personality disorders, or the many other forms of psychopathology that frequently accompany opioid dependence, nor does it have any direct effect on unemployment, poor education, or dysfunctional families. A comprehensive program of services, in which methadone is prescribed as one of the services, may have desirable effects on some or all of these by changing the balance of forces on and in the addicted individual (e.g., the addicted individual with antisocial personality disorder has to steal

less because of the methadone thus avoiding arrests, one with depression may get treatment thus freeing up energy to get a GED). The previous statements are supported by almost three decades of clinical experience and the largest scientific data base ever gathered on any biopsychosocial problem. The only proper question to pose with respect to the clinical use of methadone is whether it is achieving the goal of reducing use of nonprescribed opioids. The quality of the program in which the methadone is used, the community in which the program is embedded, funding levels, regulatory interventions, and availability of economic and educational opportunity all must be examined if other effects are in question.

Properly prescribed methadone is not intoxicating or sedating, is effective orally, suppresses narcotic withdrawal for 24–36 hours, and does not have effects that interfere with ordinary activities such as driving a car, reading a newspaper, or operating an industrial machine; thus it is not like "giving an alcoholic bour-

---

*Editor's note.* An *opiate* is any drug that is derived from opium. Although the term *opioid* was originally used for drugs with opiate-like activity but that are not derived from opium, *opioid* has gradually become the term for the entire family of natural, semisynthetic, and synthetic opiates. For the purposes of this textbook, the term *opioid* is used to refer to both the naturally occurring opiates and any drug that has opiate-like activity, unless there is need to distinguish between the two.

bon" as its critics contend. The alcoholic individual who gets bourbon gets intoxicated, whereas the methadone-maintenance (MM) patient who is intoxicated from the methadone, by definition, is getting improperly prescribed, poorly monitored doses of methadone. The successful MM patient has stopped centering his or her life on intoxication and has a daily life-style that has few, if any, differences from individuals not taking methadone.

Results from methadone programs are the familiar one-third do well, one-third vacillate between good and bad performance, and one-third show no change from a life-style centered on drugs and crime. The clinician needs to appreciate the subtle fact that before methadone there was no way to generate the one-third who do well or the successful periods of treatment for the one-third who vacillate. Methadone, for most opioid-dependent individuals, is not a cure, and to demean the substantial benefits that can flow from its proper use because they do not constitute a cure borders on the criminal in the age of HIV. Evidence indicates that methadone programs prevented many opioid injectors from getting HIV (Barthwell et al. 1989; Novick et al. 1990), and there is substantial evidence that needle use and sharing are lessened when addicted individuals enter methadone programs (Ball et al. 1988b).

Many addicted individuals develop careers marked by periods of abstinence interspersed with periods of addiction. These individuals use the treatment system to abort the episodes of addiction. Early in their career, addicted individuals use all of the treatment modalities (i.e., drug-free, therapeutic communities; MM; and detoxification). As the career lengthens, they tend to use methadone preferentially over the other modalities. The clinical reality is that addicted individuals often leave treatment before completing recovery. But they will use the system for future episodes of addiction and the net effect on their abuse is an amelioration that is significant for the addicted individual and the community.

## ▼ FEDERAL AND STATE ELIGIBILITY CRITERIA FOR METHADONE MAINTENANCE

Methadone can be used for analgesia by any licensed physician. It cannot be used for the treatment of opioid dependence unless it is used by a physician working in a treatment facility licensed by a state. States can have criteria more stringent than those established for the country by the Food and Drug Administration (FDA), but they cannot have less stringent criteria. States differ in eligibility criteria and in a variety of regulations on such matters as take-home methadone. By federal mandate each state must have a single state agency that licenses and coordinates drug treatment and prevention programs. If there are questions about eligibility criteria, these single state agencies should be consulted. The FDA's eligibility criteria for MM, defined as the use of methadone for the treatment of narcotic dependence for more than 90 days, are as follows:

### Current Physiologic Dependence on Opioids

A 1-year history of physiologic dependence on opioids must be present together with current physiologic dependence as demonstrated by positive urine tests for opioids, needle tracks, and signs and symptoms of opioid withdrawal. The regulations do not specify any particular subset of the foregoing criteria for current physiologic dependence. It is a medical judgment that physiologic dependence exists. The regulations require that the judgment be based on some of the criteria. An addicted subject, for example, may never have used needles and can still have acquired a substantial degree of physiologic dependence by "snorting" opioids. Physiologic dependence on opioids must have existed episodically or continuously for 1 year. If the addicted subject has a history of only 6–7 months of dependence, then the physician should consult with the single state agency before beginning a treatment regimen of MM.

### Individuals From Penal Institutions

A person who has been in a penal institution is eligible for MM after a period of incarceration without current physiologic dependence on opioids if their addiction met the criteria before they entered the penal institution.

### Pregnant Patients

Pregnant patients can be placed on MM if currently physiologically dependent on opioids. There is no stipulation that addicted pregnant individuals must have been dependent for 1 year but simply that physiologic dependence is current. A physician can place an addicted pregnant patient, opioid dependent in the past, on MM without current physiologic dependence if return to opioid dependence is a threat.

## Previously Treated Patients

For a 2-year period following an episode of MM, patients may be readmitted without evidence of current physiologic dependence if the physician documents that return to opioid dependence is imminent.

## Individuals Under Age 18 Years

Individuals under age 18 years must have two documented attempts at drug detoxification or drug-free treatment with a 1-week period between treatment episodes, and they must show evidence of current physiologic dependence on opioids to be eligible for MM. A parent, legal guardian, or responsible adult designated by state authority must also complete and sign *Form FDA-2635 Consent to Methadone Treatment* to complete the eligibility criteria.

The above described criteria may vary in that a state can elect to be more stringent; for example, states can require 2 years of physiologic dependence before MM is legal or they may make the rules for take-home methadone more stringent. FDA regulations permit programs to dispense one or two take-home doses of methadone after 3–6 months of good performance in treatment. Some states require longer periods of good performance, and some may not permit take-home doses at all.

If a patient has current physiologic dependence on opioids but does not meet the criteria above, then methadone can be used for detoxification for up to a 90-day period. This use is defined by FDA regulations as methadone detoxification.

## ▼ PHARMACOLOGY OF METHADONE

Methadone, first synthesized in Germany in the 1940s, is D,L-4,4-diphenyl-6-dimethylamino-3-heptanone (Jaffe and Martin 1985). The L isomer accounts for most of its activity. Subjectively, methadone is similar to morphine in that both induce dose dependent euphoria and sedation; 5–10 mg of methadone will give analgesia that is quite comparable in intensity and time course to 10–15 mg of morphine.

Methadone's effects can be achieved by oral administration. Methadone suppresses the opioid withdrawal syndrome for 12–24 hours or longer, much longer suppression than can be achieved with morphine. Day-long suppression of the abstinence syndrome and oral effectiveness define the usefulness of methadone in clinical programs because no other opioid has these characteristics.

Like other μ-agonist opioids, methadone depresses the respiratory center, has antitussive action, and produces mild hyperglycemia and hypothermia. Methadone inhibits gastrointestinal tone and propulsive activity and will cause biliary tract spasm, but it does not have effects on the pregnant uterus. Tolerance to the miotic effects of methadone develops rapidly. Methadone is well absorbed from the stomach, in most individuals, and large concentrations appear in the plasma within minutes after oral administration. The drug enters tissues throughout the body with only a small amount traversing the blood-brain barrier. Methadone appears to be bound to tissue protein; biotransformation in the liver is probably through *N*-demethylation and cyclization to form pyrolidines. The half-life of methadone in nontolerant individuals is about 15 hours.

When used as an analgesic in routine practice, methadone has effects like other μ-agonist opioids: hallucinations, delirium, and hemorrhagic urticaria have been reported rarely in ordinary clinical use of morphine. There are no reports of these rare opioid side effects in MM patients.

With chronic administration, pools of methadone are built up in body tissues, and methadone from these pools provides a steady blood concentration. After blood levels are stable, a given daily dose does not cause a sharp increase in blood levels. This accounts for the failure to produce sedation or intoxication and for the fact that methadone is not an effective analgesic in MM patients. Conversely the pool level may not decrease much following omission of a daily dose. This accounts for the common clinical observation that omission of a daily dose may not produce withdrawal. Optimal blood levels in a MM patient are between 150 and 600 ng/ml (Dole 1988). Methadone crosses the placental barrier, and chronic administration in a pregnant mother will result in a methadone-dependent fetus and neonate.

In early phases of MM treatment, several biochemical and physiological abnormalities have been observed and have been described by Kreek (1983); for example, there is a decrease in plasma levels of reproduction-related peptide hormones (e.g., follicle-stimulating hormone, luteinizing hormone). These abnormalities return to normal after a period of 2–10 months of treatment. Thyroid abnormalities and persistence of protein and immunologic abnormalities, which probably reflect years of use of unsterile needles and solutions, have also been observed. Cicero et al. (1975) found that MM patients had decreased ejaculate volume and decreased sperm counts. The time course and clinical significance of these findings are not known.

Overdose of methadone should be treated with naloxone, but it is important to remember that naloxone's actions are for 2 hours and methadone's actions are for 12–36 hours. This mandates a much longer period of observation than is the case with most other opioid overdoses; a high likelihood of repeated doses of naloxone is required in the methadone overdose.

Almost three decades of clinical experience and clinical research establish that medically prescribed methadone is safe and that its routine use is remarkably free from serious problems. Common side effects are sedation, if the dose is too high; constipation, which can be treated by increasing fluid intake and using stool softeners; occasional transient ankle edema in women; excessive sweating; and changes in libido. All these side effects tend to improve with the passage of time, but they may require dose reduction if they are very disturbing to the patient. There are four recorded cases of severe edema in MM patients in the literature (O'Connor et al. 1991).

Daily administration of opioids increases the possibility of synergism with other psychoactive drugs. Patients in many U.S. clinics who develop alcohol problems while on methadone may be required to take Breathalyzer tests before methadone is administered. If levels are 0.05 mg% or above, methadone is not administered until levels are below 0.05 mg% or perhaps until the next visit. Users of multiple drugs who are on methadone are, of course, at risk of lethal overdose because of synergism.

Studies of the biotransformation of methadone indicate wide interindividual variability in blood levels following identical dosing regimens. This research suggests that poor responders to treatment may not absorb methadone from the gastrointestinal tract normally (Kelley et al. 1978). Liver and renal disease may account for some of the individual variations. Any stress (e.g., heavy alcohol or cocaine consumption, severe weather changes, marital discord) can speed the biotransformation of methadone with associated complaints, in a previously stable dosing pattern, of withdrawal toward the end of the 24-hour cycle.

A number of investigators, as reviewed by Gritz et al. (1975), have found that methadone does not interfere with reaction time. MM patients do not appear to have memory deficits as tested by Gritz et al., but chronic administration of methadone was found to differentiate performance of patients from control subjects in that subtle recall deficits appeared on the more difficult tests. Clinically these effects are not detectable. In a study of driving records, Maddox et al. (1977) found no evidence to restrict driving privileges of MM patients. MM clinics, in our large cities, have patients from most, if not all, occupations necessary to the daily life of large urban centers.

Rifampin, barbiturates, and tricyclic antidepressants may induce liver enzymes, which speed the biotransformation of methadone. Patients taking these medications may need increases in the dose of methadone to maintain stability. Methadone can be used concurrently, with close monitoring, with therapeutic doses of antidepressants, antipsychotics, anticonvulsants, anxiolytics, sedative hypnotics, lithium, and disulfiram (Ling et al. 1983). Methadone and clonidine should not be used concurrently because of the danger of synergism of sedative effects.

## ▼ DOSE

### Initial Dose

The initial dose of methadone must be individualized. If an addicted patient gives a history of using low potency heroin in the 3-week period preceding the examination and of using just once or twice per day and, in addition, has minimal signs of opioid withdrawal, an initial dose of 5–10 mg would be indicated. If 1) use in the preceding 3 weeks has been more frequent than once or twice per day, 2) estimation of the potency of the heroin is moderate to strong, and 3) the patient is showing signs of moderate to severe opioid withdrawal, an initial dose should be in the range of 10–20 mg. If one is prescribing for someone using high doses of fentanyl or if there is obvious severe opioid withdrawal, as there may be in some communities in which high-potency heroin is being used, then an initial dose of 20–40 mg should be employed. If an addicted patient is not going to be observed for a 1- to 2-hour period after administration of an initial dose, then it is best to err on the low side because there is evidence that at least some addicted individuals entering treatment are not physiologically dependent despite the fact that they meet all the criteria for physical dependence, including positive urines for morphine and positive signs of opioid withdrawal (Kanof et al. 1991; Senay and Schick 1978; Wang et al. 1974). A dose of 30-40 mg in these patients may induce a significant degree of sedation. If there is use of heroin, alcohol, and/or other drugs, as there may be following the initial dose when the addicted patient leaves the clinic, there is a possibility of an overdose. It is good practice to observe the patient for a 1- to 2-hour period after the first dose to see what the effects of the dose are on the signs of opioid withdrawal. Adjustments can then be made on the basis of clinical observation combined with the patient's report.

All of the foregoing comments pertain to outpatients. Empirically, initial doses in hospitalized patients can be lower than is necessary in outpatient settings. Doses in hospitalized patients with medical/surgical problems can be split: for example, instead of giving a one-time-per-day dose of 30 mg of methadone, one can prescribe 10 mg three times per day, with smooth control of withdrawal (i.e., control not marked by end of the 24-hour dosing period withdrawal as may be the case in the one-time-per-day administration of 30 mg). If a patient on any dose of maintenance methadone is hospitalized, the maintenance dose should be continued throughout the hospital stay without change unless the associated stresses of medical surgical conditions precipitate opioid withdrawal. In these cases, increases in methadone dose of 5–10 mg per day will usually stabilize the situation.

## Maintenance Dose

The maintenance dose of methadone must be individualized also. The clinician and or the staff should observe the effects of a given dose with the following end points in mind: 1) suppression of narcotic withdrawal, 2) no induction of euphoria or sedation, and 3) reduction or elimination of narcotic use as measured by self and other reports and from the results of random, visually or temperature, monitored urine screens. Urine screens are particularly useful in the early phase of treatment and with relapsing patients, and they are critical in evaluating the success of programs. The exact frequency and procedures in relation to clinical use of urine screens need additional study. Havassy and Hall (1981) found no differences between urine-monitored and non-monitored groups in a 1-year study. Over half the subjects in this study were in treatment for more than 1 year and were a group in which the effects of urine screens would be less likely to produce differences than in early phase or relapsing patients.

Federal regulations prohibit doses above 120 mg per day without special permission from the FDA and/or state regulatory authorities. Most methadone clinics have patients who are successful at both ends of the dose spectrum as defined by federal regulation. Thus there will be some patients who do well on 20–50 mg per day, whereas others will require doses at the other end of the spectrum. There is no rationale for forcing those at the lower end to higher doses because this will prolong the time and increase the severity of withdrawal if they want to detoxify. If one examines large numbers of addicted subjects from a national perspective, it appears that better results are achieved at doses in excess of 60 mg per day (Hargreaves 1983).

The clinician will encounter a spectrum whose ends are defined by two different populations of addicted patients. One end of the spectrum will try to manipulate endlessly for higher and higher doses. The other will resist higher doses because of fears that methadone habits are "worse than heroin habits," "methadone gets in your bones," and the like. Most addicts will range themselves between these two poles. With the former group, it is good procedure to observe the patient for signs of withdrawal such as dilated pupils, moist skin, runny nose, and tearing 24 hours after the last dose of methadone. The signs of withdrawal should bear some relationship to the severity of complaints. One can then decide whether to increase the dose. If dose increases appear to be indicated then they may be made in increments of 5 or 10 mg depending on clinical judgment of what effects are desired. In a patient with severe complaints but no signs of withdrawal, one might prescribe a 5-mg increment; in a patient with positive signs and severe complaints, a 10-mg increment may be called for. Any change should be discussed with the patient, and the clinician should make it clear to the patient that as the dose goes up, the difficulty in withdrawing also goes up with respect to the length of time that will be necessary for the patient to accomplish detoxification and with respect to the severity of withdrawal that will likely be experienced.

Positive urine tests for opioids should lead to serious consideration of raising the dose as cessation of illegal opioid use is the first priority. Drug hunger bears no constant relationship to narcotic withdrawal, and although observation indicates few or no signs of withdrawal, an increase is justified to attempt to stop illicit opioid use. Increments of 5 mg every few days should be employed until use of illegal opioids has diminished or disappeared or legal ceilings have been reached. If the patient is willing, the clinician may request an exemption from the guidelines from the single state agency to bring the dose higher than normally permitted as it may be that the patient is a rapid metabolizer of methadone.

Clinical experience indicates that 6–24 months is an appropriate cutoff point for many addicted patients in that it appears to take that long for them to accomplish changes in life-style. For others, and they may constitute one-third or more of a given clinic population, opioid use will continue. If the continuation is at a much reduced level and particularly if it means a relative or complete cessation of needle use or sharing, then this is a legitimate clinical outcome and the maintenance program should be continued. The administration of a daily dose of methadone, at almost any level, probably lessens the urgency of pressure to use narcotics and thus gives the addicted individual a little more time for making judgments than otherwise would be the case. For example, the addicted individual may be better able to decline to use or to share needles and thus has a lower likelihood of HIV infection.

What to do about the patient who is not doing well involves a number of considerations including clinic policy, a clinical cost-benefit analysis, pressure on the clinic for services, and so on. The challenge for the clinician is to find the factors responsible for the continued drug use. An addicted individual whose family and extended family are involved in drug dealing may find family and neighborhood pressures too strong to overcome. In such a patient, a move to a new neighborhood may be the prescription. In others, a divorce, change of jobs, or entrance to a controlled environment such as a therapeutic community may be considered. Most addicted patients in MM programs will have to change friends if they want to get out of the drug culture.

In treatment failures, some clinics at the end of a 6- to 12-month period decrease the dose of methadone by 1–3 mg for each positive urine test so that the patient detoxifies him- or herself out of the program by continued drug use. In the age of HIV such policies need to be reconsidered because returning someone to needle use and sharing creates risk of contracting HIV. The scientific evidence, as reviewed by Cooper (1992), indicates that the clinician should explore dose increases in failing patients rather than the reverse. Program policies that limit the duration of MM (e.g., to 2 years) are difficult to justify in the age of HIV. Attempts to force patients who do not want to be detoxified from successful MM usually cause much suffering and in the occasional case may lead to incarceration and/or death for the individual.

There is no rationale for blind withdrawal of methadone from a legally competent adult patient without the patient's consent. In a blind detoxification, the patient's dose is changed in time and amounts, without the patient being aware of when and how much the dose is being changed. This is probably the best regimen for most addicted individuals who want to prepare to become drug free. This is effective, however, only when the patient has agreed to the contract. In blind withdrawal without patient's consent, much suffering may be induced with little or no clinical gain. The legally competent patient has a right to know his or her dose.

## ▼ STRUCTURE OF METHADONE PROGRAMS

Methadone programs commonly have cardinal rules that prohibit drug dealing or selling of goods of any kind, threats of violence, carrying of weapons, display of gang colors, and so on. The ability of the clinic administration to enforce these rules will determine the clinical context in which methadone is dispensed. Program results will not be as good as they can be if the clinic atmosphere is controlled by an uncaring administration or, alternatively, by patients who are not able to change from street life and who make the clinic an extension of the drug/street culture rather than a center governed by the culture of hope and recovery. In general, the program will have better results when the members of the staff are stable; have either training or life experience or both that provides for sensitivity on racial, ethnic, and sex issues; and when there is a board of directors that takes an active interest in the life of the clinic. Many clinics have former addicted individuals as counselors, and studies indicate that these individuals are effective in changing drug behavior but they often have no training and are therefore not effective in other areas that are important to the recovery process (of which methadone is just one component).

Comparison of the effectiveness of programs is problematic because of our inability to measure variables critical to performance. One clinic can admit a large number of patients and relatively rapidly exclude those who are difficult. After a time such a clinic can accumulate a growing fraction of the population of the clinic who are doing well. Comparing the results of this clinic with a clinic that tries to retain problem-ridden patients because of its commitment to them will make the latter clinic look bad when in fact it is refusing to give up as easily as the former clinic on what are often multiple-problem patients. Judging a clinic is a complicated exercise because, to date, we have no studies that measure the effects of clinic policies and that measure how much clinic policy has to do with what is practiced in a clinic.

The methadone system, created in the late 1960s and early 1970s, has been chronically underfunded. Its infrastructure and training needs are substantial especially in light of the fact that it is now being asked to bear the brunt of the wave of HIV infection spreading through drug users. One can see what one wants to see in most methadone programs. One-third of MM patients are not doing well even with drug problems let alone the host of other problems that exist in publicly funded program populations. They are usually responsible for diversion of methadone (i.e., selling methadone "on the street"), which can provoke draconian responses from communities. The recent cocaine epidemic, in particular, has had a serious negative effect on many MM programs. The one-third who are not doing well usually catch the public eye, and to the observer unfamiliar with the problems or outcome studies of methadone programs it appears that the programs have no value or that they are part of the problem.

The implications of the aforementioned problems for the clinician are that there is much to study and to understand about the use of methadone and the context in which it is used. A relatively brief exposure to a methadone program should be sufficient to demonstrate that there are significant contributions made by reasonably run programs while there is need for constant improvement of the technology of treatment. Current experience suggests that the addition of a mental health treatment capability and some ability to deliver elementary primary care would go a long way toward improving the fundamental treatment of drug problems. In addition, a number of behavior modification techniques have been demonstrated to have clinical usefulness, although the clinic system has not had the resources to put this new technology on line (Hall et al. 1991; O'Brien et al. 1991; Stitzer 1991). The difficulties in applying this technology are discussed in an article by Nolimal and Crowley (1990).

## ▼ METHADONE AND PREGNANCY

The pregnant opioid-dependent patient presents a dilemma because clinical experience indicates that attempts to detoxify her carry substantial risk of death for her fetus. The human adult rarely dies or has convulsions from opioid withdrawal, but this is a serious possibility for the human fetus/neonate. In the United States, several clinical centers have independently arrived at a policy of maintaining a pregnant opioid-dependent woman through her pregnancy and delivery on doses of methadone as low as possible. This regimen avoids fetal death from withdrawal and also avoids the death of neonates from withdrawal if high doses of methadone are used for maintenance throughout the pregnancy. Some centers will attempt slow withdrawal during pregnancy. With close monitoring it may be possible to lower the maintenance dose of methadone, but, even with sophisticated monitoring, success in safely reaching and maintaining zero dose is not likely (Finegan 1991).

Most neonates of MM patients will experience opioid withdrawal, but it will be mild and will not need treatment. Some neonates will have withdrawal severe enough to require treatment with paregoric and phenobarbital. The phenobarbital controls the hyperactivity and the threat of convulsions, whereas the paregoric controls the μ-opioid withdrawal. Some centers use diazepam, chlorpromazine, and methadone in various combinations, but the paregoric and phenobarbital combination appears to the most frequently used.

The fetus and neonate do not have enzyme systems mature enough to carry out the biotransformation and excretion of opioids. The result is that the onset of withdrawal is frequently delayed in comparison to that of the adult; the neonatal opioid withdrawal syndrome can last many weeks and be more variant in its form. For example, it may manifest itself solely as hyperactivity or as failure to thrive. Common symptoms of opioid withdrawal in neonates are tremor, high-pitched cry, increased muscle tone, hyperactivity, poor sleep, poor feeding, sweating, mottling, excoriation, and yawning. Less common symptoms include convulsions, fever, vomiting, markedly hyperactive Moro reflex and flapping tremor; gastrointestinal symptoms of watery stools and/or vomiting may predominate. Some clinicians feel that sudden infant death syndrome is more frequent in opioid-dependent neonates than it is in non-drug-affected infants.

The analgesic needs of the MM mothers will require usual opioid agonists in usual doses and in usual frequencies. As in other medical situations, maintenance methadone does not contribute to analgesic needs. In the event that a pregnant woman is delivering and has a heroin habit, methadone should be used to control the withdrawal symptoms. Here, as in other medical/surgical crises, one should avoid unnecessary stresses on an individual. Opioid withdrawal is a major stress and should not be added to the stress of delivery. Stress levels can be expected to be high in opioid-dependent women and will require psychological management (i.e., support, nonjudgmental attitudes, and recognition of her suffering). Additional principles of management of the drug-dependent woman are given by Finnegan and Kaltenbach (1992).

The birth weights of the neonates of MM women are elevated compared with the offspring of heroin-dependent women, although they are not normal; if methadone has teratogenic effects or major developmental effects, they are not apparent in studies carried out to date.

## ▼ METHADONE AND MEDICAL SURGICAL ILLNESS

As discussed above, one should avoid unnecessary stresses on the pregnant opioid-dependent patient. The same principle applies to medical or surgical crises in an individual dependent on either prescribed or nonprescribed opioids. In the event that a given medical or surgical patient is on MM, the dose used for maintenance should be continued throughout the medical or surgical crisis. If the opioid-addicted patient is a so-called street addict, then, in most cases, smooth control can be achieved with methadone 10–30 mg per day. Control of withdrawal is usually possible with once-a-day administration, but if there are problems at end of the 24-hour withdrawal, one can split the dose into twice or three times daily. Obviously if anesthesia is necessary, the anesthesiologist should be told about the patient's current opioid dependence. Pentazocine or other mixed agonist-antagonists, such as buprenorphine, are contraindicated for analgesia because they may have antagonist actions and cause or worsen withdrawal.

Once the medical surgical crisis has passed, a decision can be made about detoxification. If an addicted patient wants to be detoxified, referral to a drug abuse program should be the option of choice. Many patients will not want to be detoxified and will want to return to heroin use in their customary surroundings. There may be no other option as drug abuse treatment programs in many areas of the country have long waiting lists, and the option of withdrawal in medical surgical wards is problematic. The staff of these wards are not equipped by training or experience to treat addiction. More often than not, management problems (e.g., drug use, intoxication , stealing, etc.) will occur. If a given patient was on MM on admission, the patient should be discharged back to his or her MM program without alteration of dose.

In the occasional case of multiple simultaneous dependencies (e.g., heroin, alcohol), methadone may be used concurrently with other usual drugs to control withdrawal. For the patient physiologically dependent on alcohol and opioids, one could combine methadone with benzodiazepines to stabilize the patient through the medical surgical crisis. Once the crisis has passed, the methadone and the benzodiazepine can be withdrawn either sequentially or concurrently.

## ▼ PSYCHIATRIC ASPECTS OF METHADONE TREATMENT

The self-help movement defines the psychology of drug dependence as one of denial. There is abundant observation to support this view (Meyer 1986). However, in the population coming into treatment, one will see, in addition to denial, a pole of healthy striving in addition to the denial; that is, there is an intense ambivalence about the drug problem. Most addicts are aware, both acutely and chronically, of the costs of the drug problem to themselves and to others and they make repeated attempts to change. The therapist needs to identify the individually unique aspects of the healthy striving and support this pole of the ambivalence. Methadone appears to help by tilting the balance of the ambivalence toward the positive pole.

In addition to ambivalence, one will also observe that drug seeking and taking has come to take on the characteristics of a human or animal object relationship. This is reflected in the street terms for a drug habit "I've got a Jones," or "I've got a monkey on my back" in describing a heroin habit. One of the major tasks for the recovering addicted patient is to put people back in the place of the drug.

The therapist needs to identify where the recovering addicted patient is on this dimension and work to complete the process of relating to people once again. In this regard, the therapist should recognize that the addicted patient has to mourn the loss of his or her drug object relationship and that this may take some time. In many successfully maintained patients, one can observe that the subject of withdrawal is associated with phobic responses. The patient literally may not be able to think about withdrawal because of the intensity of arousal that automatically accompanies any attempt to reflect on the subject. We do not have techniques specific to this kind of phobia, but general techniques of behavior modification can be employed.

The beginning clinician probably will not know street jargon. A physician's lack of knowledge of street jargon is a nonissue if the physician cares for patients and is competent in the pharmacology of intoxicants. Addicted patients want concerned, competent care and not an extension of the drug culture. Clinicians at all levels will constantly hear new terms, for example, "ice" for smokable methamphetamine; simply asking, "What is 'ice?'" will not hurt the working relationship with the patient. If the clinician knows street jargon, it will speed workups and will not have negative consequences. (For a detailed review of history taking and relating to addicted patients see Senay 1992.)

A number of studies indicate that opioid-dependent populations have rates of depressive symptoms that are perhaps three times higher than that found in community-based samples (Ginzburg et al. 1984). The daily administration of methadone does not appear to improve or to worsen the depression. Patients studied to date appear to improve with respect to depression whether they stay in methadone treatment or drop out early (Dorus and Senay 1980). Anxiety disorders and antisocial personality disorders (ASPDs) also appear to be more frequent in opioid dependent populations than in the general population. Methadone has no effect on ASPD, but if an ASPD patient is depressed the depression may be treated and general functioning is improved. Some feel that methadone may have therapeutic effects on patients with schizophrenia or bipolar affective disorder. In my experience, if there are such effects they are quite variable from patient to patient and not dramatic in any one patient.

McClellan (1986) studied both alcoholic and drug-addicted patients in six different treatments, including an MM clinic, and found that the patients with low psychiatric severity improved in every treatment program. Patients with high psychiatric severity showed virtually no improvement in any treatment. Patients with mid-range psychiatric severity (60% of the sample) showed outcome differences from treatment and especially from patient treatment matches. In these studies, psychiatric severity was measured by the psychiatric severity scale of the Addiction Severity Index (McLellan et al. 1980), which measures needs for treatment/services in a number of areas, including psychiatric.

## ▼ EVALUATION STUDIES

It is important for the clinician to understand that the usefulness of methadone is established by two and one-half decades of clinical experience in a variety of cultural settings. In addition, the data base of studies of MM is larger and encompasses time periods longer than those related to any other biopsychosocial problem ever studied. The National Institute on Drug Abuse (NIDA) has sponsored large nationwide studies, for example, the Drug Abuse Reporting Program of Texas Christian University (DARP; Sells and Simpson 1976). DARP has a data base of over 44,000 opioid-dependent individuals, with some treatment outcome studies extending over a 12-year period. Another study, the Treatment Outcome Prospective Study (TOPS), has a data base of 12,000 patients entering treatment between 1979 and 1981. These subjects were followed prospectively, some for periods of up to 5 years (Hubbard et al. 1989). A third study by the Veterans Administration (VA) carried out a large nationwide study of MM, and its results mirror those of DARP and TOPS: illicit drug use and criminality decreased during treatment, and gains were made in social functioning both during and after treatment. These large nationwide studies have results similar to those of many city and state reports (e.g., Anglin and McGlothlin 1984 [California]; Burt Associates 1977 [New York and Washington, D.C.]; Judson et al. 1980 [Palo Alto]; Newman 1977 [New York]; Senay et al. 1973 [Illinois]) and others (Bewley et al. 1972; Blachly 1970; Bloom and Sudderth 1970; Brown et al. 1973; DuPont and Green 1973; Gearing and Schweitzer 1974; Gunne 1983; Kleber 1970; Maslansky 1970; Sheffet et al. 1980; Tuason and Jones 1974).

All of the aforementioned studies indicate that methadone reduces illicit drug use and associated crime together with other gains. However, there are reports in which these findings were not replicated (Dobbs 1971; Hallgrimsson 1980; Harms 1975; Perkins and Bloch 1970). None of these studies have the design and scope of the large national, state, or city studies; they tend to be reports from single programs with small numbers relative to those of DARP, TOPS, the VA or most of the city and state reports reviewed above.

One of the most commonly asked questions—Is MM superior to therapeutic community treatment?—cannot be answered because to date it has not been possible to assign patients randomly to these two methods. Bale et al. (1980) studied groups of addicted patients who were randomly assigned to therapeutic communities or to MM. They found that patient compliance with random assignments was so poor that the research question could not be answered.

## ▼ FUTURE DIRECTIONS FOR METHADONE MAINTENANCE

It is entirely possible that technology of legal opioid substitution therapy may be improved in the near future. The narcotic agonist/antagonist buprenorphine is being studied both for use in detoxification and in maintenance as it may have less abuse potential and may be easier to detoxify from. The use of general practitioners to care for MM patients appears to be useful for addicted patients with good performance in standard treatment (Novick et al. 1988).

L-α-acetylmethadol (LAAM) is a long-acting congener of methadone that is being explored for use in legal substitution treatment. In a LAAM regimen, the addicted patient needs only an administration of three times per week, usually on Monday, Wednesday, and Friday, with the Friday dose some 10%–15% higher than the Monday or Wednesday dose. Results with LAAM are equal to those with methadone although a different subset of addicted patients seems to be helped by LAAM.

One of the unresolved questions in MM programming is the precise role played by the various elements. As TOPS demonstrates, MM programs provide a wide range of services: legal, vocational, and social (Craddock et al. 1985), which are used and appreciated by patients. Patterns of substance abuse are changing in the direction of abuse of multiple substances, in rotating fashion, with new intoxicants added constantly to the mix. Opioids however continue to be abused. A role for legal opioid substitution therapy seems assured because, despite its controversial status, the therapy appears to offer a unique service to large numbers of addicted patients. It will be needed for the foreseeable future unless there are dramatic reductions in illicit opioid use.

## ▼ REFERENCES

Anglin MD, McGlothlin WH: Outcome of narcotic addict treatment in California, in Drug Abuse Treatment Evaluation: Strategies, Progress, and Projects, NIDA Res Monogr 51. Edited by Tims FM, Ludford JP. Washington, DC, U.S. Government Printing Office, 1984, pp 106–128

Bale RN, Van Stone WW, Kuldau JM, et al: Therapeutic communities vs methadone maintenance. Arch Gen Psychiatry 37:179–193, 1980

Ball JC, Corty E, Myers CP, et al: The reduction of intravenous heroin use, non-opiate abuse and crime during methadone maintenance treatment: further findings, NIDA Res Monogr 81 (DHHS Publ No ADM-88-1564). Rockville, MD, National Institute on Drug Abuse, 1988a

Ball JC, Lange WR, Myers E, et al: Reducing the risk of AIDS through methadone maintenance treatment. J Health Soc Behav 29:214–26, 1988b

Barthwell A, Senay E, Marks R, et al: Patients successfully maintained with methadone escaped human immunodeficiency virus infection (letter). Arch Gen Psychiatry 46:957, 1989

Bewley TH, James IP, LeFevre C, et al: Maintenance treatment of narcotic addicts (not British nor a system but working now). Int J Addict 7:597–611, 1972

Blachly PH: Progress report on the methadone blockade: treatment of heroin addicts in Portland. Northwest Medicine 69:172–176, 1970

Bloom WA Jr, Sudderth EW: Methadone in New Orleans: patients, problems and police. Int J Addict 5:465–487, 1970

Brown BS, Dupont RL, Bass UF, et al: Impact of a large-scale narcotics treatment program: a six month experience. Int J Addict 8:49–57, 1973

Burt Associates, Inc: Drug Treatment in New York City and Washington, DC: Follow-up Studies. Washington, DC, U.S. Government Printing Office, 1977

Cicero TJ, Bell RD, Wiest WG, et al: Function of the male sex organs in heroin and methadone users. N Engl J Med 292:882–887, 1975

Cooper JR: Ineffective use of psychoactive drugs. JAMA 267:281–282, 1992

Craddock SG, Bray RM, Hubbard RL: Drug use before and during drug abuse treatment: 1979–1981 admission cohorts, Treatment Research Monograph (DHHS Publ No ADM-85-1387). Rockville, MD, National Institute on Drug Abuse, 1985

Dobbs WH: Methadone treatment of heroin addicts: early results provide more questions than answers. JAMA 218:1516–1541, 1971

Dole VP: Implications of methadone maintenance for theories of narcotic addiction. JAMA 260:3025–3029, 1988

Dole VP, Nyswander ME: A medical treatment of diacetylmorphine (heroin) addiction. JAMA 193:646–650, 1965

Dorus W, Senay EC: Depression, demographics, and drug abuse. Am J Psychiatry 137:699–704, 1980

Dupont RL, Green MH: The decline of heroin addiction in the District of Columbia. National Conference on Methadone Treatment Proceedings 2: 1474–1483, 1973

Finnegan LP: Perinatal substance abuse: comments and perspectives. Semin Perinatol 15:331–339, 1991

Finnegan LP, Kaltenbach K: Neonatal abstinence syndrome, in Primary Pediatric Care, 3rd Edition. Edited by Hoekelman RA, Friedman SB, Nelson NM, et al. St. Louis, MO, CV Mosby, 1992, pp 1367–1378

Gearing FR, Schweitzer MD: An epidemiologic evaluation of long-term methadone maintenance treatment for heroin addiction. Am J Epidemiol 100: 101–112, 1974

Ginzburg HM, Allison M, Hubbard RL: Depressive symptoms in drug abuse treatment clients: correlates, treatment and changes, in Problems of Drug Dependence, 1983, NIDA Res Monogr 49 (DHHS Publ No ADM-84-1316). Edited by Harris LS. Washington, DC, U.S. Government Printing Office, 1984

Gritz ER, Shiffman SM, Jarvik ME, et al: Physiological and psychological effects of methadone in man. Arch Gen Psychiatry 32:237–242, 1975

Gunne LM: The fate of the Swedish methadone maintenance treatment programme. Drug Alcohol Depend 11:99–103, 1983

Hall SH, Wasserman DA, Havassy B: Relapse Prevention in Improving Drug Abuse Treatment, NIDA Res Monogr 106 (DHHS Publ No ADM-91-1754). Edited by Pickens RW, Leukefeld CG, Schuster CR. Rockville, MD, Department of Health and Human Services, 1991

Hallgrimsson O: Methadone treatment: the Nordic attitude. Journal of Drug Issues 10:463–474, 1980

Hargreaves W: Methadone dosage and duration for maintenance treatment, in Research on the Treatment of Narcotic Addiction: State of the Art, NIDA Treatment Research Monograph Series (DHHS Publ No ADM-83-1281). Edited by Cooper J, Altman, Brown B, et al. Washington, DC, U.S. Government Printing Office, 1983, pp 19–91

Harms E: Some shortcomings of methadone maintenance. British Journal of Addiction 70:77–81, 1975

Havassy B, Hall S: Efficacy of urine monitoring in methadone maintenance. Am J Psychiatry 138:

1497–1500, 1981

Hubbard R, Marsden M, Rachal J: Drug Abuse Treatment: A National Study of Effectiveness. Chapel Hill, NC, The University of North Carolina Press, 1989

Jaffe JH, Martin WR: Opioid analgesics and antagonists, in The Pharmacological Basis of Therapeutics, 7th Edition. Edited by Gilman AG, Goodman LS, et al. New York, Macmillan, 1985, pp 49–531

Judson BA, Ortiz S, Crouse L, et al: A follow-up study of heroin addicts five years after first admission to a methadone treatment program. Drug Alcohol Depend 6:295–313, 1980

Kanof PD, Aronson MJ, Ness R, et al: Levels of opioid physical dependence in heroin addicts. Drug Alcohol Depend 27:253–262, 1991

Kelley D, Welch R, McKneely N, et al: Methadone Maintenance; an assessment of potential fluctuations in behavior between doses. Int J Addict 13:1061–1068, 1978

Kleber HD: The New Haven methadone maintenance program. Int J Addict 5:449–463, 1970

Kreek MJ: Health consequences associated with the use of methadone, in Research on the Treatment of Narcotic Addiction: State of the Art (DHHS Publ No ADM-83-1281). Edited by Cooper JR, Altman F, Brown BS, et al. Washington, DC, U.S. Government Printing Office, 1983, pp 456–482

Ling W, Weiss DG, Charuvastra VC, et al: Use of disulfiram for alcoholics in methadone maintenance programs. Arch Gen Psychiatry 40:851–854, 1983

Maddox JF, Williams TR, Ziegler DA, et al: Driving records before and during methadone maintenance. Am J Drug Alcohol Abuse 4:91–100, 1977

Maslansky R: Methadone maintenance programs in Minneapolis. Int J Addict 5:391–405, 1970

McLellan AT, Luborsky L, Woody GE, et al: An improved diagnostic evaluation instrument for substance abuse patients: the Addiction Severity Index. J Nerv Ment Dis 168:26–33, 1980

McLellan AT: "Psychiatric severity" as a predictor of outcome from substance abuse treatments, in Psychopathology and Addictive disorders. Edited by Meyer RE. New York, Guilford, 1986, pp 97–139

Meyer RE: Psychopathology and Addictive Disorders. New York, Guilford, 1986

Newman RG: Methadone Treatment in Narcotic Addiction. New York, Academic Press, 1977

Newman RG, Whitehill WB: Double-blind comparison of methadone and placebo maintenance treatments of narcotic addicts in Hong Kong. Lancet 11:485–488, 1979

Nolimal D, Crowley TJ: Difficulties in a clinical application of methadone-dose contingency contracting. J Subst Abuse Treat 7:219–224, 1990

Novick DM, Pascarelli EF, Joseph H, et al: Methadone maintenance patients in general medical practice. JAMA 259:3299–3302, 1988

Novick DM, Joseph H, Croxson TS, et al: Absence of antibody to human immunodeficiency virus in long-term, socially rehabilitated methadone maintenance patients. Arch Intern Med 150:97–99, 1990

O'Brien CP, Childress AR, McLellan AT: Conditioning factors may help to understand and prevent relapse in patients who are recovering from drug dependence, in Improving Drug Abuse Treatment, NIDA Res Monogr 106 (DHHS Publ No ADM-91-1754). Edited by Pickens RW, Leukefeld CG, Schuster CR. Rockville, MD, Department of Health and Human Services, 1991, pp 293–312

O'Connor LM, Woody G, Yeh HS, et al: Methadone and edema. J Subst Abuse Treat 8:153–155, 1991

Perkins ME, Block HI: Survey of a methadone maintenance treatment program. Am J Psychiatry 126:33–40, 1970

Sells SB, Simpson DD: The Effectiveness of Drug Abuse Treatment, Vol 3. Cambridge, MA, Balinger, 1976

Senay EC: The diagnostic interview and mental status examination, in Substance Abuse: A Comprehensive Textbook, 2nd Edition. Edited by Lowinson JH, Ruiz P, Millman RB. Baltimore, MD, Williams & Wilkins, 1992, pp 416–424

Senay EC, Shick JF: Pupillography responses to methadone challenge: aid to diagnosis of opioid dependence. Drug Alcohol Depend 3:133–138, 1978

Senay EC, Jaffe JH, Chappel JN, et al: IDAP-five year results. Fifth National Conference on Methadone Treatment Proceedings 2:1437–1464, 1973

Sheffet A, Quinones MA, Doyle KM, et al: Assessment of treatment outcomes in a drug abuse rehabilitation network: Newark, New Jersey. Am J Drug Alcohol Abuse 7:141–173, 1980

Stitzer ML, Kirby KC: Reducing illicit drug use among methadone patients, in Improving Drug Abuse Treatment, NIDA Res Monogr 106 (DHHS Publ No ADM-91-1754). Edited by Pickens RW, Leukefeld CG, Schuster CR. Rockville, MD, Department of Health and Human Services, 1991, pp 178–203

Tuason VB, Jones WL: Methadone maintenance treatment a report on over three years experience. Minn Med 57:899–901, 1974

Wang RIH, Wiesen RL, Sofian L, et al: Rating the presence and severity of opiate dependence. Clin Pharmacol Ther 16:653–658, 1974

# CHAPTER 15

# Opioids

## Antagonists and Partial Agonists

*Charles P. O'Brien, M.D., Ph.D.*

The study of opioid drugs has been a focus of researchers since the earliest days of pharmacology because of their importance in the treatment of pain. Over the past 20 years this intense research produced discoveries in the endogenous opioid system that have increased knowledge about the way that these drugs act. It is fair to state that our understanding of the biology of opioid effects including opioid dependence is well developed and probably more complete than our understanding of any other class of drugs of abuse (see O'Brien 1992). Although there is still much to learn about the chronic changes produced in opioid receptors and second messenger systems during dependence, there is considerable knowledge about the interaction between these receptors and both opiates (derivatives of the opium plant) and opioids (synthetic substances acting at opiate receptors). This has led to the classification of drugs according to their interaction with these receptors. There are three basic categories:

▼ *Agonists* (e.g., heroin, methadone) that activate specific opioid receptors
▼ *Antagonists* (e.g., naloxone, naltrexone) that occupy opioid receptors but do not activate them
▼ *Partial agonists* (e.g., buprenorphine) that occupy opioid receptors but only activate them in a limited way and may also block the occupation of receptors by other substances thus producing both agonist and antagonist effects

Of all the medications used in the treatment of opioid dependence, methadone, a long-acting agonist at the μ subtype of opioid receptor, has clearly had the greatest impact (see Chapter 14). Naltrexone, which became available for general use in 1985, is an antagonist and therefore a distinctly different treatment from methadone. Naltrexone specifically blocks opioid receptors; while the drug is present, it prevents readdiction to heroin and other opioid drugs. Because it is so different from other available

*Editor's note.* An *opiate* is any drug that is derived from opium. Although the term *opioid* was originally used for drugs with opiate-like activity but that are not derived from opium, *opioid* has gradually become the term for the entire family of natural, semisynthetic, and synthetic opiates. For the purposes of this textbook, the term *opioid* is used to refer to both the naturally occurring opiates and any drug that has opiate-like activity, unless there is need to distinguish between the two.

treatments, naltrexone is commonly misunderstood. Clinicians tend to confuse it with disulfiram (Antabuse) in the treatment of alcoholism or methadone for agonist maintenance of opioid-addicted patients. As an antagonist, naltrexone's mechanism of action is specific, and to use this tool effectively this mechanism should be clearly understood.

Although pharmacologically distinctive, naltrexone does not change the fundamental requirements for good treatment of addiction. Rehabilitation requires a comprehensive treatment program with attention to the nonpharmacologic variables that play a critical role in the complex problem of addiction. Thus the prescription of naltrexone alone will not work. It should be part of an overall treatment program that includes individual or group psychotherapy, family therapy, contingency contracting, and possibly behavioral extinction of drug-conditioned responses.

In considering this new treatment, it should be recognized that naltrexone will not appeal to the majority of opioid-dependent individuals. Of all street heroin-addicted subjects presenting for treatment, not more than 10%–15% show any interest in a drug that "keeps you from getting high" (Greenstein et al. 1984). The vast majority prefer methadone treatment, but for those highly motivated patients who prefer to be opioid free, naltrexone is an excellent alternative. Certain patients such as health care professionals, middle-class addicts, and former addicts given an early parole from prison may find naltrexone to be the treatment of choice.

It should also be emphasized that naltrexone acts specifically only at opioid receptors. It does not block the effects of nonopioid drugs although there may be some effects on the "high" from alcohol (discussion follows later in this chapter). Cocaine abuse in association with heroin became a common problem during the 1980s. Those patients dependent on both opioids and cocaine may be treated with naltrexone, but they will need additional therapy to deal with their cocaine dependence.

## ▼ RECEPTOR INTERACTIONS WITH DRUGS

Opiates such as heroin and morphine as well as the synthetic opioids such as methadone and meperidine act through specific opioid receptors; these drugs are referred to as *agonists* (Jaffe and Martin 1990). Antagonists such as naloxone (Narcan) or naltrexone (Trexan) also bind to these receptors, but they do not activate the receptor to initiate the chain of cellular events that produce so-called *opioid effects*. Naloxone and naltrexone are relatively "pure" antagonists in that they produce little or no agonist activity at usual doses. This is in contrast to mixed partial agonists such as nalorphine or buprenorphine, which produce significant agonist effects. Not only do pure antagonists fail to produce opioid effects, but their presence at the receptor also *prevents* opioid agonists from binding to the receptor and producing opioid effects. Since the antagonist competes for a binding site with the agonist, the degree of blockade depends on the relative concentrations of each and their relative affinity for the receptor site. Naltrexone has high receptor affinity and thus it can block virtually all of the effects of the usual doses of opioids such as heroin. In the presence of naltrexone, there can be no opioid-induced euphoria, respiratory depression, pupillary construction, or any other opioid effect (Martin et al. 1973; O'Brien et al. 1975).

There are three types of medical uses for opioid antagonists:

1. To reverse the effects of an opioid, particularly in the treatment of an opioid overdose. Naloxone is commonly used to reverse the effects of high-dose morphine anesthesia and to reverse opioid-induced respiratory depression in newborns.
2. To diagnose physical dependence on opioid drugs. An antagonist such as naloxone will displace the opioid from the receptors in a dependent individual and produce an immediate withdrawal syndrome. Naloxone rather than naltrexone is typically used for this purpose because its brief duration of action will produce discomfort for only a short time.
3. To prevent readdiction in an individual who has been detoxified from opioid drugs.

### Effects of Antagonists

If a person not currently dependent on an opioid agonist receives an antagonist, there are usually no obvious effects. Theoretically, something should happen because the antagonist blocks certain endogenous opioids (endorphins) that may serve to regulate mood, pain perception, and various neuro-endocrine and cardiovascular functions. In fact, there have been reports of dysphoric reactions and endocrine changes in experimental subjects given naltrexone (Ellingboe et al. 1980; Mendelson et al. 1980). Spiegel et al. (1987) reported small decreases in appetite produced by naltrexone in human volunteers. Hollister et al. (1982) found adverse mood effects in normal volunteers given naltrexone. Crowley et al. (1985) noted similar effects in recently detoxified opioid addicts. These dysphoric effects of naltrexone were reported after brief treatment (1 day to 3 weeks), and the number of subjects was very small. In contrast, another study (O'Brien et al. 1978) of normal subjects reported no differences in mood effects between naltrexone and placebo. Moreover, most large-scale studies of recovering opioid-addicted patients have not found dysphoria or other mood changes to be a significant problem in the clinical use of naltrexone (Brahen et al. 1984; Greenstein et al. 1984; Tennant et al. 1984; Washton et al. 1984). It may be that blocking endogenous opioids with naltrexone produces mood problems in some patients, and this may explain part of the early dropout phenomenon. Those who continue on naltrexone for months or even years generally report no mood effects although careful long-term studies of mood have not been conducted.

There have been occasional reports (Sideroff et al. 1978) of reduced drug craving in naltrexone-maintained patients, but it is not clear that this is a pharmacologic effect. It may simply be a reduction in craving caused by the security that patients feel knowing that they are protected from the temptation to experience opioid effects by the pharmacologic blockade of naltrexone (Meyer et al. 1975).

On the other hand, individuals who are currently dependent on opioids are exquisitely sensitive to antagonists. This forms the basis of the naloxone test for dependence that was mentioned previously. The degree of sensitivity depends on the time since the last dose of opioid and the size of the dose. Even a very small amount of naloxone or naltrexone can rapidly displace enough opioid from opioid receptors to precipitate a withdrawal syndrome. Therefore, in starting a patient on naltrexone, it is important to make certain that the opioid-dependent patient is fully detoxified prior to the initiation of antagonist treatment.

## ▼ CLINICAL USE OF NALTREXONE

### Naloxone vs. Naltrexone

Naloxone and naltrexone differ in several important ways. Naloxone is poorly absorbed from the gut; when given parenterally, naloxone is rapidly metabolized. Naloxone, therefore, is useful only for the acute reversal of opioid effects as in the emergency treatment of opioid overdoses and in the diagnosis of physical dependence. If the presence of physical dependence is in question, a small (0.4–0.8 mg) injection of naloxone can be given. In a dependent individual, a withdrawal syndrome would immediately occur, but it would be short-lived (20–40 minutes).

In contrast, naltrexone is well absorbed when given by mouth, and it has a long-duration of action. Pharmacokinetic studies of naltrexone show a plasma half-life of the parent compound of 4 hours. An important active metabolite, 6-β-naltrexol has a plasma half-life of 12 hours. With chronic administration, there is an increase in both peak and trough levels of 6-β-naltrexol. The pharmacological duration of naltrexone is actually longer than might be predicted by the plasma kinetics. Double-blind studies showed antagonism of injected opioids up to 72 hours after a 150-mg dose, but the degree of antagonism was less than that seen at 24 and 48 hours (O'Brien et al. 1975).

Naltrexone could be used to reverse an opioid overdose, but it is usually more practical to use a short-acting drug like naloxone administered by an intravenous drip that can be titrated as needed. In this way, an overdose can be reversed by a short-acting drug without the danger of giving too much antagonist and precipitating a withdrawal reaction in an opioid-dependent individual. However, a long-acting drug such as naltrexone is ideal for use in preventing relapse to opioids. In the presence of naltrexone, heroin self-administration is no longer rewarding, and the subjects are observed to stop taking available heroin (Mello et al. 1981). In human volunteers, naltrexone has been shown to be effective in attenuating the effects of opioids for 72 hours. Patients have reported even longer activity against the relatively weak heroin purchased on the street. Although daily ingestion of naltrexone would provide the most secure protection against opioid effects, naltrexone can be given as infrequently as two or three times per week, with adequate protection against readdiction. The reduced frequency makes monitoring of the medication more practical over the long term. Tolerance does not appear to develop to the antagonism of opioid effects even after more than 1 year of regular naltrexone ingestion (Kleber et al. 1985).

## Benefits of Naltrexone

Naltrexone was approved by the Food and Drug Administration (FDA) on the basis of its clear pharmacological activity as an opioid antagonist. It has never been shown in large-scale double-blind trials that it is more effective than placebo in the rehabilitation of opioid-addicted patients. In large-scale studies, the dropout rate is very high, just as it is in drug-free outpatient treatment of heroin addiction. Naltrexone clearly is not effective when simply prescribed as a medication for street heroin-addicted patients in the absence of a structured rehabilitation program. Within a structured program, naltrexone appears to be effective, particularly with specific motivated populations. A randomized controlled study conducted with federal probationers suggests that the impressions of efficacy can be confirmed by data collected in these populations who are at risk to return to prison (Tilly et al. 1992).

Naltrexone can permit recently detoxified addicted patients to return to their usual environments secure in the knowledge that they cannot succumb to an impulsive wish to get high. For many patients, this may be the first time in years that they have been able to exist outside of a hospital or prison in an opioid-free state. The subtle manifestations of the opioid withdrawal syndrome are known to persist for months (Martin and Jasinski 1969). During this protracted withdrawal syndrome, the patient's autonomic nervous system is unstable, and symptoms such as anxiety and sleep disturbances are common. Conditioned responses to environmental cues produced by previous drug use (Wikler 1965; O'Brien et al. 1986) also may contribute to relapse. Maintenance on naltrexone provides an ideal situation to extinguish these conditioned responses (O'Brien et al. 1980, 1984) and permit the protracted withdrawal syndrome to subside.

For a recovering addicted individual who works in a field such as nursing, pharmacy, or medicine, there is an added benefit to naltrexone maintenance: it reduces suspicion about relapse. Because these medical occupations often require working with opioid drugs, there is a daily temptation to resume drug use. Of course, return to work is very important to rehabilitation, but it presents problems in a medical setting. Colleagues who are aware of the patient's struggle with addiction tend to regard any hint of unusual behavior as a sign that relapse to addiction has occurred. However, with a program of verified naltrexone ingestion as part of a comprehensive treatment program, the professional can return to work. Physicians who are recovering from addiction often cite this reduction of suspicion from colleagues as an important reason to continue naltrexone, some for 5 years or more. Of course, the opioid-free period also permits the use of psychotherapy to deal with underlying or superimposed psychosocial problems.

## Comparison With Other Treatment Approaches

As with other treatments for addiction, naltrexone works best within a comprehensive program that deals with all aspects of the patient's problems (Resnick et al. 1979). Naltrexone is similar to methadone in this sense: both are medications that can reduce relapse to illicit drug use. There are significant differences, however. Methadone has been found to be an excellent treatment for the majority of street heroin users because it satisfies their drug craving. Methadone also enables them to stop committing crimes because they no longer have an expensive drug habit to support. Former heroin users can thus stabilize their lives, take care of their families, and find legal employment. Methadone does not "block" heroin's effects, however. There is cross-tolerance between heroin and methadone, and because street heroin is relatively weak, the patient maintained on an adequate dose of methadone will get little reward from the usual dose of heroin. In addition to satisfying opioid craving, methadone may produce beneficial psychoactive effects.

In contrast to methadone, naltrexone cannot be given until all opioids have been metabolized and cleared from the body. Naltrexone does not produce opioid effects or any psychoactive benefits; patients are therefore without the feeling of opioids in their bodies. During the 24–72 hours of naltrexone's effects, it will effectively block the actions of any opioid drug; thus if the patient decides to resume heroin use, he or she cannot experience euphoria or calming from the use of heroin as in the past.

Another important distinction between methadone and naltrexone is the absence of dependence on naltrexone. Naltrexone can be stopped abruptly at any time without concern about withdrawal symptoms. In a sense, this lack of dependence is a drawback to naltrexone in clinical practice because the patient perceives no drug effect. Thus there is no built-in "reward," and there is no immediate penalty for stopping. Some clinicians have actually experimented with small monetary payments contingent on ingesting naltrexone in an effort to provide an external reward (Grabowski et al. 1979). Frequently, patients feel so good and overconfident at being opioid free that they may prematurely assume that they no longer need naltrexone. They can stop naltrexone abruptly, but several days later they are again at risk for relapse to opioid use.

Another treatment strategy that is often confused with naltrexone is disulfiram (Antabuse). The medications are similar only in that they are both taken to prevent relapse and they are both nonaddicting. Disulfiram blocks the metabolism of alcohol, not its effects. If a person receiving disulfiram ingests alcohol, the normal degradation of alcohol is inhibited and acetaldehyde accumulates. Acetaldehyde produces flushing, nausea, and other noxious symptoms. These effects, of course, can be prevented by avoiding alcohol while taking disulfiram. In contrast, no such noxious effects result from the use of opioids in association with naltrexone treatment. The opioid effects are simply blocked or neutralized in an individual receiving naltrexone treatment.

## Target Populations

**Medical professionals.** Health care professionals have generally done well in naltrexone treatment programs. For example, Ling and Wesson (1984) reported the use of naltrexone in the management of 60 health care professionals for an average of 8 months. Forty-seven were rated as "much improved" or "moderately improved" at follow-up. Washton et al. (1984) found that 74% of opioid-dependent physicians completed at least 6 months of treatment with naltrexone and were opioid free and practicing medicine at 1-year follow-up. Both of these studies involved comprehensive treatment programs, with naltrexone providing a kind of structure around which psychotherapy was built.

The comprehensive treatment program should involve a full medical evaluation, detoxification, psychiatric evaluation, family evaluation, and provision for ongoing therapy along with confirmed regular ingestion of naltrexone. Ongoing therapy usually involves marital and individual therapy. By use of this approach, the physician, whose drug use may have been discovered during a crisis, can be detoxified, started on naltrexone, and can be back at work practicing medicine in as little as 2 weeks. Of course, therapy including naltrexone may continue for several years, but the disruption of family life and medical practice is minimized.

**Employed individuals.** Studies of psychotherapy outcome consistently show that patients coming into treatment with the greatest psychosocial assets tend to respond best to treatment. Thus it is not surprising that patients with a history of recent employment and good educational backgrounds do well on naltrexone. Some patients avoid methadone because of the required daily clinic visits, especially at the beginning of treatment. Naltrexone is not a controlled substance and thus greater flexibility is permitted. Although these patients may be strongly motivated to be drug free, they are still susceptible to impulsive drug use. Using naltrexone as a kind of insurance is often a very appealing idea.

Another practical reason that naltrexone has been successful in this population is that it can be prescribed by any licensed physician. Naltrexone use is not restricted to a special program for the treatment of addiction. Middle-class patients may object to coming to such a clinic. It is recommended, however, that naltrexone be prescribed only by physicians who are familiar with the psychodynamics and behavior patterns of the addicted individual. Patients may appreciate the opportunity for treatment by an experienced practitioner from a private office rather than being restricted to a drug treatment clinic.

Tennant et al. (1984) described a group of suburban practitioners treating opioid dependence in a wide range of socioeconomic groups in southern California. They reported on 160 addicted patients with an average history of opioid use of 10.5 years. The majority (63.8%) were employed; all expressed a desire for abstinence-oriented treatment. Treatment was on an outpatient basis, and a naloxone challenge was given after completion of detoxification. After a graduated dose increase, naltrexone was given three times per week. Patients paid a fee or had the treatment covered by insurance. Each week the patients were subjected to a urine screen for all drug classes and an alcohol breath test. Counseling sessions were held weekly.

The 160 patients remained in treatment a mean of 51 days with a range up to 635 days, but the majority were in short-term treatment. Only 27 (17%) remained longer than 90 days. Tests for illicit drug or alcohol use were only 1%–3% positive during treatment. Tennant et al. (1984) considered the program, which is still in operation, to be successful. However, they pointed out that despite long remissions on naltrexone, relapse to opioid use can still occur after naltrexone is stopped. Based on follow-up results of naltrexone patients, Greenstein et al. (1983) found that while treatment with naltrexone tends to be short term, even as little as 30 days of treatment is associated with a significant improvement in overall rehabilitative status at 6-month follow-up.

A study of patients in a higher socioeconomic group predictably found even better results. Washton et al. (1984) reported on the treatment with naltrexone of 114 business executives dependent for at least 2 years on heroin, methadone, or prescription opioids. They were mainly white men of about 30 years of age, with a mean income of $42,000 per year. A critical feature of this group was that there was considerable external pressure for them to receive treatment, and almost half were in jeopardy of losing their jobs or suffering legal consequences.

The Washton et al. (1984) treatment program was oriented toward complete abstinence. It began with 4–10 weeks of inpatient treatment, during which detoxification and induction onto naltrexone was accomplished. There were also intensive individual psychotherapy and involvement in self-help groups. The importance of the posthospital phase was stressed, and all patients signed a contract for aftercare treatment.

Of the 114 patients who began the program, all completed naltrexone induction; 61% remained on the antagonist for at least 6 months with no missed visits or positive urines. An additional 20% took naltrexone for less than 6 months but remained in the program with drug-free urines. Of the entire group, at 12- to 18-month follow-up, 64% were still opioid free. Those patients who had stipulated pressure from their employers to get treatment did significantly better than the group without a clear-cut risk of loss of job.

**Probationers in a work-release program.** It is a well-known fact that a large proportion of the inmates of prisons throughout the country have been convicted of drug-related crimes. Of course, relapse to drug use and consequent crime is common among these prisoners after they are released. One way to approach this recidivism and perhaps also alleviate some of the overcrowding of our prison system is to use a work-release or half-way house program that enables prisoners to obtain an early release with the stipulation that they work in the community and live in a prison-supervised house. Naltrexone can be prescribed for those prisoners who are former heroin addicts. A pioneering model of such a program has been in existence in Nassau County, Long Island, since 1972.

Dr. Leonard Brahen, the founder and director of this program, has reported on the results of 691 former inmates whom he treated with naltrexone (Brahen et al. 1984). The treatment is set within a work-release program during which the members live in a transitional house outside the prison and obtain employment in the community. Prior to the introduction of naltrexone, the success of former opioid-addicted patients in the program was limited because of their high relapse rate when they were placed in an environment where drugs were freely available.

An inmate with a history of opioid addiction who wishes to volunteer for the program must first be stabilized on naltrexone. Random urine tests are also used to monitor the participants. Uncashed paychecks must be turned in as proof that attendance at work has been regular; a portion of the salary is applied to the cost of room and board. The participants are given supervision and counseling for problems that develop during this reentry period. Some try to use street heroin to get high despite the naltrexone, but because this fails they eventually abandon this behavior. Participants are also offered continuance in treatment after their sentences have been served.

Since the introduction of naltrexone, the rehabilitation success rate of the formerly addicted inmates is equal to that of inmates without a drug history. Although a controlled study with random assignment to naltrexone was not conducted, the staff of the work release program are enthusiastic about the benefits of naltrexone. Follow-up data suggest that even after completing their terms and leaving the program, the group treated with naltrexone had fewer drug arrests than did inmates with a history of opioid abuse who did not receive naltrexone treatment.

More recently, Cornish and colleagues (Tilly et al. 1992) did a random assignment study among federal probationers convicted of drug-related crimes in Philadelphia. The probationers all received the same amount of parole counseling, but half were randomly selected to receive naltrexone as well. After 6 months outside of prison, the group randomly selected for naltrexone had approximately half the reincarceration rate of the control group.

**Heroin-addicted patients.**   Although naltrexone can be used in the treatment of any opioid-dependent patient, it appeals most to those who are strongly motivated to become drug free. Methadone, by contrast, requires much less motivation because treatment involves only a relatively small gradual shift from the state of daily use of heroin to daily use of another opioid agonist, methadone. Naltrexone, however, requires a much bigger change; the individual must genuinely wish to remain free of opioid effects. Unfortunately, most patients who assert strongly that they want to give up drugs have not really thought through the consequences of their statements. Once they find themselves on a medication that makes it physically impossible for them to get high on heroin, they often change their minds.

The majority of street heroin-addicted individuals and participants in methadone maintenance programs are generally not interested in naltrexone treatment after learning how effectively it antagonizes opioids. Studies of the use of naltrexone in public drug treatment clinics have found that no more than 10%–15% of patients are willing to try naltrexone, and most of these drop out during the first month of naltrexone treatment (Greenstein et al. 1983; Hollister 1978; Judson and Goldstein 1984; O'Brien et al. 1975).

Among street heroin users involved in crime to support their drug habit, it is difficult to predict who will respond well to treatment with naltrexone. Certainly the proportion of former heroine-using individuals currently being treated with naltrexone is low. One possible reason for this is that publicly funded treatment programs may be discouraged by the cost of naltrexone (about $3 per tablet). Of course, the main cost of the treatment is the counseling required to support patients after detoxification. Most programs that use naltrexone have focused on patients who are employed or who have good employment prospects, have a stable relationship with spouse or

family, and express willingness to enter into long-term psychotherapy or family therapy. Surprisingly, even short-term (30 days or more) treatment with naltrexone has been shown to be associated with improved outcome at 6-month follow-up (Greenstein et al. 1983). Of course, those willing to remain on the antagonist for 6–12 months generally do well, but it is difficult to know to what degree the success is influenced by the patient's strong motivation as evidenced by remaining in treatment. Probably there is an interaction of several factors that produce a good outcome, and any single factor might not have been adequate by itself.

## ▼ HOW TO USE NALTREXONE IN A COMPREHENSIVE TREATMENT PROGRAM

### Detoxification

An abstinence-oriented program begins with detoxification. This process facilitates the performance of a complete medical evaluation and the determination of any additional health problems that may be present. Detoxification, which preferably should be accomplished on an inpatient basis, also allows opportunity for family and individual psychological evaluations.

There are several pharmacologic options for detoxification. Gradually reducing doses of methadone for 5–10 days constitutes one approach. At the other end of the spectrum, a rapid detoxification assisted by clonidine can have the patient ready for naltrexone in as little as 48 hours after being opioid dependent (Kleber and Kosten 1984). The choice depends on the type of opioid agonist the patient was using (short-acting versus long-acting), the motivation of the patient, and the need for speed in returning the patient to work. See Chapter 13 for a discussion of the different types of detoxification techniques.

### Naloxone Testing for Residual Dependence

There are various methods for beginning treatment with naltrexone (Kleber and Kosten 1984). In all cases, it is important to make certain that there is no residual physical dependence on opioid agonists. If the patient has been using a long-acting opioid such as methadone, it may be necessary to wait 7–10 days after the last dose before initiating treatment with naltrexone. With dependence on short-acting drugs such as heroin or hydromorphone, the time between detoxification and starting naltrexone can be much shorter. If naltrexone is started too soon, precipitated withdrawal will occur. Even mild withdrawal, consisting only of abdominal cramps or periods of nausea, may be enough to discourage the patient from further treatment. On the other hand, the eagerness of some patients to be protected by naltrexone and to return to work results in their willingness to tolerate mild withdrawal symptoms.

Most clinicians working with naltrexone have found that it is helpful to perform a naloxone test to determine if there is any residual physical dependence prior to giving the first dose of naltrexone. Naloxone can be given parenterally, 0.4–1.4 mg subcutaneously or intramuscularly. It can also be used intravenously if very rapid results are desired. A positive test indicating physical dependence consists of symptoms of opioid withdrawal, such as nausea or cramps that last for 20–40 minutes. A positive test indicates that the patient should wait at least another day before starting naltrexone.

Some clinicians prefer to use a very small oral dose of naltrexone rather than a naloxone injection to test for residual opioid dependence. They recommend a half or a quarter of a tablet (12.5–25 mg) as a safe dose (Greenstein et al. 1984). Certainly this approach is safe, but if even a mild withdrawal syndrome is precipitated, it will be of long duration (at least several hours and perhaps more than a day) and will possibly discourage the patient from further naltrexone treatment.

Generally, it is better to wait a longer time between the end of detoxification and the beginning of naltrexone rather than risk evoking a precipitated withdrawal reaction. This time period is critical, however, because the patient is vulnerable to relapse, as yet unprotected by naltrexone. Therefore, the clinician must exercise judgment in balancing the benefits of a rapid transition to naltrexone against the risks of discouraging the patient with a recurrence of physical withdrawal symptoms. The rapid detoxification technique of using clonidine to treat withdrawal symptoms was developed because of this problem, but well-motivated patients are required for best results.

## Naltrexone to Prevent Relapse

When the naloxone challenge is negative, naltrexone can be started with an initial dose of 25 mg (one-half tablet). If there are no side effects after an hour, another 25 mg may be administered. The recommended dose subsequently is 50 mg per day. After the first 1–2 weeks, it is usually possible to graduate to three doses per week (e.g., 100, 100, and 150 mg given on Monday, Wednesday, and Friday, respectively). It is critical that psychotherapy sessions be initiated early in treatment and that these involve family members and other significant figures in the patient's life.

It is important that ingestion of naltrexone be monitored rather than left to the patient's willpower. Confirmed dosing can occur in the clinic, but it is usually disruptive to the patient's rehabilitation to be required to come to the clinic for every dose. For this reason it is important to involve significant figures in the patient's life to observe the ingestion of naltrexone and to report periodically to the therapist. In the case of physicians, for example, a colleague may have already confronted the patient with his or her drug problem and helped steer the patient into therapy. This has sometimes been the chief of staff of the hospital where the patient works or the chairperson of the patient's department. A family member or co-worker can also be enlisted after determining the existence of a constructive relationship.

Progress in treatment is determined by engagement in psychotherapy, performance on the job, and absence of drug abuse as confirmed by urine tests. The patient should be asked to agree to random urine tests arranged by telephoning the patient and asking him or her to come in that day without prior notification. Patients who are doing well can eventually graduate to a schedule of only two doses of naltrexone per week, even though this would not provide full antagonist coverage over the entire interval between doses. However, the reduced frequency of visits reduces the patient's dependence on the therapist and decreases the treatment's interference with the patient's life. Although the degree of pharmacologic blockade is reduced by the third or fourth day after receiving the drug, at this stage of therapy the patient is less likely to be testing limits by taking opioids. Moreover, the random urine testing should detect use between naltrexone doses necessitating a return to more frequent dosing. A "slip" should not be treated as a failure of treatment, but rather as a symptom to be examined in therapy (i.e., grist for the therapeutic mill).

In private practice patients are often given a prescription for naltrexone that can be filled at a pharmacy. Patients can eventually be trusted to take doses of naltrexone at home, but it is best that some doses be taken in the physician's office under direct observation. If a patient is pretending to take naltrexone and is using opioids, a dose in the office would precipitate a withdrawal reaction. Also, there should be a supply of naltrexone tablets that the treating physician keeps in his or her office to administer to patients. Physician and pharmacist patients have been known to attempt to deactivate naltrexone tablets by treating them in a microwave oven. They could then appear to consume naltrexone in the presence of the treating physician or nurse, but they would be taking a relatively inert tablet.

## Side Effects

Considering that naltrexone is a very specific and potent drug that acts on opioid receptors throughout the body, it is surprising that there are so few side effects. Most patients report no symptoms at all; however, when the drug was first introduced in clinical trials, a variety of effects were reported. These included abdominal pain, headache, and mild increases in blood pressure. Many of these symptoms were probably related to precipitation of opioid withdrawal symptoms. Because of the recognition of naltrexone's potency in producing withdrawal in newly detoxified patients, these side effects have now become much less common.

Because naltrexone blocks endogenous opioid peptides in addition to opioid drugs that are injected, one would expect to find multiple symptoms related to blocking the wide-ranging functions of the endorphin systems. In fact, endocrine changes have been reported following naltrexone, although these are less dramatic than those produced by opioids themselves. For example, Ellingboe et al. (1980) reported a prompt rise in luteinizing hormone and a delayed rise in testosterone after naltrexone.

Most former opioid-dependent patients do not report subjective effects that can be related to naltrexone. Of course, these patients have just discontinued heroin or a similar opioid that has altered endocrine patterns, libido, mood, and pain thresh-

olds, probably for years. They could be expected to experience some rebound phenomena simply because of the absence of heroin. Some patients and their spouses report that the use of naltrexone increased sex drive, a finding that has also been reported in rodents. Others report decreased appetite; still others tend to gain weight. Thus the effects of naltrexone are probably confounded with those of protracted opioid withdrawal, and they are further influenced by the contrast with the prior life on varying doses of opioids. Even in patients who have been maintained on naltrexone for several years, consistent subjective effects have been lacking. Certainly the fear that long-term blocking of opioid receptors will lead to problems such as depression has not been realized.

## Effects on Opioid Receptors

Studies in rodents have shown that repeated doses of naloxone or naltrexone produces upregulation of $\mu$-opioid receptors (Yoburn et al. 1985) and a transient increased sensitivity to morphine. If this phenomenon were present in humans treated with naltrexone, former opioid-addicted individuals would be at risk for overdose if they stopped naltrexone and returned to their usual dose of heroin. This question was addressed in an experiment by Cornish et al. (1993) using normal volunteers. Using a test dose of morphine, they determined the degree to which the normal respiratory response to a $CO_2$ stimulus was depressed. After 2 weeks of naltrexone at 50 mg per day, the subjects were retested for morphine sensitivity. No change in morphine's effects were found, indicating lack of detectable change in receptor sensitivity. Thus the theoretical risk of overdose based on upregulation of opioid receptors does not seem to present a clinical problem for the use of naltrexone in preventing relapse to opioid dependence.

## Effects on Blood Chemistry

Changes in laboratory tests have also been examined in more than 2,000 patients involved in clinical trials with naltrexone (Hollister 1978; Pfohl et al. 1986). Despite the fact that addicted individuals are generally unhealthy to begin with, the studies in addiction treatment programs have not turned up significant laboratory abnormalities resulting from naltrexone treatment. Liver function tests are a matter of great concern due to the high frequency of hepatitis among addicted individuals. As many as 70%–80% of patients in methadone programs have some liver abnormalities, usually ascribed to past or present hepatitis.

Studies of nonaddicted groups at high-dose levels have noted dose-related increments in transaminase levels that were all reversible when the drug was stopped. These subjects generally received 300 mg of naltrexone per day, or about six times the therapeutic dose for prevention of relapse to addiction (Pfohl et al. 1986). This finding raises cautions in the treatment of addiction, although in practice transaminase elevations have not been observed at the lower dose levels used in recovering addicted patients (Arndt et al. 1986).

Opioid-addicted individuals in liver failure should not be treated with naltrexone, although those with minor abnormalities in liver function tests may receive naltrexone. Baseline laboratory tests must include a full battery of liver function studies and monthly retesting should occur for the first 3 months. If there is no evidence of rising enzymes, the tests can be repeated at 3- to 6-month intervals. Some clinicians have used as a guideline that naltrexone not be started if either the serum glutamic-oxaloacetic transaminase (SGOT) level or the serum glutamic-pyruvic transaminase (SGPT) level is greater than two times normal. Also, ongoing treatment should be stopped if the enzyme levels become greater than three times normal unless, of course, an alternative cause is found. Frequently, the alternative cause is excessive alcohol intake; when this is stopped, the enzyme levels usually return to normal.

### Safety in Women and Children

Another set of issues regarding the safety of any new drug concerns its use in pregnant women and children. There have been no clinical trials in these groups; thus no definitive statements can be made. Studies of naltrexone in animals generally have not shown signs of potential risks for pregnant patients at clinical doses (Christian 1984), but there is always the possibility of a teratogenic effect specific to humans.

### Drug Interactions

There have been no systematic studies of nonopioid drug interactions with naltrexone, but with more than 10 years of clinical trials and 7 years of post-marketing experience, much anecdotal information is available. Naltrexone has been safely used in combination with disulfiram, lithium, and tricyclic antidepressants; if these agents are indicated, they apparently can be used in their normal way at their usual doses.

One adverse interaction that has been reported is that between thioridazine (Mellaril) and naltrexone. Maany et al. (1987) reported that sedation occurred when naltrexone was added to the regimens of two patients stabilized on thioridazine. No thioridazine plasma levels were available, but a likely explanation is that naltrexone impaired the degradation of thioridazine, resulting in increased plasma levels and increased sedation. If a neuroleptic is required in combination with naltrexone, a nonsedating neuroleptic would be preferable.

### Treatment of Pain During Naltrexone Maintenance

Patients are expected to remain on naltrexone for months or years to prevent relapse to opioid abuse. During this time they may require surgery or treatment of trauma caused by an accident. The presence of naltrexone would not interfere with inhalation anesthesia, but the use of morphine would be affected. Also, opioids for immediate postoperative pain would be precluded in usual doses. If the surgery is elective, the naltrexone could be stopped several days prior to the date of the operation. For emergency surgery, nonopioid anesthesia and postoperative pain medication can be used. If opioid medication is necessary, high doses of a short-acting opioid could be used to override the competitive antagonism produced by naltrexone. As naltrexone and its active metabolites are metabolized, the problem would be resolved. In practice, this issue is rarely a problem because there are nonopioid alternatives that can be used for these patients.

### ▼ NEW THERAPEUTIC PROSPECTS

### Depot Naltrexone

A major impediment to the more widespread use of naltrexone is the early dropout rate. Often patients express an apparently genuine desire for opioid-free treatment, but during the extremely vulnerable period within the first month after detoxification, they miss an appointment, act on an impulse, and take a dose of heroin. There are no withdrawal symptoms from stopping naltrexone. Other patients simply become overconfident and feel that they do not need the protection of naltrexone. Even though the patient may later regret the sudden decision to stop naltrexone, the treatment process must start all over again with detoxification.

A delivery system for naltrexone that provides adequate antagonist protection for 30–60 days would take the patient through the period when relapse is most likely. Preclinical studies have been conducted using micronized spheres of naltrexone embedded in lactide polyglycolide, a substance that gradually dissolves releasing the medication over time. Preliminary clinical testing of a subcutaneous injection of this form of naltrexone suggests that it is not irritating to the skin and that it provides a gradual release of naltrexone for 30–60 days. Much more testing is necessary, but this delivery system holds promise for increasing the efficacy of naltrexone in the rehabilitation of opioid-addicted patients.

## Buprenorphine: Qualities of Both Methadone and Naltrexone

Buprenorphine is a partial μ-opioid agonist that is currently approved by the FDA in an injectable form to treat pain. As an agonist, it is 25–50 times more potent than morphine, but since it is a partial agonist, there is a limit to the opioid effects that it can produce. Unlike agonists such as morphine and methadone, higher doses of buprenorphine do not produce progressively greater opioid effects and thus buprenorphine is less likely to produce an overdose.

In clinical trials, buprenorphine shows some of the features of both methadone and naltrexone. The agonist properties of buprenorphine cause it to be attractive as a maintenance treatment for a large proportion of opioid-addicted patients. It blocks opioid withdrawal and satisfies craving for opioids. If buprenorphine is discontinued abruptly, the withdrawal syndrome is very mild. Heroin, in contrast, has an intense but short-lived withdrawal syndrome depending on the dose. The methadone withdrawal syndrome is milder than that of heroin, but significantly longer in duration. In addition to these opioid agonist effects,

buprenorphine antagonizes the effects of other opioids in a manner comparable to naltrexone.

Buprenorphine has certain drawbacks as well. It is only one-fifteenth as potent by oral administration compared with subcutaneous injection (Jasinski et al. 1989). By sublingual administration, it is two-thirds as potent, and this is the delivery system used in clinical trials for addiction. Buprenorphine has been found to block craving for approximately 24 hours, but this means that patients are required to come to the clinic daily and hold the medication in their mouths without swallowing for at least 3 minutes. In busy treatment programs, this can be complicated.

Based on clinical trials to date (Bickel et al. 1988; Johnson et al. 1992), it appears that buprenorphine is on track for FDA approval in the mid-1990s. It will be an important new option for the physician treating opioid-dependent patients.

## Naltrexone in the Treatment of Alcoholism

A potential new use for naltrexone in the treatment of alcoholism is included here because the mechanism is believed to involve the endogenous opioid system. There are numerous studies in animals showing that alcohol drinking produces changes in the endogenous opioid system. Opioids have been reported to increase alcohol consumption in rodents (Hubbell et al. 1987; Reid and Hunter 1984) and opioid antagonists block or antagonize preference for alcohol (DeWitte 1984; Hubbell et al. 1986; Samson and Doyle 1985; Volpicelli et al. 1986). The mechanism of these effects is not clear, but blocking opioid receptors consistently tends to decrease the ingestion of alcohol by animals previously choosing to drink this substance.

Although the effects of alcohol consumption on endogenous opioids appear to be quite complex and incompletely understood, recent experiments with naltrexone in alcoholic humans suggests a practical clinical application from this line of animal research. Volpicelli and colleagues (1990, 1992) found significant reductions in relapse to alcohol dependence in alcoholic outpatients treated with naltrexone after detoxification. The study was conducted under placebo-controlled double-blind conditions, and all patients received intensive outpatient rehabilitation counseling in addition to the study medication. Naltrexone-treated patients had about as many small slips to alcohol use as the patients randomly assigned to placebo. However, significantly fewer of the naltrexone patients continued to drink and to relapse to alcohol dependence during the 3-month trial. One interpretation of these results is that alcohol activates endogenous opioids, which form part of the reinforcement of continued alcohol drinking. Because naltrexone blocks opioid receptors, the reinforcement via the opioid system would be attenuated, and the probability of continued alcohol drinking would be reduced. In the only other trial of naltrexone in alcoholic subjects so far, O'Malley and colleagues (1991, 1992) reported results similar to those of Volpicelli and colleagues. Several additional clinical trials of naltrexone in alcoholic subjects are now in progress. If the results are similar to the first two trials, naltrexone could become an option for aiding in the treatment of alcoholism. Of course, as in the treatment of opioid dependence, medication alone would not be sufficient; rather, naltrexone would require a comprehensive treatment program including psychotherapy and attention to all facets of the alcohol dependence syndrome.

## ▼ SUMMARY

Naltrexone is a specific opioid antagonist that has a relatively long duration of action such that it can be used in aiding in the prevention of relapse to opioid dependence. Naltrexone is safe and relatively nontoxic. The antagonist treatment option is important to make available to well-motivated addicted individuals who desire to become drug free. As with all medications in the treatment of addiction, naltrexone must be used within a comprehensive treatment program, including individual or family psychotherapy and urine testing for illicit drugs. Treatment should continue for at least 3 months after detoxification and in many cases longer because there is a significant risk of relapse continuing for several years.

There is an active program in medications development currently being conducted by the National Institute on Drug Abuse. Several medications currently under study will add to the options for treatment in the next several years. The partial agonist buprenorphine combines features of both methadone and naltrexone and will probably become available in several years. A depot form of naltrexone that gives protection against relapse for 30–60 days is under study. Recent clinical trials in alcoholic subjects suggest that naltrexone may reduce the frequency of relapse among alcoholic individuals engaged in an outpatient rehabilitation program.

## ▼ REFERENCES

Arndt IO, Cacciola JS, McLellan AT, et al: A re-evaluation of naltrexone toxicity in recovering opiate addicts, in Problems of Drug Dependence, 1985, NIDA Res Monogr 67. Edited by Harris LS. Rockville, MD, U.S. Department of Health and Human Services, 1986, p 525

Bickel WK, Stitzer ML, Bigelow GE, et al: A clinical trial of buprenorphine: comparison with methadone in the detoxification of heroin addicts. Clin Pharmacol Ther 43:72–78, 1988

Brahen LS, Henderson RK, Copone T, et al: Naltrexone treatment in a jail work-release program. J Clin Psychiatry 45:49–52, 1984

Christian MA: Reproductive toxicity and teratology evaluation of naltrexone. J Clin Psychiatry 45:7–10, 1984

Cornish JW, Henson D, Levine S, et al: Naltrexone maintenance: effect on morphine sensitivity in normal volunteers. American Journal on Addictions 2:34–38, 1993

Crowley T, Wagner J, Zerbe G, et al: Naltrexone-induced dysphoria in former opioid addicts. Am J Psychiatry 142:1081–1084, 1985

DeWitte P: Nalozone reduces alcohol intake in a free-choice procedure even when both drinking bottles contain saccharin sodium or quinine substances. Neuropsychobiology 12:73–77, 1984

Ellingboe J, Mendelson JH, Kuehnle JC: Effects of heroin and naltrexone on plasma prolactin levels in man. Pharmacol Biochem Behav 12:163–165, 1980

Grabowski J, O'Brien CP, Greenstein RA: Effects of contingent payment on compliance with a naltrexone regimen. Am J Drug Alcohol Abuse 6:355–365, 1979

Greenstein RA, Evans BD, McLellan AT, et al: Predictors of favorable outcome following naltrexone treatment. Drug Alcohol Depend 12:173–180, 1983

Greenstein RA, Arndt IC, McLellan AT, et al: Naltrexone: a clinical perspective. J Clin Psychiatry

45:25–28, 1984

Hollister L: Report of the national research council committee on clinical evaluation of narcotic antagonists: clinical evaluation of naltrexone treatment of dependent individual. Arch Gen Psychiatry 33: 335–340, 1978

Hollister L, Johnson K, Boukhabza D, et al: Aversive effects of naltrexone in subjects not dependent on opiates. Drug Alcohol Depend 8:37–42, 1982

Hubbell CL, Czirr SA, Hunter GA, et al: Consumption of ethanol solution is potentiated by morphine and attenuated by nalozone persistently across repeated daily administrations. Alcohol 3: 39–54, 1986

Hubbell CL, Czirr SA, Reid LD: Persistence and specificity of small doses of morphine on intake of alcoholic beverages. Alcohol 4:149–156, 1987

Jaffe JH, Martin WR: Opioid analgesics and antagonists, in Goodman and Gilman's Pharmacological Basis of Therapeutics, 8th Edition. Edited by Gilman AG, Rall TW, Nies AS, et al. New York, Pergamon, 1990, pp 485–522

Jasinski DR, Fudala PJ, Johnson RE: Sublingual versus subcutaneous buprenorphine in opiate abusers. Clin Pharmacol Ther 45:513–519, 1989

Johnson RE, Jaffe JH, Fudala PJ: A controlled trial of buprenorphine treatment for opioid dependence. JAMA 267:2750–2755, 1992

Judson BA, Goldstein A: Naltrexone treatment of heroin addiction: one year follow-up. Drug Alcohol Depend 13:357–365, 1984

Kleber HD, Kosten TR: Naltrexone induction: psychologic and pharmacologic strategies. J Clin Psychiatry 45:29–38, 1984

Kleber HD, Kosten TR, Gaspari J, et al: Nontolerance to the opioid antagonism of naltrexone. Biol Psychiatry 2:66–72, 1985

Ling W, Wesson DR: Naltrexone treatment for addicted health-care professionals: a collaborative private practice experience. J Clin Psychiatry 45: 46–48, 1984

Maany I, O'Brien CP, Woody G: Interaction between thioridazine and naltrexone (letter). Am J Psychiatry 144:966, 1987

Martin WR, Jasinski DR: Physiological parameters of morphine in man: tolerance, early abstinence, protracted abstinence. J Psychiatr Res 7:9–16, 1969

Martin W, Jasinski D, Mansky P: Naltrexone: an antagonist for the treatment of heroin dependence. Arch Gen Psychiatry 28:784–791, 1973

Mello NK, Mendelson JH, Kuehnle JC, et al: Operant analysis of human heroin self-administration and the effects of naltrexone. J Pharmacol Exp Ther 216:45–54, 1981

Mendelson JH, Ellingboe J, Kuehnle JC, et al: Heroin and naltrexone effects on pituitary-gonadal hormones in man: interaction of steriod feedback effects, tolerance and supersensitivity. J Pharmacol Exp Ther 214:503–506, 1980

Meyer RE, Mirin SM, Altman JL: The clinical usefulness of narcotic antagonists: implications of behavioral research. Am J Drug Alcohol Abuse 2:417–432, 1975

O'Brien CP, Greenstein R, Mintz J, et al: Clinical experience with naltrexone. Am J Drug Alcohol Abuse 2:365–377, 1975

O'Brien CP, Greenstein R, Ternes J, et al: Clinical pharmacology of narcotic antagonists. Ann N Y Acad Sci 311:232–240, 1978

O'Brien CP, Greenstein R, Ternes J, et al: Unreinforced self-injections: effects on rituals and outcome in heroin addicts, in Problems of Drug Dependence 1979. Proceedings of the 41st Annual Scientific Meeting, The Committee on Problems of Drug Dependence, NIDA Res Monogr 27 (Publ No ADM-80-901). Edited Harris LS. Washington, DC, U.S. Government Printing Office, 1980, pp 275–281

O'Brien CP, Childress AR, McLellan AT, et al: Use of naltrexone to extinguish opioid-conditioned responses. J Clin Psychiatry 45:53–56, 1984

O'Brien CP, Ehrman R, Ternes J: Classical conditioning in human opioid dependence, in Behavioral Analysis of Drug Dependence. Edited by Goldberg S, Stolerman I. San Diego, CA, Academic Press, 1986, pp 329–356

O'Brien CP: Opioid addiction, in Handbook of Experimental Pharmacology. Edited by Herz A, Akil H, Simon EJ. Berlin, Springer-Verlag, 1992, pp 803–823

O'Malley SS, Jaffe A, Chang G, et al: Naltrexone in the treatment of alcohol dependence: preliminary findings, in Novel Pharmacological Interventions for Alcoholism. Edited by Naranjo CA, Sellers EM. New York, Springer-Verlag New York, 1991, pp 148–157

O'Malley SS, Jaffe A, Chang G, et al: Naltrexone and coping skills therapy for alcohol dependence: a controlled study. Arch Gen Psychiatry 49:881–887, 1992

Pfohl D, Allen J, Atkinson R, et al: TREXAN (naltrexone hydrochloride): a review of hepatic toxicity at high dosage, in Problems of Drug Dependence 1985, NIDA Res Monogr 67 (Publ No ADM-86-1448). Edited by Harris LS. Rockville, MD, U.S. Department of Health and Human Services, 1986, pp 66–72

Reid LD, Hunter GA: Morphine and naloxone modulate intake of ethanol. Alcohol 1:33–37, 1984

Resnick RB, Schuyten-Resnick E, Washton AM: Narcotic antagonists in the treatment of opioid dependence: review and commentary. Compr Psychiatry 20:116–125, 1979

Samson HH, Doyle TF: Oral ethanol self-administration in the rat: effect of nalozone. Pharmacol Biochem Behav 22:91–99, 1985

Sideroff SI, Charuvastra VC, Jarvik ME: Craving in heroin addicts maintained on the opiate antagonist naltrexone. Am J Drug Alcohol Abuse 5:415–423, 1978

Spiegel T, Stunkard AJ, Shrager E, et al: Effect of naltrexone on food intake, hunger, and satiety in obese men. Physiol Behav 40:135–141, 1987

Tennant F, Rawson R, Cohen A, et al: A clinical experience with naltrexone in suburban opioid addicts. J Clin Psychiatry 45:42–45, 1984

Tilly J, O'Brien CP, McLellan AT, et al: Naltrexone in the treatment of federal probationers, in Problems of Drug Dependence 1991, Proceedings of the 53rd Annual Scientific Meeting, The Committee on Problems of Drug Dependence, NIDA Res Monogr 119 (Publ No ADM-92-188). Edited Harris L, Washington, DC, U.S. Government Printing Office, 1992, p 458

Volpicelli JR, Davis MA, Olgin JE: Naltrexone blocks the post-shock increase of ethanol consumption. Life Sci 38:841–847, 1986

Volpicelli JR, O'Brien CP, Alterman AI, et al: Naltrexone and the treatment of alcohol dependence: initial observations, in Opioids, Bulimia, and Alcohol Abuse and Alcoholism. Edited by Reid LB. New York, Springer-Verlag New York, 1990, pp 195–214

Volpicelli JR, Alterman AI, Hayashida M, et al: Naltrexone in the treatment of alcohol dependence. Arch Gen Psychiatry 49:876–880, 1992

Washton AM, Pottash AC, Gold MS: Naltrexone in addicted business executives and physicians. J Clin Psychiatry 45:39–41, 1984

Wikler A: Conditioning factors in opiate addiction and relapse, in Narcotics. Edited by Wilner DI, Kassebaum GG. New York, McGraw-Hill, 1965, pp 85–100

Yoburn BC, Goodman RR, Cohen AH, et al: Increased analgesic potency of morphine and increased brain opioid binding sites in the rat following chronic naltrexone treatment. Life Sci 36:2325–2332, 1985

# Treatment Modalities

*Subsection 3A: Individual Treatment*

# Psychodynamics

*Richard Frances, M.D.*
*John Franklin, M.D.*
*Lisa Borg, M.D.*

Psychodynamic theory, which has its roots in psychoanalysis, has had a wide effect on the practice of psychotherapy, and its principles have been applied to understanding a broad range of treatment issues, including addiction treatment. Whereas most of what is known about psychodynamic principles has evolved from clinical applications, it has been difficult to do good treatment outcome studies that clearly demonstrate the efficacy of these approaches to specific psychiatric disorders. Some have even argued that psychodynamic treatment has no place in the treatment of substance-abusing patients (Vaillant 1981). We believe that psychodynamic understanding can add depth to work with individuals, groups, and understanding of the rehabilitation process. Attempts have even been made to understand the usefulness of 12-step programs from this perspective (Dodes 1988). This chapter will develop a rationale for the application of dynamic concepts in addiction treatment, examine its indications and contraindications, and explore how psychodynamic theory can be used to enhance the standard treatment technique and deepen the understanding of treatment of addicted patients.

## ▼ EARLY DEVELOPMENT

Freud's work in discovering the importance of unconscious phenomena; the development of a theory of the relationship between id, ego, and superego with an emphasis on resistance, defenses, and conflict; and the use of techniques such as free association, clarification, and interpretation are the basis for modern psychodynamic treatment. More recently, there has been a shift in attention from drives to ego psychology, object relations theory, and self psychology, and the importance of affective states, and these developments have added to the applicability of psychodynamic ideas to addiction treatment.

Early psychoanalytic writers, including Freud (1905/1949), Abraham (1908/1960), and Rado (1932/1981), emphasized oral cravings; regression toward infantile fixations, homosexual tendencies, and sexual and social inferiority; emotional immaturity; depressive tensions; and general insecurity (Lorand 1948). Freud (1930/1964) related the elation of intoxication that he believed causes relaxation of the superego's repression to manic states. Glover (1932/1956) emphasized the role of aggressive drives in substance use. Thus early on psychoanalysis emphasized alcohol's ability to cause regression in id, ego, and superego functions.

As far back as 1911, Bleuler (1911/1921) and Ferenczi (1911/1916) took opposing positions on whether alcoholism causes or is caused by psychological conflict. Bleuler (1911/1921) thought that drinking was more often the cause of neurotic disturbances and that clinicians should not be taken in by the "stupid excuses" of heavy drinkers. Ferenczi saw alcoholism as an "escape into narcosis" from underlying causes.

## ▼ RECENT DEVELOPMENTS

Whereas early psychoanalytic theory centered around the drives, including libidinal and aggressive drives, oral wishes, and oral aggression, psychodynamic psychotherapists recently have focused more on developmental and structural deficits. The role of ego defensive, defense deficit, and affective experience have been connected to drug abuse and alcoholism. Krystal and Rafkin (1970) have emphasized a defective stimulus barrier due to psychic trauma and the attempt to use substances to fortify against the onslaught of overwhelming affects. They describe the inability of patients to label affects, which he calls *alexithymia*, and the inability of addicted individuals to verbalize affect states.

Bean-Bayog (1988) describes the addiction itself and resultant loss of control as a sort of severe psychic trauma that results in characteristic defensive patterns. McDougall (1984) focused on drug use as a dispersion of affects into action. Wurmser (1974) and Meissner (1986) emphasize narcissistic collapse as cause for use of substances, compensating for a punctured grandiose or idealized self. Feelings of emptiness, boredom, rage, shame, depression, and guilt are symptoms of narcissistic wounds and superego regression, which prompt substance use (Wurmser 1984). These authors stress the severity of psychopathology underlying drug dependency. More recently, pathological shame, shame that effects one's core sense of self, has been highlighted as an affect associated with substance abuse (Lewis 1987). Silber (1974) emphasized the alcoholic individual's pathologic identification with destructive or psychotic parents. Kohut saw drugs in addicted individuals serving as substitute idealized selfobjects that are missing developmentally;

these symptoms were labeled as *narcissistic behavior disorders* (Kohut and Wolf 1978). Kernberg (1975), described addictive behavior as a reunion with a forgiving parent, an activation of "all good" selfobject images, and a gratification of instinctual needs. More recently, Kernberg (1991) has identified subsets of addicted individuals with *malignant narcissism,* associated with strong antisocial features.

Theorists such as Wieder and Kaplan (1969), Milkman and Frosch (1973), and Khantzian (1975) have discussed the importance of the specific effects of particular drugs on affect and the choice of a particular substance on the basis of specific sought-after effects. Khantzian (1985) highlighted this self-medication hypotheses in describing use of opioids as an attempt to assuage endpoint feelings of rage and aggression and use of cocaine to counter feelings of depressive anergic restlessness or to augment grandiosity. Alcohol has been related to deep-seated fears of closeness, dependency, and intimacy, with the alcohol effect being one of promoting toleration of loving or aggressive feelings (Khantzian et al. 1990).

Khantzian and Mack (1983) and Khantzian (1987) have emphasized affect regulation; tolerance; and self-regulation of affect, self-esteem, need satisfaction, relationships, and self-care and have related psychodynamic concepts to the total care of addicted patients including a better understanding of how 12-step programs are helpful. Substance-abusing individuals are described as lacking an internal, comforting sense of self-validation. These individuals also have difficulty obtaining nurturance and validation from others in a consistent, mature way. Self-care relates to the developmental inability to anticipate danger, worry about, anticipate, or consider the consequences of their actions, which result in self-defeating and self-destructive behavior.

Dodes (1990) has emphasized the addicted individual's sense of helplessness and powerlessness, often in the face of intolerable affects, and the need to restore a sense of power and control to which he or she feels entitled through drug use. Pharmacological control or change of one's affect state is the goal despite often unpredictable psychological, behavioral, physiological drug, or alcohol effects.

Krystal (1982) describes an inability in addicted individuals to take over the internal maternal functions that care for the self. The importance of clarifying the role of drugs and the addicted individual in the context of one's interpersonal world of relationships has been highlighted by the work of Luborsky (1984) and Klerman (1984).

Greater understanding of the addictive process and the psychology of addictions occurs through the process of dynamically oriented psychotherapy, which may add to the development of our treatment armamentarium, such as improved cognitive-behavioral techniques that take into account more complex human motivating factors and that may be specifically tailored to an individual's conflicts and defenses.

## ▼ DESCRIPTION OF APPLICATION OF PSYCHODYNAMICS TO TREATMENT

It is essential to distinguish applied psychodynamic principles, which can be used to understand individual, group, rehabilitation, and other aspects of treatment, from psychoanalysis, which is a more specific technique that may be reserved for a small number of recovering addicts who may be suitable for it. Most patients could not handle such aspects of psychoanalysis as 4–5 meetings per week, with the analyst providing relatively little feedback, being quite neutral, and providing little reassurance to the patient in order to allow frustration and permit regressive fantasies. Also generally avoided is the technical use of the couch, which also facilitates regression. In contrast, psychodynamic-oriented psychotherapy usually occurs 1–2 times per week, possibly in addition to a group psychotherapy, and the patient sits up facing the therapist. A requirement of abstinence is an essential parameter for successful treatment. Modern use of psychodynamic approaches tend to focus on current conflicts as they relate to the past rather than on childhood experience. The therapist more often takes both an active confrontive and supportive role, aware of characteristic defenses and of particular ego weaknesses and strengths of the patient. The therapist-patient relationship is openly discussed in order to facilitate working through resistances and without an effort to foster further regression. Psychodynamic techniques aimed at increased self-awareness, growth, and working through of conflicts can be combined with cognitive approaches, suggestions, education, and provision of support and reassurance where this is indicated.

## ▼ USEFULNESS OF TREATMENT OUTCOME RESEARCH

The state of the art of addiction treatment is to be aware of the results of treatment outcome studies but to select a combination of treatment that takes into account current knowledge and patient characteristics (Frances and Miller 1991). Treatment recommendations depend on a wide range of considerations of which trial results are only one factor. It is too early in addiction outcome research to make hard and fast recommendations as to what treatments should be used. Woody et al. (1983, 1990) showed us meaningful differences in efficacy between supportive-expressive psychotherapy in methadone-maintained patients. Treatment outcome studies in this volume and proposed treatment guidelines that are and will be developed provide useful information but are not definitive instructions to clinicians. Although clinicians agree in some areas (e.g., the usefulness of abstinence as a goal; the pharmacotherapy of comorbid disorders such as panic attacks; the value of adding education, cognitive, and behavioral approaches), controlled study proof of the value of treatments such as 12-step programs and psychodynamic psychotherapy are not yet strong, yet there is a common-sense rationale for each of these. Where there are not yet definite answers, clinicians need to be aware of a growing literature of outcome studies, of the methodological problems in doing good studies, and of the problems in reliability and validity in applying these results. Uncertainties as to the exact value of psychodynamic and combined treatments should not deter clinicians from using what has seemed useful, especially with patients with specific favorable characteristics such as motivation and capacity for insight, conflicts, and destructive patterns amenable to interpretation. Of course when definite conclusions about effectiveness of components of treatment are established, this will improve targeting of treatment.

## ▼ IMPLICATIONS FOR RESEARCH

New research is needed to demonstrate for which patients and which combinations with psychodynamic treatments are indicated—specifically, which Axis I or Axis II disorders, which age group, what timing, which patient characteristics, combined with what other treatment, and which among the broad range of psychodynamic intervention are most useful. It is hard to get good data bases in what are often clinically subjective material. Premature closure on any of these questions due to the challenge and expense of studying this area may lead to overly narrowly based, poorer quality treatment approaches. It will take time and the pooling of large amounts of clinical data and collaboration among many clinician researchers to get these answers. Initially, nonrandomized, noncontrolled, and descriptive studies will be needed. However, ultimately it is randomized studies that can best exclude even moderate biases, and with large numbers of patients studied, it will be possible not only to correct for false-positive but also for false-negative results.

## ▼ INDICATIONS AND RATIONALE FOR DYNAMIC PSYCHOTHERAPY

Psychodynamic principles find wide application throughout psychiatry and are relevant to the treatment of addicted patients (Karasu 1986). Insight-oriented therapy may be especially sought out by certain individuals where there is a particularly good fit for this kind of approach. Individual psychodynamic psychotherapy may be the sole treatment or combined with group, family, psychopharmacologic, self-help, cognitive-behavioral, and other treatment approaches. It may be reserved for treatment-resistant cases or may be the treatment of choice because of patient factors. Some patients refuse group or self-help programs and seek out individual psychodynamic therapy because of a wish for privacy, confidentiality, and insight. Patients with certain characteristics may especially seek out psychodynamic psychotherapy. Positive characteristics may include high intelligence, interest, and insight; psychological mindedness; a wish to understand or find meaning in behavior; a capacity for intimacy; identification with a therapist; time; money; and a wish to change aspects of self that are not acceptable. As with most forms of psychotherapy, positive prognostic indicators are higher socioeconomic status, marital stability, less severe psychopathology, and minimal sociopathy (Woody et al. 1986). Some relatively negative characteristics for other treat-

ments are social phobia with avoidance and fears that make Alcoholics Anonymous (AA) and Narcotics Anonymous (NA) attendance difficult. Initial reactions of distaste toward spirituality, which may occur in some atheists; strong negative reaction to groups in general; unwillingness to take medication in patients where it may be indicated; and a lack of a "rational approach to the world," which might benefit from cognitive-behavioral treatment are all factors that may lead some individuals to consider psychodynamic-oriented psychotherapy instead of other treatments.

Adolescents and young adults sorting out identity issues, problems in individuation, and need for independence may especially benefit from an insight-oriented approach. In some patients where denial, projection, splitting, and projective identifications are prominent defenses, consistent interpretation of defenses may be needed in order to form a working alliance that then can be used to achieve sobriety and growth.

Patients who continue to be anxious, depressed, and troubled after detoxification are more likely to seek out additional psychotherapy. In many ways the patients who benefit from psychodynamic-oriented-psychotherapy and have abused substances are very similar to those who benefit and have not abused substances. Many patients who have had failed psychodynamic psychotherapy when they were drinking find that they do benefit from this form of treatment when they are sober. Insight-oriented psychotherapy may be used to achieve or to maintain the benefits of abstinence and to prevent relapse.

Often recovering addicted patients have been survivors in families with heavy addictive behavior, and the danger of relapse is greater in those patients who have conflicts about enjoying and enhancing their success. Being more successful than an addicted parent or sibling may be feared, and insight into the sources of self-defeating behavior can be essential to prevent relapse.

For patients for whom self-care, self-destructiveness, suicidality, and masochism are a major issue, an awareness of unconscious forces of self-destructive behavior can be useful. Many patients are not aware that their alcoholism may be what Karl Menninger called "a slow form of suicide" (Menninger 1938). Awareness of risk-taking aspects of behavior may be very useful in treatment of these patients.

The rationale for using psychodynamic principles is frequently based on an in-depth clinical understanding of a particular patient's life situation. There is good evidence that alcoholism is influenced by genetic and environmental factors. The application of the study of temperament is leading to interesting treatment implications in psychiatry, including the addictions (Clonninger 1987). Psychodynamic understanding takes into account the specific childhood history of a patient; temperament; the conflict at oral/anal/phallic and genital levels; the development of the defenses; and ego and superego development, including object relations and relationships with parents, siblings, and friends.

Psychodynamics are used to deepen understanding of the rehabilitation process and group psychotherapy and make an attempt to understand how self-help groups work (Frances et al. 1989). An awareness of the importance of an unconscious wish to return to drinking, especially during periods of stress, is used in treatment. When unconscious factors have repeatedly led to relapse, this may be a special reason to use exploratory psychotherapy (Dodes and Khantzian 1991). For example, a patient's association to a "lost weekend," a drunk dream, or a planned vacation to a spot where there had been frequent relapses may all be warning signs of a possible relapse and can be used to help the patient's awareness that craving still exists and should be addressed.

An awareness of reasons not to drink and the strengthening of that side of the conflict may help, along with increased insight regarding the sources of the internal struggle. The greatest focus of attention has been on how substances may be used as self-medication for additional psychiatric disorders, self-regulation of affect, and as a symptom of an underlying deeper problem. Abusive substances may have specific meanings to patients in terms of either aiding in pushing painful areas away from consciousness and numbing feelings associated with painful knowledge or they may be used to gain access to unconscious material and facilitate experience or expression of angry and other feelings that may be avoided during sobriety. For patients for whom affect regulation is an issue, psychodynamic psychotherapy may be especially valuable. A patient with an underlying dysthymia, depression, or affective disorder may need to understand how substances have been used to cope with unmanageable feelings. Where alcohol or drugs may have caused additional life difficulties, as they invariably do, dealing with the psychosocial effects of the toxic metabolic complications may also benefit from psychodynamic approaches.

The application of psychodynamic theory to treatment of comorbid psychiatric problems such as Axis II personality disorders including borderline, narcissistic personality, and socially avoidant personality is important, especially because alcoholism and drug abuse are overrepresented in these patients. The literature on comorbidity of Axis I and II disorders is extensive and beyond the scope of this discussion. It may be especially hard to separate out the boundaries of temperament, acute substance-induced personality change, other Axis I disorders, secondary personality features, and independent personality disorders. Exploratory psychotherapy with borderline patients with a history of addiction must be informed by a good knowledge of addiction psychiatry, an emphasis on structure, and limit setting in treatment, including the vital parameter of abstinence.

Kernberg (1991) discusses the deception and projection often seen in the initial therapeutic alliance with borderline and narcissistic patients and the need to confront distorted views of reality in the therapeutic relationship. The use of insight in interpreting negative transference and acting out may deepen a positive transference and ultimately foster open expression. As a patient develops a clearer picture of his or her life through exploratory psychotherapy, the value of openness and honesty becomes apparent, and the tie to the therapist is cemented. Frequently it is the case that addicted patients have lied to themselves and others and are tired of feeling false and phony. The therapist's healthy ability to tolerate being conned by highly skilled, manipulative patients may minimize damaging countertransference reactions. If the therapist finds him- or herself doing something with a patient positive or negative that is out of the ordinary, some examination of countertransference is warranted.

During early treatment, it may be hard to tell whether personality change is due to a gradual return to better function because of physical, social, and psychological recovery from addiction effects; whether the initial diagnosis of personality disorder was correct; or whether psychodynamic and/or 12-step programs have effected change in personality. Some patients experience a rebound "high" that is analogous to Mahler et al.'s (1975) practicing subphase of development in the second year of life, when there is a burst of autonomous development.

Many addicted patients who present with narcissistic traits or personality disorder, and in whom the toxic affects of addiction heighten narcissism, suffer from a sense of specialness, entitlement, lack of empathy for others, inability to allow gratification of dependency needs, and loneliness. The experience of rehabilitation for these patients often involves acceptance of vulnerability, of being ordinary and similar to others with the same problem, a reaching out for help, and an encouragement in developing a new humility. Whether this is done through 12-step programs, application of Beck's cognitive therapy, or psychodynamic exploration of the narcissistic vulnerability, these issues should be dealt with in this substantial subpopulation.

A real danger of psychodynamic theorists has been a tendency toward reductionism that tries to apply one theory or approach to every situation. A broad and flexible use of psychodynamic thinking takes into account the total range of structural issues including id, ego, and superego; conflict theory; self psychology; affect regulation; and cognitive deficits. Perry et al. (1987) have clarified how three different models of psychodynamic theories—self psychology, object relations, and classical ego, id, and superego conflict theory—can flexibly be used to best fit the metaphor most useful to a particular patient or dynamic history.

There is evidence that alcohol problems can either cause or result from anxiety disorders and that more often than not agoraphobia, social phobia, and obsessive-compulsive disorders may precede rather than follow from an alcohol problem (Kushner et al. 1990). Although cognitive-behavioral and pharmacological approaches may be first-line treatment for panic disorder, agoraphobia, or social phobia, psychodynamic approaches are often used with patients who have been resistant or only partially successfully treated with other psychotherapies and medications (Frances and Borg 1993).

In many cases, an understanding of the specific transference of the patient that may either evoke countertransference problems or prevent compliance with treatment may be essential for good management and a successful alliance with the patient. Typical transference may result from growing up in households in which parents were addicted, inconsistent, and either overly harsh or indulgent. Children of alcoholic individuals frequently have authority problems and will often trust siblings, peers, and fellow alcoholic individuals more readily than teachers, nurses, doctors, or police. When a patient describes a therapist as cold, neglectful, uninvolved, or detached, this may be transference to a parent who fits this description.

## ▼ COUNTERINDICATIONS

Counterindications to psychodynamic-oriented psychotherapy include active use of substances, severe organicity, psychosis, and, for the most part, antisocial personality disorder. There are patients who regress too readily in individual therapy, develop psychotic transferences, or develop negative therapeutic reactions who benefit from the diffusion of transference that takes place in group therapy. If the principal problem is marital, family therapy is the treatment of choice.

## ▼ INITIATION OF TREATMENT

Although some authors recommend waiting 6 months to 1 year before beginning psychodynamic-oriented psychotherapy (Bean 1984; Zweben 1987). We believe initiation of psychodynamic-oriented treatment can successfully occur early, however timing should be tailored to the patient. The greatest opportunity to develop a treatment alliance is often early while the patient is in crisis. Supportive elements including confrontation, clarification, support of defenses, and building on ego strengths may be more prominent early in a treatment. The therapist also should take into account state-related problems of organicity, physical illness, and affective vulnerability, all of which can lead to an inability to utilize interpretations. Promoting an identification as a "recovering" person can boost self-esteem and provide stability (Brown 1985). The effects of intoxication, withdrawal, and the chronic organic effects of alcohol need to be taken into account by the dynamically oriented psychotherapist. However, during intoxication or withdrawal there are patients in whom psychodynamic-oriented interpretations are indicated from the very outset of treatment. Interpretations may help the patient work through resistances to accepting help. They may provide a meaningful explanation of destructive patterns that can inspire a wish for change.

Timing of interpretations is crucial. A patient who may need to project blame and responsibility for his or her actions onto substances early in recovery may later be able to accept responsibility for his or her actions. One patient later admitted that having an affair, embezzling money, and being abusive were things that he wanted to do anyway, and that he used alcohol and cocaine abuse as an excuse. While early into abstinence the individual may not be ready to take full responsibility for actions; over time, these things can be explored and pointed out, denial can be worked through, and acceptance of responsibility for choice can be achieved. Defenses may need to be supported at first, including denial of affect related to some of the losses, and confrontation should initially concentrate on denial surrounding addictive behaviors. Ultimately clarification, confrontation, and interpretation of denial, lying, splitting, and projective defenses in other areas needs to be gradually expanded. However, in selected cases, with repeated treatment failure, an initial intervention may require active, across-the-board confrontation and interpretation of inconsistencies and denial in order to help the patient accept a need for change. In patients with alexithymia and for patients who are affectively constricted, interpretations are aimed at increasing the patient's awareness of feeling states and helping the patient connect thoughts and feelings without the use of substances.

## ▼ FREQUENCY OF SESSIONS, SETTING, AND OTHER GENERAL FACTORS

Psychodynamic-oriented psychotherapy with alcoholic patients is usually 1–2 times a week, is often done in conjunction with group psychotherapy, and includes a parameter of abstinence and a long-term goal of sobriety. It can be done as part of an inpatient stay, organized outpatient, or office practice and can be time limited and focused or long term.

It is foolhardy for psychotherapists to offer the promise that once underlying causes of a "symptom of drinking" are dealt with that the patient will ever be able to return to controlled drinking. Similarly, it is unwise to promise that once a patient is fully treated with psychoanalytically oriented psychotherapy that

he or she will never need additional help through 12-step programs nor need additional psychotherapy.

In fact, for most alcoholic individuals, shifting dependency from a chemical such as alcohol to a therapist, group, spiritual belief, or involvement with anything human, is a major step in the direction of growth. Although issues of dependency may be worked through partially, an ongoing positive identification with a therapist, a sponsor, and/or recovering friends may be a major positive outcome in treatment. Active dialogue with the patient and an attitude of empathic concern and sharing on the part of the therapist is optimal. Issues of termination from either individual therapy or graduation from phases of treatment may resurface earlier conflicts and be triggers for relapse.

## ▼ GENERAL TECHNICAL ASPECTS

Advances in object relations theory, ego psychology, and modern psychodynamic understanding of conflicts and affect regulation can be applied to addiction treatment. Psychodynamic principles are applied in conjunction with understanding the clinical exigencies of addiction treatment. Technique needs to be modified especially in the direction of attention to issues needed to attain and sustain abstinence, and the effects of regression should be carefully monitored. However, well-established technique and principles of brief and long-term psychodynamic treatment are generally maintained. The therapist listens for themes relating to the patient's intrapsychic conflicts, developmental impairments, and defenses with special attention to how they may relate to substance abuse and relapse potential. Careful developmental history with attention to achievement of milestones of ego development; evaluation of temperament in the patient and significant caretakers; the capacity to identify with and to separate from important figures of identification, including parents, siblings, or admired peers; and exploration of affect regulation especially in relation to use of substances are important. The use of free association, "slips," and understanding of dreams to find meaning in the unconscious derivatives of behavior, such as an unconscious wish to drink expressed in a drunk dream, are tools that the therapist uses.

## ▼ TREATMENT PARAMETERS

Parameters introduced in a treatment of patients with addictions, such as a need for structure, clear boundaries, and abstinence are similar to those used effectively with borderline personality disorder. Structure and boundaries help the patient reestablish control and self-regulation, and support verbal expression of feeling rather than the patient's showing the therapist what the problems are through acting them out. The conventional practice of psychodynamic psychotherapy with limit setting is generally an aid in the treatment of these patients, although there may be rare occasions in which a more active approach may be needed. For example, a therapist may need to actively mobilize a family to bring a suicidal alcoholic patient to the emergency room or to the doctors office after a relapse.

While the therapist works through resistance and defense, there needs to be a special focus and awareness of how alcohol provides an escape, can numb or facilitate expression, and itself alter defensive operations especially heightening denial. The interplay of ego function, feeling states, and chemical effects is watched closely by the therapist.

## ▼ OTHER TOOLS OF TREATMENT

A combination of psychodynamic approaches such as clarification, interpretation, and genetic reconstruction may be used along with directive approaches such as assertiveness training, social skills training, self-efficacy groups, modeling, positive reinforcement, cognitive awareness, and suggestion. A sophisticated familiarity with typical problems that occur with alcoholic or drug-abusing individuals and their families and the use of psychoeducation about these issues aids in establishing a positive alliance. Understanding the concepts in adult children of alcoholics literature may help the therapist relate and translate these concepts for patients.

Use of combined approaches is applied in the following clinical example:

> A 42-year-old recovering alcoholic woman with panic attacks and agoraphobia had special problems around flying to another city. Psychodynamic psychotherapy was useful when added to desensitization, relaxation therapy,

exposure to flying, and closely monitoring medication of panic attacks with imipramine and benzodiazepines 2 hours before plane trips. The anxiety persisted at a significant level that frequently interfered with the patient's plans. The patient's fears of flying were related to childhood conflicts about having to take planes to visit her father after her parents divorced. She was the "apple of her father's eye" and had clearly won out over her mother, not without considerable guilt over her especially favored position. Her oedipal guilt has persisted in contributing to difficulty reaching orgasm with her husband and feeling guilty about enjoying her sexuality. The flights she currently most fears are those related to visits with her father or pleasure trips with her husband. Although none of the treatments totally have allayed her fears, she is able to travel without drinking and is better able to understand and cope with her fears of flying as a result of her enhanced insight into the roots of her fears. She is increasingly allowing herself to enjoy gradual steps toward success without relapsing.

## ▼ FINDING A FOCUS AND STAGES OF TREATMENT

The phases of intervention include initial screening, evaluation and intervention, rehabilitation, and then aftercare. The initial focus is often on conflicts around acceptance of addiction as a problem, the patient's reluctance to acknowledge dependency, and needs for treatment and conflicts that result from the complications of alcoholism, including the loss of relationships, health, jobs, and missing alcohol itself. The early goal is abstinence.

More often than is usually the case for insight-oriented psychotherapy, the patient may initially be forced into the consultation by an employer, probation officer, family member, or physician. Especially when coercion has occurred, considerable effort is needed to gradually develop trust and a working alliance with the patient. This is achieved through careful review of the patient's life and ways in which addiction has interfered with family, work, relationships and caused legal problems, all which have contributed to pain and a need to escape it. The therapist's integrity, adherence to confidentiality, and ability to be helpful all contribute to establishing trust.

The patient is helped to make a diagnosis and to accept a need for help which may lead to beginnings of a positive transference. These steps are similar to the first two AA steps in which patients admit powerlessness over alcohol and acceptance of a need for help or acknowledgment of dependency needs, which in AA is labeled a "higher power." A psychodynamic perspective may aid in the confrontation of denial and other defenses, and through interpretations patients achieve deeper understanding of certain destructive patterns that have led to the present problem. It is especially challenging to help the patient to acknowledge dependency needs that have been channeled into the addiction.

Therapy is the process in which a need for substances is shifted back into a need for people, including the therapist. Interestingly, patients who abuse drugs often refuse medications because of their fear of using them in compulsive ways, their fear of being dependent on drugs for relief, and their fear of being dependent on the therapist to obtain these medications. From early in treatment issues of trust, dependency, separation, loss, disappointment, and truthfulness are frequent themes.

In the later stages, the focus of treatment in exploratory psychotherapy should not be mechanically imposed from the outside, based on purely theoretical considerations. Rather, it should be targeted at the most pressing issue of the moment that may relate to the drinking: a particular conflict, a relationship with a family member or employer, a problem with self-esteem, self-destructiveness, or self-medication of panic or other painful affects.

Other major themes include specific conflicts over assertiveness, handling of aggression, and issues of control and inhibition. The disinhibiting role of addictions in allowing risk-taking behavior, including increased sexual activity, may be an issue. On the other hand, alcohol may play a role in distancing the individual from sexual life or substituting for sexual activity.

## ▼ WATCH FOR RELAPSE

Patients need to be carefully observed for drinking or drug use behavior. Laboratory tests may be useful aids, and meeting with family and other sources of collateral information may be essential to get a true picture and to aid in confronting patients who dissimulate.

## ▼ ACCEPTANCE OF SELF IN RECOVERY

An important part of recovery are changes in self-awareness and self-perception. One enormous shift is in accepting a diagnosis in having alcoholism as an illness. This entails not only shifting from a moral model as seeing oneself as weak, shameful, and bad for being alcoholic, but also involves an awareness that a problem exists about which a great deal is known, that it is treatable, and that it does not have to lead to hopelessness and despair. Sometimes this leads to reaction formation in which the patient feels grateful for being alcoholic and turns a disability into an advantage. There may have been real advantages in terms of broadening of experience, overcoming a vulnerability, and a pride that can occur in any group that finds a way to overcome a stigma. Just the feeling of relief from no longer suffering the consequences of alcoholism and addiction often leads to a rebound after initial abstinence that sometimes can approach euphoria. This euphoria can often be followed by a letdown when awareness of the multitude of problems that the addictions had caused becomes apparent as denial wanes.

## ▼ AN EGO PSYCHOLOGICAL MODEL OF REHABILITATION

An assessment of ego function needs to include a search for strengths, talents, and positive qualities that can be used to help the patient. All too often therapists miss opportunities to enhance self-esteem in those whose self-criticism leads to overlooking of real and potential opportunities for growth. Helping a patient recall periods in which values were in place and providing hope for a return to higher level of function is a way of combining positive insight with support. We have found that even very damaged, impaired individuals in inner city settings often had a dream in their lives that they have buried. Rekindled dreams can foster renewed hope and self-esteem. The stigma of the illness can also be lessened by discussing positive role models like Betty Ford or John Lucas who have struggled with the same illness and have worked hard at recovery.

An ego psychological model can be applied to the biopsychosocial effects of addiction and a model of rehabilitation. Chemicals and psychosocial consequences have effects and lead to regression and impairment of defenses, object relatedness, judgment, reality testing, and superego. It may take time and practice for good ego and superego function to return.

The following clinical example demonstrates recovery of function:

> A narcissistic 47-year-old man who drank heavily for 25 years had disuse atrophy of ego functions and was pushed to function better as part of rehabilitation. His wife was thought of only in terms of what she could do for him, as a part object or a need-satisfying object, and only with practice and with time sober could he relate to her in a more complex way as having needs of her own. He would idealize or devalue everyone and everything, and it took him a long time for "the glass to be seen as half full." In order to develop friendships and break isolation, it was necessary for him to practice relatedness in individual, couples therapy, group, and self-help groups. The superego had been dissolved in chemicals for years, and it took external structure and parameters to gradually awaken the "sleeping policeman" within. The program requirements and the external norms of the groups helped him regain structure. His superego was initially inconsistent and vacillated from a lack of restraint and self-indulgence to a primitive punitive masochistic rigidity. Cognitive impairment, especially in the nondominant hemisphere functions of spatial and temporal relationships, was present and this improved over time with abstinence.

Defenses initially most often encountered are the most primitive and include denial, rationalization, splitting, projection, and projective identification. With time and treatment, higher level defenses such as intellectualization, reaction formation, repression, and sublimation may be more in the forefront. For example, instead of denial of alcoholism and projection of poor self-esteem onto the group, later on a patient may feel grateful to be alcoholic and honored to have been part of a group that initially was perceived as being stigmatizing. Denial of alcohol's harmful effects on the liver, which can be addressed by a program of psychoeducation, can be replaced with curiosity and intellectualization about how liver damage occurs. Denial of losses related to addiction may over time be replaced with repression after grieving the losses has occurred.

## ▼ APPLICATIONS OF PSYCHODYNAMICS TO GROUPS AND SELF-HELP

The addition of group psychotherapy, AA, or NA is especially needed when individual therapy alone is not working at maintaining abstinence. Group treatments help diffuse some of the powerful negative transference that may be impossible to overcome early in treatment. Groups can focus on issues of self-care, self-esteem, affect regulation, sharing, exposure to feared social situations, sharing, provide social support, models for identification and coping skills, working through of family problems, and can be targeted to specific additional diagnosis in subpopulations such as anxiety disorders, the chronically mentally ill, those with medical complications, women, adolescents, and so on. The focus of groups can be quite homogeneous (e.g., recovering physicians with anxiety disorders) or heterogeneous (e.g., all patients in a detox unit). Khantzian et al. (1990) describe a model of modified dynamic group therapy for substance-abusing patients involving self-care, self-esteem, and affect regulation. Together the patient and individual therapist can look at the ways in which the patient projects and introjects feelings toward other AA, NA, or group members who for example remind them of their alcoholic relatives. Character flaws can be actively worked on with immediate and multiple feedback from group members. If the individual therapist is also the group therapist, the individual work may be used to encourage the patient to try a new behavior in the group and conversely observation of conflicts in the group can be worked on individually.

Aspects of 12-step programs may readily lend themselves to incorporation in psychodynamic treatment. These include acceptance of a diagnosis, acceptance of dependency needs, awareness that one cannot control drinking alone, taking a personal inventory (often discussed in terms of a higher power), working at change, dealing with sobriety one day at a time, acceptance of the structure of a treatment program, and enhancement of self-esteem through helping others with the problem, thus living up to an ego ideal.

The 12-step programs provide education, auxiliary ego, and superego support and powerful role models for positive identification. Steps in AA that involve taking one's inventory and making amends can be used in conjunction with the psychotherapeutic process of self-exploration and insight aimed at behavioral change. The addition of AA is especially helpful during periods of relapse and during periods of separation in which the therapist is unavailable because either the patient or the therapist is away. Because alcoholism and drug abuse are often chronic relapsing illnesses, both the patient and the therapist must be prepared for the possibility of a relapse, and the therapist should be both nonjudgmental and unafraid of confrontation when needed.

## ▼ THE PATIENT-THERAPIST RELATIONSHIP

It is helpful for the therapist to be tuned in and to be able to interpret negative transference and to know how to manage and to appropriately use therapist countertransference. Patients with alcoholism frequently will try to evoke in their therapist's feelings of fear, anger, and despair and will reenact relationships with alcoholic parents, siblings, and spouses through the transference. They may project critical attitudes onto the therapist and keep secrets out of fear that the therapist will respond like a parent. When the therapist feels like a parent, sibling, or friend, this feeling may have been evoked for specific reasons. The greater the therapist's awareness of what is happening, the more this can be brought into the treatment in a constructive way.

A second major source of countertransference problems in treating addicted patients is therapists with a weak knowledge base about addiction and its treatment. The more knowledgeable the therapist is about addiction psychiatry and about the patient, the less likely he or she is to project his or her own problems onto the patient. Attitudinal problems on the part of the therapist can be reduced by good training and an experience of having worked through issues related to stigma. The more the therapist is in command of a treatment armamentarium, the less frightened he or she is in the face of what can be a dreadful disease. It is advisable, however, for the therapist to remain a student to patients in some respects and allow the patient to inform him or her about the addictive experience, practices, and terminology.

A third source of countertransference is based on the mostly unconscious transference that the therapist may have toward the patient, related to the therapist's past or present problems. This may relate to a therapist's own attitudes about substances, present or past problems with addiction, or experience with a parent, spouse, or child with a problem. The therapist's own envy, fear, hopes, and needs can adversely affect prescribing practices and lead to over-involvement, avoidance, hopelessness, jealousy, and burnout. Seeking out second opinions or supervision with experienced practitioners is advisable with difficult patients.

Patients with addictions frequently have had early childhood trauma and stress associated with being the children of alcoholics and addicts. These families have an increase of child abuse, including sexual abuse, divorce, inconsistent parenting, economic problems, and other stresses. This may lead to specific conflicts, resistances, and transference problems that later affect treatment compliance and outcome.

## ▼ BEWARE OF MYTHS AND PITFALLS

The following is a list of myths and pitfalls to avoid in dynamic psychotherapy.

### Myths

1. One can first develop a therapeutic relationship and then gradually wean the patient off substances.
2. Substance use will disappear with understanding.
3. Once conflicts have been resolved, the patient can return safely to drinking.
4. If the problem is narcotic addiction, alcohol is safer and legal.
5. Addiction is always a symptom, not a primary problem.

**Pitfalls**

1. To believe a patient's explanation for drinking without awareness of rationalization and a patient's need for justifying his or her behavior.
2. To not check out the patient's story with collateral sources.
3. To conduct treatment as if dynamic interpretations were "golden" and other interventions less valuable. The best mix of treatment and sequence should be selected on the basis of the patient's needs.
4. To not have a healthy respect for patients' dependency needs and to have too high expectation for resolving these. It is better for patients to depend on therapists or on AA than on substances, and an endless relationship with AA is a desirable goal—not a compromise of a therapist's goal of self-reliance on the patient's part.
5. To get overinvolved or overly distant. Therapists in recovery themselves sometimes have blind spots or may share with the patient more than the patient needs to know.
6. Even moderate biases for one or another form of treatment and lack of flexibility both theoretical and practical can be a disservice to the patient.

## ▼ CONCLUSION

Psychodynamic theory can have an important role in enriching and informing substance abuse treatment and improving the therapeutic relationship. Rigid application of psychoanalytic technique however, has little place in substance treatment and can be counterproductive. Application of psychodynamic understanding, including attending to the unconscious, child development, ego function, affect regulation, efforts to enhance self-esteem and deal with shame, and other narcissistic vulnerability widens the range of patients that can be treated.

Definitive outcome studies of psychodynamic psychotherapy in substance-abusing patients will be difficult to achieve. However, there is a rich descriptive clinical experience in this area that improves our understanding of addicted patients.

## ▼ REFERENCES

Abraham K: The psychological relation between sexuality and alcoholism (1908), in Selected Papers of Karl Abraham. New York, Basic Books, 1960, pp 80–89

Bean M: Clinical implications of models for recovery from alcoholism, in The Addictive Behaviors. Edited by Shaffer HJ, Stimmel B. New York, Haworth, 1984, pp 91–104

Bean-Bayog M: Alcoholism As a Cause of Psychopathology. Hosp Community Psychiatry 39:352–354, 1988

Bleuler E: Alcohol and the Neuroses (1911). Jahrbuch für Psychoanalytisch und Psychopathologische Forschungen; Jahrbuch der Psychoanalyse 3:848. Abstracted by Blungart L. Psychoanalytic Review 8:443–444, 1921

Brown S: Treating the Alcoholic: A Developmental Model of Recovery. New York, Wiley, 1985

Cloninger CR: A systematic method for clinical description and classification of personality variants: a proposal. Arch Gen Psychiatry 44:573–588, 1987

Dodes LM: The psychology of combining dynamic psychotherapy and Alcoholics Anonymous. Bull Menninger Clin 52:283–293, 1988

Dodes LM: Addiction, helplessness, and narcissistic rage. Psychoanal Q 59:398–419, 1990

Dodes LM, Khantzian EJ: Individual psychodynamic psychotherapy, in Clinical Textbook of Addictive Disorders. Edited by Frances RJ, Miller SI. New York, Guilford, 1991, pp 391–405

Ferenczi S. On the part played by homosexuality in the pathogenesis of paranoia (1911), in Contributions to Psychoanalyse. Boston, MA, Badger, 1916

Frances RJ, Borg L: The treatment of anxiety in patients with alcoholism. J Clin Psychiatry 54 (suppl):37–43, 1993

Frances RJ, Miller SI: Clinical Textbook of Addictive Disorders. New York, Guilford, 1991

Frances RJ, Khantzian EJ, Tamerin JS: Psychodynamic psychotherapy, in Treatments of Psychiatric Disorders: A Task Force Report of the American Psychiatric Association, Vol 2. Washington, DC, American Psychiatric Association, 1989, pp 1103–1111

Freud S: Three essays on the theory of sexuality (1905), in The Standard Edition of the Complete Psychological Works of Sigmund Freud, Vol 7. Translated and edited by Strachey J. Hogarth Press, 1949, pp 125–245

Freud S: Civilization and Its Discontents (1930). New

York, WW Norton, 1964

Glover E: On the aetiology of drug addiction (1932), in Selected Papers of Psychoanalysis, Vol 1: On the Early Development of Mind. Edited by Glover E. New York, International Universities Press, 1956, pp 187–215

Karasu TB: The specificity versus nonspecificity dilemma: toward identifying therapeutic change agents. Am J Psychiatry 143:687–695, 1986

Kernberg OF: Borderline Conditions and Pathological Narcissism. New York, Jason Aronson, 1975

Kernberg OF: Transference regression and psychoanalytic technique with infantile personalities. Int J Psychoanal 72:189–200, 1991

Khantzian EJ: Self-selection and progression in drug dependence. Psychiatry Digest 10:19–22, 1975

Khantzian EJ: The self-medication hypothesis of addictive disorders: focus on heroin and cocaine dependence. Am J Psychiatry 142:1259–1264, 1985

Khantzian EJ: A clinical perspective of the cause-consequence controversy in alcohol and addictive suffering. Journal of the American Academy of Psychoanalysis 15:521–537, 1987

Khantzian EJ, Mack J: Self preservation and the care of the self. Psychoanal Study Child 38:209–232, 1983

Khantzian EJ, Halliday KS, McAuliffe WE: Addiction and the Vulnerable Self. New York, Guilford, 1990

Klerman GL, Weissman MM, Rounsaville BH, et al: The Theory and Practice of Interpersonal Psychotherapy for Depression. New York, Basic Books, 1984

Kohut H, Wolf ES: The disorders of the self and their treatment: an outline. Int J Psychoanal 59:413–425, 1978

Krystal H: Alexythmia and the effectiveness of psychoanalytic treatment. International Journal of Psychoanalytic Psychotherapy 9:353–388, 1982

Krystal H, Rafkin HA: Drug Dependence: Aspects of Ego Function. Detroit, MI, Wayne State University Press, 1970

Kushner MA, Sher KJ, Bertman BD: The relation between alcohol problems and anxiety disorders. Am J Psychiatry 147:685–695, 1990

Lewis HB: Shame and the narcissistic personality, in The Many Faces of Shame. Edited by Nathanson DL. New York, Guilford, 1987, pp 93–132

Lorand J: A summary of psychoanalytic literature on problems of alcoholism. Yearbook of Psychoanalism 1:359–378, 1948

Luborsky L: Principles of Psychoanalytic Psychotherapy: A Manual for Supportive-Expressive Treat-

ment. New York, Basic Books, 1984

Mahler M, Pine R, Bergman A: The Psychological Birth of the Human Infant: Symbiosis and Individuation. New York, Basic Books, 1975

McDougall J: The "dis-affected" patient: reflections on affect pathology. Psychoanal Q 53:366–409, 1984

Meissner WW: Psychotherapy and the Paranoid Process. New York, Jason Aronson, 1986

Menninger KA: Man Against Himself. New York, Harcourt Brace, 1938

Milkman H, Frosch WA: On the preferential abuse of heroin and amphetamine. J Nerv Ment Dis 156:242–248, 1973

Perry S, Cooper A, Michels R: The psychodynamic formulation: its purpose, structure, and clinical application. Am J Psychiatry 144:543–550, 1987

Rado S: The psychoanalysis of pharmacothymia (1932), in Classic Contributions in the Addictions. Edited by Shaffer H, Burglass ME, New York, Brunner/Mazel, 1981

Silber A: Rationale for the technique of psychotherapy with alcoholics. International Journal of Psychoanalytic Psychotherapy 3:28–47, 1974

Vaillant GE: Dangers of psychotherapy in the treatment of alcoholism, in Dynamic Approaches to the Understanding and Treatment of Alcoholism. Edited by Bean MH, Zinberg NE. New York, Free Press, 1981, pp 36–54

Wieder H, Kaplan EH: Drug use in adolescents. Psychoanal Study Child 24:399–431, 1969

Woody GE, Luborsky L, McLellan AT, et al: Psychotherapy for opiate addicts: does it help? Arch Gen Psychiatry 40:639–648, 1983

Woody GE, McLellan AT, Luborsky L, et al: Psychotherapy for substance abuse. Psychiatr Clin North Am 9:547–562, 1986

Woody G, Luborsky L, McLellan AT, et al: Corrections and revised analyses for psychotherapy in methadone maintenance patients (letter). Arch Gen Psychiatry 47:788–789, 1990

Wurmser L: Psychoanalytic considerations of the etiology of compulsive drug use. J Am Psychoanal Assoc 22:820–843, 1974

Wurmser L: The role of superego conflicts in substance abuse and their treatment. International Journal of Psychoanalytic Psychotherapy 10:227–258, 1984

Zweben JE: Recovery-oriented psychotherapy: facilitating the use of 12-step programs. J Psychoactive Drugs 19:243–251, 1987

# etwork Therapy
# for the Office Practitioner

*Marc Galanter, M.D.*

This chapter defines aspects of addiction relevant to ambulatory therapy and then describes a treatment modality that was designed to address them. This approach, called *network therapy* (Galanter 1993), was developed specifically to bring addicted patients to a successful recovery, whereas conventional office therapy often fails in this task. *Network therapy* can be defined as an approach to rehabilitation in which specific family members and friends are enlisted to provide ongoing support and to promote attitude change. Network members are part of the therapist's working "team" and not subjects of treatment themselves. The goal of this approach is the prompt achievement of abstinence with relapse prevention and the development of a drug-free adaptation.

Most mental health professionals are ill-prepared to help the alcoholic or drug-abusing individual achieve recovery, even though addicted individuals and their families regularly turn to them for help. In one survey of general psychiatrists practicing primarily with this modality alone, over half reported no success with any alcoholic patients (Hayman 1956). Those who reported any success said that it occurred in no more than 10% of their patients. Furthermore, few alcoholic and addicted individuals are willing to go to Alcoholic Anonymous (AA) until they have suffered very long, and most drop out before becoming involved. A pointed question inevitably arises: How can we engage and treat these troubled individuals more effectively?

Furthermore, how can we make treatment more efficient? In recent years we have witnessed the proliferation of inpatient rehabilitation facilities for substance-abusing patients. These programs are useful in that they terminate the patient's access to drugs and create a safe environment for detoxification and education. Nonetheless, they require weeks of hospital-

This chapter was adapted in part from articles by the author in Galanter M: "Cognitive Labelling: Psychotherapy for Alcohol and Drug Abuse: An Approach Based on Learning Theory. *Journal of Substance Abuse Treatment and Evaluation* 5:551–556, 1983; Galanter M: "Social Network Therapy for Cocaine Dependence." *Advances in Alcoholism and Substance Abuse* 6:159, 1987; Galanter M: "Management of the Alcoholic in Psychiatric Practice." *Psychiatric Annals* 19:226–270, 1989; and Galanter M: "Network Therapy for Addiction: A Model for Office Practice." *Am J Psychiatry* 150:28–36, 1992.

ization and often disrupt family and social ties while patients are hospitalized. They also remove patients from the opportunity of learning to deal with the cues to drinking while treatment supports are greatest. It seems more reasonable to support a patient's rehabilitation by means of the social ties available in his or her own community.

This latter point is supported by the finding that augmentation of treatment by group and family therapy in the multimodality clinic setting has led to considerably more success in alcoholism treatment (Gallant et al. 1970). Groups such as AA also offer invaluable adjunctive support. A model for enhancing therapeutic intervention in the context of insight-oriented individual therapy would be of considerable value, given the potential role of the individual practitioner as primary therapist for many patients with addictive problems.

In enhancing the effectiveness of ambulatory therapy, an individual's immediate network might draw on his or her spouse, friends, or family of origin, and perhaps a friend from work. Components of the network are only parts of the natural support systems that usually operate without professional involvement, but if they can be brought to act in concert, the strength of their social influence can serve as a therapeutic device. It can complement individual or group therapy as well as AA.

## ▼ ADDRESSING THE PROBLEMS OF RELAPSE AND LOSS OF CONTROL

To frame a social therapy using network support, we must first define the target problem clearly and then consider the particulars of how the network bears its influence. From a clinician's perspective, the problems of *relapse* and *loss of control*, embodied in the third and fourth criteria for substance dependence in the DSM-IV (American Psychiatric Association 1994), are central to the difficulty of treating addiction. Because addicted patients are typically under pressure to relapse to ingestion of alcohol or drugs, they are seen as poor candidates for stable attendance and tend to drop out. *Loss of control* has been used to describe the addicted individual's inability to reliably limit consumption once an initial dose is taken (Gallant 1987).

These clinical phenomena are generally de-scribed anecdotally but can be explained mechanistically as well by recourse to the model of conditioned withdrawal, which relates the psychopharmacology of dependency-producing drugs to the behaviors they produce. Wikler (1973), an early investigator of addiction pharmacology, developed this model to explain the spontaneous appearance of drug craving and relapse. He pointed out that drugs of dependence typically produce compensatory responses in the central nervous system at the same time that their direct pharmacologic effects are felt, and these compensatory effects partly counter the drug's direct action. Thus when an opioid antagonist is administered to addicted subjects who are maintained on morphine, latent withdrawal phenomena are unmasked. Similar compensatory effects are observed in alcoholic subjects who are maintained on alcohol, who evidence evoked response patterns characteristic of withdrawal while still clinically intoxicated (Begleiter and Porjesz 1979).

In the laboratory, O'Brien et al. (1977) demonstrated the conditioning of addict subjects of opioid withdrawal responses to neutral stimuli, such as sound and odor. This conditioning, produced in a laboratory setting, provided experimental corroboration of Wikler's hypothesis. Ludwig et al. (1974) have demonstrated the direct behavioral correlates of such conditioned stimuli in relation to alcohol administration. They found that for the alcoholic subject, the alcohol dose itself might serve as a conditioned stimulus for enhancing craving, as could the appropriate drinking context.

Clinical interviews demonstrate that withdrawal feelings, and hence craving, could be elicited by cues previously associated with the addicted subject's use of the drug. Hence, exposure to the smell of liquor in a bar could precipitate the "need" to drink; seeing the "works" for injecting heroin, or going by a "shooting gallery," could lead a heroin-addicted individual to relapse.

Importantly, the conditioned stimulus of a drug or environmental cue, or even the affective state regularly associated with the drug, can lead directly to the behavioral response before the addicted individual consciously experiences withdrawal feelings. The individual may therefore automatically seek out drugs upon experiencing anxiety or depression, or narcissistic injury, all of which may have become conditioned stimuli.

Very often, modulations in mood state are the

conditioned stimuli for drug seeking as well, and the substance-abusing individual can become vulnerable to relapse through reflexive response to a specific affective state. Such phenomena have been described clinically by Khantzian (1985) as *self-medication*. Such mood-related cues, however, are not necessarily mentioned spontaneously by the patient in a conventional therapy because the triggering feeling may not be associated with a memorable event, and the drug use may avert emergence of memorable distress.

More dramatic is the phenomenon of affect regression, which Wurmser (1977) observed among addicted patients studied in a psychoanalytic context. He pointed out that when addicted subjects suffer narcissistic injury, they are prone to a precipitous collapse of ego defenses and the consequent experience of intense and unmanageable affective flooding. In the face of such vulnerability, these subjects handle stress poorly and may turn to drugs for relief. This vulnerability can be considered in light of the model of conditioned withdrawal, whereby drug seeking can become an immediate reflexive response to stress, undermining the stability and effectiveness of a patient's coping mechanisms. This can occur quite suddenly in patients who have long associated drug use with their attempts to cope with stress, as illustrated in the following case.

> **Case 1.** In the course of his therapy, it was found that the drinking of one alcoholic lawyer had often been precipitated by situations that threatened his self-esteem. After 6 months of sobriety, he suffered a relapse that was later examined in a session as follows: immediately prior to his relapse he had received an erroneous report that his share of the partnership's profits would be cut back, which he took to be an evidence of failure. He reported experiencing feeling humiliated and then very anxious. Without weighing the consequences, he went out to purchase a bottle of liquor, returned to his office, and began drinking. He said that he had not thought to control this behavior at the time.

This model helps to explain why relapse is such a frequent and unanticipated aspect of addiction treatment. Exposure to conditioned cues, ones that were repeatedly associated with drug use, can precipitate reflexive drug craving during the course of therapy, and such cue exposure can also initiate a sequence of conditioned behaviors that lead addicted individuals to relapse unwittingly into drug use.

Loss of control can be the product of conditioned withdrawal, as described by Ludwig et al. (1978). The sensations associated with the ingestion of an addictive drug, like the odor of alcohol or the euphoria produced by opioids, are temporally associated with the pharmacologic elicitation of a compensatory response to that drug and can later produce drug-seeking behavior. For this reason, the "first drink" can serve as a conditioned cue for further drinking. These phenomena yield patients with very limited capacity to control consumption once a single dose of drug has been taken.

## Application to Treatment

What, then, will serve as a minimally noxious aversive stimulus that would be specific for the conditioned stimuli associated with drug craving, thereby providing a maximal useful learning experience? To answer this, we may look at Wikler's (1971) initial conception of the implications of his conditioning theory. He pointed out that,

> The user would become entangled in an interlocking web of self-perpetuating reinforcers, which perhaps explain the persistence of drug abuse, despite disastrous consequences for the user, and his imperviousness to psychotherapy which does not take such conditioning factors into account, because neither the subject nor the therapist is aware of their existence (p. 611).

Since Wikler's time, specific techniques have been developed to overcome this problem. The model of conditioned drug seeking has been applied to training patients to recognize drug-related cues and avert relapse. Annis (1986), for example, has used a self-report schedule to assist patients in identifying the cues, situations, and moods that are most likely to lead them to alcohol craving. Marlatt evolved the approach he described as *relapse prevention* (Marlatt and Gordon 1985), whereby patients are taught strategies for avoiding the consequences of the alcohol-related cues they have identified, and a similar conception has been used to extinguish cocaine craving through cue exposure in a clinical laboratory (Childress et al. 1988).

These approaches can be introduced as part of a

single-modality behavioral regimen, but they also can be used in expressive and family oriented psychotherapy. For example, Ludwig et al. (1978) suggested the approach of *cognitive labeling*, namely associating drinking cues with readily identified guideposts to aid the patient in consciously averting the consequences of prior conditioning. Similarly, the author (Galanter 1983) described a process of guided recall to explore the sequence of antecedents of given episodes of craving or drinking "slips" that were not previously clear to a patient. These approaches can be conducted concomitant with an examination of general adaptive problems in an exploratory therapy.

There is a problem in application, though. If a patient is committed to achieving abstinence from an addictive drug, but is in jeopardy of occasional slips, cognitive labeling can facilitate consolidation of an abstinent adaptation. Such an approach is less valuable, however, in the context of inadequate motivation for abstinence, fragile social supports, or compulsive substance abuse unmanageable by the patient in his or her usual social settings. Hospitalization or replacement therapy (e.g., methadone) may be necessary here because ambulatory stabilization through psychotherapeutic support is often not feasible. Under any circumstances, cognitive labeling is an adjunct to psychotherapy and not a replacement for group supports such as AA, family counseling, or ambulatory therapeutic community programs, where applicable.

## ▼ THE USE OF NETWORK THERAPY

Having examined the need for introducing behavioral techniques into ongoing treatment of the addicted patient, we can now consider the model of network therapy for addiction. This model offers a pragmatic approach to augmenting conventional individual therapy that draws on these recent advances in order to enhance the effectiveness of office management.

This conception has been validated in general terms. In an evaluation of family treatment for alcohol problems reported by the Institute of Medicine, McCrady concluded that "research data support superior outcomes for family involved treatment, enough so that the modal approach should involve family members and carefully planned interventions" (Institute of Medicine 1990, p. 84). Indeed, the idea

of the therapist's intervening with family and friends to start treatment was introduced by Johnson (1986) as one of the early ambulatory techniques in the addiction field (Gallant 1987; Gitlow and Peyser 1980). More broadly, the availability of greater social support to patients has been shown to be an important predictor of positive outcome in addiction (McLellan et al. 1983).

The author (Galanter, in press) reported a positive outcome for this approach in a clinical trial in a series of 60 patients treated in network therapy. It involved one network session per week for an initial month, with subsequent sessions held less frequently, typically on a bimonthly basis after a year of ambulatory care. Individual therapy was carried out concomitantly on a once- or twice-weekly basis. On average, the networks had 2.3 members, the most frequent participants being mates, peers, parents, or siblings.

### The Couple As a Network

A cohabiting couple will provide an initial example of how natural affiliative ties can be used to develop a secure basis for rehabilitation. Couples' therapy for addiction has been described in both ambulatory and inpatient settings, and a favorable marital adjustment is found to be associated with a diminished likelihood of dropout and a positive overall outcome (Kaufman and Kaufman 1979; McCrady et al. 1986; Stanton and Thomas 1982).

The use of disulfiram has yielded relatively little benefit overall in controlled trials when it is prescribed for patients to take on their own recognizance (Fuller and Williford 1980). This is largely because this agent is only effective insofar as it is ingested as instructed, typically on a daily basis. Alcoholic patients who forget to take required doses will likely resume drinking in time. Indeed, such forgetting often reflects the initiation of a sequence of conditioned drug-seeking behaviors.

Although patient characteristics have not been shown to predict compliance with a disulfiram regimen (Schuckit 1985), changes in the format of patient management have been found to be beneficial (Brubaker et al. 1987). For example, the involvement of a spouse in observing the patient's consumption of disulfiram yields a considerable improvement in outcome (Azrin et al. 1982; Keane et al. 1984). Patients alerted to taking disulfiram each morning by this external reminder are less likely to experience conditioned drug seeking when exposed to addictive cues and are more likely to comply in subsequent days with the dosing regimen.

The technique also helps in clearly defining the roles in therapy of both the alcoholic patient and spouse (typically the wife), by avoiding the spouse's need to monitor drinking behaviors he or she cannot control. The spouse does not actively remind the alcoholic to take each dose. The spouse merely notifies the therapist if he or she does not observe the pill being ingested on a given day. Decisions on managing compliance are then allocated to the therapist, thereby avoiding entanglement of the couple in a dispute over the patient's attitude and the possibility of drinking in secret.

A variety of other behavioral devices demonstrated to improve outcome can be incorporated into this couple's format. For example, it has been found that setting the first appointment as soon as possible after an initial phone contact improves outcome by undercutting the possibility of an early loss of motivation (Stark et al. 1990). Spouses can also be engaged in history taking at the very outset of treatment to minimize the introduction of denial into the patient's presentation of his or her illness (Liepman et al. 1989). The initiation of treatment with such a regimen is illustrated in the following case.

> **Case 2.** A 39-year-old alcoholic man was referred for treatment. Both patient and spouse were initially engaged in an exchange on the phone by the psychiatrist, so all three could plan for the patient to remain abstinent on the day of the first session. They agreed that the wife would meet the patient at his office at the end of the work day on the way to the appointment. This would ensure that cues presented by his friends going out for a drink after work would not lead him to drink. In the session, an initial history was taken from the spouse as well as the patient, allowing her to expand on ill consequences of the patient's drinking, thereby avoiding his minimizing the problem. A review of the patient's medical status revealed no evidence of relevant organ damage, and the option of initiating his treatment with disulfiram at that time was discussed. The patient, with the encouragement of his wife, agreed to take his first dose that day and continue under her observation. Subsequent sessions with the couple were dedicated to

dealing with implementation of this plan, and concurrent individual therapy was initiated.

## The Network's Membership

Networks generally consist of a number of members. Once the patient has come for an appointment, establishing a network is a task undertaken with active collaboration of patient and therapist. The two, aided by those parties who join the network initially, must search for the right balance of members. The therapist must carefully promote the choice of appropriate network members, however, just as the platoon leader selects those who will go into combat. The network will be crucial in determining the balance of the therapy. This process is not without problems, and the therapist must think strategically of the interactions that may occur among network members. The following case illustrates the nature of the therapist's task.

> **Case 3.** A 25-year-old graduate student had been abusing drugs since high school, in part drawing in funds from his affluent family, who lived in a remote city. At two points in the process of establishing his support network, the reactions of his live-in girlfriend were particularly important. Both he and she agreed to bring in his 19-year-old sister, a freshman at a nearby college. He then mentioned a "friend" of his, a woman whom he had apparently found attractive, even though there was no history of an overt romantic involvement. The expression on his girlfriend's face suggested that she was uncomfortable with this option. The therapist deferred on the idea of the "friend," and moved on to evaluating the patient's uncle. Initially the patient was reluctant; it later turned out that he perceived the uncle as a potentially disapproving representative of the parental generation. The therapist and girlfriend encouraged him to accept the uncle as a network member nonetheless to round out the range of relationships within the group. In matter of fact, the uncle was caring and supportive, particularly after he was helped to understand the nature of the addictive process.

## The Network's Task

The therapist's relationship to the network is one of a task-oriented team leader rather than a family therapist oriented toward restructuring relationships. The network is established to implement a straightforward task, that of aiding the therapist to sustain the patient's abstinence. It must be directed with the same clarity of purpose that a task force is directed in any effective organization. Competing and alternative goals must be suppressed or at lease prevented from interfering with the primary task.

Unlike family members involved in traditional family therapy, network members are not led to expect symptom relief or self-realization for themselves. This prevents the development of competing goals for the network's meetings. It also ensures the members protection from having their own motives scrutinized and thereby supports their continuing involvement without the threat of an assault on their psychological defenses. Because network members have kindly volunteered to participate, their motives must not be impugned. Their constructive behavior should be commended. It is useful to acknowledge appreciation for the contribution they are making to the therapy. There is always a counterproductive tendency on their part to minimize the value of their contribution. The network must, therefore, be structured as an effective working group with good morale.

> **Case 4.** A 45-year-old single woman served as an executive in a large family held business, except when her alcohol problem led her into protracted binges. Her father, brother, and sister were prepared to banish her from the business but decided first to seek consultation. The father was a domineering figure who intruded in all aspects of the business, evoking angry outbursts from his children. The children typically reacted with petulance, provoking him in return. The situation came to a head when both the patient's siblings angrily petitioned the therapist to exclude the father from the network, 2 months into the treatment. This presented a problem because the father's control over the business made his involvement important to securing the patient's compliance. The patient's relapse was still a real possibility. This potentially coercive role, however, was an issue that the group could not easily deal with. The therapist supported the father's membership in the group, pointing out the constructive role he had played in getting the therapy started. It was clear to the therapist that the father could not deal with a situation where he was not accorded sufficient respect

and that there was no real place in this network for addressing the father's character pathology directly. The children became less provocative themselves, as the group responded to these pleas for civil behavior.

## Some Specific Techniques

Yalom (1974) has described anxiety-reducing tactics that he used in therapy groups with alcoholic patients in order to avert disruptions and promote cohesiveness. These tactics include setting an agenda for the session and using didactic instruction. In the network format, a cognitive framework can be provided for each session by starting out with the patient recounting events related to cue exposure or substance use since the last meeting. Network members are then expected to comment on this report to ensure that all are engaged in a mutual task with correct, shared information. Their reactions to the patient's report are addressed as well.

> **Case 5.** An alcoholic man began one of his early network sessions by reporting a minor lapse to drinking. This was disrupted by an outburst of anger from his older sister. She said that she had "had it up to here" with his frequent unfulfilled promises of sobriety. The psychiatrist addressed this source of conflict by explaining in a didactic manner how behavioral cues affect vulnerability to relapse. This didactic approach was adopted in order to defuse the assumption that relapse is easily controlled and to relieve consequent resentment. He then led members in planning concretely with the patient how he might avoid further drinking cues in the period preceding their next conjoint session.

Patients undergoing detoxification from chronic depressant medication often experience considerable anxiety, even when a gradual dose reduction schedule is undertaken (American Psychiatric Association 1990). The expectancy of distress, coupled with conditioned withdrawal phenomena, may cause patients to balk at completing a detoxification regimen (Monti et al. 1988). In individual therapy alone, the psychiatrist would have little leverage at this point. When augmented with network therapy, however, the added support can be invaluable in securing compliance under these circumstances.

**Case 6.** A patient elected to undertake detoxification from chronic use of diazepam, approximately 60 mg qd. In network meetings with the patient, her husband, and her friend, the psychiatrist discussed the need for added support toward the end of her detoxification. As her daily dose was brought to 2 mg tid, she became anxious, said that she had never intended to stop completely, and insisted on being maintained permanently on that low dose. Network members supportively but explicitly pointed out that this had not been the plan. She then relented to the original detoxification agreement, and her dose was reduced to zero over 6 weeks.

Contingency contracting as used in behavioral treatment stipulates that an unpalatable contingency will be applied should a patient carry out a prohibited symptomatic behavior (Hall et al. 1977). Crowley successfully applied this technique to rehabilitating cocaine-addicted patients by preparing a written contract with each patient that indicated a highly aversive consequence would be initiated for any use of the drug (Crowley 1984). For example, for an addicted physician, a signed letter was prepared for mailing to the state licensing board admitting addiction. The approach can be adapted to the network setting as well.

Patients are strongly inclined to deny drinking problems during relapse. The network may be the only resource in providing the psychiatrist with the means to communicate with a relapsing patient and assist in reestablishing abstinence.

**Case 7.** A patient suffered a relapse to drinking after 6 months of abstinence. One of the network members consulted with the psychiatrist and then stayed with the patient in his home for a day to ensure that he would not drink. He then brought the patient to the psychiatrist's office along with the other network members to reestablish a plan for abstinence.

### The Use of Alcoholics Anonymous

The use of AA is desirable whenever possible. For the alcoholic individual, certainly, participation in AA is strongly encouraged. Groups such as Narcotics Anonymous, Pills Anonymous, and Cocaine Anonymous are modeled after AA and play a similarly useful role for drug-abusing individuals. One approach

is to tell the patient that he is expected to attend at least two AA meetings a week for at least 1 month so as to familiarize him- or herself with the program. If after a month the patient is quite reluctant to continue, and other aspects of the treatment are going well, his or her nonparticipation may have to be accepted.

Some patients are more easily convinced to attend AA meetings. Others may be less compliant. The therapist should mobilize the support network as appropriate in order to continue pressure for the patient's involvement with AA for a reasonable trial. It may take a considerable period of time, but ultimately a patient may experience something of a conversion wherein he or she adopts the group ethos and expresses a deep commitment to abstinence, a measure of commitment rarely observed in patients who experience psychotherapy alone. When this occurs, the therapist may assume a more passive role in monitoring the patient's abstinence and keep an eye on his or her ongoing involvement in AA.

### Contrasts With Family Therapy

Like family and group therapy, network therapy brings several people together to address a psychological problem. Approaches vary among practitioners of group and family modalities, as therapists may focus on the individual patient or try to shape the family or group overall. In the network, on the other hand, the focus is always kept on the individual patient and his or her addictive problem.

In network therapy, unlike family therapy, the practitioner avoids focusing on the patient's family history in the network sessions themselves because an involvement in family conflicts can be disruptive to the network's primary task of helping to maintain the patient's abstinence. Such a focus would establish an additional agenda and set of goals, potentially obliging the therapist to assume responsibility for resolving conflicts that are not necessarily tied to the addiction itself. Family and interpersonal dynamics can be addressed individually with the patient on his or her own.

**Case 8.** One patient brought his estranged wife and his brother as network members in embarking on treatment of his prescription drug abuse. The tension between patient and his spouse was considerable, as both were competitive and controlling in their own ways. She interrupted too often, offering her opinions, and he was dismissive of her and sat with his back to her. His brother tried his best to remain neutral. By listening with interest and respect to both husband and wife, letting each play a positive role in framing the treatment, the therapist could tap their initiative and their desire to "shine" in the session. This created the option of drawing on the wife's knowledge as a historian of the patient's drug use and focussed all three participants on the task of considering more members of this emerging network. The very traits that might have served as grist for a family therapist were not discussed.

One technique of family therapy that does bear considerable similarity to network format is the "strategic" family approach identified with Haley (1977). As in network therapy, his approach focuses directly on the presenting problem rather than the dynamics of the family system. Treatment is begun with a careful examination of the nature of the symptoms, their time course, and the events that take place as they emerge. As in other behaviorally oriented therapies, the focus is a relatively narrow one, and an understanding of behavioral sequences associated with the problematic situation is of primary importance. This identification of the circumstances surrounding the emergence of the problem can be likened to ferreting out conditioned cues that lead to the addicted subject's sequence of drug use. Both strategic family therapy and the behavioral approach assume that these will suggest options for bringing about the problem's resolution. Indeed, as he developed this strategic model, Haley observed that certain behaviors within a family can unintentionally promote the very symptoms they are designed to suppress, clearly similar to the conception of the alcoholic subject's spouse unwittingly serving as an enabler.

## ▼ THE RULES OF NETWORK THERAPY: A SUMMARY

At its heart, network therapy is meant to be straightforward and uncomplicated by theoretical bias. In this light, the author has summarized the main points to be observed in treatment.

### Who Needs Network Therapy?

1. Network therapy is appropriate for individuals who cannot reliably control their intake of alcohol or drugs once they have taken their first dose, those who have tried to stop and relapsed, and those who have not been willing or able to stop.
2. Individuals whose problems are too severe for the network approach in ambulatory care include those who cannot stop their drug use even for a day or comply with outpatient detoxification.
3. Individuals who can be treated with conventional therapy and without a network include those who have demonstrated the ability to moderate their consumption without problems.

### Start a Network As Soon As Possible

1. It is important to see the alcohol- or drug-abusing patient promptly because the window of opportunity for openness to treatment is generally brief.
2. If the patient is married, engage the spouse early on, preferably at the time of the first phone call. Point out that addiction is a family problem. For most drugs, the therapist can enlist the spouse in ensuring that the patient arrives at the therapist's office with a day's sobriety.
3. In the initial interview, frame the exchange so that a good case is built for the grave consequences of the patient's addiction, and do this before the patient can introduce a system of denial. That way you are not putting the spouse or other network members in the awkward position of having to contradict a close relation. Then make clear that the patient needs to be abstinent, starting now.
4. When seeing an alcoholic patient for the first time, start him or her on disulfiram as soon as possible, in the office if you can. Have the patient continue taking disulfiram under observation of a network member.
5. Start arranging for a network to be assembled at the first session, generally involving a number of the patient's family or close friends.
6. From the very first meeting you should consider whatever is necessary to ensure sobriety until the next meeting, and plan that with the network. Initially, the plan might consist of their immediate company and a plan for daily AA attendance.

7. Include people who are close to the patient, have a long-standing relationship with him or her, and who are trusted. Avoid members with substance problems because they will let you down when you need their unbiased support.

8. Get a balanced group. Avoid a network composed solely of the parental generation, or of younger people, or people of the opposite sex.

9. The tone should be directive. Give explicit instructions to support and ensure abstinence.

## Three Priorities in Running the Ongoing Therapy

1. *Maintaining abstinence.* The patient and the network members should report at the outset of each session any events related to the patient's exposure to alcohol and drugs. The patient and network members should be instructed on the nature of relapse and plan with the therapist how to sustain abstinence. Cues to conditioned drug seeking should be examined.

2. *Supporting the network's integrity.* The patient is expected to make sure that network members keep their meeting appointments and stay involved. The therapist sets meeting times explicitly and summons the network for any emergency, such as relapse; he or she does whatever is necessary to secure stability of the membership if the patient is having trouble with this.

3. *Securing future behavior.* The therapist should combine any and all modalities necessary to ensure the patient's stability, such as a stable, drug-free residence; avoidance of substance abusing friends; attendance at 12-step meetings; compliance in taking medications such as disulfiram or blocking agents; observed urinalysis; and ancillary psychiatric care.

4. Also, meet as frequently as necessary to ensure abstinence, perhaps once a week for a month, every other week for the next few months, and every month or two by the end of a year. Individual sessions run concomitantly. Make sure that the mood of meetings is trusting and free of recrimination. Explain issues of conflict in terms of the problems presented by addiction, rather than getting into personality conflicts. Once abstinence is stabilized, the network can help the patient plan for a new drug-free adaptation.

### Ending the Network Therapy

1. Network sessions can be terminated after the patient has been stably abstinent for at least 6 months to 1 year. This should be done after discussion of the patient's readiness for handling sobriety without a network in the group.

2. An understanding is established with the network members that they will contact the therapist at any point in the future if the patient is vulnerable to relapse. The members can be summoned by the therapist as well. This should be made clear with the patient before termination in the presence of the network but applies throughout treatment as well.

## ▼ REFERENCES

American Psychiatric Association: Diagnostic and Statistical Manual of Mental Disorders, 4th Edition. Washington, DC, American Psychiatric Association, 1994

American Psychiatric Association Task Force on Benzodiazepine Dependence, Toxicity, and Abuse: A Task Force Report of the American Psychiatric Association. Washington, DC, American Psychiatric Association, 1990

Annis HM: A relapse prevention model for treatment of alcoholics, in Treating Addictive Behaviors: Processes of Change. Edited by Miller WR, Heather NH. New York, Plenum, 1986, pp 407–434

Azrin NH, Sisson RW, Meyers R: Alcoholism treatment by disulfiram and community reinforcement therapy. J Behav Ther Exp Psychiatry 13:105–112, 1982

Begleiter H, Porjesz B: Persistence of a "subacute withdrawal syndrome" following chronic ethanol intake. Drug Alcohol Depend 4:353–357, 1979

Brubaker RG, Prue DM, Rychtarik RG: Determinants of disulfiram acceptance among alcohol patients: a test of the theory of reasoned action. Addict Behav 12:43–52, 1987

Childress AR, McLellan AT, Ehrman R, et al: Classically conditioned responses in opioid and cocaine dependence: a role in relapse? in Learning Factors in Substance Abuse, NIDA Res Monogr 84. Edited by Ray BA. Rockville, MD, U.S. Department of Health and Human Services, 1988

Crowley TJ: Contingency contracting treatment of drug-abusing physicians, nurses, and dentists, in

Behavioral Integration Techniques in Drug Abuse Treatment. Edited by Grabowski J, Stitzer ML, Henningfeld JF. NIDA Res Monogr 46. Rockville, MD, Department of Health and Human Services, 1984

Fuller RK, Williford WO: Life-table analysis of abstinence in a study evaluating the efficacy of disulfiram. Alcohol Clin Exp Res 4:298–301, 1980

Galanter M: Cognitive labelling: psychotherapy for alcohol and drug abuse: an approach based on learning theory. Journal of Substance Abuse Treatment and Evaluation 5:551–556, 1983

Galanter M: Network Therapy for Addiction: A New Approach. New York, Basic Books, 1993

Galanter M: Network therapy for substance abuse: a clinical trial. Psychotherapy (in press)

Gallant DM: Alcoholism: A Guide to Diagnosis, Intervention, and Treatment. New York, WW Norton, 1987

Gallant DM, Rich A, Bey E, et al: Group psychotherapy with married couples: a successful technique in New Orleans Alcoholism Clinic patient. J La State Med Soc 122:41–44, 1970

Gitlow SE, Peyser HS (eds): Alcoholism: A Practical Treatment Guide. New York, Grune & Stratton, 1980

Haley J: Problem Solving Therapy. San Francisco, CA, Jossey-Bass, 1977

Hall SM, Cooper JL, Burmaster S, et al: Contingency contracting as a therapeutic tool with methadone maintenance clients. Behav Res Ther 15:438–441, 1977

Hayman M: Current attitudes to alcoholism of psychiatrists in Southern California. Am J Psychiatry 112:484–493, 1956

Institute of Medicine: Broadening the Base of Treatment for Alcohol Problems. Washington, DC, National Academy Press, 1990

Johnson VE: Intervention: How To Help Someone Who Doesn't Want Help. Minneapolis, MN, Johnson Institute Books, 1986

Kaufman E, Kaufman PN: Family Therapy of Drugs and Alcohol Abuse. New York, Gardner Press, 1979

Keane TM, Foy DW, Nunn B, et al: Spouse contracting to increase Antabuse compliance in alcoholic veterans. J Clin Psychol 40:340–344, 1984

Khantzian EJ: The self-medication hypothesis of addictive disorders: focus on heroin and cocaine dependence. Am J Psychiatry 142:1259–1264, 1985

Liepman MR, Nierenberg TD, Begin AM: Evaluation of a program designed to help family and significant others to motivate resistant alcoholics to recover. Am J Drug Alcohol Abuse 15:209–222, 1989

Ludwig AM, Wikler A, Stark LM: The first drink: psychobiological aspects of craving. Arch Gen Psychiatry 30:539–547, 1974

Ludwig AM, Bendfeldt F, Wikler A, et al: "Loss of control" in alcoholics. Arch Gen Psychiatry 35:370–373, 1978

Marlatt GA, Gordon J (eds): Relapse Prevention: Maintenance Strategies in the Treatment of Addictive Behaviors. New York, Guilford, 1985

McCrady BS, Noel NE, Abrams DB, et al: Comparative effectiveness of three types of spouse involvement in outpatient behavioral alcoholism treatment. J Stud Alcohol 47:459–467, 1986

McLellan AT, Woody GE, Luborsky L, et al: Increased effectiveness of substance abuse treatment: a prospective study of patient-treatment "matching." J Nerv Ment Dis 171:597–605, 1983

Monti PM, Rohsenow DJ, Abrams DB, et al: Social learning approaches to alcohol relapse: selected illustrations and implications, in Learning Factors in Substance Abuse, NIDA Res Monogr 84. Edited by Ray BA. Rockville, MD, U.S. Department of Health and Human Services, 1988, pp 141–159

O'Brien CP, Testa T, O'Brien TJ, et al: Conditioned narcotic withdrawal in humans. Science 195:1000–1002, 1977

Schuckit MA: A one-year follow-up of men alcoholics given disulfiram. J Stud Alcohol 46:191–195, 1985

Stanton MD, Thomas TC (eds): The Family Therapy of Drug Abuse and Addiction. New York, Guilford, 1982

Stark MJ, Campbell BK, Brinkerhoff CV: "Hello, may we help you?" A study of attrition prevention at the time of the first phone contact with substance-abusing clients. Am J Drug Alcohol Abuse 16:67–76, 1990

Wikler A: Some implications of conditioning theory for problems of drug abuse. Behav Sci 16:92–97, 1971

Wikler A: Dynamics of drug dependence: implications of a conditioning theory for research and treatment. Arch Gen Psychiatry 28:611–616, 1973

Wurmser L: Mrs. Pecksniff's horse? Psychodynamics of compulsive drug use, in NIDA Res Monogr 12. Edited by Blaine JD, Julius DS. Rockville, MD, U.S. Government Printing Office, 1977, pp 36–72

Yalom ID: Group therapy and alcoholism. Ann N Y Acad Sci 233:85–103, 1974

# Individual Psychotherapy

## *Alcohol*

*Sheldon Zimberg, M.D.*

sychotherapy of alcoholism has in the past been considered ineffective by most psychiatrists. This has been due to the fact that *psychoanalytic* psychotherapy for alcoholism has been largely a failure (Zimberg 1982). Also, the rationale for psychoanalysis has been the mistaken belief that alcoholism is always a symptom of underlying psychological disorders, and by uncovering this disorder and providing insight into its role in abusive drinking the drinking problem would cease. This has not proven to be the case because alcoholism is a disorder of multicausality, including biological (genetic), sociocultural, and psychological factors. The ineffectiveness of psychoanalysis and the psychodynamic rationale has resulted in psychotherapists' avoidance of alcoholic patients and a bias against psychiatry by those in the addictive disorder field and by many members of Alcoholics Anonymous (AA).

However, there are many forms of psychotherapy other than psychoanalysis. In fact, any form of verbal interaction between a therapist or counselor and patient designed to change behavior and feelings can be called psychotherapy. The verbal process of AA is a form of psychotherapy.

A modified form of psychodynamic psychotherapy in the treatment of alcoholism was pioneered by Tiebout (1962) and Fox (1965). They used a psychodynamic understanding of alcoholism in their approach to psychotherapy but avoided uncovering early in treatment and gave priority to the elimination of alcohol use as the first and necessary step in the psychotherapeutic approach. Discussion follows on the rationale for this modified psychodynamic psychotherapy of alcoholism.

In most treatment programs for alcoholism, group therapy is often the treatment of choice. Much of the counseling is modeled on the 12-step, self-help approach of AA, which has been found to be effective for many alcoholic individuals.

However, an interventionist and directive approach of psychotherapy of alcoholism has been found to be effective. Interpretations of unconscious thoughts and feelings are not used early in treatment; rather, direction, guidance, and suggestions regarding the need to maintain sobriety and avoid triggers for relapse are used extensively. This approach must be based on a great deal of knowledge of the patients and their psychological needs and vulnerabilities. Intense transference and countertransference issues emerge that can be used therapeutically.

In group therapy, patients are generally not known as well by the group leader, and there is little control of the responses of other group members to a particular patient. Therefore, the precision of the interventions in issues other than alcohol use is much less than in individual therapy. Patients with coexisting psychiatric disorders will often not do well in group therapy unless their psychiatric problems are diagnosed and treated as well as the alcoholism.

Individual therapy is underutilized in alcoholism but can be the most effective approach with individuals who are resistant to treatment or who have coexisting psychiatric disorders. The transference can develop into a dependent relationship to the therapist that can be used to influence the drinking as well as the changes in self-perception and self-destructive behavior that characterizes the alcoholic individual's life. Individual therapy can be the preferred approach for those who feel uncomfortable in groups or who fear the disclosure of very sensitive information. Alcoholic individuals are a heterogeneous group, and no one modality of treatment can be effective for all patients.

## ▼ PSYCHODYNAMICS OF ALCOHOLISM

A number of authors have indicated that the conflict with dependent needs is a major psychological factor that contributes to alcoholism (Bacon et al. 1965; Blane 1968; McCord and McCord 1962).

This conflict relates to histories of childhood rejection by one or both parents, overprotection, or forcing premature responsibility on a child, particularly if a parent is alcoholic. The literature on children of alcoholics also discusses these issues (Ackerman 1983; Kern 1985).

The psychological conflict observed in alcoholic individuals consists of low self-esteem along with feelings of worthlessness and inadequacy. These feelings are denied and repressed and lead to unconscious needs to be taken care of and accepted. Because these dependent needs cannot be met in reality, they lead to anxiety and compensatory needs for control, power, achievement, and elevated self-esteem. There is denial of this conflict with development of reactive

grandiosity and excessive narcissism as defense mechanisms. Alcohol tranquilizes the anxiety; more importantly, it creates pharmacologically induced feelings of power, omnipotence, and invulnerability in men (McClelland et al. 1972) and enhanced feelings of womanliness in women (Wilsnack 1976). When alcoholic individuals wake up after a drinking episode, they experience guilt and despair because they have not achieved anything more than before they drank and their problems remain. They have a primitive, punishing superego, and their feelings of worthlessness are intensified and the conflict continues in a vicious circle, often with a progressive downward spiral leading to psychological dependence and eventually physiological dependence on alcohol with addiction.

Alcohol provides an artificial feeling state of power, control, and elevated self-esteem that cannot be achieved in reality. The very act of producing this feeling of power at will feeds the alcoholic individual's conscious grandiose self-image.

An individual with such a psychological conflict will become alcoholic if there is a *genetic* predisposition to alcoholism and if the individual lives in a society in which the use of alcohol is *sanctioned* as a way to feel better or in which there is considerable ambivalence regarding the use of alcohol. In any particular individual, one or more of these etiologic factors may predominate and lead to alcoholism.

AA is effective because the alcoholic individual's narcissism is sublimated by the rescuing of other alcoholic individuals, therefore the grandiosity becomes fulfilled and socially useful, and much of the alcoholic individual's dependent needs are met by the acceptance of the group.

AA members recognize that their support of other alcoholic individuals helps them maintain their own sobriety. Therefore, the successful development of AA was based on an intuitive understanding of alcoholic individuals' psychological conflict and needs.

In the traditional psychoanalytic approach to treating alcoholism, the therapist attempts to work from the defenses to uncover the underlying psychological conflicts. The very technique of uncovering therapy produces anxiety, which results in the need to drink and thus is ineffective. Also, insight alone cannot affect physiologic addiction.

The central problem in the psychotherapy of the alcoholic individual is breaking through the reactive grandiosity that produces the massive denial of profound feelings of inferiority and dependence that permit the pattern of self-destructive drinking to continue. Alcoholic individuals destroy not only themselves but also their loved ones without perceiving their lack of control of their behavior pattern. The typical response of an alcoholic individual without insight into this behavior is, "I can stop drinking any time I want to," despite overwhelming evidence to the contrary. This self-deception must be penetrated if rehabilitation is to succeed.

## ▼ DIFFERENTIAL DIAGNOSIS AND TREATMENT OF COEXISTING PSYCHIATRIC DISORDERS

A cardinal rule of treating alcoholic patients is the recognition that they are not a homogeneous group. There are a number of subpopulations of alcoholic individuals that require specific treatment. There is no *one* treatment approach that will be successful for *all* alcoholic patients, including AA.

The various subpopulations include problem drinkers with related developmental problems in which the abusive drinking is part of an adjustment reaction. Such groups include adolescent problem drinkers and alcoholic elderly. The manifestation of alcoholism in these groups is different and related to the adjustment problems in adolescents (Fischer 1985) or the stresses of aging in alcoholic elderly (Zimberg 1990).

Another large subpopulation of alcoholic individuals include those with coexisting psychiatric disorders, called *dual diagnosis patients* or *mentally ill chemical abusers* (MICA). The high prevalence of these patients (Regier 1990) and the difficulty in treating them has recently become apparent. Also, today many alcoholic individuals are involved with other substances of abuse.

In order to successfully treat alcoholic patients and determine problems other than alcoholism, a complete psychiatric history, mental status examination, and developmental and family history are essential parts of the initial evaluation.

Another cardinal rule in alcoholism therapy is that if there are signs and symptoms of psychiatric disorder in an actively drinking alcoholic patient, the patient must be detoxified from alcohol and observed to be alcohol free for 3–6 weeks before a coexisting psychiatric disorder can be effectively diagnosed. This is essential because the excessive use of alcohol can produce a great variety of organic and functional psychiatric symptoms. The understanding of these psychiatric complications is required for appropriate treatment. The following is a discussion of these various psychiatric complications and how they can be treated.

The complicating problems found in alcoholic individuals include the acute and chronic organic mental syndromes associated with alcoholism. Other conditions found to coexist with alcoholism include attention-deficit disorder, residual type; schizophrenia; borderline syndrome; affective disorders; and other personality and neurotic disorders such as anxiety. Individual assessment and individual therapy can best determine over time the differential diagnosis in an outpatient setting and provide the appropriate and specific treatment in an integrated way.

The alcohol withdrawal syndrome includes tremulousness, withdrawal seizures, hallucinosis, and alcohol withdrawal delirium (DTs). Tremulousness can, in most cases, be managed with ambulatory detoxification using diazepam 15–20 mg per day decreased over 7–10 days. The other more serious withdrawal manifestations should be treated in a hospital with the use of benzodiazepines in a detoxification regimen.

Alcohol amnestic disorder (Korsakoff's psychosis), an acute and chronic organic mental disorder with coexisting neurological disorders, is due to thiamine deficiency and is seen rarely today. Such patients should be hospitalized and treated with parenteral thiamine.

Dementia associated with alcoholism is a chronic organic mental disorder with memory impairment and intellectual and cognitive defects. This disorder results from a relatively long history of excessive alcohol consumption. Cerebral atrophy, found with a CAT scan of alcoholic individuals' brains, is not generally correlated with the presence of this disorder (Lusins et al. 1980). Diagnosis has to be established by a precise mental status examination and neuropsychological testing. Individuals with this disorder should be hospitalized or treated in long-term residential treatment so as to improve their mental functioning to some degree.

Patients with significant cerebral atrophy often are not responsive to verbally oriented therapy until sobriety has been achieved for at least 3–6 months.

Protracted withdrawal syndrome, although not an official diagnosis, has been noted in many alcoholic individuals. This is a disorder characterized by irritability, emotional lability, insomnia, and anxiety that persists for weeks to months after alcohol withdrawal. It is due to the residual effects of alcohol toxicity on the central nervous system. It generally clears spontaneously after prolonged abstinence. In AA it has been called a "dry drunk." Many alcoholic individuals return to drinking because of the persistence of these unpleasant symptoms. Patients should be warned about this condition and be told that it will pass in time. Small doses of thioridazine (Mellaril) 50–100 mg at bedtime may be helpful.

Some alcoholic individuals have been found to have a history of attention-deficit hyperactivity disorder from childhood, with the disorder continuing into adulthood. As adults, they developed alcoholism but retained the disorder in a modified form characterized by defects in attention and impulsivity. The diagnosis can be established by taking a careful history that includes a developmental history and determining if hyperactivity as well as attention defects and impulsivity were present in the individuals as children. The diagnosis is established by history and observation of the alcohol-free patient for 6–8 weeks. Such patients must be treated for their alcoholism, but the addition of stimulating drugs such as imipramine, magnesium pemoline, or methylphenidate can be helpful in reducing the symptoms of the attention-deficit disorder, residual type and facilitate recovery. Often, such patients abuse cocaine as well as alcohol, and the stimulant drugs can be a useful substitute for the cocaine.

Patients with schizophrenia have been noted to use and abuse alcohol as self-medication. Such patients when observed while alcohol free for 3–4 weeks can be noted to have persistent functional psychotic symptoms and usually give a history of prolonged duration of these symptoms and psychiatric hospitalizations prior to their drinking problem. The schizophrenia should be treated with injectable, long-acting fluphenazine or haloperidol and the involvement of the patients in social and vocational rehabilitation programs. When the schizophrenia is effectively treated, the alcohol abuse generally clears up. Such patients generally do not do well at AA meetings but may do better at Double Trouble self-help groups that deal with the alcoholism and psychiatric problems in a self-help, 12-step context.

A significant number of patients with borderline syndrome abuse alcohol and become alcoholic. The borderline patients give a history of mood and behavioral disturbances that exist prior to the alcoholism. Such disturbances include impulsive behavior, very poor interpersonal relationships, inappropriate and intense anger, poor self-identity, physical self-mutilation, and having long-term feelings of depression, emptiness, boredom, loneliness, and intense anxiety. Such patients should be specifically treated for their alcoholism and involved in AA. Supportive psychotherapy is necessary as well as use of small doses of thioridazine at 50 mg per day for the depression and anxiety. Benzodiazepine drugs should be avoided in these patients because they will be often abused. AA can supply many of the dependency needs for these patients and reduce their severe feelings of social isolation and loneliness. A period of 4–6 weeks of alcohol-free observation, plus the history of these symptoms, is necessary to establish the diagnosis.

Anxiety is a common symptom among alcoholic individuals. However, in primary alcoholic patients, it generally clears up within 4 weeks of detoxification with the maintenance of abstinence. In some alcoholic patients, it will persist longer as part of the protracted withdrawal syndrome. Some alcoholic patients will present themselves with a long history of episodic bouts of intense anxiety characterized as panic reactions, at which time they drink to relieve the anxiety. Such patients have panic-anxiety disorder and are secondary alcoholics. These patients should be maintained alcohol free and treated with imipramine or nortriptyline for the panic disorder. Once the panic disorder is effectively treated, the alcohol abuse generally lessens and clears up.

Alcoholism can coexist with other neurotic or personality disorders. In such situations, the alcoholism must be initially addressed until sobriety is well established for 6 months to 1 year before any uncovering therapy is attempted for the existing neurotic or personality disorder.

Depression is a common symptom in alcoholic patients. In most cases, the feelings of depression will lessen or disappear with 4 weeks of abstinence. However, in a small number of alcoholic men (less than 5%) and in a substantial number of alcoholic women (25%–50%), the depression will persist in the alcohol-free state (Zimberg 1982). Such individuals have a major affective disorder and should be treated with lithium carbonate if there is a history of recurrent depression or episodes of mania. Antidepressants should be used if the current depression is the first episode. It should be pointed out to the patient that this medication is used for the mood disorder and not the alcoholism to avoid bad reactions of AA members to the patients use of a mood-altering drug.

One must be able to provide an effective differential diagnosis and appropriate treatment for alcoholic patients with coexisting major psychiatric disorders. Most of these patients are primary alcoholic individuals and do not require psychiatric treatment. However, for those that do, such a multitreatment approach is essential if the alcoholic patient is to recover. Individual therapy is the most effective way to determine any coexisting psychiatric disorder and provide the appropriate treatment. If the therapist is a psychiatrist, medication and individual therapy can be provided by one clinician. If the therapist is not a psychiatrist, referral to a psychiatrist who is knowledgeable about alcoholism for psychiatric medication is necessary.

## ▼ INDICATIONS AND ADVANTAGES OF INDIVIDUAL THERAPY

Individual therapy provides distinct advantages compared with the more commonly used modality of group therapy. These advantages include the ability to observe and scrutinize patients more closely to permit the differential diagnosis of coexisting psychiatric disorders as indicated. When such psychiatric disorders are present, it is essential to provide the necessary treatments or the patient will not recover.

Individual therapy can facilitate a dependent transference with the therapist. This dependent relationship can be useful to influence the patient to change his or her drinking behavior and other maladaptive approaches to life and problems. Because the early stages of treatment require suggestions, guidance, advice, and role model for changes to occur, a dependent relationship will facilitate such approaches in individual therapy. The therapist is able to learn more about the patient more quickly, and this information enables the therapist to target interventive suggestions at a time when the patient may be receptive. Premature interventions can cause anger and avoidance and in extreme situations cause the patient to leave therapy. The art of alcoholism psycho-

therapy that is active and interventionist is to know when to intervene and when not. This takes experience and a great deal of knowledge of the patient that can only come in individual therapy. Knowledge of the patient is also important regarding cues or triggers that could to relapse drinking. Therefore, individual therapy can facilitate cognitive relapse prevention strategies *specific* for the patient rather than the discussion of general principles that occurs in groups.

Individual therapy can be more effective for individuals who fear groups and/or are unwilling to disclose very sensitive life traumas such as rape, incest, or illegal activities in a group setting.

Individual therapy, however, cannot provide the peer support and identification with recovering alcoholic patients that occurs in group therapy if the group is made up of patients at various levels of recovery. However, the combination of individual therapy with AA participation can provide the peer support so helpful to recovery.

The use of disulfiram, 250 mg per day, can be useful to patients who have difficulty maintaining sobriety initially. Individual therapy can facilitate the monitoring of disulfiram use and help in the maintenance of sobriety early in treatment.

## ▼ STAGES OF TREATMENT AND RECOVERY

The treatment has been observed to progress through several stages. Although the stages can be observed in group therapy and in AA involvement, they are most apparent in individual therapy. The first stage involves the situation in which the alcoholic patient enters treatment with the feeling that "I cannot drink." This situation exists when there is external pressure on the patient to stop drinking, such as the threat of loss of job or his or her spouse's leaving or with the use of disulfiram. In a sense, the alcoholic patient is forced to stop drinking for at least a short time. His or her attitudes toward drinking and the denial of drinking as a serious problem have not changed. The alcoholic patient has stopped not because he or she sees it as necessary, but because someone else does. The patient must be helped by directive counseling to face problems and stress without resorting to alcohol. During this stage, patients should be directed cognitively to recognize cues that might lead to drinking so that they can develop alternative coping mechanisms. Forgetting to take a disulfiram tablet can be such a cue, and therefore the use of disulfiram can serve as an early warning system.

Often patients who have stopped drinking early in treatment feel extremely confident about their newly acquired sobriety and experience a feeling of euphoria. This feeling is a reaction-formation to an unconscious lack of control over their drinking, which is now experienced as a certainty of control over their not drinking as well as control over other aspects of their lives. Patients should be warned to expect such inappropriate feelings. This situation is by its nature very unstable because there has been no significant change in the patients' attitude about drinking nor reduced grandiosity. This situation can easily lead to a return to drinking or, through individual therapy, to a stage where the alcoholic patient believes, "I won't drink."

This is the stage at which the controls on the compulsion to drink have become internalized and there is no longer a serious conscious conflict about whether or not to drink. At this stage, the patients' attitude toward the necessity of drinking and the deleterious consequences in resuming drinking are apparent; they have experienced a considerable attitudinal change toward drinking. The conflict about drinking is still present but at an unconscious level. Evidence of the continued existence of this conflict is present in fantasies and dreams. This stage is the level successful AA members have achieved. Discontinuation or the intermittent use of disulfiram in stressful situations can be considered. Further help in developing alternative coping mechanisms for stress and unpleasant feelings should be provided. This stage represents a reasonably good stage of recovery and is fairly stable, only occasionally leading to a "slip" after years of sobriety. The reactive grandiosity has now been sublimated (redirected) in the ego-enhancing feelings of control over a previously uncontrollable problem, or for active AA members, their work with other alcoholic patients serves as an additional outlet for the need for grandiosity. At least 6 months to 1 year of directive psychotherapy is required to achieve this stage of recovery.

The third stage of recovery involves the situation in which the alcoholic individual "does not have to drink." This stage can be achieved only through insight into the individual's personality problems and conflicts and his or her resolution to a major degree. The alcoholic individual's habitual use of alcohol in the past can be understood as a way of dealing with his or her conflicts. With the resolution of the conflicts through insight, the individual can achieve more adaptive ways of coping with internal and external problems. This stage can be achieved effectively through psychoanalytically oriented psychotherapy and self-understanding.

The third stage is a stable stage as long as the alcoholic individual refrains from drinking. Abstinence is relatively easy to maintain at this stage. The duration of treatment required to achieve this stage of recovery has, in my experience, been about 1–2 years after reaching stage 2.

After reaching stage 2 or 3, some patients enter a situation in which they believe, "I can return to social drinking." Possibly a small percentage of alcoholic individuals can achieve this (Pattison 1968), but at our present level of knowledge it is impossible to predict which patients these might be. All alcoholic individuals believe during the initial stages of treatment that they can return to controlled drinking. Alcoholic individuals who have achieved recovery (stage 2 or 3) in most cases do not desire to resume social drinking because of the risk involved. For all practical purposes at the present time, abstinence should be a necessary goal in the treatment of all alcoholic individuals. Alcohol is not necessary to life, and it is quite possible to live and even be happy without consuming alcohol even in our drinking society. This fact should be part of the attitudinal change an alcoholic individual experiences during the process of recovery.

The termination of treatment with an alcoholic patient is critical. If the treatment process has been successful, the alcoholic patient will have established a dependent, trusting relationship with the therapist, and therefore termination will produce anxiety and the possibility of a return to drinking. This termination should be based on mutual agreement between the therapist and patient, a termination date determined, and the final period of therapy involved with the issue of termination.

Termination can occur at stage 2 or 3 because both are relatively stable stages regarding control of drinking. A decision has to be made, however, when a patient reaches stage 2, whether further treatment to achieve insight into the psychological conflict related to his or her drinking problem and moving to reach stage 3 in treatment is important to the patient. This option should be decided by the patient. Nonpsychiatric physicians can provide the directive counseling and the use of disulfiram, where indicated, to help alcoholic patients reach stage 2. More traditional psychotherapy is required to reach stage 3, and nonpsychiatric physicians and alcoholism counselors might consider referral of such patients to psychotherapists.

Regardless of whether the patient terminates in stage 2 or 3, the door to return to therapy should be left open. A patient who stops treatment after stage 2 may determine after a while that not drinking is not enough to help him or her deal with feelings and conflicts and might wish to return to treatment to try to achieve insight into his personality conflicts. A patient terminated after stage 2 may have a slip, and a return to treatment should be available. This slip, however, should not be viewed as a treatment failure but as part of a rehabilitation process that is not yet complete. Patients who slip in stages 2 and 3 generally do not return to continuous uncontrolled drinking because their awareness of their problem and control mechanisms are such that controls can be quickly reinstated. The slip can be looked at as a psychological maladaptation to conflict and anxiety or as a transference reaction, and it is possible to help the patient gain more understanding of his or her need to drink by analyzing such slips.

The approach to individual psychotherapy of alcoholic patients, presented in terms of stages of progression of treatment in relations to varying abilities to control the impulse to drink, provides a framework for a complex and often amorphous treatment process. It provides a goal-directed approach to achievable levels of improvement. Complex therapeutic decisions regarding involvement of the family in treatment, starting or stopping of disulfiram, attendance at AA meetings, use of uncovering techniques, discontinuation of therapy, and others can be considered in relationship to these fairly predictable stages in the recovery process. It is possible to make predictions of outcome of therapeutic intervention or lack of intervention based on knowledge of the stage of recovery the patient has entered. Therefore, such an awareness can make the complex psychotherapeutic process with alcoholic patients potentially understandable and subject to a certain degree of predictability. Individual therapy can facilitate this understanding and predictability.

# ▼ TECHNIQUES OF INDIVIDUAL THERAPY

This discussion will center on the techniques used in each of the stages of recovery from early, middle, to late stage 3 recovery.

The basis of the early stage of treatment is *intervention* with regard to drinking. It must be established in the therapeutic contract that the goal of treatment is to achieve abstinence. Most patients in early-stage treatment will reluctantly agree to this goal, although testing of it will occur with slips or provocative drinking. This behavior must be confronted and used as helping the patient see his or her inability to control the impulse drink. Suggesting the use of disulfiram to control the impulse drink should be introduced. If the patient refuses disulfiram at this time, a contract should be established that if the patient can remain alcohol free, there is no problem; however, if there is one more slip, use of disulfiram is mandatory if treatment is to continue.

Patients should be encouraged to attend AA meetings. They should be helped to find meetings where they feel comfortable with other members who should be their peers. Although the AA message and settings are very similar, the membership will vary greatly from group to group. Although some alcoholic individuals can recover without AA, it can be extremely helpful for most individuals through its peer support, alcoholism education, opportunities to identify with recovering alcoholic individuals, and education on how live without alcohol in our drinking society.

The family should be involved early and encouraged to attend Al-Anon. They should learn about their *enabling* behavior, should encourage sobriety with their support and interest, and should avoid covering up or excusing the drinking.

Thus early in treatment a structure should be provided to the alcoholic patient in the form of *scaffolding*. The scaffolding erected around a building under renovation does not itself provide structural support for the building's foundation but provides the ability for workers to enter the building from different directions and provide the renovations inside. The changes produced are from *outside in*. In psychoanalytic treatment, the changes occur through insight and are from *inside out*.

The scaffolding erected include the therapist,

family involvement, AA participation, and use of disulfiram and provides the structural components of *scaffolding therapy*.

The verbal interactions involve the therapist providing direction and guidance and cognitive suggestions to help the alcoholic patient learn to cope with unpleasant feelings, conflicts, problems, and stress without resorting to alcohol. Cognitive-behavioral suggestions are made to encourage the patient to avoid situations, interpersonal relationships, and places that have been triggers to drinking in the past. Such triggers are very individual, so that one must learn about these unique drinking triggers in each patient. The more one learns, the more effective this approach will be. This avoidance behavior is extremely useful early in therapy but can be modified at later stages as the patient has developed better coping skills and the attitude about the need for alcohol has changed. Anxiety and stress reduction techniques other than cognitive-behavioral approaches can be used early in therapy and can include meditation, self-hypnosis, biofeedback, and other relaxation techniques.

The major goals of the scaffolding therapy are to help patients accept the problem with alcohol and learn to cope with their lives and its problems without using alcohol. In some patients, the absence of the anesthetic effects of alcohol will make the problems that were once neglected more apparent and more painful. Patients should be helped to recognize that only with sobriety can they successfully deal with their problems. In some patients, early sobriety can produce a feeling of euphoria and omnipotence that is called the "pink cloud" in AA. Giving up alcohol successfully seems to suggest that they can do anything. Patients should be guided through this reaction-formation defense by helping them recognize their limitations as well as the possibilities for feeling and functioning better without alcohol in the future if sobriety is maintained.

Defenses observed in patients and the transference should not be interpreted at this stage of recovery but if possible utilized and redirected in the recovery process. Sublimation of the feelings of omnipotence with involvement in AA and helping others by qualifying to speak at meetings is an example of such redirection. Wallace (1985) gives an excellent discussion of managing the "preferred defense structure of the alcoholic."

This early stage of treatment with its active inter-vention in relation to drinking and helping the alcoholic individual adapt to life and its problems without drinking takes about 6 months to 1 year to produce stability. The overt conflict of whether to drink becomes internalized, and the alcoholic individual enters the next stage of recovery with the belief that "I won't drink."

In this second stage of recovery, the therapeutic effort should help the individual gain more independence and the scaffolding system can be partially dismantled. Disulfiram can be discontinued but might only be used intermittently when the patient expects some severe stress. The patient should have this option to use disulfiram when his or her control over the impulse to drink feels threatened by external or internal drink signals.

Attendance at AA should continue, but its frequency might diminish from daily to 2–3 times a week. Patients should be encouraged to actively speak at AA meetings to reinforce their determination to stay sober. In AA there is a saying: "You can't keep it unless you give it away."

The therapeutic approach should be supportive but the emphasis should shift to the patient's opportunities to change aspects of behavior that contributed to the drinking. Greater attention to problems in dealing with feelings such as anger and the need for control should be discussed. Some interpretation of behavior and feelings could be made but with avoidance of uncovering approaches and interpretation of the dependent transference.

Helping develop the patient's ability to empathize with other individuals' feelings can reduce the egocentrism and increase a more mature recognition of one's own limitations and well as the limitations of others to respond to all the patient's needs. More anxiety will result, but the patient is usually able to cope without drinking because of stable internalized control over the impulse to drink. Drinking dreams and fantasies are common during this stage. Interpretation regarding them should deal with issues of controlling the impulse to drink.

After 1–1½ years in the second stage, the alcoholic individual has generally established very good internalized controls over the impulse to drink. This is the stage that has been achieved by most successful AA members. These individuals will not have insight into the psychological sources of the dependency conflict or understanding of serious interpersonal problems or profound feelings of anger that may exist, but they have good sobriety.

Patients with severe anxiety, episodes of depression, or serious characterological problems are candidates for treatment in the third stage of recovery, in which "I don't have to drink" is the goal. This stage is not necessary to maintain sobriety but can produce longer term, better outcomes through conflict resolution. At this stage, the focus of therapy is on uncovering and reconstruction and less supportive, directive, and cognitive. The transition should be gradual because as the therapist becomes more passive and analytical, transference issues will surface and should be interpreted at this time. Dreams and fantasies should be used to a greater degree, and memories and feelings from childhood should be examined as they relate to past and present behavior and feelings. Thus a more traditional psychoanalytic approach can be used. The duration of this phase of treatment is indefinite but usually lasts an additional 1–2 years.

Drinking slips can occur in the second and third stage of recovery but are usually of short duration and without serious consequences. If they occur during the second stage, the issues of drinking cues and control issues are reviewed. If they occur in the third stage, the unconscious conflicts' role in the slip should be explored to produce insight and greater control of the impulse to drink with conflict resolution.

Successful termination can occur in the second stage or at any point in the third stage when it is mutually agreed the patient has good internalized controls over the impulse to drink and has experienced significant improvement in functioning. Because alcoholism is a lifelong condition and no one is ever cured, the door to return to treatment should be left open. Patients involved in AA should be encouraged to maintain the involvement, and those not involved should be encouraged to consider trying again to observe role models of successful recovery.

## ▼ TRANSFERENCE AND COUNTERTRANSFERENCE

The transference relationship in individual therapy is intensified. It is usually based on dependent needs but with some mistrust and hostility based on previous rejections and is therefore ambivalent. There may be testing of the therapeutic relationship, which

alcoholic patients usually do by drinking early in therapy. If these episodes can be dealt with in an understanding and not a judgmental and punitive way, the transference can be shifted to a dependent relationship that is necessary for it to be successful. In a dependent transference, the patient is more receptive to the guidance and suggestion as part of the scaffolding therapy.

At times the ambivalent feelings may be acted out by the patients even after achieving months of sobriety. The therapist must still be supportive and nonjudgmental and explore these slips not as transference reactions but as responses to insufficiently established controls and as responses to signals of which the patient may not be aware. Thus cognitive approaches should be used early in therapy rather than uncovering techniques and interpretation of the transference.

A supportive and nonjudgmental, nonpunitive therapeutic relationship will produce a "corrective emotional experience" as described by Alexander (1946) and lead to the maintenance of long-term sobriety. After sobriety has become well stabilized up to 1-1½ years, the transference relationship can be regarded as part of the uncovering approaches used in stage 3 of treatment. Entering stage 3 should be by mutual agreement, and the transition should be a slow process over weeks rather than an abrupt transition from support to uncovering.

*Countertransference* is described as the therapist's reaction to the patient as if the patient were an important person in the therapist's life and/or as a reaction to the behavior of the patient in relation to the feelings, needs, and self-image of the therapist. The early and provocative drinking of the patient and later slips can cause the therapist to feel frustrated and angry because of the therapist's need for the gratification of successful treatment. This anger and frustration is very common in therapists and is the major reason many therapists refuse to treat alcoholic patients.

The reality is that the therapist cannot force, control, or seduce patients into achieving abstinence but only can offer them the tools to assist them in achieving abstinence for themselves. The therapist's omnipotent need for successful treatment cannot be arrayed against the patient's unconscious psychological need for omnipotence and control or the treatment will fail. Only the patient can decide to work toward abstinence, using the help and guidance of the therapist. Every therapist working with alcoholic patients must adopt this stance of recognition of one's own limitations or burnout, avoidance of alcoholic patients, and other adverse psychological reactions will result.

In the early stage of treatment, the therapist can discuss his or her responses to feelings and problems as a role model for the patient. The therapist should not discuss negative countertransference reactions early in therapy, but in stage 3 interpretations using the therapists reactions is appropriate and helpful.

The treatment of alcoholic patients can be quite rewarding. There are many successes but also some failures. It can not be determined early in treatment who will succeed or fail to achieve long-term abstinence and improvement in other aspects of their lives. However, patients are ultimately responsible for the success of the treatment if provided in this alcoholism-specific method.

## ▼ OUTCOME STUDIES

There have been few controlled studies comparing outcomes of individual and group therapy of alcoholic individuals. A review article of this issue (Solomon 1982) reported slightly better outcomes for group therapy. However, patient characteristics seemed more predictive of outcome than the modality of treatment. A study by Woody et al. (1983) indicated the efficacy of individual therapy in opioid-addicted patients.

A number of clinical reports including my experience has indicated the value of individual therapy (Kaufman 1989; Khantzian 1982; Wurmser 1984; Zimberg 1989). Group therapy is more widely practiced in alcoholism treatment, particularly in hospital- and institution-based programs. This is because group therapy, with its peer involvement, can be very effective, is generally more cost efficient, and it more closely resembles the group model of the self-help programs. However, the great heterogeneity of the alcoholic population suggests that no one modality of treatment can be the most effective for all patients. Recent literature suggests that there are different typologies of alcoholism, requiring differing treatment approaches (Meyer 1989; Schuckit 1989). In this regard, individual therapy is neglected in spite of the fact that it can be extremely effective in selected patients. Often a combination of individual therapy with

peer involvement in AA can be the most effective combination for many alcoholic patients.

Patients who drop out of group therapy or who do not respond to group therapy should not be considered treatment failures unless they have been given an opportunity for individual therapy in which a more profound patient-therapist attachment can be established that can help the patient recover. These reports suggest that patients, particularly those with a coexisting major psychiatric disorder and those reluctant to disclose information about themselves in groups, are more likely to do better when treated in individual therapy.

## ▼ REFERENCES

Ackerman RJ: Children of Alcoholics: A Guide Book for Educators, Therapists, and Parents. Holmes Beach, FL, Learning Publications, 1983

Alexander F, French TM: Psychoanalysis Therapy: Principles and Application. New York, Ronald Press, 1946

Bacon MK, Barry H, Child IL, et al: A cross-cultural study of drinking; II: relation to other features of culture. Quarterly Journal of Studies on Alcohol 3:29–48, 1965

Blane HT: The Personality of the Alcoholic: Guises of Dependency. New York, Harper & Row, 1968

Fischer J: Psychotherapy of adolescent alcohol abusers, in Practical Approaches to Alcoholism Psychotherapy, 2nd Edition. Edited by Zimberg S, Wallace J, Blume SB. New York, Plenum, 1985, pp 295–313

Fox R: Psychiatric aspects of alcoholism. Am J Psychother 19:408–416, 1965

Kaufman E: The psychotherapy of dually diagnosed patients. J Subst Abuse Treat 6:9–18, 1989

Kern JC: Management of children of alcoholics, in Practical Approaches to Alcoholism Psychotherapy, 2nd Edition. Edited by Zimberg S, Wallace J, Blume SB. New York, Plenum, 1985, pp 315–345

Khantzian EJ: Some treatment implications of the ego and self disturbance in alcoholism, in Dynamic Approaches to the Understanding and Treatment of Alcoholism. Edited by Bean MH, Zinberg NE. New York, Free Press, 1982, pp 103–188

Lusins J, Zimberg S, Smokler H, et al: Alcoholism and cerebral atrophy: a study of 50 patients with CT SCAN and psychologic testing. Alcohol Clin Exp Res 4:406–411, 1980

McClelland DC, Davis WW, Kalin R, et al: The Drinking Man. New York, Free Press, 1972

McCord W, McCord J: A longitudinal study of the personality of alcoholics, in Society, Culture, and Drinking Patterns. Edited by Pittman DJ, Snyder CR. New York, Wiley, 1962, pp 186–201

Meyer R: Typologies, in Treatments of Psychiatric Disorders: A Task Force Report of the American Psychiatric Association, Vol 2. Washington, DC, American Psychiatric Association, 1989, pp 1065–1072

Pattison EM: Abstinence criteria: a critique of abstinence criteria in the treatment of alcoholism. Int J Soc Psychiatry 14:268–276, 1968

Regier DA, Farmer ME, Rae DS, et al: Comorbidity of mental disorders with alcohol and other drug abuse. JAMA 264:2511–2518, 1990

Schuckit MA: Goals of treatment, in Treatments of Psychiatric Disorders: A Task Force Report of the American Psychiatric Association, Vol 2. Washington, DC, American Psychiatric Association, 1989, pp 1072–1076

Solomon SD: Individual versus group therapy: current status in the treatment of alcoholism. Advances in Alcohol and Substance Abuse 2:69–86, 1982

Tiebout HM: Intervention in psychotherapy. Am J Psychoanal 22:1–6, 1962

Wallace J: Working with the preferred defense structure of the recovering alcoholic, in Practical Approaches to Alcoholism Psychotherapy, 2nd Edition. Edited by Zimberg S, Wallace J, Blume SB. New York, Plenum, 1985, pp 23–36

Wilsnack SC: The impact of sex roles and women's alcohol use and abuse, in Alcoholism Problems in Women and Children. Edited by Greenblat N, Shuckit MA. New York, Grune & Stratton, 1976

Woody GE, Luborsky L, McLellan AT, et al: Psychotherapy for opiate addicts: does it help? Arch Gen Psychiatry 40:639–645, 1983

Wurmser L: More respect for the neurotic process: comments on the problem of narcissism in severe psychopathology; especially the addictions. J Subst Abuse Treat 1:37–45, 1984

Zimberg S: The Clinical Management of Alcoholism. New York, Brunner/Mazel, 1982

Zimberg S: Individual management and psychotherapy, in Treatments of Psychiatric Disorders: A Task Force Report of the American Psychiatric Association, Vol 2. Washington, DC, American Psychiatric Association, 1989, pp 1093–1103

Zimberg S: Management of alcoholism in the elderly. Addiction Nursing Network 1:4–6, 1990

# Individual Psychotherapy

## *Other Drugs*

*George E. Woody, M.D.*
*Delinda Mercer, M.S.*
*Lester Luborsky, Ph.D.*

Psychotherapeutic treatments for substance use disorders are very widely used. Individual therapy or drug counseling is available in about 99% of the drug-free, methadone-maintenance, and multiple-modality drug treatment units and about 97% of the detoxification units in this country (National Drug and Alcoholism Treatment Unit Survey 1982). The types of psychotherapy for treating addiction include individual, family, and group therapies, each with a variety of orientations.

Despite the widespread use of psychotherapeutic approaches to treat chemical dependence, it is only within the last two decades that these approaches have begun to be scientifically evaluated. Most of the research on addiction treatment has focused on pharmacological rather than psychosocial interventions, even though some form of psychosocial intervention is at least a part of virtually every addiction treatment program. Often psychosocial interventions make up

the entire program (Onken and Blaine 1990). This insufficiency of research on psychosocial treatments for substance abuse/dependence is due to the numerous difficulties in attempting to conduct scientific research in this area (Onken and Blaine 1990). The methodological problems faced in doing research on psychotherapy for addiction treatment have been discussed in depth (Beutler 1990; Borkovec 1990; Carroll and Rounsaville 1990; Crits-Christoph et al. 1990; Howard et al. 1990; Lambert 1990).

The numerous approaches to using psychotherapy in the treatment of substance use disorders, and the different orientations of the therapies themselves, make it difficult to write a brief yet comprehensive chapter on this topic. We have attempted to draw together significant contributions from the vast clinical literature and from our own experience and blend them with the relatively few research findings to provide a selection of meaningful guidelines for those who wish to use psychotherapy with patients who have substance use disorders.

## ▼ DEFINITION OF PSYCHOTHERAPY

Throughout this chapter, the term *psychotherapy* is used to describe a psychological treatment that aims to change problematic thoughts, feelings, and behaviors through creating a new understanding of the thoughts and feelings that appear to be causally related to the presenting difficulty. When psychotherapy is used in the treatment of addiction, it must address the addictive behaviors and the thoughts and feelings that appear to promote, maintain, or occur as a result. Along with the goals specific to addiction, which, by definition, involve cessation of drug self-administration, psychotherapy addresses issues related to other aspects of patients' lives, both past and present, under the assumption that some of these contribute to their current drug use.

Addiction counseling, not psychotherapy, is the most widely used psychosocial intervention in substance abuse treatment. In contrast to psychotherapy, counseling is much less focused upon identifying and changing internal, intrapsychic processes and is much more focused on managing current problems, especially those related to drug use. *Counseling* is perhaps best defined as the regular management of addicted patients, primarily through giving support, providing structure, monitoring behavior, encouraging abstinence, and providing concrete services such as referral for job counseling, medical services, or legal aid. This approach constantly addresses the addictive behavior, often using the language and concepts of the 12-step program developed by Alcoholics Anonymous. It attempts to modify the dependence and/or abuse by identifying daily problems and behaviors that contribute to drug self-administration, and by delivering concrete services aimed to overcome these problems. Counseling, like psychotherapy, attempts to assist the patient in dealing with addiction-related consequences that have often become a part of the patients' lives. However, the approach taken in counseling is concrete and specific and does not have the more indirect and intrapsychic focus that is seen in psychotherapy.

## ▼ A RATIONALE FOR USING PSYCHOTHERAPY WITH SUBSTANCE ABUSE PATIENTS

Psychotherapy has been used in the treatment of addiction because problematic psychological factors seem to contribute to, and result from, chemical dependence and because some of the drugs that are used will reduce subjective distress. This relationship is probably best observed in the case of opioids, in which the drug has potent sedative and analgesic effects. In this sense, psychological factors serve as course modifiers for the dependence in that their presence may encourage drug use as an attempt to escape from painful subjective experiences.

One of the major theories about the relationship between addiction and comorbid psychiatric symptoms is the self-medication hypothesis. This hypothesis suggests that some types of drug abuse may begin, continue, or be otherwise fostered as a form of self-medication to treat anxiety, depression, or other psychiatric disorders (Khantzian 1985; Khantzian and Khantzian 1984). This apparent relationship between psychological symptoms and substance abuse/addiction provides a rationale for the use of psychotherapy in the treatment of addiction—if the accompanying psychiatric symptoms can be reduced, the person has a better chance to reduce or stop drug self-administration. Of course, there may also be physiological as well as medical factors that predispose one to addiction. For this reason, comprehensive addiction treatment should involve both medical and psychological evaluation and treatment as necessary, based on a biopsychosocial assessment.

Research has shown that there is a high level of comorbidity between substance use disorders and a wide range of psychiatric symptoms, many of which meet symptomatic and duration criteria for DSM-III-R (American Psychiatric Association 1987) diagnoses (Khantzian and Treece 1985; Rounsaville et al. 1982, 1991; Weiss et al. 1986; Woody et al. 1983; Woody et al. 1990). The most common of these are major depression, dysthymia, and most of the anxiety disorders. Because chronic use of most drugs of abuse (with the exception of opioids and nicotine) will magnify or even produce psychiatric symptoms, it is often difficult to determine which of these symptoms and syndromes represent independent psychiatric disorders versus drug-induced/organic conditions.

However, whether these symptoms are drug-related or whether they represent independent psychiatric disorders (and provided they persist beyond the immediate period associated with intoxication or withdrawal), a number of studies have shown that they have prognostic significance. This finding is especially relevant to psychotherapeutic approaches for treating individuals with substance use disorders, as the psychotherapies have been adapted specifically to address such problems. In contrast, drug counseling has been developed to address drug problems directly. Thus counseling does not focus on the psychiatric symptoms as contributors but rather sees them as consequences of the dependence and treatable primarily by cessation of drug use.

When viewed in this way, the presence of psychiatric symptoms in the context of a substance use disorder identifies a subgroup of patients that may benefit from an approach that combines psychotherapy and drug counseling. The length of time during which psychotherapy may be a useful adjunct can vary, depending on the duration of the associated symptoms/disorders.

Psychological symptoms that often coexist with addiction and are well treated by individual psychotherapy include anxiety and depression associated with low self-esteem, shame and guilt, fear and loneliness, or isolation. These problems may result in psychiatric diagnoses only in their more severe forms but even in milder forms clearly diminish one's quality of life and may contribute to drug administration.

In this chapter, we will emphasize a "how to do it" approach and thus will draw heavily on data obtained from studies that have provided evidence for the efficacy of psychotherapy with this population. The chapter will consist of four parts: 1) a description of general factors with which it is important to be familiar when providing psychotherapeutic treatment for addiction, 2) a description of the settings in which addiction treatment is provided, 3) a discussion of the modalities of individual psychotherapy for addiction and their relative efficacy, and 4) implications for the provision of treatment.

## ▼ GENERAL FACTORS IN ADDICTION TREATMENT

### Knowledge of Abused Drugs

It is important for psychotherapists who treat individuals with substance use disorders to become familiar with the main and adverse effects of the drugs that are abused, routes of administration, drug combinations often used, and typical patterns of use.

An experienced therapist knows that substance-abusing patients sometimes come to treatment while under the influence of drugs. This probably occurs most often on initial visits, but it can occur at any time. Obviously, the patient's mental state can vary considerably, depending on whether he or she is intoxicated, withdrawing, or in the more "normal" state that is found between these two extremes. The therapist needs to recognize whether the patient's mood is altered by recent drug use or withdrawal and whether problematic mental symptoms are present. Drug-induced organic mental disorders are usually temporary but may need to be treated aggressively with medication or containment to ensure the patient's safety. On the other hand, psychiatric disorders can be masked by drug intoxication and thus may become evident only when the acute drug effects disappear.

In an outpatient setting, when a patient comes for a scheduled therapy session intoxicated on either alcohol or drugs, therapists' immediate responses should be guided by their own judgment, but usually it is best to strongly discourage the patient from coming to treatment intoxicated. This often involves rescheduling the session for a time when the patient agrees to at least try to come in a sober condition because little psychotherapy can be done under the influence of a drug. If the patient is unable to comply with this request, it is probably an indicator of the severity of the addiction and of the need for hospitalization or for some other controlled setting involving more structure and safety for the patient.

It is worth noting that some patients use drugs in combination and become addicted to multiple substances. Common drug combinations are cocaine and alcohol; amphetamines and sedatives of any kind; alcohol and marijuana; heroin and cocaine, amphetamines, benzodiazepines, or alcohol; and ritalin and talwin. Also, characteristic patterns of use are associated with certain of these multiple substances. For example, individuals who are dependent on cocaine and alcohol usually use these drugs in combination. They commonly report that they drink to reduce anxiety that is produced by the cocaine. Methadone patients who abuse benzodiazepines commonly report that they take the benzodiazepine immediately before or after the methadone in an attempt to produce a "high." Individuals having such complex patterns of use can be unusually difficult to treat because they may be under the influence of opposing pharmacological effects in addition to having other psychiatric problems. For example, such a patient may be withdrawing from one drug and intoxicated with another while also experiencing symptoms of a major depressive disorder.

### Subculture of Addiction and Life-Styles of Addicted Individuals

It is helpful for the psychotherapist to be knowledgeable about the life-styles of addicted individuals and the subculture in which addiction prevails. Alcoholic patients may often be able to function well enough in society to retain employment and family relationships. Although these things are damaged by the dependence, alcohol-dependent individuals may not be disengaged from society. On the other hand, heroin-addicted individuals usually live in a subculture of their own, and much of their time is spent in drug-related activities like obtaining the drug, preparing to shoot up, "nodding out," becoming "normal," and then experiencing withdrawal symptoms until their next dose. Many cocaine-addicted individuals' life-styles appear to be midway between these two points; they enter treatment when still functioning in society, they have a job, a family, etc. However, severe cocaine addiction rapidly disintegrates one's connections to the non-drug-using society, and there is a definite subculture, typically associated with "crack" cocaine, in which the individual becomes increasingly involved as the dependence progresses.

Familiarity with the varied life-styles of individuals with substance use disorders can be gained by talking to paraprofessionals or psychotherapists who have experience treating them or by the first-hand experience gained through treating patients. Hanson et al. (1985) provide excellent descriptive information about opioid-addicted individuals and their life-styles; descriptions of the cocaine/crack subculture are widely available in medical journals and the lay press.

### Knowledge of Self-Help Programs

For a therapist treating addicted patients, it is important to be familiar with self-help programs, especially the 12-step programs. These programs, which are free of charge and widely available, are extremely popular and appear to be a part of most successful drug-free addiction recovery programs. The 12-step programs are very supportive, abstinence-oriented, espouse the disease model of addiction, and foster a network of healthy social support. In addition, the 12-step philosophy imparts some psychological and spiritual ideas that many find helpful in dealing with everyday life stressors and that appear to help these individuals establish and maintain a sober life-style.

## ▼ TREATMENT SETTINGS

Psychotherapy is appropriate for use in almost any type of treatment setting. Although the trend in recent years has been to shift treatment for substance use disorders away from inpatient and into outpatient settings, much treatment continues to be done in residential settings. There are six settings in which treatment is typically provided: 1) inpatient within psychiatric or general hospitals, 2) inpatient within penal institutions, 3) outpatient in clinics or private practice settings, 4) intensive day treatment programs, 5) halfway houses, and 6) therapeutic communities. The philosophy of treatment varies somewhat by treatment setting and psychotherapy may fit better into some programs than others.

The therapeutic community modality is probably the only treatment setting into which psychotherapy may not be easily integrated. Here, the typical program is a peer-regulated milieu with an emphasis on self-government, individual responsibility, group meetings, and strict behavioral controls. Psychotherapy is beginning to be used in some such programs as an ancillary treatment that is targeted to patients with persistent and overt psychiatric symptoms.

Psychotherapy probably has the best chance to work in any setting when it is integrated into an ongoing program that focuses directly on reducing or eliminating drug use, along with psychiatric symptoms that may accompany the dependence. Washton (1989) describes the components of such a program. It includes a structured, progressive treatment program that is abstinence oriented, provides education about the effects of drugs, encourages family involvement, does frequent urine testing, provides group and individual therapy, supports 12-step participation, and encourages good physical health. In Washton's program, drug-focused counseling and psychotherapy are provided by the same person. Khantzian (1987) advocates this type of role in which the therapist has the primary responsibility for meeting all the treatment needs of the patient.

Another model is to assign the patient an addiction counselor and a psychotherapist. The counselor handles the patient's more concrete needs such as talking about current problems, supporting and encouraging efforts to reduce drug use, monitoring progress, providing liaison or consultation with medical personnel, making job referrals, obtaining legal advice, encouraging limit setting by enforcing program rules, and keeping accurate records. This model allows the psychotherapist to focus on therapy, but it also requires coordination of services. This is facilitated by good personal relations between the psychotherapist and the counseling staff. Helpful in this regard is commitment to the overall program through activities such as having the therapist work within the facility and interact with other treatment staff, be involved in making decisions regarding the patient's treatment program, and be familiar with the overall program procedures and policies.

Psychotherapy, regardless of the setting in which it is conducted, is most effective when combined with the structure imposed by frequent urine testing. Urinalysis for the presence of drugs of abuse encourages honesty and helps to hold the patient accountable for his or her behavior. Prompt feedback on drug-positive and drug-negative urine samples helps the patient to feel that the therapist is concerned with and is monitoring his or her progress in recovery. Appropriate confrontation and analysis of what led to the use is important in the case of any lapse to drug use, whether it is discovered through urine testing or the patient's self-report. Positive feedback, given for clean urine samples is a powerful reinforcer for abstinence.

Many clinicians have found that involvement of significant family members in the treatment process is also helpful. Family members are usually informed of the nature and consequences of addiction and of the treatment process, and their support is usually enlisted through occasional family meetings. Most counselors and therapists pay special attention to any factors that exist in the family that may undermine treatment. These factors could be addiction in a family member or other more subtle factors such as the development of family crises in response to improvements in the patient's dependence. If such factors exist, family therapy may be necessary as well. At least one controlled study of structural family therapy, used in combination with drug counseling for patients on methadone maintenance, showed positive results (Stanton and Todd 1982).

Drug treatment programs exhibit tremendous variability in basic aspects of service delivery such as availability of medical services, control of behavioral problems, level of illicit drug use, safety and sanitary conditions, use of psychotropic drugs, level of staff morale, educational level of staff, and types of patients treated (Ball et al. 1986). These programmatic qualities may play a major but, as yet, undefined role in the feasibility, efficacy, or relative importance that psychotherapy may have in different settings.

## ▼ THERAPIST QUALITIES

Therapist qualities appear to have an impact upon success in therapy (Luborsky et al. 1985, 1986). Kleinman et al. (1990), in investigating crack- and cocaine-abusing subjects, found that therapist assignment was the strongest predictor of treatment retention, an important measure of success in treatment.

Little evidence is available to indicate the type of therapist who may best treat substance-abusing patients, thus it is difficult to comment with certainty on this issue, perhaps partly because substance-abusing individuals are such a heterogeneous group. However, some guidelines can be offered from the few available studies that examine therapist qualities as they relate to psychotherapy outcome in general.

Three therapist qualities appear to be predictive of outcome: adjustment, skill, and interest in helping patients (Luborsky et al. 1985). Another factor that predicts outcome in psychotherapy is quality of the therapist-patient relationship. Therapists who from the beginning of treatment form a positive relationship that is perceived by the patient as "helping" appear to have a better chance of success than those who form less positive bonds (Luborsky et al. 1985).

In treating patients with substance use disorders, the therapist should be interested in and comfortable with certain kinds of problems. Some therapists have strong negative reactions to the manipulative, sociopathic, impulsive, or demanding behavior that is often seen in drug-abusing individuals. Others react negatively to the self-induced quality of substance abuse, which sets it apart from many other medical disorders in which the patient has relatively little to do with the onset or continuation of the illness. Therapists with such predominantly negative reactions will probably not do well with these patients.

Some clinicians feel that therapists occasionally need to extend themselves a little more with addicted patients than with other types of adult psychiatric patients. The dependency needs of the patients often express themselves in the doctor-patient relationship, and an occasional appropriate, concrete supportive response is probably useful, especially in the early phases of treatment. This may consist of greeting the patient warmly on entering the office, actively seeking to reestablish contact when an appointment is missed, recognizing improvements when they occur, or seeing the patient occasionally at unscheduled times if the need is present and the time is available.

## ▼ INDIVIDUAL PSYCHOTHERAPY FOR SUBSTANCE ABUSE

Many of the techniques and principles of psychotherapy used with substance-abusing patients are similar to those used in psychotherapy with other patients. However, to treat addicted patients effectively, it is important to combine general knowledge of psychotherapy with knowledge of the general factors mentioned previously, and have some understanding of the loss of control that accompanies the addiction and of the biopsychosocial consequences of addiction. In modifying the supportive-expressive form of psychotherapy for use with substance-abusing patients, Luborsky et al. (in press) identified certain special emphases that are particularly important in treating individuals with substance use disorders. These emphases, shown in the following list, are also relevant for other orientations of psychotherapy.

1. The therapist must devote much time and energy to introduce the patients to treatment and to engage them in it.
2. The treatment goals must be formulated early and kept in sight.
3. The therapist must give much attention to developing a positive relationship and supporting the patient.
4. The therapist has to keep abreast of the patient's compliance with the overall drug treatment program, which includes adherence to rules and avoiding nonprescribed drug taking. This information should come from the patient's self-report and urinalysis and may also be provided by family, friends, and other treatment staff.
5. If the patient is receiving methadone, attention should be given as to when the patient feels therapy is best, before or after the daily dose. Methadone usually is such a central part of the patient's life, that establishing an agreed-upon time for therapy around the dosing schedule could determine whether the patient engages or drops out of therapy.

Psychotherapeutic techniques from several orientations have been adapted to focus specifically on the treatment of addiction. Psychodynamic approaches to therapy for the treatment of addiction have been written about extensively (Khantzian 1985, 1986, 1987; Levin 1987). Supportive-expressive psychotherapy (Luborsky 1984), which derives from psychoanalytic therapy has been modified to address substance abuse/addiction, specifically opioid and cocaine dependence (Luborsky et al., in press; Mark and Luborsky, in press). Interpersonal psychotherapy, another supportive/dynamic model, has also been adapted for use in the treatment of opioid dependence (Rounsaville et al. 1983) and cocaine abuse/dependence (Rounsaville et al. 1985). Cognitive therapies have also addressed substance use disorders. The most prominent contributions to addiction treatment in the cognitive area are cognitive therapy (Beck and Emery 1977; Beck et al. 1990), relapse prevention (Carroll et al. 1991; Gorski 1990; Gorski and Miller 1986; Marlatt and Gordon 1985), and social learning theory (Annis 1990). Behavioral strategies have been used in combination with other treatment to aid the patient in coping with drug craving (Childress et al. 1988; O'Brien et al. 1990). Family therapy (Stanton and Todd 1982) and group therapy (LaRosa et al. 1974; Willett 1973) have also been used to treat addiction, either alone or in combination with individual therapy.

## ▼ PSYCHOTHERAPY EFFICACY WITH SUBSTANCE–ABUSING PATIENTS

It is only in the last two decades that the psychosocial components of drug abuse treatment have been the subject of scientific investigation. The vast majority of research on the efficacy of psychotherapy in the treatment of substance use disorders has concluded that psychotherapy is an effective treatment modality (Carroll et al. 1991; LaRosa et al. 1974; McLellan et al. 1986; Resnick et al. 1981; Woody et al. 1983). These studies and reviews have examined individual, family, and group psychotherapies.

The comparison of specific models of therapy for substance use disorders has become the focus of much interest. One study compared supportive-expressive psychotherapy and cognitive-behavioral therapy with standard drug counseling for opioid-addicted patients (Woody et al. 1983). It was concluded that the professional psychotherapies in addition to the drug counseling benefited patients with higher levels of psychopathology more than the drug counseling alone; however, drug counseling alone was adequately helpful for patients with low levels of psychopathology. Further, neither of the two psychotherapy models was found to be superior to the other. A cross-validation of these results showed similar trends (Woody et al. 1991).

Structural family therapy (Stanton et al. 1982) and supportive-expressive psychotherapy (Luborsky et al., in press) have been compared in the treatment of cocaine-abusing patients. It was concluded that once-a-week therapy, of either type, did not provide the necessary treatment intensity. This finding has been confirmed in later studies, as seen in a project examining once-per-week family therapy versus weekly supportive-expressive psychotherapy (Kang et al. 1991; Kleinman et al. 1990). Here, dropout rates were high, and overall abstinence did not appear to differ from that that would be expected to result from spontaneous remission. Thus several studies indicate that participation in treatment must be relatively intense, at least initially, for patients attempting to recover from addiction.

Relapse prevention and interpersonal psychotherapy, provided once per week for 12 weeks, were compared in the treatment of ambulatory cocaine-abusing patients (Carroll et al. 1991). Relapse prevention was found to be more effective than interpersonal therapy among patients with severe levels of cocaine dependence, although overall the research did not find statistically significant differences between the two types of treatment. Generally, no one type of therapy has been found to be more effective than any other in the treatment of addiction; this is consistent with much of the psychotherapy outcome research for other psychiatric disorders (Luborsky et al. 1975; Smith and Glass 1977; Smith et al. 1980).

At 6-month follow-up, Alterman (1990) reported a 50%–60% abstinence rate among cocaine-abusing patients treated in either inpatient or intensive day treatment for 1 month followed by twice-per-week therapy compared with the 19% abstinence rate for once-per-week outpatient therapy found by Kang et al. (1991). Of course, the intensity of treatment needed varies with the specific drug, the severity of the dependence, and the patient's psychosocial stability. A related study (McLellan et al. 1993) has recently examined three levels of treatment services in methadone-maintained opioid addicts: minimal services (10 minutes of counseling once per month), standard services (one full counseling session once per week), or enhanced services (standard counseling plus psychotherapy, family therapy, and vocational services available on site). Only approximately 30% of patients receiving minimum services in addition to daily methadone did well; two-thirds did very poorly and had to be administratively transferred to the standard condition. Upon transfer, most improved substantially within 6 weeks. Patients receiving enhanced services did somewhat better than those randomly assigned to the standard treatment condition. Thus there was a stepwise progression of improvement associated with receiving psychosocial services, including professional psychotherapy.

This line of research, combining methadone with psychosocial treatments, is consistent with other studies that suggest that only some substance abuse patients can be successfully treated with a purely psychotherapeutic approach (Carroll et al. 1991). This is especially true for many detoxification programs in which pharmacological intervention in addition to psychosocial treatment is usually necessary (Alterman et al. 1991).

## ▼ IMPLICATIONS FOR TREATMENT

It seems clear that psychotherapy can be effective in the treatment of substance abuse/addiction (Carroll et al. 1991; LaRosa et al. 1974; McLellan et al. 1986; Resnick et al. 1981; Woody et al. 1983). However, certain other conditions must be met in order for positive outcomes to occur.

Usually, the chemically dependent patient requires more structure and greater frequency of visits than traditional psychotherapy provides. As described previously, pharmacological treatments are often indicated in addition to psychotherapy and other psychosocial treatments. In many instances, psychotherapy appears to be most effective when combined with other treatment services, either within the context of a structured addiction treatment program (McLellan et al. 1993) or organized as needed by the individual psychotherapist (Khantzian 1987). In addition, the more traditional psychotherapies, such as cognitive-behavior, supportive-expressive, or interpersonal, may be useful only for patients experiencing clinically significant psychiatric symptoms in addition to their drug problem (Woody et al. 1985). This finding is not surprising because these psychotherapies were developed to treat anxiety, depression, and other non-drug-related psychiatric disorders and symptoms.

Thus far, research has not indicated that one kind of psychotherapy is superior to any other for the treatment of addiction, although the different models of psychodynamic, cognitive, and behavior therapy all offer some helpful strategies. It may be, however, that certain patient characteristics or comorbid psychiatric disorders suggest one model of psychotherapy over another. For example, one study found that alcoholic patients who scored high on measures of sociopathy or global psychopathology had better outcomes in coping skills treatment, whereas patients low on these dimensions did better in interactional treatment (Cooney et al. 1991). Additionally, earlier studies show that both therapist and patient qualities, including comorbid psychiatric symptoms and disorders, have a moderate influence on treatment outcome (Luborsky et al. 1985, 1986, 1988; McLellan et al. 1988). These findings highlight the importance of exploring further the question of patient-treatment matching (McLellan et al. 1980).

The following are guidelines that the clinician who is interested in treating chemically dependent patients with psychotherapy may find helpful:

1. Be familiar with the pharmacology of abused drugs, the subculture of addiction, and self-help programs.
2. Formulate clear goals early in treatment; establish a positive, supportive relationship; and keep abreast of the patient's success with abstinence and compliance in other aspects of the treatment.
3. Understand that the recovering addicted patient usually requires treatment resources in addition to psychotherapy, so the therapy is most effective when it is provided within the context of a structured treatment program or when the individual therapist takes the responsibility for connecting the patient to other services as needed.
4. Target the psychotherapy to the most psychiatrically symptomatic patients. It is this subgroup that may benefit the most from the additional resources.

## ▼ REFERENCES

Alterman AI: Day hospital verses inpatient cocaine dependence rehabilitation: an interim report, in Problems of Drug Dependence 1990, NIDA Res Monogr 105. Edited by Harris L. Rockville, MD, Department of Health and Human Services, 1990, pp 363–364

Alterman AI, O'Brien CP, McLellan AT: Differential therapeutics for substance abuse, in Clinical Textbook of Addictive Disorders. Edited by Frances RJ, Miller SI. New York, Guilford, 1991, pp 369–390

American Psychiatric Association: Diagnostic and Statistical Manual of Mental Disorders, 3rd Edition Revised. Washington, DC, American Psychiatric Association, 1987

Annis HM: Relapse to substance abuse: empirical findings within a cognitive-social learning approach. J Psychoactive Drugs 22:117–124, 1990

Ball JC, Corty E, Petroski SP, et al: Medical services provided to 2394 patients at methadone programs in three states. J Subst Abuse Treat 3:203–209, 1986

Beck AT, Emery G: Cognitive Therapy of Substance Abuse. Philadelphia, PA, Center for Cognitive Therapy, 1977

Beck AT, Wright FD, Newman CF: Cognitive Therapy of Cocaine Abuse. Philadelphia, PA, Center for Cognitive Therapy, 1990

Beutler LE: Methodology: What are the design issues involved in the defined research priorities? in Psychotherapy and Counseling in the Treatment of Drug Abuse, NIDA Res Monogr 104. Edited by Onken LS, Blaine JD. Rockville, MD, Department of Health and Human Services, 1990, pp 105–118

Borkovec TD: Control groups and comparison groups in psychotherapy outcome research, in Psychotherapy and Counseling in the Treatment of

Drug Abuse, NIDA Res Monogr 104. Edited by Onken LS, Blaine JD. Rockville, MD, U.S. Department of Health and Human Services, 1990, pp 50–65

Carroll KM, Rounsaville BJ: Can a technology model of psychotherapy research be applied to cocaine abuse treatment? in Psychotherapy and Counseling in the Treatment of Drug Abuse, NIDA Res Monogr 104. Edited by Onken LS, Blaine JD. Rockville, MD, Department of Health and Human Services, 1990, pp 91–104

Carroll KM, Rounsaville BJ, Treece FH: A comparative trial of psychotherapies for ambulatory cocaine abusers: relapse prevention and interpersonal psychotherapy. Am J Drug Alcohol Abuse 17:229–247, 1991

Childress AR, Ehrman R, McLellan AT, et al: Conditioned craving and arousal in cocaine addiction: a preliminary report, in Problems of Drug Dependence, NIDA Res Monogr 81. Rockville, MD, Department of Health and Human Services, 1988, pp 74–80

Cooney NL, Kadden RM, Litt MD, et al: Matching alcoholics to coping skills or interactional therapies: two-year follow-up results. J Consult Clin Psychol 59:598–601, 1991

Crits-Christoph P, Beebe KL, Connolly MB: Therapist effects in the treatment of drug dependence: implications for conducting comparative treatment studies, in Psychotherapy and Counseling in the Treatment of Drug Abuse, NIDA Res Monogr 104. Edited by Onken LS, Blaine JD. Rockville, MD, Department of Health and Human Services, 1990, pp 39–48

Gorski TT: The CENAPS model of relapse prevention: basic principles and procedures. J Psychoactive Drugs 22:125–133, 1990

Gorski TT, Miller MM: Staying Sober: Guide to Relapse Prevention. Independence, MO, Herald House, 1986

Hanson B, Beschner G, Walters JM: Life With Heroin: Voices from the Inner City. Lexington, MA, DC Heath and Company, 1985

Howard KI, Cox WM, Saunders SS: Attrition in substance abuse comparative treatment research: the illusion of randomization, in Psychotherapy and Counseling in the Treatment of Drug Abuse, NIDA Res Monogr 104. Edited by Onken LS, Blaine JD. Rockville, MD, Department of Health and Human Services, 1990, pp 66–79

Kang SY, Kleinman PH, Woody GE, et al: Outcomes for cocaine abusers after once-a-week psychosocial therapy. Am J Psychiatry 148:630–635, 1991

Khantzian EJ: The self-medication hypothesis of addictive disorders: focus on heroin and cocaine dependence. Am J Psychiatry 142:1259–1264, 1985

Khantzian EJ: A contemporary psychodynamic approach to drug abuse treatment. Am J Drug Alcohol Abuse 12:213–222, 1986

Khantzian EJ: The primary care therapist and patient needs in substance abuse treatment. Am J Drug Alcohol Abuse 14:159–167, 1987

Khantzian EJ, Khantzian NJ: Cocaine addiction: is there a psychological predisposition? Psychiatric Annals 14:753–759, 1984

Khantzian EJ, Treece C: DSM-III psychiatric diagnosis of narcotic addicts. Arch Gen Psychiatry 42:1067–1071, 1985

Kleinman PH, Woody GE, Todd TC, et al: Crack and cocaine abusers in outpatient psychotherapy, in Psychotherapy and Counseling in the Treatment of Drug Abuse, NIDA Res Monogr 104. Edited by Onken LS, Blaine JD. Rockville, MD, Department of Health and Human Services, 1990, pp 24–34

Lambert MJ: Conceptualizing and selecting measures of treatment outcome, in Psychotherapy and Counseling in the Treatment of Drug Abuse, NIDA Res Monogr 104. Edited by Onken LS, Blaine JD. Rockville, MD, Department of Health and Human Services, 1990, pp 80–90

LaRosa JC, Lipsius JH, LaRosa JH: Experience with a combination of group therapy and methadone maintenance in the treatment of heroin addiction. Int J Addict 9:605–617, 1974

Levin JD: Treatment of Alcoholism and Other Addictions: A Self-Psychology Approach. Northvale, NJ, Jason Aronson, 1987

Luborsky L: Principles of Psychoanalytic Psychotherapy: A Manual for Supportive-Expressive Treatment. New York, Basic Books, 1984

Luborsky L, McLellan AT, Woody GE, et al: Therapist success and its determinants. Arch Gen Psychiatry 42:602–611, 1985

Luborsky L, Crits-Christoph P, McLellan AT: Do therapists vary in their effectiveness? Findings from four outcome studies. Am J Orthopsychiatry 66:501–512, 1986

Luborsky L, Crits-Christoph P, Mintz J, et al: Who Will Benefit From Psychotherapy—Predicting Therapeutic Outcomes. New York, Basic Books, 1988

Luborsky L, Woody GE, Hole A, et al: Special adaptation of SE psychotherapy for drug dependence, in Manuals for Dynamic Psychotherapy. Edited by Barber J, Crits-Christoph P. New York, Basic Books (in press)

Mark D, Luborsky L: Manual for supportive-expressive psychotherapy for cocaine abuse, in Manuals for Dynamic Psychotherapy. Edited by Barber J, Crits-Christoph P. New York, Basic Books (in press)

Marlatt GA, Gordon J (eds): Relapse Prevention: Maintenance Strategies in the Treatment of Addictive Behaviors. New York, Guilford, 1985

McLellan AT, O'Brien CP, Luborsky L, et al: Certain types of substance abuse patients do better in certain types of treatment, in Problems of Drug Dependence, NIDA Res Monogr 34. Edited by Harris LS. U.S. Government Printing Office, USPHS, 1980, pp 123–130

McLellan AT, Childress AR, Ehrman R, et al: Extinguishing conditioned responses during opiate dependence treatment: turning laboratory findings into clinical procedures. J Subst Abuse Treat 3:33–40, 1986

McLellan AT, Woody GE, Luborsky L, et al: Is the counselor an "active ingredient" in methadone treatment? An examination of treatment success among four counselors. J Nerv Ment Dis 176:423–430, 1988

McLellan AT, Arndt IO, Metzger DS, et al: Are psychosocial services necessary in substance abuse treatment? JAMA 269:1953–1959, 1993

National Drug and Alcoholism Treatment Unit Survey (DHHS Publ No ADM-89-1626). Rockville, MD, Department of Health and Human Services, 1982

O'Brien CP, Childress AR, McLellan AT, et al: Integrating systematic cue exposure with standard treatment in recovering drug dependent patients. Addict Behav 15:355–365, 1990

Onken LS, Blaine JD: Psychotherapy and counseling research in drug abuse treatment: questions, problems, and solutions, in Psychotherapy and Counseling in the Treatment of Drug Abuse, NIDA Res Monogr 104. Edited by Onken LS, Blaine JD. Rockville, MD, Department of Health and Human Services, 1990, pp 1–5

Resnick RB, Washton AM, Stone-Washton N, et al: Psychotherapy and naltrexone in opioid dependence, in Problems of Drug Dependence, NIDA Res Monogr 34. Edited by Harris LS. Rockville, MD, U.S. Department of Health and Human Services, 1981, pp 109–115

Rounsaville BJ, Weissman MM, Kleber HD, et al: Heterogeneity of psychiatric diagnoses in treated opiate addicts. Arch Gen Psychiatry 39:161–166, 1982

Rounsaville BJ, Glazer W, Wilber CH, et al: Short-term interpersonal psychotherapy in methadone maintained opiate addicts. Arch Gen Psychiatry 40:629–636, 1983

Rounsaville BJ, Gawin FH, Kleber HD: Interpersonal psychotherapy adapted for ambulatory cocaine abusers. Am J Drug Alcohol Abuse 11:171–191, 1985

Rounsaville BJ, Foley S, Carroll KM, et al: Psychiatric diagnoses of treatment-seeking cocaine abusers. Arch Gen Psychiatry 48:43–51, 1991

Smith ML, Glass GV: Meta-analysis of psychotherapy outcome studies. Am Psychol 32:752–760, 1977

Smith M, Glass G, Miller T: The Benefits of Psychotherapy. Baltimore, MD, Johns Hopkins University, 1980

Stanton MD, Todd TC: The Family Therapy of Drug Abuse and Addiction. New York, Guilford, 1982

Washton AM: Cocaine Addiction: Treatment, Recovery, and Relapse Prevention. New York, WW Norton, 1989

Weiss RD, Mirin SM, Michael JL, et al: Psychopathology in chronic cocaine abusers. Am J Drug Alcohol Abuse 12:17–29, 1986

Willett EA: Group therapy in a methadone treatment program: an evaluation of changes in interpersonal behavior. Int J Addict 8:33–39, 1973

Woody GE, Luborsky L, McLellan AT, et al: Psychotherapy for opiate addicts: does it help? Arch Gen Psychiatry 40:639–645, 1983

Woody GE, McLellan AT, Luborsky L, et al: Psychiatric severity as a predictor of benefits from psychotherapy. Am J Psychiatry 141:1172–1177, 1985

Woody GE, McLellan AT, O'Brien CP: Research on psychopathology and addiction: treatment implications. Drug Alcohol Depend 25:121–123, 1990

Woody GE, McLellan AT, Luborsky L, et al: Psychotherapy for methadone maintained opiate addicts: a validation and cross-validation. Article presented at the annual meeting of the Society for Psychotherapy Research, Lyon, France, 1991

# elapse Prevention

*G. Alan Marlatt, Ph.D.*
*Kimberly Barrett, Ed.D.*

In this chapter, we present an overview of the relapse prevention (RP) model of treatment for substance use disorders. Because this chapter is intended to provide a general discussion of the RP model, we emphasize practical applications of the assessment and treatment techniques presented. Background research and theory leading to the development of this model can be found in earlier publications on the RP approach (Marlatt 1979, 1982; Marlatt and George 1984; Marlatt and Gordon 1985; Sandberg and Marlatt 1991). Much of the material presented in this chapter is drawn from these sources.

## ▼ WHAT IS RELAPSE PREVENTION?

*Relapse prevention* is a cognitive-behavioral treatment (Kendall and Hollon 1979) that combines behavioral skill-training procedures with cognitive intervention techniques to assist individuals in maintaining desired behavioral changes. Based in part on the principles of health psychology (e.g., Stone et al.

1979) and social-cognitive theory (Bandura 1986), RP uses a psychoeducational self-management approach to substance abuse designed to teach patients new coping responses (e.g., alternatives to addictive behavior), to modify maladaptive beliefs and expectancies concerning substance use, and to change personal habits and life-styles.

Initially, the RP model was developed as a behavioral maintenance program for use in the treatment of addictive behaviors (Marlatt 1978; Marlatt and Gordon 1980). In the addictions, the typical treatment goals are either to refrain totally from performing a target behavior—the abstinence model—or to reduce the harm or risk of ongoing habits—the harm-reduction model (Marlatt and Tapert 1993). Although the material presented in this chapter is primarily directed toward substance use disorders, the RP model may have additional applications that extend beyond drug addiction. Problems such as excessive drinking, smoking, overeating, gambling, and high-risk sexual behaviors may be considered collectively as *addictive behaviors* (Donovan and Marlatt 1988). Addictive behaviors include those acts leading to a state of immediate reward; with many addictive behaviors (especially substance abuse), the experience of immediate reinforcement (the pleasure, "high," tension-reduction, or relief associated with the act itself) is followed by delayed negative consequences such as physical discomfort or disease, social disapproval, financial loss, and decreased self-esteem. Because many treatment programs for these kinds of problems have high recidivism rates, the RP model has been applied to an increasingly broad range of behaviors (Daley 1989; Laws 1989; Wilson 1992).

## ▼ TREATMENT GOALS AND TREATMENT PHILOSOPHY

RP is one of several behavior therapy approaches to the treatment of addictive behaviors (e.g., Cox 1987; Hester and Miller 1989; Monti et al. 1989). Behavior therapists have been active in developing and evaluating a variety of empirically based techniques. *Aversion therapy* (Wilson 1987), and *covert sensitization* (Cautella 1977) have been applied in the treatment of alcohol dependence. *Cue exposure,* designed to extinguish reactivity or "craving" to substance-use cues (e.g., exposure to drug-taking paraphernalia) has been explored as a behavioral approach to smoking, drinking, and abuse of other substances such as cocaine and the opioids (Blakey and Baker 1980; Childress et al. 1986; Cooney et al. 1987). Other operant procedures, such as contingency contracting (Bigelow et al. 1981) and community reinforcement methods (Azrin et al. 1982; Hunt and Azrin 1973) have also been evaluated. In the community reinforcement method, access to family, jobs, and friends is made contingent upon continued sobriety.

The cornerstone of behavior therapy for substance abuse problems is *skills training* (Chaney et al. 1978; Monti et al. 1989). In this approach, patients are taught behavior and cognitive skills such as resisting social pressure, increased assertiveness, relaxation and stress management, and interpersonal communication (Shiffman and Wills 1985).

RP procedures can be applied in prevention and treatment designed to prevent relapse or to manage ongoing relapse problems. Maintenance strategies are designed both to anticipate and prevent the occurrence of relapse following treatment (e.g., to prevent a recent drug abuser from returning to habitual drug use) and to help patients cope with relapse if it occurs. Because RP was designed as a posttreatment

*maintenance* program, the methods can be applied regardless of the particular program or approach used during the initial stages of treatment. Once an alcoholic patient has stopped drinking, for example, RP methods can be applied toward the effective maintenance of abstinence, regardless of the methods used to initiate abstinence (e.g., attending Alcoholics Anonymous meetings, Antabuse, group therapy, aversion therapy, voluntary cessation, or some other means). RP can also be used to direct the alcoholic patient to other useful treatment modes, such as couples therapy (e.g., identification of interpersonal conflicts that may trigger drinking). One important goal of RP is to train the patient to become his or her own therapist and thus carry on the thrust of the initial treatment program after the termination of the formal therapeutic relationship. The RP model is fundamentally a self-control program in which patients are taught how to anticipate and cope effectively with problems as they arise during the posttreatment or follow-up period.

The RP model is also used to facilitate changes in personal habits and life-style to reduce the risk of physical disease or other harm associated with the addictive behavior. In this instance, the aim of the RP program is much broader in scope: to teach the individual how to reduce life-style health risks and prevent the formation of additional unhealthy habit patterns. The central motif of this approach is one of *moderation,* a balanced life-style that is midway between the opposing extremes of behavioral excess and restraint. Viewed from this more global perspective, RP can be considered as a component of the developing public health model of *harm reduction*—behavior-change programs designed to reduce the risk of ongoing addictive behavior problems (Marlatt and Tapert 1993).

The following sections present an overview of the RP model. We begin with a general discussion of the relapse process and the theoretical model as it applies specifically to the treatment of substance abuse. First, we outline high-risk situations that may trigger a lapse and the cognitive and affective reactions associated with its occurrence. Second, we describe predispositional factors or covert antecedents that may set the stage for relapse. In the final sections, we discuss assessment of intervention strategies derived from the RP model that can be used either to prevent the occurrence of relapse or to cope with the aftermath should relapse occur.

## ▼ DEFINITION OF LAPSE AND RELAPSE

Broadly considered, *relapse* is defined as any discrete violation of a self-imposed rule or set of rules governing the rate or pattern of a selected target behavior. Total abstinence, the most stringent rule one can adopt, is thus violated by a single instance of a target behavior (e.g., the first drink or use of a substance). Viewed from this absolute black/white perspective, a single *lapse* is equated with total relapse (see Figure 20–1). Although violation of the abstinence rule is the primary form of relapse we have studied in our research in substance abuse, other forms of relapse would also be included within the above definition. Violation of rules governing caloric intake imposed by a diet would also constitute a relapse, as would exceeding alcohol-consumption limits imposed in a drinking moderation program. Within this general definition of relapse, we distinguish between the first violation of the rules (the initial *lapse*) and the subsequent secondary effects in which the behavior may increase toward the original pretreatment baseline level (a full-blown *relapse*). This distinction between lapse and relapse is shown in Figure 20–2, showing the gray area of a lapse experience.

In the RP approach, relapse is viewed as a transitional process rather than an outcome failure. The relapse process consists of a series of events that may or may not be followed by a return to pretreatment baseline levels of the target behavior. It is possible to view the alcoholic individual who takes a single drink after a period of abstinence as someone who has made a single excursion over the border between abstinence and relapse. Whether this excursion or lapse is followed by a return to abstinence depends in part

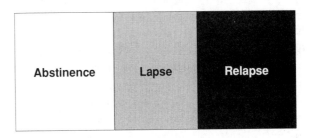

**Figure 20–2. The "gray area" model of abstinence, lapse, and relapse.**

on the expectations and attributions of the individual involved. One of the goals of RP is to provide an individual with the necessary skills and cognitive strategies to prevent a lapse from escalating into a total relapse. Rather than looking pessimistically on a lapse as a dead-end failure, the RP approach views each lapse as a fork in the road, one path returning to the former problem behavior (relapse) and the other continuing in the direction of positive change (see Figure 20–3). Instead of being viewed as an indication of failure, a lapse can be viewed more optimistically as a challenging mistake or error, an opportunity for new learning to occur.

## ▼ OVERVIEW OF HIGH-RISK SITUATIONS FOR RELAPSE

In the following overview, only the highlights of the RP model are presented. Further details on background research and theory leading to the assessment of high-risk situations can be found in studies by Cummings et al. (1980), Donovan and Marlatt (1988), and Marlatt and Gordon (1985). A schematic representation of the relapse model is shown in Figure 20–4.

To begin, we assume that the individual experiences a sense of perceived control while maintaining abstinence (or complying with other rules governing the target behavior). The target behavior is "under control" so long as it does not occur. For example, the longer the period of successful abstinence, the greater the individual's perception of self-control. This perceived control will continue until the individuals encounters a *high-risk situation*, defined broadly as any situation that poses a threat to the individual's sense of control and increases the risk of potential relapse. In an analysis of 311 initial relapse episodes

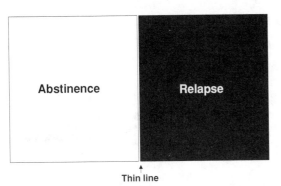

**Figure 20–1. Black-white model of abstinence versus relapse.**

obtained from patients with a variety of problem behaviors (i.e., problem drinking, smoking, heroin addiction, compulsive gambling, and overeating), three primary high-risk situations were associated with almost 75% of all the relapses reported (Cummings et al. 1980; Marlatt and Gordon 1985). A brief description of the high-risk situations associated with the highest relapse rates follows.

*Negative emotional states* (35% of all relapses in the sample): situations in which the individual is experiencing a negative (or unpleasant) emotional state, mood, or feeling such as frustration, anger, anxiety, depression, boredom, etc., prior to or occurring simultaneously with the first lapse. For example, a smoker in the sample gave the following description of a relapse episode: "It had been raining continually all week. Saturday I walked down to the basement to do laundry and I found the basement filled with a good 3 inches of water. To make things worse, as I went to turn on the light to see the extent of the damage, I got shocked from the light switch. Later that same day I was feeling real low and knew I had to have

a cigarette after my neighbor, who is a contractor, assessed the damage at over $4,000. I went to the store and bought a pack."

*Interpersonal conflict* (16% of the relapses): situations involving an ongoing or relatively recent conflict associated with any interpersonal relationship such as marriage, friendship, family members, or employer-employee relations. Arguments and interpersonal confrontations occur frequently in this category. For example, a recovering alcoholic father confronts his teenage son about having stayed out all night with the car. His son then accuses him of being "on his case all the time." The son leaves the house slamming the door. The father reports becoming angry and taking his first drink in 4 months.

*Social pressure* (20% of the sample): situations in which the individual is responding to the influence of another individual or group of individuals who exert pressure on the individual to engage in the proscribed behavior. Social pressure may be either direct (e.g., interpersonal contact with verbal persuasion) or indirect (e.g., being in the presence of others who

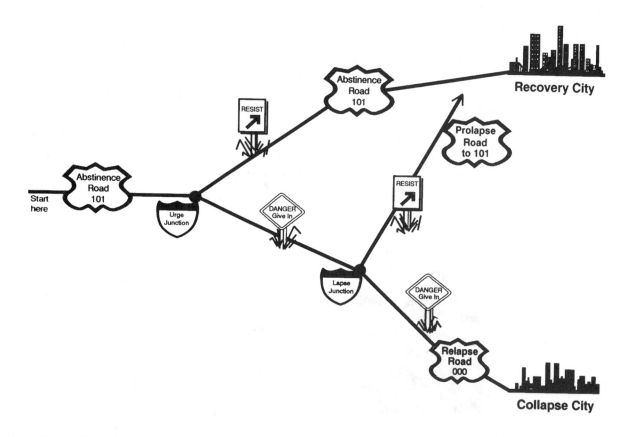

**Figure 20–3.** Forks along the road to recovery.

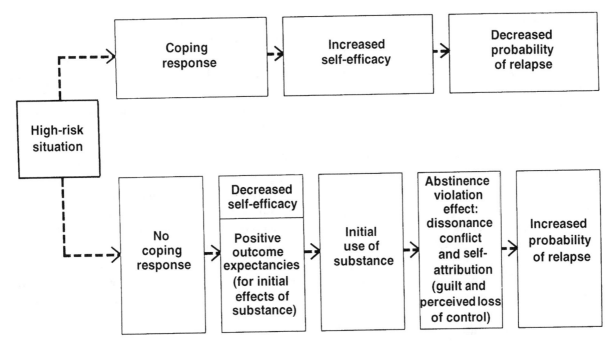

Figure 20–4. Cognitive-behavioral model of the relapse process.

are engaging in the same target behavior, even though no direct pressure is involved). Here is an example of direct social pressure given by a formerly abstinent problem drinker in our sample: "I went to my boss's house for a surprise birthday dinner for him. I got there late and as I came into the living room everyone had a drink in hand. I froze when my boss's wife asked me what I was drinking. Without thinking, I said, 'J & B on the rocks.'"

In our analyses of relapse episodes, these same three high-risk situations are frequently found to be associated with relapse, indicative of a common risk factor for a variety of addictive behaviors (i.e., problem drinking, smoking, gambling, heroin use, or overeating). Other high-risk situations described by Marlatt and Gordon (1985) include negative physical states (withdrawal), testing personal control, and responsivity to substance cues (craving, urges). This pattern of findings lends support to our hypothesis that there are common triggers that frequently initiate the relapse process.

If an individual is able to execute an effective coping response in a high-risk situation (e.g., is assertive in countering social pressures), the probability of relapse decreases. An individual who copes successfully with a high-risk situation is likely to experience a sense of mastery or perception of control. Successful

mastery of one problematic situation is often associated with an expectation of being able to cope successfully with the next challenging event. The expectancy of being able to cope with successive high-risk situations as they develop is closely associated with Bandura's notion of *self-efficacy* (Bandura 1977), defined as the individual's expectation concerning the capacity to cope with an impending situation or task. A feeling of confidence in one's abilities to cope effectively with a high-risk situation is associated with an increased perception of self-efficacy, a kind of "I know I can handle it" feeling. As the duration of the abstinence (or period of controlled use) increases, and an individual is able to cope effectively with more and more high-risk situations, perception of control increases in a cumulative fashion; the probability of relapse decreases accordingly.

What happens if an individual is unable or unwilling to cope successfully with a high-risk situation? Perhaps the individual has never acquired the coping skills involved, or the appropriate response has been inhibited by fear or anxiety. Or, perhaps the individual fails to recognize and respond to the risk involved before it is too late. For others, the anticipated rewards for indulgence may undermine motivation to resist temptation in the high-risk situation. Whatever the reason, if a coping response is not performed, the individual is likely to experience a decrease in self-efficacy, frequently coupled with a sense of helplessness and a tendency to passively give in to the situation. "It's no use, I can't handle this," is a common reaction. As self-efficacy decreases in the precipitating high-risk situation, one's expectations for coping successfully with subsequent problem situations also suffer. If the situation also involves the temptation to engage in the prohibited behavior (substance abuse) as a means of attempting to cope with the stress involved, the stage is set for a probable relapse. The probability of relapse is enhanced if the individual holds positive expectancies about the effects of the substance involved. Often the individual will anticipate the euphorogenic effects of the substance, positive effects based on past experience, while simultaneously ignoring or not attending to the delayed negative consequences involved. The lure of immediate gratification looms dominantly as the reality of the full consequences of the act recedes. For many individuals, smoking a marijuana cigarette or taking a drink has long been associated with coping with stress. "A drink would sure help me get through this," or, "If only I could have a joint, I would feel more relaxed," are commonly held beliefs. Positive outcome expectancies are a primary motivational determinant of alcohol and drug use (Marlatt and Rohsenow 1980).

The combination of being unable to cope effectively in a high-risk situation coupled with positive outcome expectancies for the effects of the habitual coping behavior (substance use) greatly increases the probability that an initial lapse will occur. On the one hand, the individual is faced with a high-risk situation with no coping response available; self-efficacy decreases as the individual feels less able to exert control. On the other hand, there is the lure of the old coping response—the drink or the drug. At this point, unless a last-minute coping response or a sudden change of circumstances occurs, the individual may cross over the abstinence border. Whether the first lapse is followed by a total relapse depends in part on the individual's attributions as to the "cause" of the lapse and the reactions that are associated with its occurrence.

The requirement of abstinence is an absolute dictum. Once someone has crossed over the line, there is no going back. From this black/white perspective (see Figure 20–1), a single drink or use of a drug is sufficient to violate the rule of abstinence: once committed, the deed cannot be undone. Unfortunately, many individuals who attempt to stop a habit, such as using drugs or drinking, perceive quitting in this "once and for all" manner. To account for the reaction to the transgression of an absolute rule, we have postulated a mechanism called the *Abstinence Violation Effect* or AVE (Curry et al. 1987; Marlatt and Gordon 1985). The AVE is postulated to occur under the following conditions. Prior to the first lapse, the individual is personally committed to an extended or indefinite period of abstinence. The intensity of the AVE varies as a function of several factors, including the degrees of prior commitment or effort expended to maintain abstinence, the duration of the abstinence period (the longer the period, the greater the effect), and the subjective value or importance of the prohibited behavior to the individual. We hypothesize that the AVE is characterized by two key cognitive-affective elements: cognitive dissonance (conflict and guilt) and a personal attribution effect (blaming the self as the cause of the relapse). Individuals who experience an intense AVE following a lapse often experience a motivation crisis (demoralization reaction) that undermines their commitment to abstinence goals.

## ▼ COVERT ANTECEDENTS OF RELAPSE

In the foregoing discussion of the immediate determinants and reactions to relapse, the high-risk situation is viewed as the precipitating or triggering situation associated with the initial lapse or first "slip" following a period of abstinence or controlled use. In many of the relapse episodes we have studied, the first lapse is precipitated in a high-risk situation that the individual unexpectedly encounters. In most of these instances, the individual is not expecting the high-risk situation to occur and/or is generally ill-prepared to cope effectively with the circumstances as they arise. Quite often, the individual will suddenly find him- or herself in a rapidly escalating situation that cannot be dealt with effectively. For example, one of our patients who had a serious drinking problem experienced her first lapse after several weeks of abstinence when she treated a new friend to lunch. A last-minute change of plans led them to eat at a restaurant that served alcoholic beverages. Just moments after their arrival, a cocktail waitress approached their table and asked for drink orders. Our patient's friend ordered a cocktail first, and then the waitress turned to the patient saying, "And you?" She too ordered a drink, the first of a series of events that culminated in a full-blown relapse. As the patient said later, "I didn't plan it and I wasn't prepared for it."

In other relapse episodes, however, the high-risk situation appears to be the last link in a chain of events preceding the first lapse. For example, another patient was a compulsive gambler who came to us for help in controlling his habit, a habit that had caused him numerous marital and financial problems (Marlatt and Gordon 1985). Before coming to us, he had managed to abstain from all gambling for approximately 6 months, followed by a relapse and an inability to regain abstinence. We asked the patient, a resident of Seattle, Washington, to describe this last relapse episode. "There's nothing much to talk about," he began. "I was in Reno and I started gambling again." Obviously, Reno, Nevada, is a high-risk city for any gambler trying to maintain abstinence. We then asked him to describe the events preceding his arrival in Reno. A close analysis of this chain of events led us to conclude that this patient had covertly set up or "planned" his relapse. Although he strongly denied his responsibility in this covert planning process, there were clearly a number of choice-points (forks in the road) preceding the relapse where the patient "chose" an alternative that led him closer to the brink of relapse. He finally ended up in a downtown Reno casino putting a dollar in a slot machine, an event that triggered a weekend-long binge of costly gambling. It was as if he had placed himself in a situation so risky that it would take a "moral Superman" to resist the temptation to resume gambling.

Why do some patients appear to set up their own relapse? From a cost-benefit perspective, a relapse can be seen as a rational choice (or a justified gamble). The benefit is swift in coming: a payoff of immediate gratification. The reward of instant gratification is seen to outweigh the cost of potential negative effects that may or may not occur sometime in the distant future. Why not take a chance when this time the outcome might be different? Cognitive distortions such as *denial* and *rationalization* make it much easier to set up one's own relapse episode; one may deny both the intent to relapse and the importance of long-range negative consequences. There are also many excuses

one can use to rationalize the act of indulgence.

*Denial* and *rationalization* are cognitive distortion mechanisms that go hand in hand in the covert planning of a relapse episode. These two defense mechanisms may combine to influence the individual to make certain uninformed choices or decisions as part of a chain of events leading ultimately to relapse. We hypothesize that an individual headed for a relapse often makes a number of mini-decisions over time, each of which brings the individual closer to the brink of succumbing to or creating a high-risk situation. The term *apparently irrelevant decisions* is used to describe these choices. An example is that of the abstinent drinker who buys a bottle of sherry to take home, "just in case guests drop by." In our gambler case study, a last-minute decision was made to expand a driving trip to eastern California to include a visit to Lake Tahoe, just a few miles from Reno. In these examples, the individual sets the stage for relapse through a series of apparently irrelevant decisions, each moving him or her one step closer to relapse. A final advantage in setting up a relapse in this manner is that the individual may attempt to avoid assuming personal responsibility for the relapse episode itself. By putting oneself in an impossibly tempting high-risk situation, one can claim being "overwhelmed" by external circumstances that are "impossible" to resist. There is almost nothing a gambler can do to resist the temptation of a "downtown Reno" situation, but he or she can accept responsibility for plotting the chain of events that led to Reno. By doing so, it is possible to train an individual to recognize early warning signals that precede a relapse and how to plan and execute a series of intervention strategies before it is too late to do anything.

One of the most tempting rationalizations is that the desire to yield to temptation is justified. Our research findings and clinical experience suggest that the degree of *life-style balance* has a significant impact on the individual's desire for indulgence or immediate gratification (Marlatt and Gordon 1985). Here, we are defining *balance* as the degree of equilibrium that exists in one's daily life between those activities perceived as external demands (or "shoulds") and those perceived as activities engaged in for pleasure or self-fulfillment (the "wants"). Paying bills or performing routine chores or menial tasks at work would count highly as shoulds for many individuals. At the other end of the scale are the wants, activities the individual enjoys or likes to perform (e.g., going fishing, taking time off for lunch with a friend, engaging in a creative work task). Other activities represent a mixture of wants and shoulds. We find that if a patient's life-style is encumbered with a preponderance of perceived shoulds, this is often associated with an increased perception of self-deprivation and a corresponding desire for indulgence and gratification. It is as if the individual who spends his or her entire day engaged in activities high in external "should" demands then attempts to balance this disequilibrium by engaging in an excessive want or self-indulgence at the end of the day (e.g., drinking to excess in the evening). The patient may rationalize this behavior by saying, "I owe myself a drink or two—I deserve a break today!"

## ▼ ASSESSMENT AND SPECIFIC INTERVENTION STRATEGIES

In this section, we present highlights of RP assessment and intervention strategies. We first discuss strategies designed to teach the patient to recognize and cope with high-risk situations that may precipitate a lapse, and to modify cognitions and other reactions to prevent a single lapse from developing into a full-blown relapse. Explicitly focused on the high-risk situations for relapse, these procedures are referred to collectively as *specific RP intervention strategies*. Second, we go beyond the micro-analysis of the initial lapse and present strategies designed to modify the patient's life-style and to identify and cope with covert determinants of relapse. We refer to these procedures as *global RP self-control strategies*. In selecting techniques from the material to be presented in the remaining sections, it should be kept in mind that the RP model can be applied either as an "add-on" program, in which techniques are introduced as an addition to an already existing substance abuse treatment program, or as a general self-control approach designed to develop and maintain a balanced life-style. A complete application of the RP model would integrate both global (life-style) and specific intervention techniques.

Both specific and global RP strategies can be grouped in three main categories: skill training, cognitive reframing, and life-style intervention. *Skill-training strategies* include both behavioral and cognitive responses to cope with high-risk situations.

*Cognitive reframing* procedures are designed to provide the patients with alternative cognitions concerning the nature of the habit-change process (i.e., to view it as a learning process), to introduce coping imagery to deal with urges and early warning signals, and to reframe reactions to the initial lapse (restructuring of the AVE). Finally, *life-style balancing strategies* (e.g., meditation, mindfulness, and exercise) are designed to strengthen the patient's global coping capacity and to reduce the frequency and intensity of urges and cravings that are often the product of an unbalanced life-style.

Which of the various intervention techniques should be applied with a particular patient? It is possible to combine techniques into a standardized package, with each patient receiving identical components, if the purpose is to evaluate the effectiveness of a package RP program. Most therapists, however, will be adapting the RP model with patients in an applied clinical setting. In contrast with those who deal with the demands of treatment outcome research, those working in the clinical area typically prefer to develop a tailor-made program of techniques for each patient. The individualized approach is the one we recommend for implementation of RP with most patient problems. Particular techniques should be selected based on a carefully conducted assessment program (Donovan and Marlatt 1988). Therapists are encouraged to select intervention procedures based on their initial evaluation and assessment of the patient's substance abuse problem and general life-style pattern.

The possibility of moderation as an alternative to abstinence is the single most controversial issue associated with treatment planning. Resistance to controlled drinking in the treatment of alcohol abuse and dependence has intensified in the traditional *disease model* or *chemical dependency* programs in the United States. Because a complete discussion of the controversy is beyond the scope of this chapter, the reader is referred to other publications on the topic (e.g., Heather and Robertson 1987; Marlatt 1983; Marlatt et al., in press). As a form of secondary prevention or harm reduction, controlled drinking may work best for those who are beginning to develop problems with their drinking rather than as a remedial treatment program for individuals who have developed a long-term dependence on alcohol (Baer et al. 1992; Kivlahan et al. 1990). Initial reduction of alcohol use rather than abstinence may also be used as a motivational tool (Miller and Rollnick 1991) to motivate otherwise resistant patients to seek help.

When abstinence has been identified as the goal of treatment, the overall aim of specific intervention procedures is to teach the patient to anticipate and cope with the possibility of relapse, to recognize and cope with high-risk situations that may precipitate a slip, and to modify cognitions and other reactions to prevent a single lapse from developing into a full-blown relapse. Figure 20–5 shows a schematic overview of the specific RP intervention techniques. The first step in the prevention of relapse is to teach the patient to recognize high-risk situations that may precipitate or trigger a relapse. Here, the earlier one becomes aware of being involved in a chain of events that increases the probability of a slip or lapse, the sooner one can intervene by performing an appropriate coping skill. Patients are taught to recognize and respond to warning signals (*discriminative stimuli*) associated with entering a high-risk situation and to use these signals as reminders to engage in alternative or remedial action.

An essential aspect of teaching patients to better handle high-risk situations is to help them to identify and anticipate these situations. Earlier we discussed prototypic kinds of high-risk situations. However, ultimately the identification of high-risk situations is an individualized question requiring ideographic assessment procedures. *Self-monitoring procedures* (keeping a diary or daily tally) offer an effective method for assessing high-risk situations whenever it is possible to have patients keep a record of their addictive behavior for a baseline period prior to treatment. As little as 10 days of self-monitoring data can often highlight situational influences and skill deficits that underlie an addictive behavior pattern. If the patient is already abstinent, monitoring strong urges or cravings can provide similar information.

Determining the adequacy of preexisting coping abilities is a critical assessment target. In a treatment outcome investigation aimed at teaching alcoholic patients to handle situational temptations, Chaney et al. (1978) devised the Situational Competency Test to measure coping ability. In this technique, the patient is presented with a series of written or audiotaped descriptions of potential relapse situations. Each description ends with a prompt for the patient to respond. Later, the patient's responses to the scenes can be scored on a number of dimensions, including

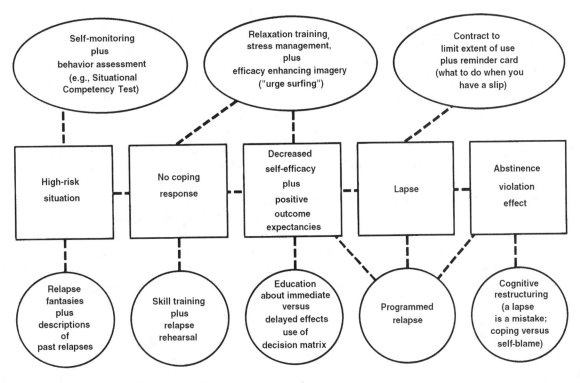

**Figure 20–5.  Relapse prevention: specific intervention strategies.**

response duration and latency, degree of compliance, and specification of alternative behaviors. A similar technique involved the use of *self-efficacy ratings,* in which the patient, and perhaps spouse, are presented with a list of potential relapse situations (Annis and Davis 1988). For each situation, the patient uses a rating scale to estimate the subjective expectation of successful coping. Ratings across a wide range of situations enable the individual to identify both problematic situations and skill deficits in need of remedial training. Results from these types of assessment tools can later dictate the focus of skill-training procedures.

Carefully administered assessment procedures will enable the individual to identify many high-risk situations. The patient must then learn an alternative approach for responding to these situations. A first step in this new approach is to recognize that high-risk situations are best perceived as discriminative stimuli signaling the need for behavior change in the same way that road signs signal the need for alternative action. Viewed in this way, high-risk situations can be seen as junctures where choices are made rather than as inevitable and uncontrollable challenges that must be endured. In this light, the choice to simply avoid or take a detour around risky situations becomes more available to the individual. However, routine avoidance of particular high-risk situations is unrealistic. Therefore, patients must acquire coping skills that enable them to cope with these situations as they arise. The specific coping skills to be taught will depend on whether the existing deficiencies are due to actual skill deficits or response inhibition. An individual who has never learned or mastered the skills required to better cope with the high-risk situation needs remedial skill-training. In response inhibition, an individual has already acquired the skills needed to cope with the situation but is unable to execute them because of inhibiting anxiety and/or conflicted motivation. In this instance, skill-training focuses on interventions designed to disinhibit the appropriate behavior, either by reducing anxiety (e.g., relaxation training) or by working on motivational resistance to active coping.

Remedial skills training necessitated by identification of coping skill deficits is the cornerstone of the RP treatment program. When the individual lacks coping skills, a variety of coping skills can be taught. The content of the skill-training program is variable and will depend on the needs of the individual. Pos-

sible content areas include assertiveness, stress management, relaxation training, anger management, communication skills, marital therapy, and general social and/or dating skills.

Along with education about the long-range negative effects of excessive substance use on physical health and social well-being, a *decision matrix* allows patients to examine both the immediate and delayed effects of substance usage, which may help counter the tendency of patients to think only of the initial pleasant short-term effects. In skill-training, the actual teaching procedures are based on the work of McFall (1976) and other investigators. The range of methods includes behavior rehearsal, instruction, coaching, evaluative feedback, modeling, and role playing. In addition, cognitive self-instructional methods introduced by Meichenbaum (1977) have proven especially valuable. For troubleshooting and consolidating the newly acquired skills, regular homework assignments are an essential ingredient in skill training.

In some instances, it is impractical to rehearse the new coping skills in real-life situations. This problem can be surmounted through *relapse rehearsal methods.* In this procedure, the patient is instructed to imagine being involved in actual high-risk situations and performing more adaptive coping behaviors and thoughts. The emphasis here is on active coping rather than on resisting temptation. The patient is thus encouraged to visualize that he or she is successfully handling the difficult situation through effective coping instead of exercising willpower. To emphasize self-efficacy enhancement, the patient can be instructed to imagine that the rehearsed experience is accompanied by mounting feelings of competence and confidence.

That the patient may fail to effectively employ these coping strategies and experience a slip must be anticipated. The patient's postslip reaction is a pivotal intervention point in the RP model because it determines the degree of escalation from a single, isolated lapse to a full-blown relapse. The first step in anticipating and dealing with this reaction is to devise an explicit therapeutic contract to limit the extent of use if a lapse occurs. The actual specifications of the contract can be worked out individually with the patient. However, the fundamental method of intervention after a lapse is the use of cognitive restructuring to counteract the cognitive and affective components of the AVE. It may be helpful in this regard to have the patient carry a wallet-sized reminder card with instructions to read and follow in the event of a slip. The text of this card should include the name and phone number of a therapist or treatment center to be called as well as the cognitive reframing antidote to the AVE.

## ▼ GLOBAL LIFE-STYLE STRATEGIES

The final thrust in the RP self-management program is the development of global intervention procedures for life-style change. It is insufficient to just teach patients mechanistic skills for handling high-risk situations and regulating consumption. A comprehensive RP self-management program also should attempt to improve the patient's overall life-style to increase the capacity to cope with more pervasive stress factors serving as antecedents to high-risk situations. To accomplish this training, a number of treatment strategies have been devised to short-circuit the covert antecedents to relapse and promote mental and physical wellness. A schematic representation of the global self-control strategies used in the RP approach is shown in Figure 20–6.

As discussed previously, a persistent and continuing disequilibrium between shoulds and wants can pave the way for relapse by producing a chronic sense of deprivation. As these feelings mount, the individual may experience a growing desire for self-indulgence. For some patients, substance use is viewed as a means of restoring balance in an "unfairly" lopsided equation. This desire for indulgence translates into urges, cravings, and distortions that permit a patient to "unintentionally" meander closer to the brink of relapse.

An effective way to induce patients to view this disequilibrium as a precursor of relapse is to have them self-monitor wants and shoulds. By keeping a daily record of duties and obligations on the one hand and enjoyable pleasures on the other, the patient becomes aware of the sources of imbalance. Next, the patient is encouraged to seek a restoration of balance by engaging daily in healthy life-style habits or *positive addictions* (Glasser 1976). The advantage of this shift from negative (substance abuse) to positive addiction lies in the latter's capacity to contribute to-

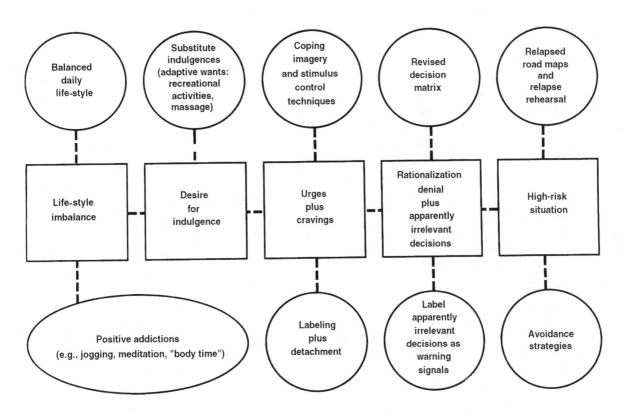

**Figure 20–6.** Relapse prevention: global life-style strategies.

ward the individual's long-term health and well-being while also providing an adaptive coping response for life stressors and relapse situations. As long-range health benefits accrue, the individual begins to develop more self-confidence and self-efficacy.

Despite the efficacy of these techniques for counteracting feelings of deprivation that would otherwise predispose the individual toward relapse, occasional urges and cravings may still surface from time to time. As indicated in Figure 20–6, various *urge control procedures* are recommended. Sometimes urges and cravings are directly triggered by external cues such as the sight of one's favorite beer mug in the kitchen cabinet. The frequency of these externally triggered urges can be substantially reduced by employing simple *stimulus control* techniques aimed at minimizing exposure to these cues. In some instances, avoidance strategies offer the most effective way of reducing the frequency of externally triggered urges.

In teaching patients to cope with urge and craving experiences, it is important to emphasize that the discomfort associated with these internal events is natural. Indeed, urges can be likened to waves in the sea: they rise, crest, and fall. Using this "urge-surfing" metaphor, we encourage the patient to wait out the urge, to look forward to the downside, and to maintain balance when the urge wave is peaking.

Recall that urges and cravings may not always operate at a conscious level but may become masked by cognitive distortions and defense mechanisms. As such, they still exert a potent influence by allowing for apparently irrelevant decisions that inch the individual closer to relapse. To counter this, we train the patient to see through these self-deceptions by recognizing their true meanings. Explicit self-talk can help in making apparently irrelevant decisions seem more relevant. By acknowledging to oneself that certain mini-decisions (e.g., keeping a bottle of wine at home for friends dropping over) actually increase the risk of relapse, the patient may be able to identify these decisions as early warning signals. An important objective in these urge-control techniques is to enable the individual to externalize urges and cravings and to view them with objective detachment. Another way to achieve this detachment is to encourage the patient to deliberately label the urge as soon as it registers into consciousness. Urges should be viewed as natural occurrences in response to environmental and life-style forces rather than as signs of treatment failure and indicators of future relapse.

## ▼ SOCIAL SUPPORT IN COUPLES AND FAMILIES

The importance of family involvement and social support in recovery from alcoholism had been emphasized by a number of authors (Catalano and Hawkins 1985; Jacob et al. 1983; Kaufman 1985; Kaufman and Kaufmann 1979; Moos et al. 1990; Steinglass 1979).

Several clinicians and researchers have recently extended the RP model to treatment with couples and families (Cawthra et al. 1991; Daley and Raskin 1991; McCrady 1989; O'Farrell 1991). Myers and Brown (1990) report improved outcome in adolescent abstinence when social support, situational appraisal, and problem-focused coping skills are used in potential relapse situations. O'Farrell (1991) summarizes promising results with couples who were treated with methods that used behavioral marital therapy (BMT) in conjunction with RP. This combination of interventions with couples can be used to help facilitate the initial motivation to change in the alcoholic individual and to promote the use of problem solving and communications skills to increase positive interactions between spouses. The program is designed to stabilize the marriage while the alcoholic individual is trying to maintain sobriety and to teach both members of the couple how to recognize and cope with triggers that could potentially lead to relapse. Available data show more days of abstinence and marital gains made in the recovery process when BMT and RP are combined.

Cawthra et al. (1991) discuss the use of family group therapy with RP. Participants include alcoholic patients and their family members, meeting in a format in which emotional warnings of relapse are discussed, as well as using the shared expertise of the group to develop problem solving skills that focus on emotional, cognitive, and behavioral aspects of the relapse process in families. Patient attendance in the RP program was improved through the use of family involvement in the group.

Steinglass (1987) provides an extensive analysis of both variations and similarities in alcoholic family process. In an approach that integrates both a family systems and developmental view of alcoholism, Steinglass emphasizes the heterogeneous nature of these families while also discussing the discrete, alcohol-centered regulatory mechanisms that govern alcoholic family interactions and short-term problem-solving efforts. The expression of affect is often a cue that problem solving must occur; however, it is the use of alcohol that provides a means by which both positive and/or negative affect can be expressed (Jacob et al. 1985; Steinglass 1987). For example, consider a husband who arrives home late for dinner and complains to his wife and children about his job dissatisfaction. His wife, in turn, voices her upset about the excessive number of hours that he is working and thus unavailable to the family. As their parents begin to argue, the children leave the table and disappear to their rooms. Dad opens a bottle of wine. After he has a few drinks, he apologizes to his wife for his frequent evenings away from home. She accepts his apology, and they retire to the living room to talk affectionately about past romantic times when life was not so hectic. The recognition of these distinctive, short-term problem-solving behaviors, and repetitive interactional sequences described in family systems models of alcoholism, provide new directions for helping families to understand, recognize, and change behavioral patterns that lead to relapse and vulnerability to future alcohol use.

## ▼ CONCLUSION

The empirical underpinnings of the RP model have been reviewed by Marlatt and Gordon (1985). Additional recent applications of the RP model have been presented as well (Brownell et al. 1986; Chiauzzi 1991; Daley 1989; Daley and Raskin 1991; Wanigaratne et al. 1990). Research is currently under way on the treatment efficacy of RP, expanding the model to work with couples, families, and adolescents. Research on the role of expectancies (self-efficacy and outcome expectancies) and coping skills in the habit-change process (Shiffman and Wills 1985) provide general support for the RP model.

## ▼ REFERENCES

Annis HM, Davis CS: Assessment of expectancies in alcohol dependent clients, in Assessment of Addictive Behaviors: Behavioral, Cognitive, and Physiological Processes. Edited by Donovan DM, Marlatt GA. New York, Guilford, 1988, pp 84–111

Azrin NH, Sisson RW, Meyers RW, et al: Alcoholism treatment by disulfiram and community reinforcement therapy. J Behav Ther Exp Psychiatry 13:105–112, 1982

Baer JS, Marlatt GA, Kivlahan DR, et al: An experimental test of three methods of alcohol risk-reduction with young adults. J Consult Clin Psychol 60:974–979, 1992

Bandura A: Self-efficacy: toward a unifying theory of behavior change. Psychol Rev 84:191–215, 1977

Bandura A: Social Foundations of Thought and Action: A Social Cognitive Theory. Englewood Cliffs, NJ, Prentice-Hall, 1986

Bigelow G, Stitzer ML, Griffiths RR, et al: Contingency management approaches to drug self-administration and drug abuse: efficacy and limitations. Addict Behav 6:241–252, 1981

Blakey R, Baker T: An exposure approach to alcohol abuse. Behav Res Ther 18:319–325, 1980

Brownell KD, Marlatt GA, Lichtenstein E, et al: Understanding and preventing relapse. Am Psychol 41:765–782 1986

Catalano RF, Hawkins JD: Project skills: preliminary results from a theoretically based aftercare experiment. NIDA Res Monogr 58:157–181, 1985

Cautella JR: The treatment of alcoholism by covert sensitization. Psychotherapy: Theory, Research, and Practice 7:86–90, 1977

Cawthra E, Borrego N, Emrick C: Involving family members in the prevention of relapse: an innovative approach. Alcoholism Treatment Quarterly 8:101–112, 1991

Chaney EF, O'Leary MR, Marlatt GA: Skills training with alcoholics. J Consult Clin Psychol 46:1092–1104, 1978

Chiauzzi EJ: Preventing Relapse in the Addictions: A Biopsychosocial Approach. New York, Pergamon, 1991

Childress RF, McLellan AT, O'Brien CP: Role of conditioning factors in the development of drug dependence. Psychiatr Clin North Am 9:413–425, 1986

Cooney NL, Gillespie RA, Baker LH, et al: Cognitive changes after alcohol cue exposure. J Consult Clin Psychol 55:150–155, 1987

Cox WM (ed): Treatment and Prevention of Alcohol Problems: A Resource Manual. Orlando, FL, Academic Press, 1987

Cummings C, Gordon JR, Marlatt GA: Relapse: strategies of prevention and prediction, in The Addictive Behaviors: Treatment of Alcoholism, Drug

Abuse, Smoking, and Obesity. Edited by Miller WR. London, Pergamon, 1980

Curry SJ, Marlatt GA, Gordon JR: Abstinence violation effect: validation of an attributional construct with smoking cessation. J Consult Clin Psychol 55:145–149, 1987

Daley DC (ed): Relapse: Conceptual, Research, and Clinical Perspectives. New York, Haworth, 1989

Daley D, Raskin M: Relapse prevention and treatment effectiveness studies, in Treating the Chemically Dependent and Their Families. Edited by Daley D, Raskin M (eds). Newbury Park, CA, Sage, 1991

Donovan DM, Marlatt GA (eds): Assessment of Addictive Behaviors: Behavioral, Cognitive, and Physiological Processes. New York, Guilford, 1988

Glasser W: Positive Addiction. New York, Harper & Row, 1976

Heather N, Robertson I (eds): Controlled Drinking, 2nd Edition. London, Methuen, 1987

Hester R, Miller W: Handbook of Alcoholism Treatment Approaches: Effective Alternatives. New York, Pergamon, 1989

Hunt GM, Azrin NH: A community-reinforcement approach to alcoholism. Behav Res Ther 11:91–104, 1973

Jacob T, Dunn NJ, Leonard K: Patterns of alcohol use and family stability. Alcohol Clin Exp Res 7:382–385, 1983

Jacob T, Dunn NJ, Leonard K, et al: Alcohol-related impairments in male alcoholics and the psychiatric symptoms of their spouses: an attempt to replicate. Am J Drug Alcohol Abuse 11:55–67, 1985

Kaufman E: Substance Abuse and Family Therapy. Orlando, FL, Grune & Stratton, 1985

Kaufman E, Kaufmann P: Family Therapy of Drug and Alcohol Abuse. New York, Gardner Press, 1979

Kendall PC, Hollon SD (eds): Cognitive-Behavioral Interventions: Theory, Research, and Procedures. New York, Academic Press, 1979

Kivlahan DR, Marlatt GA, Fromme K, et al: Secondary prevention with college drinkers: evaluation of an alcohol skills training program. J Consult Clin Psychol 58:805–810, 1990

Laws R (ed): Relapse Prevention With Sex Offenders. New York, Guilford, 1989

Marlatt GA: Craving for alcohol, loss of control and relapse: a cognitive-behavioral analysis, in Alcoholism: New Directions in Behavioral Research and Treatment. Edited by Nathan PE, Marlatt GA, Loberg T. New York, Plenum, 1978, pp 271–314

Marlatt GA: Alcohol use and problem drinking: a cognitive-behavioral analysis, in Cognitive-Behavioral Interventions: Theory, Research, and Procedures. Edited by Kendall PC, Hollon SD. New York, Academic Press, 1979, pp 319–355

Marlatt GA: Relapse prevention: a self-control program for the treatment of addictive behaviors, in Adherence, Compliance, and Generalization in Behavioral Medicine. Edited by Stuart RB. New York, Brunner/Mazel, 1982, pp 329–378

Marlatt GA: The controlled drinking controversy: a commentary. Am Psychol 38:1097–1110, 1983

Marlatt GA, George WH: Relapse prevention: introduction and overview of the model. British Journal of Addiction 79:261–273, 1984

Marlatt GA, Gordon JR: Determinants of relapse: implications for the maintenance of behavior change, in Behavioral Medicine: Changing Health Lifestyles. Edited by Davidson PO, Davidson SM. New York, Brunner/Mazel, 1980, pp 410–452

Marlatt GA, Gordon J (eds): Relapse Prevention: Maintenance Strategies in the Treatment of Addictive Behaviors. New York, Guilford, 1985

Marlatt GA, Rohsenow DR: Cognitive processes in alcohol use: expectancy and the balanced placebo design, in Advances in Substance Abuse, Vol 1. Edited by Mello NK. Greenwich, CT, JAI Press, 1980, pp 159–199

Marlatt GA, Tapert SF: Harm reduction: reducing the risk of addictive behavior, in Addictive Behaviors Across the Lifespan. Edited by Baer JS, Marlatt GA, McMahon B. Newbury Park, CA, Sage Publications, 1993, pp 243–273

Marlatt GA, Larimer ME, Baer JS, et al: Harm reduction with alcohol problems: moving behind the controlled drinking controversy. Behavior Therapy (in press)

McCrady B: Extending relapse models to couples. Addict Behav 14:69–74, 1989

McFall RM: Behavioral Training: A Skill-Acquisition Approach to Clinical Problems. Morristown, NJ, General Learning Press, 1976

Meichenbaum D: Cognitive-Behavioral Modification. New York, Plenum, 1977

Miller WR, Rollnick S: Motivational Interviewing. New York, Guilford, 1991

Monti PM, Abrams DB, Kadden RM, et al: Treating Alcohol Dependence. New York, Guilford, 1989

Moos RH, Finney JW, Cronkite RC: Alcoholism Treatment: Process and Outcome. New York, Oxford

University Press, 1990

Myers, MG, Brown SA: Coping responses and relapse among adolescent substance abusers. J Subst Abuse 2:117–189, 1990

O'Farrell T: Using couples therapy in the treatment of alcoholism. Family Dynamics of Addiction Quarterly 1:39–45, 1991

Sandberg GG, Marlatt GA: Relapse prevention, in Clinical Manual of Chemical Dependence. Edited by Ciraulo DA, Shader RI. Washington, DC, American Psychiatric Press, 1991, pp 377–399

Shiffman S, Wills TA (eds): Coping and Substance Abuse. New York, Academic Press, 1985

Steinglass P: Family therapy with alcoholics, in Family Therapy of Drug and Alcohol Abuse. Edited by Kaufman E, Kaufmann P. New York, Gardner Press, 1979, pp 147–187

Steinglass P: The Alcoholic Family. New York, Basic Books, 1987

Stone GC, Cohen F, Adler NE: Health Psychology. San Francisco, CA, Jossey-Bass, 1979

Wanigaratne S, Wallace W, Pullin J, et al: Relapse prevention for addictive behaviors: a manual for therapists. London, Blackwell Scientific, 1990

Wilson GT: Chemical aversion conditioning as a treatment for alcoholism: a re-analysis. Behav Res Ther 25:503–516, 1987

Wilson PH (ed): Principles and Practice of Relapse Prevention. New York, Guilford, 1992

# Treatment Modalities

*Subsection 3B: Group and Family Therapy*

# Group Therapy

*Sarah J. Golden, Ph.D.*
*Edward J. Khantzian, M.D.*
*William E. McAuliffe, Ph.D.*

The group therapy approach in the treatment of addiction has traditionally served as the most popular solution to the problem of addiction and is currently the treatment of choice as addictions are increasingly recognized in our society. The suffering and disruption of lives caused by substance abuse and dependence, and the heightened awareness of "hidden" addictive disorders, such as eating, sex, and gambling, and of the comorbidity and substitution of one addiction for another (Flores 1988) have trained our attention anew on the question of what is to be done. Whereas the controversy over the etiology and conceptualizations of addiction continues unabated, there appears to be an often unacknowledged consensus about the advantages of group treatment over individual approaches in addressing this problem. Thus whereas the origins of addiction to substances may be diversely viewed as physiological, intrapsychic, social and environmental, or moral and volitional, almost all these conceptual rivals have advocated the group approach as a remedy.

Group approaches are as wide ranging in form as the theories that give rise to them. Self-help "fellowships" of Alcoholics Anonymous (AA); time-limited psychoeducational and cognitive-behavioral models; and open-ended, psychodynamic group therapies adhere not only to different assumptions about the nature of addiction but also to different practices in the management of and recovery from addiction.

What all group approaches share is an appreciation of the healing power of the connection with others, what Herman (1992) has called "the restoration of social bonds" that "begins with the discovery that one is not alone" (p. 215). Psychoanalytic thinking holds that the group experience addresses the "universal need to belong, to establish a state of psychological unity with others, [representing] a covert wish to restore an earlier state of unconflicted well-being inherent in the exclusive union with the mother" (Tuttman describing the work of Scheidlinger in Roth et al. 1990, pp. 15–16). Yalom (1983), an existential group theorist, holds that in a group the "disconfirmation of the feeling of uniqueness offers considerable relief and a 'welcome to the human race' experience" (p. 41). Orford (1985) sees the self-help group and therapeutic community as using public testimony, social support, and social coercion to guide the individual through a "moral passage" to forge a new social identity. In the respite from the shame, isolation, and loneliness of addiction that the group offers (Khantzian 1986), and in the possibilities for both support and confrontation that it provides, the group approach continues to hold its own as a force for managing and changing addictive behavior.

## ▼ GROUPS AND ADDICTION

Historically, the most widely accepted approach to addiction is the group, with the kind of group reflecting a particular view of addiction. Orford attributes the popularity and success of the self-help group, epitomized by AA, to its ability to "fuse the disease and the moral perspectives," to offer both a practical explanation and a corrective spiritual and moral approach to the problem of addiction (Orford 1985 p. 309). Significantly, AA was founded in 1935 by two men, Bill Wilson and Dr. Bob, in an attempt to help each other. Their fledgling organization derived from the model of a Christian fellowship, with its "ideas of self-examination, acknowledgment of character defects, restitution for harm done to others, and working with others" (Orford 1985, p. 309).

Change in the self-help group takes place in a public forum. Orford (1985) emphasizes that, beyond support, this forum promotes the expectation to conform to certain values: the group provides this "new set of attitudes and values, and it is to the group's ideology or 'will' that the novice must submit if he or she is to become a successful member" (p. 303). A wider range of group processes are described by Khantzian and Mack (1989) as accomplishing change in the group: they see support, surrender, spirituality, and altruism serving as the therapeutic and transformational elements. After enjoying five decades of growth, AA has more recently served as a model for 12-step programs addressing many other addictive behaviors such as drug taking and gambling.

The concept of the individual's submission to the group's ideology has perhaps found its fullest expression in therapeutic communities for the treatment of addiction. Synanon, established in the 1960s to address heroin addiction, aggressively used the group to change attitudes through confinement, structure, daily work assignments, and often demanding interpersonal confrontation (Cherkas 1965). This "total"

group approach, in which every aspect of daily life is regimented, continues to thrive in such programs as Daytop and Phoenix House. The therapeutic community model, with group therapy as its mainstay, is also to be found in shorter-term "detox" and intensive inpatient treatments for a wide range of addictions, including cocaine, narcotics, eating disorders, and gambling.

Other major group approaches in the treatment of addiction have developed from the cognitive-behavioral and psychoanalytic, psychodynamic clinical traditions. From these schools of thought have emerged both individual and group therapies for addiction. We will focus here on the group models.

Cognitive-behavioral theory holds that addiction is learned behavior that is reinforced by such contingencies as the pleasurable effects of drugs (McAuliffe and Ch'ien 1986). The addictive behavior is conditioned and then generalized to a range of stimuli in the environment that continue to perpetuate it. The treatment for addiction thus involves learning to recognize and avoid these stimuli and thus to extinguish conditioned responses to these stimuli. The aim of cognitive-behavior therapy is to develop alternative thoughts and behaviors to the conditioned, "addictive" responses.

The psychoeducational group is one form of cognitive-behavior group therapy. This model uses the group format to inform and teach addicted individuals about the behavioral, medical, and psychological consequences of their addiction. Such groups are a staple of most rehabilitation programs (Nace 1987) and are often seen as the first step of a more comprehensive treatment program. By raising awareness of the consequences of addictive behavior through informational materials, didactic presentations, and group discussions, this method is both educational and at the same time intended as persuasion, an attempt to show the group members how the addiction complicates their lives (Drake et al. 1991). As persuasion, the psychoeducational group intends to prepare the group members to make a commitment to further treatment.

McAuliffe and Ch'ien (1986) have developed a cognitive-behavioral group treatment for substance abuse (recovery training and self-help) that uses a curriculum in a highly structured, didactic group format to teach group members about the cognitive and behavior factors involved in drug use (e.g., to recognize the social and environmental cues that can lead to relapse). Restructuring life-styles that have been associated with the addictive use of substances, anticipating obstacles to recovery, and finding alternative ways to manage problems that have triggered drug use are systematically addressed in the group. Whereas the focus of this method is on managing and modifying one's own behavior, the group setting emphasizes the commonality of certain situations and responses in both the addicted and recovering lifestyles. This group model was studied experimentally in the Harvard Cocaine Recovery Project (Khantzian et al. 1990).

An outpatient cessation model for early recovery from cocaine addiction, also developed in the Harvard Cocaine Recovery Project, is described by McAuliffe and Albert in *Clean Start* (1992). From the initiation of recovery, the model is a group one in which chemical rewards are replaced with social ones (McAuliffe and Albert 1992, p. 27). The group serves as an arena for social learning and social backing: "Seeing others make changes gives clients a clear picture of how change is accomplished, and provides motivation to try a little harder" (p. 28). Group members experience nonexploitative friendships, perhaps for the first time, and are prepared by this "prosocial abstinent culture" for participation in the larger recovering community (p. 28).

A number of group models have emerged from the psychoanalytic, psychodynamic tradition. Most relevant for the treatment of addiction have been groups that have a psychodynamic, interpersonal focus and that address the particular needs of the addicted individual for safety and structure in the group setting (Brown and Yalom 1977; Khantzian et al. 1990; Matano and Yalom 1991; Vannicelli 1982, 1988; Yalom 1974).

In the psychoanalytic, psychodynamic tradition, addiction is understood as the individual's "solution" to the problem of psychological vulnerability. Contemporary psychoanalytic theory has elaborated on these vulnerabilities as defects of self, both intrapsychic and characterological, that can lead to addiction in an attempt to regulate and medicate the distress caused by the defect (Kohut 1977; Meissner 1986; Wurmser 1978). Khantzian's work (1974, 1978, 1985) addresses the particular psychological and narcissistic vulnerabilities of the potential addict: his *self-medication* hypothesis holds that addictions result when an individual seeks to relieve the suffering and distress resulting from deficits in ego capacities involving af-

fects, self-esteem, self-care, and relationships with others as they play themselves out in everyday life. Heightening awareness of self and changing characteristic patterns of handling these vulnerabilities in everyday situations is addressed in the psychodynamic group treatment of addiction.

Perhaps the most important aspect of Khantzian's model is that it is modified dynamic group therapy (MDGT; Khantzian et al. 1990). The modifications mean that the vulnerabilities and difficulties of the addicted individual are recognized in the format of the treatment: the group model is one that establishes maximum safety for addicted individuals in requiring and helping to maintain abstinence, in providing outreach and support, in an active style of leadership, and in always addressing the potential for drug and psychological relapse. Structure and containment are emphasized rather than confrontation. This group model has also been recently studied experimentally as part of the Harvard Cocaine Recovery Project (Khantzian et al. 1990).

## ▼ EFFICACY

The literature on the efficacy of the group therapy of addiction is notably sparse, and there is an especial need for controlled studies of treatment outcome. The Harvard Cocaine Recovery Project, a NIDA-funded study carried out at Harvard Medical School at the Cambridge Hospital from 1987 to 1990, compares two group treatments (cognitive-behavioral and psychodynamic) and a no-group treatment for cocaine-addicted individuals in a controlled clinical trial. This study promises to yield much-needed guidance in our use of the group modality. Other recent studies, although less comprehensive in their conception, shed light on the efficacy issues of abstinence, tenure in treatment, the matching of the patient and the treatment, the type of group, and maintenance of improvement.

Kang et al. (1991), in a recent study comparing individual and family therapy and group treatment for cocaine use disorders, found that improvement was most strongly related to abstinence and also concluded that an intense level of therapy is needed to sustain this abstinence. Bowers and al-Redha (1990), studying alcoholic individuals and their spouses, found that group therapy for couples was superior to individual therapy for the couple in lowering alcohol consumption for the alcoholic partner. They also found a trend for the conjointly treated couples to report better marital adjustment and higher relationship ratings than the individually treated couples. Hellerstein and Meehan (1987) reporting on a group treatment for schizophrenic substance-abusing patients found that over 1 year group members had a marked decrease in days of hospitalization. These studies provide evidence for the group modality's need to address the particular addictive behavior and its capacity to address other life issues and problems beyond the addiction.

A study by Yalom et al. (1978) comparing interactional groups of alcoholic patients with groups of neurotic patients found no significant differences in outcome but did find that despite a higher initial number of dropouts for the alcoholic patients, their tenure in therapy was greater than for the neurotic group members. A recent study by Cooney et al. (1991) comparing outcomes of coping skills groups and interactional group therapies reports that individuals scoring high on sociopathy or global pathology have better outcomes in coping skills groups, whereas patients scoring low on these dimensions did better in the interactional groups. Poldrugo and Forti (1988) conclude from their study that group treatment for alcoholic patients is most useful for those diagnosed with dependent personality disorders and is not beneficial to antisocial patients. These studies begin to address the particular needs of addicted individuals in group therapy and the nature of the group treatment most beneficial to them.

Although more definitive studies of outcome and efficacy of the group treatment of addiction are needed, a wide diversity of group treatments have conceptually and practically gained prominence in recent years.

## ▼ GROUP THERAPY AS TREATMENT OF CHOICE

Group psychotherapy recently has been described as "the definitive treatment for producing character change" (Alonso 1989, p. 1). This is because in a group setting, the "cost of character defenses is illuminated and presents a conflict which can render the same traits dystonic and thus available to interpretation and change" (Alonso 1989, p. 8). Sim-

ilarly, group therapy recently has been described as "the treatment of choice for chemical dependency" (Matano and Yalom 1991, p. 269). Matano and Yalom attribute this choice to the "power of groups—the power to counter prevailing cultural pressures to drink, to provide effective support to those suffering from the alienation of addiction, to offer role modeling, and to harness the power of peer pressure, an important force against denial and resistance" (pp. 269–270).

The rapidly growing focus of mental health professionals on the dually diagnosed patient, one who is diagnosed both with a major mental illness and an addiction (usually a substance use disorder), has opened up new possibilities for the treatment of these individuals (Minkoff and Drake 1991). In acknowledging that addicted individuals often suffer as well from a range of psychological and characterological problems and that both the addiction and the psychological difficulties need to be actively addressed if there is to be improvement in either domain, access to adequate treatment becomes available for the first time. Paradoxically, the acceptance of a dual diagnosis may mean that an individual's treatment can be unified, coherent, and integrated rather than fragmented or divided between care systems, systems that have often worked at cross-purposes to each other.

In this context, *dual diagnosis* does not apply only to the severely and chronically mentally ill individual. Klein et al. (1991) hold that individuals suffering from severe personality disorders, disorders diagnosed on Axis II of the DSM-III-R (American Psychiatric Association 1987), and who are also actively abusing substances, are most accurately considered to be dually diagnosed. Klein et al.'s conceptualization of *Axis II therapy groups* addresses the special problems of providing group therapy for these severely personality-disordered and substance-abusing individuals. The supportive, holding environment of the group facilitates treatment of the addiction. At the same time, the group is tailored to manage the characterological difficulties of these patients. In the same manner, the MDGT model developed for cocaine-addicted patient by Khantzian et al. (1990) actively addresses both the substance abuse and the psychological and character problems of the group members. Group therapies for substance-abusing patients based on the interpersonal model, variants of this same conceptualization, are described by Vannicelli (1988) and by Matano and Yalom (1991). Here the attempt is to make available to substance-abusing patients in groups "a very powerful therapeutic element: the interactive group process" (Matano and Yalom 1991, p. 270). The group is seen as an adaptation of "regular" interactive group therapy, in which a focus on the here-and-now interpersonal relationships in the group as "social microcosm" offers a rich source of learning and change.

## ▼ SPECIAL NEEDS OF ADDICTED INDIVIDUALS IN GROUP THERAPY

Whether individuals are seen as vulnerable to addiction because they are narcissistically compromised through early experiences of deprivation and damage, with the persistent feelings of shame, loneliness, depression, defectiveness, and emptiness described by Kohut (1977), Wurmser (1978), and Meissner (1986); whether they are understood to be narcissistically vulnerable and impaired *secondary* to the addiction (Vaillant 1983); or whether some common shared factor is responsible for both addiction and character problems (Flores 1988), the addicted individual faces particular difficulties in the therapeutic process. A narcissistically vulnerable individual may on the one hand crave empathy and contact with others yet fear and reject it (Liebenberg 1990). The characteristically uneven and inconsistent way in which cocaine-addicted patients relate suggests their dilemma upon entering therapy. As Khantzian et al. (1990) reported, "They may be alternately charming, seductive, and passively expectant, or they may act aloof, as if they do not need other people. Their supersensitivity may be evident in deferential attitudes and attempts to gain approval and acceptance, but they may rapidly shift and become ruthless and demanding in their dealings with others" (p. 40).

Klein et al. (1991) outline the relevant issues in providing outpatient group psychotherapy for character-disordered individuals with addictions: they must be viewed as dually diagnosed; the "recurrent dangers these individuals pose to themselves and/or to others" must be recognized; "their intense demands, during repeated crises," "their propensity for acting out anxiety and aggression, and tendency to split clinicians and systems," and the difficult countertransference these patients can evoke must all be addressed (Klein et al. 1991, p. 99). Action, rather than bearing affect or anxiety or talking about things, is the preferred expressive mode, and the acting out may well involve relapsing to the addictive behavior—drinking, using drugs, gambling. Other characteristic acting out behaviors may involve splitting, violations of boundaries, and of the group contract (e.g., attempting to do group business outside the group either with therapists or with other group members).

Matano and Yalom (1991), writing about the group treatment of alcohol-abusing patients, have identified their tendency to externalize, to "see themselves as being influenced or controlled primarily by external events," and by way of compensation to employ the defenses of "defiance, grandiosity, and counterdependency" (pp. 288–289). Because the patients do not experience themselves as being effective or in control, they rebel against control experienced as coming from outside. These defenses, or characteristic ways of coping, are taken into account in tailoring group therapy to the needs of the addicted patient.

Khantzian (1985) has identified four areas of psychological vulnerability in the addicted individual that may be seen as disturbances or deficits in ego functioning and that potentiate characterological problems. These four areas are 1) regulating affects, 2) self-care (the capacity to protect oneself from undue risk or danger), 3) relationships with others, and 4) self-esteem. The difficulty in regulating affects manifests itself in an intensity of unmodulated feeling, often dysphoric, or in being unable to identify one's own emotions. Self-care deficits find their expression in poor attention to health, engaging in risky behaviors such as unsafe sex, and a general lack of concern for emotional and physical self-preservation. Relationships with others can be problematic in many ways—tumultuous, dependent, or lacking because of the individual's isolation and withdrawal. Finally, self-esteem is compromised or shaky and may manifest as idealization or devaluing of others, feelings of shame and inadequacy, or bravado and grandiosity.

In modifying group treatment for the special needs of the addicted individual, these four dimensions of everyday intrapsychic and social life become the organizing foci for understanding the individual's distress, behavioral difficulties, characteristic ways of handling problems, and possibilities for change. The dimensions provide clarity and structure for handling complex issues with action-oriented, crisis-prone, and affectively constricted or volatile group members.

## ▼ THE TRADITION OF EXCLUSION

Whereas group therapy has acknowledged advantages in the treatment of the addicted, character-disordered individual, the addicted individual has often been excluded from group therapy on the grounds of being too unstable, disruptive, or too unmotivated. His or her difficulty in tolerating affect and managing anxiety; the characteristic postures of self-sufficiency, disavowed need, and bravado (Khantzian 1986); the tendency toward using more primitive defenses (splitting, denial); and the propensity for action rather than reflection have often made the addicted individual an unwelcome group candidate. The addicted individual as candidate for therapy can easily be seen as one of the "difficult" patients described by Rice and Rutan (1987) who can make the therapist feel "puzzled, overwhelmed, depressed, angry, [and] confused" and on whom "all our skill and knowledge has little impact" (p. 131).

Negative countertransference responses, often unacknowledged and resulting in a reluctance to work with addicted individuals, has been a problem in providing adequate individual or group treatment for them (Levy 1987). Levy reports, for example, that the therapist may "not be able to tolerate the alcoholic's repeated 'falls off the wagon' and might, in subtle ways, castigate the patient, adding to the alcoholic's already low self-esteem and causing the alcoholic to continue drinking as a way to cope with such feelings" (p. 786). The ongoing possibility of relapse, *both* relapse to the addictive behavior and psychological relapse to the unadaptive, problematic emotional state, must be tolerated and actively addressed. The characteristic "difficult" postures, attitudes, and behaviors of addicted patients must be understood and worked with. The propensity for impulsive action leads to crisis, instability, and lack of safety, continually testing the therapist's empathy, objectivity, and steadiness. As Klein et al. (1991) point out, these difficulties are geometrically increased in a group. The group, like its individual members, can change rapidly, verge on dissolution, and regroup in the nick of time.

The exclusion from treatment can be rationalized from either the viewpoint of the addictions approach or from the mental health perspective. A situation develops in which an individual is either excluded from both systems, shuttled back and forth to the other, or in which parallel—yet potentially unco-ordinated—treatments take place.

Sciacca (1991) distinguishes between the characteristics of traditional *addiction* treatment versus traditional *mental health* treatment approaches. Programs to treat addictions stress willingness and motivation (with the exception of hospitalization for detoxification) and often involve highly confrontational encounters that attempt to break down denial of the problematic consequences of addiction and about one's own behavior. In a similar vein, addiction treatment may emphasize the necessity of "hitting bottom." Sciacca (1991) reported that "patients must experience severe losses or deterioration in order to perceive that they need help for addiction" (p. 72). Otherwise, addicted patients are seen as not ready for treatment. The addicted patient must be willing and motivated by dint of having hit bottom and thus ripe for confrontation.

On the other hand, mental health or psychotherapeutic approaches, according to Sciacca, characteristically require first of all that there be a diagnosable mental illness. If addiction is the most salient presenting feature of the individual coming for treatment, it may be seen as reason to refer for addiction treatment rather than considering a larger, more comprehensive, psychological picture. Mental health approaches, however, are less likely than addiction programs to emphasize motivation or even awareness or acceptance of the addiction as a prerequisite for treatment. This is seen as the work of the therapy itself, and the approach is more likely to be supportive in nature than confrontational; it is less interested in breaking down defenses than in shoring them up (Sciacca 1991, p. 73). Finally, the mental health professional may be unaccepting of addictive problems, either unaware and unable to easily identify them or judgmental and critical in response to recognizing them.

Thus the traditional mental health approach to the character-disordered, addicted individual may offer more emphasis on outreach and engagement, understanding and tolerance of defensive structures, and support during treatment. However, because of lack of awareness of the psychological aspects of addictive suffering—the way in which the addiction expresses the vulnerable, compromised ego or self—the traditional approach may see addiction as *the* problem and be unwilling to provide therapy. Negative prejudices about the addicted individual may result in exclusion from mental health or psychotherapeutic services. Therapy programs specializing in addiction, on the other hand, while welcoming the most desperate of addicts, tend to want them to come to treatment with a degree of prior preparation and readiness, to underplay the importance of psychological factors and defenses, and to confront rather than support. The addicted individual is assumed to have certain strengths to sustain the treatment and a capacity for individual responsibility or to be just "not ready."

Failure to appreciate the whole of the addicted individual's experience leads to fragmented, exclusionary, and ineffective treatments. Getting caught between two systems is a real possibility. Taking into account the strengths and shortcomings of both traditional addiction and mental health approaches, as in Sciacca's schema, can serve as a guide for developing an integrated treatment. Conceptually and practically, these two traditions can then both inform the treatment of choice for the character-disordered, addicted patient—the specially modified group therapy.

## ▼ FEATURES OF THE GROUP

Specific features of group therapy for the addicted individual derive from the consideration of the addict's special needs and have been discussed by several authors in the literature of addiction and group psychotherapy (Brown and Yalom 1977; Flores 1988; Golden et al. 1993; Khantzian et al. 1990; Khantzian et al. 1992; Matano and Yalom 1991; McAuliffe and Albert 1992; Vannicelli 1982, 1988; Yalom 1974). In addition, the emerging literature of group psychotherapy of the difficult patient, one whose character defenses and acting-out behavior challenge the traditional group therapy format, contributes to our understanding of what is needed (Fenchel and Flapan 1985; Klein et al. 1991; Leszcz 1989; Rice and Rutan 1987; Roth et al. 1990; Stone and Gustafson 1982). Finally, the literature of dual diagnosis of major mental illness and substance use disorder offers guidance in modifying group therapy for this population (Levy and Mann 1988; Minkoff and Drake 1991).

### Pregroup Preparation

Group therapy in the treatment of addiction begins pregroup with outreach and preparation. The goal of this preparation is to provide a welcome that will increase motivation for the treatment, reduce premature dropouts, ease fears and resistance to the group modality, and increase self-awareness. Sciacca (1991) emphasizes the supportive, collaborative nature of the pregroup contacts: the potential group member's level of motivation and readiness is accepted and he or she is encouraged to keep an open mind regarding him- or herself and others. A clear therapeutic contract is presented, including guidelines regarding boundaries between group members and between therapist and group member, and "the necessity for therapist communication and collaboration with other treaters" (Klein et al. 1991, p. 99).

Khantzian et al. (1990) state that the therapist "can play a critical role at this point in establishing optimistic and realistic member expectations regarding the efficacy" of the group. The therapist (in this case for a psychodynamic group treating cocaine addiction) not only "acquaints the new members with the established ground rules, which include strict confidentiality, attendance and promptness, and abstinence from drugs and alcohol," but also discusses the benefits of group therapy, the focus of the group, acknowledges the difficulty of joining groups, "explains the work of therapy," and identifies the new members' personal goals (Khantzian et al. 1990, pp. 46–48).

Reaching out to the prospective group member, anticipating what will follow, and concretely outlining the expectations provides necessary structure to allay overwhelming anxiety.

### Structure

Structure in the group for addicted patients is provided in several ways. The group contract serves as an organizing feature initially and as the group progresses. It is a given that the contract will be tested and perhaps hotly debated; this is part of the work of the group. Matano and Yalom (1991) caution against an overly authoritarian stance and advise a sensitivity of the group therapist to the addicted patient's feeling of loss of personal control, which evokes defiant and counterdependent reactions.

Shared norms, explicitly stated and reiterated, also provide structure. Abstinence from the problematic, addictive behavior; a commitment to talking about feelings and problems rather than acting on them in the group; and agreement about the goals of the treatment are important. Vannicelli (1988), in describing a group for alcoholic patients, emphasizes that the shared understanding "about what it means to be working on one's drinking problem" and "what it means to be getting better" is necessary to the integrity of the group (Vannicelli 1988, p. 349). These norms are essential to dealing with the regression to the addictive behavior—relapse and "slips"—as well as with providing a vision of progress, improvement, and recovery.

Didactic and psychoeducational groups, self-help and 12-step programs, and cognitive-behavioral groups are all models with a high degree of inherent structure. This chapter's focus is thus on the less-structured, psychodynamic and interpersonal groups and how they can be modified to provide adequate containment and comfort for the addicted group member. Enhanced structure in a psychodynamically oriented group means explicitly endorsing certain group norms, an active leadership style for the therapist, and, as in Khantzian's MDGT model, a focus on specific character and interpersonal problems.

## Safety

Safety considerations in the group setting include immediate physical safety during the meetings of the group, ensuring safety for therapeutic exploration and change by establishing the norm of abstinence, and promoting an atmosphere of enough interpersonal comfort and psychological security for the interactive work of the group to proceed. Physical safety is a consideration in selection of the meeting place, the group leadership, and the strongly upheld norm of putting things into words instead of actions.

In the treatment of addiction, especially in the beginning stages, as Matano and Yalom (1991) put it, "Nothing takes precedence over recovery—it is a life or death issue" (p. 273). In their interpersonal group model for alcoholic patients, they advocate the active facilitation of achieving and maintaining sobriety. Thus early on in the group, any interpersonal interaction is "gentle, supportive, and directly supportive of sobriety" (p. 274). Vigilance for any threats to the recovery process is counseled. Safety is also of paramount importance in the MDGT group (Khantzian et al. 1992). One of the four foci of MDGT—self-care—addresses the self-defeating, destructive, and dangerous nature of the addictive involvement: the addicted individual's poor capacity for self-preservation plays itself out through the addiction. Cognitive-

behavioral and psychoeducational groups emphasize the risks that are external to the individual, such as dangerous companions who are active in their addictive behavior or environments that can stimulate cravings or actual relapse. The individual learns in the group to recognize and avoid these dangers and to find new, safe friends and activities to replace them. McAuliffe and Albert's model (1992) emphasizes the building of "walls" and a "foundation" by detailing a "system of steps that creates a life space that is free of drugs and that ensures support for recovery" (p. 33). Attention to the real dangers of the addiction and relapse in everyday life and the strengthening of the motivation for abstinence are necessary from the inception of the group therapy.

Discovering what increases the safety for individual group members may lead to directing members to other, concomitant treatments. Some individuals, for example, may need support between weekly group meetings and find the accessibility of AA meetings vitally important. As one group member who attends a weekly Cocaine Anonymous meeting and a psychodynamic group meeting for cocaine-addicted individuals each week put it, "I need to keep seeing guys who are right at the beginning so I don't forget, and some who have a lot of recovery, but I want to talk about *all* the problems in my life." Some may need concurrent individual and group treatment. Others may need to use emergency or crisis intervention services. Developing an individualized combination of services to increase safety is an ongoing aspect of the work of the group therapist for addicted patients.

Within the group, safety is maintained by attending to the ever-possible psychological relapse or relapse to the addictive behavior. In a group for pathological gamblers, for example, the ongoing stress of overwhelming debt, often compounded by the unfamiliar tension of paying back slowly, over time, puts the abstinent gambler at continuing risk that must be monitored in the group. It may be common to find the group struggling with the question of what constitutes gambling (running a game at a carnival, buying a raffle ticket for a good cause, investing in stock for the children's college education) long after "the last bet." The question of openness versus keeping secret the extent of the ongoing debt also persists and may add to the risk. Even as self-awareness grows in the group, new stressors appear (e.g., long-term debt, the family's anger), and the risk of relapse remains high.

The atmosphere of the group must also be maintained as one safe for listening and disclosure: accepting, empathic, respectful of varying amounts of awareness and motivation, encouraging of participation, and understanding of resistance. Modeling this accepting stance, the group leader maintains safety by protecting members from attack, shame, or premature self-disclosure, such as of traumatic material (Khantzian et al. 1990). Acknowledging the possible discomfort and anxiety of being in a group, the group leader assists the group in managing these feelings and in sticking with it.

## Confrontation Versus Support

Matano and Yalom (1991) point to the dangers of an overly confrontational approach in the group. Although the necessity of increasing the addicted patient's honesty with him- or herself and others is real, the attempt to break down denial can backfire, causing the patient to leave the treatment program or to "dissemble compliance while inwardly retreating" (p. 291). The key is to treat addicted patients like other patients—that is, by relating to them in an empathic, supportive, and understanding manner. A central task of the group leader is thus to manage the anxiety that the group process, particularly confrontation, inevitably stimulates in the group members and to keep it at a tolerable level.

Leszcz (1989), writing about the group treatment of the characterologically difficult patient, sees the group as first of all providing a holding environment, a place that is reliable, constant, and accepting, a place where group members can "relate in a non-related way, until they are able to ascertain that it is safe . . ." (p. 326). The confrontation itself is spelled out as "a forceful, but supportive pressure on the patient to acknowledge something that is conscious or preconscious, but avoided because of the distress that it involves" (p. 327).

The group model of Khantzian et al. (1990) encourages an understanding of addictive behavior as an attempt to deal with feelings and experiences, an adaptation that has outlived its usefulness, and an understanding of resistance to change: group members are guided "to appreciate how their ways of coping and the crises they precipitate are linked to the past; they need to acknowledge their painful feelings from the past and in the present, and to support each other in finding alternative ways to cope with their painful

feeling states and problems in living" (p. 76). In other words, the group members, although they are held responsible for their choices and actions and are asked to look squarely at themselves, are not blamed and judged.

The group modality offers a particular advantage when it comes to confrontation: group members are more likely to respond to confrontation by their peers. As Leszcz (1989) puts it, "[G]roup members are less restricted in their range of responses and may be better able to use humor, cajole, or shock one another to force attention to a disavowed issue" (p. 327). In a psychodynamic group led by one of the authors, a group member who kept his distance from others, refusing to "come clean" with his family about the extent of his addictive behavior, never removed his coat during the group meetings for many months, stating he was "too cold." After other group members had "worked" on him for awhile, he not only began to consider the problem of his secretiveness, but actually shed his coat for the first time, which was greeted by pleased laughter and a fellow group member's remark: "We *must* be hot tonight if Bob is taking off his coat!" Bob's joining in was acknowledged, gladly but lightly, without making him unduly self-conscious.

Perhaps the question of responsibility lies at the heart of the balancing of confrontation and support. Matano and Yalom (1991) distinguish between the *addictive process* (called the *disease* in AA terms) and the recovery process. Although they do not hold the alcoholic patient responsible for the addiction itself, for the "psychological loss of control," or for his or her culturally learned beliefs about drinking, they do "demand that patients assume responsibility for their recovery" (pp. 277–278). Clarity about responsibility is crucial in the group therapy of addiction, especially as this treatment may represent the confluence of the mental health and the addiction traditions that have so widely diverged on the question.

## Cohesion and the "Addict Identification"

Cohesiveness in group therapy has been likened to the importance of the relationship or therapeutic alliance in individual therapy (Yalom 1985). Cohesiveness, or the attraction of the members to the group and their sense of belonging, has been correlated with tenure in the group (prevention of early dropout), with the stability necessary for any kind of long-term therapeutic work to occur (Yalom 1985), and as the central mediator of outcome (Budman et al. 1989). Matano and Yalom (1991), in their work specifically addressing group therapy for the alcoholic patient, link the individual's identification as an "alcoholic" as well as the emphasis on sameness among the group members with feeling connected to the group and the growth of group cohesion and safety (p. 275). Vannicelli (1988) warns against overdoing the bonding that occurs by talking about the addiction. War stories about the glory days of drinking and how bad things finally got, for example, can also serve as a defense against further development of the group, a way to avoid other emotionally charged issues (p. 346). Group members, even while seeking mutuality and safety in their identification as "addicts," can withdraw in this way from other contact with their fellow group members.

Khantzian et al. (1990) describe the group process in the modified psychodynamic group for substance-abusing individuals as moving toward the discovery of common ground. Initially, the group bonds around the identity as an addict. Many dually diagnosed patients see their addicted status as preferable, more socially acceptable than other labels. To call oneself an alcoholic or a drug addict and to belong to a group for addicted individuals is a less stigmatized identity than that of mental patient, borderline personality disorder, or narcissist. The "outlaw" life of the addicted individual and the desperate extremities of addiction bring the group together, idealized even as they are now disavowed. Self-esteem is maintained, and cohesion is established.

However, the group must progress to find common bonds in some larger, universal human experience if the members are to grow and begin to see themselves are part of the human mainstream. For addicted individuals in group therapy, the common ground to seek is the middle ground about which they may be ambivalent, "as if the price of ordinary life were one of unremitting drudgery and joyless obligation" (Khantzian et al. 1990, p. 95). The personal material shared at first after the initial identification as an addict may be equally extreme or grandiose or may be withheld as not worthy of exposure in the group. Here is where the work of the group on awareness of self and others and on addressing problems of living can proceed.

The very nature of the psychodynamic or interpersonal group, with an emphasis on interpersonal interactions in the here-and-now and on the understanding of individual characterological patterns as they emerge within the group, provides a way to talk about ordinary life. Thus a member of a group for cocaine-addicted individuals offered her group members a chance for greater involvement with each other when she remarked that she felt closer to them than to her family. This led to a discussion of alienation from neglectful or intrusive parents instead of the usual accounts of past ruthless quests for cocaine and the enumeration of the pitfalls of addiction. Ordinary problems, everyday life beyond the addiction, offer the group members a way into the ordinary world.

## The Group Therapist

The therapist in the group therapy of addiction has an active, demanding role to play. Concerns for safety and structure require an alert presence, a readiness to manage and help to modulate anxiety, to address acting-out behavior, and to intervene if necessary by setting limits and upholding the group contract, even as building cohesion and developing the work of the group proceeds. This active mode of leadership is important because, as reported by Khantzian et al. (1990), addicted individuals with histories of neglect and trauma "do not respond well to the traditions of therapeutic passivity . . . instead they need therapists who can actively and empathically help to engage them and each other around their vulnerabilities and the self-defeating defenses and behaviors they adopt to avoid their distress and suffering" (p. 162).

The therapist may become the focus of anger and dependency, the mediator of struggles, and the unintentional voice of the superego. Cotherapists are split into good and evil. Countertransference feelings may be difficult, especially when helplessness and fear are evoked, as they often are in these groups (Klein et al. 1991). Supervision, opportunities to share the work, concurrent therapies, or supports for the group members—working as part of a team or a program— all help to make the group therapy of addiction possible and effective.

## ▼ SUMMARY

Current group approaches to addiction have emerged from several traditions: self-help fellowships; the psychoeducational, cognitive-behavioral modality; and the psychodynamic, interpersonal tradition. Although the group approach has evolved from these diverse theoretical and ideological viewpoints, there is a dearth of controlled studies of efficacy and outcome that could support a particular school of thought. Conceptually and pragmatically, practitioners working with addicted individuals have come to similar conclusions regarding their special needs in a group setting. If addicted individuals are to receive the full benefit of treatment, their characterological and psychological vulnerabilities must be recognized and addressed. Traditional treatments are then modified, particularly if they do not already provide the high degree of structure and safety necessary for engaging and holding the addicted individual. The group approach, in its powerful capacity to support and confront, to comfort and to challenge, and to involve its members in encounters that vividly heighten awareness of interpersonal and characterological problems and provide a safe place for change, is now viewed as the treatment of choice for the individual who suffers from addiction. Special features of group therapy for the treatment of addiction are an emphasis on outreach and preparation for involvement in the group, a high degree of structure and active leadership, a concern for safety (particularly an awareness of the risk of relapse to the addictive behavior), a balance between confrontation and support, and a goal of moving beyond the initial cohesiveness of the group members' identification as addicts to helping them discover common bonds in living ordinary life.

## ▼ REFERENCES

Alonso A: Character Change in Group Therapy. Paper presented at Psychiatric Grand Rounds, The Cambridge Hospital, Cambridge, MA, September 1989

American Psychiatric Association: Diagnostic and Statistical Manual of Mental Disorders, 3rd Edition, Revised. Washington, DC, American Psychiatric Association, 1987

Bowers TG, al-Redha MR: A comparison of outcome with group/marital and standard/individual therapies with alcoholics. J Stud Alcohol 51:301–309, 1990

Brown S, Yalom ID: Interactional group therapy with alcoholics. J Stud Alcohol 38:426–456, 1977

Budman SH, Soldz S, Demby A, et al: Cohesion, alliance and outcome in group psychotherapy. Psychiatry 52:339–350, 1989

Cherkas MS: Synanon foundation—a radical approach to the problem of addiction (editorial). Am J Psychiatry 121:1065, 1965

Cooney NL, Kadden RM, Litt MD, et al: Matching alcoholics to coping skills or interactional therapies: two year follow-up results. J Consult Clin Psychol 59:598–601, 1991

Drake RE, Antosca LM, Noordsy DL, et al: New Hampshire's specialized services for the dually diagnosed, in Dual Diagnosis of Major Mental Illness and Substance Disorder. Edited by Minkoff K, Drake RE. San Francisco, CA, Jossey-Bass, 1991, pp 57–67

Fenchel GH, Flapan D: Resistance in group psychotherapy. Group 9:35–47, 1985

Flores PJ: Group Psychotherapy With Addicted Populations. New York, Haworth, 1988

Golden S, Halliday K, Khantzian EJ, et al: Dynamic group therapy for substance abuse patients: a reconceptualization, in Group Therapy in Clinical Practice. Edited by Alonso AA, Swiller HI. Washington, DC, American Psychiatric Press, 1993, pp 271–287

Hellerstein DJ, Meehan B: Outpatient group therapy for schizophrenic substance abusers. Am J Psychiatry 144:1337–1339, 1987

Herman JL: Trauma and Recovery. New York, Basic Books, 1992

Kang SY, Kleinman PH, Woody GE, et al: Outcomes for cocaine abusers after once-a-week psychosocial therapy. Am J Psychiatry 148:630–635, 1991

Khantzian EJ: Opiate addiction: a critique of theory and some implications for treatment. Am J Psychother 131:160–164, 1974

Khantzian EJ: The ego, the self, and opiate addiction: theoretical and treatment considerations. International Review of Psychoanalysis 5:189–198, 1978

Khantzian EJ: The self-medication hypothesis of addictive disorders: focus on heroin and cocaine dependence. Am J Psychiatry 142:1259–1264, 1985

Khantzian EJ: A contemporary psychodynamic approach to drug abuse treatment. Am J Drug Alcohol Abuse 12:213–222, 1986

Khantzian EJ, Mack JE: Alcoholics anonymous and contemporary psychodynamic theory, in Recent Developments in Alcoholism, Vol 7: Treatment Research. Edited by Galanter M. New York, Plenum, 1989, pp 67–89

Khantzian EJ, Halliday K, McAuliffe WE: Addiction and the Vulnerable Self. New York, Guilford, 1990

Khantzian EJ, Halliday KS, Golden S, et al: Modified group therapy for substance abusers: a psychodynamic approach to relapse prevention. American Journal on Addictions 1:67–76, 1992

Klein RH, Orleans JF, Soule CR: The Axis II group: treating severely characterologically disturbed patients. Int J Group Psychother 41:97–115, 1991

Kohut H: Preface, in Psychodynamics of Drug Dependence, NIDA Res Monogr No 12 (DHEW Publ No ADM-77-470). Edited by Blaine JD, Julius DA. Washington, DC, U.S. Government Printing Office, 1977, pp vii–ix

Leszcz M: Group psychotherapy of the characterologically difficult patient. Int J Group Psychother 39: 311–335, 1989

Levy MS: A change in orientation: therapeutic strategies for the treatment of alcoholism. Psychotherapy: Research and Practice 24:786–793, 1987

Levy MS, Mann DW: The special treatment team: an inpatient approach to the mentally ill alcoholic patient. J Subst Abuse Treat 5:219–227, 1988

Liebenberg B: The unwanted and unwanting patient: problems in group psychotherapy of the narcissistic patient, in The Difficult Patient in Group. Edited by Roth B, Stone W, Kibel H. Madison, CT, International Universities Press, 1990, pp 311–322

Matano RA, Yalom ID: Approaches to chemical dependency: chemical dependency and interactive group therapy—a synthesis. Int J Group Psychother 41:269–293, 1991

McAuliffe WE, Ch'ien JMN: Recovery training and self help: relapse prevention program for treated opiate addicts. J Subst Abuse Treat 3:9–20, 1986

McAuliffe WE, Albert J: Clean Start. New York, Guilford, 1992

Meissner WW: Psychotherapy and the Paranoid Process. New York, Jason Aronson, 1986

Minkoff K, Drake RE (eds): Dual Diagnosis of Major Mental Illness and Substance Disorder. San Francisco, CA, Jossey-Bass, 1991

Nace EP: The Treatment of Alcoholism. New York, Brunner/Mazel, 1987

Orford J: Excessive Appetites: A Psychological View of Addictions. New York, Wiley, 1985

Poldrugo F, Forti B: Personality disorders and alcoholism treatment outcome. Drug Alcohol Depend 21:171–176, 1988

Rice CA, Rutan JS: Inpatient Group Psychotherapy. New York, Macmillan, 1987

Roth B, Stone W, Kibel H (eds): The Difficult Patient in Group. Madison, CT, International Universities Press, 1990

Sciacca K: An integrated treatment approach for severely mentally ill individuals with substance disorders, in Dual Diagnosis of Major Mental Illness and Substance Disorder. Edited by Minkoff K, Drake RE. San Francisco, CA, Jossey-Bass, 1991, pp 69–84

Stone W, Gustafson JP: Technique in group psychotherapy of narcissistic and borderline patients. Int J Group Psychother 32:29–47, 1982

Tuttman S: Principles of psychoanalytic group therapy applied to the treatment of borderline and narcissistic disorders, in The Difficult Patient in Group. Edited by Roth B, Stone W, Kibel H. Madison, CT, International Universities Press, 1990, pp 7–29

Vaillant GE: The Natural History of Alcoholism. Cambridge, MA, Harvard University Press, 1983

Vannicelli M: Group psychotherapy with alcoholics. J Stud Alcohol 43:17–37, 1982

Vannicelli M: Group therapy aftercare for alcoholic patients. Int J Group Psychother 38:337–353, 1988

Wurmser L: The Hidden Dimension: Psychodynamics of Compulsive Drug Use. New York, Jason Aronson, 1978

Yalom ID: Group psychotherapy and alcoholism. Ann N Y Acad Sci 233:85–103, 1974

Yalom ID: Inpatient Group Psychotherapy. New York, Basic Books, 1983

Yalom ID: The Theory and Practice of Group Psychotherapy. New York, Basic Books, 1985

Yalom ID, Bloch S, Bond G, et al: Alcoholics in interactional group therapy: an outcome study. Arch Gen Psychiatry 35:419–25, 1978

# Family Therapy

## Alcohol

*Peter Steinglass, M.D.*

During the past two decades, a growing clinical and research literature on family issues in alcoholism has pointed to the important role of family factors in the onset and clinical course of this condition (Lawson et al. 1983; Steinglass and Robertson 1983). Considerable interest has been generated not only in investigating family aspects of alcoholism but also in applying family therapy techniques to its treatment. Twenty-five years ago, families were by and large ignored by alcoholism clinicians. The current picture is dramatically different. One is now hard pressed to find a credible alcoholism treatment program that does not at least give lip service to the importance of including family members in the treatment plan.

At least five factors can be thought of as having contributed to this growing interest in family issues in alcoholism.

First, after many years of public and professional perceptions of the typical alcoholic individual as one who is homeless, with no family, and living out his or her life in a "skid-row" setting, we now know that the vast majority of alcoholic individuals live in intact families. Further, within these families the most telling

consequences of chronic alcohol abuse are not the biomedical sequelae suffered by the individual with alcoholism but rather the impact of drinking on marital, social, and work relationships. The staggering figures estimating the financial costs of alcoholism to industry can also be viewed from a family perspective in that they also represent lost income, job loss, and so on. The growing evidence of a strong associational relationship between alcohol use and family violence (Gelles and Straus 1979; Gondolf and Foster 1991; Hindman 1979), paralleled by equally strong associational data regarding child abuse (Hindman 1979), incest (Herman 1992; Sheinberg 1992), and significantly higher divorce rates (Schuckit and Morrissey 1976), all represent powerful consequences to families of the presence of an alcoholic member. Faced with these various challenges, over time most of these families must develop strategies for managing the stresses of chronic alcoholism, and their response patterns therefore must be considered as possible factors in determining the differential chronic course of the condition.

Second, although compelling data now exist suggesting that at least some forms of alcoholism are genetically transmitted, it is also clear that individually based biomedical models of alcoholism (including genetic transmission models) account for at most considerably less than half of the expressed variance in incidence and course of the condition (Plomin 1990). Taking these two factors into account, it seems reasonable to assume that intergenerational transmission of alcoholism is at least partially accounted for by environmental variables, and surely family behavioral factors are prominent candidates in this regard. Although research in this area is still quite primitive, a number of interesting initial leads are emerging. For example, the work of Wolin and Bennett has pinpointed family rituals as one such environmental variable that might account for differential expression of alcoholism across generations (Bennett et al. 1987; Wolin et al. 1980). These findings, in turn, could conceivably point to family-based prevention strategies, yet another area in which a focus on the family might prove quite profitable.

Third, improvements in research methods for studying family interaction—including direct observation of interactional behavior as well improved techniques of conjoint interviewing—have generated a wealth of new findings and ideas about alcoholism and the family, including family-based clinical typologies of alcoholism and identification of specific family environmental factors that impact on clinical course issues related to alcoholism (Finney et al. 1983; Jacob and Seilhamer 1987; Jacob et al. 1983; Moos et al. 1989; Steinglass 1980; Steinglass et al. 1987). These ideas about clinical course issues have in turn generated experimentation regarding how treatment interventions aimed at the family might be integrated into comprehensive treatment programs for alcoholism (Kaufman 1985; Lawson et al. 1983; Steinglass et al. 1977). (I will be expanding on many of these issues in a later section.)

Fourth, the increasing use of family-oriented treatment approaches to alcoholism (and parenthetically, the growing evidence of the efficacy of these approaches) has added a wealth of clinical data to more systematic research findings regarding alcoholism and the family. Further, pressure on the part of the nonpatient members of alcoholic families for increased services (the dramatic growth of the Adult Children of Alcoholics movement is perhaps the best example here) has brought home the need for alcoholism specialists to master family interviewing skills and to be able to provide therapeutic services to families as well as individuals.

Finally, a change away from the focus on the family as an *etiological* factor in alcoholism (the position taken by many family-oriented clinicians in the 1960s and 1970s) has significantly broadened the clinical appeal of family-based models of alcoholism. That is, as long as the emphasis was on delineating the characteristics of the "addiction-prone" family (a family psychopathology model), the implication was that family factors might play an etiological role in the emergence of all substance abuse problems, including chronic alcoholism. More recently, family clinicians have been urging a less pejorative stance vis-à-vis these families (Steinglass et al. 1987). Instead of viewing family environmental factors as causative agents in the development of alcoholism, seemingly dysfunctional family behavior is viewed as a reaction to the stresses associated with chronic alcohol abuse by one or more family members. As this new view has come to dominate thinking in the alcoholism/family field, the concept of the alcoholism-prone family is no longer thought to be credible. Instead, most family researchers and clinicians are comfortable with multifactorial models of alcoholism that acknowledge predisposing factors (e.g., genetic transmission) but also include a focus on the family environment as significantly affecting the clinical course of these conditions (Cronkite et al. 1990; Jacob and Leonard 1988; Moos and Moos 1984; Steinglass et al. 1985). These models also form the rationale for multipronged treatment approaches that include, as an important component, an attempt to alter these family environmental variables, hence the growing interest in family therapy as an integral component of comprehensive alcoholism treatment programs. But in addition to these research-based and conceptual reasons for incorporating the family in alcoholism treatment, this trend has also been reinforced by clinical experience. As Collins (1990) has noted, clinical wisdom has increasingly concluded that 1) the alcoholic individual's response to treatment is better when family members are included (this seems particularly true when spouses are incorporated in the treatment process); 2) isolation of the alcoholic individual from his or her family, which is often a concomitant of chronic alcoholism, is reversed by using a family therapy approach; and 3) the inclusion of the family unit allows for the identification of parallel problems such as sexual difficulties, parenting issues, and family violence, thereby making the treatment more comprehensive.

Nevertheless, despite this growing interest in the family on the part of alcoholism specialists, and the widespread perception that family therapy is being offered as a standard component of most treatment programs, there is still considerable confusion as to how this "family component" should be implemented. It is not unusual, for example, for treatment programs to count as their family therapy component a few educational experiences for family members along with some encouragement to participate in an Al-Anon group. This is particularly true in comprehensive care programs (e.g., HMOs) in which family therapy clinics and addiction programs are organizationally separated and are staffed by professionals who know very little about each other's perspective. In such settings, once alcoholism is identified as an issue, it is not uncommon for the "identified alcoholic" family member to be referred to the addiction program for detoxification and rehabilitation, while the family therapy work, if it continues at all, does so without directly addressing the alcoholism.

In this chapter, I approach the alcoholism treatment issue primarily from the vantage point of a systems-oriented family therapist. At issue here is how to conceptualize a rationale for a genuine family therapy approach to alcoholism, what are the core issues that such a therapist must be aware of, how would assessment issues play themselves out within such a therapy framework, what are the central therapeutic components of such an approach, and to what extent do we have outcome data available regarding efficacy of these treatment approaches. But in doing so, I also want to caution the reader that it would be rare to find such an approach practiced in "pure" form in an alcoholism treatment setting. Instead the approaches should be looked on as examples of how treatment for alcoholism has been carried out when a family therapist has taken on this clinical population.

## ▼ FAMILY THERAPY TREATMENT APPROACHES TO ALCOHOLISM

### General Issues

As will be discussed shortly, family-oriented clinicians have proposed a wide variety of models for incorporating family perspectives into both the assessment/diagnostic and intervention phases of treatment. However, whatever the theoretical orientation, all clinicians working with alcoholism from a family perspective have had to keep in mind four aspects of the condition that invariably impact on family life:

1. *Its chronicity.* Clinicians usually encounter alcoholism problems many years after they have reached pathologic proportions. Relationships between the condition itself, the alcoholic family member, and the rest of the family have usually reached some steady state. The precipitating event leading to a request for treatment is often a crisis that has temporarily disrupted this steady state (e.g., a medical crisis, a drunk-driving arrest, a confrontation by an employer because of job performance). However, therapy, to be successful, must combat and overcome long-standing patterns of behavior that have become rigidified over time. These obviously include family interaction patterns.

2. *The use of a psychobiologically active drug.* Because the family's alcoholic member is chronically ingesting a psychobiologically active drug that is both a depressant and a drug that significantly impairs cognition and verbal communication, family behavior patterns have gradually been adopted to accommodate for these defects. These patterns are often not immediately apparent and therefore are a challenge to the family therapist during the initial phases of treatment.

3. *Sober-intoxicated cycling.* Direct observations of interactional behavior of alcoholic families have indicated that these families manifest two quite distinct interactional styles—one that occurs when the alcoholic member is sober and another that occurs when the alcoholic member is intoxicated (Steinglass et al. 1977). It has been suggested, therefore, that a unique feature of the alcoholic family is its dual-state, interactional style. It has further been suggested that family therapists must develop strategies for accessing information about the intoxicated interactional state in order to appreciate behaviors that have developed in these families. (One such approach that was developed by Liepman and colleagues, will be described in the next section.)

4. *Intergenerational transmission of alcoholism.* Alcoholism is a familial condition. Most likely, both genetic and psychosocial factors contribute to the intergenerational transmission of alcoholism.

Family therapists must appreciate that their interventions are appropriately directed not only at containing alcoholic behavior as it is currently being manifested but also in attending to the needs of children within the family toward the goal of disrupting possible intergenerational transmission of the condition. Thus family therapy might be considered unique among the various psychological therapies for alcoholism in that it explicitly addresses prevention of alcoholism in at-risk children as well as intervening in currently existing alcoholism problems.

## Overview of Treatment Models

In response to the above issues, over the past three decades family therapists have used a number of conceptual models for designing treatment strategies for alcoholism. The best known of these is the *family systems* approach, a model that applies principles of general systems theory to families. Particular attention is paid here to ways in which families, as behavioral systems, regulate their internal and external environments, and how patterns of interactional behavior change over time. Both the structural and strategic approaches to family therapy, as well as newer constructivist approaches, use family system theory as their conceptual base.

A second approach that has also been widely utilized is a *family behavioral* model that extends classical conditioning principles to interpersonal behavior. Concepts of reciprocity, coercion, and reinforcement are applied to an analysis of the contingencies that help explain patterns of interactional behavior.

A third approach focuses particular attention on constructs of *stress* and *coping*, as applied this time to families rather than just to individuals. Constructs such as social support and social networks, and stressful life events are used to understand the factors that either assist or interfere with the ability of families to problem solve in the face of stressful events. Many of the highly successful psychoeducational family therapy models owe their conceptual basis to these notions of family coping styles and resources, such as social support networks.

Although family therapy approaches to alcoholism have lagged behind family therapy for other psychiatric and medical conditions (e.g., schizophrenia, eating disorders, child behavioral disorders), by now virtually every one of the above conceptual approaches has been applied to alcoholism treatment. For example, the family systems approach forms the underpinnings for the therapy approaches suggested by Steinglass et al. (1987), Treadway (1989), and Berenson (1979), among others. Behavioral approaches, on the other hand, are the basis for the marital therapy approach advocated by McCrady and colleagues (McCrady et al. 1982, 1986). Family stress and coping concepts are perhaps best represented by the family functioning model proposed by Kaufman and Pattison (1981, 1982) and the network therapy approach advocated by Galanter (1993). In each of these areas, these different conceptual models have been used both to suggest strategies for assessment in which family data become important components of the diagnostic process and also to guide the treatment intervention approaches.

At the same time, however, it is also the case that these conceptual models have not become fully integrated into mainstream thinking about alcoholism. One reason is that they do not fit well with current conventions for diagnosing alcoholism. Thus although there is widespread acknowledgment of the importance of family factors in the onset and course of chronic alcoholism, no widely accepted schema exist for integrating a family prospective with DSM-IV (American Psychiatric Association 1994) criteria sets for diagnosing alcohol abuse and alcohol dependence. Instead, what we currently have available are a variety of descriptive models based on family systems, behavioral, and stress/coping concepts that together form the conceptual rationale for the various family therapy approaches currently in use in alcoholism treatment settings.

With that caveat, let us briefly summarize of the main tenets of these different conceptual models of alcoholism.

## The Family Systems Model

The family systems model of alcoholism, as described in greatest detail by Steinglass et al. (1987), centers around the concept of the *alcoholic system*, defined as a behavioral system in which alcohol acquisition and/or consumption is a major organizing principle for patterns of interactional behavior within the system. *Bottle gangs* (Rubington 1968), groups of alcoholic individual who converge in a common location such as a park or alley for the specific purpose of consuming wine or whiskey, are perhaps the purest examples of such drinking systems. But families can also become alcoholic systems in that chronic alcoholism occupies a central position as a core identity issue for many families dealing with chronic alcoholic problems. The term *alcoholic family* has been suggested to describe such a situation, and within the family systems typology of alcoholism is contrasted with a second type of family, the *family with an alcoholic member,* the latter subtype being a family still faced with the challenges of chronic alcoholism but one that has not reorganized in substantive ways to accommodate these challenges. Thus the basic distinction being made in this typology centers around the extent to which the family has become altered in its behavior patterns by the presence of a chronic alcoholic member.

In tracking this process of reorganization of families around alcoholism, the family systems model focuses particular attention on two aspects of family life: 1) a set of regulatory behaviors that families typically use to structure the pattern of everyday life, to establish family priorities, and to ensure stability; and 2) the course of family development. In terms of family regulatory behaviors, the interest is in whether family behavior has been altered by inordinate attention to the demands of alcoholism. Three areas of family life have been suggested as foci for assessing this question: daily routines; family rituals (e.g., holidays, vacations, dinnertime); and short-term, problem-solving strategies. For each area, the central question is the extent to which family behavior patterns have been *invaded* (substantively changed) to accommodate the unique demands generated by the family's alcoholic member.

This focus on family regulatory behaviors as vehicles for assessment of the role of alcoholism in family life has also received considerable research validation. Empirical studies of problem-solving behavior in alcoholic families have consistently demonstrated the striking differences in interactional behavior in the presence versus the absence of alcohol (Billings et al. 1979; Davis et al. 1974; Frankenstein et al. 1985; Jacob and Krahn 1988; Steinglass et al. 1977). Detailed studies of family daily routines have demonstrated that these behaviors are closely linked to highly significant clinical course issues related to alcoholism (Jacob and Leonard 1988; Steinglass 1981). Finally, studies of alcoholic family rituals have yielded important findings about the relationship between family environmental factors and intergenerational transmission of alcoholism (Bennett et al. 1987; Wolin et al. 1980).

Regarding the second major focus of systems-oriented models, that of family development, the critical question here is whether the inordinate attention being given to alcoholism-related issues within the family is taking the family away from competing developmental issues (e.g., the needs of an adolescent member for differentiation). Within this model, it is posited that often family development is *distorted* when alcoholism is introduced into family life because the family typically skews its focus in the direction of an emphasis on short-term stability at the expense of long-term growth. It is this process that in turn gives the family the appearance of rigidity or narrowness, a characteristic frequently mentioned in the clinical literature.

Clinicians using this systems approach have recommended family therapy as the treatment of choice whenever this reorganization around the alcoholic symptom has occurred in the family. Further, it has been suggested that this reorganization process may substantively increase the likelihood of cross-generational transmission of alcoholism, whether or not a genetic predisposition is concurrently present.

It should also be noted that the family systems approach to alcoholism also draws links between alcoholism and other conditions, emphasizing that the alcoholic family is an example of a more general phenomenon characteristic of all chronic illnesses. That is, families dealing with such chronic conditions as diabetes, end-stage renal disease, heroin addiction, traumatic injuries leading to permanent disabilities, mental retardation, or chronic psychosis all have this capacity to become organized around strategies for accommodating to or maintaining the chronic illness process.

## Behavioral Family Models

As noted above, behaviorally oriented marital and family therapy is an extension of the basic constructs of learning theory to behavior in families. Central here is the tenet that behaviors, including interactional behaviors, are learned and maintained via positive and negative reinforcements of these behaviors. In the alcoholism field, behaviorally oriented treatment approaches have been based primarily on social learning theory, a variant of behavior theory that starts with the basic stimulus-response models of operant and classical conditioning but also incorporates the role of cognitive processes.

As outlined by one of the major proponents of the use of behavior therapy techniques for the treatment of alcoholism, Barbara McCrady, Ph.D., reinforcement patterns involving families struggling with alcoholism issues take on three major forms (i.e., types of responses or consequences families establish for drinking behavior): 1) reinforcement for drinking behavior in the form of attention or caretaking, 2) shielding the alcoholic from experiencing the negative consequences, and 3) punishing drinking behavior (McCrady 1986, p. 310).

Faced with this clinical situation, the behavior therapist would attempt to do the following:

1. Identify specific sequences of behavior toward identifying the stimulus-response patterns associated with repetitive drinking episodes.
2. Categorize these response patterns (consequences) as either positively or negatively reinforcing drinking behavior.
3. Introduce interventions to increase and reinforce positive behavioral interactions at the spousal or family level and concomitantly decrease negative behavioral response patterns related to drinking. The terms *positive* and *negative* here connote consequences that seem to further increase drinking behavior (negative reinforcers) or those that reinforce or reward decreased drinking (positive reinforcers).

Toward these goals the assessment phase of treatment focuses on identification of specific behaviors that can be targeted for subsequent interventions. Treatment approaches use the now familiar techniques of monitoring behavior, establishing and rehearsing alternative behavioral sequences, and establishing specific behavioral goals regarding positive reinforcement patterns (Jacobson et al. 1989; McCrady 1990; O'Farrell and Cutter 1984).

## The Family Functioning Model

The third major conceptual scheme offered by family-oriented alcoholism clinicians is one that places greater emphasis on the overall functionality of the family system. As described by its main proponents, Kaufman and Pattison (1982), it can be thought as primarily a typological model. Four different family types are described, each based on a descriptive analysis of the behavioral responses of the family to the stresses and challenges posed by chronic alcoholism.

The family types are as follows: 1) the functional family system, in which alcoholic drinking is thought to be the product primarily of personal neurotic conflict or individual social strains but not of family systemic malfunction; 2) the neurotic, enmeshed family system, in which drinking behavior interrupts normal family tasks, causes conflict, shifts roles, and demands adjustive and adaptive responses from family members who do not know how to respond appropriately; 3) the disintegrated family system, in which family functioning has largely collapsed as the result of failure to cope adequately with drinking behavior; and 4) the absent family system, thought of as a final severing of the bonds between the family and the alcoholic member, either as a result of extrusion or of family dissolution.

This classification scheme, which bears obvious analogous features to the family systems model described above, seems to be particularly useful as a guide to treatment planning. For example, functional family systems are thought to respond well to treatment plans that engage them in a supportive plan aimed mainly at the identified alcoholic member, such as the use of disulfiram (Antabuse), group therapy for the alcoholic member, and Alcoholics Anonymous (AA). The neurotic, enmeshed family system, on the other hand, usually is in need of a treatment program that aims at restructuring the entire family system, and may call for hospitalization of the drinking member as an initial step in order to involve the family in therapy. In the disintegrated family system, separate but concurrent treatment programs for the identified alcoholic and the family are often recommended. Here the family might be engaged in supportive treatment and/or Al-Anon while a largely independent, individually oriented treatment program is instituted for the alcoholic member. Finally, the absent family system is, by definition, usually not available to the therapist, and treatment centers entirely on the alcoholic individual.

## Social Network Therapy

The fourth approach, based on a social systems model (Colletti and Brownell 1982; Galanter 1993; Moos et al. 1989), uses a variety of family interventions in support of a treatment plan targeted at the alcoholic individual as the primary patient. Here, the involvement of the family is undertaken with one or more of the following goals in mind:

1. To obtain more accurate and complete historical data regarding alcoholism history of the identified patient
2. To increase the likelihood of engagement of the patient in the treatment process
3. To increase compliance rates, especially as regards disulfiram therapy and detoxification strategies
4. To increase the social supports available to the alcoholic individual, especially during the postdetoxification period
5. To provide independent counseling to family members regarding their own coping strategies and psychological sequelae attendant to the impact of chronic alcoholism on family life

Typically, these goals are achieved by establishing a concurrent program for family members parallel to and integrated with the treatment program for the identified alcoholic member of the family. For example, family sessions (often without the alcoholic member present) might occur on a regular basis during the time when the alcoholic member is engaged in a residential detoxification program. Another popular approach has been the use of multiple family group psychotherapy, groups that focus on issues presumably relevant to the nonalcoholic members of the family, including supportive approaches that are geared to assist families in dealing with common difficulties they face as a result of having an alcoholic member. In some instances these are established for spouses and/or children that meet concurrently with groups for the alcoholic family members. In other instances the alcoholic members are included in the group, but the focus remains a social systems one.

## Al-Anon Groups

It is important to include a word here about the use of self-help groups designed for family members as part of treatment planning. The above four models of family therapy for alcoholism have all been proposed by family therapy specialists. For the most part, they are also designed to be implemented by family therapy clinicians.

However, by far the most active family-oriented program for alcoholism is a self-help one: the Al-Anon family group. Al-Anon is an indigenous self-help movement that arose spontaneously as a parallel but separate movement to AA in the 1940s. Al-Anon family groups are modeled after AA (i.e., a group fellowship of peers sharing a common problem). In the case of Al-Anon, the peers are spouses, children, and close relatives of alcoholic individuals who are usually, but not necessarily, part of an AA group.

Ablon (1977), who has extensively studied the Al-Anon movement, suggested that successful Al-Anon members must accept one basic didactic lesson and three principles for operating in the groups themselves. The didactic lesson is the acceptance of the AA concept of alcoholism as "an obsession of the mind and an allergy of the body," implying that the alcoholic is suffering from a disease that is totally outside his or her control. The three operating principles are the following: first, a "loving detachment from the alcoholic," in which family members accept as a given that they are powerless to intervene constructively in the behavior of the alcoholic family member; second, the reestablishment of the individual's self-esteem and independence; and third, a reliance on a "higher power," a spiritual emphasis that, of course, also closely parallels AA.

Family therapists are divided about combining traditional family therapy approaches with concurrent involvement in AA or Al-Anon groups. Some have argued that the two approaches work at cross-purposes in that AA and Al-Anon clearly see the alcoholic individual, not the family, as the "patient." The prevailing view, however, is that participation in self-help groups is a useful adjunctive experience to family therapy for many families (Berenson 1976), especially as a component of the rehabilitation (relapse-prevention) phase of treatment.

## Integration of Models

Although I have separately delineated the main principles of family systems therapy, behavioral family therapy, the family functioning model, social network therapy, and self-help approaches, it should also be stated that it would be most unusual to find any of these approaches being practiced in "pure" form in an alcoholism treatment program. In part, this is because there are major conceptual and technical overlaps between these various approaches. For example, systems therapists routinely analyze interactional sequences of behaviors as part of their assessment procedures and also use techniques such as behavioral monitoring as part of their treatment armamentarium. In like fashion, behavioral family therapists rely heavily on systems concepts in extending notions of social learning theory to marital and family units. Another factor is that alcoholism treatment programs tend to be eclectic in their organization, with frequent mixing of psychodynamically oriented treatments alongside 12-step programs, and biomedically oriented detoxification and psychopharmacological approaches side by side with marital sessions and family education.

Nevertheless, as research efforts increasingly focus on the development of meaningful clinical typologies of the different subtypes of alcoholism, it is likely that the primary goal of treatment evaluation research will be to determine which treatment approach seems most efficacious for each of the subtypes of alcoholism identified within the different typologies. A concomitant of this process will be a need to more clearly delineate the core constructs of each of the therapy approaches. It is not unlikely, therefore, that the next decade will see an increasing emphasis placed on attempts to clarify those components of the different family therapy treatment approaches that contribute uniquely to efficacy for a specific pattern or subtype of alcoholism.

## ▼ FAMILY SYSTEMS APPROACHES TO ASSESSMENT AND DETOXIFICATION

Of the various family therapy approaches to alcoholism treatment outlined above, the family systems approach is perhaps the most unique. I will therefore describe in somewhat greater detail how the first two phases of treatment—assessment and detoxification—are implemented if one is using a family systems therapy approach.

### Assessment Strategies

In the typical clinical situation, therapists are guided in their assessment approaches by the need to answer two fundamental questions: 1) what is wrong here (i.e., the question of diagnosis), and 2) how should the clinical problem be treated. Treatment evaluation typically includes assessment of patient strengths and weaknesses, as well as a review of treatment options.

Family therapists undertake the same assessment process, but in the family systems approach particular emphasis is placed on family-level evaluation. Toward that goal, the assessment phase is typically carried out via conjoint interviews of the whole family and/or important subunits (especially the marital dyad). In many regards, the material covered parallels that of an individual assessment of an alcoholic patient. But in this approach, one has available the multiple perspectives of all family members, and the data base therefore tends to be both richer and far more reliable than is the case with assessment of the alcoholic individual alone.

In one area in particular, this ability to obtain multiple perspectives has proven especially valuable—that is, in assessing the impact of intoxicated behavior on family regulatory mechanisms (as discussed previously, these mechanisms include family problem-solving styles, daily routines, and family rituals). A key aspect of the family systems model of alcoholism treatment posits that differences in patterns of interactional behavior in the presence versus absence of active drinking must be understood *as a preliminary* to undertaking detoxification. Otherwise, the complex ways in which alcohol-related behaviors have become incorporated in family life will not be understood, and as a consequence removal of alcohol may inadvertently destabilize rather than improve family life.

Consequently, an interest has been generated in the development of assessment techniques for specifically addressing these differences. In some instances an opportunity to assess behavior under "wet" conditions is afforded by the alcoholic family member appearing for a treatment session in an intoxicated state. The therapist can use this opportunity to observe differences in interaction patterns regarding such variables as activity/passivity of various family members, interaction rates, range of affective expression, levels of direct conflict, verbal content (especially as regards raising of problem areas not previously mentioned), interactional distance, prevailing mood, and degree of interpersonal engagement. For example, an observation that a marital couple seems more emotionally engaged during such a session might lead to speculations that the couple is inadvertently using this engagement to carry out problem solving during periods of intoxication, a factor that might presumably then become a reinforcer of subsequent episodes of drinking.

At the same time, it is important to note that studies of such differences in patterns of interactional behavior under wet versus dry conditions, although having established that such differences do exist, have remained speculative as to the functional or adaptive consequences of this biphasic quality of family life (Davis et al. 1974; Liepman et al. 1989b; Steinglass et al. 1977). Also important to underscore here is that individual families differ in their response to the presence of an intoxicated member (e.g., one family might forcefully engage the intoxicated member; another might avoid or isolate the drinker). This also suggests that the direction of changes in interactional patterns during wet conditions may vary considerably from family to family as well.

Further, it might also be the case that the concept that alcohol use might have adaptive consequences for family behavior would be true only for certain *subtypes* of alcoholic families (e.g., the "neurotic/enmeshed" or "disintegrated" families described by Kaufman [1985], or the "stable wet" families described by Steinglass [1980]). However, for these families, at least, an assessment strategy that allows the therapist to carefully observe and delineate behavior sequences in families under wet conditions might be quite useful.

One such technique for more systematically carrying out such an enterprise has been suggested by Liepman et al. (1989a), a technique they have called "family behavior loop mapping." In this technique, sequential behaviors are mapped to construct circular loops, with particular emphasis placed on determining which aspects of the sequence occur as the alcoholic family member moves from dry to wet to dry conditions in cyclical fashion.

An analysis of these loops is then useful not only in developing a better appreciation of the interface between drinking behavior and patterns of family interaction but also in identifying specific behavioral sequences that might be addressed in a behaviorally oriented or systemically oriented family therapy approach. An example of such a loop, as described by Liepman et al. (1989c) is the following:

1. Son misses nurturing behavior and becomes angry.
2. Son acts out anger by doing something destructive.

3. Mother detects son's misbehavior and decides to punish him.
4. Mother asks Dad to punish son.
5. Dad agrees to do this despite his fear of his large son.
6. Dad drinks alcohol to relieve fear, which reinforces drinking.
7. Dad whips son fiercely.
8. Son cries out in pain.
9. Mother responds to cries by interrupting Dad's punishment.
10. Dad feels undermined and retreats while Mother hugs son.
11. Son is reinforced by hugging for acting out anger and Mother is reinforced for rescue behavior.
12. Dad yells over resentment toward Mother's undermining of discipline and toward son's destructive acts.
13. Mother yells back at Dad for being so rough on son but yells at son for being bad.
14. In context of yelling and put downs, son misses nurturing behavior and becomes angry.

Again, the critical issue here is the clinician's ability to clearly demonstrate the shifts in *interactional* behavior that are consistently tied to cycling between "drinking on" versus "drinking off" states in the family. Only by having a clear picture of these patterns can the clinician fully appreciate the ways in which alcohol-related behaviors are now integral parts of family routines and problem-solving sequences.

## Family Detoxification

The family systems model of alcoholism treatment shares with virtually all other treatment approaches the belief that meaningful psychotherapeutic work can only proceed after the alcoholic family member (the identified patient [IP]) has stopped drinking. However, its approach to detoxification is fundamentally different in two regards: 1) that the goal for this treatment phase is *family level* detoxification (including, of course, abstinence on the part of the IP), and 2) that the central technique for accomplishing detoxification is the establishment of a contract *with the entire family* to achieve an alcohol-free environment at a family level, as well as individual level. (The most complete description of this approach to treatment can be found in Steinglass et al. 1987.)

The underlying rationale for family detoxification could be stated as follows: Whether or not alcoholism started because of the behavior of one individual within the family, by the time it reaches its chronic phase it has become a central organizer of important aspects of family life. For the marital couple being treated, it is likely that important aspects of their interaction patterns are now inexorably linked to patterns of alcohol consumption on the part of the IP. Daily routines may be paced to drinking patterns. Interaction rates, problem solving, and so forth, all have been shaped by the types of behaviors the couple manifests when drinking is occurring. Each spouse has developed strong opinions and feelings about the reasons for and implications of alcoholic drinking, and these views have become fixed. Associated behaviors (e.g., physical violence, sexual behavior, employment records) and their exigencies have required family attention and responses. These responses may also have placed heavy demands on family emotional and financial resources. In all these ways, alcoholism has invaded family life and dictated the shape and flavor of life within the family.

The cessation of drinking by the IP will therefore have profound implications for all members of the family. Hence, the entire family has a stake in how the detoxification process unfolds. Further, because chronic alcoholism is now driving (organizing) much of family life, detoxification will initially at least be a *destabilizing* event for the family. For these reasons, it is important that the detoxification process be framed from a family as well as IP perspective—hence the establishment of the twofold goal of first, facilitating a cessation of drinking by the alcoholic family member, and second, establishing an "alcohol-free" psychosocial environment for the family. It is this second goal that differentiates the family systems approach from more traditional individually oriented treatments. The term *psychosocial environment* as applied to the family refers to all settings in which the family is interacting and behaving as a unit, including its home and relationships with friends and relatives.

To accomplish the above aims, Steinglass et al. suggest a multiphase process that centers on the development of a written contract that is conjointly constructed by the family and the therapist—the *family detoxification contract*. The process begins with the therapist explaining to the couple the rationale and need for detoxification as the first step in successful treatment and then proceeds through a series of steps in which the couple identifies what has to be done to achieve an alcohol-free environment and assigns tasks to accomplish these goals.

As a first step, a contract is developed that is intended to ensure that no drinking occurs at home and that the household environment is made totally alcohol free. Once this first step has been accomplished (a contract has been designed *and* successfully implemented), the family environment metaphor is expanded to include the environments of the extended family and the family's social and work networks. A simpler way of saying it is that the contract first aims at detoxifying the family's daily routines, then moves on to ensure that the family's external boundaries are protected from any new alcohol invasion, and finally, when the family moves into the outside world it does so within a protective bubble that still keeps it alcohol free (i.e., they take the alcohol-free environment with them as they as a family unit venture out into the world).

Once the contract moves beyond the simple extrapolation of the family environment concept as analogous to the household and daily routines, complexity increases. The number of possible combinations and permutations exceed the ability of the contract to anticipate all possible situations, so instead the contract focuses on a delimited number of "model" exchanges between the family and the outside world that serve as examples of how the contract terms should be interpreted in such circumstances. Critical here is the therapist's ability to identify with the couple two or three situations that in the past would have been high-risk situations for drinking. Once identified, the couple then rehearses with the therapist an alternative way of handling the situation that will protect the alcohol-free family environment.

Finally, the therapist uses two additional techniques throughout the process of contracting that are designed to reinforce and solidify the terms of the contract itself. These techniques are 1) making the terms of the contract public by sharing with friends or relatives that the contract has been established and is in effect, and 2) using *rehearsing* techniques to *anticipate* any problems the couple might have with implementation of the details of the contract.

To summarize, the success of family level detoxification depends on six integrated components: 1) the detoxification contract; 2) the use of a core set of metaphors around which the detoxification contract is framed; 3) a multistage strategy for implementing the scope of detoxification; 4) the use of public disclosure to reinforce the meaning and importance of the detoxification contract; 5) the use of a prospective, anticipatory stance to identify potential challenges to abstinence; and 6) ample rehearsal of strategies to effectively meet these potential challenges to abstinence.

The family detoxification component is the most unique aspect of the systems treatment model. By asking the couple to work together on the framing of the contract, and by establishing as the treatment goals the metaphor of an alcohol-free family environment, the therapist is automatically reframing the entire alcoholism issue in family rather than individual terms. Although the therapist is not challenging that it is the IP who has actually been consuming the alcohol, he or she is dramatically reinforcing the concept that alcoholism has in important ways taken over family life. Thus at the same time that this phase of treatment is aimed at the important goal of cessation of drinking as a necessary prerequisite for further treatment, one is also carrying out the essential reframing work that will place the couple in a position to subsequently reevaluate how to reorganize family life to put in place the necessary relapse prevention tools and structures.

## ▼ EFFICACY

Although there are still few controlled clinical trials of family therapy approaches to alcoholism and drug abuse treatment, studies carried out to date have consistently indicated the superiority of marital and/or family therapy over individual therapy approaches (Collins 1990; Orford 1984; Steinglass and Robertson 1983). Further, involvement of family members substantially increases patient engagement in both detoxification and rehabilitation phases of treatment (Jacobson et al. 1989; Keane et al. 1984; Liepman et al. 1989a; Sisson and Azrin 1986). Thus the importance of family involvement in substance abuse treatment has solid empirical support.

At the same time, reviews of the family therapy literature make it clear that a wide array of family treatment techniques (e.g., family systems therapy, behavioral family therapy, multiple couples and multiple-family group therapy) have been used with this population of families, and all have their strong advocates. It is also the case that these different family therapy approaches are only beginning to be tested against each other. Nevertheless, there are by now a body of studies suggesting that most family-oriented treatment approaches are efficacious for treatment of alcoholism, and we are just now beginning to see the undertaking of studies using treatment match designs. This new generation of studies, which take advantage of the clinical models that propose different typologies of alcoholism (already discussed above) are likely to yield interesting data that in turn would form the basis of informed treatment assignments of different types of alcoholic patients to not only individual versus family-oriented treatments, but perhaps even to different types of family treatments.

### The Treatment Outcome Literature

A modest literature now exists examining the efficacy of a wide variety of family therapy approaches for the treatment of alcoholism. Although somewhat artificial, it is possible to divide the studies that have been published into a four-step sequence, with stages that roughly build on one another.

The first stage focused on an examination of the marital dynamics of alcoholic men and their wives (Edwards et al. 1973). This stage is primarily of historical significance only, in that it for some time supported pejorative attitudes toward wives of alcoholic men (i.e., it implied that these women subsidized the drinking behavior of their husbands for their own psychopathological reasons) but failed to identify useful structural and/or interactional patterns in families associated with chronic alcoholism.

The second stage comprised a series of treatment outcome studies focusing on concurrent group psychotherapy as a treatment approach for alcoholism (Ewing et al. 1961; Gliedman 1956). Although findings were uniformly positive, this type of family therapy approach has been largely supplanted by more systemically oriented programs and hence also is only of historical interest at this point.

The third stage focused attention largely on systems theory and model-building (rather than on formal treatment outcome studies). These systems approaches were also pivotal in stimulating the growing application of family therapy techniques to the treatment of alcoholic families. These techniques included conjoint family therapy (Esser 1971; Kaufman and Pattison 1981; Usher et al. 1982), marital group therapy (Arieli 1981; Gallant et al. 1970), and conjoint hospitalization of marital couples (Steinglass 1979).

The fourth stage, a natural outgrowth of the increasing experimentation with family therapy approaches, has been the formal testing of these treatments in a small series of case history treatment outcome studies and controlled clinical trials done during the 1970s and 1980s (e.g., Cadogan 1973; McCrady et al. 1982; O'Farrell et al. 1985; Zweben et al. 1988).

The following generalizations about this treatment evaluation literature seem warranted:

1. Both clinical reports and controlled studies are overwhelmingly favorable to the use of family therapy for the treatment of alcoholism. However, with rare exceptions, all studies published to date must be characterized as pilot in nature. Sample sizes are small, random assignment of patients has been carried out in only a few studies, and details regarding treatment programs and qualifications of therapists tend to be scanty. On the other hand, there are no reports in the literature suggesting that family therapy is either less effective than an alternative treatment approach to which it has been compared or that inclusion of family members in a treatment program has had detrimental effects. Nevertheless, we have yet to see a completed treatment outcome study carried out by experienced family therapists incorporating sound research principles (although one such study is currently under way at the University of California, Santa Barbara, under the direction of Dr. Larry Beutler). Nor do we have any data at this point about the comparative efficacy of the different family therapy approaches, one against the other.

2. A wide variety of family treatment approaches have been tried, including conjoint family therapy, behavioral marital therapy, concurrent group therapy, multiple couples therapy, and multiple family therapy. All have been reported to be efficacious; none has occupied a dominant position in the field.

3. There is compelling evidence that the involvement of a nonalcoholic spouse in a treatment program significantly improves the likelihood that the alcoholic individual will participate in treatment as well. Although here also sample sizes tend to be small in each of the studies reported, the consistency of this finding coupled with the magnitude of reported differences in dropout rates when spouses are included in treatment versus when they are not suggests that this finding would survive replication in a large-scale study.

Further, more detailed studies are now beginning to emerge suggesting that specific behavioral techniques may be useful in helping nonalcoholic spouses to motivate their alcoholic husbands or wives to begin treatment (Sisson and Azrin 1986). That this study also demonstrated the usefulness of specific behavioral strategies focusing on reinforcement of positive consequences for not drinking and negative consequences for intoxication as useful in contributing to positive treatment outcome further underscores how important spousal involvement may be in overall treatment efficacy.

A related theme is that of overall compliance with ongoing treatment, even when the treatment is biomedically oriented. For example, around the critical issue of compliance with disulfiram use, Keane et al. (1984) demonstrated an unusually high rate of compliance with the disulfiram regimen (88%) when the treatment regimen included a contract to take the disulfiram in the presence of the spouse and subsequent positive reinforcement for taking disulfiram. That compliance should improve if spouses can be appropriately involved as active members of treatment planning and implementation would surely have considerable face validity. It is thus encouraging to see the emergence of data supportive of this notion.

4. There is little evidence in the treatment outcome literature that clinicians are approaching alcoholism with a sophisticated sense of family dynamics or family systems principles. Nor is there evidence that clinicians appreciate the heterogeneity of this interesting group of families. Instead, the dominant model in clinical practice remains heavily influenced by the AA/Al-Anon philosophy of "separate but equal" treatment. For example, it would be unusual to find an alcoholism treatment program that incorporates a sophisticated family assessment as a mandatory part of its workup and then designs a treatment program based on the finding of such a workup. Much more likely, a standard program exists and the alcoholic individual and family are pushed and squeezed to fit the preconceived notions, treatment schedule, and goals of this already-established program.

5. Overall, therefore, the alcoholism field is receptive to the notion that family intervention has an appropriate place in the overall treatment process but is still struggling to define the scope and form this intervention should take.

## ▼ SUMMARY: OBSTACLES TO FAMILY THERAPY IMPLEMENTATION

Despite the clear-cut advances in the development of clinical models incorporating family systems principles (noted above), and despite the compelling evidence of the profound impact of chronic alcoholism on family life, family therapy is not widely used in traditional alcoholism treatment programs. Several factors are likely contributors to this situation:

The current politics of substance abuse treatment have undermined the ability of experienced family therapists and experienced substance abuse clinicians to meet on a common ground. Typically, therefore, the family component offered in an alcoholism or drug abuse rehabilitation program is being administered by therapists with only elementary level training in family interview skills and conjoint therapy techniques. Particular concern must be expressed about the tendency to provide uniform, prepackaged treatment modules for families, as if all families with alcoholism/drug abuse problems have comparable issues and psychodynamics.

Further, these family treatment modules are rarely informed by either advances in family systems treatment approaches or the growing body of research findings about alcoholism and the family. For example, we have already discussed that family researchers have delineated major within-group differences in alcoholic families and have proposed interesting typologies of families based on drinking patterns (Dunn et al. 1987; Jacob et al. 1983), family developmental issues (Steinglass et al. 1987), or family functional status (Kaufman and Pattison 1982). The clinical relevance and implications of these typologies have also been thoroughly described. However, few treatment programs seem cognizant of these research-based clinical treatment models, preferring instead to impose standardized programs on families independent of the heterogeneity of this clinical population.

Finally, the tendency in many treatment programs to compartmentalize individual and family-focused treatment components precludes the implementation of systems-oriented treatment techniques. For example, in many treatment programs psychiatrists work exclusively with the individual patient, leaving to other professionals the tasks of evaluating and providing services for families. Often themselves poorly trained in family interviewing techniques, psychiatrists are therefore more comfortable treating the index patient alone. Because of this separation of treatment responsibilities, the psychiatrist is likely to view the family as adjunctive to the treatment process and more likely to focus attention on the clinical parameters of the individual substance abuser alone. For the family, however, their issues center around how to cope with the challenges of a chronic, episodic illness. Although they can usually be co-opted into supporting a treatment plan designed to address the needs of the substance abuse, they often do so at the expense of their own needs and developmental priorities. In this sense, treatment success for the substance-abusing family member can at the same time result in developmental distortions and arrest for the rest of the family.

## ▼ REFERENCES

Ablon J: Perspectives on Al-Anon family groups, in Alcoholism: Development, Consequences, and Interventions. Edited by Estes NJ, Heinemann, ME. St. Louis, MO, CV Mosby, 1977

American Psychiatric Association: Diagnostic and Statistical Manual of Mental Disorders, 4th Edition. Washington, DC, American Psychiatric Association, 1994

Arieli A: Multi-couple group therapy of alcoholics. Int J Addict 16:773–782, 1981

Bennett LA, Wolin SJ, Reiss D, et al: Couples at risk for alcoholism recurrence: protective influences. Fam Process 26:111–129, 1987

Berenson D: Alcohol and the family system, in Family Therapy: Theory and Practice. Edited by Guerin PJ. New York, Gardner Press, 1976, pp 284–297

Berenson D: The therapist's relationship with couples with an alcoholic member, in Family Therapy of Drug and Alcohol Abuse. Edited by Kaufman E, Kaufmann P. New York, Gardner Press, 1979, pp 233–242

Billings AG, Kessler M, Gomberg CA, et al: Marital

conflict resolution of alcoholic and non-alcoholic couples during sobriety and experimental drinking. J Stud Alcohol 40:183–195, 1979

Cadogan DA: Marital group therapy in the treatment of alcoholism. Quarterly Journal of Studies on Alcohol 34:1187–1194, 1973

Colletti G, Brownell KD: The physical and emotional benefits of social support: application to obesity, smoking, and alcoholism, in Progress in Behavior Modification. Edited by Hersen M, Eisler RM, Miller PM. New York, Academic Pres, 1982, pp 109–178

Collins RL: Family treatment of alcohol abuse: behavioral and systems perspectives, in Alcohol and the Family: Research and Clinical Perspectives. Edited Collins RL, Leonard KE, Searles JS. New York, Guilford, 1990, pp 285–308

Cronkite RC, Finney JW, Nekich J, et al: Remission among alcoholic patients and family adaptation to alcoholism: a stress and coping perspective, in Alcohol and the Family: Research and Clinical Perspectives. Edited by Collins RL, Leonard KE, Searles JS. New York, Guilford, 1990, pp 309–337

Davis, DI Berenson D, Steinglass P, et al: The adaptive consequences of drinking. Psychiatry 37:209–215, 1974

Dunn NJ, Jacob T, Hummon N, et al: Marital stability in alcoholic-spouse relationships as a function of drinking pattern and location. J Abnorm Psychol 96:99–107, 1987

Edwards P, Harvey C, Whitehead PC: Wives of alcoholics: a critical review and analysis. Quarterly Journal of Studies on Alcohol 34:112–132, 1973

Esser PH: Evaluation of family therapy with alcoholics. British Journal of Addiction 66:251–255, 1971

Ewing JA, Long V, Wenzel GG: Concurrent group psychotherapy of alcoholic patients and their wives. Int J Group Psychother 11:329–338, 1961

Finney JW, Moos RH, Cronkite RC, et al: A conceptual model of the functioning of married persons with impaired partners: spouses of alcoholic patients. Journal of Marriage and Family Therapy 45:23–34, 1983

Frankenstein W, Hay WM, Nathan PE: Effects of intoxication on alcoholics' marital communication and problem solving. J Stud Alcohol 46:1–6, 1985

Galanter M: Network Therapy for Alcohol and Drug Abuse. New York, Basic Books, 1993

Gallant DM, Rich A, Bey E, et al: Group psychotherapy with married couples: a successful technique in New Orleans clinic patients. J La Med Soc 122: 41–44, 1970

Gelles RJ, Straus MA: Determinants of violence in the family: toward a theoretical integration, in Contemporary Theories About the Family. Edited by Burr WR, Hill R, Nye FI, et al. New York, Free Press, 1979, pp 549–581

Gliedman LH, Rosenthal D, Frank JD, et al: Group therapy of alcoholics with concurrent group meetings with their wives. Quarterly Journal of Studies on Alcohol 17:655–670, 1956

Gondolf EW, Foster RA: Wife assault among VA alcohol rehabilitation patients. Hosp Community Psychiatry 42:74–79, 1991

Herman JL: Trauma and Recovery. New York, Basic Books, 1992

Hindman M: Family violence. Alcohol Health and Research World 1:1–11, 1979

Jacob T, Krahn GL: Marital interaction of alcoholic couples: comparison with depressed and nondepressed couples. J Consult Clin Psychol 56:73–79, 1988

Jacob T, Leonard KE: Alcoholic-spouse interaction as a function of alcoholism subtype and alcohol consumption interaction. J Abnorm Psychol 97:231–237, 1988

Jacob T, Seilhammer R: Alcoholism and family interaction, in Family Interaction and Psychopathology: Theories, Methods and Findings. Edited by Jacob T. New York, Plenum, 1987, pp 535–580

Jacob T, Dunn N, Leonard K: Patterns of alcohol abuse and family stability. Alcohol Clin Exp Res 7:382–385, 1983

Jacobson NS, Holtzworth-Munroe A, Schmaling KB: Marital therapy and spouse involvement in the treatment of depression, agoraphobia, and alcoholism. J Consult Clin Psychol 57:5–10, 1989

Kaufman E: Family system variables in alcoholism. Alcohol Clin Exp Res 8:4–8, 1985

Kaufman E, Pattison EM: Different methods of family therapy in the treatment of alcoholism. J Stud Alcohol 42:951–971, 1981

Kaufman E, Pattison EM: Family and network therapy in alcoholism, in Encyclopedia Handbook of Alcoholism. Edited by Pattison EM, Kaufman E. New York, Gardner Press, 1982

Keane TM, Foy DW, Nunn B, et al: Spouse contracting to increase Antabuse compliance in alcoholic veterans. J Clin Psychol 40:340–344, 1984

Lawson G, Peterson JS, Lawson A: Alcoholism and the

Family: A Guide to Treatment and Prevention. Rockville, MD, Aspen, 1983

Liepman MR, Nirenberg TD, Begin AM: Evaluation of a program designed to help families and significant others to motivate resistant alcoholics into recovery. Am J Drug Alcohol Abuse 15:209–221, 1989a

Liepman MR, Nirenberg TD, Doolittle RH, et al: Family functioning of male alcoholics and their female partners during periods of drinking and abstinence. Fam Process 28:239–249, 1989b

Liepman MR, Silvia LY, Nirenberg TD: The use of family behavior loop mapping for substance abuse. Family Relations 38:282–287, 1989c

McCrady BS: The family in the change process, in Treating Addictive Behaviors: Processes of Change. Edited by Miller WR, Heather NH. New York, Plenum, 1986, pp 305–318

McCrady BS: The marital relationship and alcoholism, in Alcohol and the Family: Research and Clinical Perspectives. Edited by Collins RL, Leonard KE, Searles JS. New York, Guilford, 1990, pp 338–355

McCrady BS, Moreau J, Paolino TJ, et al: Joint hospitalization and couples therapy for alcoholism: a four year follow-up. J Stud Alcohol 43:1244–1250, 1982

McCrady BS, Noel NE, Abrams DB, et al: Comparative effectiveness of three types of spouse involvement in outpatient behavioral alcoholism treatment. J Stud Alcohol 47:459–467, 1986

Moos RH, Moos BS: The process of recovery from alcoholism; III: comparing families of alcoholics and matched control families. J Stud Alcohol 45:111–118, 1984

Moos R, Fenn C, Billings A, et al: Assessing life stressors and social resources: applications to alcoholic patients. J Subst Abuse 1:135–152, 1989

O'Farrell TJ, Cutter HSG: Behavioral marital therapy couples groups for male alcoholics and their wives. J Subst Abuse Treat 1:191–204, 1984

O'Farrell TJ, Cutter HSG, Floyd FJ: Evaluating behavioral marital therapy for male alcoholics: effects of marital adjustment and communication from before to after treatment. Behavior Therapy 16:147–167, 1985

Orford J: The prevention and management of alcohol problems in the family setting: a review of work carried out in English-speaking countries. Alcohol Alcohol 19:109–122, 1984

Plomin R: The role of inheritance in behavior. Science 248:183–188, 1990

Rubington E: The bottle gang. Quarterly Journal of Studies on Alcohol 29:943–955, 1968

Schuckit MA, Morrisey ER: Alcoholism in women: some clinical and social perspectives with an emphasis on possible subtypes, in Alcoholism Problems in Women and Children. Edited by Greenblatt M, Schuckit M. New York, Grune & Stratton, 1976, pp 5–35

Sheinberg M: Navigating treatment impasses at the disclosure of incest: combining ideas from feminism and social constructionism. Fam Process 31: 201–216, 1992

Sisson RW, Azrin NH: Family member involvement to initiate and promote treatment of problem drinkers. J Behav Ther Exp Psychiatry 17:15–21, 1986

Steinglass P: An experimental treatment program for alcoholic couples. J Stud Alcohol 40:159–182, 1979

Steinglass P: A life history model of the alcoholic family. Fam Process 19:211–225, 1980

Steinglass P: The alcoholic family at home: patterns of interaction in dry, wet, and transitional stages of alcoholism. Arch Gen Psychiatry 38:578–584, 1981

Steinglass P, Bennett L, Wolin SJ, et al: The Alcoholic Family. New York, Basic Books, 1987

Steinglass P, Robertson A: The alcoholic family, in The Biology of Alcoholism, Vol 6. The Pathogenesis of Alcoholism: Psychosocial Factors. Edited by Kissin B, Begleiter H. New York, Plenum, 1983, pp 243–307

Steinglass P, Tislenko L, Reiss DS: Stability/instability in the alcoholic marriage: the interrelationships between course of alcoholism, family process and marital outcome. Fam Process 24:365–376, 1985

Steinglass P, Davis DI, Berenson D: Observations of conjointly hospitalized "alcoholic couples" during sobriety and intoxication: implications for theory and therapy. Fam Process 16:1–16, 1977

Treadway D: Before It's Too Late: Working With Substance Abuse in the Family. New York, WW Norton, 1989

Usher ML, Jay J, Glass DR: Family therapy as a treatment modality for alcoholism. J Stud Alcohol 43:927–938, 1982

Wolin SJ, Bennett LA, Noonan DL, et al: Disrupted family rituals: a factor in the intergenerational transmission of alcoholism. J Stud Alcohol 41:199–214, 1980

Zweben A, Pearlman S, Li S: A comparison of brief advice and conjoint therapy in the treatment of alcohol abuse: the results of the Marital Systems study. British Journal of Addiction 83:899–916, 1988

# Family Therapy

## *Other Drugs*

*Edward Kaufman, M.D.*

Substance abuse has a profound effect on the family, and the family is a critical factor in the treatment of a substance-abusing individual. In this chapter, I will focus on the role of the family in substance abuse treatment. Family therapy cannot stand alone in the treatment of individuals with a serious substance abuse problem. However, it is a valuable and often necessary adjunct to treatment, particularly when integrated into a comprehensive program. In family therapy, there are three basic phases of the family's involvement in treatment: 1) developing a system for establishing and maintaining a drug-free state, 2) establishing a workable method of family therapy, and 3) dealing with the family's readjustment after the cessation of substance abuse. These three phases will be discussed in detail, with an emphasis on a variation in treatment techniques to meet the needs of the different types of substance-abusing individuals. The variations are based on the following factors: drug(s) abused, ethnicity, family type, stage of disease, and sex of the individual. Before this material is presented, I will review the effi-cacy of family treatment of substance-abusing individuals to date.

## ▼ EFFICACY OF FAMILY THERAPY WITH SUBSTANCE ABUSE

A major problem in assessing family therapy is that all family therapy is not the same. Thus it is difficult to generalize success for failure from one program or individual to another or to the field in general.

Hersch (1961) advocated group therapy with the parents of addicted adolescents. Granger and Shug-art (1966) conducted family therapy with more than 100 addicted males. They concluded that the treatment of choice was to treat the addicted male within his family unit.

Several family therapy outcome studies were performed in the 1970s, generally characterized by a lack of methodological sophistication. Silver et al. (1975) have described a methadone program for addicted

The author wishes to acknowledge the assistance of Laura Lowe in the preparation of this manuscript.

pregnant women and their addicted spouses; 40% of the women in treatment have become drug free and the employment rate of the men has increased from 10%–55%. Both rates are higher than those achieved by traditional methadone programs without family treatment. A problem with this study, as with most evaluations of family approaches to drug abuse, is the lack of follow-up data or control groups.

Ziegler-Driscol (1977) reported a study conducted at Eagleville Hospital that found no difference between treatment groups with family therapy and those without at 4–6 month follow-up. However, the therapists were new to family therapy and the supervisors new to substance abuse. As the therapist became more experienced, their results improved.

Hendricks (1971) found at 1-year follow-up that narcotic-addicted subjects who had received 5½ months of multiple family therapy (MFT) were twice as likely to remain in continuous therapy as addicted subjects who did not respond to MFT. Kaufman and Kaufmann's (1977) work has shown that addicted adolescents with MFT have half the recidivism rate of patients without it.

Stanton (1979) noted that of 68 studies of the efficacy of the family therapy of drug abuse, only 14 quantify their outcome. Only six of these provided comparative data with other forms of treatment of control groups. Four of the six (Hendricks 1971; M. A. Scopetta et al., unpublished observations, 1979; Stanton and Todd 1982; Wunderlich et al. 1974) showed family treatment to be superior to other modes. Winer et al. (1974) and Ziegler-Driscoll (1977) found no superiority of family treatment. Stanton (1979) concluded that "family treatment shows considerable promise for effectively dealing with problems of drug abuse" (p. 10).

Stanton and Todd (1982) have provided the field with the best documented controlled study of the family therapy of drug abuse to date. They emphasized concrete behavioral changes, which include a focus on family rules about drug-related behavior and the use of weekly urine tests to give tangible indications of progress. They were concerned with interrupting and altering the repetitive family interactional patterns that maintain drug taking.

In their family treatment groups, Stanton and Todd found on 1-year follow-up that days free of methadone, illegal opioids, and marijuana all shifted favorably, compared with a nonfamily treatment group. However, there was no significant decrease in alcohol abuse or increase in work or school productivity. They noted a high mortality rate in nonfamily therapy cases (10%) and only 2% in those who received family therapy.

However, lack of success in certain aspects of outcome is troubling. Even their best treatment group (paid family) had 31% of days on methadone, 19% illegal opioids, 12% nonopioid illegal drugs, 25% marijuana, 44% alcohol, and 63% of possible work or school days not attended or involved (an important parameter of individuation).

McCrady et al. (1986) compared the effectiveness of family therapy on drinking behavior and life satisfaction in three treatment groups: 1) minimal spouse involvement with interventions directed toward the drinker, although the spouse was present; 2) alcohol-focused spouse involvement in which coping skills for alcohol-related situations were emphasized, and 3) alcohol behavioral marital therapy in which the need to modify the marital relationship was also addressed in addition to alcohol-focused spouse involvement. Results showed better compliance, faster decrease of drinking, and a greater likelihood of staying in treatment and marital satisfaction posttreatment in the subjects receiving alcohol behavior marital therapy.

Family therapy evaluation has now reached a high level of sophistication. Since 1985, the National Institute on Drug Abuse has funded several studies of systemic-structural family therapy using comprehensive evaluation techniques. These evaluations focus on patient characteristics and heterogeneity, technique variability, deleterious or beneficial aspects of other components, patient and therapist treatment goals, therapist attributes, sample selection and attrition, patient experiences outside of and after treatment, psychiatric diagnosis in all family members, quantification of substance abuse evaluation in relation to treatment, and analysis and interpretation of data.

The family therapy techniques in two of these studies by Joanning et al. and Liddle et al. are described in detail in Kaufman and Kaufman 1992.

## ▼ DEVELOPING A SYSTEM FOR ESTABLISHING AND MAINTAINING ABSTINENCE

The family treatment of substance abuse begins with developing a system to achieve and maintain abstinence. This system, together with specific family therapeutic techniques and knowledge of family patterns commonly seen in families with a substance-abusing member, provides a workable, therapeutic approach to substance abuse.

Family treatment of substance abuse must begin with an assessment of the extent of substance dependence as well as the difficulties it presents for the individual and the family. The quantification of substance abuse history can take place with the entire family present; the substance-abusing member often will be honest in this setting, and "confession" is a helpful way to begin communication. Moreover, other family members can often provide more accurate information than the substance-abusing member (also known as the identified patient [IP]). However some IPs will give an accurate history only when interviewed alone. In taking a drug-abuse history, it is more important to know what current and past use has been of every type of abusable drug as well as alcohol. IPs also should be asked about quantity, quality, duration, expense, how intake was supported and prevented, physical effects, tolerance, withdrawal, and medical complications. At times, other past and present substance-abusing family members are identified, and their use and its consequences should be quantified without putting the family on the defensive. It is also essential to document the families' patterns of reactivity to drug use and abuse. The specific method necessary to achieve abstinence can only be decided on after the extent and nature of substance abuse is quantified.

## Early Establishment of a System for Achieving Abstinence

It is critical first to establish a system for enabling the substance-abusing individual to become drug free so that family therapy can take place effectively. The specific methods employed to achieve abstinence vary according to the extent of use, abuse, and dependence. Mild to moderate abuse in adolescents can often be controlled if both parents can agree on clear limits and expectations and how to enforce them. Older abusing individuals may also stop if they are aware of the medical or psychological consequences to themselves or the effects on their family.

If substance abuse is moderately severe or intermittent and without physical dependence, such as intermittent use of hallucinogens or weekend cocaine

abuse, then the family is offered a variety of measures, such as regular attendance at Narcotics Anonymous (NA) or Cocaine Anonymous (CA) for the IP and Al-Anon or Narcanon for family members.

Some mild to moderate substance-abusing individuals who are resistant to self-help groups may find that another system (e.g., religion, exercise regime, relaxation techniques, career change) helps them stay off of drugs (Kaufman 1985). If these methods fail, then short-term hospitalization or treatment in a 20-hour weekly intensive outpatient program may be necessary to establish abstinence and to begin effective treatment even with nondependent patients. In more severe cases of drug abuse and dependence, more aggressive methods are necessary to establish abstinence. Heroin-addicted individuals can be detoxified as outpatients with clonidine or methadone, the latter only in specialized 21-day programs. However, if substance abuse is so severe that the IP is unable to attend sessions without being under the influence of drugs, if social or vocational functioning is severely impaired, if there is drug-related violence, or if there is physical dependence, then the first priority in treatment is to stop substance abuse immediately. This involves persuading the family to pull together to achieve at least temporary abstinence. Generally, this is best done in a hospital setting. Thus if the abuse pattern is severe, hospitalization will be set as a requirement very early in therapy.

## Establishing a Method for Maintaining Abstinence

The family is urged to adopt some system that will enable the abusing individual to continue to stay free of abusable substances. This system is part of the therapeutic contract made early in treatment. A lifetime commitment to abstinence is not required. Rather, the "one day at a time" approach of Alcoholics Anonymous (AA) is recommended; the patient is asked to establish a system for abstinence, which is committed to for only one day at a time but which is renewed daily using the basic principles of NA and CA. When the patient has a history of past or present drug dependence, therapy is most successful when total abstinence is advocated.

Many individuals initially have to shop for CA or NA groups in which they feel personally comfortable. Every recovering patient is strongly encouraged to attend small study groups, which work on AA's 12 Steps, as well as larger open meetings that often have speakers and that anyone can attend. Abstinence can also be achieved in heroin-addicted individuals by drug-aided measures such as methadone maintenance or naltrexone blockade. These medications work quite well in conjunction with family therapy, as work with the family enhances compliance and the blocking effects on the primary drug of abuse helped calm down the family system so that family and individual therapy can take place. Hospitalization also calms down an overreactive family system. Another advantage of hospitalization is that it provides an intensive 24-hour-a-day orientation to treatment. This total immersion in treatment for a 14- to 30-day period may provide the impetus for the patient to get off and stay off drugs, particularly if there is effective, comprehensive aftercare. Individuals who have been dependent on illicit drugs for more than a few years generally do not do well in short-term programs, although these programs may buy time so that effective individual and family therapy can occur. For drug-dependent patients who fail in outpatient and short-term hospital programs, insistence on long-term residential treatment is the only workable alternative. Most families, however, will not accept this until other methods have failed. To accomplish this end, a therapist must be willing to maintain long-term ties with the family, even through multiple treatment failures. On the other hand, it may be more helpful to terminate treatment if the patient continues to abuse chemicals, as continued family treatment implies that change is occurring when it is not. One way to continue therapist-family ties while not condoning substance abuse is to work with the family without the patient present (discussion follows). In other cases, it is more effective to terminate treatment until all family members are willing and able to adopt a workable program for reinforcing abstinence. Families that believe that therapy is being terminated in their best interest often return a few months or years later, ready and willing to commit to abstinence from drugs of abuse (Kaufman 1985).

## Working With Families With Continued Drug Abuse

The family therapist is in a unique position in regard to continued substance abuse and other manifestations of the IP's resistance to treatment, including total nonparticipation. The family therapist still has a workable and highly motivated patient(s): the family. One technique that can be used with an absent or highly resistant patient is the *intervention* (Johnson 1973), which was developed for use with alcoholic patients but can be readily adapted to work with drug-abusing patients, particularly those who are middle class, involved with their nuclear families, and employed.

In this technique, the family (excluding the drug-abusing patient) and significant network members (e.g., employer, fellow employees, friends, neighbors) are coached to confront the patient with concern, but without hostility, about the destructiveness of his or her drug abuse and behavior. They agree in advance about what treatment is necessary and then insist on it. As many family members as possible should be included because the breakthrough for acceptance of treatment may come from an apparently uninvolved family member such as a grandchild or cousin. The involvement of the employer is crucial, and in some cases, may be sufficient in and of itself to motivate the patient to seek treatment. The employer who clearly makes treatment a precondition of continued employment, who supports time off for treatment, and who guarantees a job on completion of the initial treatment course is a very valuable ally. The employer's model is also a very helpful one for the family who needs to be able to say "we love you and because we love you we will not continue to live with you if you continue to abuse drugs. If you accept the treatment being offered to you and continue to stay off drugs, we will renew our lifetime commitment to you" (Kaufman 1985).

If the drug-abusing patient does not meet the above criteria for an intervention or if the intervention has failed, we are left with the problems of dealing with a substance-abusing family. Berenson (1979) offered a workable, three-step therapeutic strategy for dealing with the spouses or other family members of individuals who continue to abuse substances or who are substance dependent. Step 1 is to calm down the family by explaining problems, solutions, and coping mechanisms. Step 2 is to create an external supportive network for family members so that the emotional intensity is not all in the relationship with the substance-abusing patient or redirected to the therapist. There are two types of support systems available to these spouses. One type is a self-help group in the Al-Anon model, Narcanon or Cocanon, and the other is a significant others (SO) group led by a trained therapist. In the former, the group and sponsor provide emotional support, reinforce detachment, and help calm down the family. An SO group may provide more insight and less support for remaining with a substance-abusing spouse. Step 3 involves giving the spouse three choices: 1) keep doing exactly what you are doing, 2) detach or emotionally distance yourself from the patient, or 3) separate or physically distance yourself. When the patient does not change, it is labeled an overt choice 1. When the patient does not choose 2 or 3, the therapist can point out that he or she is in effect choosing not to change. If not changing becomes a choice, then the spouse can be helped to choose to make a change. In choice 2, spouses are helped to avoid overreacting emotionally to drug abuse and related behavior and are taught strategies for emotional detachment. Leaving, choice 3, is often difficult to carry out when the family is emotionally or financially dependent on the substance-abusing patient.

Each of these choices seems impossible to carry out at first. The problem of choosing may be resolved by experiencing the helplessness and powerlessness in pursing each choice.

As part of the initial contract with a family, it is suggested that the patient's partner continue individual treatment, Al-Anon, Cocanon, or a spouse group even if the patient drops out. Other family members are also encouraged to continue in family therapy and support groups. It should be reemphasized that whenever the therapist maintains therapy with a family where serious drug abuse continues, he or she has the responsibility of not maintaining the illusion that a family is resolving problems while in fact they are really reinforcing them. On the other hand, even when the substance-abusing patient does not participate in treatment, the therapist may be quite helpful to the rest of the family.

## Motivating the Entire Family to Participate

Although I describe above how to deal with a family when the IP is resistant to treatment participation, it should be obvious that treatment works best when the entire family is available for therapy. Once the family therapist has knowledge of the substance-abusing family, a program for dealing with substance abuse, and a workable personal method of family therapy, it becomes remarkably easy to get the entire

family to come in for treatment. The individual who calls for an initial appointment is generally the one who is best able to get the entire household to come in for therapy. However, in some cases, the therapist may have to contact one or more family members directly. If a reluctant family member claims to no longer be involved with the family, the therapist can truthfully point out that he or she would be valuable because of objectivity. If the member says his or her relationship with the family is too painful, then the therapist can emphasize the potential helpfulness of that individual in joining the family therapy. The therapist my emphasize his or her own inability to help the family unless the member attends. Reluctant family members can also be asked to attend to protect their interest, to prevent a skewed view, to ensure that all views are expressed, to preserve fairness, and to attend a therapy session without any obligation to participate (Bauman 1981). Most family members will agree to a single evaluative visit. It then becomes imperative for the therapist to establish a contract with the family that all members feel will relieve their pains as well as that of the IP.

Stanton and Todd (1982) have been successful in getting 70% of the families of methadone-maintenance patients, a generally unreachable group, into an initial interview. Of those who attended the initial session, 94% continued with treatment. Stanton and Todd presented 21 valuable, basic, facilitatory principles. For example, the therapist should deliver a non-blaming message that focuses on helping the patient rather than the family. Family treatment should be presented in such a way that, in opposing it, family members would be stating that they want the IP to remain symptomatic. The program should be structured in a way that does not allow the therapist to back down from enlisting whole families.

More recently, Szapocznik et al. (1988) have also used structural-strategic family therapy techniques in order to engage families in treatment. They were successful in getting 93% of experimental families into treatment compared with only 42% in a treatment-as-usual group. In addition, 77% of experimental subjects completed treatment compared with 25% of families in the control condition.

The concept of the family as a multigenerational system necessitates that the entire family be involved in treatment. The family members necessary to perform optimum treatment consist of the entire household and any relatives who maintain regular (approximately weekly) contact with the family. Relatively emancipated family members who have less than weekly contact may be very helpful to these families; sessions that include them should be scheduled around their visits home.

The use of a multigenerational approach involving grandparents, parents, spouse, and children at the beginning of family therapy as well as certain key points throughout the therapy is advised. However, the key unit with substance-abusing patients younger than about age 24 is the IP with siblings and parents. The critical unit with married patients older than 24 is the IP and spouse. However, the more dependent the IP is on the parents, the more critical is work with the parents. The majority of sessions should be held with these family units; the participation of other family members is essential to more thorough understanding and permanent change in the family.

Family therapy limited to any dyad is most difficult. The mother–addicted son dyad is almost impossible to treat; someone else, such as a lover, grandparent, or uncle should be brought in if treatment is to succeed. If there is absolutely no one else available from the natural family network, then surrogate family members in multiple family therapy groups can provide support and leverage to facilitate restructuring maneuvers (Kaufman and Kaufmann 1977).

Treatment for drug-addicted individuals and their spouses has been less effective than treatment for alcoholic couples (Kaufman 1985). This led Stanton and Todd (1982) to suggest that family treatment of narcotic-addicted males begin with their parents, and that the addict-spouse couple should not be worked with until the addicted patient's parents can "release" the patient to the spouse. In the experience of Phoenix House, there has been so much difficulty with addicted couples that they insist on separate residential treatment sites for such couples as a matter of program policy. But, at a therapeutic community at Metropolitan State Hospital in California (The Awakening Family), addicted couples have been successfully treated in the same program by insisting on couples therapy throughout their stay. Another essential aspect of treating couples with children is focusing on their functions as parents, and therapy involving children has the distinct advantage of developing parenting skills.

Substance-abusing women with young children are often best treated in programs that can house the children jointly, provide child care, and attend directly to parenting and child care issues.

## ▼ AN INTEGRATED APPROACH TO A WORKABLE SYSTEM OF FAMILY TREATMENT

### Family Diagnosis

Accurate diagnosis is as important a cornerstone of family therapy as it is in individual therapy. In family diagnosis, we look at family interactional and communication patterns and relationships. In assessing a family, it is helpful to construct a map of their basic alliances and roles (Minuchin 1974). We also examine the family rules, boundaries, and adaptability. We look for coalitions (particularly transgenerational ones), shifting alliances, splits, cutoffs, and triangulation. We observe communication patterns, confirmation and disconfirmation, unclear messages, and conflict resolution. We note the family's stage in the family life cycle. We note mind reading (predicting reactions and reacting to them before they happen, or knowing what someone thinks or wants), double binds, and fighting styles. It is helpful to obtain an abbreviated three-generation genogram that focuses on the IP, his or her parents and progeny, and the spouse's parents.

The genogram, another contribution of Bowen (1971), has become a basic tool in many family therapy approaches. A genogram is a pictorial chart of the people involved in a three-generational relationship system; it marks marriages, divorces, and births, and geographical dysfunctions may be added to it. The genogram is used to examine relationships in the extended family complex (Geurin and Pendagast 1976). Other members of the household and any other significant relatives with whom there is regular or important current contract are also included. In stepfamilies, the initial genogram must include the noncustodial parent(s) and the geographical location and family situation of all children from prior marriages; these may be extremely significant. As therapy progresses, a full but informal family genogram may be gradually developed as other important family members from the past and present are discussed. The genogram provides a cast of significant characters in the family so that a diagnostic map may be constructed. Obviously, the diagnostic frame of reference of the therapist is greatly influenced by the therapeutic system(s) used.

## An Overview of Family Treatment Techniques

Each of the systems of family therapy presently in use will be briefly summarized in this chapter, with an emphasis on the application of these techniques to substance-abusing individuals. They are classified into four schools: *structural-strategic, psychodynamic, Bowen's systems theory,* and *behavioral.* Any of these types of family therapy can be applied to substance-abusing patients if their common family patterns are kept in mind and if a method to control substance abuse is implemented.

### Structural-strategic therapy

In this approach, the structural and strategic types of therapy are combined because they were developed by many of the same practitioners, and shifts between the two are frequently made by these therapist, depending on the family's needs. The trust of structural family therapy is to restructure the system by creating interactional change within the session. The therapist actively becomes a part of the family, yet retains sufficient autonomy to restructure the family (Stanton 1981).

According to strategic therapists, symptoms are maladaptive attempts to deal with difficulties that develop a homeostatic life of their own and continue to regulate family transactions. The strategic therapist works to substitute new behavior patterns for the destructive repetitive cycles. Techniques used by strategic therapists (Stanton 1981) include the following:

1. Using tasks with the therapist responsible for planning a strategy to solve the family's problems.
2. Putting the problem in solvable form.
3. Placing considerable emphasis on change outside the sessions.
4. Learning to take the path of least resistance so the family's existing behaviors are used positively.
5. Using paradox, including restraining change and exaggerating family roles.
6. Allowing the change to occur in stages. The therapist may create a new problem so that solving it leads to solving the original problem. The family hierarchy may be shifted to a different, abnormal one before reorganizing it into a new functional hierarchy.
7. Using metaphorical directives in which the family members do not know they have received a directive.

Stanton and Todd (1982) successfully used an integrated structural-strategic approach with heroin-addicted patients who were on methadone maintenance.

### Psychodynamic therapy

Psychodynamic therapy approach has rarely been applied to substance-abusing patients because they usually require a more active, limit-setting emphasis on the here and now than is usually associated with psychodynamic techniques. However, if certain basic limitations are kept in mind, psychodynamic principles can be extremely helpful in the family therapy of these patients. As Gurman and Kniskern (1981) noted, most psychodynamic family therapists are pragmatic psychodynamic in that they use a broad-based workable system that includes psychodynamic principles and techniques.

The symptoms of the IP are viewed in the context of his or her own historical past as well as that of every family member. Psychodynamic family therapy and strategic therapies have a common ultimate goal: achieving second-order change. In other words, the goal is to change the entire family system so that dysfunction does not occur in other family members once the symptoms of the IP have been alleviated.

There are two cornerstones for the implementation of psychodynamic techniques: the therapist's self-knowledge and a detailed family history. Every family member will internalize a therapist's good qualities, such as warmth, trust, trustworthiness, assertion, empathy, and understanding. Likewise, they may incorporate less desirable qualities such as aggression, despair, and emotional distancing. It is absolutely essential that a therapist thoroughly understand his or her own emotional reactions as well as those of the family.

Important elements of psychodynamic family therapy include the following:

**Countertransference.** The therapist may have a countertransference problem toward the entire family or any individual member of the family and may get into power struggles or may overreact emotionally to affect, content, or personality. There are several common countertransference reactions to substance-abusing patients and their families. The IP's dependency, relationship suction and repulsion, manipulativeness, denial, impulsivity, and role abandonment may readily provoke countertransference reactions in the therapist. However, family therapists view their emotional reactions to families in a systems framework as well as a countertransference context. Thus they must be aware of how families will replay their problems in therapy by attempting to detour or triangulate their problems onto the therapist. The therapist must be particularly sensitive about becoming an enabler who, like the family, protects or rejects the substance-abusing patient.

**The role in interpretation.** Interpretations can be extremely helpful if they are made in a complementary way, without blaming, guilt induction, or dwelling on the hopelessness of longstanding, fixed patterns. Repetitive patterns and their maladaptive aspects to each family member can be pointed out, and tasks can be given to help them change these patterns. Some families need interpretations before they can fulfill tasks. An emphasis on mutual responsibility when making any interpretation is an example of a beneficial fusion of structural and psychodynamic therapy (Kaufman 1985).

**Overcoming resistance.** *Resistance* is defined as behaviors, feelings, patterns, or styles that prevent change (Anderson and Steward 1983). In substance-abusing families, key resistance behaviors that must be dealt with involve the failure to perform functions that enable the abuser to stay "clean."

Every substance-abusing family has characteristic patterns of resistant behavior in addition to individual resistances. This family style may contribute significantly by resistance; some families may need to deny all conflict and emotion and are almost totally unable to tolerate any displays of anger or sadness; others may overreact to the slightest disagreement. It is important to recognize, emphasize, and interpret the circumstances that arouse resistance patterns (Anderson and Steward 1983). However, early on, the therapist must avoid labeling the behavior as resistance or directly confronting it because this increases hostility and, in turn, enhances resistance. The reciprocal family interactions that lead to resistant behaviors should be pointed out.

Resistance can be focused on in the treatment contract; each family member agrees to cooperate in overcoming resistance. If a family is willing to perform its assigned tasks, then most resistances are irrelevant or can be overcome. Resistances such as blaming, dwelling on past injustices, and scapegoating can be directly discouraged by the therapist. The therapist may overcome resistance by joining techniques, including minimizing demands on the family to change so that the family moves more slowly but in the desired direction.

**Working through.** This important concept, derived from psychoanalysis, is quite similar to the structural concept of isomorphic transactions. It underscores the need to work repeatedly on many different overt issues, all of which stem from the same dysfunctional core. Thus to have real change, a family must deal with a problem over and over until it has been worked through.

This process is much quicker in family than individual therapy because when an appropriate intervention is made, the entire family system may reinforce the consequent positive change. If the system later pulls the family's behavior back to old maladaptive ways, then it becomes necessary to work the conflicts through in many different transactions until stable change takes placer. A specific psychodynamic technique that is often helpful with substance-abusing patients is the *family of origin technique* as developed by Framo (1981). In this technique, the family of origin of substance-abusing adults is worked with to understand how past difficulties are being replayed in the present and to begin to shift these transferential problems.

### Bowen's systems family therapy

In Bowen's (1971) approach, the cognitive is emphasized and the use of affect is minimized. Systems theory focuses on triangulation, which implies that whenever there is emotional distance or conflict between two individuals, tensions will be displaced onto a third party, issue, or substance. Drugs are frequently the subject of triangulation.

*Behavioral family therapy*

This approach is commonly used with substance-abusing adolescents. Its popularity may be attributed to the fact that it can be elaborated in clear, easily learned steps.

Noel and McCrady (1984) developed seven steps in the therapy of alcoholic couples that can readily be applied to married drug-abusing adults and their families:

1. *Functional analysis.* Families are taught to understand the interactions that maintain drug abuse.
2. *Stimulus control.* Drug use is viewed as a habit triggered by certain antecedents and maintained by certain consequences. The family is taught to avoid or change these triggers.
3. *Rearranging contingencies.* The family is taught techniques to provide reinforcement for efforts at achieving a drug-free state by frequent reviewing of positive and negative consequences of drug use and self-contracting for goals and specific rewards to achieving these goals. Covert reinforcement is done by rehearsing in fantasy a scene in which the IP resists a strong urge to use drugs.
4. *Cognitive restructuring.* IPs are taught to modify their self-derogatory, retaliatory, or guilt-related thoughts. IPs question the logic of these "irrational" thoughts and replace them with more "rational" ideation.
5. *Planning alternatives to drug use.* IPs are taught techniques for refusing drugs through role-playing and covert reinforcement.
6. *Problem solving and assertion.* The IP and family are helped to decide if a situation calls for an assertive response and then, through role-playing, develop effective assertive techniques. IPs are to perform these techniques twice daily as well as use them in a difficult situation that would have previously triggered the urge to use drugs.
7. *Maintenance planning.* The entire course of therapy is reviewed, and the new armamentarium of skills emphasized. IPs are encouraged to practice these skills regularly as well as reread handout materials that explain and reinforce these skills.

Families can also be taught through behavioral techniques to become aware of their nonverbal communication to make the nonverbal message concordant with the verbal and to learn to express interpersonal warmth nonverbally as well as verbally (Stuart 1980).

## ▼ SPECIFIC STRUCTURAL TECHNIQUES

In this section, I will emphasize the family therapy techniques that I have found most useful in my work with substance-abusing individuals. Many of these techniques evolve from the structural family work of Minuchin (1974) and Haley (1977). This approach also borrows from systems and psychoanalytic techniques and integrates these disparate treatment methods into one system. The reader is advised to choose those methods that are compatible with his or her personality, to learn and practice these techniques by rote, and finally to use them in a spontaneous manner. These techniques will be described individually, although most techniques are a fusion of several others as they are implemented in clinical practice. These techniques include the contract, joining, actualization, marking boundaries, assigning tasks, reframing, the paradox, balancing and unbalancing, and creating intensity. Lastly, the use of a cotherapist will be discussed.

### The Contract

The *contract* is an agreement to work on mutually agreed on, workable issues. The contract should always promise help with the IP's problem before it is expanded to other issues.

The primary contract is drafted with the family at the end of the first interview. In subsequent sessions, the concept of a contract is always maintained so that family assignments and tasks are agreed on and their implementation contracted by the family. When an individual or agency chooses an initial assessment period of more than one session, then the contract at the end of the first session may include only an agreement by the family to participate in the planned evaluation. However, the likelihood that the family will return after the first session is greatly enhanced by a contract that develops measures for problem resolution. In establishing a contract, the family must choose a system to achieve abstinence and agree to pursue that system after it has been agreed on as part of the initial evaluation.

The family should be provided with the beginnings of a system of shifting overreactivity to substance abuse in the initial contract. They may be coached to disengage from the IP, using strength gained from support groups and the therapist. At times, this disengagement can only be accomplished by powerful restructuring or paradoxical interventions. Later in therapy, contingency contracting principles can be used to facilitate mutual trust, particularly in areas such as adolescent individuation (e.g., a child agrees to be more respectful if his or her curfew is extended).

## Joining

In *joining*, the therapist adjusts himself or herself in a number of different ways to affiliate with the family system. Joining enhances the therapist's leverage to change the system. The therapist alternates between joining that supports the family system and its members and joining that challenges it. Joining with only one part of a family may severely stress or change the rest of the family. The therapist must make contact with all family members so that they will comply with the therapist even when they sense that the therapist is being unfair (Kaufman 1985). The therapist should join by respecting and not challenging the initial defensiveness so common in these families.

Joining begins in the first moment of the session when the therapist makes the family comfortable through social amenities and chatting with each member. There are three types of joining techniques: maintenance, tracking, and mimesis (Minuchin 1974). Joining can also be classified by proximity.

### Maintenance

*Maintenance* requires supporting the family structures and behaving according to the family rules. In its most extreme form, this includes accepting the family scapegoats as the problem when another family member is much more problematic. Maintenance operations include supporting areas of family strength, rewarding, affiliating with a family member, complimenting or supporting a threatened member, and explaining a problem. The therapist uses the family's metaphors, expressions, and language.

### Tracking

In *tracking*, the therapist follows the content of the family's interactions by listening carefully to what everyone has to say and by providing comments and expressions that help each member know he or she has been heard and understood.

### Mimesis

*Mimesis* involves the therapist's adopting the family's style and affect. If a family uses humor, so should the therapist. If a family communicates through touching, then the therapist can also touch. The therapist supports family members or the entire family by means of nonverbal identifications.

### Joining classified by proximity

In joining families from a position of closeness, the therapist must push to find positive aspects in all family members, particularly ones who are disliked (Minuchin and Fishman 1981). A therapist who finds something positive in someone unlikable will find that he or she then begins to like that individual. Being able to help difficult patients change positively also helps therapists to like them. Another technique is for therapists to look into their own personality and find similar characteristics. By confirming these positives, the therapist will enhance the individual's self-esteem and help make that individual more likable. In general, pointing out several individuals' complementary responsibility for negative behaviors will help the therapist join with the entire system. In joining from a middle position, the therapist gathers important information by observing his or her own ways of interacting with the family without being incorporated into the family system. Here it is often important to shift emphasis by tracking from content to process. In joining from a disengaged position, the therapist may have the role of an expert or director.

## Actualization

Patients usually direct their communications to the therapist. They should be trained to talk to each other rather than to the therapist. They should be asked to enact transactional patterns rather than describe them. Manipulating space is a powerful tool for generating actualization. Changing seating may create or strengthen boundaries. Asking two members who have been chronically disengaged or communicating through a third party to sit next to each other can actualize strong conflicts and emotions.

Many families try to look as good as possible when they enter therapy. Actualizations unleash sequences that are beyond their control and permit the therapist to see the family as it really is. Three progressively elaborated types of actualization are used (Minuchin and Fishman 1981). The first involves sequences that evolve spontaneously as families are permitted to be themselves in session. In the second, therapist-planned scenarios permit further natural interactions; these may use latent issues that are close to the surface and are beginning to evolve in session. The third, the most change-oriented type of actualization, has the family reenacting in session a pattern that is outside of their repetitive, maladaptive system and that demonstrates new ways of problem solving.

## Marking Boundaries

All individuals and subsystems are encouraged to preserve their appropriate boundaries. Each individual should be spoken to, not about, and no one should talk, feel, think, answer or act for anyone else. Each family member is encouraged to tell his or her own story and listen to and acknowledge the communications of others. Nonverbal checking and blocking of communications should also be observed and, when appropriate, pointed out and halted. "Mind reading" is very common, and is strongly discouraged because even if the mind reader is correct it almost always starts an argument. No one likes his or her reactions to be anticipated.

Symbolic boundaries are established in the session by the therapist placing his or her body, an arm, or a piece of furniture between members, by rearranging members, or by avoiding eye contact. These boundaries are supported and strengthened by tasks outside of the session. The most important boundary shift in family therapy is weakening the ties between an overinvolved parent and child and strengthening the boundary that protects the parents as a unit and supports them against parents, in-laws, affairs, and the rest of the world external to the nuclear family.

If a role or tie is removed from a family member, this relationship should be replaced by building ties with other family members or individuals outside of the family. When boundaries are strengthened around a system, it's functioning invariably improves.

## Assigning Tasks

Tasks help gather information, intensify the relationship with the therapist, continue the therapy outside of sessions, and give family members the opportunity to behave differently (Haley 1977). Tasks that work in the framework of family goals, particularly those involving changing the symptoms of the IP, should be chosen. Tasks should involve everyone in the family and bring gains to each member. A task should be successfully completed in session before one is assigned as homework.

When tasks are given they should be specific, clear, and concise. If tasks are performed successfully, they will restructure the family toward optimal functioning. Tasks that fail are used as valuable learning experiences that reveal family dysfunction. Still, the family should not be left off easily, and the reasons for their failing themselves should be explored.

## Reframing

In *reframing* (Minuchin and Fishman 1981), the therapist takes information received from the family and transforms it into a format that will be most helpful to changing the family. Reframing begins at the start of the first session as the therapist receives information from the family, molding it so that the family members feel that their problems are clear and solvable. Reframing is achieved by focusing material as it is received, selecting the elements that will facilitate change, and organizing the information in such a way as to give it new meaning. Perhaps the most common use of reframing occurs when the symptoms of an IP are broadened to include the entire family system. Another common reframing is describing the positive function of the IP's symptoms for the family.

## The Paradox

*Paradoxical* techniques work best with chronically rigid, repetitive, circular, highly resistant family systems, particularly ones that have had many prior therapeutic failures (Papp 1981).

Paradox is not used when family motivation is high, resistance is low, and the family responds readily to direct interventions. Paradox is not used in crisis situations such as violence, suicide, incest, or child abuse; here the therapist needs to provide structure and control. Paradox is often used to show progress so that a family is chafing at the bit to move faster or to exaggerate a symptom to emphasize the family's need to extrude it. A symptom that is an externalized acting-out of family conflicts (e.g, stealing, secret drug taking) can be prescribed to be performed within the family so that the family can deal with it. An individual's behavior is not prescribed without relating it to its function in the family system. At times, psychodynamic interpretations can be made in a paradoxical way that gives greater impact to reach and change the family.

### Balancing and Unbalancing

*Balancing* techniques, which tend to support a family, are conceptually similar to Minuchin and Fishman's (1981) complementary technique. They challenge the family's views of symptoms as part of a linear hierarchy and emphasize the reciprocal involvement of symptom formation while supporting the family. In using balancing as a technique, mutual responsibility is emphasized, and tasks that involve change in all parties should be given.

*Unbalancing* involves changing or stressing the existing hierarchy in a family. The therapist unbalances by affiliating with a family member of low power so this individual can challenge his or her prescribed family role, or by escalating a crisis, emphasizing differences, blocking typical transactional patterns, developing implicit conflict, and rearranging the hierarchy (Minuchin and Fishman 1981). Unbalancing should be attempted only after the therapist has achieved a great deal of power through joining.

### Creating Intensity

*Creating intensity* techniques are verbal devices used to ensure that the therapist's message is heard and incorporated by the family. One simple way to be heard is to repeat either the same phrase or different phrases that convey the same concept. Another way of creating intensity is through isomorphic transactions that use many different interventions to attack the same underlying dysfunctional pattern.

The amount of time a family spends on a transaction can be increased or decreased, as can the prox-

imity of members during an interaction. Intensity can also be created by resisting the family's pull to get the therapist to do what they want.

### Individual Versus Cotherapy

*Cotherapy* is very helpful in work with these families for a number of reasons. One therapist can join with one segment of the family (e.g., parents) while the other joins with the sibling subsystem. One therapist can join from very close proximity while the other can maintain sufficient distance to remain objective. Cotherapy pairing can also provide the breadth of male-female or professional–ex-addict perspectives. The relationship between cotherapists may be conflictual, and it is essential that time be set aside both pre- and postsession for therapists to work through these conflicts or at times to agree to disagree.

Strategic therapists advocate that there should only be one therapist in the room with the family but that the cotherapist, treatment team, or supervisor all remain outside of the room, viewing the session through a one-way mirror. This procedure provides for objectivity for the team and a place for the primary therapist to retreat from the family tension to receive consultation. Two therapists or a team is obviously more expensive than one, but the benefits of the former may outweigh its short-term expense.

## ▼ VARIATIONS IN TREATMENT FOR DIFFERENT TYPES OF DRUG–ABUSING PATIENTS

I will now consider the modification of treatment typologies necessary for optimal treatment of abusers of various types of drugs and their families. In family treatment we must consider the needs of at least one other individual and, in most cases, many others as we adapt our treatment techniques to each individual family. It is not the drug of abuse that demands modifications in techniques but other variables such as extent and severity of substance abuse, psychopathology, ethnicity, family reactivity, stage of disease, and sex (Kaufman 1985).

### Drug Type and Family Treatment

Most of the modifications in family treatment that are based on drug type occur in the first phase of treatment when a system is developed for establishing and maintaining a drug-free state. Family self-help support groups are extremely helpful adjuncts to family therapy. Cocanon is extremely helpful in dealing with the specific problems of the relatives of cocaine-abusing individuals. Some relatives of abusers of minor tranquilizers can participate well in Al-Anon, whereas the relatives of abusers of other types of drugs may find it difficult to relate to the relatives of alcoholic individuals and would work best in a specialized group. In most areas, groups such as Cocanon and Narcanon do not exist, and it is helpful to use groups of significant others that may be organized according to substance of abuse as well as by other factors such as social class and ethnicity.

Substance abuse choice may interact with a variety of factors, such as ethnicity and life-cycle stage. For example, white adolescents abuse mainly alcohol and marijuana and are less involved in the use of heroin and barbiturates that nonwhites (Carlisi 1979). Other studies have found that whites are more likely than blacks to have tried alcohol, marijuana, barbiturates, amphetamines, psychedelics, and inhalants, but are less likely to have tried cocaine or heroin (Kandel et al. 1978). As drug trends have changed, more and more white youths have at least tried cocaine. Mexican Americans are more likely to use phencyclidine, East Coast Hispanic youths to use inhalants, and so on. Younger substance-abusing individuals are more likely to abuse inhalants, hallucinogens, and marijuana; young adults, heroin; middle-age persons, tranquilizers and alcohol. With younger drug-abusing patients, we focus on the family of origin; with older patients, we focus on their nuclear family of procreation. When the drug abuse pattern is associated with a high level of criminality or antisocial personality, more intense and prolonged family treatment efforts are necessary, although the prognosis is poorer than with less antisocial patients. When there is drug dependence rather than abuse, family therapy must be more intensive and prolonged.

## Ethnicity

Ethnicity exerts a powerful effect on family function, styles, roles, and communication patterns, which supersede the differential effects of various drugs. The effects of ethnicity depend on how many generations of the family have lived in the United States and the homogeneity of the neighborhood in which

they live. In describing ethnic characteristics, we must realize that we risk overgeneralizing because of individual variations among ethnic groups (e.g., northern urban versus southern rural blacks, northern versus southern Italian family of origin).

### Italian-American families

In Italian-American families, the family of origin has the highest priority, often creating difficulties for the spouse, who must cope with a mate's intense and exclusive ties to the family of origin. Therapy with Italian-American families should focus on the renegotiation of their rigid system boundaries, which keep the extended family out of contact with the outside world (Rotunno and McGoldrick 1982). They talk openly and with exaggerated feeling, yet hide their family secrets, which are plentiful. Secrets must be dealt with delicately, as their being made known to the therapist may constitute family betrayal (McGoldrick 1982a).

The therapist must overcome being distrusted as an outsider so that the authority that is necessary to change the family can be established. The therapy then can focus on helping the IP differentiate from his or her family in more adaptive ways than through substance abuse, yet permit a face-saving way to remain within the family (Rotunno and McGoldrick 1982).

Multiple family groups (Kaufman and Kaufmann 1977) can be very helpful in providing Italian-American families the support that they need to let their children individuate. Given the insularity of the Italian-American extended family, their willingness to open up and change in a group of other families is surprising. The use of an Italian-American cotherapist, their view of the doctor as respected expert, and other Italian-American families in the group who supported the letting-go process were also helpful (Kaufman 1985).

### Jewish-American families

There is a very strong family orientation in Jewish-American families, with marriage and children central (Herz and Rosen 1982). There is also a strong sense of family democracy, with consensual decision making and diffuse generational boundaries (McGoldrick 1982b). They place a high value on verbal explanation and reassurance in child rearing and do not use strong threats (McGoldrick 1982b).

Jewish-American families value credentials and education, and the therapist should not feel threatened by questions about these issues. When credentials are established, they readily consult with the therapist as a wise person, but still retain the right to make the final judgment about which interventions they will or will not use. They prefer complex, sophisticated interventions and consider behavioral types of techniques to be superficial (McGoldrick 1982b). Talking and expressing their feelings is more important to Jewish-American families than actively changing; thus they prefer analytic techniques to strategic ones (Herz and Rosen 1982). However, tasks are essential to shift from intellect to action, and they can be given in the families' own complex terms, using their language and rituals.

The therapist must respect the rules that support enmeshed togetherness at the same time as he or she facilitates some essential boundary making.

### White Anglo-Saxon families

White Anglo-Saxon families place a strong emphasis on independence, which extrudes children from the family early and neglects the extended family. They have difficulties in communication and have an inadequate sense of self-worth if they do not meet the expectations of the Calvinistic work ethic (McGill and Pearce 1982).

In these families, the IP's difficulties are perceived as the patient's problem, not the family's (McGill and Pearce 1982). Thus white Anglo-Saxon families should be encouraged to stay involved, to provide support, and to assume control of the problem. The patient is encouraged to share his or her pain with the family members so they are able to share the responsibility (McGill and Pearce 1982). Because asking for help is so difficult for these families, the therapist should support rather than confront them in the early stage of therapy and should build trust so that their feelings of vulnerability will not be intensified (McGill and Pearce 1982). Once the problem is clearly defined and a treatment contract is made, they will proceed with hard work in therapy, with the belief that this will be sufficient for success in therapy as it is in life.

### Irish-American families

Irish-American families tend to view therapy in the same way they view confession; relating sins and gaining forgiveness (McGoldrick 1982a). Yet if the therapist uncovers their sins, they will feel embarrassed. They do not let the therapist know if they are inconvenienced or uncomfortable. Because of their politeness and loyalty, they may comply with the therapist without really changing. They view the therapist like a priest/authority and thus will respond best to a structured, problem-oriented approach or to a specific, clearly spelled-out plan such as behavior therapy (McGoldrick 1982a).

Involving a distant father is often essential to correcting the maternally dominated imbalance that is so common in Irish-American families. Some Irish-American fathers have become so totally removed from the family that it has been impossible to get them to come into therapy. Although the actual therapy may be very uncomfortable for these families, a deep sense of personal responsibility leads them to continue therapeutic work on their own after termination of formal therapy.

### Black-American families

The constant impact of racism and discrimination is a continuing and pervasive aspect of black-American family systems and is a crucial factor in their family therapy. Disciplining of children is strict and direct, but the lack of positive support by social structures leads to a high incidence of substance abuse in youth. Talking-oriented therapy is not effective or acceptable in black-American families, particularly those that have become underorganized as a result of social pressures (McGoldrick 1982b). In these families, structural therapy, which strengthens family organization while adding to its flexibility, is the most effective model.

## Family Reactivity

Substance-abusing families have been categorized according to four types: functional, enmeshed, disintegrated, and absent, each with different needs for family therapy (Kaufman and Pattison 1981).

## Functional families

Functional families have minimal overt conflict and a limited capacity for insight as they protect their working homeostasis. Thus the therapist should not be too ambitious to crack the defensive structure of the family, which is likely to be resistant. The initial use of family education is often well received. Explanation of the medical effects of drugs provides a concrete way for the family to face up to the consequences of substance abuse (Kaufman and Pattison 1981). These families can usually be taught appropriate family rules and roles. Cognitive modes of interaction are usually acceptable; more uncovering and emotional interactions may be resisted.

If abstinence and equilibrium are achieved, the therapist should be content even if the family members continue to use a great deal of denial and emotional isolation.

The achievement of a "dry system" is usually feasible. Short-term hospitalization may be required. Drug-abusing patients from functional families are often resistant to long-term residential treatment because they are protected by the family homeostasis.

## Enmeshed families

The therapeutic approach with enmeshed families is much more difficult and prolonged than with functional families. Educational and behavioral methods may provide some initial relief but are not likely to have much impact on the enmeshed neurotic relationships. Often these families are resistant to ending substance abuse, and the therapist is often faced with working with the family while substance abuse continues.

Although initial hospitalization or detoxification may achieve temporary abstinence, the IP is highly vulnerable to relapse. Therefore, long-term family therapy with substantial restructuring is required to develop an affiliated family system free of substance abuse. An integrated synthesis of several schools of family therapy techniques may be required.

Because of the enmeshment and explosiveness of these families, it is usually necessary to reinforce boundaries, define personal roles, and diminish reactivity. The therapist will have to be active and directive to keep the emotional tensions within workable limits. Disengagement can be assisted by getting family members involved with external support groups.

## Disintegrated families

In disintegrated families, there is a prior history of reasonable vocational function and family life but a progressive deterioration of family function, and finally separation from the family. The use of family intervention might seem irrelevant in such a case. However, many of these marriages and families have fallen apart only after severe drug-related behavior. Further, there is often only pseudoindividuation of the patient from marital, family, and kinship ties. These families cannot and will not reconstitute during the early phases of rehabilitation. Early therapeutic sessions are usually characterized by apathy or by intense hostility toward the IP. Thus the early stages of treatment should focus primarily on the substance-abusing patient. However, potential ties to spouse, family, relatives, and friends should be explored early in treatment, and some contact should be initiated. When abstinence and personal stability have been achieved over several months, the family can be worked with to reestablish family ties, but reconstitution of the family unit should not be a necessary goal.

## Absent families

In absent family systems, there is a total loss of the family of origin and a lack of other permanent relationships. Nevertheless, there are two types of social network interventions possible. The first is the elaboration of still-existing friend and relative contacts. Often these social relationships can be revitalized and provide meaningful social support. Second, in occasional younger patients, there is a positive response to peer group approaches, such as long term-therapeutic communities, NA, church fellowships, and recreational and avocational clubs, which draw them into social relationships and vocational rehabilitation. These patients can develop new skills and the ability to engage in satisfactory marriage and family life.

## Life-Cycle Phase of the Family

Often therapists must deal with several phases of the family cycle simultaneously because of the high frequency of substance abuse in many generations of the same family. The therapy of 15 year olds will be quite similar regardless of the substance being abused. The treatment of a 45-year-old corporate executive alcoholic individual may be quite different from that of a 45-year-old heroin-addicted individual because their individual styles and family systems have evolved so differently over a long period of time.

Family therapy with an adolescent IP differs from one with an adult in the following ways: less chronicity and severity, peer group involvement that is insusceptible to parental influence, less criminal activity, and fewer involvements in extrafamilial systems. Families with an adolescent IP invariably experience difficulties setting appropriate limits on adolescent individuation. The major therapeutic thrust in these families is to help the parents remain unified when setting limits while permitting flexibility in their negotiating these limits (Fishman et al. 1982).

For a drug-abusing young adult offspring, separation from the family is often a more desirable goal. To achieve this, the therapist must create intensity, escalate stress, and use other strategic unbalancing techniques. In dealing with older adults, the structural-dynamic techniques that were described in the beginning of this chapter are more often indicated.

The family therapy of a substance-abusing grandparent is just beginning to be addressed. Here it may be critical to involve their children and grandchildren to facilitate the IP's entry into treatment. Once a substance-free state is achieved, the IP grandparent can work toward achieving or reestablishing an executive or consultant position in the hierarchy (Kaufman 1979).

## Stages of Family's Reaction to IPs

Every family goes through various phases or cycles in their reactions to substance abuse. After an initial phase of denial, but still early in a substance-using career, families tend to overreact in an enmeshed and chaotic way to drug-related behavior, particularly during periods of intoxication and heavy use. Later on, there is usually more of a tendency to form a new family homeostasis, one that excludes the IP. Unfortunately, some families may stay enmeshed with the IP, and family members may be dragged down to severe depression and substance abuse themselves. Families may also cycle between disengagement and enmeshed reactivity (Steinglass 1980). During highly reactive, enmeshed stages, boundaries must be demarcated to calm down the

system. In disengaged families, trust and closeness need to be gradually rebuilt. However, the therapist must realize that repetitive cycling from enmeshed to distant may continue whether the family is in therapy or not and that these cycles must be expected. This is a strong argument for long-term therapy as well as for maintaining a positive alliance after treatment so that the family can return as needed.

## Variations According to Sex of the IP

Traditionally, substance abuse treatment in the United States has been male oriented. In countering this one-sided approach, family therapists must be aware that the families of chemically dependent women demonstrate much greater disturbance that those of male patients seeking treatment. These disturbances include greater incidence of chemical dependency of other family members, mental illness, suicide, violence, and both physical and sexual abuse. Family-related issues also bring far more women than men into treatment, with potential loss of custody of minor children heading the list (Sutker 1981).

In view of the differences in the families of substance-abusing women, family intervention strategies with women must differ from those for men. Family therapy may be more essential for substance-abusing women because of these symbolic or often actual losses of spouse and children. The therapist should not impose a stereotyped view of femininity on female patients; this could intensify the conflicts that may have precipitated their substance use (Sandmeier 1980). The therapist should be sensitive to the specific problems of women and substance-abusing women in our society and address these issues in treatment.

Substance-abusing women have special concerns about their children and child care. Family therapy may assist them to see how the parenting role fits into their lives and how to establish parenting skills, perhaps for the very first time. Many women have been victimized in a number of ways in the past, including incest, battering, and rape. Catharsis and understanding of these feelings may be essential before a woman can build new relationships or improve her present ties (Kaufman 1985).

With male patients, special issues such as pride and accepting their own dependency strivings often need to be addressed.

## ▼ FAMILY READJUSTMENT AFTER THE CESSATION OF SUBSTANCE ABUSE

Once the substance abuse has stopped, the family may enter a honeymoon phase in which major conflicts are denied. The family may maintain a superficial harmony based on relief and suppression of negative feeling. On the other hand, when the drug-dependent individual stops using drugs, other family problems may be uncovered, particularly in the parent's marriage or in other siblings. These problems, which were present all along but obscured by the IP's drug use, will be "resolved" by the IP's return to symptomatic behavior if not dealt with in family therapy. In the latter case, the family then reunites around their problem person, according to their old, familiar pathologic style.

Too many treatment programs in the substance abuse field focus their efforts on the 28-day inpatient program, neglecting aftercare. Many of these programs include a 1-week intensive family educational and therapeutic experience but with even less focus on the family in aftercare or on the IP. These intensive short-term programs have great impact on the family system but only temporarily. The pull of the family homeostatic system will draw the IP and/or other family members back to symptomatic behavior. The family must be worked with for months and often years after substance abuse first abates if a drug-free state is to continue. In addition, ongoing family therapy is also necessary for the emotional well-being of the IP and other family members.

In my experience, family therapy as described in this chapter, reduces the incidence of premature dropouts, acts as a preventive measure for other family members, serves as an extended "healthy family," and creates structural family changes that interdict the return of both drug and alcohol abuse.

## ▼ REFERENCES

Anderson CM, Stewart S: Mastering Resistance: A Practical Guide to Family Therapy. New York, Guilford, 1983

Bauman MH: Involving resistant family members in therapy, in Questions and Answers in the Practice of Family Therapy. Edited by Gurman AS. New York, Guilford, 1981, pp 16–19

Berenson D: The therapist's relationship with couples with an alcoholic member, in Family Therapy of Drug and Alcohol Abuse. Edited by Kaufman E, Kaufmann P. New York, Gardner Press, 1979, pp 233–242

Bowen M: Family therapy and family group therapy, in Comprehensive Group Psychotherapy. Edited by Kaplan H. Sadock B. Baltimore, MD, Williams & Wilkins, 1971

Carlisi JA: Unique aspects of white ethnic drug use, in Youth Drug Abuse: Problems, Issues, and Treatment. Edited by Beschner GM, Friedman AS. Lexington, MA, Lexington Books, 1979

Fishman HC, Stanton MD, Rossman BL: Treating families of adolescent drug abusers, in The Family Therapy of Drug Abuse and Addiction. Edited by Stanton MD, Todd TC. New York, Guilford, 1982

Framo JL: Integration of martial therapy with sessions with family of origin, in Handbook of Family Therapy. Edited by Gurman AJ, Kniskern DP. New York, Brunner/Mazel, 1981, pp 133–158

Granger R, Shugart G: The heroin addict's pseudoassertive behavior and family dynamics. Social Caseworks 47:643–649, 1966

Guerin PJ, Pendagast EF: Evaluation of family system and genogram, in Family Therapy: Theory and Practice. Edited by Guerin PJ. New York, Gardner Press, 1976, pp 450–464

Gurman AS, Kniskern DP: Handbook of Family Therapy. New York, Brunner/Mazel, 1981

Haley J: Problem Solving Therapy. San Francisco, CA, Jossey-Bass, 1977

Hendricks WJ: Use of multifamily counseling groups in treatment of male narcotic addicts. Int J Group Psychother 21:34–90, 1971

Hersch R: Group therapy with parents of adolescent drug addicts. Psychiatr Q 35:702–710, 1961

Herz FM, Rosen EJ: Jewish families, in Ethnicity and Family Therapy. Edited by McGoldrick M, Pearce JK, Giordano J. New York, Guilford, 1982, pp 364–392

Johnson VE: I'll Quit Tomorrow. New York, Harper & Row, 1973

Kandel D (ed): Longitudinal Research on Drug Use: Empirical Findings and Methodological Issues. Washington, DC, Hemisphere, 1978

Kaufman E: The application of the basic principles of family therapy to the treatment of drug and alcohol abusers, in Family Therapy of Drug and Alcohol Abuse. Edited by Kaufman E, Kaufmann P. New York, Gardner Press, 1979

Kaufman E: Substance Abuse and Family Therapy. New York, Grune & Stratton, 1985

Kaufman E, Kaufmann P: Multiple family therapy: a new direction in the treatment of drug abusers. Am J Drug Alcohol Abuse 4:467–468, 1977

Kaufman E, Kaufmann P (eds): Family Therapy of Drug and Alcohol Abuse, 2nd Edition. Boston, MA, Allyn & Bacon, 1992

Kaufman E, Pattison EM: Different methods of family therapy in the treatment of alcoholism. J Stud Alcohol 42:951–971, 1981

McCrady B, Noel NE, Abrams DB, et al: Comparative effectiveness of three types of spousal involvement in outpatient behavioral alcoholism treatment. J Stud Alcohol 14:459–467, 1986

McGill D, Pearce JK: British families, in Ethnicity and Family Therapy. Edited by McGoldrick M, Pearce JK, Giordano J. New York, Guilford, 1982, pp 457–479

McGoldrick M: Irish families, in Ethnicity and Family Therapy. Edited by McGoldrick M, Pearce JK, Giordano J. New York, Guilford, 1982a, pp 310–340

McGoldrick M: Normal families: an ethnic perspective, in Normal Family Processes. Edited by Walsh F. New York, Guilford, 1982b

Minuchin S: Families and Family Therapy. Cambridge, MA, Harvard University Press, 1974

Minuchin S, Fishman HC: Family Therapy Techniques. Cambridge, MA, Harvard University Press, 1981

Noel NE, McGrady BS: Behavioral treatment of an alcohol abuser with the spouse present, in Power to Change: Family Case Studies in the Treatment of Alcoholism. Edited by Kaufman E. New York, Gardner Press, 1984, pp 23–77

Papp P: Paradoxical strategies and countertransference, in Questions and Answers in the Practice of Family Therapy. Edited by Gurman AS. New York, Brunner/Mazel, 1981

Rotunno M, McGoldrick M: Italian families, in Ethnicity and Family Therapy. Edited by McGoldrick M, Pearce JK, Giordano J. New York, Guilford, 1982, pp 340–363

Sandmaier M: The Invisible Alcoholics: Women and Alcohol Abuse in America. New York, McGraw-Hill, 1980

Silver FC, Panepinto WC, Arnon D: A family approach in treating the pregnant addict, in Developments in the Field of Drug Abuse. Edited by Senay E. Cambridge, MA, Schenkman Publishers, 1975

Stanton MD: Family treatment approaches to drug abuse problems: a review. Fam Process 18:251–280, 1979

Stanton MD: An integrated structural/strategic approach to family therapy. Journal of Marital and Family Therapy 7:427–439, 1981

Stanton MD, Todd TC: The Family Therapy of Drug Abuse and Addiction. New York, Guilford, 1982

Steinglass P: A life history model of the alcoholic family. Fam Process 19:211–216, 1980

Stuart RB: Helping Couples Change. New York, Guilford, 1980

Sutker PB: Drug dependent women: an overview of the literature, in Treatment Services for Drug Dependent Women, Vol 1 (NIDA Publ ADM-81-1177). Edited by Beschner GM, Reed B, Mondanaro J, et al. Rockville, MD, National Institute on Drug Abuse, 1981, pp 25–51

Szapocznik J, Perez-Vidal A, Brinkman AL, et al: Engaging adolescent drug users and their families in treatment: a strategic structural systems approach. J Consult Clin Psychol 56:552–557, 1988

Winer LR, Lorio JP, Scrofford I: Effects of Treatment on Drug Abusers and Family. Report to SOADAP, 1974

Wunderlich RA, Lozes J, Lewis J: Recidivism rates of group therapy participants and other adolescents processed by a juvenile court. Psychotherapy: Research and Practice 11:243–245, 1974

Ziegler-Driscoll G: Family research study at Eagleville hospital and rehabilitation center. Fam Process 16:175–189, 1977

# Treatment Modalities

*Subsection 3C: Special Programs*

# Alcoholics Anonymous and Other 12-Step Groups

*Chad D. Emrick, Ph.D.*

Since its founding in 1935, Alcoholics Anonymous (AA) has grown into a worldwide organization with more than 1 million active members in more than 87,000 groups in over 100 countries. Its success as a social movement is indisputable, exercising considerable influence on the professional community, government agencies and programs, as well as the general public (Makela 1991). The shape of public policy and opinion has been substantially determined by the depiction in film, television, and the print media (including AA's numerous publications; Littlefield 1988) of AA's primacy and potency in helping "alcoholics" "recover" from "alcoholism." Within the context of AA's exceedingly high profile, health care providers can easily fall prey to the comforting belief that any patient who suffers from a problem with alcohol or other drug needs to go to AA or other appropriate 12-step group. Should the patient not go, he or she is thought of as "in denial," "resistant to treatment," and unlikely to make any change in his or her relationship with mood-altering chemicals.

In actuality, a sizable body of quantitative research, undertaken to explore the suitability and ef-

fectiveness of AA and its corollary organizations, offers a disturbing challenge to the comfort gained from such reasoning. The purpose of this chapter is to inform health care providers about pertinent findings from this quantitative research and then to apply these findings to the practice of caregivers as they strive to make the best use of AA and other 12-step groups.

## ▼ WHEN TO REFER TO AA OR OTHER 12-STEP GROUPS

Primary caregivers are repeatedly faced with the responsibility of making recommendations to patients who are known to have or are suspected of having a problem with alcohol or other drugs. As will be documented later in this chapter, it is inadvisable to tell every such patient that AA or another 12-step group will be necessary or even helpful in dealing with his or her chemical dependency problem. Inasmuch as these groups are not for everyone, how can the primary caregiver decide when to advise a patient to pursue them?

A recently completed meta-analysis of the quantitative research literature on the affiliation with AA (Emrick et al. 1993) offers some help at least with respect to the alcohol-dependent patient. This meta-analysis reported that alcohol-troubled individuals with certain characteristics have been found consistently across samples to be more likely to become involved with AA. More likely to affiliate were those who had a history of using external sources of support to stop drinking, experienced loss of control of drinking behavior itself as well as of behavior when under the influence of alcohol, consumed large quantities of alcohol on days when drinking occurred, suffered anxiety about drinking behavior, been obsessively, compulsively involved with drinking, believed that drinking had enhanced their mental functioning, and engaged in religious/spiritual activity.

Health care providers should not act heedlessly on these findings, however, inasmuch as with the exception of the variable, using external sources of support to deal with drinking, all of the personal characteristics identified in the meta-analysis related only modestly at best with AA affiliation. This means that even though a patient may have the characteristics of an individual who is likely to affiliate with AA, there is no certainty that he or she will become a member. Likewise, individuals who do not possess the characteristics of the probable affiliate as identified by the results of the meta-analysis may nevertheless become actively involved in the organization.

Furthermore, an array of variables have been measured with respect to their possible association with AA affiliation in but a single study. Although such data do not enable us to determine if a specific variable is a reliable correlate of affiliation with AA, they do offer intriguing suggestions about additional characteristics that might be associated with an individual's becoming a member of AA and might therefore further enlighten the health care provider about the type of patient he or she should most assertively encourage to seek membership in AA. Among these suggested correlates are the following:

▼ Having an Irish background (found in a Boston sample)
▼ Having a less flexible thinking style
▼ Having poorer psychosocial adjustment
▼ Being more likely to label the self as "alcoholic"
▼ Possessing more of an authoritarian attitude
▼ Having a shorter duration of drinking problems

▼ Having consumed alcohol in a greater number of situations
▼ Experiencing one's religious life more intrinsically
▼ Having less conflict regarding one's religious life
▼ Being more likely to view God as being in control of life's events
▼ Having less of a general internal control orientation
▼ Being more likely to perceive control as resting with both self and with God
▼ Being less prone to think of God as a passive influence in one's life with oneself being in control
▼ Being more given to thinking of God as being in control of life's experience with oneself being in a passive role
▼ Being more likely to have experienced an intense personal religious experience
▼ Being more ready to perceive that one's drinking problems have caused social/interactional problems rather than vice versa
▼ Having experienced a warm childhood environment
▼ Having lived in a childhood environment in which adults engaged in alcohol and drug use

Two or more investigators have explored still other affiliation variables with one of two results: Either the samples reported no or at best low correlations between the variable and AA affiliation, or the samples found substantially different correlations for the variable, with the differences not being attributable to chance fluctuation about a single population parameter. Demographic characteristics such as sex, age, education, intelligence, marital status, employment status, and socioeconomic status accounted for a sizable portion of these findings, suggesting that the demographics of a patient may be of little value in deciding who to direct to AA.

Given the complexity of currently available data, for what then should the health care professional look to guide him or her in identifying those individuals who might be advised most wisely to attend AA? It looks like the best bet is to concentrate on obtaining a good understanding of the patient's drinking problem itself (e.g., the quantity of alcohol consumed, degree of anxiety about drinking, previous efforts to get support to stop drinking) as well as certain facets of the patient's psychological functioning (e.g., perceived locus of control, spiritual/religious orientation, thinking style, attitude toward formal authority). Most suitable for strong encouragement to go to AA seems to be the patient who suffers from a relatively strong degree of alcohol problem characterized by loss of control of drinking behavior and loss of control of behavior when drinking, drinking large amounts of alcohol on those days when drinking occurs, having more worry and anxiety about drinking, being more preoccupied with and compulsively involved with drinking, and more often espousing beliefs about how alcohol use improves his or her ability to function mentally. If this patient has had a history of seeking out help from others to stop drinking and has been active in the spiritual/religious domain of life, his or her candidacy for the "go-to-AA" advice is even greater. Further markers for possible successful affiliation include having an inflexible cognitive style, having a readiness to accept formal authority, and being less likely to believe that what occurs in life is under the patient's control.

Although health care professionals are advised to focus most sharply on these patient characteristics, they would nevertheless be smart to remember that *all* alcohol-troubled individuals are both possible acceptors of and potential rejecters of the organization. This advice can in all probability be extended to the acceptance or rejection of other 12-step groups by chemically dependent patients. Any further refinement of the assessment process for chemically dependent patients must await good quality prospective and longitudinal studies of affiliation with AA or other 12-step groups using complex multivariate analyses (see Glaser 1993). In the meantime, caregivers can help rejecters of these groups explore recently established alternatives to 12-step programs such as Rational Recovery and Secular Organizations for Sobriety. These alternatives may not be attractive either, but rejecters of 12-step programs would be well served by encouragement to investigate them.

## ▼ WHAT TO ENCOURAGE PATIENTS TO DO IN AA OR OTHER 12-STEP GROUPS

Once a patient has started going to AA or another 12-step group, what aspects of the experience should health care providers stress for the patient to maximize the beneficial effects of the organization? Obviously, a 12-step group is a highly complex, multifaceted entity that interacts in diverse ways with chemically dependent individuals. Any inflexible expectations or prescriptions concerning a patient's participation in a 12-step organization is therefore improper. Some patients may find benefit in attending meetings daily or even several times per day, whereas others may receive effective help from only a weekly meeting or less. Some individuals may create an entire social life within the 12-step community; others may attend meetings, have individual meetings with a sponsor, and otherwise live their lives outside of the community. Certain patients will find optimal benefit in attending meetings for only a few months, others will participate for a few years and then "mature out" of the organization, and still others will decide that only a lifetime of involvement will ensure their living without dependence on major mood altering chemicals.

On the surface, 12-step groups take a rather doctrinaire approach to participation. Members are encouraged to attend meetings very frequently in the first 3 months of participation (i.e., to attend 90 meetings in 90 days) and are urged to commit ultimately their very identity to the organization. One sociological observer, in fact, described AA as "greedy," inasmuch as it asks for "total allegiance" from its members (Rudy 1986). Nevertheless, some seasoned members recognize that certain individuals will do quite well with a considerably smaller amount of investment than what is formally stated.

Even though chemically dependent patients take widely divergent approaches to 12-step groups, there are perhaps certain activities that are consistently and sufficiently associated with a successful membership to merit their being monitored and supported by health caregivers. Once again, the results of the recent meta-analysis of the quantitative literature on AA reported by Emrick et al. (1993) can serve to enlighten us. Quantitative research has found several components of participation in AA that are consistently and positively, although modestly, related to having a good outcome with respect to drinking behavior. These variables are 1) having an AA sponsor, 2) engaging in 12th Step work, 3) leading a meeting, and 4) increasing one's degree of participation in the organization compared with a previous time (e.g., being more involved in AA after an alcohol treatment experience than before professional treatment). Other variables found to be consistently and positively, although even more modestly, associated with having a good drinking outcome are sponsoring other AA members and "working" the last seven of the 12 Steps. Although these findings can potentially inform us about the most therapeutically active ingredients in AA, they were based, with the exception of having an AA sponsor, on samples that appear to have consisted of mostly good prognosis patients. Only a wary application of these findings in the clinical setting can therefore be considered appropriate.

Two additional variables were noted by Emrick et al. (1993) as possible covariates of drinking outcome among AA members—merely possible because they have been reported only once in the quantitative literature. These variables are 1) having the AA member reach out to other members for help in the time of need and 2) working Steps 1 and 2.

A particularly intriguing study that was not included in the meta-analysis by Emrick et al. (1993), an investigation of Step activity by Tuite and Luiten (1986), led to the identification of Steps 4 and 5 as the only ones having any therapeutic power. A combination of the findings of Emrick et al. (1993) and Tuite and Luiten (1986) thus leaves the clinician with some empirical support for encouraging AA patients to take all of the 12 Steps, with the exception of Step 3; it is reasonable to speculate that with future research even this step will get empirical support in at least some samples.

Interestingly enough, the quantitative evidence concerning the role of frequency of meeting attendance on drinking outcome has been inconsistent. Perhaps attendance frequency covaries more strongly during the initial phase of AA involvement than during later phases, but only future research will tell us if this is so. In the meantime, health caregivers are on unstable ground should they insist indiscriminately on a high frequency of attendance for all of their patients who go to AA.

In fact, the quantitative data accumulated to date concerning the relationship between drinking outcome and participation in AA leave the health care professional with but one activity that he or she can assuredly promote with patients who are members: "get a sponsor." At the same time, the data suggest that caregivers encourage their AA patients to partic-

ipate actively in the organization in terms of leading meetings, working the steps, sponsoring others, reaching out to others for help at a time of need, and—for those who have gone to AA in the past but without a stable good drinking outcome—increasing the degree of their participation in the organization. In brief, health care providers may contribute to a member's good drinking outcome by encouraging active membership. No doubt this recommendation can be extended to any chemically dependent patient who attends a 12-step group.

## ▼ HOW EFFECTIVE IS AA?[1]

Although AA is widely hailed as an effective, if not absolutely necessary, intervention for dealing with alcohol-dependent individuals, quantitative research invites the health care provider to give the organization a qualified endorsement—qualified because AA is not always helpful to, is often not necessary for, and is frequently rejected by the alcohol-troubled patient.

### AA Is Not Always Helpful

With respect to AA's limited helpfulness, a body of pertinent data has emerged from investigations into the drinking outcome of individuals who have had specialized alcohol treatment and who have participated in AA before, during, or after such treatment. The drinking outcome of these patients has been compared with the outcome of patients in specialized alcohol treatment who have not participated in AA.

The data from these research efforts tell us that attendance at AA prior to professional alcohol treatment is either unrelated or negatively related to drinking outcome (Emrick et al. 1993). This is not a surprising finding inasmuch as those individuals who need professional treatment after going to AA make up a group of AA members for whom the organization has not been sufficient in overcoming their dependence on alcohol. At the same time, that such individuals may do worse than patients who have not had exposure to AA prior to specialized treatment

---

[1]This section pertains only to AA because the bulk of quantitative research on 12-step organizations has been conducted solely or predominately on AA members. Speculation concerning the effectiveness of other 12-step groups appears in the immediately succeeding section.

suggests that health care professionals should be cautious in referring their patients to AA without first getting them involved in some form of alcohol treatment (either brief intervention or specialized care, depending on the severity of the alcohol problem; see Institute of Medicine 1990). A recent randomized clinical trial (Walsh et al. 1991) demonstrates the wisdom of this suggestion. In this study of employer-referred individuals with alcohol problems, those who were assigned professional treatment before joining AA had substantially better outcome on several alcohol-related measures over a 24-month follow-up period than did those who were simply assigned to AA attendance in the community. Subjects who had been abusing cocaine in addition to alcohol were particularly poor responders to the AA-only intervention. *Referring alcohol-troubled individuals to AA only without careful consideration of the particular needs of the patient and without close monitoring of the patient's response to the organization is simply inadequate treatment.*

Contrary to the findings pertaining to AA involvement prior to professional alcohol treatment, individuals who participate in AA during or after professional treatment have, on average, a somewhat greater chance of improvement in drinking behavior. Mean correlations between AA membership and drinking outcome have hovered around the .20 level in the published quantitative research literature (Emrick et al. 1993). Although this level of relationship is indeed modest, the finding does suggests that AA is most likely effective, an interpretation that is bolstered by the fact that the .20 correlation is not a sample statistic but rather an estimate of a population parameter that is based on more than 10,000 subjects. At the same time, much of the variance in drinking outcome has not, as yet, been explainable by participation in AA, at least with the quantitative research methods employed and published to date. This finding has led Emrick et al. (1993) to suggest that "professionally treated patients who attend AA during or after treatment are more likely to improve in drinking behavior than are patients who do not attend AA, although the chances of drinking improvement are not overall a great deal higher" (p. 57).

Improvement in drinking behavior may be positively, although modestly related to AA involvement during or after professional treatment, but what impact does participation in the organization have on other outcome measures? Quantitative research studies reveal only weak positive relationships on average between AA attendance and a problem drinker's employment situation, social/family/marital adjustment, religious activity, legal situation, and internal locus of control orientation (Emrick et al. 1993). Similarly weak, although inverse, relationships have been found between attendance and the number of physical symptoms reported by individuals with alcohol problems. Psychological adjustment measures have been observed to be more than weakly related to AA participation, yet here, as with drinking outcome, the relationships have been positive but on average of only modest size.

Given that the correlations between AA involvement and outcome measures (both drinking and otherwise) are related modestly at best, caregivers will step into a quagmire should they insist indiscriminately on their patients joining AA and making this group the core of their initial or aftercare treatment. Consistent with this advice, Patek and Hermos (1981) reported that only 9% of their liver clinic patients who had improved in drinking behavior for 1 year or more had tried AA and found it to contribute to their abstinence or "marked, sustained decrease in alcohol intake" (p. 782). Likewise, only 7% of a Swedish sample (Nordstrom and Berglund 1986) of 42 "recovered" male alcoholics considered a Swedish equivalent of AA to be a contributor to their improvement in drinking behavior. Obviously, some formally treated patients do well without AA.

Adding further strength to the advice against indiscriminate prescriptions to attend AA is the possibility that membership may actually have negative effects on some individuals who suffer from alcohol problems (see Emrick 1989; Glaser 1993; Peele 1989; Ragge 1991). Any intervention that holds the power to help some people possesses the potential to harm others, AA not excluded. Should a health care provider assume that AA participation "can't hurt," he or she may fail to intervene appropriately if a patient claims to be worsening through his or her involvement in AA. Quite often the complaint is an expression of resistance to a beneficial membership, in which case helping the patient to overcome his or her resistance to active membership is appropriate. On the other hand, the organization may truly be impacting the patient negatively as evidenced by increased drinking or the exacerbation of depressive symptoms such as helplessness, guilt, or inadequacy perceptions. In this situation the caregiver needs to work with the patient to pursue alternative treatments. To

**Alcoholics Anonymous and Other 12-Step Groups**

insist on the latter patient's continued attendance at AA meetings is equivalent to instructing a patient to stay on a medication that is not only failing to improve his or her condition but is also causing harmful side-effects. Good medical practice proscribes the latter. Such practice needs to prohibit the former as well. Supporting this position, Kasl (1992), in her recent book, *Many Roads, One Journey: Moving Beyond the Twelve Steps*, avers that "to help find a program that is right for [problem drinkers] would probably save countless people from relapse and pain because they would be free to put their energy into uncovery [sic] and discovery rather than adapting to a program that doesn't feel right" (p. 165). These are words to the wise.

### Treatment Is Not Always Necessary

Although many alcohol-troubled individuals need some type of formal treatment (AA or otherwise) in order to stop drinking, ample evidence exists for the phenomenon of improvement in drinking behavior without formal treatment in a substantial proportion of problem drinkers (Institute of Medicine 1990). Available information (see Fillmore et al. 1988) indicates that among young problem drinkers about 50%–60% of men and 70% of women experience improvement without formal treatment. For middle-aged drinkers in trouble with alcohol, the rates of improvement without formal treatment are approximately 30%–40% for men and 30% for women. For older drinkers the rates for improvement without formal treatment are about 60%–80% for men and 50%–60% for women. Improvement rates of this magnitude make it compellingly clear that AA, or any type of formal intervention for that matter, is often unnecessary in an individual's efforts to overcome a problem with alcohol. Natural healing processes are frequently adequate. The wise health care provider will seek to activate or enhance "naturally occurring factors that facilitate the remission of alcohol problems" (Institute of Medicine 1990, p. 158). Only when such factors are not sufficient for overcoming a drinking problem should the health care provider consider the option of referring a patient to formal treatment, including AA.

### AA Is Often Rejected

Psychotherapy researchers have long observed that a substantial portion of consumers of professional treatment reject therapy outright or leave treatment after at most a very few treatment contacts. The phenomenon of rapidly dropping out of treatment appears to extend to AA as well. Triennial surveys conducted by the General Service Office of AA have consistently found a pattern of about a 50% dropout rate by the fourth month of participation and about a 75% dropout rate by the 12th month (Alcoholics Anonymous 1990). Either dropouts experience AA as being no longer necessary in staying away from alcohol dependence or they reject the organization for a variety of reasons. A recent survey of members of Rational Recovery, an alternative community group for alcohol-troubled individuals, provide clues as to some of the sources of rejection: conflicts concerning spirituality, disagreement with the concept of powerlessness, disagreement with the belief that chemical dependency is a lifelong disease, feeling mistreated by members of the organization, and not relating to the "program" of AA (Willis et al. 1992).

In addition to dropouts, untold numbers of alcohol-dependent individuals never attend any meeting of AA, believing that they do not need help of any sort or at least the sort they imagine that AA provides. One observer of AA estimated that as little as 5% of all alcohol-troubled individuals ever "darken the doors" of AA (Tournier 1979).

When one combines the fact that many individuals with alcohol problems never go to AA at all with the finding that a sizable number of those who do try the organization drop out fairly quickly, the limited use and applicability of AA become incontrovertible.

## ▼ JUDICIOUS USE OF OTHER 12-STEP GROUPS

Because the program of AA has been adapted to an estimated more than 100 other diseases besides alcoholism (Ragge 1991), the health care provider will often be invited to consider encouraging a patient to become active in one or more 12-step groups that address that patient's specific problems. The quantitative research on AA can help the caregiver place the suitability and efficacy of these other 12-step groups in perspective. It appears sensible and wise to regard these organizations as being of help to some individuals. At the same time, certain patients will probably not get better by participation in these groups and others may actually deteriorate.

Still others (and probably a substantial number at that) are likely to improve in their disease without specialized treatment of any sort, including 12-step organizations. As suggested by research on smoking behavior (Russell et al. 1979), brief, authoritative confrontation by a primary caregiver can effectively turn large numbers of patients away from self-destructive diseases. For these individuals, 12-step groups are simply unnecessary.

Inasmuch as improvement in a patient's disease has an uncertain relationship with 12-step group participation, the advice of a contemporary sage (Glaser 1993) in alcohol treatment might wisely be followed for now in approaching patients concerning other 12-step groups: "Never require, always encourage." It is left to future research to inform us more precisely about when the health caregiver needs to require, needs to encourage, needs to discourage, and needs to prohibit 12-step group involvement. Such information can only improve the ability of health care providers to help their patients who suffer from a broad spectrum of troubling and destructive disorders.

## ▼ CONCLUSION

It is hoped that the reader of this chapter is left with enhanced circumspection concerning the role of AA and other 12-step organizations in the healing of those who suffer from psychoactive substance abuse disorders. To the strong advocate of 12-step programs, this chapter may seem unduly critical of, if not outright wrong about, the parameters concerning AA's and other 12-step groups' applicability, benefits, and even essentiality. Gainsayers of 12-step groups may well see this chapter as endorsing too strongly the suitability and effectiveness of such groups. If this is so, then the chapter will have served its purpose of stimulating health care providers to approach such groups with cautious optimism—optimism because great numbers of chemically dependent individuals are helped by 12-step groups, and cautious because as we have seen such groups are at times unhelpful, let alone often not necessary, and they can have deleterious effects. The health care professional can not be reminded too often of Hippocrates's admonition: *"primum non nocere"*—the first duty of the treater is to do no harm (Institute of Medicine 1990, p. 160). May this chapter constitute such a reminder.

## ▼ REFERENCES

Alcoholics Anonymous: Comments on AA's Triennial Surveys. New York, Alcoholics Anonymous World Services, 1990

Emrick CD: Alcoholics Anonymous: emerging concepts: overview, in Recent Developments in Alcoholism, Vol 7: Treatment Research. Edited by Galanter M. New York, Plenum, 1989, pp 3–10

Emrick CD, Tonigan JS, Montgomery H, et al: Alcoholics Anonymous: what is currently known? in Research on Alcoholics Anonymous: Opportunities and Alternatives. Edited by McCrady BS, Miller WR. Piscataway, NJ, Rutgers Center of Alcohol Studies, 1993, pp 41–76

Fillmore KM, Hartka E, Johnstone BM, et al: Spontaneous Remission from Alcohol Problems: A Critical Review. Paper prepared for the Institute of Medicine Committee for the Study of Treatment and Rehabilitation Services for Alcoholism and Alcohol Abuse, Washington, DC, June 1988

Glaser FB: Alcoholics Anonymous and the matching hypothesis, in Research on Alcoholics Anonymous: Opportunities and Alternatives. Edited by McCrady BS, Miller WR. Piscataway, NJ, Rutgers Center of Alcohol Studies, 1993, pp 379–395

Institute of Medicine: Broadening the Base of Treatment for Alcohol Problems. Washington, DC, National Academy Press, 1990

Kasl CD: Many Roads, One Journey: Moving Beyond the Twelve Steps. New York, Harper Collins, 1992

Littlefield WC: Some key literature of Alcoholics Anonymous. Reference Quarterly 28:156–161, 1988

Makela K: Social and cultural preconditions of Alcoholics Anonymous (AA) and factors associated with the strength of AA. British Journal of Addiction 86:1405–1413, 1991

Nordstrom G, Berglund M: Successful adjustment in alcoholism: relationships between causes of improvement, personality, and social factors. J Nerv Ment Dis 174:664–668, 1986

Patek AJ Jr, Hermos JA: Recovery from alcoholism in cirrhotic patients: a study of 45 cases. Am J Med 70:782–785, 1981

Peele S: Diseasing of America: Addiction Treatment

Out of Control. Lexington, MA, Lexington Books, 1989

Ragge K: More Revealed: A Critical Analysis of Alcoholics Anonymous and the Twelve Steps. Henderson, NV, Alert Publishing, 1991

Rudy DR: Becoming Alcoholic: Alcoholics Anonymous and the Reality of Alcoholism. Carbondale, IL, Southern Illinois University Press, 1986

Russell MA, Wilson C, Taylor C, et al: Effect of general practitioners' advice against smoking. BMJ 2:231–235, 1979

Tournier RE: Alcoholics Anonymous as treatment and as ideology. J Stud Alcohol 40:230–239, 1979

Tuite DR, Luiten JW: 16PF research into addiction: meta-analysis and extension. Int J Addict 21:287–323, 1986

Walsh DC, Hingson RW, Merrigan DM, et al: A randomized trial of treatment options for alcohol-abusing workers. N Engl J Med 325:775–782, 1991

Willis C, Gastfriend DR, Meyer S: Rational Recovery: A Self-Help Alternative to Alcoholics Anonymous. Paper presented at the 145th annual meeting of the American Psychiatric Association, Washington, DC, May 1992

# Inpatient Treatment

*Roger D. Weiss, M.D.*

In recent years, few subjects in the field of addiction research have generated as much debate as the role of inpatient treatment for patients with substance use disorders. This controversy has been fueled, in part, by the enormous cost of alcoholism treatment in the United States. It has been estimated, for example, that in 1988, more than $6 billion was spent on treating alcohol-related problems in a wide variety of health care settings. On the other hand, the cost to society of alcohol-related problems themselves has been estimated at over $100 billion per year (Institute of Medicine 1990). Therefore, establishing effective treatment methods for patients with substance use disorders represents both a public health and a financial priority. Moreover, because the resources available to tackle this issue are finite, treatment should be not only effective but also cost effective. Because the cost differential between inpatient and outpatient treatment is substantial, and because there is wide variation in per diem costs even among inpatient facilities, determining the proper role of hospital treatment is critical.

Unfortunately, discussions regarding inpatient treatment have often been fueled by political and financial considerations rather than clinical research data. This has sometimes led to the promulgation of extremist positions from proponents of various viewpoints. As a result, arguments are alternately presented that support either the extraordinary effectiveness (McElrath 1988) or the virtual lack of need (Miller and Hester 1986) for inpatient treatment. This debate has been sharpened by the fact that in the late 1970s and early 1980s, private sector (much of it for-profit) hospital treatment of substance-abusing individuals expanded dramatically at the same time that the number of public hospital units declined. By the mid-1980s, however, inpatient treatment of substance use disorders became the focus of cost containment efforts. As clinicians, researchers, government officials, and entrepreneurs attempted to develop less costly alternatives to hospitalization, the rationale for inpatient treatment was questioned, and it has remained a subject of considerable controversy.

In this chapter, I will present an overview of inpatient treatment, discuss current thinking about the indications for hospital care, and review research on the efficacy of this treatment modality.

Supported by National Institute on Drug Abuse Grant 1-R29 DA05944 and a grant from the Engelhard Foundation.

## ▼ WHAT IS INPATIENT TREATMENT?

The term *inpatient treatment* actually refers to a variety of forms of treatment that may take place in one of a number of different settings. Inpatient treatment may involve detoxification, rehabilitation, a combination of the two, or one followed sequentially by the other. The treatment may take place either in a medical or general psychiatric setting or on a specialized chemical dependency unit, located either in a general hospital, a psychiatric hospital, or a free-standing chemical dependency facility. Many clinicians who work with addicted patients recommend that they be treated in a specialized setting because of the availability of peer support and confrontation, the presence of a knowledgeable and dedicated clinical staff, and the fact that substance-abusing patients and patients with other psychiatric disorders may feel uncomfortable around each other. However, I am aware of no studies that have compared the effectiveness of treating chemically dependent patients on a specialized unit as opposed to a general psychiatric setting.

The recognition during the past decade of the frequent comorbidity of addictive disorders and other psychiatric illness (Meyer 1986; Mirin et al. 1991; Ross et al. 1988) has led to the creation of numerous *dual diagnosis* inpatient units, which are devoted to the treatment of patients with coexisting mental illness and chemical dependency. One problem with the use of the term *dual diagnosis patients* is the fact that it connotes more similarities among this population than actually exist (Weiss et al. 1992). In fact, patients with coexisting mental illness and chemical dependency are quite heterogeneous. Thus although such patients may be grouped together for the purpose of creating greater cohesion on an inpatient unit, this desired result may not, in fact, occur. For example, a young, bulimic cocaine-dependent patient will not necessarily feel commonality with an elderly, depressed alcoholic patient merely because they each have two disorders. Thus although treating dually diagnosed patients together may make programmatic sense in a particular institution, it is important to recognize the potential pitfalls inherent in this approach.

Dual diagnosis treatment may occur on a unit with a primary psychiatric focus, on a substance abuse unit with a psychiatric consultant (who may either be peripherally involved or well integrated), or on a unit that attempts to integrate principles of psychiatric and chemical dependency treatment. Minkoff (1989), for example, has argued that substance-abusing patients, psychiatric patients, and individuals with both types of disorders are best treated together in an integrated therapeutic model. He has posited that many of the concepts that have traditionally been associated with chemical dependency treatment (e.g., acceptance of and recovery from a chronic illness, the need to overcome denial and shame, the importance of asking for help, using treatment actively, developing new coping skills) are equally useful in the treatment of patients with other primary psychiatric disorders.

Virtually all inpatient substance abuse programs in the United States stress the importance of abstinence from all drugs of abuse, including alcohol, as the cornerstone of successful treatment. The most common form of inpatient treatment in this country is the *Minnesota Model* (Cook 1988a), so named because of its development in that state in the 1950s. A Minnesota Model treatment program often has a standardized, fixed length of stay, commonly lasting 4 weeks (although the latter aspect of such programs has changed recently in favor of more flexibility). After initial detoxification, patients attend educational lectures based on the disease concept of chemical dependency. In addition to learning about the harmful psychological and medical consequences of drugs and alcohol, patients are typically taught about the natural history of alcoholism, the effects of substance abuse on the family, conditioned cues and relapse prevention techniques, the importance of making life-style changes, and alternative coping mechanisms. Patients are often asked to recount their drug and alcohol histories in front of other patients and staff members in a forum similar to Alcoholics Anonymous (AA) meetings. The purpose of this exercise is to help patients confront and accept the adverse effects of their substance use; minimization or denial of the severity of their problems is common among patients admitted to inpatient units. Minnesota Model programs rely strongly on group therapy and peer confrontation and heavily employ recovering alcoholic individuals as primary counselors. Systems interventions, including involvement of employers and family members, are also frequently used in these programs.

Many therapy groups in Minnesota Model programs are based on principles of AA and Narcotics Anonymous. Indeed, orienting patients to AA and establishing their continued AA and group therapy involvement after discharge are major goals of such programs.

Psychiatrists may be involved to a variable extent in Minnesota Model treatment programs, often playing a consultative role in dealing with patients who have clear coexisting psychiatric disorders. The degree of integration between the psychiatric and counseling staff is variable, and can range from cooperation and integration to mutual distrust.

Minnesota Model programs provide an intense immersion in an environment that is dedicated to challenging addictive thoughts and beliefs through group therapy, peer evaluation, and meetings with counselors who themselves are recovering from substance use disorders. One of the most powerful tools in these programs is the instillation of hope in many individuals who have felt trapped in their addiction. To this end, these programs generally emphasize the importance of spirituality in the recovery process.

Cook (1988b) has referred to the "comprehensive and dogmatic ideology" of Minnesota Model programs as one of their most powerful therapeutic tools. This aspect of these programs, however, has also been a target of criticism. For example, some patients who have objected to the spiritual aspects of these programs or who have found AA distasteful, for whatever reason, have felt that treatment staff members have given up on them. Some such patients are accused of being resistant to treatment, when in fact, they are merely being resistant to AA. Indeed, alternative self-help groups such as Rational Recovery and Secular Organization for Sobriety have arisen, in part, in response to this complaint. Despite these criticisms, however, Minnesota Model programs remain extraordinarily popular in the United States.

A small number of hospitals in this country practice chemical aversion counterconditioning therapy (Institute of Medicine 1990). In this form of treatment, which is more widely used in Russia, an emetic drug is paired with the patient's favored alcoholic beverage in order to induce him to associate drinking with nausea and vomiting. Although uncontrolled research on this procedure has reported favorable outcome (Neuberger et al. 1980), controlled investigations have been less encouraging (Richard 1983). At present, there is some disagreement regarding the overall efficacy of chemical aversive countercondi-

tioning in the inpatient treatment of substance use disorders (Thurber 1985; Wilson 1987).

## ▼ THE RATIONALE FOR INPATIENT TREATMENT

Inpatient treatment offers several advantages over less intensive programs. First, a hospital setting offers a high level of medical supervision and safety for individuals who require intensive physical and/or psychiatric monitoring. Thus for patients with medically dangerous conditions, or for those who represent an acute danger to themselves or others, inpatient treatment in a hospital setting is indicated. The intensity of inpatient treatment may also be helpful to patients who, for whatever reason, do not respond to lesser measures. For example, hospital treatment may benefit those who are too discouraged or unmotivated to regularly attend outpatient treatment on their own. Moreover, inpatient treatment may benefit some individuals by increasing their awareness of the internal triggers that place them at risk to return to substance abuse. For example, the intensity and degree of discomfort that some patients feel in a 24-hour-per-day treatment setting may precipitate drug urges. Experiencing these in a protected setting, where they are not in danger of acting on their urges, may help patients to learn enough about their vulnerability to either avoid such situations in the future or cope with them effectively. Moreover, inpatient treatment can help to interrupt a cycle of drug use even in the absence of medically dangerous withdrawal symptoms. For some individuals, the safety of an inpatient environment and a period of respite from a barrage of conditioned cues may help them in their attempt to make treatment and life decisions that are in their best interest.

The protectiveness of an inpatient treatment unit also represents one of its potential disadvantages, however. Because one of the major determinants of craving is drug availability (Meyer and Mirin 1979), patients admitted to inpatient units may not experience drug urges simply because they are living in a drug-free environment. Therefore, they may not be fully prepared to handle the drug urges that they will surely encounter after discharge upon returning to a setting in which drugs are once again available. As a result, many inpatient programs gradually expose patients to such triggers by granting them brief passes during their hospital stay.

The other disadvantages of inpatient treatment, in addition to those mentioned above, are obvious. First, hospital treatment is quite expensive, typically costing upwards of several hundred dollars per day. Second, patients who enter a hospital are unable to work, care for their families, study, or conduct their normal daily activities. Finally, patients may unfortunately be stigmatized as the result of having been hospitalized. Thus inpatient treatment should not be recommended lightly and generally should be used only when less intensive treatment methods have either failed or are considered too risky to attempt.

## ▼ WHEN SHOULD PATIENTS BE HOSPITALIZED?

The implementation of cost containment efforts, when combined with data challenging the effectiveness of inpatient treatment, has led clinicians to hospitalize chemically dependent patients more sparingly than they previously had. Lists of indications for inpatient treatment have been developed by a variety of health care insurers, managed care companies, hospitals, and professional groups. For example, one recent attempt to define criteria for inpatient treatment (Hoffman et al. 1991) listed six areas that should be assessed in determining whether a patient requires inpatient treatment, partial hospital care, or less intensive ambulatory treatment. The areas recommended for assessment were 1) acute intoxication and/or withdrawal potential, 2) biomedical conditions and complications, 3) emotional and behavioral conditions or complications, 4) treatment acceptance/resistance, 5) relapse potential, and 6) recovery environment. Although one may argue with the emphasis placed on specific criteria in this or any other document, it is important to recognize the importance of a multidimensional assessment in determining the optimal treatment plan for a chemically dependent patient.

When this assessment has been completed, the clinician must ultimately consider two major issues in deciding whether or not to hospitalize a patient: 1) the danger that the patient might be imminently harmful to him- or herself or others, and 2) the likelihood that the patient would achieve treatment success in a less restrictive environment. These issues can sometimes be extremely difficult to evaluate in patients abusing substances. For example, although patients with active homicidal ideation and/or a recent suicide attempt might be considered clear candidates for hospitalization, danger to self or others may occur in substance-abusing patients in the absence of overt threats or self-destructive or violent acts. Patients who regularly drive while intoxicated, share needles with others, or commit violent crimes in order to finance their drug habit may also represent a substantial risk to themselves and to society. Because one of the functions of inpatient treatment is to protect the chemically dependent patient and/or the people around him or her during a period of acute danger, decisions regarding the timing of hospitalizing those individuals who represent a chronic recurrent danger are quite complicated.

Another area in which an inpatient setting may provide safety is in the process of detoxification. This is particularly true for patients who are being detoxified from alcohol and/or sedative-hypnotics drugs because withdrawal from these agents may be accompanied by serious medical consequences, including grand mal seizures, delirium, and death. A number of studies have shown that outpatient alcohol detoxification can be accomplished safely and effectively in selected settings (Collins et al. 1990; Hayashida et al. 1989). However, inpatient detoxification is still commonly employed because of the risk of potentially serious medical sequelae of withdrawal in combination with the potential unreliability of this patient population. For example, some patients undergoing outpatient detoxification may concomitantly use alcohol or other drugs, such as cocaine, which lowers seizure threshold. Although detoxification from therapeutic doses of benzodiazepines is frequently performed on an outpatient basis, patients with mixed benzodiazepine and alcohol dependence or patients who have been abusing benzodiazepines are often detoxified as inpatients. Moreover, although opioid withdrawal is generally less medically dangerous than sedative-hypnotic or alcohol withdrawal, the discomfort that many opioid-addicted patients experience in attempting detoxification may diminish the effectiveness of outpatient treatment because of frequent relapses. Some patients who are unable to successfully detoxify from opioids on an ambulatory basis may thus be admitted to a hospital to complete the withdrawal process. Complicated detoxification regimens such as those that are prescribed for patients who are dependent on two or more classes of drugs should generally be administered in a hospital because of the need for frequent reevaluation and adjustment of such regimens. Similarly, patients with significant organ (e.g., cardiac, cerebral, hepatic) dysfunction should generally be detoxified in the hospital.

As can be seen in the latter examples of indications for hospitalization, there is frequently an overlap between the use of the hospital as a protective environment and the use of the hospital in order to reap the benefits of a maximally intensive treatment program. As described above, some individuals are treated as inpatients because of their actual or perceived inability to benefit from less intensive forms of treatment. Although hospitalization was frequently recommended as an initial treatment modality a decade ago, patients are currently recommended for hospital care either in the case of imminent danger (as described above) or after previous outpatient or partial hospital treatment efforts have failed.

Studies comparing inpatients and outpatients typically show that the former group have more severe substance use histories and a greater prevalence rate of medical, psychosocial and vocational difficulties, including less social stability, more unemployment, and a greater preponderance of medical and psychiatric disorders (Harrison et al. 1988; Skinner 1981). Of course, these data in part reflect referral patterns and do not necessarily indicate which populations fare best in which settings. Indeed, there have now been a number of studies in which alcohol- or drug-dependent patients were randomly assigned to inpatient treatment or a less intensive alternative. Although these studies have generally shown little difference between inpatient treatment and other modalities (Longabaugh 1988; Miller and Hester 1986), methodological flaws in some of these studies may have affected their results (Nace 1990). For example, one frequently cited study by Longabaugh et al. (1983) concluded that individuals treated as inpatients or in a partial hospital setting had similar outcomes. However, both groups of patients in this study were initially treated as inpatients. Another well-known study, by Edwards et al. (1977), concluded that a session of outpatient "advice" was as effective as inpatient treatment. However, later analysis of the data from this study showed that patients with more severe alcohol dependence responded better to inpatient treatment than to outpatient treatment (Nace 1990).

More recent studies of randomized treatment have again shown some disagreement regarding the role of inpatient treatment. Although Walsh et al. (1991) showed inpatient treatment to be more effective than assignment to AA meetings for alcohol-dependent individuals referred for treatment by their employee assistance program, O'Brien et al. (1990) showed partial hospital treatment of cocaine-addicted patients to be as effective as inpatient treatment. At this time, studies are needed to determine patient-treatment matching characteristics (McLellan et al. 1983) so that we can better identify which groups of patients are most likely to respond best to which specific types of treatment.

# ▼ INPATIENT TREATMENT: OUTCOME

## General Findings

A number of follow-up studies that have been performed on patients treated in hospital programs have shown impressive success rates. For example, Gilmore et al. (1986) conducted 6-month and 12-month follow-up questionnaire assessments on patients who had been treated at the Hazelden Foundation (a well-known Minnesota Model treatment center) and two other facilities. They found that 73% of those who completed the questionnaires (approximately half of the total sample) were abstinent from alcohol at the time of the 6-month assessment, and 58% of respondents were abstinent 1 year following discharge. Wallace et al. (1988) presented similarly favorable results among patients treated at Edgehill Newport, an analogous facility. They found that 57% of patients interviewed had been continuously abstinent from alcohol and drugs for 6 months following discharge. However, in both treatment samples, patients who were discharged prematurely or (in the case of the latter study) were unmarried were excluded from the follow-up study. In a 4-year follow-up of inpatients treated at the Carrier Foundation, approximately half of the study sample had favorable outcomes (Pettinati et al. 1982). However, fluctuations in outcome status were common, and only one-fourth of patients were continuously abstinent for all 4 years.

Unfortunately, all of the studies mentioned above are uncontrolled and are therefore subject to the biases inherent in uncontrolled research. It is because of these concerns that an increasing number of controlled studies have taken place recently. Unfortunately, as mentioned above, controlled studies have also been not immune to methodological flaws. Thus continued research on this topic is needed.

## Patient Characteristics in Inpatient Treatment Outcome Research

Although, as mentioned above, some authors have written that inpatient treatment of substance-abusing individuals is often not superior to less intensive treatment, some subgroups of patients do appear to respond best to hospitalization. Specifically, patients with greater severity of substance-related problems, less social stability, and greater psychiatric comorbidity appear to benefit preferentially from inpatient treatment (McKay et al. 1991). In general, most studies of inpatient treatment have found that the following groups have a better prognosis: patients who are older, married, abusing alcohol rather than other drugs, and whose families participate in treatment (Harrison et al. 1991). Patients with histories of intravenous drug use or antisocial behavior tend to fare less well in treatment outcome studies (Harrison et al. 1991).

## Program Characteristics in Inpatient Treatment Outcome Research

Although a number of studies have focused on the contribution of patient factors in substance abuse treatment outcome, there has long been a relative paucity of research on characteristics of inpatient treatment programs that affect prognosis. Although some authors have argued that programmatic variables are less important than patient characteristics in determining treatment outcome (Armor et al. 1976), Cronkite and Moos (1978) conducted a path analysis of treatment outcome for 429 alcoholic patients treated in five different programs and concluded that program-related characteristics did influence treatment outcome substantially.

A number of different characteristics of inpatient substance abuse treatment have been examined to determine their impact on treatment outcome (Adelman and Weiss 1989), although many of these studies have either been uncontrolled or have not included a carefully matched control group. In a study of the

impact of the referral process on outcome, employed alcoholic individuals who were forced by their employers to enter treatment fared better than individuals who volunteered for treatment (Chopra et al. 1979). Moberg et al. (1982) also found that involving a patient's employer during hospitalization had a beneficial effect on treatment outcome.

There is some evidence that the milieu orientation of a treatment center may affect treatment efficacy as well. Stinson et al. (1979) randomly assigned 466 patients to two alcoholism treatment programs, one of which emphasized intensive individualized treatment, with a high staff-to-patient ratio, whereas the other program had a lower staff-to-patient ratio and emphasized peer group interaction. Patients who entered the latter program had better treatment outcome, thus suggesting the potential importance of peer support in alcoholism treatment programs.

Characteristics of staff members have been examined in several studies. Valle (1981) found that the interpersonal skills of alcoholism counselors in an inpatient treatment facility had a significant effect on treatment outcome of their patients. McLellan et al. (1988) obtained similar results in a study of counselors in an outpatient methadone maintenance program, thus adding weight to the argument that characteristics of specific counselors may significantly affect treatment outcome within a given treatment setting. Studies of inpatient substance abuse programs have also shown that degree of medical orientation may affect treatment outcome. Smart and Gray (1978) studied 792 alcoholic patients in five different inpatient treatment programs and attributed 30% of the variance in dropout rates to treatment variables. They found that patients who were treated in facilities that were more medically oriented were most likely to complete treatment.

Psychiatric assessment has also been shown to be an important part of treatment. For example, in a well-known series of studies, McLellan et al. (1986) showed the importance of severity of psychopathology as a predictor of outcome in patients with substance use disorders. They found that patients with moderate levels of psychiatric severity, as measured by the Addiction Severity Index (McLellan et al. 1980), had the best response to inpatient treatment. Thus such assessments may help facilitate patient-treatment matching and thus improve outcome. As part of this series of studies, McLellan et al. (1983) also found that patients with employment problems fared better when treated in the hospital than when treated as outpatients.

One of the major components of virtually all inpatient treatment programs is an emphasis on group therapy and attendance at AA meetings. Because of the near ubiquity of these aspects of inpatient treatment, little research has actually been done on their relative contribution to treatment outcome. However, some specific types of groups have been examined, and positive results have been reported for client-centered groups (Ends and Page 1959) and social skills training groups (Eriksen et al. 1986). Other specific interventions that have been reported as beneficial include the administration of thermal and electromyogram biofeedback (Denney et al. 1991) and the use of patient-authored treatment contracts (as opposed to staff-authored or mutually authored contracts) in treatment planning (Vannicelli 1979). Physical exercise has also been shown in one study to reduce state and trait anxiety and depression in chemically dependent inpatients, although long-term effects of exercise on outcome are not clear (Palmer et al. 1988).

Aftercare has long been considered an essential part of inpatient treatment; several studies have shown the positive impact of aftercare attendance on treatment outcome. Some researchers have questioned whether the aftercare program itself improves treatment outcome or whether the patients who are likely to have good treatment outcome are also those who attend aftercare more often. Two studies using cross-lagged analyses have supported the former hypothesis (Costello 1980; Vannicelli 1978). More recently, however, McLatchie and Lomp (1988) disputed this theory. They randomly assigned 155 patients who had completed a 4-week inpatient alcoholism treatment program to one of three aftercare groups: 1) mandated aftercare; 2) voluntary aftercare, in which patients could decide on their own whether or not to attend; and 3) a condition in which patients were dissuaded from attending aftercare. No differences were found among groups with respect to relapse to drinking, life-style, satisfaction, or level of anxiety. However, it should be noted that 66% of patients in the voluntary group did request aftercare.

Finally, the correlation between length of stay and inpatient treatment outcome has long been a controversial subject. Although some research, as mentioned above, found that inpatient treatment offered no more benefit than a session of outpatient advice (Edwards et al. 1977), and one study (Rae 1972) correlated longer hospital stays with poorer outcome, other studies (Finney et al. 1981; McLellan et al. 1982) have reported a positive correlation between length of stay and treatment response. However, many of these are difficult to evaluate because of lack of randomization or poor comparability of study groups. One recent study (Gottheil et al. 1992) examined 131 alcoholic male veterans who were treated in an inpatient program with a recommended length of stay of 90 days. The authors found that patients with less severe impairment, as measured by the Addiction Severity Index, fared best. Moreover, in these patients, a longer hospital stay resulted in better treatment outcome. Patients with the most severe problems, on the other hand, did not benefit from increased length of stay. The results of this study are similar to those of Simpson (1979), who found that drug-dependent patients who received less than 90 days of treatment either in inpatient or outpatient programs did less well than patients who received 90 days or more of treatment. Indeed, Gottheil et al. (1992) posited that the more severely psychiatrically ill patients may have failed to benefit from treatment because even 90 days of hospitalization was insufficient to meet their needs.

## ▼ FUTURE IMPLICATIONS

The role of inpatient treatment for patients with substance use disorders remains a complex and controversial issue, with public health, political, philosophical, moral, and financial implications attached to its discussion. It is clear, however, that attempting to formulate simplistic guidelines about the use of this treatment modality serves no one's best interest. Thus the question "Is inpatient treatment effective?" should continue to shift to a more difficult but critical question: "For which patients is inpatient treatment effective, at what time(s), and for how long?" To that end, current research in this area, particularly that being performed by McLellan et al. (1992), is attempting to define the *active* and *inert* ingredients of inpatient (and outpatient) treatment in order to more clearly discern those aspects of inpatient treatment that are truly effective for which subgroups of patients. As future research helps to clarify these issues, it is hoped that inpatient treatment can reach a more stable and defined place in the therapeutic approach to patients with substance use disorders.

## ▼ REFERENCES

Adelman SA, Weiss RD: What is therapeutic about inpatient alcoholism treatment? Hosp Community Psychiatry 40:515–519, 1989

Armor DJ, Polich JM, Stambul H: Alcoholism and Treatment. Santa Monica, CA, Rand Corporation, 1976

Chopra KS, Preston DA, Gerson LW: The effect of constructive coercion on the rehabilitative process: a study of the employed alcoholics in an alcoholism treatment program. J Occup Med 21: 749–752, 1979

Collins MN, Burns T, Van Den Berk PAH, et al: A structured programme for out-patient alcohol detoxification. Br J Psychiatry 156:871–874, 1990

Cook CCH: The Minnesota Model in the management of drug and alcohol dependence: miracle, method or myth? Part I: the philosophy and the programme. British Journal of Addiction 83:625–634, 1988a

Cook CCH: The Minnesota Model in the management of drug and alcohol dependence: miracle, method or myth? Part II: evidence and conclusions. British Journal of Addiction 83:735–748, 1988b

Costello RM: Alcoholism aftercare and outcome: cross-lagged panel and path anaylsis. British Journal of Addiction 75:49–53, 1980

Cronkite RC, Moos RH: Evaluating alcoholism treatment programs: an integrated approach. J Consult Clin Psychol 46:1105–1119, 1978

Denney MR, Baugh JL, Hardt HD: Sobriety outcome after alcoholism treatment with biofeedback participation: a pilot inpatient study. Int J Addict 26:335–341, 1991

Edwards G, Orford J, Egert S, et al: Alcoholism: a controlled trial of "treatment" and "advice." J Stud Alcohol 38:1004–1031, 1977

Ends EJ, Page CW: Group Psychotherapy and Concomitant Psychological Change: Psychological Monographs, Vol 73, No 480. Washington, DC, American Psychological Association, 1959

Eriksen L, Bjornstad S, Gotestam KG: Social skills training in groups for alcoholics: one-year treatment outcome for groups and individuals. Addict Behav 11:309–330, 1986

Finney JW, Moos RH, Chan DA: Length of stay and program component effects in the treatment of alcoholism: a comparison of two techniques for process analyses. J Consult Clin Psychol 49:120–131, 1981

Gilmore K, Jones D, Tamble L: Treatment Benchmarks. Center City, MN, Hazelden, 1986

Gottheil E, McLellan AT, Druley KA: Length of stay, patient severity and treatment outcome: sample data from the field of alcoholism. J Stud Alcohol 53:69–75, 1992

Harrison PA, Hoffman NG, Gibb L, et al: Determinants of chemical dependency treatment placement: clinical, economic, and logistic factors. Psychotherapy 25:356–364, 1988

Harrison PA, Hoffmann NG, Streed SG: Drug and alcohol addiction treatment outcome, in Comprehensive Handbook of Drug and Alcohol Addiction. Edited by Miller NS. New York, Marcel Dekker, 1991, pp 1163–1197

Hayashida M, Alterman AI, McLellan AT, et al: Comparative effectiveness and costs of inpatient and outpatient detoxification of patients with mild-to-moderate alcohol withdrawal syndrome. N Engl J Med 320:358–365, 1989

Hoffman NG, Halikas JA, Mee-Lee D, et al: Patient Placement Criteria for the Treatment of Psychoactive Substance Use Disorders. Washington, DC, American Society of Addiction Medicine, 1991

Institute of Medicine: Broadening the Base of Treatment for Alcohol Problems. Washington, DC, National Academy Press, 1990

Longabaugh R, McGrady B, Fine E, et al: Cost effectiveness of alcoholism treatment in partial vs inpatient settings: six-month outcomes. J Stud Alcohol 44:1049–1071, 1983

Longabaugh R: Longitudinal outcome studies, in Alcoholism: Origins and Outcome. Edited by Rose RM, Barrett J. New York, Raven, 1988, pp 267–280

McElrath D: The Hazelden Treatment Model. Testimony Before the U.S. Senate Committee on Governmental Affairs, Washington, DC, June 16, 1988

McKay JR, Murphy RT, Longabaugh R: The effectiveness of alcoholism treatment: evidence from outcome studies, in Psychiatric Treatment: Advances in Outcome Research. Edited by Mirin SM, Gossett JT, Grob MC. Washington, DC, American Psychiatric Press, 1991, pp 143–158

McLatchie BH, Lomp KGE: An experimental investigation of the influence of aftercare on alcoholic relapse. British Journal of Addiction 83:1045–1054, 1988

McLellan AT, Luborsky L, Woody GE, et al: An improved diagnostic evaluation instrument for substance abuse patients: the Addiction Severity Index. J Nerv Ment Dis 168:26–33, 1980

McLellan AT, Luborsky L, O'Brien CP, et al: Is treatment for substance abuse effective? JAMA 247:1423–1428, 1982

McLellan AT, Luborsky L, Woody GE, et al: Predicting response to alcohol and drug abuse treatments: role of psychiatric severity. Arch Gen Psychiatry 40:620–625, 1983

McLellan AT, Luborsky L, O'Brien CP: Alcohol and drug abuse treatment in three different populations: is there improvement and is it predictable? Am J Drug Alcohol Abuse 12:101–120, 1986

McLellan AT, Woody GE, Luborsky L, et al: Is the counselor an "active ingredient" in substance abuse rehabilitation? An examination of treatment success among four counselors. J Nerv Ment Dis 176:423–430, 1988

McLellan AT, O'Brien CP, Metzger D, et al: Is substance abuse treatment effective—compared to what? in Addictive States. Edited by O'Brien CP, Jaffe JH. New York, Raven, 1992, pp 231–252

Meyer RE: Psychopathology and Addictive Disorders. New York, Guilford, 1986

Meyer RE, Mirin SM: The Heroin Stimulus: Implications for a Theory of Addiction. New York, Plenum, 1979

Miller WR, Hester R: Inpatient alcoholism treatment: who benefits? Am Psychol 41:794–805, 1986

Minkoff K: An integrated treatment model for dual diagnosis of psychosis and addiction. Hosp Community Psychiatry 40:1031–1036, 1989

Mirin SM, Weiss RD, Griffin ML, et al: Psychopathology in drug abusers and their families. Compr Psychiatry 32:36–51, 1991

Moberg DP, Krause WK, Klein PE: Post-treatment drinking behavior among inpatients from an industrial alcoholism program. Int J Addict 17:549–567, 1982

Nace EP: Inpatient treatment of alcoholism: a necessary part of the therapeutic armamentarium. The Psychiatric Hospital 21:9–12, 1990

Neuberger OW, Matarazzo JD, Schmitz RE, et al: One-year follow-up of total abstinence in chronic alcoholic patients following emetic countercondi-

tioning. Alcoholism 4:306–312, 1980

O'Brien CP, Alterman A, Walter D, et al: Evaluation of treatment for cocaine dependence, in Problems of Drug Dependence 1989, NIDA Res Monogr 95 (DHHS Publ No ADM-90-1663). Edited by Harris LS. Washington, DC, U.S. Government Printing Office, 1990, pp 78–84

Palmer J, Vacc N, Epstein J: Adult inpatient alcoholics: physical exercise as a treatment intervention. J Stud Alcohol 49:418–421, 1988

Pettinati HM, Sugerman AA, DiDonato N, et al: The natural history of alcoholism over four years after treatment. J Stud Alcohol 43:201–215, 1982

Rae JB: The influence of wives on the treatment outcome of alcoholics: a follow-up study at two years. Br J Psychiatry 120:601–613, 1972

Richard GP: Behavioral treatment of excessive drinking. Unpublished dissertation, University of New South Wales, 1983

Ross HE, Glaser FB, Germanson T: The prevalence of psychiatric disorders in patients with alcohol and other drug problems. Arch Gen Psychiatry 45:1023–1031, 1988

Simpson DD: The relation of time spent in drug abuse treatment to posttreatment outcome. Am J Psychiatry 136:1449–1453, 1979

Skinner HA: Comparison of clients assigned to inpatient and outpatient treatment for alcoholism and drug addiction. Br J Psychiatry 138:312–320, 1981

Smart RG, Gray G: Multiple predictors of dropout from alcoholism treatment. Arch Gen Psychiatry 35:363–367, 1978

Stinson DS, Smith WG, Amidjaya I, et al: Systems of care and treatment outcomes for alcoholic patients. Arch Gen Psychiatry 36:535–539, 1979

Thurber S: Effect size estimates in chemical aversion treatments of alcoholism. J Clin Psychol 41:285–287, 1985

Valle SK: Interpersonal functioning of alcoholism counselors and treatment outcome. J Stud Alcohol 42:783–790, 1981

Vannicelli M: Impact of aftercare in the treatment of alcoholics: a cross-lagged panel analysis. J Stud Alcohol 39:1875–1886, 1978

Vannicelli M: Treatment contracts in an inpatient alcoholism treatment setting. J Stud Alcohol 40:457–471, 1979

Wallace J, McNeill D, Gilfillan D, et al: Six-month treatment outcomes in socially stable alcoholics: abstinence rates. J Subst Abuse Treat 5:247–252,

1988

Walsh DC, Hingson RW, Merrigan DM, et al: A randomized trial of treatment options for alcohol-abusing workers. N Engl J Med 325:775–782, 1991

Weiss RD, Mirin SM, Frances RJ: The myth of the typical dual diagnosis patient. Hosp Community Psychiatry 43:107–108, 1992

Wilson GT: Chemical aversion conditioning as a treatment for alcoholism: a re-analysis. Behav Res Ther 25:503–516, 1987

# Employee Assistance Programs

*Paul M. Roman, Ph.D.*
*Terry C. Blum, Ph.D.*

## ▼ THE DISCOVERY OF EMPLOYED SUBSTANCE–ABUSING INDIVIDUALS

One of the main ingredients in the expansive growth of the American alcoholism movement during the 1970s was a broadening of the definition of the alcohol-troubled population. This "new epidemiology" (Roman and Blum 1987) characterizes the entire population as being at risk for developing patterns of alcohol abuse or alcoholism. This characterization was in part a reaction to one of the curious residues that followed after the repeal of National Prohibition in 1933. This was the subtle but pervasive characterization of the American alcoholic as a "skid row bum."

The importance and persistence of this image is reflected in the extensive efforts within the voluntary alcoholism movement, centered on the medicalization of alcohol problems (Schneider 1978). Through the 1950s and 1960s, many of these energies were centered on changing the management of the public inebriate from imprisonment to treatment. Thus the establishment of public treatment facilities was seen a major aspect of successful decriminalization of the alcoholic individual (Rubington 1991).

Custody of public inebriates, decriminalized or not, made up a somewhat feeble political constituency as a basis for attracting public interest, involvement, and support. Successful mainstreaming of alcoholism into the health care management system in the United States required a refocus of attention away from the lower status, disenfranchised public inebriate. In many ways this was accomplished through the early emphases of the National Institute on Alcohol Abuse and Alcoholism (NIAAA) following its founding in 1970. Both overtly and subtly, the social construction of the "hidden alcoholic" began in earnest (Roman 1991). Distinctive themes are evident today in the continuing effort to institutionalize the definition of the typical American alcoholic individual as employed with a stable residence and family who heretofore had been "hidden" by both social ignorance and the absence of effective means of identification and intervention.

The authors gratefully acknowledge partial support from National Institute on Drug Abuse Research Grant R01 DA07417 and National Institute on Alcohol Abuse and Alcoholism Research Grant R01 AA07250.

In the 1990s, Employee Assistance Programs (EAPs) are prominent as a principal response to this new epidemiology and as a means for dealing with the population of employed (and still largely hidden) alcoholic individuals. EAPs may be seen as comprising two main components in a given workplace setting. First is access to some form of professional assistance for implementing the various aspects of EAP technology (i.e., identification, intervention, motivation, referral, and follow-up). Second is a set of written policies and procedures whereby the core techniques of EAP work are integrated with the operative bureaucratic features of the workplace.

There is considerable variation in the manner in which these two principal components are represented in given workplaces. In some instances, access to professional assistance may be fairly "distant," using contractual services of an external provider organization located outside the workplace. Such contracts vary greatly in their scope of services and in the relative control over service delivery exercised by the contractor and by the patient work organization. In other instances there are fully staffed EAP departments, which are distinctive as integral activities of the organization's medical department or human resource management function. Obviously the variations in EAP organization are functions of workplace size and of the physical/geographic distribution of employees.

Increasingly common in a large multisite organization is an EAP that is comprised of an internal EAP that is staffed by corporate employees, the duties of whom include direct services to employees at corporate headquarters. In addition to these traditional EAP activities are the internal EAP staff's responsibility for the coordination and the monitoring of contracts with external EAP service providers that operate programs in the geographically dispersed locations of the organizations.

An important variation is the manner in which quality is emphasized and the EAP is seen as a significant organizational investment. The extent of investment in the major program components is mirrored in the degree to which a given EAP is an active and effective means for dealing with employee substance abuse. As is elaborated throughout this chapter, the level of investment and the consequent quality of an EAP relates to its specific effectiveness in targeting employee substance abuse (Roman 1989), which is only one of many targets of EAPs.

## ▼ EAPs AND MAINSTREAMING SUBSTANCE ABUSE TREATMENT

Compared with other substance abuse–related interventions, EAPs have a curious and important history relative to their mainstreaming of substance abuse problems (Roman and Blum 1987). The concept of an EAP stems from industrial alcoholism programming that began in the early 1940s as a direct spin-off of knowledge and influence of Alcoholics Anonymous (AA) and its members (Trice and Schonbrunn 1981). Indeed, a treasured piece of lore in the specialty is that the first industrial alcoholism program, founded at the Dupont Chemical Company, stemmed directly from an unplanned and casual conversation between a Dupont executive and Bill Wilson, cofounder of AA, as they rocked on the front porch of a Massachusetts inn where they both happened to be vacationing.

A key idea that has been embellished in a variety of ways over the years is that in the early or early middle (using Jellinek-type concepts) stages of serious dependence, an individual developing alcoholism will manifest visible job performance deterioration that can be used by supervisors as a basis for motivating behavioral change (Sonnenstuhl and Trice 1986). Undergirding this concept is the idea that through its control over continued employment, the workplace possesses unique leverage in terms of being able to motivate and direct behavior change. Further, it is reasoned, the workplace presents the opportunity for earlier intervention than would be the case if the progression of alcoholic behavior were to continue until employment was lost (Maxwell 1960).

Additional advantages of this type of intervention center on the savings rendered to employers by the curbing of alcoholic behavior early in its progression before serious losses occur in association with quality or quantity of job output. At the same time the intervention may allow for conservation of employees in whom there may be substantial investment. Somewhat independent of productivity, it is also evident that employers may save substantially in reducing on-the-job safety risks and reducing the impact of alcoholic behavior on fellow employees and supervisors.

As attractive as these concepts for reaching employed alcoholic individuals may seem, their diffusion in the form of workplace programs was very limited through the 1950s and 1960s. There are many possible explanations for this, most obvious of which is the relatively low priority of alcohol-related issues in the public interest during this period. In retrospect it appears that there were at least two major barriers that were difficult to overcome in workplaces: first, the adoption of this type of program within a workplace required willingness to admit the presence of alcohol problems in that workplace, and second, if it was believed that there were such problems, workplace decision makers needed to be substantially committed to the belief that recovery was a viable possibility once identification had occurred.

A somewhat more subtle barrier was one of feasibility of program implementation. The suggested design implied that such a program required diagnostic skills on the part of supervisors if the alcoholic employee was to be accurately identified. Encouraging their supervisors to become involved in such identification, with all the implications that that might bear, was not attractive to many employers.

Through its early efforts to emphasize intervention strategies directed toward employed persons, the leadership of NIAAA attempted to remedy the problems with the industrial alcoholism model that were then only vaguely perceived. In concert with a series of trial and error experiences in which the acceptance of the industrial alcoholism model seemed very limited, NIAAA ultimately moved toward the promotion of a somewhat different concept that ultimately became embellished as the philosophy of the EAP (Roman 1975, 1981, 1988; Roman and Trice 1976).

This programming strategy deemphasized the substance-abusing employee per se. It instead suggested that work settings are characterized by costly disruptions and productivity loss due to a wide variety of *behavioral-medical problems,* of which substance abuse is only one category, albeit a very significant category. Although it might be difficult for an employer to deny the presence of alcoholic employees, it would be much less credible to claim that none of the range of disruptive behavioral-medical problems was represented in a given work force.

To sidestep employer's problems with empowering their supervisors to identify alcoholism within the work force, the EAP strategy firmly stated that problem employees were to be identified based on performance problems, not behavioral symptoms. Within the EAP philosophy, the emphasis moved away from the supervisor's knowledge of the signs and symptoms of alcoholism. Substituted was the presence of

professional expertise capable of specifying and diagnosing the nature of employee problems that underlay the job performance problems. Upon receiving a referral, the EAP expert was to assess, motivate, and direct those employees to the treatment resources in the community most appropriate for their needs.

Thus the EAP represented an early and continuing form of mainstreaming of substance abuse problems into consideration of broader health care and behavioral management issues. One of the immediate consequences of the adoption of this model was the need for a particular combination of workplace and clinical expertise to be incorporated in the roles of the EAP coordinator. This comprehensive set of requirements slowly eroded the heretofore central role of recovering alcoholic individuals as the administrators of workplace programs. To a degree, this change in the occupational opportunities within workplace interventions, although it can be seen as a partial break with the alcoholism movement, was one cost of mainstreaming. However, it did not preclude the upgrading of clinical and other formal skills among recovering alcoholic individuals who wanted to continue this work. A related change was that alcoholism treatment was only one of many resources needed by an EAP, reducing the extent to which the alcoholism treatment movement would have opportunities to "colonize" EAPs. However, a significant problem associated with this pattern of mainstreaming is the possibility that an emphasis on substance abuse may be minimized or lost within the broader stream of employee problems that are presented to an EAP, especially problems that are less stigmatic and less resistant to intervention.

## ▼ THE EAP PROCESS

To bring this part of the discussion out of history and into the present: an EAP is a workplace-based intervention strategy by which employee substance abuse problems are dealt with through a broad-based employee problem identification policy. Identification and referral to an EAP can occur through supervisory documentation of deteriorated job performance or through self-referral. After entry into the program, it is the task of the EAP professional to identify the nature of the presenting problem. Especially important is the professional's skills in detecting at this point whether what is presented is a genuine behavioral problem or an outcome of a poor fit between abilities and job demands, workplace conflict, or work group politics. Thus along with clinical expertise, workplace familiarity and knowledge of organizational behavior are important for the effective performance of EAP roles.

Following the identification of the problem, the EAP professional links the individual with the community resources most appropriate for dealing with the problem. The essence of the "EAP contract" between the employer and the employee (with the EAP professional acting as "broker") is that it is the employee's responsibility to cooperate with this regimen in order to resolve the work performance problems that precipitated the referral. In a great many instances in which problems less serious than substance abuse are involved, self-referrals may not involve evidence of job performance problems. Here there is less emphasis on agreements with employees about their responsibilities for behavior change.

Following these steps, it is appropriate for the EAP professional to monitor individuals' progress in counseling or treatment. Sometimes this includes coordinating the involvement of individuals' supervisors in treatment if the treatment plans are so designed. Finally, it is a typical responsibility of the EAP to engage in structured follow-up with employees after treatment. Such follow-up involves not only dealing with the short-term problems of workplace reentry and encouragement of a firm self-help group affiliation but also with longer term issues of successful rehabilitation and relapse prevention.

The promise of EAPs in dealing with substance abuse problems as well as other employee problems is great. Their attractiveness to employers is demonstrated by data indicating that over 40% of the American work force is covered by such programs as of 1991 (Blum and Roman 1992). Such coverage is considerably more likely in medium sized and larger workplaces but tends to be fairly uniform across industry types, with a somewhat greater likelihood of program presence in manufacturing settings.

## ▼ WORKPLACE FUNCTIONS SERVED BY EAPs

For employers concerned about dealing with employee substance abuse, there are at least five basic functions that can be served by EAPs.

The first dates back to the earliest industrial alcoholism programs: *the retention of employees who have developed substance abuse problems but in whom the organization has a substantial training investment.* The intervention strategies embedded in EAPs can be used to reduce or eliminate the job performance problems of substance-abusing employees through motivating them to receive counseling or treatment. The image that workplace management would like to identify and dismiss all employees with substance abuse problems is inaccurate. By contrast, most managements view employee turnover as expensive, even when employees with seemingly low levels of skill are involved. Especially when dismissals occur, turnover is also disruptive to the morale and efficiency of work groups. Thus turnover prevention or employment conservation can be markedly valuable for the work organization.

Further, the use of constructive intervention has a humanitarian dimension. Under an EAP policy, the employer's efforts to support the recovery process may include extending treatment opportunities with benefit coverage, affording use of sick leave when appropriate, and suspending the steps of progressive discipline when employees' performance problems have led to discipline and when such employees agree to undertake diligently counseling or treatment that may resolve their substance abuse problems. Such support by employers recognizes employees' personal investments, commitments, and contributions to the work organization. Depending on the extent to which EAP substance abuse referrals become known to other employees (which is not uncommon following return from treatment), the employer's supportive actions may reflect positively on the employer's image within the work force.

A second function is *reducing supervisory and managerial responsibility for and involvement in counseling employees with substance abuse problems* (Roman 1988). There is a long-standing stereotype that in the absence of a constructive policy, supervisors and managers facing a substance-abusing employee engage in denial and try their best to cover up and ignore the problem. Although this may be true in the early stages of the development of an employee's pattern of substance abuse, in fact there is a marked degree of activity relative to the problem as it progresses (Roman et al. 1992). The key point is that in the absence of an EAP and the expert resources that it offers for management in dealing with troubled workers, there is an implicit policy that delegates these responsibilities to supervisors and managers. Where a union is present, these implicit expectations also devolve upon union shop stewards.

In undertaking these counseling responsibilities by default, it must be recognized that supervisors and managers may sometimes be effective in leading an employee to rehabilitation. But there is little reason to expect such outcomes. Without policy guidelines or assistance from professional expertise, attempts at intervention will be notably inefficient. Without knowing the "right" thing to do, significant others in the workplace will be hesitant and often inconsistent in trying to deal with problems that typically become increasingly visible and demanding over time. The recognition that supervisors, managers, and shop stewards will engage in these frustrating counseling attempts is an idea that substitutes for the earlier observation that, without an EAP, supervisors will engage in mindless cover-up efforts, which result in "killing the employee with kindness" (Wrich 1973). Trying to build upon a more positive base may be more attractive for demonstrating to supervisors that an EAP can help them in dealing with issues that they will otherwise attempt to deal with themselves.

When an EAP is implemented, educational materials accompanying its diffusion need not caricature the behavior of supervisors toward substance-abusing employees as inept or harmful. EAP implementation should, however, gently discourage supervisors and managers from attempting to counsel or treat the substance-abusing employee and to instead seek consultative assistance from an EAP specialist when it is evident that they are dealing with such a problem. Such an approach continues to include the supervisor in the process of dealing with the employee rather than emphasizing an immediate "handing over" to the expertise of the EAP. Experience indicates that an approach that focuses on the EAP as a resolution for the frustrations of managing substance-abusing subordinates without external support meets with an enthusiastic reception from most supervisors. Few of them have had successful outcomes in dealing with such employees, and it is the kind of situation that practically anyone would want to avoid.

Beyond the relief that an EAP may offer to supervisors and managers who are forced into counseling roles by default is a phenomenon recognized by EAP practitioners in the mid-1970s (Phillips and Older 1977). Pivoting from the hypothesis that the behavior of alcoholic individuals engenders mirror-like behaviors among their significant others (a hypothesis since translated into "fact" within parts of the substance abuse treatment community) is the concept of the "troubled supervisor." According to Phillips and Older, the supervisor attempting to deal with a substance-abusing employee commonly develops a parallel troubled behavior pattern, marked by doubts and ambivalence that may come to undermine the supervisor's own job performance and his or her relationship with other subordinates. Such ambivalence had been revealed in an early research study focused on supervisors who had dealt with a variety of troubled employees (Trice 1965). Phillips and Older suggest that the performance problems of the troubled supervisor could be as costly to the organization as those of the troubled employee. EAP implementation may be seen as a means for the primary prevention of this troubled supervisor syndrome.

Turning to the third function that EAPs may serve, it should be recognized that the contemporary environment within which work organizations operate is characterized by the following:

▼ A multitude of legal protections that have developed around the employment relationship
▼ Many instances in which labor-management relationships are governed by collective bargaining agreements
▼ The organization's own possibly complex guidelines regarding employees' rights, benefits, responsibilities, and the steps in the implementation of progressive discipline

An EAP function that responds to this environment of rules and regulations is that *the EAP policy provides for due process for those employees whose substance abuse is affecting the quality and/or quantity of their work performance.*

In a very broad sense, the provision of offers of assistance for employees with substance abuse problems is not only humanitarian but may protect the employer against subsequent legal action. Part of the logic behind these decisions is that because a health-based technology exists for dealing with substance abuse and mental health problems, employees should be given the opportunity to access such technology before their employment is terminated due to substandard job performance. This principle is becoming more pervasive in court decisions in which employees charge their employers with discriminatory behavior vis-à-vis a substance abuse issue (Sonnenstuhl and Trice 1986). A further consideration is the matter of ensuring that steps taken toward problem employees occur in an appropriate context of employees' rights and responsibilities (i.e., that through the offer of assistance through an EAP, an employer is not committed to ensuring employees' recovery or their permanent employment).

Most recently, EAPs have demonstrated their value as a referral outlet for employees who produce positive results on random or for-cause screening for the use of illegal drugs (Roman and Blum 1992). Firing such employees, despite its promotion by national leadership, is not a reasonable alternative, and invites litigation that in the long run may serve neither the employee's nor the employer's interest (Blum 1989). The presence of an EAP encourages approaches that offer assistance but place responsibility for adequate job performance after receiving assistance squarely on the shoulders of the substance-abusing employee. Equitable implementation of the EAP policy is a critical dimension for due process. When the EAP is part of written human resource management policy, the likelihood of equitable implementation is enhanced. EAP sensitivity to due process also fosters an atmosphere in which unions can work cooperatively with management in EAP implementation.

A fourth function is that *through encouraging treatment of substance abuse among employees and their dependents, EAPs may contribute to overall health care cost containment.* Evidence has accumulated that employees with alcohol problems in particular are heavy users of health care services. As a group, untreated alcoholic individuals show levels of health care use that exceed the levels of their nonalcoholic peers at markedly high levels of statistical significance. This heavy use pattern extends to their families as well (Fein 1984; Holder 1987; Holder and Hallan 1986). Data indicate further that these levels of health care usage, both by the substance-abusing individual and his or her family members, decline markedly following successful interventions to deal with substance abuse problems.

It should be noted that these reductions in service use do not occur immediately but usually require several years. However, in light of the earlier discussion, it is evident that in the absence of an EAP, employees with substance abuse problems are not readily dismissed. Thus their high health care costs will not be avoided through a do-nothing approach. Thus although the initial investment in providing treatment for substance abuse problems may appear high, follow-up studies indicate that these investments have the ultimate effect of health care cost containment (Smith and Mahoney 1989). It is interesting to note that although the pattern of over-use of services (with a drop in service use following substance abuse treatment) has been confirmed in a number of different studies across different populations, there is little in the way of theoretical explanation to account for these patterns of change.

A fifth function served by EAPs is of substantial contemporary importance as the costs of substance abuse treatment are increasingly monitored: *the role of EAPs in providing gatekeeping and channeling in employees' use of health care services for substance abuse problems, including the channeling to proper treatment of dependents who are covered by employer-provided health care benefits.* It is evident that most employees do not have access to criteria by which they can select the most effective substance abuse treatment providers when they perceive that they or a family member have a problem requiring such assistance. Advice and direction about such resource use by EAP professionals can result in more efficient use of more effective services. This in turn leads to cost savings for the employer as well as for the employee when copayments are involved. This function is being extended in many organizations with EAPs through the establishment of preferred provider organization (PPO) arrangements. In these arrangements, community resources are evaluated in terms of both their effectiveness and their cost efficiency, with both the employer and employee benefiting from direction to these services.

With or without PPO arrangements, organizations are rapidly moving toward the requirement of precertification of employees' use of inpatient substance abuse services in order for the employee to minimize the copayment or in some instances to eliminate the copayment altogether. In other settings, managed care services have been adopted to review EAP-based recommendations for treatment referrals. In some instances these reviews lead to disagreements, conflicts, and the termination of treatment that has already begun. Conflict and the withholding of care is not a necessary consequence of using managed care and utilization review devices. Establishing clear lines of communication and coordination, reasonable outcome-oriented data bases, and mutual professional respect are all necessary ingredients if EAPs and managed care devices are to produce the desired outcomes of the more effective use of care.

A sixth function is embedded in the possibility that *EAPs may have a major impact in transforming workplaces' organizational cultures in regard to their images of substance abuse and its proper management*. Specifically, the implementation of an EAP and its effective use with substance-abusing employees can promote cultural norms within the organization that treatment rather than punishment is the appropriate approach to dealing with instances of substance abuse in which it is evident that the individual has little control over the patterning of use. Further, through the presence of individuals who are recovering from substance abuse problems, the reality of effective rehabilitation can be communicated to those who are skeptical about recovery. Such immediate exposure among workplace peers stands in contrast to the messages that employees and their families may receive through the mass media and other sources in which claims are based on hypothetical cases.

Although difficult to measure, it is also possible that there may be primary preventive impacts of EAPs through their sensitizing employees to broad issues associated with the use of alcohol and other drugs, sensitivity that may lead in some instances to the moderation of individual behaviors or to constructive reactions to substance abuse observed among family members or friends in settings outside the workplace.

# ▼ THE DYNAMICS OF EAP IMPLEMENTATION

For the remainder of this chapter we review how effectively EAPs may fulfill these six functions within workplaces. As substance abuse interventions, EAPs are quite new and have diffused quite rapidly in many different forms. It is therefore difficult to identify research data that allow for conclusive generalizations across a wide range of EAP settings. In very general terms, there is evidence that EAPs "work" in relation to resolving problems of employee substance abuse. There is much less information on how various combinations of these components work in concert or their sustained impact over a long period. We return to the discussion of efficacy and

its appropriate application to understanding EAPs in the last section of this chapter.

EAPs may be seen as a seedbed for role conflict for EAP administrators. In the early days of industrial alcoholism programs, coordinators were often "two-hatters" who needed to balance their personal commitments to AA with the bureaucratic features of their jobs as semiprofessional counselors (Blum 1988). Today, as employees of workplaces either directly or through contract, EAP administrators are called upon to maximize the extent of "smoothing" of organizational functioning in their dealing with employed substance abusers (i.e., the identification and management of these employees should minimally interfere with ongoing organizational functioning). On the other hand, as human services professionals, many EAP administrators feel bound to their commitments to maximize the welfare of individuals who have sought help. Thus the macro-level issues associated with the multiplicity of evaluation criteria that might be used to judge EAP effectiveness may be reflected in ethical issues at the level of individual practitioners. These issues are presently unresolved. We turn now to examining individual components of the EAP implementation process.

## Policy Statements

Although some companies have reportedly supported EAPs for many years without the presence of a written policy statement, in practically all instances the development and promulgation of such a policy is the initial step in a workplace's implementation of an EAP. Such a policy may be seen as serving at least three functions:

1. It is the basis for introducing the program, explaining its purpose and philosophy, and generating support for it at all levels of the work organization.
2. The policy spells out the roles of individuals who may be faced with dealing with a substance abuser or other troubled employee. Usually the policy urges that supervisors or managers contact the EAP for assistance before attempting a referral on their own.
3. The policy statement may be a means of ensuring equity. By providing rules and guidelines, it ensures that all employees will have equal opportunities to use the services of the program if

necessary. Further it ensures that in that process all will be provided with the benefits of confidentiality and the suspension of disciplinary procedures where applicable.

In settings in which unions are present, the development of the components of the policy statement can provide the opportunity for labor and management to work together (Trice and Roman 1972). This can be the foundation for "jointness" throughout the implementation process. Joint support of the program by labor and management can be very important in encouraging utilization, ensuring supervisors and managers that they are not generating conflict through using the policy but instead encouraging direct involvement of union stewards and other representatives as appropriate.

The written policy statement also provides a vehicle for top management of the organization to indicate both symbolically and tangibly its support for this new program. Ideally, as a personnel policy, the EAP policy is introduced in a fashion in which it is seen as something that should be used by supervision in dealing with problem employees. At best, it signals a shift in organizational culture to the formal acceptance of substance abuse as a health problem to be dealt with in the same fashion as other health issues. This hopefully constitutes a major step toward destigmatization of substance abuse problems at both collective and individual levels.

## Policy Diffusion and Training

Diffusion of the policy is essential for program use. The policy can be introduced into personnel manuals, and it can be diffused to all employees through various forms of internal communication. However, since the early days of industrial alcoholism programs, there has been a general belief that specific training of supervisors and managers is necessary in order for effective program implementation to occur (Trice and Roman 1972). Although such training might occur before the program is actually implemented, the typical pattern is for such training to be introduced over a long period, with different segments of the managerial work force scheduled for training attendance as time permits. Such spacing is also typically required because the training is carried out by EAP personnel who must otherwise be available to perform their direct service functions.

For an EAP to be effective in dealing with substance-abusing employees, there must be a reasonable degree of "readiness" to use the program on the part of supervisors and affected individuals. At the same time, efforts must be made to reduce or eliminate barriers to program use. The extent to which these issues are problematic is reflected in the proportion of the work force and demographic distributions found in the caseload of the EAP.

## EAP Referral Routes

Obviously, there are many barriers within the context of social interaction that preclude or delay supervisors from taking definitive actions toward subordinates (Roman et al. 1992). These factors include a variety of beliefs that may be embedded in organizational cultures:

▼ The problem will eventually diminish or "go away"
▼ The referral might damage the subordinate
▼ The referral might reflect badly on the supervisor
▼ It is simply easier to put up with the troublesome situation than to get involved in embarrassing and unpredictable referral actions

As mentioned previously, it is not at all uncommon for supervisors themselves to undertake to counsel an employee in attempt to correct deviant behavior for a considerable period of time before seeking outside assistance. Indeed, there are many principles of supervisory performance management that call upon supervisors to engage in such corrective counseling prior to seeking outside assistance. Although encouragement of supervisory counseling may be useful in dealing with a variety of problematic behaviors directly associated with job tasks and interpersonal relationships with work peers, it seems likely that it constitutes an invitation for the supervisor and subordinate to become enmeshed in a cycle of enabling and denial when employee substance abuse is at issue. Nonetheless, regardless of the effectiveness of supervisory training and other means of encouraging referral, it is typical for knowledge of problematic employee behavior to have persisted for some time before supervisory referrals occur.

The self-referral is, of course, a very different matter. The principal emphasis here is confidentiality, with employees referring themselves to the program without the knowledge of the supervisor or co-workers. Although such self-referrals are very common in dealing with a variety of employees' personal troubles, the extent of genuine self-referral for employees' personal substance abuse is low. Accumulated knowledge about substance abuse suggests that cases of significant alcohol and drug dependency would be well known to supervisors and co-workers as well as to the affected individual well before job-based crises occur.

Data from an ongoing study of EAP referral routes indicate that most events involving employee substance abuse that are recorded as self-referrals are indeed the result of informal "nudges" by supervisors and other significant others (Blum and Roman 1992). In these circumstances the supervisor does not undertake a formal referral of the employee but threatens that a formal referral will be forthcoming unless the employee undertakes a self-referral. Such procedures minimize the likelihood of the supervisor becoming enmeshed in red tape or interpersonal complications. On the other hand, the supervisor's failure to become formally involved reduces the likelihood that leverage will be available to be used subsequently to motivate the individual to engage in genuine behavior change if referral to treatment is successful.

It is also possible individuals may be pressed toward seeking assistance for their problems through the action of peers or family members. If one looks at the broader picture of barriers to seeking treatment for substance abuse problems, it is clear that the EAP can be a mechanism for greatly reducing the distance between individuals and access to help. It appears that over time the existence of the EAP becomes well known to family members such that they may play a more significant role in motivating what appear to be employee self-referrals than has previously been assumed (Blum and Roman 1992). At the same time, it is also possible, particularly in settings involving professional and technical occupations, that peers may play significant roles in the referral process.

Thus there are many routes by which substance-abusing employees may access an EAP for assistance. There are barriers to such referrals, both those embedded in the nature of relationships in the workplace as well as problems associated with an understanding of the EAP or particular aspects of its image in a given workplace. EAP administrators are called upon to deal both with the direct service needs of employee referrals (and sometimes referrals of employee dependents as well) and also deal with issues of organizational image and information diffusion. This complex of ongoing demands that are not easily prioritized oftentimes outruns the time and resources available to the individuals assigned to EAP coordinator positions, enhancing the risks for stress within these jobs.

## Diagnosis and Use of Treatment

Once a referral has occurred, it is essential that the EAP administrator develop an adequate level of rapport with the referred individual in order that an adequate assessment may be made. Although there is sometimes a temptation to follow such assessments by direct counseling proffered to the employee by the EAP professional, most adhere to EAP principles that referrals to appropriate resources in the community are essential if conflicts of interest are to be avoided, especially in terms of the EAP contract discussed previously.

If these referrals are to be carried out effectively, it is obvious that an adequate and correct diagnosis needs to be made. Although some EAPs equip their professional staff with adequate diagnostic skills through requiring appropriate credentials and licensure, there are other settings in which a central diagnostic and referral agency is used as a means for reaching a decision as to what the individual's problem happens to be.

Use of such a central agency has advantages in that it takes the employer out of the role of supporting a diagnostic function and the conflicts of interest that diagnosis of one organizational employee by another may entail. Further, use of a central diagnostic agency allows for a lower level of clinical skills in the EAP administrative position, perhaps increasing the likelihood that the incumbent will be highly skilled in understanding the organizational dynamics vital to EAP success. On the other hand, adding this step to the referral process requires particular skills in keeping referred employees motivated to stay within the system and to go through the various steps that are being prescribed for them.

Following diagnosis, suggestions are made to the employee as to the type of counseling or treatment that may be necessary in order to help him or her deal with the diagnosed problem. According to EAP principles, these are suggestions rather than directives to the employee, making certain that the entry into a treatment regimen is an individual choice and that the success of that treatment rests heavily with individual responsibility.

It is critical to note that these recommendations should be made on the basis of knowledge of the most effective facility available in the community. Such knowledge does not refer to impressionistic ideas about community-based facilities acquired through "networking" or other informal means but to data-based assessments of effectiveness. Further, the referring agent, be it an internal employee or an external provider, needs to have full knowledge of the health benefits coverage associated with a particular employee's position in the workplace. This is vital so that a recommended referral will be adequately covered by health insurance so that the services can be used without undue hardship or without demotivating the employee from seeking assistance because of the expense. Thus a careful matching process is typically necessary, often made more complicated when employees at a given workplace are covered under different types of health insurance or HMO (health maintenance organization) policies.

Thus the referral decision needs to be highly informed not only in terms of the effectiveness of the external agency but also in terms of the changing provisions in employee insurance coverage. This often means that EAP administrators need to be fully acquainted with the benefits structure of their organization and any changes that may occur in benefits provisions. It also means that EAP administrators must spend a good deal of their working time becoming acquainted with the quality of services available in the community and the appropriateness of these services for the needs of their particular work force.

At the same time, the referral function is made increasingly complicated in many work settings by the involvement of managed care agents who review referral suggestions. The manner in which workplaces have linked their EAP with managed care and utilization review processes varies greatly. In some instances the EAP administrator has reasonable control in this process and is in a position to negotiate disagreements. In other instances, especially where the EAP has not established an effective data base on which to justify its referral suggestions, the EAP administrator's referral suggestions may be completely altered by the review process built into managed care. Further complexities can be added to this when the managed care processes are delayed such that the in-

dividual is already in treatment when a decision is made that alters the third-party payments that will be guaranteed for that particular placement.

It is important for the EAP administrator to monitor the individual's passage through the substance abuse treatment process. Here it is clear that some degree of clinical skills on the part of the EAP administrator are necessary if he or she is to effectively communicate with the treatment center. On the other hand, it is clear that treatment center personnel must understand the particular nature of EAP referrals and the contingencies associated with the employed individual's job if they are to effectively communicate with the EAP administrators, ideally including them as part of the treatment team both symbolically and in actuality.

## Posttreatment

As mentioned, it may be that workplace personnel, particularly immediate supervisors, may be called in to be part of the treatment process as a means of enhancing effective reentry of the treated substance-abusing individual into the workplace. There is every reason to expect the various dynamics that are associated with family members' adaptation to the recovering substance-abusing individual would also apply to the immediate supervisor and other members of the work group. The EAP administrator is crucial in making sure that these linkages are made and that appropriate participation occurs.

Although reentry may be usefully viewed as part of the treatment process, long-term follow-up and aftercare is probably not effectively viewed in this context. From observations in our own research (Blum and Roman 1992), effective follow-up with employees who have received counseling or treatment at external agencies is an area of marked weakness in the operation of most EAPs. At the same time it might be said that follow-up associated with most substance abuse treatment programs is notably weak. The problem of poor follow-up is compounded when the EAP and the treatment center each assume that the other is effectively managing follow-up.

One of the greatest advantages of EAP policies is their typical intention to maintain the substance-abusing individual's employment throughout the course of treatment and recovery (i.e., a structure within which follow-up is a ready possibility compared with patients who are dispersed across the community following treatment). The workplace also provides a substantial set of opportunities for relapse prevention. Follow-up regarding self-help group participation or brief follow-up counseling sessions can be crucial during this first year following treatment and beyond.

Follow-up counseling may highlight necessities for considering changes within the work role assignment, assuming such changes are a possibility. Follow-up activities may or may not involve the employee's supervisor, depending on the nature of the referral and the manner in which confidentiality guidelines may be breached by such involvement if releases have not been obtained. This highlights the delicacy of follow-up in situations of self-referral in which confidentiality to the employee has been part of the guarantee that may have motivated the individual's accessing of treatment.

From our observations, the lack of attention to follow-up is not a consequence of a lack of follow-up skills, but rather stems from inadequate time by the EAP staff to pursue these cases. Given the obvious value of follow-up as insurance on the investment in treatment, this is regrettable. Unfortunately, its relative neglect stems from the manner in which most EAPs are monitored by upper level workplace managers. Given its obvious face validity, the rate of initial use or intake is the datum most commonly used to monitor EAP performance on a periodic basis. It is clearly a convenient statistic with much face validity, yet few EAP administrators appear to realize how their encouragement of the use of such data actually shapes their job performance. Most significant is that this emphasis inadvertently can reduce the critical visibility of long-term payoffs, such as recovery from substance abuse that is enhanced by careful attention to routine, long-term follow-up of existing patients as an alternative to a steady emphasis on new referrals.

## Staffing and Program Design

This brief overview of the dynamics of EAP functioning in dealing with substance-abusing employees provides some insights into the array of skills needed to be an effective EAP administrator whose caseload is going to include an adequate representation of these individuals. Individuals doing such work need to have a comprehensive knowledge of a variety of clinical issues and broad-based knowledge of personnel practices and internal culture of a particular

workplace. These comprehensive EAP expectations are especially demanding on individuals' time. However such a range of roles can provide a diversity of work activities that may prove more stimulating than substance abuse intervention occupations that are assigned a rather narrow division of labor.

As mentioned early in this chapter, there is considerable variation in the extent to which employers elect to operate EAPs with their own employees versus contracting with external agencies for EAP services (Roman 1990). There are obvious advantages in either type of arrangement. The internal personnel are more likely to have a clear acquaintance with a particular workplace and its rules and practices. Further, they are more likely to be accessible and known to members of the work force. Over time, they may build up substantial credibility that constitutes another stimulus for both supervisory and self-referral and may increase the likelihood of effective follow-up.

External agencies on the other hand may be more flexible in their ability to be staffed with different personnel representing the different types of expertise necessary for effective EAP operation. The external agency may also have more flexibility in increasing its allocation of professional resources to the contracting workplace, assuming that the contract can be adjusted to pay for such additional personnel when the demand proves that it is necessary. On the other hand, the external agency may be more strongly motivated toward minimizing services in the interest of maximizing its profits than is the case with an internal program.

Finally, although the internal program might be directly controlled by a human resource administrator without EAP experience on a day-to-day basis, the external staff would be more likely under the direction of individuals with EAP experience that more effectively equips them to evaluate staff performance and provide program direction.

## ▼ THE EFFICACY OF EAPs

A natural question to be raised about EAPs is their efficacy. One way to respond is to refer to the oft-quoted figure of 70% "success," based on the 1985 reports of coordinators of 317 internal programs and the contract monitors of 126 external programs (Blum and Roman 1989; Blum et al. 1992), as well as a range of other summaries of discrete studies of program functioning (Sonnenstuhl and Trice 1986). Another way to look at outcome is to examine the operation of discrete components of EAPs. Here a classic study reported by Trice and Beyer (1984) establishes that constructive confrontation was highly efficacious for alcoholic subordinates described by a sample of supervisors in several locations of a large corporation. There is some evidence indicating the impact of supervisory training associated with EAPs (Colan and Schneider 1992; Gerstein et al. 1989). There are data from several different sources confirming the cost-effectiveness of EAPs (Foote et al. 1978; Smith and Mahoney 1989).

Elsewhere there are criticisms of the methodology employed in the evaluations of all workplace programs that have attempted alcohol problem intervention, both before and since the introduction of the EAP model (Kurtz et al. 1984; Walsh 1982). One partial review that was restricted mainly to the human resource management literature claims that there is no evidence that EAPs work (Luthans and Waldersee 1989). There are also critiques that claim that EAPs are simply social control mechanisms designed to coerce employees into stricter conformity with employers' demands (Weiss 1986).

Speaking both generally and strictly, there is no answer to the question of whether EAPs are efficacious or how efficacious they are under different circumstances. In several respects this is the wrong question to ask. It is the wrong question because it approaches EAPs as if they were a treatment modality, which they distinctively are not. The outcomes of most substance abuse referrals to EAPs are tied to the treatment and aftercare that is provided completely independent of the auspices of the EAP. Thus examining outcomes associated with EAPs is to focus on the consequences of multiple inputs wherein it is impossible to disentangle the positive or negative influences of EAP inputs, treatment inputs, or aftercare/follow-up inputs.

It is also the wrong question because it presumes that EAPs are primarily focused on patient outcomes. Research indicates that EAP personnel spend substantial amounts of their time in resolving problems between supervisors and subordinates that do not lead to referral, in giving advice to individuals that is not recorded in case records, or in attempting to motivate providers to upgrade the quality of treatment services in order to improve treatment efficacy, just to cite a few examples (Blum and Roman 1989; Blum et al. 1992; Roman and Blum 1987).

Returning to the data that indicate a 70% success rate, these can be challenged on many grounds. Most important is the fact that the patients represent only those who agreed to be treated by the EAP service. These individuals were somehow successfully motivated to become EAP intakes. These success data say nothing about the potential patients who remained at their jobs, quit, were fired, or died. Likewise, data indicating a high level of efficacy for constructive confrontation are based only on those patients that made it to this point in the EAP process, indicating that as a subgroup they were considerably "ready" as compared with those whose recalcitrance prevented them from entering the system in the first or who dropped out at a point prior to formal confrontation.

This is not to devalue this body of research or to discourage its further development and replication. But there is a repeated set of difficulties in discussing EAP efficacy within a framework that EAPs are another genre of treatment programs. EAPs do far more than deal with patients; they control access to their patients only for very brief periods and generally are not correctly viewed in an input/outcome framework. At the same time, it must be recognized that there is little standardization in design and process across EAPs for two very basic reasons.

First, EAPs must be adapted to both the work forces they serve and the workplaces within which they are developed, defying standardization in either structure or process.

Second, with the exception of the transportation and nuclear power industries in the United States, EAPs are implemented voluntarily by employers who make independent decisions about the level of investment they desire to make in their respective programs. Thus although there is pressure for conformity to standards developed by EAP personnel, such conformity will be almost totally voluntary for the foreseeable future.

In sum, asking about the efficacy of EAPs is similar to asking about the efficacy of employers' provision of health insurance benefits or the efficacy of pension plans for retirees. These questions seem absurd because the immediate and obvious responses are "efficacious for accomplishing what?" and, perhaps, "what kind of health insurance coverage or pension plan?"

What health insurance and pension plans have in common with EAPs is that they are human resource management practices based in the workplace, not freestanding human service programs. This means that they do not lend themselves to typical evaluations of efficacy because there is such a broad range of outcomes of interest to different constituency groups and there is such variation in their structure and design. Concepts of program evaluation assume commonalities across programs and program ingredients, coupled with the opportunity for some form of quasiexperimental design to ascertain program impact.

Although human resource management strategies do not easily lend themselves to typical program evaluations, this does not mean that their efficacy is to be ignored or simply assumed on faith. The more appropriate approach is to examine the effectiveness of the structure and process of an individual program, often called an *audit*. An audit requires on-site examination of the presence and quality of program ingredients, including review of data generated through management information systems wherein auditors can examine the efficiency of the use of resources assigned by the work organization to the particular program.

To demonstrate how this applies to the efficacy of an EAP, a hypothetical scenario may be helpful. An audit of an EAP in a large for-profit manufacturing firm might reveal that the rate of supervisory referrals to the EAP of employees with substance abuse problems is low relative to EAPs situated in workplaces of similar type and size. Further examination may reveal that rates of such referrals were substantially higher 2 years earlier when the EAP staff routinely conducted orientation and refresher programs about the EAP for new and continuing supervisors and managers. Interviews may reveal that an increase in caseload led to decisions to sharply curtail the supervisory training. Such decisions in turn reflected the denial of an earlier request by the EAP for an additional staff position. This denial occurred because of an overall freeze on hiring that had occurred across the organization.

Placing these results in an evaluation framework might suggest that this EAP is relatively ineffective in dealing with employee substance abuse. The strategy of an audit however, reveals that the internal political economy of a particular workplace led to the observed outcome, an outcome that might be seen as beyond the control of a particular EAP staff. In contrast to outcome data generated by an evaluation, an audit provides a firmer base on which to assess the realities of different alterations that might be made to the program that is being examined.

Returning to the earlier discussion of the functions that may be served by an EAP, issues of efficacy as examined through an audit may center on the extent to which each of these functions are being served in a given workplace. An audit will likely also offer an explanation for shortfalls. Such shortfalls should not suggest the abandonment of the EAP because there is no alternative with which to replace the EAP (i.e., no parallel to the way in which outpatient treatment of substance abuse can be an alternative to inpatient care). Thus EAPs' effectiveness is relative to their workplace settings, their integration within these settings, and the extent to which the EAP attracts the investment of organizational resources. It is impossible to specify EAP efficacy in dealing with employee substance abuse or other employee problems independent of considering the relatively complex context within which given EAPs function.

## ▼ CONCLUSION

In conclusion, the voluntary adoption of EAPs over the past 20 years to the point where their coverage extends to over 40% of the work force is testimony to their perceived value by workplace managers and labor unions. That EAPs are better than some alternative is impossible to address because EAPs are essentially "value-added" human resource management practices in the workplace rather than substitutes or replacements for preexisting structures or programs. Organizational audits can establish the EAP design that appears most effective for a given work site, a design that might need to be altered over time in response to changes in a particular workplace and the composition of its work force.

Because EAPs are widely involved in mainstreaming the management of substance abuse problems with other types of behavioral problems, the community of EA workers lies outside the broader community of substance abuse interventionists. EAPs are not well understood in this broader community, and their perception as work-based treatment programs leads to frustrations for those who demand simple analyses of the program efficacy. As human resource management practices adapted to particular workplace settings, EAPs require a different frame of reference for understanding their value in dealing with substance abuse issues. EAPs are, however, unique in their access to the employed population, which includes the vast majority of society's recovering, active, and potential substance-abusing individuals. A better understanding of their roles by substance abuse interventionists as well as interventionists primarily focused on psychiatric and family problems is critical if the range of such interventions is to significantly affect consequences of behaviors linked to substance abuse.

## ▼ REFERENCES

Blum TC: New occupations and the division of labor in workplace alcoholism programming, in Recent Developments in Alcoholism, Vol 6. Edited by Galanter M. New York, Plenum, 1988

Blum TC: The presence and integration of drug abuse intervention in human resource management, in Drugs in the Workplace: Research and Evaluation Data, NIDA Res Monogr 91. Edited by Guste S. Washington, DC, U.S. Government Printing Office, 1989, pp 271–286

Blum TC, Roman PM: Employee assistance and human resources management, in Research in Personnel and Human Resources Management, Vol 7. Edited by Rowland K, Ferris G. Greenwich, CT, JAI Press, 1989, pp 258–312

Blum TC, Roman PM: Identifying alcoholics and persons with alcohol-related problems in the workplace: a description of EAP clients. Alcohol, Health and Research World 16:120–128, 1992

Blum TC, Martin JK, Roman PM: A research note on EAP prevalence, components and utilization. Journal of Employee Assistance Research 1:209–229, 1992

Colan NB, Schneider R: The effectiveness of supervisor training: one-year follow-up. Journal of Employee Assistance Research 1:83–95, 1992

Fein R: Alcohol in America: The Price We Pay. Minneapolis, MN, Care Institute, 1984

Foote A, Erfurt J, Strauch P, et al: Cost Effectiveness of Occupational Employee Assistance Programs. Ann Arbor, MI, Institute of Labor and Industrial Relations of the University of Michigan, 1978

Gerstein L, Eichenhofer D, Bayer G, et al: EAP referral training and supervisors' beliefs about troubled workers. Employee Assistance Quarterly 4:15–30, 1989

Holder HD: Alcoholism treatment and potential health care cost savings. Med Care 25:52–71, 1987

Holder HD, Hallan JB: Impact of alcoholism treatment on total health care costs: a six-year study. Advances in Alcohol and Substance Abuse 6:1–15, 1986

Kurtz NR, Googins B, Howard WC: Measuring the success of occupational alcoholism programs. J Stud Alcohol 45:33–45, 1984

Luthans F, Waldersee R: What do we really know about EAPs? Human Resource Management 28:385–401, 1989

Maxwell MA: Early identification of problem drinkers in industry. Quarterly Journal of Studies on Alcohol 21:655–678, 1960

Phillips DA, Older HJ: A model for counseling troubled supervisors. Alcohol, Health and Research World 2:24–30, 1977

Roman PM: Secondary prevention of alcoholism: problems and prospects in occupational programming. Journal of Drug Issues 5:327–343, 1975

Roman PM: From employee alcoholism to employee assistance: an analysis of the de-emphasis on prevention and on alcoholism problems in work-based programs. J Stud Alcohol 42:244–272, 1981

Roman PM: Growth and transformation in workplace alcoholism programming, in Recent Developments in Alcoholism, Vol 6. Edited by Galanter M. New York, Plenum, 1988, pp 131–158

Roman PM: The use of employee assistance programs to deal with drug abuse in the workplace, in Drugs in the Workplace: Research and Evaluation Data, NIDA Res Monogr 91. Edited by Guste S. Washington, DC, U.S. Government Printing Office, 1989, pp 245–270

Roman PM: Strategic considerations in designing interventions to deal with alcohol problems in the workplace, in Alcohol Problem Intervention in the Workplace: Employee Assistance Programs and Strategic Alternatives. Edited by Roman PM. Westport, CT, Quorum Press, 1990, pp 371–406

Roman PM: Problem definitions and social movement strategies: the disease concept and the hidden alcoholic revisited, in Alcohol: The Development of Sociological Perspectives on Use and Abuse. Edited by Roman PM. New Brunswick, NJ, Center of Alcohol Studies, Rutgers University, 1991, pp 235–254

Roman PM, Blum TC: Notes on the new epidemiology of alcoholism in the USA. Journal of Drug Issues 11:321–332, 1987

Roman PM, Blum TC: Employee assistance and drug screening programs, in Treating Drug Problems, Vol 2. Edited by Gerstein DR. Washington, DC, National Academy of Sciences Press, 1992

Roman PM, Trice HM: Alcohol abuse in work organizations, in The Biology of Alcoholism, Vol 4: Social Aspects of Alcoholism. Edited by Kissin B, Begleiter H. New York, Plenum, 1976, pp 445–518

Roman PM, Blum TC, Martin JK: "Enabling" of male problem drinkers in work groups. British Journal of Addictions 87:275–289, 1992

Rubington E: The chronic drunkenness offender: before and after decriminalization, in Society, Culture and Drinking Patterns Reexamined. Edited by Pittman DJ, White H. New Brunswick, NJ, Rutgers Center for Alcohol Studies, 1991, pp 733–752

Schneider J: Deviant drinking as disease: alcoholism as a social accomplishment. Social Problems 25:361–372, 1978

Smith D, Mahoney J: McDonnell Douglas Corporation's EAP produces. The ALMACAN 19:18–26, 1989

Sonnenstuhl W, Trice HM: Strategies for Employee Assistance Programs: The Crucial Balance, Key Issues No 30. Ithaca, NY, ILR Press, 1986

Trice HM: Alcoholic employees: a comparison of psychotic, neurotic, and "normal" personnel. J Occup Med 7:94–99, 1965

Trice HM, Beyer J: Work-related outcomes of constructive confrontation strategies in a job-based alcoholism program. J Stud Alcohol 45:393–404, 1984

Trice HM, Roman PM: Spirits and Demons at Work: Alcohol and Other Drugs on the Job. Ithaca, NY, Publications Divisions of the New York State School of Industrial and Labor Relations at Cornell University, 1972

Trice HM, Schonbrunn M: A history of job-based alcoholism programs, 1900–1955. Journal of Drug Issues 11:171–198, 1981

Walsh D: Employee assistance programs. Milbank Q 60:492–517, 1982

Weiss R: Managerial Ideology and the Social Control of Deviance in Organizations. New York, Praeger, 1986

Wrich J: The Employee Assistance Program. Center City, MN, Hazleden Foundation, 1973

# CHAPTER 27

# Community-Based Treatment

*James H. Shore, M.D.*

This chapter reviews and updates community-based treatment resources for substance abuse, with a special focus on alcohol abuse and dependence (Shore 1989; Shore and Kofoed 1984b). Although many of the significant issues that are related to community-based treatment for addictions are discussed in other chapters, there are several unique features not covered elsewhere that will be reviewed here. These features include the important influence of social supports on community treatment outcome, the impact of local ordinances, workplace factors, community case finding, community detoxification, and significant nontreatment factors. While considering each of these variables, it is critical that the psychiatrist maintain a flexible approach and define a therapeutic plan that is specifically tailored to individual patient needs.

It is important that the clinical psychiatrist in community-based practice appreciate the dichotomy between models of substance abuse treatment. For clarification of treatment models the psychodynamic psychiatric model for the treatment of alcoholism is compared with an addiction model. These two models can be contrasted somewhat stereotypically to highlight psychiatry's earlier approach to substance abuse and the recent clarity that is associated with the addiction model of treatment. Historically psychia-

trists used a psychodynamic model to define and treat alcoholism, focusing on the disorder as a symptom of an underlying psychiatric etiology. The primary therapeutic goal was to diagnose and treat the underlying disorder with an intensive psychodynamic approach and with considerable permissiveness. The psychiatrist assumed responsibility for the treatment and did not necessarily encourage the patient to participate in self-help groups. Coercion or surveillance were carefully avoided. This approach included a concept of cure. In contrast, the addiction model defines alcoholism or drug abuse as a primary disorder. This approach has significant implications for the behavior of the therapist and the patient. The psychiatrist treats the addiction directly, often with confrontation and a strict adherence to abstinence from substance use. The responsibility is primarily assigned to the patient, who also may be encouraged or required to join Alcoholics Anonymous (AA) or other self-help groups. In special circumstances, surveillance for compliance is a component of treatment. For certain risk groups coercion is seen to be useful. Although the treatment goals include abstinence and symptom relief with psychosocial rehabilitation, they do not include a concept of cure. It should be obvious that any treatment model used rigidly or exclusively can lead to serious errors in the development of an individualized diagnosis and therapeutic plan. Fortunately, we have reached a point in the treatment of substance abuse that an addiction model incorporates an integrated biopsychosocial perspective with focused attention on the needs of each individual patient (Frances et al. 1989; Frances and Miller 1991).

## ▼ SOCIAL SUPPORTS

Social support is a critical issue for the outcome of community-based alcohol and drug abuse treatment. In 1992, Booth et al. evaluated the influence of social support on community adjustment following an inpatient alcoholism treatment admission. The important variables included support from the treatment environment and support from family and friends. In a follow-up of these patients, the study demonstrated that reassurance of worth from family and friends and number of previous hospitalizations were independent and both significant predictors of relapse and time to readmission. Higher levels of reassurance of worth or support for self-esteem significantly lengthened time to readmission. A specific finding from this study suggested that the particular sources and forms of social support, that is from family and friends, are important to the recovering alcoholic individual. The effect of social support on treatment outcome is independent of the alcoholic individual's prior history including treatment failure. This work substantiated the work of Billings and Moos (1981), who demonstrated that stress, coping responses, and family environment as posttreatment factors also were important predictors of alcoholism treatment outcome.

In addition to the importance of social supports, the type of service delivery system that is accessible to any patient is often first determined in the way a patient's alcoholism or drug addiction is identified by the community. The means of case identification and the availability of services often is more influential than the patient's individual needs in determining the treatment plan. Obviously, other variables such as comorbidity, socioeconomic class, cultural orientation, and patient preference also are important determinants for successful entry into a particular system. In 1975, Emrick conducted a comprehensive review and demonstrated that specific differences in treatment methods were not significantly related to the long-term outcome. This review included 384 studies

of psychologically oriented community alcohol programs in which the nonspecific factors were more important. Armor et al. (1976) summarized the Rand Report of alcoholism treatment in the community. They demonstrated that consistent alcoholism treatment programs had a general effectiveness at a 70% improvement rate.

## ▼ LOCAL ORDINANCES

Changes in local ordinances that affect access to alcohol and programs for drunken driver diversion have received widespread attention in the news media and with public policy development (Ogborne et al. 1991; Ogborne et al. 1992). Dull and Giacopassi (1988) studied the correlates and presumed consequences of local alcohol ordinances in the State of Tennessee, where 28% of the population reside in "dry" jurisdictions that forbid the sale of alcohol to the public. They compared dry and "wet" communities with respect to accessibility of alcohol, population demographics, mortality rates from auto accidents, liver disease and cirrhosis, suicide, and homicide. The results suggested that alcohol availability played both a direct and indirect role in influencing these serious consequences. Their analysis revealed a complex interrelationship between variables. No simple conclusions could be drawn concerning the effectiveness of a particular type of alcohol ordinance or its relationship to a particular population in determining the outcome. May (1992) also has published a comprehensive study of local ordinances on American Indian reservations and demonstrated a significant relationship between the social pathologies and the availability of alcohol.

Maghsoodloo et al. (1988) evaluated the impact of legislation revision for driving while under the influence (DUI) in Alabama after a major revision of the state DUI laws in 1980. This revision resulted in an increase in the proportion of DUI convictions, a reduction in the number of DUI citations reduced to reckless driving, a reduction in the proportion of offenders acquitted and/or dismissed, an increase in the proportion of revocations, and an increase in court referrals to an educational program on the first offense. However, in spite of the changes the revision also was accompanied by a significant increase in alcohol-related accidents. A second revision was effected in 1983 with more stringent penalties and had a positive impact on all six alcohol-related measures, plus significantly decreasing the proportion of alcohol-related accidents by almost 3%. Lange and Green (1990) evaluated in case vignettes how Colorado judges sentenced DUI offenders. Colorado judges gave more serious sentences to offenders with prior records and to those with higher blood alcohol levels. A prior record had the greatest impact on sentencing. These findings demonstrated that for DUI offenders the judges treated the repeat offenders differently, regardless of intoxication level at arrest.

In 1984 Shore and Kofoed (1984a) conducted an extensive review of the literature, analyzing the outcome evaluation of first time offender programs and repeater offender programs. From this review there were a few significantly positive results. The review identified wide variation in evaluation methods and illustrated the problems in comparing such research. This comparison of research studies demonstrated significant variability in the choice of outcome measures. Alcohol consumption, arrests for driving while intoxicated, and accidents did not appear to be related in the studied populations. Follow-up outcome in all the studies varied considerably. In the 1980s, the introduction of the 55 mile per hour speed limit also occurred during many program evaluations; this complicated outcome interpretation because highway fatalities dropped significantly during this time.

## ▼ THE WORKPLACE

An important setting for community-based treatments is the workplace. (Employee assistance programs are covered in Chapter 26.) The development of drug testing in the workplace has been widely reported. In a review of drug testing in the workplace and its objectives, pitfalls, and guidelines, Schottenfeld (1989) identified and discussed seven potential problems that resulted. Because this issue is critical in a consideration of community-based treatments and employment settings, Schottenfeld's seven factors are outlined here.

1. Workplace testing may lead to the abandonment of effective and less problematic approaches
2. Workplace drug-testing may focus on drug abuse and divert attention from alcohol abuse
3. Workplace testing may be used to intimidate employees

4. Workplace testing may mistakenly identify as substance-abusing individuals employees and applicants who do not have drug or alcohol problems
5. Workplace testing may detect medically prescribed drug use unrelated to an employee's job performance and thereby may lead to discrimination against employees with medical problems
6. Workplace testing programs may result in the creation of a pool of unemployable individuals
7. Workplace testing programs may unintentionally infringe on the private lives of employees

The impact of monitoring recovery in the workplace is particularly important but difficult to evaluate because there are no controlled studies. Follow-up data with various occupations have reported 89%–90% success rates for certain monitored employee groups. Two groups of particular interest for recovery monitoring are airline pilots and physicians. Obviously, both professions are associated in the eyes of the public with significant responsibility for human life. Each have dramatic and publicized examples of addicted individuals whose behavior has led to tragic outcomes for passengers and patients. Because both professions have a higher degree of governmental control through the licensing authority, there is significant coercion for treatment compliance and participation in monitoring. Harper (1983) reported the outcome with 120 treated pilots and demonstrated a 93% success rate. Shore (1987) reported an 8-year follow-up for 63 addicted or impaired physicians who had been on probation with the Oregon Board of Medical Examiners. Seventy-five percent were rated as stable or improved at 8-year evaluation. There was a significant correlation between treatment with monitoring and improvement for addicted physicians, with a 96% positive outcome at 8 years. The high rehabilitation success rates for pilots and physicians associated with careful treatment supervision and monitoring cannot necessarily be generalized to other treatment populations. Both of these professional groups identify specific workplace settings where compliance and outcome have been significantly affected and where treatment outcome is outstanding.

## ▼ COMMUNITY CASE FINDING

Throughout the 1980s, a series of reports focused on the reliability of community case finding beginning in the psychiatric emergency room (Jones 1979; Rund et al. 1981; Solomon et al. 1980). The estimates of the treatment prevalence for alcoholism in the general emergency room population ranged as high as 20%. In the early 1980s, the studies demonstrated that physicians generally recognized less than 50% of patients as alcoholic. These studies were usually conducted with an independent assessment using an alcohol abuse scale such as the Michigan Alcoholism Screening Test (MAST; Selzer 1971). In a 1980 study, Murphy (1980) demonstrated an important principle in a community case finding for alcoholic patients by showing that patients were unlikely to discuss the subject or their problem drinking spontaneously. Of 51 alcoholic patients who had come to their family physicians for care, only two specifically asked for substance abuse treatment. Eighteen others mentioned some aspect of their drinking problem. Murphy's most interesting finding was that the physicians themselves suggested alcoholic treatment for only 8 of the 18 patients. It is no surprise that most patients felt their physician should both recognize and spontaneously discuss their alcoholism even if the patients did not raise the issue. Studying the same issue, Briggs and Huettner (1983) demonstrated that 42% of patients in their sample who had a positive MAST score had not been identified by their physicians as alcoholic.

By 1985 a study by Lieberman and Baker (1985) reported a more optimistic picture, at least in relationship to emergency room identification of alcoholic individuals. These authors compared the diagnoses of 50 emergency room patients with those made during a subsequent inpatient hospitalization for the same patients. They found an acceptable level of reliability for broad diagnostic categories, with the highest agreement for alcoholism. However, the diagnosis of other specific subtypes of psychiatric disorders were not reliably made in the emergency room, including nonalcoholic substance abuse disorders. Other diagnoses that also were less reliable included schizophrenia, other psychotic disorders, and organic brain syndrome. The practice of underdiagnosing substance abuse disorders has continued. Szuster et al. (1990) studied the diagnostic patterns of emergency room psychiatrists making alcohol- and drug-related diagnoses before and after answering a standardized substance use questionnaire. The questionnaire significantly increased the recognition and the number of diagnosed substance use disorders.

There was a concomitant significant decrease in the frequency of psychotic disorder diagnosis as substance abuse was more reliably identified. In fact, psychoactive substance-induced organic mental disorder diagnosis increased by one-half to one-third of the total patient group with the addition of the questionnaire. Although the diagnosis of alcohol abuse alone increased only slightly, the diagnosis of alcohol in combination with other drugs and nonalcoholic substance abuse diagnoses doubled with the use of the standardized questionnaire, significantly increasing the diagnostic yield of substance-induced disorders in this psychiatric emergency room. A review of these studies indicates that the change in the 1980s was for an improvement in the reliable identification and diagnosis of alcoholism in the community in the setting of the emergency room. It appeared that other substance abuse disorders continue to be disproportionately unrecognized in community settings.

## ▼ COMMUNITY TREATMENT PROGRAMS

As reimbursement for hospital substance abuse programs has become more limited, it is remarkable that the program evaluation and research literature has not expanded significantly since 1985. At the same time there continues to be a major emphasis on the need for new addiction treatment alternatives to provide quality care at reduced cost. These treatments include outpatient and social detoxification as well as an addiction day treatment approaches in community and local hospital settings. Different types of outpatient patient community detoxification treatments have been extensively evaluated. The findings demonstrate that in all patient groups, but especially high-risk, lower socioeconomic patients, outpatient and social detoxification for alcoholism can be highly effective and safe. Shore and Kofoed (1984a) summarized several studies that reported no mortality, evaluating hundreds of patients. Only a small proportion of less that 5% in these combined studies required a subsequent hospitalization for medical and withdrawal complications. Bachman et al. (1992) evaluated and demonstrated a successful community treatment program for substance-abusing patients in a model addiction day treatment program. In their study substance-abusing patients were randomly assigned to the day treatment or a traditional inpatient treatment program. The day treatment approach was as effective as the traditional inpatient care for up to 18 months after discharge and was significantly less expensive with a higher level of patient satisfaction.

Certain high-risk groups continue to demonstrate remarkably elevated recidivism rates in spite of intensive community treatment resources. One of the most affected subcultures are American Indians. They have been carefully studied by both Westermeyer and Walker. In a 10-year follow-up of 45 alcoholic American Indians, Westermeyer and Peake (1983) demonstrated that 58% continued to have a significant drinking problem despite repeated inpatient and community treatment approaches and 20% were deceased. In Seattle, Kivlahan et al. (1985) followed 50 alcoholic American Indians into the community after their medical detoxification. They also reported a discouraging recovery rate with high recidivism. Ninety-four percent demonstrated recent alcohol-dependent symptoms or episodic alcohol abuse. These American Indian patients had continued to experience serious alcohol-related problems in spite of repeated treatment attempts in the community and with inpatient rehabilitation settings. Certainly, for many patient groups, a continued high morbidity, mortality, and revolving-door process continues despite well-meaning initiatives and community programming. These outcomes highlight the need for additional research focusing on the issues of continuity of care and an attempt to identify more innovative and effective treatment alternatives.

## ▼ NONTREATMENT FACTORS IN THE COMMUNITY

Important nontreatment factors have a significant implication for the effectiveness of community treatments in addictions. In a review of the literature, Westermeyer (1989) identified 50 articles that evaluated nontreatment factors influencing treatment outcome. Those factors include self-help in social affiliations, community reinforcement approaches, life-change events and residential change, demographic characteristics, coercion, involuntary treatment, compliance, and monitoring. For example, although random assignment to AA has not been

demonstrated to be effective, descriptive studies continue to demonstrate a positive association between AA attendance and improved outcome. *Social reinforcers*, including special training in problem-solving, behavioral family therapy, social counseling, training in finding a job, a "buddy" system, and nondrinking social clubs, correlated positively in all studies in multiple measures of improved status. In focusing on stressful life events and residential change, Maddux and Desmond (1982) demonstrated that abstinence rates were tripled in the year after relocation. Important demographic characteristics included employment, marital status, living with others, subcultures, church or community activities, and social class. Westermeyer also concluded that although nonlegal coercion as a treatment motivator has seldom been studied, legal coercion has been comprehensively assessed in multiple studies, demonstrating some positive outcomes. However, most of the studies involving coercion have failed to include a longer term follow-up or assessment after parole or mandated supervision. A general conclusion is that occupational work is needed to interact positively with the role of coercion. Concerning the monitoring of recovery, most studies are uncontrolled observations on highly selected population samples such as the airline pilots and physicians previously discussed. Lastly, Westermeyer suggests that researchers have tended to view these nontreatment community factors as secondary issues. This approach should be changed, and these factors should be viewed as a critical part of the community treatment perspective.

A review of selected community treatment issues highlights the significance of these multiple variables. The factors include both the global and specific, ranging for sociocultural, to legal, to treatment systems, to so-called nontreatment issues. These variables are usually incompletely evaluated in research and often overlooked in treatment planning. The community-based treatment context should be a central focus in the treatment of substance abuse.

## ▼ REFERENCES

Armor DJ, Polich JM, Stambul HB: Alcoholism and treatment. Santa Monica, CA, Rand Corporation, 1976

Bachman SS, Batten HL, Minkoff K, et al: Predicting

success in a community treatment program for substance abusers. American Journal on Addictions 1:155–167, 1992

Billings AG, Moos RH: The role of coping responses and social resources in attenuating the stress of life events. J Behav Med 4:139–157, 1981

Booth BM, Russell DW, Soucek S, et al: Social support and outcome of alcoholism treatment: an exploratory analysis. Am J Drug Alcohol Abuse 18:87–101, 1992

Briggs TG, Huettner J: The alcoholism task force. Minn Med 66:245–248, 1983

Dull R, Giacopassi D: Dry, damp, and wet: correlates and presumed consequences of local alcohol ordinances. Am J Drug Alcohol Abuse 14:499–514, 1988

Emrick CD: A review of psychologically oriented treatment in alcoholism. J Stud Alcohol 36:88–108, 1975

Frances RJ, Miller SI: Addiction treatment: the widening scope, in Clinical Textbook of Addictive Disorders. Edited by Frances RJ, Miller SI. New York, Guilford, 1991, pp 3–22

Frances RJ, Galanter M, Miller SI: Psychosocial approaches to treatment and rehabilitation, in American Psychiatric Press Review of Psychiatry, Vol 8. Edited by Tasman A, Hales RE, Frances AJ. Washington, DC, American Psychiatric Press, 1989, pp 341–358

Harper CR: Airline pilot alcoholism: one airline's experience. Aviat Space Environ Med 54:590–591, 1983

Jones GH: The recognition of alcoholism by psychiatrists in training. Psychol Med 9:789–791, 1979

Kivlahan DR, Walker RD, Donovan DM, et al: Detoxification recidivism among urban American Indian alcoholics. Am J Psychiatry 142:12:1467–1470, 1985

Lange TJ, Greene E: How judges sentence DUI offenders; an experimental study. Am J Drug Alcohol Abuse 16 (1 and 2):125–133, 1990

Lieberman PB, Baker FM: The reliability of psychiatric diagnosis in the emergency room. Hosp Community Psychiatry 36:291–293, 1985

Maddux JF, Desmond DP: Residence relocation inhibits opioid dependence. Arch Gen Psychiatry 39:1313–1317, 1982

Maghsoodloo S, Brown DB, Greathouse PA: Impact of the revision of DUI legislation in Alabama. Am J Drug Alcohol Abuse 14:97–108, 1988

May P: American Indian Drinking and Prohibition. Boulder, CO, CU Press, 1992

Murphy HBM: Hidden barriers to the diagnosis and treatment of alcoholism and other alcohol misues. J Stud Alcohol 41:417–428, 1980

Ogborne AC, Manuella A, Newton-Taylor B, et al: Long-term trends in male drunkenness arrests in metropolitan Toronto: effects of social-setting detoxication centers. Am J Drug Alcohol Abuse 17:187–197, 1991

Ogborne AC, Kapur BM, Newton-Taylor B: Characteristics of drug users admitted to alcohol detoxication centers. Am J Drug Alcohol Abuse 18: 177–186, 1992

Rund DA, Summers WK, Levin M: Alcohol use and psychiatric illness in emergency patients. JAMA 245:1240–1245, 1981

Schottenfeld RS: Drug and alcohol testing in the workplace—objectives, pitfalls, and guidelines. Am J Drug Alcohol Abuse 15:413–427, 1989

Shore JH: The Oregon experience with impaired physicians on probation: an eight-year follow-up. JAMA 257:2931–2934, 1987

Shore JH: Community-based treatment, in Treatments of Psychiatric Disorders: A Task Force Report of the American Psychiatric Association, Vol 2. Washington, DC, American Psychiatric Association, 1989, pp 1147–1151

Shore JH, Kofoed L: Community intervention in the treatment of alcoholism. Alcohol Clin Exp Res 8:151–159, 1984a

Shore JH, Kofoed L: The treatment of alcoholism in the community, in Psychosocial Treatment of Alcoholism. Edited by Galanter M, Pattison EM. Washington, DC, American Psychiatric Press, 1984b, pp 57–67

Solomon J, Vanga N, Morgan JP: Emergency-room physicians' recognition of alcohol misuse. J Stud Alcohol 41:583–586, 1980

Szuster RR, Schanbacher BL, McCann SC, et al: Underdiagnosis of psychoactive substance-induced organic mental disorders in emergency psychiatry. Am J Drug Alcohol Abuse 16 (3 and 4):319–327, 1990

Westermeyer J: Nontreatment factors affecting treatment outcome in substance abuse. Am J Drug Alcohol Abuse 15:13–29, 1989

Westermeyer J, Peake E: A ten-year follow-up of alcoholic Native Americans in Minnesota. Am J Psychiatry 140:189–194, 1983

# Therapeutic Communities

*George De Leon, Ph.D.*

Therapeutic communities (TCs) have been treating substance-abusing patients for three decades. Originating as an alternative to conventional medical and psychiatric approaches, the TC has established itself as a major psychosocial treatment for thousands of chemically involved patients. This chapter provides a comprehensive overview of the residential TC approach to the treatment of chemical dependency and related problems and is a substantial revision of an earlier version describing TC treatment (De Leon and Rosenthal 1989).

In this revision, the description of the basic TC model and approach is the same, although some theoretical elements are amplified and further clarified. The original sections on applications of the TC model and research are considerably expanded to highlight recent treatment developments and the impressive growth of research in TCs. Discussion of these additions is necessarily limited within the format of a single chapter. However, the extended reference section reflects the scope of the new material and can guide the reader to original sources.

## ▼ HISTORY

Drug-free residential programs for substance abuse appeared a decade later than TCs in psychiatric hospitals pioneered by Jones (1953) and others in the United Kingdom. The name *therapeutic community* evolved in these hospital settings, although the two models arose independently. The TC for substance abuse emerged in the 1960s as a self-help alternative to existing conventional treatments. Recovering alcoholic and drug-addicted individuals were its first participant-developers. Although its modern antecedents can be traced to Alcoholics Anonymous (AA) and Synanon, the TC prototype is ancient, existing in all forms of communal healing and support.

Contemporary TCs have evolved much beyond their origins into sophisticated human services institutions. Today, the term *therapeutic community* is generic, describing a variety of short- and long-term residential programs, as well as day treatment and ambulatory programs, that serve a wide spectrum of drug- and alcohol-abusing patients. Although the TC model has been widely adapted, it is the traditional long-term residential prototype that has documented effectiveness on rehabilitating substance-abusing individuals.

## ▼ THE TRADITIONAL TC

Traditional TCs are similar in planned duration of stay (15–24 months), structure, staffing pattern, perspective, and rehabilitative regime, although they differ in size (30–600 beds) and patient demography. Staff are composed of TC-trained clinicians and other human service professionals. Primary clinical staff are usually former substance-abusing individuals who themselves were rehabilitated in TC programs. Other staff consist of professionals providing, medical, mental health, vocational, educational, family counseling, fiscal, administrative, and legal services.

TCs accommodate a broad spectrum of drug-abusing patients. Although they originally attracted narcotic-addicted individuals, a majority of their patient populations are nonopioid drug-abusing individuals. Thus this modality has responded to the changing trend in drug use patterns, treating patients with drug problems of varying severity, different life-styles, and various social, economic, and ethnic/cultural backgrounds.

The TC views drug abuse as a deviant behavior, reflecting impeded personality development or chronic deficits in social, educational, and economic skills. Its antecedents lie in socioeconomic disadvantage, in poor family effectiveness, and in psychological factors. Thus the principal aim of the TC is a global change in life-style: abstinence from illicit substances, elimination of antisocial activity, development of employability, and prosocial attitudes and values. The rehabilitative approach requires multidimensional influence and training, which for most can only occur in a 24-hour residential setting.

The traditional TC can be distinguished from other major drug treatment modalities in three broad ways. First, the TC coordinates a comprehensive offering of interventions and services in a single treatment setting. Vocational counseling, work therapy, recreation, group and individual therapy, educational, medical, family, legal, and social services all occur within the TC. Second, the primary "therapist" and teacher in the TC is the community itself, consisting of peers and staff who role model successful personal change. Staff members also serve as rational authorities and guides in the recovery process. Thus the community as a whole provides a crucial 24-hour context for continued learning in which individual changes in conduct, attitudes, and emotions are monitored and mutually reinforced in the daily regime. Third, the TC approach to rehabilitation is based on an explicit perspective of the drug abuse disorder, the patient, the recovery process, and healthy living. It is this perspective that shapes its organizational structure, staffing, and treatment process.

## ▼ THE TC PERSPECTIVE

More complete accounts of the TC perspective are given elsewhere (De Leon, in press [b]; De Leon and Rosenthal 1989; De Leon and Ziegenfuss 1986). Although expressed in a social psychological idiom, this perspective evolved directly from the experience of recovering participants in TCs and is organized in terms of four interrelated views, each of which is briefly outlined.[1]

### View of the Disorder

Drug abuse is viewed as a disorder of the whole person, affecting some or all areas of functioning. Cognitive and behavioral problems appear, as do mood disturbances. Thinking may be unrealistic or disorganized; values are confused, nonexistent, or antisocial. Frequently there are deficits in verbal, reading, writing, and marketable skills. Whether couched in existential or psychological terms, moral or even spiritual issues are apparent.

Abuse of any substance is viewed as overdetermined behavior. Physiologic dependency is secondary to the wide range of influences that control the

---

[1] Descriptive accounts of the TC for substance-abusing patients, which are less formal than that presented here, are contained in the literature (e.g., Casriel 1966; Deitch 1972; Yablonsky 1965, 1989), and formal accounts of the TC from a sociological and anthropological perspective are contained in Sugarman 1986 and Frankel 1989.

individual's drug use behavior. Thus the problem is the individual, not the drug. Addiction is a symptom, not the essence of the disorder. In the TC, chemical detoxification is a condition of entry, not a goal of treatment. Rehabilitation focuses on maintaining a drug-free existence.

## View of the Person

TCs distinguish individuals along dimensions of psychological dysfunction and social deficits rather than according to drug-use patterns. Many patients have never acquired conventional life-styles. Vocational and educational problems are marked; middle-class mainstream values are either missing or unpursued. Usually these patients emerge from a socially disadvantaged sector, where drug abuse is more a social response than a psychological disturbance. Their TC experience is better termed *habilitation*, the development of a socially productive, conventional life-style for the first time in their lives.

Among patients from more advantaged backgrounds, drug abuse is more directly expressive of psychological disorder or existential malaise. For these, the word *rehabilitation* is more suitable, emphasizing a return to a life-style previously lived, known, and perhaps rejected.

Notwithstanding these social differences, substance-abusing patients in TCs share important similarities. Either as cause or consequence of their drug abuse, all reveal features of personality disturbance and impeded social function (see the Other Addicted Individual Characteristics section). Thus all patients in the TC follow the same regime. Individual differences are recognized in specific treatment plans that modify the emphasis, not the course, of their experience in the TC.

## View of Recovery

In the TC's view of recovery, the aim of rehabilitation is global, involving both a change in life-style and personal identity. The primary psychological goal is to change the negative patterns of behavior, thinking, and feeling that predispose drug use; the main social goal is to develop the skills, attitudes, and values of a responsible drug-free life-style. Stable recovery, however, depends on a successful integration of these social and psychological goals. For example, healthy behavioral alternatives to drug use

are reinforced by commitment to the values of abstinence; acquiring vocational or educational skills and social productivity is motivated by the values of achievement and self-reliance. Behavioral change is unstable without insight, and insight is insufficient without felt experience. Thus conduct, emotions, skills, attitudes, and values must be integrated to ensure enduring change. The rehabilitative regime is shaped by several broad assumptions about recovery.

### Motivation

Recovery depends on pressures to change, positive and negative. Some patients seek help, driven by stressful external pressures; others are moved by more intrinsic factors. For all, however, remaining in treatment requires continued motivation to change. Thus elements of the rehabilitation approach are designed to sustain motivation or to detect early signs of premature termination. Although the influence of treatment depends on the individual's motivation and readiness, change does not occur in a vacuum. Rehabilitation unfolds as an interaction between the patient and the therapeutic environment.

### Self-help and mutual self-help

Strictly speaking, treatment is not provided but made available to the individual in the TC environment, its staff and peers, the daily regime of work, groups, meetings, seminars, and recreation. However, the effectiveness of these elements depends on the individual, who must constantly and fully engage in the treatment regime. Self-help recovery means that the individual makes the main *contribution* to the change process. Mutual self-help emphasizes the fact that the main messages of recovery, personal growth, and "right living" are mediated by peers through confrontation and sharing in groups; by example as role models; and as supportive, encouraging friends in daily interactions.

### Social learning

A life-style change occurs in a social context. Negative patterns, attitudes, and roles were not acquired in isolation nor can they be altered in isolation. Thus recovery depends not only on what has been learned but how and where learning occurs. This assumption is the basis for the community itself serving as teacher. Learning is active, by doing and participating. A socially responsible role is acquired by acting the role. What is learned is identified with the individuals involved in the learning process, with peer support and staff as credible role models.

New ways of coping with life that are learned in the TC are threatened by isolation and its potential for relapse outside of the TC. Thus a sustained recovery requires a perspective on self, society, and life that must be continually affirmed by a positive social network of others within and beyond residency in the TC.

### Treatment as an episode

Residency in the TC is a relatively brief period in an individual's life, and its influence must compete with the influences of the years before and after treatment. For this reason, unhealthy "outside" influences are minimized until the individual is better prepared to engage these on his or her own. Thus the treatment regimen is designed for high impact. Life in the TC is necessarily intense, its daily regime demanding, and its therapeutic confrontations unmoderated.

### View of Right Living

TCs adhere to certain precepts that constitute a view of healthy, personal, and social living. Although somewhat philosophical in its focus, these precepts concern moral behavior, values, and a social perspective that are intimately related to the TCs view of the individual and of recovery. For example, TCs hold unambiguous "moral" positions regarding social and sexual conduct. Explicit right and wrong behaviors are identified for which there are appropriate rewards and sanctions. These include antisocial behaviors and attitudes; the negative values of the street, jails, or negative peers; and irresponsible or exploitative sexual conduct.

Guilts to self, significant others, and the larger community outside of the TC are central issues in the recovery process. Although they refer to moral matters, guilts are special psychological experiences that if not addressed maintain the individual's disaffiliation from peers and block the self-acceptance that is necessary for authentic personal change.

Values are stressed as essential to social learning and personal growth. These include truth and honesty (in word and deed), work ethic, self-reliance, earned rewards and achievement, personal accountability, responsible concern ("brother's/sister's keeper"), social manners, and community involvement.

On a broader philosophical level, treatment focuses the individual on the personal present (here and now) versus the historical past (then and when). Past behavior and circumstances are explored only to illustrate the current patterns of dysfunctional behavior, negative attitudes, and outlook. Individuals are encouraged and trained to assume personal responsibility for their present reality and destiny.

## ▼ WHO COMES FOR TREATMENT

The majority of entries have histories of are multiple drug use including marijuana, opioids, alcohol, and pills, although in recent years most report cocaine/crack as their primary drug of abuse. However, research has documented that TC admissions reveal a considerable degree of psychosocial dysfunction in addition to their substance abuse.

### Social Profiles

Patients in traditional programs are usually men (70%–75%), but admissions of women are increasing in recent years. Most community-based TCs are integrated across sex, race/ethnicity, and age, although the demographic proportions differ by geographic regions and in certain programs. In general, Hispanics, Native Americans, and patients under 21 years of age represent smaller proportions of admissions to TCs.

About half of all admissions are from broken homes or ineffective families; a large majority have poor work histories and have engaged in criminal activities at some time in their lives. Among adult admissions, less than one-third are employed full-time in the year before treatment, more than two-thirds have been arrested, and 30%–40% have had prior drug treatment histories (e.g., De Leon 1984; Hubbard et al. 1984; Simpson and Sells 1982).

Among adolescents, 70% have dropped out of school, and more than 70% have been arrested at least once or involved with the criminal justice system.

More have histories of family deviance, fewer have had prior treatment for drug use (De Leon and Deitch 1985; Holland and Griffen 1984), but more of the younger adolescents have had treatment for psychological problems (Jainchill and De Leon 1992).

These social profiles of admissions to traditional TC programs are similar regardless of drug preference, and they do not differ significantly from patient profiles in special TC facilities implemented exclusively for certain groups such as adolescents, women, ethnic minorities, and criminal justice referrals.

## Psychological Profiles

Patients differ in demography, socioeconomic background, and drug-use patterns, but psychological profiles obtained with standard instruments appear remarkably uniform, as evident in a number of TC studies (e.g., Biase 1982; Biase et al. 1986; Brook and Whitehead 1980; De Leon 1976, 1980, 1984, 1989; De Leon et al. 1973; Holland 1986; Kennard and Wilson 1979; Zuckerman et al. 1975).

Typically, symptom measures on depression and anxiety are deviantly high, socialization scores are poor, and IQ is in the dull–normal range. On the Tennessee Self-Concept Scales, the self-esteem segment is markedly low and confusion and contradiction concerning self-perception is high, as is the level of the maladjustment segment. The Minnesota Multiphasic Personality Inventory scales are deviant, with prominent peaks reflecting confusion (high F), character disorder (Pd), and disturbed thinking and affect (high Sc). Smaller but still deviant peaks are seen on depression (D) and hypomania (Ma).

The psychological profiles reveal drug abuse as the prominent element in a picture that mirrors features of both psychiatric and criminal populations. For example, the character disorder characteristics and poor self-concept of delinquent and repeated offenders are present, along with the dysphoria and confused thinking of emotionally unstable or psychiatric populations.

These psychological profiles vary little across age, sex, race, primary drug, or admission year and are not significantly different from drug-abusing patients in other treatment modalities. Thus the drug-abusing individuals who come to the TC do not appear to be sick, as do patients in mental hospitals, nor are they simply "hard-core" criminal types, but they do reveal a considerable degree of psychological disability.

## Other addicted individual characteristics

Although the personality inventory studies provide rather uniform findings, they do not necessarily capture the behavioral and attitudinal characteristics that make up the TC's guide for treating substance-abusing patients (see, De Leon 1986, 1989). This view has emerged from experience with the more severe opioid-abusing patients who require long-term residential treatment. Regardless of drug preference or severity, however, these features are shared by most addicted individuals.

The main characteristics center around immaturity and/or antisocial dimensions. They include, for example, low tolerance for all forms of discomfort and delay of gratification; problems with authority; inability to manage feelings (particularly hostility, guilt, and anxiety); poor impulse control (particularly sexual or aggressive); poor judgment and reality testing concerning consequences of actions; unrealistic self-appraisal in terms of a discrepancy between personal resources and aspirations; prominence of lying, manipulation, deception as coping behaviors; personal and social irresponsibility (i.e., inconsistency or failures in completing expected obligations). Additionally, significant numbers have marked deficits in education, marketable, and communication skills.

These clinical characteristics do not necessarily depict an "addictive personality," although many of these features are typical of conduct disorder in the younger substance-abusing individual, which later evolves into adult character disorder. Nevertheless, whether antecedent or consequent to serious drug involvement, these characteristics are commonly observed to be correlated with chemical dependency. More importantly, TCs consider a positive change in these characteristics to be essential for stable recovery.

## Psychiatric Diagnoses

There are a few recently completed diagnostic studies of admissions to the TC using the Diagnostic Interview Schedule. In these, over 70% of the admission sample revealed a lifetime nondrug psychiatric disorder in addition to substance abuse or dependence. A third had a current or continuing history of mental disorder in addition to their drug abuse. The most frequent nondrug diagnoses were phobias, generalized anxiety, psychosexual dysfunction, and antisocial personality. There were only few cases of schizophrenia, but lifetime affective disorders occurred in over one-third of those studied (De Leon 1988a, in press [a]; Jainchill 1989, in press; Jainchill et al. 1986).

That the psychological and psychiatric profiles reveal few psychotic features, and relatively low variability in symptoms or personality characteristics reflects several factors: the TC exclusionary criteria at admissions, the common characteristics among all substance-abusing individuals, and to some degree the self-selection among those who seek admission to residential treatment. Nevertheless, patients do differ; this is evident in their dropout and success rates, which are discussed later. Rather than fixed background or psychopathologic characteristics, patient diversity points to such factors as motivation for personal change, readiness, and suitability for TC treatment.

## Contact and Referral

Patients voluntarily contact TCs through several sources: self-referral, social agencies, treatment providers, and active recruitment by the program. Outreach teams (usually trained graduates of TCs and selected human services staff) recruit patients in hospitals, jails, courtrooms, social agencies, and the street, conducting brief orientations or face-to-face interviews to determine receptivity to the TC.

Approximately 30% of all admissions to TCs are under some form of legal pressure, parole, probation, or another court-mandated disposition (De Leon 1988b; National Institute on Drug Abuse 1980), although surveys of earlier samples of opioid admissions to TCs yield higher percentages of those legally involved. Among adolescents, 40%–50% have been legally referred to treatment compared with 25%–30% of adults; for some programs, legal referrals consist of considerably higher percentages of all admissions (e.g., Pompi and Resnick 1987).

Although the majority of entries to TCs are voluntary, many of these come to treatment under various forms of perceived pressures from family/relationships, employment difficulties, or anticipated legal consequences (De Leon 1988b).

## Admission Interview

A full admission evaluation establishes a disposition for the patient for referral within the TC treatment system, either outpatient or residential, or referral outside the TC system (e.g., psychiatric, hospital, private counseling). The admissions procedure is a structured interview conducted by trained paraprofessionals. Initial interviews last 60 minutes and may be followed with a second interview, often including significant others. Additionally, records of previous legal, medical, psychiatric, and drug treatment histories are evaluated.

## Detoxification

With few exceptions, admissions to residential treatment do not require medically supervised detoxification. Thus traditional TCs do not usually provide this service on the premises. Most primary abusers of opioids, cocaine, alcohol, barbiturates, and amphetamines have undergone self- or medical detoxification before seeking admission to the TC. A small proportion require detoxification during the admission evaluation, and they are offered the option of a detoxification at a nearby hospital. Barbiturate users are routinely referred for medically supervised detoxification, after which they are assessed for admission. A minor percentage of admissions to TCs have been primarily involved with hallucinogens or phencyclidine (PCP). Among those who appear compromised, a referral is made for psychiatric service, after which they can return for residential treatment.

## Criteria for Residential Treatment

Traditional TCs maintain an open-door policy with respect to admission to residential treatment. This understandably results in a wide range of treatment candidates, not all of whom are equally motivated, ready, or suitable for the demands of the residential regime. Relatively few are excluded because the TC policy is to accept individuals who elect residential treatment, regardless of the reasons influencing their choice.

However, there are two major guidelines for excluding patients: suitability and community risk. *Suitability* refers to the degree to which the patient can meet the demands of the TC regime and integrate with others. This includes participation in groups, fulfilling work assignments, and living with minimal privacy in an open community, usually under dormitory conditions. *Risk* refers to the extent to which patients present a management burden to the staff or pose a threat to the security and health of the community of others.

Specific exclusionary criteria most often include histories of arson, suicide, and serious psychiatric disorder. Psychiatric exclusion is usually based on documented history of psychiatric hospitalizations or prima facie evidence of psychotic symptoms on interview (e.g., frank delusions, thought disorder, hallucinations, confused orientation, signs of serious affect disorder). An important differential diagnostic issue concerns drug-related mood or mental states. For example, disorientation, dysphoria, and thought or sensory disorders clearly associated with hallucinogens, PCP, and sometimes cocaine may not exclude an otherwise suitable individual from the TC. Where diagnosis remains in question, most TCs will use a psychiatric consultation after admission. Appropriate referral, however, is based on the patient's suitability or risk rather than on diagnosis alone.

Generally, patients on regular psychotropic regimes will be excluded because use of these usually correlates with chronic or severe psychiatric disorder. Also, the regular administration of medication, particularly in the larger TCs, presents a management and supervisory burden for the relatively few medical personnel in these facilities.

Medication for medical conditions is acceptable in TCs, as are handicapped patients or those who require prosthetics, providing they can meet the participatory demands of the program. A full medical history is obtained during the admission evaluation, which includes questions on current medication regimes (e.g., asthma, diabetes, hypertension), and the necessity for prosthetics. Physical examinations and laboratory workups (blood and urine profiles) are obtained after admission to residency. Although test results occasionally require removal of a patient from residency, such cases are relatively rare. Because of concern about communicable disease in a residential setting, some TCs require tests for conditions such as hepatitis prior to entering the facility or at least within the first weeks of admission.

Policy and practices concerning testing for HIV status and management of AIDS and AIDS-related complex (ARC) have recently been implemented by most TCs. These emphasize voluntary testing with counseling, special education seminars on health management and sexual practices, and special support groups for residents who are HIV-positive or have a clinical diagnosis of AIDS or ARC. Further clarification is needed with respect to the recent influx of patients with medication-resistant tuberculosis.

## The Residential Patient

Although there is no typical profile of the residential patient, the need for long-term treatment in TCs is based on several indicators. These can be briefly summarized across five main areas: health and social risk status, abstinence potential, social and interpersonal function, antisocial involvement, and suitability for the TC.

### Health and social risk status

*Health and social risk status* refers to the extent of chronic-acute stress concerning physical, psychological, and social problems associated with drug use. Some indicators are out-of-control behavior with respect to drug use, criminality, or sexuality; suicidal potential threat through overdose; threat of injury or death through other drug-related means; degree of anxiety or fear concerning violence, jail, illness, or death; and extent of personal losses (e.g., financial, relationships, employment).

Most patients who seek treatment in the TC experience acute stress. They may be in family or legal crisis or at significant risk to harm themselves or others such that a period of residential stay is indicated. However, the patients suitable for long-term treatment reveal a more chronic pattern of stress that induces treatment seeking and when relieved, usually results in premature dropout. They require longer term residential treatment because they are a constant risk threat and they must move beyond relief seeking to initiate a genuine recovery process.

### Abstinence potential

*Abstinence potential* is a specific component of risk and refers to the individual's ability to maintain complete abstinence in a nonresidential treatment setting. Some indicators are previous treatment experiences (i.e., number, type, and outcomes), previous self-initiated attempts at abstinence (i.e., frequency and longest duration), and current active drug use versus current abstinence.

In the TC's view of substance abuse as a disorder of the whole individual, abstinence is a prerequisite for recovery. Among chronic users, the risk of repeated relapse can subvert any treatment effort regardless of the modality. Thus the residential TC is needed to interrupt out-of-control drug use and to stabilize an extended period of abstinence in order to facilitate a long-term recovery process.

### Social and interpersonal function

*Social and interpersonal function* refers to the current capability to function in a responsible way. Some indicators are involvement in the drug life-style (e.g., friends, places, activities) and impaired ability to maintain employment or school responsibility or to maintain social relations and responsibilities (e.g., parental spouse, filial, friendships).

Inadequate social and interpersonal function not only results from drug use but often reveals a more general picture of immaturity or an impeded developmental history. Therefore, a setting such as the TC is needed that focuses on the broad socialization and/or habilitation of the individual.

### Antisocial involvement

*Antisocial involvement* refers to the extent to which the individual's drug use is embedded in an antisocial life-style. Some indicators are active and past criminal history in terms of type and frequency of illegal activities; frequency and duration of incarceration; existing legal pressures for treatment; and assessment of the long-term pattern of antisocial behavior, including juvenile contact with the criminal justice system and early school problems.

In the TC view, the term *antisocial* also suggests characteristics that are highly correlated with drug use. These include behaviors such as exploitation, abuse and violence, attitudes of mainstream disaffiliation, and the rejection or absence of prosocial values. Modification of these characteristics requires the intensive resocialization approach of the TC setting.

### Suitability for the TC

A number of those seeking admission to the TC may not be ready for treatment in general or suitable for the demands of a long-term residential regime. Assessment of these factors at admission provides a basis for treatment planning in the TC or sometimes appropriate referral. Some indicators of motivation, readiness, and suitability for TC treatment are acceptance of the severity of drug problem; acceptance for the need for treatment ("can't do it alone"); willingness to sever ties with family, friends, and current life-style while in treatment; and willingness to surrender a private life, meeting the expectations of a structured community. Although motivation, readiness, and suitability are not criteria for admission to the TC, the importance of these factors often emerges after entry to treatment and if not identified and addressed are related to early dropout (De Leon and Jainchill 1986; Schoket 1992).

## ▼ THE TC APPROACH

The TC uses the diverse elements and activities of community to foster rehabilitative change. These can be outlined in terms of the TC structure or social organization and its process in terms of the individual's passage through stages of change within the context of community life.

### TC Structure

The TC structure is composed of relatively few staff and stratified levels of resident peers—junior, intermediate, and senior—who constitute the community or family in the residence. This peer-to-community structure strengthens the individual's identification with a perceived, ordered network of others. More importantly, it arranges relationships of mutual responsibility to others at various levels in the program.

The daily operation of the community itself is the task of the residents, working together under staff supervision. The broad range of resident job assignments illustrates the extent of the self-help process. These include conducting all house services (e.g., cooking, cleaning, kitchen service, minor repair), serving as apprentices, running all departments, and conducting house meetings, certain seminars, and peer-encounter groups.

The TC is managed by staff who monitor and evaluate patient status, supervise resident groups, assign and supervise resident job functions, and oversee house operations. Clinically, the staff conduct therapeutic groups (other than peer encounters), provide individual counseling, organize social and recreational projects, and confer with significant others. They decide matters of resident status, discipline, promotion, transfers, discharges, furloughs, and treatment planning.

The new patient enters a setting of upward mobility. The resident job functions are arranged in a hierarchy, according to seniority, clinical progress, and productivity. Job assignments begin with the most menial tasks (e.g., mopping the floor) and lead vertically to levels of coordination and management. Indeed, patients come in as patients and can leave as staff. This social organization of the TC reflects the fundamental aspects of its rehabilitative approach: *work as education and therapy, mutual self-help, peers as role models*, and *staff as rational authorities*.

## Work as education and therapy

In the TC, work mediates essential educational and therapeutic effects. Work and job changes have clinical relevance for substance-abusing patients in TCs, most of whom have not successfully negotiated the social and occupational world of the larger society. Vertical job movements carry the obvious rewards of status and privilege. However, lateral job changes are more frequent, providing exposure to all aspects of the community. Typically, residents experience many lateral job changes that enable them to learn new skills and to negotiate the system. This increased involvement also heightens their sense of belonging and strengthens their commitment to the community.

Job changes in the TC are singularly effective therapeutic tools, providing both measures of and incentives for behavioral and attitudinal changes. In the vertical structure of the TC, ascendancy marks how well the patient has assimilated what the community teaches and expects; hence the job promotion is an explicit measure of the resident's improvement and growth.

Conversely, lateral or downward job movements also create situations that require demonstrations of personal growth. A resident may be removed from one job to a lateral position in another department or dropped back to a lower status position for clinical reasons. These movements are designed to teach new ways of coping with reversals and change that appear to be unfair or arbitrary.

## Mutual self-help

The essential dynamic in the TC is mutual self-help. The day-to-day activities of a TC are conducted by the residents themselves. In their jobs, groups, meetings, recreation, and personal and social time, it is residents who continually transmit to each other the main messages and expectations of the community.

## Peers as role models

Peers as role models and staff as role models and rational authorities are the primary mediators of the recovery process. Indeed, the strength of the community as a context for social learning relates to the number and quality of its role models. All members of the community are expected to be role models— roommates; older and younger residents; and junior, senior, and directorial staff. TCs require these multiple role models to maintain the integrity of the community and ensure the spread of social learning effects. Members who demonstrate the expected behaviors and reflect the values and teachings of the community are viewed as role models. This is illustrated in two main attributes:

1. *Resident role models "act as if."* They behave as the individual they should be, rather than as the individual they have been. Despite resistances, perceptions, or feelings to the contrary, they engage in the expected behaviors and consistently maintain the attitudes and values of the community. These include self-motivation, commitment to work and striving, positive regard for staff as authority, and an optimistic outlook toward the future—in the TC's view, acting as if it is not just an exercise in conformity but an essential mechanism for more complete psychological change. Feelings, insights, and altered self-perceptions often follow rather than precede behavior change.

2. *Role models display responsible concern.* This concept is closely akin to the notion of "I am my brother's/sister's keeper." Showing *responsible concern* involves willingness to confront others whose behavior is not in keeping with the rules of the TC, the spirit of the community, or the knowledge that is consistent with growth and rehabilitation. Role models are obligated to be aware of the appearance, attitude, moods, and performances of their peers, and confront negative signs in these. In particular, role models are aware of their own behavior in the overall community and the process prescribed for personal growth.

**Therapeutic Communities**

## Staff as rational authorities

Staff foster the self-help learning process through their managerial and clinical functions described above and in their psychological relationship with the residents as role models, parental surrogates, and rational authorities. TC patients often have had difficulties with authorities who have not been trusted or who have been perceived as guides and teachers. Thus they need a successful experience with an authority figure who is viewed as credible (recovered), supportive, corrective, and protective in order to gain authority over themselves (personal autonomy). Implicit in their role as rational authorities, staff provide the *reasons* for their decisions and explain the *meaning* of consequences. They exercise their powers to teach and guide, facilitate and correct, rather than to punish, control, or exploit.

## The TC Process: Basic Program Elements

The recovery process may be defined as the interaction between treatment interventions and patient change. Unlike other treatment approaches, however, the TC treatment intervention is the *community milieu*, which consists of the daily regime of structured and unstructured activities and social intercourse occurring in formal and informal settings.

The typical day in a TC begins at 7 A.M. and ends at 11 P.M. It includes a variety of meetings, job functions (work therapy), encounter and other therapeutic groups, individual counseling, and recreation. The interplay of these activities contribute to patient change and may be grouped into three main elements: *therapeutic-educative, community enhancement,* and *community and clinical management.*

### Therapeutic-educative element

Therapeutic-educative activities consist of various group processes and individual counseling. They provide settings for expressing feelings, divert negative acting-out, permit ventilation of feeling, and resolve personal and social issues. They increase communication and interpersonal skills, examine and confront behavior and attitudes, and offer instruction in alternate modes of behavior.

There are four main forms of group activity in the TC: encounters, probes, marathons, and tutorials.

These differ somewhat in format, objectives, and method, but all attempt to foster trust, personal disclosure, intimacy, and peer solidarity to facilitate therapeutic change. The focus of the *encounter* is behavioral. Its approach in confrontation, and its objective is to modify negative behavior and attitudes directly. *Probes* and *marathons* have as their primary objective significant emotional change and psychological insight. *Tutorials* stress the learning of concepts and specific skills.

*Encounters* are the cornerstone of group process in the TC. The term *encounter* is generic, describing a variety of forms that use confrontational procedures as their main approach. The basic encounter is a peer-led group composed of 12–20 residents; it meets at least three times weekly, usually for 2 hours in the evening, and is followed by an additional 30 minutes for snacks and socializing. Although often intense and profoundly therapeutic, the basic objective of each encounter is modest and limited: to heighten individual awareness of specific attitudes or behavioral patterns that should be modified.

*Probes* are staff-led group sessions composed of 10–15 residents, conducted to obtain in-depth clinical information on patients early in their residency (2–6 months). They are scheduled when needed and usually last from 4–8 hours. Their main objectives are to increase staff understanding of the individual's background for the purposes of treatment planning and to increase openness, trust, and mutual identification. Unlike the encounter, which stresses confrontation, the probe emphasizes the use of support, understanding, and the empathy of the other group members. Probes go much beyond the here-and-now behavioral incident, which is the material of the encounter, to past events and experiences.

*Marathons* are extended group sessions, the objective of which is to initiate resolution of life experiences that have impeded the individual's development. During their 18 months of residence, every patient participates in several marathons. These groups are conducted by all staff, assisted by senior residents with marathon experience ("shepherds"). Marathons are usually composed of large groups of selected residents and meet for 18–36 hours. Considerable experience, both personal and professional, is required to ensure safe and effective marathons.

The general approach of the marathon is to dissipate defensiveness and resistance to painful but meaningful experiences. The intimacy, safety, and bonding in the setting facilitate emotional processing ("working through") of a significant life event and encourage the individual to continue to address the importance of certain life-altering issues of the past. These issues are identified in counseling, probes, or other groups and may include catastrophic events of violence, sexual abuse, abandonment, illness, deaths of significant others, and so on. A wide variety of techniques are employed, including elements from psychodrama, primal therapy, and pure theater, to produce its impact.

*Tutorials* are primarily directed toward training or teaching, as opposed to correcting behavior or facilitating of emotional catharsis and psychological insight. Tutorial groups, usually staff led, consist of 10–20 residents, are scheduled as needed, and address certain themes for purposes of teaching including personal growth, recovery, and right-living concepts (e.g., self-reliance, maturity, relationships); job skill training (e.g., managing the department or the reception desk); and clinical skill training (e.g., use of encounter tools).

*Ad hoc groups* supplement the four main groups, and they convene as needed. These vary in focus, format, and composition. For example, sex, ethnic, or age-specific theme groups may use encounter or tutorial formats. Dormitory, room, or departmental encounters may address issues of daily community living. Additionally, sensitivity training, psychodrama, and conventional gestalt and emotionality groups are employed to varying extents.

*One-to-one counseling* balances the needs of the individual with those of the community. Peer exchange is ongoing and is the most consistent form of informal counseling in TCs. Staff counseling sessions are both formal and informal and are usually conducted as needed. The staff counseling method in the TC is not conventional, as is evident in its main features: transpersonal sharing, direct support, minimal interpretation, didactic instructions, and concerned confrontation.

## Community enhancement element

Community enhancement activities, which facilitate assimilation into the community, include the four main facility-wide meetings (the morning meeting, seminars, and the house meeting are held each day), and the general meeting is called when needed.

*Morning meetings* convene all residents of the facility and the staff on the premises after breakfast, usually for 30 minutes, to initiate the day's activities with a positive attitude, motivate residents, and strengthen unity. Teams of residents conduct the morning meeting as a planned program of recitation of the philosophy, songs, readings, and skits. This meeting is particularly relevant because most residents of TCs have never adapted to the routine of an ordinary day.

*Seminars* convene every afternoon, usually for 1 hour. The seminar collects all the residents together at least once during the working day. Thus staff observation of the entire facility is regularized because the seminar in the afternoon complements the daily morning meeting and the house meeting in the evening. A clinical aim of the seminar, however, is to balance the individual's emotional and cognitive experience. Most seminars are led by residents, although sometimes led by staff and outside speakers. Of the various meetings and group processes in the TC, the seminar is unique in its emphasis on listening, speaking, and conceptual behavior.

*House meetings* convene nightly, after dinner, usually for 1 hour, and are coordinated by a senior resident. The main aim of these meetings is to transact community business, although they also have a clinical objective. In this forum, social pressure is judiciously employed to facilitate individual change through public acknowledgment of positive or negative behaviors among certain individuals or subgroups.

*General meetings* convene only when needed, usually to address negative behavior, attitudes, or incidents in the facility. All residents and staff (including those not on duty) are assembled at any time and for indefinite duration. These meetings, conducted by multiple staff, are designed to identify problem individuals or conditions or to reaffirm motivation and reinforce positive behavior and attitudes in the community. A variety of techniques may be employed in the general meeting (e.g., special sessions to relieve guilt, staff lecturing and testimony, dispensing sanctions for individuals or groups).

## Community and clinical management element

Community and clinical management activities maintain the physical and psychological safety of the environment and ensure that resident life is orderly and productive. They protect the community as a whole and strengthen it as a context for social learning. The main activities are privileges, disciplinary sanctions, surveillance, and urine testing.

**Privileges.** In the TC, privileges are explicit rewards that reinforce the value of achievement. Privileges are accorded by overall clinical progress in the program. Displays of inappropriate behavior or negative attitude can result in loss of privileges, which can be regained by demonstrated improvement.

The type of privilege is related to the degree of personal autonomy achieved at different stages of treatment. These may range from phone and letter writing earlier in treatment to overnight furloughs later in treatment. Successful movement through each stage earns privileges that grant wider personal latitude and increased self-responsibility.

Privileges acquire importance because they are earned through investment of time, energy, self-modification, risk of failure, and disappointment. Thus the earning process establishes the value of privileges and gives them potency as social reinforcements. Although the privileges offered in the TC are quite ordinary, it is their social and psychological relevance to the patient that enhances their importance.

Because privilege is equivalent to status in the vertical social system of the TC, loss of even small privileges is a status setback that is particularly painful for individuals who have struggled to raise their low self-esteem. Moreover, because substance-abusing patients often cannot distinguish between privilege and entitlement, the privilege system in the TC teaches that productive participation or membership in a family or community is based on an earning process.

Finally, privileges provide explicit feedback in the learning process. They are tangible rewards that are contingent on individual change. This concrete feature of privilege is particularly suitable for those with histories of performance failure or incompletion.

**Discipline and sanctions.** TCs have their own specific rules and regulations that guide the behavior of residents and management of facilities. The explicit purpose of these is to ensure the safety and health of the community; however, their implicit aim is to train and teach residents through the use of discipline.

In the TC, social and physical safety are prerequisites for psychological trust. Therefore, sanctions are invoked against any behavior that threatens the safety of the therapeutic environment. For example, breaking one of the TC's cardinal rules—such as no violence or threat of violence—can bring immediate expulsion. Even a minor deviance such as the unapproved borrowing of a book is a threat that must be addressed.

The choice of specific disciplinary action, or "contract," depends on the severity of the infraction, time in the program, and history of infractions. For example, verbal reprimands, loss of privileges, or speaking bans may be selected for less severe infractions. Job demotions or loss of residential time may be invoked for more serious infractions. Expulsion may be appropriate for behavior that is incorrigible or dangerous to others.

Although often perceived as punitive, the basic purpose of contracts is to provide a learning experience by compelling residents to attend to their own conduct, to reflect on their own motivation, to feel some consequence of their behavior, and to consider alternate forms of acting under similar situations.

Contracts also have important community functions. The entire facility is made aware of all disciplinary actions. Thus contracts deter violations. They provide vicarious learning experiences for others. As symbols of safety and integrity, they strengthen community cohesiveness.

**Surveillance: the house run.** The TC's most comprehensive method for assessing the overall physical and psychological status of the residential community is the *house run*. Several times a day, staff and senior residents walk through the entire facility from top to bottom, examining its overall condition. This single procedure has clinical implications as well as management goals. House runs provide global "snapshot" impressions of the facility: its cleanliness, planned routines, safety procedures, morale, and psychological tone. They illuminate the psychological and social functioning of individual residents and peer collections. House runs provide observable, physical indicators of self-management skills, attitudes toward self and the program, mood and emotional status, and the resident (and staff) general level of awareness of self and the physical and social environment.

The actions taken for departures from house regulations or expectations vary with the infraction but are consistent with the TC's management and clinical goals. Actions include, for example, deferring the issue to later encounter groups or house meetings; instruction and reprimands on the spot; and bans (restrictions) on roommates, floor mates, or individual residents. Expulsion may be invoked for serious violations of safety, health, and cardinal rules.

**Urine testing.** Most TCs use unannounced random urine testing or incident-related urine-testing procedures. Residents who deny the use of drugs or refuse urine testing on request are rejecting a fundamental expectation in the TC, which is to trust staff and peers enough to disclose undesirable behavior. The voluntary admission of drug use initiates a learning experience, which includes exploration of conditions precipitating the infraction. Denial of actual drug use, either before or after urine testing, can block the learning process and may lead to termination or dropout.

Random urine procedures in the TC usually consist of weekly sampling of urines on an unannounced basis, either routinely or based on suspicions of a "dirty house." The more usual procedure is urine testing on incident or observation. Thus staff's suspicion of drug use in the facility or, more likely, of a patient's return from furlough could result in a urine test.

When positive urines are detected, the action taken depends on the drug used, time and status in the program, previous history of drug and other infractions, and locus and condition of use. Actions may involve expulsion, loss of time, radical job demotions, or loss of privileges for specific periods. Review of the "triggers" or reasons for drug use is also an essential part of the action taken.

## The Change Process

Rehabilitation and recovery in the TC unfold as a developmental process occurring in a social learning setting. Values, conduct, emotions, and cognitive understanding (insight) must be integrated toward the goals of a new life-style and a positive personal-social identity. Achievement of the goals of the process reflects the individual's relationship to the community and acceptance of its teachings. This relationship can be characterized as *compliance, conformity,* and *commitment.*

*Compliance* refers to adherence to norms and expectations of the community primarily to *avoid* negative consequences in the program, such as disciplinary sanctions, or undesirable alternatives, such as discharge to the street or return to jail or home situation. *Conformity* refers to adherence to the expectations and norms primarily to *maintain* affiliation with the community, personal relationships, or simply the acceptance of peers and staff. *Commitment* refers to adherence to a *personal resolve* to remain in the change process that reflects an internalization of the therapeutic and educational teachings in TC.

Although the behavior profile of the individual may appear similar in compliance, conformity, and commitment, the factors *influencing* the profile differ significantly. If commitment or internalization is not attained, recovery is incomplete and the potential is greater for premature dropout, relapse, or recidivism after leaving treatment.

## Program Stages and Profiles

The developmental process itself can be understood as a passage through stages of incremental learning. The learning that occurs at each stage facilitates change at the next, and each change reflects movement toward the goals of recovery. There are three major program stages that characterize change in long-term residential TCs: orientation-induction, primary treatment, and reentry, although additional substages or phases are included. The typical profiles of each stage are briefly outlined.

*Stage 1: orientation-induction*
*(0–60 days)*

The main objectives of this initial phase of residency are further assessment and orientation to the TC. The admission evaluation does not always yield a complete picture of the patient, which is evident in the high early dropout rates. Thus clinical assessment of the patient continues during the first 2 months of residency to clarify specific treatment needs and overall suitability for the long-term residential TC.

The objective of orientation in the initial phase of residency is to assimilate the individual into the community through full participation and involvement in all of its activities. Rapid assimilation is crucial at this point when patients are most ambivalent about the long tenure of residency. Thus the new resident is immediately involved in the daily regime, which emphasizes role induction into the community.

Formal seminars and informal peer instruction focus on reducing anxiety and uncertainty through information and instruction concerning cardinal rules (i.e., no use of drugs, no violence, or threat of physical violence); house regulations (e.g., no leaving the facility, stealing, borrowing or lending; maintaining manners) or expected conduct (such as speaking, dressing, punctuality, attendance); program essentials (e.g., structure organization, job functions, the privilege system, its process stages, its philosophy and perspective); and TC tools (e.g., encounter and other groups). The overall intensity of treatment in this stage in terms of program demands and confrontations is moderate in order to avoid elevating individual fear. Group process is designed to facilitate involvement and acceptance of the regime and to train patients in using the group itself.

Successful passage through the initial stage is reflected mainly in retention. The fact that patients remain for 30–60 days indicates that they have adhered to the rules of the program enough to meet the orientation objectives of this stage and have passed the period of highest vulnerability to early dropout. At the end of this period the new residents are expected to know the structure and to work at maintaining compliance.

### Stage 2: primary treatment (2–12 months)

Primary treatment consists of three phases that roughly correlate with time in the program (2–4, 5–8, and 9–12 months). These phases are marked by plateaus of stable behavior that signal the need for further change. The daily therapeutic-educational regimen of meetings, groups, job functions, peer and staff counseling remains the same throughout the year of primary treatment. However, progress is reflected at the end of each phase in terms of three interrelated dimensions of change: community member development/maturity, and overall psychological adjustment.

**Four-month resident.** Four-month residents have junior status in the TC, limited freedom, and lower-level jobs. These residents display a general knowledge of the TC approach. They may not completely accept the perspective and regime, but they act as if they understand, and they comply with the program, participating fully in daily activities. They follow directions, engage in basic expected behaviors (e.g., getting up in the morning, making the bed, keeping the area clean, attending all meetings). They adhere to the cardinal and house rules and accept disciplinary contracts.

Developmentally, 4-month residents accept the seriousness of their drug use and show awareness of their other life problems and personal growth issues. They reveal some separation from their previous lifestyle (e.g., the language and attitudes of the drug culture or street code). Psychologically, 4-month residents reveal measurable decreases in the dysphoria that are usually present at admission. Their participation in groups increases, although communication and group skills are not fully acquired. They display limited personal disclosure in groups and in one-on-one sessions.

**Eight-month resident.** Eight-month residents "set an example." Their elevated status in the social structure is evident in their privileges and job functions. They have earned greater personal freedom, including the right to leave the facility without escort when going to prescribed places for brief periods and for specific reasons. They have ascended the job hierarchy and can hold special positions that pay a modest stipend (e.g., $5–$10 weekly). Their involvement in the community is evident in attitudes that reflect their acceptance of the values of right living (e.g., honesty and responsibility, importance of role models).

In terms of development, personal growth in 8-month residents is shown in their adaptability to job changes, acceptance of staff as rational authorities, and ability to contain their negative thoughts and emotions. For the 8-month resident, the precept to "act as if" has become a personal mode of learning, not merely a tactic of compliance or conformity. This picture reveals some degree of internalization of the TC's perspective on recovery and the early signs of a personal commitment to remain in the change process.

Psychologically, these residents reveal elevated self-esteem based on the status and progress through the previous 8 months. This is most evident in the positive assertions about next steps. Self-awareness is manifest in identification of their characteristic images. More importantly, although they may not indicate special understanding or insight into the origins or "dynamics" of their problems, they accept full responsibility for their behavior, problems, and solutions. For 8-month residents, personal disclosure is less restrained. When confronted, these residents quickly drop defenses and reveal honest emotional expression. They have acquired group skills and are expected to assist facilitators in the encounter group process.

**Twelve-month resident.** Twelve-month residents are established role models in the program. Privileges reflect the increasing degree of personal autonomy. They enjoy more privacy and can obtain regular furloughs. Although they cannot hold jobs outside the facility, their positions within the residence indicate that they effectively run the house. As senior coordinators, for example, they are responsible for arranging resident movement, trips, and seminars, under staff supervision. Similarly, their stipend status is also elevated; they are eligible to be staff-in-training in executive management offices, special ancillary services, or as junior counselors. They are expected to assist staff in monitoring the facility overnight and on weekends. Those beginning vocational-educational programs are experiencing the pressures and challenges of academic or training demands. They accept responsibility for themselves and for other members in the community.

Developmentally, the maturity of the 12-month residents is most evident in their emotional self-management and increased autonomy. Job performance is consistent, and self-assessment is realistic as is goal setting. Their social interactions with staff are more spontaneous and relaxed, and they socialize with a network of positive peers during recreation and furlough. Their movement past conformity is evident in their ability to adapt to new situations and teach others TC teachings.

Twelve-month residents display some insight into their drug problems and personalities. These residents also display paradoxical signs of positive change. Although confident and eager to move forward, there is a certain degree of anxiety and insecurity that emerges associated with their uncertainty about the future. Their openness about anticipated problems in the future is considered a positive psychological sign. After a year, residents are fully trained participants in the group process and often serve as facilitators. A high level of personal disclosure is evident in groups, in peer exchange, and in their increased use of staff counseling.

## Stage 3: reentry (13–24 months)

Reentry is the stage at which the patient must strengthen skills for autonomous decision making and the capacity for self-management, with less reliance on rational authorities or a well-formed peer network. There are two phases of the reentry process: early reentry and later reentry.

**Early reentry phase (13–18 months).** The main objective of the early reentry phase, during which patients continue to live in the facility, is to prepare for healthy separation from the community. Emphasis on rational authority decreases under the assumption that the patient has acquired a sufficient degree of self-management. This is reflected in more individual decision making about privileges, social plans, and life design. The group process involves fewer leaders at this stage, fewer encounters, and more shared decision making. Particular emphasis is placed on life-skills seminars, which provide didactic training for life outside the community. Attendance is mandated for sessions on budgeting, job seeking, use of alcohol, sexuality, parenting, use of leisure time, and so on.

During this phase individual plans are a collective task of the patient, a key staff member, and peers. These plans are comprehensive blueprints for long-term psychological, educational, and vocational efforts, which include goal attainment schedules, methods of improving interpersonal and family relationships, and social and sexual behavior. Patients may be attending school or holding full-time jobs, either within or outside of the TC. Still, they are expected to participate in house activities when possible and to carry some community responsibilities (e.g., facility coverage at night).

**Later reentry phase (18–24 months).** The objective of this phase is to complete a successful separation from residency. Patients are on "live-out" status, involved in full-time jobs or education, and maintaining their own households, usually with live-out peers. They may attend such aftercare services as AA or Narcotics Anonymous (NA) or take part in family or individual therapy. This phase is viewed as the end of residency but not of program participation. Contact with the program is frequent at first and only gradually reduced to weekly phone calls and monthly visits with a primary counselor.

## Graduation

Completion marks the end of active program involvement. Graduation itself, however, is an annual event conducted in the facility for completers at usually a year beyond their residency. Thus the TC experience is preparation rather than a cure. Residence in the program facilitates a process of change that must continue throughout life, and what is learned in treatment are the tools to guide the individual on a steady path of continued change. Completion, or graduation, therefore, is not an end but a beginning.

## Aftercare

Although aftercare is not a stage of the residential treatment process, it does underscore the continuing, perhaps lifelong process of recovery. Until recently, long-term TCs have not formally acknowledged aftercare as a definable period following program involvement. Nevertheless, TCs have always appreciated the patients' efforts to maintain sobriety and a positive life-style beyond graduation. In most TCs, key clinical and life adjustment issues of aftercare are addressed during the reentry stages of the 2-year program. As discussed in the later section on modifications, however, many contemporary TCs now offer explicit aftercare components within their systems or through linkages with outside agencies.

## ▼ RESEARCH: EFFECTIVENESS AND RETENTION

### Success Rates

A substantial evaluation literature documents the effectiveness of the TC approach in rehabilitating drug-abusing individuals (e.g., De Leon 1984, 1985; Hubbard and Condelli, in press; Hubbard et al. 1984; Institute on Medicine 1990; Simpson 1990; Simpson and Sells 1982; Tims et al., in press; Tims and Ludford 1984). The findings on short- and long-term posttreatment follow-up status from single program and multiprogram studies are summarized briefly.

Significant improvements occur on separate outcome variables (i.e., drug use, criminality, and employment) and on composite indices for measuring individual success. Maximum to moderately favorable outcomes (which are based on opioid, nonopioid, and alcohol use; arrest rates; retreatment; and employment) occur for more than half of the sample of completed patients and dropouts (De Leon 1984; Hubbard et al. 1989; Simpson and Sells 1982).

There is a consistent positive relationship between time spent in residential treatment and posttreatment outcome status. For example, in long-term TCs success rates (on composite indices of no drug use and no criminality) at 2 years posttreatment approximate 90%, 50%, and 25%, respectively for graduates/completers, dropouts who remain more than 1 year, and dropouts who remain less than 1 year in residential treatment; improvement rates over pretreatment status approximate 100%, 70%, and 40%, respectively (De Leon et al. 1982).

In a few studies that investigated psychological outcomes, results uniformly showed significant improvement at follow-up (e.g., Biase et al. 1986; De Leon 1984; Holland 1983). A direct relationship has been demonstrated between posttreatment behavioral success and psychological adjustment (De Leon 1984; De Leon and Jainchill 1981–1982).

The outcome studies reported were completed on an earlier generation of chemical-abusing individuals, primarily opioid-addicted individuals. Since the early 1980s, however, most admissions to residential TCs have been multiple-drug–abusing individuals, primarily involving, cocaine, crack, and alcohol, with relatively few primary heroin users (e.g., De Leon 1988a, TCA Therapeutic Community Research Facts 1988). New studies are needed to evaluate the effectiveness of the TC for this recent generation of abusers. In this regard, two large-scale evaluation efforts funded by the National Institute on Drug Abuse are under way: the Drug Abuse Treatment Outcome Study (DATOS) and the multisite program of research carried out in a recently established Center for Therapeutic Community Research (CTCR; 1991).

### Retention

Dropout is the rule for all drug treatment modalities. For TCs, retention is of particular importance because research has established a firm relationship between time spent in treatment and successful outcome. However, most admissions to TC programs leave residency, many before treatment influences are presumed to be effectively rendered.

Research on retention in TCs has been increasing in recent years. Reviews of the TC retention research are contained in the literature (e.g., De Leon 1985, 1991a; Lewis and Ross, in press). Studies focus on several questions, retention rates, patient predictors of dropout, and attempts to enhance retention in treatment. The key findings from these are briefly summarized:

### Retention rates

Dropout is highest (30%–40%) in the first 30 days of admission but declines sharply thereafter (De Leon and Schwartz 1984). This temporal pattern of dropout is uniform across TC programs (and other modalities). In long-term residential TCs, completion rates range from 10%–25% of all admissions. One-year retention rates range from 20%–35%, although more recent trends suggest gradual increases in annual retention compared with the period before 1980 (De Leon 1989).

### Predictors of dropout

There are no reliable patient characteristics that predict retention, with the exception of severe criminality and/or severe psychopathology, which are correlated with earlier dropout. Recent studies point to the importance of dynamic factors in predicting retention in treatment, such as perceived legal pressure, motivation, and readiness for treatment (e.g., Condelli and De Leon 1993; Condelli and Dunteman 1993; De Leon 1988a; De Leon and Jainchill 1986; Hubbard et al. 1988; Schoket 1992; Siddiqui 1989).

Only a few studies have assessed self-reported reasons for leaving treatment prematurely. Findings from these studies suggest the importance of patient perception factors as reasons for early dropout. These mainly reflect low readiness for treatment in general or perceived unsuitability for the TC life in particular (e.g., De Leon 1988a).

### Enhancing retention in TCs

Some experimental attempts to enhance retention in TCs have used supportive individual counseling, improved orientation to treatment by experienced staff ("senior professors"), and family alliance strategies to reduce early dropout (e.g., De Leon 1988a, 1991a). Other efforts provide special facilities and programming for mothers and children (N. Arbiter, personal communication, 1989; Coletti 1989) and curriculum-based relapse prevention methods (Lewis and Ross, in press) to sustain retention throughout residential treatment. Although results are promising, these efforts require replication in multiple sites.

Although a legitimate concern, retention should not be confused with treatment effectiveness. TCs are effective for those who remain long enough for treatment influences to occur. Obviously, however, a critical issue for TCs is maximizing holding power to benefit more patients.

## ▼ THE EVOLUTION OF THE TC: MODIFICATIONS AND APPLICATIONS

The traditional TC model described in this chapter is actually the prototype of a variety of TC-oriented programs. Today, the TC modality consists of a wide range of programs serving a diversity of patients who use a variety of drugs and present complex social-psychological problems in addition to their chemical abuse. Patient differences as well as clinical requirements and funding realities have encouraged the development of modified residential TCs with shorter planned durations of stay (3, 6, and 12 months) as well as TC-oriented day treatment and outpatient ambulatory models. Correctional, medical and mental hospital, and community residence and shelter settings, overwhelmed with alcohol and illicit drug abuse problems, have implemented TC programs within their institutional boundaries. The following sections highlight some of the key modifications and applications of the TC treatment approach for different patient populations in different settings.

### Current Modifications of the TC Model

Most community-based traditional TCs have expanded their social services or have incorporated new interventions to address the needs of its diverse admissions. In some cases, these additions enhance but do not alter the basic TC regime; in others they significantly modify the TC model itself.

### Family services approaches

The participation of families or significant others has been a notable development in TCs for both adolescents and adults. Some TCs offer programs in individual and multiple family therapy as components of their adolescent programs, nonresidential, and (more recently) short-term residential modalities. However, most traditional TCs do not provide a regular family therapy service because the patient in residence rather than the family unit is viewed as the primary target of treatment.

Experience has shown that beneficial effects can occur with forms of significant-other participation other than family therapy (e.g., De Leon 1988a). Seminars, support groups, open houses, and other special events focus on how significant others can affect the patient's stay in treatment; they teach the TC perspective on recovery and provide a setting for sharing common concerns and strategies for coping with the patient's future reentry into the larger community. Thus family psychoeducational and participation activities enhance the TC's rehabilitative process for the residential patient by establishing an alliance between the significant others and the program.

### Primary health care and medical services

Although funding for health care services remains insufficient for TCs, these agencies have expanded services for the growing number of residential patients with sexually transmitted and immune compromising conditions, including HIV seropositivity, AIDS, syphilis, hepatitis B, and recently for tuberculosis. Screening, treatment, and increased health education have been sophisticated, both on site and through linkages with community primary health care agencies.

### Aftercare services

Currently, most long-term TCs have linkages with other service providers and 12-step groups for their graduates. However, the TCs with shorter-term residential components have instituted well-defined aftercare programs both within their systems and through linkages with other non-TC agencies. There are limits and issues concerning these aftercare efforts concerning discontinuities between the perspectives of the TC and other service agencies. These are outlined along with a fuller discussion of aftercare in TCs in other writings (De Leon 1990–1991).

### Relapse prevention training

Based on its approach to recovery, traditional TCs have always focused on the key issues of relapse prevention. The 24-hour TC communal life fosters a process of learning how to resist drug taking and negative behavior. In its social learning setting the individual engages many of the social, emotional, and circumstantial cues for and influences on drug use that exist in the larger macrosociety. This broad context of social learning essentially provides continual relapse prevention training (RPT; De Leon 1990–1991).

Currently, however, a number of TCs include special workshops on RPT, using the curriculum, expert trainers, and formats developed outside of the TC area (e.g., Marlatt 1985). These workshops are offered as formal additions to the existing TC protocol, usually in the reentry stage of treatment. However, some programs incorporate RPT workshops in earlier treatment stages, and in a few others RPT is central to the primary treatment protocol (e.g., Lewis and Ross, in press). Clinical impressions supported by preliminary data of the efficacy of RPT within the TC setting are favorable, although rigorous evaluation studies are still in progress (Lewis and Ross, in press).

### Twelve-step components

Historically, TC graduates were not easily integrated into AA meetings for a variety of reasons (see De Leon 1990–1991). In recent years, however, there has been a gradual integration of AA/NA/CA (Cocaine Anonymous) meetings during and following TC treatment given the wide diversity of users socially and demographically and the prominence of alcohol use regardless of the primary drug. The common genealogical roots found in TCs and the 12-step groups are evident to most participants of these, and the similarities in the self-help view of recovery far outweigh the differences in specific orientation. Today, 12-step groups may be introduced at any stage in residential treatment but are considered mandatory in the reentry stages of treatment and in the aftercare or continuance stages of recovery after leaving the residential setting.

## Mental health services

Among those seeking admission to TCs, increasing numbers reveal documented psychiatric histories (e.g., De Leon 1989; Jainchill 1989; Jainchill et al. 1986). Certain subgroups of these patients are treated within the traditional TC model and regime, which requires some modification in services and staffing. For example, psychopharmacologic adjuncts and individual psychotherapy are used for selected patients at appropriate stages in treatment. Nevertheless, the traditional community-based TC models still cannot accommodate the substance-abusing patients with serious psychiatric disorders. As described in a following section on mentally ill chemical-abusing individuals, these primary psychiatric substance-abusing individuals require specially adapted forms of the TC model.

## Multimodal TC and patient-treatment matching

Traditional TCs are highly effective for a certain segment of the drug-abuse population. However, those who seek assistance in TC settings represent a broad spectrum of patients, many of whom may not be suitable for a long-term residential stay. Improved diagnostic capability and assessment of individual differences have clarified the need for options other than long-term residential treatment.

Many TC agencies are multimodality treatment centers, which offer services in their residential and nonresidential programs depending on the clinical status and situational needs of the individual. The modalities include short- (less than 90 days), medium- (6–12 month), and long-term (1–2 years) residential components; drug-free outpatient services (6–12 months). Some TCs operate drug-free day treatment and methadone maintenance programs. Assessments attempts to match the patient to the appropriate modality within the agency. For example, the spread of drug abuse in the work place, particularly in cocaine use, has prompted the TC to develop short-term residential and ambulatory models for the employed, more socialized patients.

To date, the effectiveness of TC-oriented multimodality programs has not been systematically evaluated, although several relevant studies are currently under way. Of particular interest is the comparative effectiveness and cost benefits of long- and short-term residential treatment. Thus far, however, there is no convincing evidence supporting the effectiveness of short-term treatment in any modality, residential or ambulatory.

Given what is known about the complexity of the recovery process in addiction and the importance of length of stay in treatment, there is little likelihood that shorter-term treatment components alone will be sufficient to yield stable positive outcomes. In the multimodality TCs, for example, combinations of residential and outpatient services are needed to provide a long-term treatment involvement and impact.

## Current Applications with Special Populations

A significant sign of the evolution of the TC is its application to special populations and special settings. It is beyond the purview of this chapter to detail the modifications of these adapted TC models. In the main examples of these models, the mutual self-help focus is retained along with basic elements of the community approach, meetings, groups, work structure, and perspective on recovery and right living.

## TCs for adolescents

The prominence of youth drug abuse and the unique needs of the adolescent has led to adaptations of the traditional TC approach that appear more appropriate for these patients. These include age-segregated facilities, with considerable emphasis on management and supervision, educational needs, family involvement, and individual counseling. Fuller accounts of the treatment of adolescents in TCs and effectiveness are contained in other writings (e.g., De Leon 1986; De Leon and Deitch 1985; Jainchill 1989).

## Addicted mothers and their children

Several TCs have adapted the model for the chemically dependent mothers with their children. The profile of the addicted mother in residence is generally not different from other abusers, although it reflects more social disadvantage, poor socialization, and a predominance of crack/cocaine abuse. Most evident is that these women need a life-style change and an opportunity for personal maturation. Thus within the context of the basic TC regime, additional services and modifications are provided that address their specific needs and those of their recovery. These include family unit housing for mothers and children, medical and psychological care, parental training, and child care. Further accounts of clinical issues in TC programs for women in general and addicted mothers in particular are contained in other writings (e.g., N. Arbiter, personal communication, 1989; Coletti 1989; De Leon and Jainchill 1992; Stevens et al. 1989).

### TCs for incarcerated substance-abusing individuals

In recent years TC models have been adapted for incarcerated substance-abusing individuals in prison settings. This development has been fostered by overcrowded prisons, the influx of drug offenders, and the documented success of an early TC prison model in reducing recidivism to crime and relapse drug use (Wexler and Williams 1986). Modifications of the TC model are shaped by the unique features of the correctional institution (i.e., its focus on security, its goal of early release, its limited physical and social space, and the prison culture itself). Nevertheless, a peer-managed community for social learning is established for the inmates who volunteer for the program. A prominent feature of the modified prison model is the mutual involvement of correctional officers, prison administrators, and mental health and TC treatment paraprofessionals. For inmates who leave these prison TCs, models for continuance of recovery have recently been established outside the walls in TC-oriented halfway houses.

### TCs for mentally ill chemical-abusing individuals

Special TC-adapted models have been developed to exclusively treat the more seriously disturbed mentally ill chemical-abusing individuals (e.g., MICA [mentally ill chemical abuser] patients). Several of these have been developed by community-based TC agencies as special programs in separate facilities; others have been implemented as innovative research demonstration projects in the mental hospital (e.g., Galanter et al. 1991) and in community residence settings for the homeless, mentally ill chemical-abusing patient (e.g., Sacks et al. 1992).

In these models for the dually disordered, the basic peer orientation and elements of the daily regime are retained, although there is more focus on individual differences evident in a greater flexibility in planned duration of stay, structure, and phase format. Specific modifications include the standard psychotropic medication regime, moderated intensity of groups, a less demanding work structure, significant use of individual psychotherapy, case management, and skills training.

The effectiveness of the TC for special populations has not yet been sufficiently evaluated. Currently, however, multisite studies are under way of adolescents in various adaptations of the community-based TC (De Leon and Jainchill 1992; Hubbard 1989; Jainchill and De Leon 1992); inmates in prison TCs (Wexler and Williams 1986); mentally ill chemical-abusing individuals (Sacks et al. 1992); addicted mothers and their children (Coletti 1989; Stevens et al. 1989); and, although not described, methadone patients in a day-treatment TC (De Leon et al. 1993).

## The TC in Human Services

The modifications of the traditional model and its adaptation for special populations and settings are redefining the TC modality within mainstream human and mental health services. Most contemporary TC programs adhere to the perspective and approach described earlier. However, the basic peer/social learning framework has been amplified to include additional social, psychological, and health services. Staffing compositions have altered to reflect a mix of traditional professionals—correctional, mental health, medical and educational, family and child care specialists; social workers; and case managers—to serve along with the with the experientially trained TC professionals.

These changes in patients, services, and staffing have also surfaced complex issues particularly concerning staff divergence and integration. Some relate to the TC's drug-free philosophy and self-help perspective, others to differences in vernacular, academic education, experience with addiction, and roles and functions within the unique context of a peer-community model.

The issues of integration have been addressed through vigorous training and orientation efforts guided by a common perspective of recovery (Carroll and Sobel 1986; Deitch and Solit, in press; De Leon 1985; Galanter 1992; Galanter et al. 1991). Indeed, the cross-fertilization of personnel and methods from the traditional TC and mental health and human services portends the evolution of a new TC: a general treatment model applicable to a broad range of populations for whom affiliation with a self-help community is the foundation for effecting the process of individual change.

## ▼ REFERENCES

Biase DV: Daytop Miniversity: Advancement in Drug-Free Therapeutic Community Treatment (Evaluation Report No 1-H81-DA-01911-01A1). Rockville, MD, National Institute on Drug Abuse, 1982

Biase DV, Sullivan AP, Wheeler B: Daytop miniversity—phase 2—college training in a therapeutic community: development of self concept among drug free addict/abusers, in Therapeutic Communities for Addictions: Readings in Theory, Research, and Practice. Edited by De Leon G, Ziegenfuss JT. Springfield, IL, Charles C Thomas, 1986

Brook RC, Whitehead IC: Drug-Free Therapeutic Community. New York, Human Sciences Press, 1980

Carroll JFX, Sobel BS: Integrating mental health personnel and practices into a therapeutic community, in Therapeutic Communities for Addictions: Readings in Theory, Research, and Practice. Edited by De Leon G, Ziegenfuss JT. Springfield, IL, Charles C Thomas, 1986, pp 209–226

Casriel D: So Fair a House: The Story of Synanon. New York, Prentice Hall, 1966

Center for Therapeutic Community Research: Findings from NIDA Grant No P50 DA07700-01, awarded to National Development and Research Institutes, New York, NY, 1991

Coletti SD: Eliminating Barriers: Residential Treatment of Addicted Mothers With Their Infants. Findings from NIDA Grant No R18 DA06369-01, awarded to PAR, Inc., St. Petersburg, FL, 1989

Condelli WS, De Leon G: Fixed and dynamic predictors of retention in therapeutic communities for substance abusers. J Subst Abuse Treat 10:11–16, 1993

Condelli WS, Dunteman GH: Issues to consider when

predicting retention in therapeutic communities. J Psychoactive Drugs 25:239–244, 1993

Deitch DA: Treatment of Drug Abuse in the Therapeutic Community: Historical Influences, Current Considerations, and Future Outlooks, Vol 4. Washington, DC, Report of the National Commission on Marihuana and Drug Abuse, 1972, pp 158–175

Deitch DA, Solit R: Training drug abuse workers in a therapeutic community. Psychotherapy: Theory, Research and Practice (in press)

De Leon G: Psychological and Socio-Demographic Profiles, Final Report of Phoenix House Project Activities (NIDA Grant No DA00831-01). Rockville, MD, National Institute on Drug Abuse, 1976

De Leon G: Therapeutic Communities: Training Self-Evaluation, Final Report of Project Activities (NIDA Grant No 1-H81 DA01976). Rockville, MD, National Institute on Drug Abuse, 1980

De Leon G: The Therapeutic Community: Study of Effectiveness (NIDA Treatment Res Monogr Ser ADM-84-1286). Rockville, MD, National Institute on Drug Abuse, 1984

De Leon G: Adolescent Substance Abusers in the Therapeutic Community: Treatment Outcomes. Proceedings of the Ninth World Conference on Therapeutic Communities, Montreal, Canada, 1985

De Leon G: The therapeutic community for substance abuse: perspective and approach, in Therapeutic Communities for Addictions: Readings in Theory, Research, and Practice. Edited by De Leon G, Ziegenfuss JT. Springfield, IL, Charles C Thomas, 1986, pp 5–18

De Leon G: The Therapeutic Community: Enhancing Retention in Treatment. Final Report on National Institute on Drug Abuse Project No R01 DA03860, 1988a

De Leon G: Legal pressure in therapeutic communities, in Compulsory Treatment of Drug Abuse: Research and Clinical Practice (NIDA Res Monogr No 86). Edited by Leukefeld CG, Tims FM. Rockville, MD, National Institute on Drug Abuse, 1988b, pp 160–177

De Leon G: Psychopathology and substance abuse: what we are learning from research in therapeutic communities. J Psychoactive Drugs 21:177–188, 1989

De Leon G: Aftercare in therapeutic communities. Int J Addict 25 (9A–10A):1225–1237, 1990–1991

De Leon G: Retention in drug free therapeutic communities, in Improving Drug Treatment (NIDA Res Monogr No 106). Edited by Pickens RW, Leukefeld CG, Schuster CR. Rockville, MD, National Institute on Drug Abuse, 1991a, pp 218–244

De Leon G: Cocaine abusers in therapeutic community treatment, in Advances in Cocaine Treatment. Edited by Tims FM. Rockville, MD, National Institute on Drug Abuse Monograph (in press [a])

De Leon G: Therapeutic communities: diversity and theory, in Therapeutic Community Research. Edited by Tims FM, De Leon G, Jainchill N. Rockville, MD, National Institute on Drug Abuse Monograph (in press [b])

De Leon G, Deitch D: Treatment of the adolescent substance abuser in a therapeutic community, in Treatment Services for Adolescent Substance Abusers, NIDA Research Monograph (DHHS Publ No ADM-85-1342). Edited by Friedman A, Beschner G. Rockville, MD, National Institute on Drug Abuse, 1985, pp 216–230

De Leon G, Jainchill N: Male and female drug abusers: social and psychological status 2 years after treatment in a therapeutic community. Am J Drug Alcohol Abuse 8:465–497, 1981–1982

De Leon G, Jainchill N: Circumstances, motivation, readiness, and suitability (CMRS) as correlates of treatment tenure. J Psychoactive Drugs 8:203–208, 1986

De Leon G, Jainchill N: Adolesent Drug Abusers in Therapeutic Communities: Evaluation of Effectiveness, Final Report of Project Activities (NIDA Grant No R01 DA05192). Rockville, MD, National Institute on Drug Abuse, 1992

De Leon G, Rosenthal MS: Treatment in residential therapeutic communities, in Treatments of Psychiatric Disorders: A Task Force Report of the American Psychiatric Association, Vol 2. Washington, DC, American Psychiatric Association, 1989, pp 1379–1397

De Leon G, Schwartz S: The therapeutic community: what are the retention rates? Am J Drug Alcohol Abuse 10:267–284, 1984

De Leon G, Ziegenfuss JT (eds): Therapeutic Communities for Addictions: Readings in Theory, Research, and Practice, Springfield, IL, Charles C Thomas, 1986

De Leon G, Skodol A, Rosenthal MS: Phoenix House: changes in psychopathological signs of resident drug addicts. Arch Gen Psychiatry 23:131–135, 1973

De Leon G, Jainchill N, Wexler H: Success and improvement rates 5 years after treatment in a therapeutic community. Int J Addict 17:703–747, 1982

De Leon G, Sacks S, Hilton R: Passages: a modified therapeutic community day treatment model for methadone clients, in Innovative Approaches to the Treatment of Drug Abuse, Vol 1: Program Models and Strategies. Edited by Inciardi JA, Tims FM, Fletcher B. New York, Greenwood Press, 1993, pp 126–148

Frankel B: Transforming Identities, Context, Power, and Ideology in a Therapeutic Community. New York, Peter Lang, 1989

Galanter M: Addressing the Cocaine Crisis: A Model for Ambulatory Treatment in the General Hospital. Status report for the New York State Division of Substance Abuse Services, IFIP Contract C-0002121 with Bellevue Hospital Center, New York, 1992

Galanter M, Egelko S, De Leon G, et al: Crack/cocaine abusers in the general hospital: assessment and initiation of care. Am J Psychiatry 149:810–815, 1991

Holland S: Evaluating community based treatment programs: a model for strengthening inferences about effectiveness. International Journal of Therapeutic Communities 4:285–306, 1983

Holland S: Measuring process in drug abuse treatment research, in Therapeutic Communities for Addictions: Readings in Theory, Research, and Practice. Edited by De Leon G, Ziegenfuss JT. Springfield, IL, Charles C Thomas, 1986, pp 169–181

Holland S, Griffen A: Adolescent and adult drug treatment clients: patterns and consequences of use. J Psychoactive Drugs 16:79–90, 1984

Hubbard RL: Drug Abuse Treatment Outcome Study (DATOS), Contract No 271-89-8233 (9/29/89–9/30/94), awarded by the National Institute on Drug Abuse to the Research Triangle Institute, Research Triangle Park, NC, 1989

Hubbard RL, Condelli W: Client outcomes from therapeutic communities, in Therapeutic Community Research, National Institute on Drug Abuse Monograph. Edited by Tims FM, De Leon G. Rockville, MD, National Institute on Drug Abuse (in press)

Hubbard RL, Rachal JV, Craddock SG, et al: Treatment outcome prospective study (TOPS): client characteristics and behaviors before during, and after treatment, in Drug Abuse Treatment Evaluation: Strategies, Progress and Prospects (NIDA Res Monogr No 51), RAUS, Special Issue on Research Analysis and Utilization System. Edited by Tims FM, Ludford JP. Rockville, MD, National Institute on Drug Abuse, 1984, pp 42–68

Hubbard RL, Collins JJ, Rachael JV, et al: The criminal justice client in drug abuse treatment, in Compulsory Treatment of Drug Abuse: Research and Clinical Practice (NIDA Res Monogr No 86, DHHS Publ ADM-88-1578). Edited by Leukefeld CG, Tims FM. Rockville, MD, National Institute on Drug Abuse, 1988, pp 57–80

Institute on Medicine: Treating Drug Problems: A Study of the Evolution, Effectiveness, and Financing of Public and Privated Drug Treatment Systems: Report by the Institute of Medicine Committee for the Substance Abuse Coverage Study, Division of Health Care Services. Washington, DC, National Academy Press, 1990

Jainchill N: The relationship between psychiatric disorder, retention in treatment, and client progress among admissions to a residential drug-free modality. Unpublished doctoral dissertation, New York University, New York, 1989

Jainchill N: Co-morbidity and therapeutic community treatment, in Therapeutic Community Research, National Institute on Drug Abuse Monograph. Tims FM, De Leon G, Jainchill N. Rockville, MD, National Institute on Drug Abuse (in press)

Jainchill N, De Leon G: Therapeutic community research: recent studies of psychopathology and retention, in Drug Abuse Treatment Research: German and American Perspectives. Edited by Buhringer G, Platt JJ. Malabar, FL, Krieger Publishing, 1992, pp 367–388

Jainchill N, De Leon G, Pinkham L: Psychiatric diagnosis among substance abusers in therapeutic community treatment. J Psychoactive Drugs 18:209–312, 1986

Jones M: Therapeutic Community: A New Treatment Method in Psychiatry. New York, Basic Books, 1953

Kennard D, Wilson S: The modification of personality disturbance in a therapeutic community for drug abusers. Br J Med Psychol 52:215–221, 1979

Lewis BF, Ross R: Retention in therapeutic communities: challenges for the 90s, in Therapeutic Community Research, National Institute on Drug Abuse Monograph Series. Edited by Tims FM, De Leon G, Jainchill N. Rockville, MD, National Institute on Drug Abuse (in press)

Marlatt GA: Relapse prevention: theoretical rationale and overview of the model, in Relapse Prevention. Edited by Marlatt GA, Gordon JR. New York, Guilford, 1985

National Institute on Drug Abuse: CODAP (Client Oriented Data Acquisition Process): 1979 Annual Data, NIDA Statistical Series E, No 17 (DHEW Publ ADM-81-1-25). Rockville, MD, National Institute on Drug Abuse, 1980, p 395

Pompi KF, Resnick J: Retention in a therapeutic community for court referred adolescents and young adults. Am J Drug Alcohol Abuse 13:309–325, 1987

Sacks S, Sacks J, Bernhardt A: Halsey House: A Modified Therapeutic Community for Homeless MICA Clients. Presentation to CTCR Colloquium, New York, June 1992

Schoket D: Circumstances, motivation, readiness and suitability for treatment in relation to retention in a residential therapeutic community: secondary analysis. Unpublished doctoral dissertation, New York University, New York, 1992

Siddiqui Q: The relative effects of extrinsic and intrinsic pressure on retention in treatment. Unpublished doctoral dissertation, City University of New York, New York, 1989

Simpson DD: 12-year follow-up: outcomes of opioid addicts treated in therapeutic communities, in Therapeutic Communities for Addictions: Readings in Theory, Research, and Practice. Edited by De Leon G, Ziegenfuss JT. Springfield, IL, Charles C Thomas, 1990, pp 109–120

Simpson DD, Sells SB: Effectiveness of treatment for drug abuse: an overview of the DARP research program. Advances in Alcohol and Substance Abuse 2:7–29, 1982

Stevens S, Arbiter N, Glider P: Women residents: expanding their role to increase treatment effectiveness in substance abuse programs. Int J Addict 24:425–434, 1989

Sugarman B: Structure, variations, and context: a sociological view of the therapeutic community, in Therapeutic Communities for Addictions: Readings in Theory, Research, and Practice. Edited by De Leon G, Ziegenfuss JT. Springfield, IL, Charles C Thomas, 1986, pp 65–82

TCA Therapeutic Community Research Facts: What We Know. TCA News, Spring, 1988, pp 2–3

Tims FM, De Leon G, Jainchill N: Therapeutic Community Research, National Institute on Drug Abuse Research Monograph Series. Rockville, MD,

National Institute on Drug Abuse (in press)

Tims FM, Ludford JP (eds): Drug Abuse Treatment Evaluation: Strategies, Progress, and Prospects (NIDA Res Monogr No 51), RAUS, Special Issue on Research Analysis and Utilization System. Rockville, MD, National Institute on Drug Abuse, 1984

Wexler H, Williams R: The Stay'n Out therapeutic community: prison treatment for substance abusers. J Psychoactive Drugs 18:221–230, 1986

Yablonsky L: Synanon: The Tunnel Back. New York, Macmillan, 1965

Yablonsky L: The Therapeutic Community. New York, Gardner Press, 1989

Zuckerman M, Sola S, Masterson J, et al: MMPI patterns in drug abusers before and after treatment in therapeutic communities. J Consult Clin Psychol 43:286–296, 1975

# CHAPTER 29

# Adolescent Substance Abuse

*Yifrah Kaminer, M.D.*

Childhood and adolescence are not only critical phases for normal development but are also periods when various behaviors are first recognized. For example, psychoactive substance use was detected among latency age children (Johnston et al. 1987), and the median age of substance abuse and dependence has dropped to 19 years (Christie et al. 1988). Child and adolescent substance use (CASU)[1] and child and adolescent psychoactive substance use disorders (CAPSUD)[2] in the United States are widespread and were reported to be the highest in the industrialized world (Johnston et al. 1987).

It is generally recognized that in preadulthood, treatment cannot be discussed without first addressing prevention because prevention is expected to be the most effective means of deterring CASU. Only after prevention efforts fail should a treatment program for CAPSUD be considered (Schinke et al. 1991). Although primary and secondary prevention appear to be an appealing solution for CASU, there have been few methodologically sound studies that

may be able to support such an assumption. Moreover, systematic successful prevention programs have been scarcely available, and in most reports they have been neither clearly defined nor tailored to the needs of the target heterogeneous populations or individuals (Kaminer and Bukstein 1989). Also in contrast to the relatively large body of literature on adult substance abuse treatment, there has been a paucity of empirical studies evaluating the efficacy of CAPSUD treatment outcome (Kaminer 1991a).

The objectives of this chapter are to describe the present status of prevention and treatment of CASU and CAPSUD, respectively. A biopsychosocial orientation is used to demonstrate the special needs of this population.

At the outset, it is imperative to assess the magnitude of CASU and CAPSUD from an epidemiological perspective in the general adolescent population. This information is needed to quantify the demand for prevention and treatment services. The meaning of nosological changes and their clinical implications on CASU and CAPSUD are then discussed. In the

The author gratefully acknowledges the editorial assistance of Ms. Eileen McMurrer and Ms. Melissa Tatum.

[1] *CASU* refers to a nonpathological use (i.e., use that does not meet DSM-III-R criteria for psychoactive substance use disorders [PSUD]).

[2] *CAPSUD* refers to a pathological use (according to DSM-III-R criteria for PSUD).

next section, the nature of age appropriate drug experimentation in the context of developmental process versus pathological use is illuminated, with an additional emphasis on the clinical differences between CAPSUD and adult psychoactive substance use disorders (PSUD). This is followed by present and future implications for prevention approaches. A large section is devoted to a generic description of present treatment modalities and facilities and to treatment outcome studies. Then a model for referral, assessment, treatment, and aftercare process is described. This model takes into consideration the interaction between individual characteristics, environmental factors, and treatment variables. The needs of special populations, especially dually diagnosed adolescents and pregnant adolescent women and their offspring, are addressed, and ethnic and sexual minorities are noted. Finally, future suggestions to improve prevention and treatment outcome are outlined.

# ▼ EPIDEMIOLOGY

The measurement of CASU and CAPSUD is complicated by the fact that the desired information pertains to an illegal behavior and that populations of interest may not volunteer to cooperate. A pivotal source in the United States is the Annual National High School Survey, which has been conducted by Johnston and colleagues since 1975 (Johnston et al. 1992). In 1991, 15,500 seniors were surveyed in 136 high schools.

The survey includes neither the 15%–20% of dropouts nor absentees on the day of survey at each school. However, the stability of the survey provides a good measurement of trends in that seniors who are frequently truant are similar in many respects to dropouts.

It has been reported that in 1991 the general downward trend in the prevalence of drug use that had started in the early 1980s has continued (Johnston et al. 1992). Excluding cigarettes, this information is pertinent to the three most commonly used drugs: alcohol, marijuana, and cocaine and other stimulants (crystal methamphetamine not included). Johnston et al. (1992) suggest that an increase in peer disapproval and perceived risk and not a reduction in supply, as reflected by a high rate of perceived availability of these drugs, are responsible for the downturn in drug use. However, a considerable segment of

high school seniors still use these illicit drugs.

Most of the other illicit drug use rates are down by less than statistical significance or have remained fairly stable at a quite low level of use. These include stimulants, anabolic steroids, inhalants, crystal methamphetamine, phencyclidine (PCP), heroin, barbiturates, sedatives, methaqualone, and tranquilizers.

Lysergic acid diethylamide (LSD) is a growing source of concern due to the increase in its use since the mid-1980s. Another major reason for concern is the arrest in the mild downward trend in cigarette smoking. The survey reports that the decline in 30-day and daily prevalence in the last 10 years amounts only to 10% and 1.8%, respectively. Despite this encouraging report that in general adolescents continue to move away from drug use, these findings may represent a decline mainly in nonpathological use only (CASU).

What are the clinical implications of the results of the Johnston et al. (1992) epidemiological study, and how could experimental and recreational use of drugs by adolescents be differentiated from abuse and dependence according to the present DSM-IV nosology (American Psychiatric Association 1994)?

The data provided regarding trends in lifetime and annual prevalence use of drugs by high school seniors (Johnston et al. 1992) have no clear clinical significance. The majority of individuals, while beginning cigarettes, alcohol, and marijuana use in preadolescence and adolescence, merely experiment occasionally with other substances and most often mature out of use of illicit substances, except for very occasional social use (Tubman et al. 1991). The noted figures serve at best as a periodic "snapshot" of the target population. The survey (Johnston et al. 1992) does not indicate how many of the seniors are polydrug users. A number of studies among adolescents have shown associations between substance use and adjustment problems, most notably depression and psychological distress (Aneshensel and Huba 1983; Kashani et al. 1985; Tanaka and Huba 1989). Also, it was indicated that individuals consistently using the highest amounts of multiple substances exhibited the lowest levels of psychological adjustment (Tubman et al. 1991). Psychological adjustment measured in late childhood appears to be related to substance use, including the number of substances used and the level of use (Newcomb and Bentler 1988).

The data regarding trends in 30-day prevalence of drug use and most importantly the trends in 30-day prevalence of daily use may represent the adolescent population segment that is most likely to develop or has already developed CAPSUD according to DSM-IV criteria.

## ▼ NOSOLOGY

It is necessary to clarify the nosological implications of the natural history of CASU, the changing phenomenology, and the differences in patterns of CASU and CAPSUD among children and adolescents versus adults with PSUD.

The ideal diagnostic label indicates the cause of a disorder, the most likely prognosis, and the best available treatment (Schuckit et al. 1985). However, in the DSM-III-R the same diagnostic criteria were used for the diagnosis of substance abuse and dependence for adolescents and adults. Substance abuse was a residual category in the DSM-III-R. It was considered a less maladaptive disorder than substance dependence, and criterion B for abuse required that "some symptoms of the disturbance have persisted for at least one month, or have occurred repeatedly over a longer period of time" (American Psychiatric Association 1987, p. 169).

This category of substance abuse appeared to be suitable for a majority of adolescents identified with a pathological pattern of substance use. The DSM-III-R dependence category was more appropriate for the diagnosis of adolescents than DSM-III criteria (American Psychiatric Association 1980). Substance dependence was based on the presence of three or more criteria out of nine. None of the classic, restrictive symptoms of tolerance, withdrawal, or withdrawal avoidance was necessary for diagnosis. Adolescents infrequently manifest these three traditional symptoms.

The implications in differentiating treatment of either psychoactive substance abuse or dependence have recently gained a cardinal importance due to empirical evidence provided by Hasin et al. (1990). They concluded that a majority of individuals diagnosed as abusers had never progressed to dependence. These findings advocated for the change in the status of abuse from a residual category to a distinct and specific set of behaviors in DSM-IV (American Psychiatric Association 1994). Such a move should service substance-abusing adolescents better by playing up the importance of this category.

## ▼ CASU VERSUS CAPSUD

Adolescence has long been recognized as a developmental phase when the individual is expected to test and modify cognitive and social skills (Erikson 1968). As Newcomb and Bentler (1988) concluded, "One defining feature of adolescence is a quest for or establishment of independence and autonomous identity and functioning. This may involve experimentation with a wide range of behaviors, attitudes, and activities before choosing a direction and way of life to call one's own. This process of testing attitudes and behavior may include drug use. In fact, experimental use of various drugs, both licit and illicit, may be considered a normative behavior among teenagers in terms of prevalence, and form a developmental task perspective" (p. 214). Any drug use by a child can be considered abuse unless it is a "guided experimentation," which is quite prevalent (e.g., taking a sip of parent's alcoholic drink; Newcomb and Bentler 1989).

Shedler and Block (1990) reported in a longterm longitudinal study of children through their 18th birthday that those who had experimented with drugs were psychologically healthier than either abstainers or frequent users. An inverted *U* shape characterized the relation between drug use and psychological adjustment in the study. The above-noted researchers (Newcomb and Bentler 1988; Shedler and Block 1990) indicated that the efforts aimed at eliminating adolescent experimentation are likely to be costly and only partially successful. Moreover, the education campaign trivializes the factors underlying drug abuse and pathologizes normative experimentation and limit testing. Avoidance of experimentation with drugs among the abstainers was related to relative alienation from peers, lack of social skills, and relatively high anxiety level and not a result of a successful drug education or better "moral fiber" (Shedler and Block 1990).

In summary, although it is important to delay the onset of regular drug use as long as possible in order to allow time for the development of adaptive skills, it may be less important to prevent drug use than drug abuse (Newcomb and Bentler 1989). In addition, the adolescent who occasionally uses alcohol or marijuana does not need to be treated. He or she is part of a large section of society that in most cases will not qualify for the abuse category and will probably "grow out" of the habit or will become a social drinker as an adult.

## ▼ PSUD IN ADOLESCENTS VERSUS ADULTS

Adolescents with PSUD differ from adults with PSUD by factors that have significant implications for treatment. The adolescent is usually characterized by a shorter history of PSUD. Tolerance, craving, and withdrawal symptoms are less common and, in most cases, less severe. The need for detoxification is relatively rare, and long-term physical effects are usually not yet manifested. Therefore, descriptions of hitting "rock bottom" ("once a junky, always a junky") and a simplistic cause-effect disease model without additional developmental stage-oriented interventions do not apply well to adolescents and may be ineffective (Kaminer and Frances 1991).

Many adolescents, especially those at early and middle adolescence, have yet to achieve the stage of formal operational thinking (Piaget 1962). Incomplete attainment of this cognitive capacity leads to major difficulties in understanding and internalizing abstract values and concepts that are so predominant in the addiction field (e.g., denial, higher power, responsibility). Many frustrated addiction specialists who do not specialize in mental health struggle with substance-abusing adolescents without acknowledging that the adolescent is not resisting treatment but simply cannot understand it. Add to this the fact that many substance-abusing adolescents have concomitant learning disabilities, hyperactivity, attention problems, and other psychopathology, and the magnitude of the problem increases even more (Kaminer 1991a).

More than any other age group, adolescents rely on role modeling, imitation, and peer pressure as part of the process of achieving independence and identity. This concept also applies to the initiation, maintenance, and stoppage of CASU and CAPSUD. The adolescent culture is based on action, immediate gratification, and an all-or-nothing approach to life. This includes relationships, self-esteem, interpretation of social status, academic success, and more. It is also important to consider the adolescent's false sense of invulnerability, narcissistic approach to life, and lack of fully developed empathy, which leads to

an assumption that adults cannot understand adolescents and therefore cannot help them.

These above-noted factors need to be considered in developing "here-and-now"–oriented prevention and treatment programs for children and adolescents who are interested not in the end result of their substance use or abuse but in the present relationships between substance use and abuse and the social, academic, family, and legal aspects of their lives (Kaminer 1991a).

## ▼ PREVENTION

There is a growing recognition that the present prevention approaches of CASU and CAPSUD are deficient. The greatest concern is that the multifactorial determinants that contribute to the manifestation of the disorders are not fully recognized and/or acknowledged (Tarter 1992). Furthermore, the paucity of studies that carefully define the target population and the outcome goals for prevention by addressing specific behaviors leave the arena to simplistic and mostly untested prevention strategies that do not serve the most needy youth at risk for PSUD.

The most common approaches to primary or early prevention are media campaigns and education programs. The goal of primary prevention among children and adolescents is to defer or preclude initiation of drug use, especially cigarettes, alcohol, and marijuana. These targeted "gateway" drugs (Kandel 1982) serve as "villains," based on the fear-arousal model of prevention (Goodstadt 1980). Even experimental use of these drugs is portrayed as dangerous, especially in mass media campaigns. Films and videos that dramatize the risks associated with drug use are usually used. The traditional education program attempts to prevent drug use through use of information dissemination, which aims to increase knowledge about the consequences of drug use and promote an antidrug attitude, in a classroom setting accompanied by displays of substances and relevant literature. These approaches to prevention among children and adolescents were found to be ineffective by empirical studies as reviewed by Schinke et al. (1991). The assumption that increased knowledge will decrease drug use was found to be invalid. In fact, there were reports that this approach may serve to increase adolescents' curiosity, which may initiate substance use (Swisher 1979).

Media campaigns may tackle prevention by aiming at reducing harmful behaviors related to drinking. The success in the decrease of injuries related to drunk driving suggest that media intervention with motivated individuals is effective (Nathan 1990). At the same time, however, media indirectly provokes the adolescent to seek out cigarettes and alcohol by portraying the products as harmless and "cool" to use, (e.g., Joe Camel, beer commercials, etc.). Coate and Grossman (1987) reported that use of alcohol by youths declines when either the price of alcoholic beverages or the legal drinking age increases. This finding should encourage community efforts to influence appropriate legislations.

Affective education that increases self-esteem and enhances responsible decision making and personal growth was another approach to prevention presented in the 1970s. No information on drugs was included in the program and yet the expectations were that the youngsters would be able to make the right decision regarding drug use (Swisher 1979). Also, the idea that alternative activities offered to adolescents would substitute drug use was presented in the early 1980s (Swisher and Hu 1983). Athletic, academic, and vocational programs were the most commonly offered alternatives. Both approaches (i.e., affective education and alternative activities) were found to be ineffective in the prevention of drug use. In fact, in the quest for a "natural high" as experienced in wilderness programs and in some entertainment and vocational programs there were reports of increase in substance abuse (Schinke et al. 1991). The above-noted reports regarding the ineffectiveness of these approaches to primary prevention were supported by two recent publications (Pentz et al. 1989; Tobler 1986). It was concluded that an unidimensional approach to prevention in an extremely heterogenous population is likely to be ineffective for a large percentage of participants (Tarter 1992).

A more advanced strategy to prevention is based on a psychosocial approach. The prevention programs are aimed at enhancing self-esteem (Schaps et al. 1986) and social skills (Botvin et al. 1990). These strategies, employed as part of primary, secondary, and tertiary prevention strategies, usually use manuals in group settings. Such strategies are rooted in social-learning theory (Bandura 1977) and problem-behavior theory (Jessor and Jessor 1977).

According to the social-learning theory, individuals learn how to behave according to a four-compo-nent model: 1) role modeling, 2) reinforcement, 3) establishment of normative expectations, and 4) coping with social pressure. A fifth component is sometimes employed (i.e., training for generalization). A program entitled "Life Skills Training" was developed based on the social-learning theory (Botvin et al. 1984). The program was taught to 6th and 7th graders, at times led by peers, and resulted in significant improvements. The problem-behavior theory derives from a sociopsychological framework and recognizes the importance of the complex interaction of personal factors (cognition, attitudes, beliefs), physiological genetic factors, and perceived environmental factors on problems occurring during adolescence, such as drug use, precocious sexual behavior, and delinquency (Donovan and Jessor 1985). A problem behavior is one that is identified as a problem within the context of a particular value system and elicits a social response designed to control it. Substance use therefore helps the adolescent to achieve personal goals such as peer group approval and alleviating discomfort in interpersonal or intrapersonal conflicts.

Programs that increase awareness of social influence to use drugs, anxiety reduction, social and assertive skills, resistance to substance use, and changing attitudes and beliefs were reported to reduce smoking initiation by 50% in 1-year follow-up studies (Botvin et al. 1990). Other reports of substantial reduction (from 42% to 75%) in experimental smoking have used prevention approaches based on the social-learning theory and the problem-behavior theory (Schinke and Gilchrist 1983).

A critical review of the above-noted results was provided by two well-designed studies of prevention programs based on the socialization model (Ellickson and Bell 1990; Pentz et al. 1989). These findings indicated that although previous reports were able to demonstrate reduction of experimental use, they failed to be successful in enhancing secondary prevention. An earlier review by Flay (1985) supports these findings.

Walter et al. (1991) found that most of the theories accountable for various aspects of drug using behavior can be organized into three primary models of substance use: socialization, stress/strain, and disaffiliation. The researchers reported that in a sample of 1,091 10th-grade students, the measured risk factors most strongly associated with the use of drugs were derived from these three models (mainly from the socialization model).

Walter et al.'s study emphasizes that risk status is not necessarily the same for all individuals. It appears that the drawback in prevention programs based on social-learning theory and the problem-behavior theory is the underlying assumption that these adolescents' characteristics or deficiencies are somehow linked casually to drug use initiation (Tarter 1992). This assumption that drug consumption is prompted by one or more highly salient risk factors, such as low self-esteem, lack of social skills, or emotional distress in different individuals, negates logic for the prevention program implemented (i.e., the same menu to all participants). Not surprisingly, these types of prevention programs alone have not yet proven to be effective in follow-up.

So far, it appears that primary prevention programs to defer or prevent initiation of drug use among children and adolescents in the form of experimental or recreational use has had modest success at best, especially among children and adolescents who are not at high risk for substance abuse and dependence. However, in addressing secondary prevention (aimed to deter further use and avoiding abuse) and tertiary prevention (aimed to end abuse and dependence or to ameliorate its effects through treatment), no clinically and statistically meaningful results have been demonstrated.

The reason for the poor success rate in secondary prevention may be that prevention requires individualized intervention due to the adolescent's specific vulnerabilities that predispose him or her to substance abuse. To date, individualized prevention interventions have not been adopted despite the recognition of drug abuse etiology as multifactorial (biopsychosocial) in nature. Tarter (1992) argues that there are at least three reasons for this: "1) the emphasis has been on program content rather than on characteristics of individuals, 2) the state of professional development of prevention specialists has not progressed to a level at which skills are easily adapted for individualized interventions, and 3) institutional and professional environments are neither sensitized to nor prepared for detection of individuals at high risk for drug abuse" (p. 4).

Before starting any individualized program, it is important to identify children and adolescents at risk for CAPSUD. A late detection of these youngsters after substance abuse has initiated will require treatment. Children whose biological parent was diagnosed with PSUD are at up to 10-fold greater risk of developing the same disorder (Tarter 1992). The transmission of genetic vulnerability to Type II alcoholism (male limited) was presented by Cloninger et al. (1981). This subpopulation of alcoholic men, characterized by an early onset of problematic drinking, aggressive behavior, high sensation-seeking behavior, low harm avoidance, and low reward dependence, calls for prevention—intervention as early as possible, preferably before aggressive behavior has been manifested.

Children with conduct disorder that continues to express itself as antisocial personality disorder in adulthood have an odds ratio of greater than 21 to be diagnosed with substance abuse (Helzer and Pryzbeck 1988). About 25% of children diagnosed with attention-deficit hyperactivity disorder (ADHD) develop conduct disorder (Mannuzza et al. 1991) and are therefore at increased risk for substance abuse (Kaminer 1992a). Early intervention programs are needed to decrease the odds of developing conduct disorders and PSUD in the high-risk population of children and adolescents with ADHD and their families.

Children and/or their parents diagnosed with mood disorders, schizophrenia, anxiety disorders, bulimia, and antisocial personality disorder (adults only) and adolescents with cluster B personality disorders are also at high risk to develop PSUD (Bukstein et al. 1989). Traumatized children and adolescents who have been exposed to aggression (physically and/or sexually) in the family or in their immediate environment or those who have come from a dysfunctional family are at risk for PSUD as well.

The intervention in children and adolescents at risk should start by enhancing the motivation of the child or adolescent and the caretakers to participate in a prevention program before the initial drug use. The objective of the intervention is to change both the specific components of vulnerability within the individual and the environment. A stable remission of a psychiatric disorder in the adolescent and/or the caretaker is a key to meaningful intervention. In conclusion, a hypothesis to be tested is that prevention for individuals at risk for PSUD appears to command the same principles for intervention and a comparable but less intense curriculum as treatment of PSUD. Research has yet to report the results of a study that will aim at prevention intervention for children at risk for PSUD and their caretakers. A control group of matched children and caretakers without a known family history of PSUD and other risk factors for

CAPSUD may improve the scientific merit of such a study.

## ▼ TREATMENT

The literature on the treatment of CAPSUD is replete with descriptive publications regarding various treatment facilities, philosophies, and modalities. No studies have yet been targeted on the natural course and outcome of adolescents who meet diagnostic criteria for PSUD, and very little documented research has been reported regarding treatment outcome.

In many treatment programs for adolescents the treatment philosophy and curriculum are identical to those of facilities for substance-abusing adults. Moreover, a "mixture" of adolescents and adults in the same facility is not uncommon. Length of stay and type of facility are still emphasized over patient needs and individualized treatment factors, as had been the case in the 1970s (Simpson 1979), and regardless of the evidence that among adult patients treatment setting had no clear bearing on outcome (Holden 1987). This resistance to change is related to 1) the historical-conceptual roots of substance abuse treatment according to the disease model and 2) the scarcity of child and adolescent health professionals in the addictions field.

It has been recognized that the interaction between adolescent variables, treatment variables, and to a lesser degree environmental factors defines the therapeutic process (Kaminer 1991a). This is most probably responsible for a substantial proportion of the variance in treatment outcome. Before answering the question of how to treat CAPSUD and what is a favorable treatment outcome, we have to define the needs of the heterogenous population of adolescents with PSUD.

## ▼ THE NEEDS OF SPECIAL POPULATIONS

There is a growing recognition of the need to stress the consideration of different patient viewpoints in CAPSUD treatment. Such viewpoints take into consideration the attributes that the patient brings from the specific population with which he or she identifies. The psychosocial factors that ought to be considered in the etiology, prevention, and treatment of

CASU and CAPSUD include sex, ethnic, and cultural differences.

Adolescent females as well as sexual and ethnic minorities require special attention in designing prevention programs for them and their families as target populations, as well as when they are identified patients in treatment programs.

The rationale and suggestions for planning treatment and prevention of substance abuse for black, Native American, and Hispanic communities; women; and gay or lesbian individuals were extensively reviewed (Lawson and Lawson 1989). However, there has been considerable speculation regarding the adolescent age group. The few studies conducted on special adolescent populations focus mainly on epidemiology and etiology with suggestions regarding primary prevention (Oetting and Beauvais 1989).

Two special populations to be discussed in this chapter are pregnant adolescents and substance-abusing adolescents with comorbid psychiatric disorders (to be referred to as hereafter dually diagnosed).

## ▼ PATIENT VARIABLES

A large segment of adolescents with PSUD are dually diagnosed. This is true for untreated as well as treated populations as reviewed by Bukstein et al. (1989) and Kaminer (1991b). The two most prevalent Axis I diagnoses according to DSM-III-R are mood disorders (especially major depression) and conduct disorders. Anxiety disorders, schizophrenia, adjustment disorders, bulimia nervosa, ADHD, and cluster B personality disorders (Axis II) are less commonly diagnosed.

The high rates of dually diagnosed adolescents appear to be the rule rather than the exception, especially among adolescents with PSUD in treatment (Kaminer 1991b). Keller et al. (1992) conducted the only study that investigated the clinical course and outcome of substance abuse disorders in a non-treatment-seeking cohort of adolescents. Eighty-nine percent of the adolescents diagnosed with DSM-III diagnoses of substance use disorders had received one or more additional diagnoses.

Lifetable estimates of time to recovery show that after 3 years from onset, 42% of the adolescents had not recovered. Of the recovered adolescents, almost one-half had remitted from a previous episode of substance use prior to the assessment. Friedman and

Glickman (1986) reported that 28% of substance-abusing adolescents sought help for emotional and psychiatric problems.

The purpose of emphasizing the importance of dually diagnosed adolescents is fourfold:

1. To introduce and increase awareness, recognition, and understanding of the concept of dual diagnosis in substance-abusing adolescents among mental health professionals, communities, schools, the judicial system, and other relevant parties
2. To explore and suggest treatment and aftercare options for these adolescents and their families
3. To enhance training designed to improve clinical care and research of these patients
4. To advocate for allocation of resources and improve reimbursement for the treatment of these youngsters

It is also important to note that PSUD among adolescents is considered to be a high-risk factor for suicidal behavior. The typical adolescent at risk for suicide is a white male who is likely to be intoxicated and to attempt suicide with a firearm without ever seeking treatment. Psychopathologies such as depression and conduct disorder accompanied by precipitating events are frequently present (Kaminer 1992c).

Most studies have found that psychiatric disorders and behavior traits associated with substance abuse in adolescents and young adults precede the use of drugs (Buydens-Branchey et al. 1989; Christie et al. 1988; Kandel 1982).

Patients' problems in other domains such as school performance, peer-social relationships, family function, and legal issues may develop before or after the initiation of substance abuse or may be exacerbated as a consequence of drug abuse.

Studies conducted in the late 1970s and early 1980s were designed to assess types of adolescents in treatment (Beschner 1985). Seventy-five percent were white and 11.5% were black; also white adolescents were more likely to abuse multiple drugs than minority adolescents.

## ▼ TREATMENT CHARACTERISTICS

Few drug treatment programs are designed specifically to serve adolescents. About 20% of all patients in substance abuse treatment programs are under age 19 years (Beschner 1985); only 5% of programs have adolescents as their main clientele.

The most prevalent levels of treatment care noted for CAPSUD are outpatient treatment, day or evening treatment (also known as partial hospitalization), inpatient treatment, and various types of residential treatment (e.g., halfway house, group home).

Some or all of the following interventions may be provided to adolescents at any levels of treatment to be described, depending on philosophy and/or goals of treatment, resources, accreditation demands, and so on. Basic components for a drug-free adolescent treatment program include individual counseling, individual therapy, self-help groups for the patients and caretakers (e.g., Alcoholics Anonymous [AA], Narcotics Anonymous, Al-Anon, Alateen), substance abuse education, random urine analysis for psychoactive substances, Breathalizer testing, family therapy and/or involvement, relapse prevention techniques, educational or vocational counseling, legal assistance, various types of group activities or therapies, contingency contracting, medications, and written assignments related to the recovery process.

## ▼ OUTPATIENT AND PARTIAL HOSPITALIZATION TREATMENT

Most adolescents (81.5%) are admitted to drug-free outpatient programs (Beschner 1985). These programs range from unstructured "drop-in" centers to clinics with a more structured environment where a demanding curriculum is followed.

These programs offer one or more of the following services: individual, group, family, and vocational counseling and a strong support for attendance at community self-help groups. These programs are usually run by a municipal or state agency. Programs affiliated with mental health centers may offer additional services that include follow-up after discharge from an inpatient or residential treatment program, psychiatric evaluation, and treatment including medications and medical workup and random urine screening. Outpatient treatment is the least expensive treatment service. The consensus in the literature on adults is that patients with low to medium severity of alcohol dependence may equally benefit from such a program at one-tenth the cost of an inpatient program (Hayashida et al. 1989).

Partial hospitalization in the form of a day or evening program is an alternative form of more intensive outpatient treatment or a form of step down from an inpatient setting. Such a program can offer the adolescent more interventions after school/work or may have a school component as an integral part of a day program. The adolescent attends this program for a few hours each day. Length of stay and interventions provided vary and depend on the match between patient variables and program characteristics. Partial hospitalization improves continuity of care between outpatient and inpatient treatment and can also be provided for first-time treatment. The advantages for an outpatient program and partial hospitalization are low cost, easy accessibility, and high level of acceptability among adolescents and their caretakers.

The criteria frequently cited that rule out outpatient treatment for adolescents with acute or chronic medical and acute psychiatric problems are not defined and appear to be unnecessarily restrictive (Semlitz and Gold 1986). Most adolescents with these problems at a moderate or lower severity or those who are neither suicidal nor prone to other physical morbidities can benefit from an outpatient or partial hospitalization treatment program.

## ▼ INPATIENT TREATMENT

Most inpatient programs are short-term, hospital-based units. They are usually more structured and more expensive than other services. A commonly used treatment model is the one designed according to the Minnesota Model (MM; Laundergan 1982). The MM addresses chemical dependency only and does not recognize age differences and other comorbid problems or psychiatric disorders. Four key elements are identified in this AA-oriented philosophy: 1) the possibility of change, 2) the disease concept, 3) long-term treatment goals of abstinence and improvement of life-style, and 4) acceptance of self-help group principles and traditions.

There are four short-term goals that are used as indicators of progress: 1) the need to recognize the illness and its implications, 2) admitting the need for help, 3) the need to identify specifically what needs to be changed in order to meet the second short-term goal, and 4) developing a new life-style. The length of stay is usually 28 days as dictated in most cases by re-

imbursement tradition. Customary program variables include attendance at self-help group meetings, a therapeutic drug-free milieu, and counselors who have been in recovery from substance abuse for at least 2 years. Work assignments include reading the "big book" of AA and presenting one's life history with a special emphasis on drug use. The adolescent is expected to complete up to 5 of the 12 steps. Group therapy sessions are focused on breaking the denial system. The techniques used vary from problem solving to the "hot seat" confrontation approach. Aftercare following discharge involves weekly meetings for several months to a year, accompanied by continued attendance at self-help groups.

Another model that is gaining recognition and acceptance recently is the dimensional multidisciplinary treatment program. This treatment philosophy recommends treating the adolescent as a patient with various problems in multiple domains. The treatment curriculum is comprehensive and is also tailored to address dual diagnosis patients. Individualized treatment matches the adolescent's needs in additional domains such as family function, peer-social relationships, legal issues, and school or employment function (Kaminer 1991a).

A multidisciplinary team that includes mental health professionals experienced in substance abuse treatment attends to the patient's needs from the assessment stage through the entire treatment period.

Inpatient treatment of dually diagnosed adolescents may be constructed in three manners: 1) *parallel treatment*, in which the patient attends selected therapies alternately on either a substance abuse or a psychiatric unit while being hospitalized on one or the other unit; 2) *sequential treatment*, in which the patient completes treatment on either a psychiatric unit or on a substance abuse treatment unit, then proceeding to the other unit; and 3) *integrated treatment*, which combines both substance abuse and psychiatric therapies within one unit.

## ▼ RESIDENTIAL TREATMENT AND THERAPEUTIC COMMUNITIES

Residential treatment programs and therapeutic communities strive to provide the adolescent with PSUD with a long-term, drug-free, structured, and therapeutic environment. These programs are less intensive than inpatient programs and may employ a diversity of approaches. The spectrum of approaches available includes a long-term family program, which demands intensive caretaker participation and processing of addiction, sexual, and physical abuse in the family. Others put the emphasis on social skills learning in the form of residential job functions and training or wilderness experience. Involvement in the immediate community and educational services and participation in self-help groups exist in various levels. Therapeutic communities are considered to be more restrictive and structured than residential treatment programs at large.

These programs are cheaper than inpatient treatment and accommodate the patients for 6 months to sometimes more than a year. Religious treatment programs or sponsorship and halfway houses are alternatives or variants to residential treatment and therapeutic communities programs (Kusnetz 1985).

It is unfortunate that during this era of limited resources a referral or a decision for triage to treatment programs is based on the program's availability and not necessarily according to the patient's needs.

## ▼ TREATMENT OUTCOME STUDIES

Questions regarding the effectiveness of treatment of CAPSUD are embedded in complex methodologic issues, which obscure clear conclusions. A small number of studies investigating treatment outcome in adolescents with PSUD were conducted. Most studies did not employ valid and reliable criteria for the diagnosis of substance abuse. Also, personal and demographic variables such as sex, age, race, and socioeconomic factors have not been researched to the extent that would allow a determination of the need for specialized treatment program components. Lastly, from among the limited available studies, the treatment setting or time in treatment were neither controlled nor comparable across studies (Simpson 1979). It is generally recognized that the criteria for treatment outcome can be defined either per treatment program or as compared with the individual patient. The two criteria commonly used in program evaluation are attrition rate and/or length of stay versus planned stay.

*Individual outcome* refers exclusively to complete abstinence of the adolescent with PSUD. Rush (1979) indicated that productivity (an index score combining education, training, and employment) is another goal that defines outcome in addition to abstinence. Reduction in the severity of PSUD and/or PSUD-related problems is not an index for treatment outcome commonly reported among adolescents. Also the use of severity indices of assessment instruments designed to measure CAPSUD has not been common (Tarter 1990).

Attrition, rather than completion of treatment, is considered to be the rule rather than the exception for most programs for adolescents with PSUD (De Leon and Schwartz 1984).

Rush (1979) conducted research on adolescents and young adults in the Pennsylvania substance abuse system in order to predict treatment outcomes. This large sample included approximately 2,940 adolescents. Most of them were enrolled in outpatient programs, and 17% were treated in residential facilities.

Predictors of treatment success for adolescents in drug-free outpatient clinics were enrollment in education and employment programs on admission. Delinquency at admission was inversely correlated with productivity at discharge. Delinquency is reflected in the following predictor variables as indicated by Rush (1979): more felony arrests, a longer drug habit (in years of continuous use), and early initiation of drug use. The abuse of only one drug and the abuse of nonopioid drugs were positively correlated with productivity. It is interesting to note that time in outpatient treatment accounted for very little of the variance and had a negative effect on treatment outcome.

An important criterion to consider was treatment completion in terms of meeting the goals of the program. Significant factors at admission positively related to completion of treatment were being 1) enrolled in an education program, 2) a nonopioid-abusing individual, 3) white, and 4) older when the drug of abuse was first tried. Delinquency was inversely correlated with completion of treatment (Rush 1979).

Two large-scale national studies have been designed to assess adolescent treatment outcome. The Drug Abuse Reporting Program (DARP) assessed treatment outcomes of 5,405 patients under the age of 19 from a large number of mixed ages programs. Reduction in the use of opioids but not alcohol and marijuana was recorded among patients from outpatient clinics and therapeutic communities (Sells and Simpson 1979). No data that might indicate an optional patient-treatment match were noted. The Treatment Outcome Prospective Study (TOPS) evaluated treatment outcome for 11,750 adolescents in outpatient clinics and residential treatment facilities (Hubbard et al. 1985). The results of this study were comparable to the DARP study, although lack of an untreated control group in the TOPS study makes it difficult to determine the meaning of treatment. (The DARP study employed an "intake only" control group.) A few Scandinavian studies (Benson 1985; Holsten 1980; Vaglum and Fossheim 1980) provide information about overall treatment results and their relationships to patient variables. However, lack of information about the specific interventions in treatment limits the utility of these data in developing matching criteria (Hester and Miller 1988). Szapocznik et al. (1983) reported that adolescents who received a small number of brief strategic family therapy sessions, in addition to individual sessions, reported overall reductions in drug use and delinquent behavior at 6 month follow-up. Also, temporary placement of adolescents with a family of an adolescent who had progressed further in the day program appeared to be helpful in reducing PSUD (Friedman et al. 1989).

The best predictor of productivity at discharge was involvement in an educational program at admission, followed by time spent in treatment. Employment status lacked statistical significance. Also the same two variables that predicted productivity were found to be related to treatment completion. DeJong and Henrich (1980) and Langrod et al. (1981) published studies that evaluated treatment program effectiveness among mixed populations of adolescents and young adults. The design of these studies could be classified as having a "posttest only" follow-up design. As in the study conducted by Rush (1979), no control group was employed and psychiatric comorbidity issues were not investigated. DeJong and Henrich (1980) conducted a 2-year follow-up study of 89 young addicted individuals in a behavior modification program who attended a rehabilitation center for at least 7 days. They reported that one-third of the total sample was drug free. Langrod et al. (1981) studied a residential, religious intervention program and reported a 24% abstinence rate at outcome. No research methodology on this study was reported.

Amini et al. (1982) reported a random assignment controlled study of inpatient versus outpatient treatment of 74 delinquent drug-abusing adolescents. Results at 1 year of treatment effectiveness showed no significant difference in outcome.

Grenier (1985) used a waiting-list control-group experimental design to empirically assess the efficacy of adolescent residential treatment. The age of patients in this study was 9–21 years. The abstinence rate for the treatment group (65%) was significantly higher than the abstinence rate for the waiting list control group (14% of spontaneous remission).

Studies published in the second half of the 1980s indicated the growing awareness of dually diagnosed adolescents and of patient treatment matching (i.e., individualized treatment objectives). Also, emphasis on the differences between dropouts and patients engaged in treatment illuminated the importance of retention in treatment. One basic difficulty in the comparison of the findings and rates of attrition reported by the different studies is that attrition occurred at different phases of the referral treatment process.

It is generally recognized in child and adolescent psychiatry that dropout from an outpatient clinic is primarily a function of referral source expectations and the caretaker's symptomatology (Gould et al. 1985).

The effects of psychiatric symptomatology on treatment outcome for drug-abusing adolescent males were studied (Friedman and Glickman 1987). A total of 130 court-referred, substance-abusing delinquent boys of ages 14–18 years were engaged in a day treatment program. The inconclusive findings were that a number of psychiatric symptoms were positively correlated with treatment outcome. These findings are different from those reported in the literature on adults.

Another recent study (Kaminer et al. 1992a) investigated the psychiatric and demographic characteristics that may distinguish completers from noncompleters among hospitalized dually diagnosed adolescents. Mood and adjustment disorders were more prevalent among 50 treatment completers, whereas noncompleters were more likely to be diagnosed with conduct disorder. There were no differences between the groups with respect to demographic and legal status, education level and lifetime psychiatric diagnosis in the parents or caretakers, living arrangements, treatment history, and perception of treatment benefits. A higher percentage of treatment completers than noncompleters received psychotropic medications.

Friedman and Glickman (1986) reported on outpatient program characteristics for successful treatment of adolescent drug abuse, as measured by reduction in drug use. Adolescents in 30 programs were assessed, and 50% of them ($n = 5,789$) dropped out before completion of treatment. The following characteristics of programs were found to predict the outcome to a statistically significant degree: having a special school for school dropouts; employing experienced counselors; providing vocational, recreational, and birth control services; using therapies such as crisis intervention, gestalt therapy, music/art therapy, and group confrontation; and being perceived by the patient as allowing and encouraging free expression and spontaneous action.

Another approach to the assessment of the contribution of treatment variables to treatment outcome among adolescents with PSUD at an inpatient unit for dually diagnosed patients was reported by Kaminer et al. (1992b). They compared unit staff, treatment completers, and noncompleters (21% of the unit population) on their perception of the efficacy of treatment modalities.

Results indicated statistically significant and clinically meaningful differences in perception of the value of three therapeutic modalities: individual treatment contracting, therapeutic community meeting, and educational counseling. Seven other variables did not differentiate the three groups.

The findings of this study suggest that patients' involvement in the above-noted interventions should be encouraged and that staff ability to provide these services should be improved.

The small number of studies on treatment outcome among adolescents with PSUD and various methodological problems hamper the efforts to generalize the conclusions drawn. More studies are needed in this population.

## ▼ THE ASSESSMENT OF CAPSUD

The assessment of psychopathology including PSUD in children and adolescents has typically lagged behind that of the general population. The introduction of rating scales, usually in the form of self-report questionnaires and interviews, compensates for deficiencies in the recognition of PSUD in clinical settings based on observations and nonstructured evaluations only.

Assessment instruments are devised either for diagnostic purposes or for the recognition of the severity of the problems/disorders measured. Commonly used psychiatric diagnostic interviews for children and adolescents are the Diagnostic Interview Schedule for Children-Revised (DISC-R; Costello et al. 1985), the Kiddie Schedule for Affective Disorders and Schizophrenia (K-SADS; Orvaschel et al. 1982), and the Diagnostic Interview for Children and Adolescents (Wellner et al. 1987). Each of these interviews also has a version to be administered to a parent in order to compare the information obtained from multiple informants. These three instruments cover the range of psychiatric disorders including PSUD in accordance with the DSM-III and DSM-III-R systems, and they have acceptable psychometric support regarding their reliability and validity.

Only a handful of instruments for the clinical assessment of CAPSUD have been described; most of them are not widely tested and accepted as yet. Most of these instruments were reviewed by Tarter (1990).

The instruments to be reviewed here have been chosen because of their relative popularity in publications or based on their promise for use in clinical settings.

The first instrument, the Adolescent Alcohol Involvement Scale (AAIS; Mayer and Filstead 1979), is a 14-item, self-report scale used for screening. It is not meant for diagnostic purposes but to identify adolescents who are misusing drugs. Riley and Klockars (1984) critically examined the AAIS and discouraged its use because of a lack of common variance among its items. They concluded that revision of the poorly constructed and unordered response options to items be made in order to produce meaningful results.

The Personal Experience Inventory (PEI) and the Chemical Dependency Assessment Scale (CDAS) are the two best-developed instruments for evaluation of suspected drug-using adolescents. Both instruments have been validated, with the PEI being more suitable for a clinical population. The PEI, developed by Winters and Henly (1988), is a standardized measure of substance abuse in adolescents. It covers all forms of PSUD and identifies the personal risks that may precipitate or sustain PSUD. This is a self-report inventory for 12- to 18-year-old subjects, which also assesses drug-related problems. The CDAS (Oetting et al. 1984) was specifically designed to describe and quantify drug use behavior in adolescents. The scale is self-administered and provides information about current and prior history of 11 classes of drugs used. The instrument also measures psychological adjustment according to various domains of the patient's life and interaction with the environment.

Three other instruments follow the same multidimensional approach. The Teen Addiction Severity Index (T-ASI) is an age-appropriate modification of the ASI (McLellan et al. 1980). The T-ASI (Kaminer et al. 1991) is a semistructured interview that includes the following six domains: 1) substance use, 2) school or employment status, 3) family function, 4) peer-social relationships, 5) legal status, and 6) psychiatric status. This is not a diagnostic instrument but a severity measurement questionnaire that may be best used periodically to measure progress in treatment and aftercare. Reliability and validity studies of the T-ASI generated good results (Kaminer et al. 1991, 1993).

The Drug Use Screening Inventory (DUSI) is a self-report measure that profiles substance use involvement in conjunction with severity of disturbance in 9 spheres of everyday functioning (Tarter 1990). The following three domains of the DUSI are added to the six domains assessed by the T-ASI: 1) recreation, 2) health status, and 3) behavior patterns.

The Problem Oriented Screening Instrument for Teenagers (POSIT) is an instrument similar to the DUSI regarding the problematic functional areas represented. The POSIT (E. Rahdert, unpublished observations, 1990) has been field tested and is available for use and psychometric tests.

In summary, based on the assessment information, a treatment plan or an aftercare formulation can be tailored for each patient.

## ▼ A SUGGESTED MODEL FOR EVALUATION AND TREATMENT OF CAPSUD

### The Referral-Assessment Process

In order to develop a referral system for a treatment program, the community needs to know at least the following minimum information: 1) the goals of the treatment program, 2) the population to be served, and 3) how to communicate with the referral system. Other questions can be answered once communication channels have been established. On the other end, the treatment service is obligated to assess the needs of the community in order to ensure a successful program and its appropriateness to the environment. Needs assessment surveys, certificate of need procedures, and marketing strategies are beyond the scope of this chapter. However, it is important to get acquainted with the following services: school systems, D and A agencies (private, county, municipal, state, etc.), children and youth services, the juvenile-justice system, mental health services, pediatricians, and private practitioners.

The referral may start by having an intake coordinator accept phone calls for screening. An intake questionnaire is recommended even for phone calls (15–20 minutes of administration preferred). Substance use patterns and psychiatric status, family function, school performance, and legal problems are the pivotal domains addressed. A scheduled outpatient multidisciplinary evaluation should follow, based on the urgency and severity of the case involved. Dispositional options (triage) involve a variety of possibilities, depending on service availability (see Figure 29–1).

Adolescents with PSUD seen on an urgent basis in an emergency room or according to the above-noted procedures can subsequently be admitted directly to an inpatient unit. Appropriate referrals to an inpatient unit may include 1) adolescents with PSUD who have failed or do not qualify for outpatient treatment; 2) dually diagnosed adolescents with moderate or severe psychiatric disorders; 3) adolescents who display a potentially morbid or mortal behavior toward themselves or others (e.g., suicidal behavior, self-injurious behavior); 4) adolescents who are intravenous drug abusers, drug dependent, or need to be detoxified; 5) patients with accompanying moderate to severe medical problems; 6) adolescents that need to be isolated from their community to ensure treatment without interruptions; and 7) pregnant adolescents who manifest PSUD that endangers the fetus. Enrollment criteria in a drug-free outpatient or partial hospitalization setting include 1) severity of CAPSUD and other psychiatric disorders that do not require inpatient treatment (i.e., PSUD severity less than moderate); 2) previous successful outpatient treatment or follow-up after completion of inpatient treatment; 3) agreement for a contingency contract that will delineate frequency of visits, compliance with curriculum including random urine screening, consequences of noncompliance and relapse, and participation in the community network including self-help groups.

The admission process to an inpatient unit is very stressful to the adolescent and the caretaker(s). It is imperative to find out what their expectations from treatment are and to describe to them the program's operations including rules and regulations. The high anxiety level of the caretakers and patient need to be considered, therefore the explanation should be brief and clear. Dropout from treatment occurs more frequently during the first week following admission; many times it is because of unrealistic expectations from treatment or lack of knowledge about the unit milieu (e.g., smoke-free environment, random urine analysis and searches, restrictions on visitations and phone calls). Patient and caretaker manuals prove to be helpful in enhancing adjustment to the unit milieu.

A thorough body and belongings search is mandatory upon entry to the unit. Recommended laboratory work upon admission includes Breathalizer test; urine toxicology screen; urinalysis and urine-specific gravity; human chorionic gonadotropin (B-HCG) to sexually active females; hepatitis B and HIV screen for

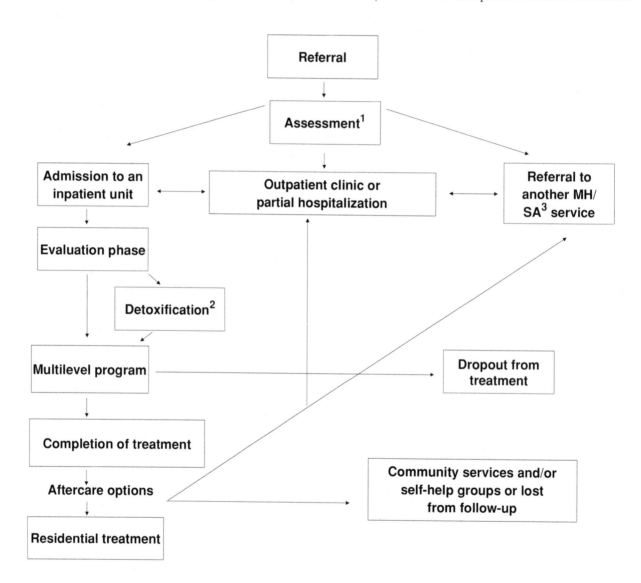

**Figure 29–1. Options for the treatment of an adolescent with PSUD (dual diagnosis included).**
[1]Assessment can be done through an assessment coordination team and can combine a preliminary phone evaluation and/or use questionnaires followed by an interview with the patient and caretaker(s).
[2]Detoxification is the exception rather than the rule with adolescents.
[3]MH = mental health; SA = substance abuse; PSUD = psychoactive substance use disorder.

*American Psychiatric Press Textbook of Substance Abuse Treatment*

suspected intravenous drug abusers, those with a history of multiple sex partners, homosexual males, and patients who request the test; and chest X ray and creatine phosphokinase for suspected inhalant abusers.

Areas for multidisciplinary evaluation include 1) substance use history, 2) psychiatric status and history, 3) family function and history, 4) medical status and developmental history, 5) school status and cognitive-intellectual function or employment status, 6) peer-social function, and 7) legal status.

Use of assessment rating scales as described earlier may be helpful.

### Legal Aspects of Admission and Treatment

Facilities that treat minors have to follow some basic common rules with minor differences. Consent for admission to an inpatient unit must be provided by the caretaker and child (unless the child or adolescent has been committed). Any patient under 18 years of age who is married, a parent, or emancipated has the right to consent on his or her own behalf. Prior to rendering any care without parental consent, the facility must obtain a written acknowledgment from the minor stating that he or she was 1) advised of the purpose and nature of such treatment services, 2) told that he or she may withdraw the signed acknowledgment and cease participation in the treatment service at any time, 3) told that the facility will make attempts to convince the child of the need for involvement of other family members in treatment and the facility's preference for parental consent for the rendering of treatment services, and 4) told that a medical/clinical record of his or her treatment services will be made and maintained by the facility.

For overnight treatment, parental consent is always required unless the parents refuse consent, in which case the family court may substitute its consent.

The provisions of various laws and regulations establish that parental consent is usually, but not always, required to deliver drug or alcohol abuse treatment to minors. However, the release of information regarding such treatment is governed by the strict federal rules regarding education and medical records. Regardless of state laws granting parents unilateral rights to consent to treatment, the federal rules require both a parent's and a minor patient's prior consent to the release of medical record information that would identify the patient as an alcohol or drug abuser. Whenever state law does permit a minor to consent unilaterally to treatment, the federal rules require that only the patient's consent be obtained prior to the release of medical record information. Also, drug or alcohol abuse patients must be notified of the protections afforded by the federal rules upon admission (C. Weinberg, personal communication, 1991).

## ▼ TREATMENT ELEMENTS

This chapter does not extensively elaborate on interventions that have received special description elsewhere in this book. However, some key interventions will be briefly described in order to note their applicability and importance, primarily for the inpatient treatment of PSUD in adolescents (Kaminer and Frances 1991).

### Individualized Treatment Contract

This treatment component is based on a contract developed from a problem list conjointly prepared by the patient and the therapist during the evaluation phase. The contract specifies long-term goals according to the T-ASI (Kaminer et al. 1991). The goals are sensible, achievable, and measurable and are divided into weekly objectives according to the following domains: substance abuse, psychiatric symptomatology, family issues, legal status, peer-social relationships, and school or vocational problems. Individual treatment is provided by a team led by a psychiatrist who supervises the primary therapists who contract with the patients. Progress on the multilevel system is dependent on the periodic presentation of the contract.

Continued staff development and increased awareness regarding the importance of negotiating treatment goals and developing a contract with patients is of great importance (Kaminer et al. 1992b). Tackling violations of contract and regulations on the unit vary little from procedures followed on an adult unit. However, the treatment team is responsible for communicating with the caretakers frequently, especially when a patient has been disciplined. A clear protocol on how to handle such situations with minors may prevent legal hazards.

## Social Skills Training (SST) and Relapse-Prevention Group (RPG)

SST and RPG consist of behavioral and cognitive therapy-oriented group activities. SST addresses the following areas: anger control, assertiveness training, and communication. RPG tackles the high-risk situations that may lead to drug-using behavior and relapse based on the self-efficacy paradigm of relapse prevention (Marlatt and George 1984). The development of a coping skills manual according to various sessions is helpful (Kaminer and Bukstein 1992). Monti et al.'s (1989) guide may serve as an example of the development of such a manual. The Inventory of Using Situations (IUS) and the Situations Confidence Questionnaire (SCQ), developed by Annis (1986) for alcoholic adults, have been found appropriate for use among adolescents (based on my clinical experience). However, versions specific for adolescents are being developed (H. Annis, personal communication, 1989).

## Family Therapy

Family therapy consists of 1) individual family therapy (in which all significant family members and the patient attend therapy); 2) multiple-family group therapy, which is offered to all the parents/caretakers and patients in a supportive peer-group atmosphere (to increase understanding and adaptation to the common problems of these families in the form of lectures, therapeutic interventions, and skill training to parents/caretakers and patients); and 3) family weekends, which are offered on a monthly basis and provide an extension of the multiple-family group therapy experience.

## Therapeutic Group Meetings

The therapeutic group meeting is an intervention based on modified dynamic group therapy (MDGT). Four primary dimensions of MDGT, namely self-care, relationship conflict, self-esteem, and affect regulation, are explored (Khantzian et al. 1992). MDGT may focus on PSUD-related behaviors, or on a unit with parallel programs MDGT could tackle other problems, which will enable the group to relate to the four primary dimensions.

## Self-Help Groups

Adolescents involvement in self-help groups of mixed age populations need to be supervised to prevent unwarranted risky behaviors. Staff attendance is mandatory, and meetings on hospital grounds are helpful (e.g., AA, NA). Alateen and Al-Anon meetings are of significant help to these youngsters and their families.

## Medications

Psychotropic medications for comorbid psychiatric disorders are administered to patients as necessary, based on strict psychiatric criteria and usually only after a medication-free evaluation phase. Detoxification of adolescents from alcohol, barbiturates, benzodiazepines, and opioids should follow the same therapeutic format as that of adults (Kaminer 1994). Also, treatment of withdrawal symptoms from cocaine in an adolescent was successfully completed with desipramine (Kaminer 1992b). Methadone maintenance under age 18 years has not been approved in most states and demands special authorization or two documented detoxification failures.

## ▼ DISCHARGE AND AFTERCARE

It is generally agreed that aftercare is necessary to solidify and maximize treatment gains and to minimize relapse. Aftercare also ensures the transfer and generalization of treatment results to the patient's community. Lack of follow-up services may essentially nullify the positive effects of treatment. It would appear worthy to explore the hypothesis that adolescents who drop out of treatment and especially those with a comorbid diagnosis of conduct disorder could be better served in a facility other than a psychiatric hospital. Also, because no therapeutic intervention appears yet to be superior to another in the treatment of CAPSUD, specialized interventions may be necessary to increase retention in treatment of this high-risk population for dropout. Special techniques to improve the capability of tracking adolescents after discharge from treatment were suggested by Kaminer et al. (Y. Kaminer, unpublished manual that accompanies the T-ASI questionnaire, 1989).

Most patients return to school, therefore school-based tertiary prevention in the form of counseling and support group for "recovered" adolescents is warranted. Adolescents enrolled in these programs may also be instrumental as role models in school-based primary and secondary prevention groups for high-risk youth (Kaminer and Bukstein 1989). Also continued participation in self-help groups, follow-up with an outpatient clinic, and rigorous maintenance of a contingency discharge contract is helpful for relapse prevention.

Parents/caretakers should be encouraged to support the recovery process and to maintain a risk-free life-style for the adolescent (e.g., be aware of ominous signs of relapse, keep curfew hours, avoid enabling behavior).

In accord with the adult aftercare guidelines, the difference between lapse and relapse and how to initiate therapeutic contact in stressful situations should be clarified to the youngster and the family.

## ▼ MATERNAL PSUD IN ADOLESCENTS

### Epidemiology and Phenomenology

Adolescent PSUD and unplanned pregnancy are two major present public health problems. According to the problem-behavior theory (Donovan and Jessor 1985; Jessor and Jessor 1977), adolescents who are prone to problematic behavior may experience several harmful behaviors (e.g., precocious sexual activity, substance use, delinquency). About one-fourth of adolescent females who are sexually active will become pregnant before age 18. More than 1 million adolescent females in the United States become pregnant annually, and approximately 60% of pregnant adolescents carry their pregnancies to term (Hechtman 1989).

The overall incidence of substance abuse in pregnancy was found to be 11% (Chasnoff 1989), about 20% of whom were reported to be adolescents (Marques and McKnight 1991). Adolescents who carry their pregnancies to term are more likely than aborters to be poor, younger at first intercourse, less educated, and at higher risk for multiple pregnancies and substance abuse (Gilchrist et al. 1990). Pregnant adolescents who abuse drugs frequently have other health problems (e.g., anemia, malnutrition) and psychiatric comorbidities such as depression and anxiety.

None of the major national studies supply data about psychoactive drug use among pregnant adolescents. Alcohol consumption was found to decrease from 32% to 20% among pregnant women between the years 1985 and 1988. The study conducted in 21 states surveying pregnant women older than age 18 years concluded that no decline was observed among women younger than 25 (Serdula et al. 1991).

The prenatal effects of psychoactive drugs on the fetus, especially on the central nervous system, are seen as creating biologic vulnerability (Zuckerman and Bresnahan 1991). Fetal alcohol syndrome is only one of the various morbid effects inflicted on the fetus in utero. Effects on children born to mothers abusing various substances during pregnancy include intrauterine growth retardation and neonatal neurobehavioral dysfunction (e.g., irritability, difficulty in the self-regulation of attention and alertness states [Chasnoff 1988]). Polydrug abuse, poor nutrition, poor health, and other risk factors make it difficult to isolate the effects of one specific drug, especially after 2–4 years of follow-up.

Cocaine's vasoactive effects have been reported to cause abruptio placentae, preterm labor, hemorrhagic and cystic lesions in the brain, seizures, congenital anomalies in the urogenital and gastrointestinal tracts, and limb deformities (Chavez et al. 1989; Hoyme et al. 1990). Sudden infant death syndrome, transient abnormalities, and neurobehavioral abnormalities have been reported by some studies as reviewed by Zuckerman and Bresnahan (1991).

Opioids affect the fetus and newborn directly (decreased somatic growth and neonatal abstinence syndrome [NAS]). Subacute NAS may continue up to 6 months. It is important to note that many pregnant heroin-addicted individuals also abuse cocaine. Opioids and cocaine are excreted in small amounts in breast milk and cause or continue infant dependency on these drugs (Chasnoff 1988).

Marijuana use in pregnancy was associated with decreased fetal growth, arm or muscle mass, and nonfat mass. This pattern is consistent with the findings on infants exposed to maternal cigarette smoking (Zuckerman and Bresnahan 1991).

These infants are also at high risk for various sexually transmitted diseases, including AIDS. Fifty-one percent of children with AIDS have at least one parent who used intravenous drugs (Jaffe et al. 1983). Intravenous drug use has been the probable source of infection in 80% of children infected in utero (Des

Jarlais and Friedman 1987). Women with positive HIV status are at substantial risk (50%) of transmission to the fetus in utero (Abrams 1987). Between 38% to 67% of women terminated their pregnancies after learning they were seropositive (Schleifer et al. 1991). Also, PSUD is associated with increased physical abuse of the mother and fetus. These children continue to be at high risk after birth for abuse and neglect (Zuckerman and Bresnahan 1991).

## Prevention Intervention

Substance use declined voluntarily and substantially among a segment of pregnant adolescents (Gilchrist et al. 1990). Moss and Hensleigh (1988) reported that most substance use ceased after 12–16 weeks of pregnancy among Hispanic and white pregnant adolescents. Among the group who persisted in substance use, continued use was found to positively correlate with high stress, lack of social support, and parental substance use. However, these factors were independent of ethnicity, thus suggesting that ethnicity-dependent intervention may not be efficient (Moss and Hensleigh 1988). The implications of this study are that a supportive environment such as the inclusion of social network members in pregnancy care of adolescents contributes significantly to the self-care behavior of the pregnant adolescent, which also influences perinatal outcome.

If prevention of continued substance abuse during pregnancy fails, the need for continued follow-up of the mother and child after delivery intensifies. Mothers who did not attend prenatal clinics, and who are being diagnosed as substance abusers during the hospitalization for delivery, are also at high risk for dropout from follow-up. The age, ethnicity, and marital status of the mother; the type of drug used during pregnancy; and the length, number, and type of addiction problems are not significantly different between dropouts and active participants in pediatric clinic for substance abuse mothers. Dropouts were different in many aspects, including lack of prenatal care and no previous children at home at the time of the present birth (Chan et al. 1986). The dropouts' newborns were found to have lower birth weight and shorter gestation. The relatively positive outcome of children whose mothers remained in the research/ intervention programs underscores the importance of multifaceted interventions that are not limited to drug treatment (Zuckerman and Frank 1992).

It is important to point out that the most dysfunctional families/mothers may fail to return for follow-up, leading to bias toward retaining children with more favorable outcome. Even among children exposed in utero to opioids or cocaine, the quality of the postnatal environment in the form of mothers' participation in programs appears to be crucial for developmental outcome (Chasnoff et al. 1992; Lifschitz et al. 1985).

Children born to adolescent mothers are at higher risk than those born to adult mothers. Physical health, and cognitive, emotional, and behavioral effects are the most affected (Hechtman 1989). Therefore, the National Commission on Infant Mortality recommends the provision of services in a model of "one-stop shopping" for all services rendered especially to the segment who live in poverty (Zuckerman and Frank 1992). This plan provides substance abuse treatment, health care, family planning, parental skills training, and other services to the mother-child dyad and to other children in the family. Incentives for compliance with appointments are provided (e.g., food, clothing, laundry services) to improve the chances of the family to maximize the benefits of the service.

A special emphasis on psychopharmacological treatment to the mother-child dyad is needed in maternal opioid dependence. Maintenance with low dosages of methadone during pregnancy is recommended in order to reduce infant morbidity and mortality (Connaughton et al. 1977). Witmann and Segal (1991) recommended split-dose methadone to single dose during pregnancy based on fetal distress in ultrasound evaluation. Infants born to mothers addicted especially (although not exclusively) to opioids, barbiturates, and tranquilizers should be considered at high risk during the withdrawal period and therefore should be cared for in an intensive care nursery. Finnegan (1986), who developed a NAS scoring system of neonatal behavior, suggests that when pharmacologic intervention is recommended, the treatment of choice is paregoric (tincture of opium) or phenobarbital.

Treatment can best be summarized by Zuckerman and Frank (1992), who stated the following:

> [P]renatal drug exposure should be conceptualized as one of multiple treatable or preventable biologic and social stressors experienced mainly by children living in poverty. By focus-

ing on cocaine (as an example) and not on lack of adequate nutrition, health care, and education, we conveniently can blame mothers and not the conditions of poverty. Prenatal care coordinated with drug treatment and postnatally for other needed services exemplifies the need for programs for the whole child and the whole family (p. 338).

It is generally recognized that competent care of the child born to a mother who abused psychoactive substances can improve developmental outcome.

Finally, criminal charges against women abusing drugs during pregnancy is not a solution. More treatment facilities for adolescent mothers, pregnant women, and their offspring are needed. Failing to develop them will result in more women avoiding possible treatment due to fear of prosecution and consequential increases in morbidity of mothers and infants.

## ▼ CONCLUSION

The prevention and treatment of CAPSUD is still underdeveloped and constitutes a challenge for clinicians and researchers. Improved awareness and understanding of the magnitude of the problem is the first step.

More resources and an increased number of training programs to develop prevention and treatment specialists are needed.

It is also noteworthy to caution politicians and other influential community leaders who may draw an erroneous conclusion that CASU and CAPSUD are decreasing and that the "War on Drugs" is being won. The simplistic shotgun approach, in the form of the slogan "Say No to Drugs," ignores the complexity of the problem and especially the existence of high-risk groups for CAPSUD. Diversity and not reduction of resources for continued research of the needs of various child and adolescent subpopulations for prevention services and treatment should be continued.

Continued research on the biopsychosocial aspects of high-risk behaviors (substance use and PSUD included) is warranted, and improved individualized prevention intervention and treatment programs are a necessity. Other areas to be explored include program design, treatment variable strength, patient-treatment matching, treatment outcome research, and aftercare assessment.

Improved design of controlled prospective studies can be invaluable in designing effective intervention programs for these youngsters.

## ▼ REFERENCES

Abrams E: New York City Collaborative Study Group of Maternal Transmission of Human Immunodeficiency Virus: Longitudinal Study of Infants Born to Women at Risk of AIDS; One Year Report. Paper presented at the 27th Interscience Conference on Antimicrobial Agents and Chemotherapy, New York, 1987

American Psychiatric Association: Diagnostic and Statistical Manual of Mental Disorders, 3rd Edition. Washington, DC, American Psychiatric Association, 1980

American Psychiatric Association: Diagnostic and Statistical Manual of Mental Disorders, 3rd Edition, Revised. Washington, DC, American Psychiatric Association, 1987

American Psychiatric Association: Diagnostic and Statistical Manual of Mental Disorders, 4th Edition. Washington, DC, American Psychiatric Association, 1994

Amini F, Zilberg NJ, Burke EL, et al: A controlled study of inpatient vs outpatient treatment of delinquent drug abusing adolescents: one year results. Compr Psychiatry 23:436–444, 1982

Aneshensel CS, Huba GJ: Depression, alcohol use and smoking over one year: a four wave longitudinal causal model. J Abnorm Psychol 92:134–150, 1983

Annis HM: A relapse prevention model for treatment of alcoholics, in Treating Addictive Behaviors: Processes of Change. Edited by Miller WR, Heather NH. New York, Plenum, 1986, pp 407–434

Bandura A: Social Learning Theory. Englewood Cliffs, NJ, Prentice-Hall, 1977

Benson G: Course and outcome of drug abuse and medical and social condition in selected young drug abusers. Acta Psychiatr Scand 71:48–66, 1985

Beschner G: The problem of adolescent drug abuse: an introduction to intervention strategies, in Treatment Services for Adolescent Substance Abusers (NIDA-DHHS Publ No ADM-85-1342). Edited by Friedman AS, Beschner GM. Washington, DC, U.S. Department of Health and Human Services, 1985, pp 1–12

Botvin G, Baker E, Renick N, et al: A cognitive behavioral approach to substance abuse prevention. Addict Behav 9:137–147, 1984

Botvin G, Baker E, Filazzola A, et al: A cognitive behavioral approach to substance abuse prevention: one year follow-up. Addict Behav 15:47–63, 1990

Bukstein OG, Brent DA, Kaminer Y: Comorbidity of substance abuse and other psychiatric disorders in adolescents. Am J Psychiatry 146:1131–1141, 1989

Buydens-Branchey L, Branchey MH, Noumair D: Age of alcoholism onset; I: relations to psychopathology. Arch Gen Psychiatry 46:225–230, 1989

Chan LS, Wingert WA, Wachsman L, et al: Differences between dropouts and active participants in a pediatric clinic for substance abuse mothers. Am J Drug Alcohol Abuse 12:89–99, 1986

Chasnoff IJ: Drug use in pregnancy: parameters of risk. Pediatr Clin North Am 35:1403–1412, 1988

Chasnoff IJ: Drug use and women: establishing a standard of care. Ann N Y Acad Sci 562:208–210, 1989

Chasnoff IJ, Griffith DR, Freier C, et al: Cocaine/polydrug use in pregnancy: two-year follow-up. Pediatrics 89:284–289, 1992

Chavez GF, Mulinare J, Cordero JF: Maternal cocaine use during early pregnancy as a risk factor for congenital urogenital anomalies. JAMA 262:795–798, 1989

Christie KA, Burke JD, Regier DA, et al: Epidemiologic evidence for early onset of mental disorders and higher risk of drug abuse in young adults. Am J Psychiatry 145:971–975, 1988

Cloninger CR, Bohman M, Sigvardsson S: Inheritance of alcohol abuse. Arch Gen Psychiatry 38:861–871, 1981

Coate D, Grossman N: Change in alcoholic beverage prices and legal drinking age. Alcohol Health Research World Fall 11:22–25, 1987

Connaughton JF, Reeser D, Schut J, et al: Perinatal addiction: outcome and management. Am J Obstet Gynecol 129:679–686, 1977

Costello A, Edelbrock C, Costello AJ: Validity of the NIMH Diagnostic Interview Schedule for Children: a comparison between pediatric and psychiatric referrals. J Abnorm Child Psychol 13:579–595, 1985

Des Jarlais DC, Friedman S: HIV infection among intravenous drug users: epidemiology and risk reduction. AIDS 1:67–76, 1987

DeJong R, Henrich G: Follow-up results of a behavior modification program for juvenile drug addicts. Addict Behav 5:49–57, 1980

De Leon G, Schwartz S: Circumstances, motivation, readiness and suitability as correlates of treatment tenure. J Psychoactive Drugs 18:203–208, 1984

Donovan JE, Jessor R: Structure of problem behavior in adolescence and young adulthood. J Consult Clin Psychol 53:890–904, 1985

Ellickson PL, Bell RM: Drug prevention in junior high: a multi-site longitudinal test. Science 247:1299–1305, 1990

Erikson EH: Identity: Youth and Crisis. New York, Plenum, 1968

Finnegan LP: Neonatal abstinence syndrome: assessment and pharmacotherapy, in Neonatal Therapy: An Update. Edited by Rubaltelli FF, Granati B. New York, Elsevier, 1986, pp 122–146

Flay BR: Psychosocial approaches to smoking prevention: a review of findings. Health Psychol 4:449–488, 1985

Friedman AS, Glickman NW: Program characteristics for successful treatment of adolescent drug abuse. J Nerv Ment Dis 174:669–679, 1986

Friedman AS, Glickman NW: Effects of psychiatric symptomatology on treatment outcome for adolescent male drug abusers. J Nerv Ment Dis 175:425–430, 1987

Friedman AS, Schwartz R, Utada A: Outcome of a unique youth drug abuse program: a follow-up study of clients of Straight, Inc. J Subst Abuse Treat 6:259–268, 1989

Gilchrist LD, Gillmore MR, Lohr MJ: Drug use among pregnant adolescents. J Consult Clin Psychol 58:402–407, 1990

Goodstadt MS: Drug education: a turn on or a turn off? J Drug Educ 10:89–99, 1980

Gould MS, Shaffer D, Kaplan D: The characteristics of dropouts from a child psychiatry clinic. Journal of the American Academy of Child Psychiatry 24:316–328, 1985

Grenier C: Treatment effectiveness in an adolescent chemical dependency treatment program: a quasi-experimental design. Int J Addict 20:381–391, 1985

Hasin DS, Grant B, Endicott J: The natural history of alcohol abuse implications for definitions of alcohol use disorders. Am J Psychiatry 147:337–341, 1990

Hayashida M, Alterman AI, McLellan AT, et al: Comparative effectiveness and costs of inpatient and outpatient detoxification of patients with mild to moderate alcohol withdrawal syndrome. N Engl J Med 320:358–365, 1989

Hechtman L: Teenage mothers and their children: risks and problems. Can J Psychiatry 34:569–575, 1989

Helzer JE, Pryzbeck TR: The co-occurrence of alcoholism with other psychiatric disorders in the general population and its impact on treatment. J Stud Alcohol 49:219–224, 1988

Hester RK, Miller WR: Empirical guidelines for optimal client-treatment matching, in Adolescent Drug Abuse: Analyses of Treatment Research (NIDA Res Monogr No 77). Edited by Rahdert E, Grabowski J. Washington, DC, U.S. Department of Health and Human Services, 1988, pp 27–39

Holden C: Is alcoholism treatment effective? Science 236:20–22, 1987

Holsten F: Repeat follow-up studies of 100 young Norwegian drug abusers. Journal of Drug Issues 10: 491–504, 1980

Hoyme HE, Jones KL, Dixson SD, et al: Prenatal cocaine exposure and fetal vascular disruption. Pediatrics 85:743–747, 1990

Hubbard RL, Cavanough ER, Craddock SG, et al: Characteristics, behaviors, and outcomes for youth in the TOPS, in Treatment Services for Adolescent Substance Abusers (NIDA-DHHS Publ No ADM-85-1342). Edited by Friedman AS, Beschner GM. Washington, DC, U.S. Department of Health and Human Services, 1985, pp 49–65

Jaffe HW, Bregman DJ, Selik RM: AIDS in the US: the first 100 cases. J Infect Dis 148:339–345, 1983

Jessor R, Jessor SL: Problem Behavior and Psychosocial Development: A Longitudinal Study of Youth. New York, Academic Press, 1977

Johnston L, Bachman JG, O'Malley PM: National trends in drug use and related factors among American high school students and young adults 1975–1986 (NIDA-DHHS Publ No ADM-87-1587). Washington, DC, U.S. Department of Health and Human Services, 1987

Johnston L, Bachman JG, O'Malley PM: Details of Annual Drug Survey. Ann Arbor, MI, University of Michigan News Information Services, January 1992

Kaminer Y: Adolescent substance abuse, in Clinical Textbook of Addictive Disorders. Edited by Frances RJ, Miller SI. New York, Guilford, 1991a, pp 320–346

Kaminer Y: The magnitude of concurrent psychiatric

disorders in hospitalized substance abusing adolescents. Child Psychiatry Hum Dev 22:89–95, 1991b

Kaminer Y: Clinical implications of the relationship between attention-deficit hyperactivity disorder and psychoactive substance use disorders. American Journal on Addictions 1:257–264, 1992a

Kaminer Y: Desipramine facilitation of cocaine abstinence in an adolescent. J Am Acad Child Adolesc Psychiatry 31:312–317, 1992b

Kaminer Y: Psychoactive substance abuse and dependence as a risk factor in adolescent-attempted and -completed suicide: a review. American Journal on Addictions 1:21–29, 1992c

Kaminer Y: Understanding and Treating Adolescent Substance Abuse. New York, Plenum, 1994

Kaminer Y, Bukstein OG: Adolescent chemical use and dependence: current issues in epidemiology, treatment and prevention. Acta Psychiatr Scand 79:415–424, 1989

Kaminer Y, Bukstein OG: Inpatient behavioral and cognitive therapy for substance abuse in adolescents, in Inpatient Behavior Therapy for Children and Adolescents. Edited by Van Hasselt VB, Kolko DJ. New York, Plenum, 1992, pp 313–339

Kaminer Y, Frances RJ: Inpatient treatment of adolescents with psychiatric and substance abuse disorders. Hosp Community Psychiatry 42:894–896, 1991

Kaminer Y, Bukstein OG, Tarter RE: The Teen Addiction Severity Index (T-ASI): Rationale and Reliability. Int J Addict 26:219–226, 1991

Kaminer Y, Tarter RE, Bukstein OG, et al: Comparison between completers and non-completers among dually diagnosed substance abusing adolescents. J Am Acad Child Adolesc Psychiatry 31: 1046–1049, 1992a

Kaminer Y, Tarter RE, Bukstein OG, et al: Adolescent substance abuse treatment: staff, treatment completers', and noncompleters' perception of the value of treatment variables. American Journal on Addictions 1:115–120, 1992b

Kaminer Y, Wagner E, Plummer B, et al: Validation of the Teen Addiction Severity Index (T-ASI): preliminary findings. American Journal on Addictions 2:250–254, 1993

Kandel DB: Epidemiological and psychosocial perspective on adolescent drug use. Journal of the American Academy of Child Psychiatry 21:328–347, 1982

Kashani JH, Keller MB, Solomon N, et al: Double depression in adolescent substance users. J Affect Disord 8:153–157, 1985

Keller MB, Lavori PW, Beardslee W, et al: The clinical course and outcome of substance abuse disorders in adolescents. J Subst Abuse Treat 9:9–14, 1992

Khantzian EJ, Halliday KS, Golden S, et al: Modified group therapy for substance abusers: a psychodynamic approach to relapse prevention. American Journal on Addictions 1:67–76, 1992

Kusnetz S: An overview of selected adolescent substance abuse treatment programs, in Treatment Services for Adolescent Substance Abusers (NIDA-DHHS Publ No ADM-85-1342). Edited by Friedman AS, Beschner GM. Washington, DC, U.S. Department of Health and Human Services, 1985, pp 31–48

Langrod L, Alksne L, Gomez E: A religious approach to the rehabilitation of addicts, in Substance Abuse Clinical Problems and Perspectives. Edited by Lowinson J, Ruiz P. Baltimore, MD, Williams & Wilkins, 1981, pp 408–420

Laundergan JC: Easy Does It. Center City, MN, Hazelden Foundation, 1982

Lawson GW, Lawson AW: Alcoholism and Substance Abuse in Special Populations. Rockville, MD, Aspen, 1989

Lifschitz MH, Wilson GS, Smith EO, et al: Factors affecting head growth and intellectual function in children of drug addicts. Pediatrics 75:269–274, 1985

Mannuzza S, Klein RG, Bonaguran P, et al: Hyperactive boys almost grown up v. replication of psychiatric status. Arch Gen Psychiatry 48:77–83, 1991

Marlatt GA, George WH: Relapse prevention: Introduction and overview of the model. British Journal of Addiction 79:261–275, 1984

Marques PR, McKnight AJ: Drug abuse risk among pregnant adolescents attending public health clinics. Am J Drug Alcohol Abuse 17:399–414, 1991

Mayer J, Filstead WJ: The adolescent alcohol involvement scale. J Stud Alcohol 40:291–300, 1979

McLellan AT, Luborsky L, Woody GE, et al: An improved diagnostic evaluation instrument for substance abuse patients: the Addiction Severity Index. J Nerv Ment Dis 168:26–33, 1980

Monti PM, Abrams DB, Kadden RM, et al: Treating Alcohol Dependence: A Coping Skills Training Guide. New York, Guilford, 1989

Moss N, Hensleigh PA: Substance use by Hispanic and white non-Hispanic pregnant adolescents: a pre-liminary survey. Journal of Youth and Adolescence 17:531–541, 1988

Nathan PE: Integration of biological and psychosocial research on alcoholism. Alcohol Clin Exp Res 14:368–374, 1990

Newcomb MD, Bentler PM: Consequences of Adolescent Drug Use: Impact on the Lives of Young Adults. Newbury Park, CA, Sage, 1988

Newcomb MD, Bentler PM: Substance use and abuse among children and teenagers. Am Psychol 44:242–248, 1989

Oetting ER, Beauvais F: Epidemiology and correlates of alcohol use among Indian adolescents living on reservations, in Epidemiology of Alcohol Use and Abuse Among US Ethnic Minorities (NIAAA Publ No ADM-89-1435). Washington, DC, U.S. Department of Health and Human Services, 1989 pp 323–373

Oetting ER, Beauvais F, Edwards RV, et al: The Drug and Alcohol Assessment System. Fort Collins, CO, Rocky Mountain Behavioral Sciences Institute, 1984

Orvaschel H, Puig-Antich J, Chambers W, et al: Retrospective assessment of prepubertal major depression with the Kiddie-SADS-E. J Am Acad Child Psychiatry 21:392–397, 1982

Pentz MA, Dwyer JH, MacKinnon DP, et al: A multicommunity trial for primary prevention of adolescent drug abuse. JAMA 261:3259–3266, 1989

Piaget J: The Moral Judgment of the Child. New York, Collier, 1962

Riley K, Klockars AJ: A critical reexamination of the Adolescent Alcohol Involvement Scale. J Stud Alcohol 45:184–187, 1984

Rush TV: Predicting treatment outcome for juvenile and young adult clients in the Pennsylvania substance abuse system, in Youth Drug Abuse: Problems, Issues, and Treatment. Edited by Beschner GM, Friedman AS. Lexington, MA, Lexington Books, 1979, pp 629–656

Schaps E, Moskowitz J, Malvin J, et al: Evaluation of seven-school based prevention programs: a final report on the Napa project. Int J Addict 21:1081–1112, 1986

Schinke SP, Gilchrist LD: Primary prevention of tobacco smoking. J Sch Health 53:416–419, 1983

Schinke SP, Botvin GJ, Orlani MA: Substance Abuse in Children and Adolescent: Evaluation and Intervention. Newbury Park, CA, Sage, 1991

Schleifer SJ, Delaney BR, Tross S, et al: AIDS and addictions, in Clinical Textbook of Addictive Disorders. Edited by Frances RJ, Miller SI. New York, Guilford, 1991, pp 299–319

Schuckit MA, Zisook S, Mortola J: Clinical implications of DSM-III diagnoses of alcohol abuse and alcohol dependence. Am J Psychiatry 142:1403–1404, 1985

Sells SB, Simpson DD: Evaluation of treatment outcome for youths in the drug abuse reporting program (DARP): a follow-up study, in Youth Drug Abuse: Problems, Issues, and Treatment. Edited by Beschner GM, Friedman AS. Lexington, MA, Lexington Books, 1979, pp 571–628

Semlitz L, Gold MS: Adolescent drug use: diagnosis, treatment, and prevention. Psychiatr Clin North Am 9:455–473, 1986

Serdula M, Williamson DF, Kendrick JS, et al: Trends in alcohol consumption by pregnant women 1985 through 1988. JAMA 265:876–879, 1991

Shedler J, Block J: Adolescent drug use and psychological health. Am Psychol 45:612–630, 1990

Simpson DD: Relation of time spent in drug abuse treatment to treatment outcome. Am J Psychiatry 136:1449–1453, 1979

Swisher JD: Prevention issues, in Handbook On Drug Abuse. Edited by Dupont RL, Goldstein A, O'Donnell J. Rockville, MD, National Institute on Drug Abuse, 1979, pp 49–62

Swisher JD, Hu TW: Alternatives to drug abuse: some are and some are not, in Preventing Adolescent Drug Abuse: Intervention Strategies (NIDA-DHHS Publ No ADM-83-1280). Edited by Glynn TS, Leukefeld CG, Ludford JP. Washington, DC, U.S. Department of Health and Human Services, 1983

Szapocznik J, Kurtines WM, Foote F, et al: Conjoint versus one person family therapy: some evidence for the effectiveness of conducting family therapy through one person. J Consult Clin Psychol 51:881–889, 1983

Tanaka JS, Huba GJ: Confirmatory hierarchical factor analysis of psychological distress measures. J Pers Soc Psychol 46:621–635, 1989

Tarter RE: Evaluation and treatment of adolescent substance abuse: a decision tree method. Am J Drug Alcohol Abuse 16:1–46, 1990

Tarter RE: Prevention of drug abuse: theory and application. American Journal on Addictions 1:2–20, 1992

Tobler NS: Meta-analysis of 143 adolescent drug prevention programs: quantitive outcome results of program participants compared to a control or comparison group. Journal of Drug Issues 16:537–567, 1986

Tubman JG, Vicary JR, Von-Eye A, et al: Qualitative changes in relationships between substance use and adjustment during adolescence. J Subst Abuse 3:405–414, 1991

Vaglum P, Fossheim I: Differential treatment of young abusers: A quasi-experimental study of a therapeutic community in a psychiatric hospital. Journal of Drug Issues 10:505–516, 1980

Walter HJ, Vaughan RD, Cohall AT: Risk factors for substance use among high school students: implications for prevention. J Am Acad Child Adolesc Psychiatry 30:556–562, 1991

Wellner Z, Reich W, Herjanic B, et al: Reliability, validity and parent-child agreement studies of the Diagnostic Interview for Children and Adolescents (DICA). J Am Acad Child Adolesc Psychiatry 26:649–653, 1987

Winters K, Henly G: Personal Experience Inventory Test and Manual. Los Angeles, CA, Western Psychological Services, 1988

Witmann BK, Segal S: A comparison of the effects of single and split methadone administration of the fetus: ultrasound evaluation. Int J Addict 26:213–218, 1991

Zuckerman B, Bresnahan K: Developmental behavioral consequences of prenatal drug and alcohol exposure. Pediatr Clin North Am 38:1387–1406, 1991

Zuckerman B, Frank DA: "Crack kids": not broken. Pediatrics 89:337–339, 1992

# iagnostic Criteria for Substance-Related Disorders From DSM-IV

## ▼ CRITERIA FOR SUBSTANCE DEPENDENCE

A maladaptive pattern of substance use, leading to clinically significant impairment or distress, as manifested by three (or more) of the following, occurring at any time in the same 12-month period:

(1) tolerance, as defined by either of the following:
    (a) a need for markedly increased amounts of the substance to achieve intoxication or desired effect
    (b) markedly diminished effect with continued use of the same amount of the substance

(2) withdrawal, as manifested by either of the following:
    (a) the characteristic withdrawal syndrome for the substance (refer to Criteria A and B of the criteria sets for Withdrawal from the specific substances)
    (b) the same (or a closely related) substance is taken to relieve or avoid withdrawal symptoms

(3) the substance is often taken in larger amounts or over a longer period than was intended

(4) there is a persistent desire or unsuccessful efforts to cut down or control substance use

(5) a great deal of time is spent in activities necessary to obtain the substance (e.g., visiting multiple doctors or driving long distances), use the substance (e.g., chain-smoking), or recover from its effects

(6) important social, occupational, or recreational activities are given up or reduced because of substance use

(7) the substance use is continued despite knowledge of having a persistent or recurrent physical or psychological problem that is likely to have been caused or exacerbated by the substance (e.g., current cocaine use despite recognition of cocaine-induced depression, or continued drinking despite recognition that an ulcer was made worse by alcohol consumption)

*Specify* if:
**With Physiological Dependence:** evidence of tolerance or withdrawal (i.e., either Item 1 or 2 is present)

**Without Physiological Dependence:** no evidence of tolerance or withdrawal (i.e., neither Item 1 nor 2 is present)

*Course specifiers* (see text for definitions):
**Early Full Remission**
**Early Partial Remission**
**Sustained Full Remission**
**Sustained Partial Remission**
**On Agonist Therapy**
**In a Controlled Environment**

## ▼ CRITERIA FOR SUBSTANCE ABUSE

A. A maladaptive pattern of substance use leading to clinically significant impairment or distress, as manifested by one (or more) of the following, occurring within a 12-month period:

(1) recurrent substance use resulting in a failure to fulfill major role obligations at work, school, or home (e.g., repeated absences or poor work performance related to substance use; substance-related absences, suspensions, or expulsions from school; neglect of children or household)

(2) recurrent substance use in situations in which it is physically hazardous (e.g., driving an automobile or operating a machine when impaired by substance use)

(3) recurrent substance-related legal problems (e.g., arrests for substance-related disorderly conduct)

(4) continued substance use despite having persistent or recurrent social or interpersonal problems caused or exacerbated by the effects of the substance (e.g., arguments with spouse about consequences of intoxication, physical fights)

B. The symptoms have never met the criteria for Substance Dependence for this class of substance.

## ▼ CRITERIA FOR SUBSTANCE INTOXICATION

A. The development of a reversible substance-specific syndrome due to recent ingestion of (or exposure to) a substance. **Note:** Different substances may produce similar or identical syndromes.

B. Clinically significant maladaptive behavioral or psychological changes that are due to the effect of the substance on the central nervous system (e.g., belligerence, mood lability, cognitive impairment, impaired judgment, impaired social or occupational functioning) and develop during or shortly after use of the substance.

C. The symptoms are not due to a general medical condition and are not better accounted for by another mental disorder.

## ▼ CRITERIA FOR SUBSTANCE WITHDRAWAL

A. The development of a substance-specific syndrome due to the cessation of (or reduction in) substance use that has been heavy and prolonged.

B. The substance-specific syndrome causes clinically significant distress or impairment in social, occupational, or other important areas of functioning.

C. The symptoms are not due to a general medical condition and are not better accounted for by another mental disorder.

## ▼ DIAGNOSTIC CRITERIA FOR 303.00 ALCOHOL INTOXICATION

A. Recent ingestion of alcohol.

B. Clinically significant maladaptive behavioral or psychological changes (e.g., inappropriate sexual or aggressive behavior, mood lability, impaired judgment, impaired social or occupational functioning) that developed during, or shortly after, alcohol ingestion.

C. One (or more) of the following signs, developing during, or shortly after, alcohol use:

(1) slurred speech

(2) incoordination

(3) unsteady gait

(4) nystagmus

(5) impairment in attention or memory

(6) stupor or coma

D.  The symptoms are not due to a general medical condition and are not better accounted for by another mental disorder.

## ▼ DIAGNOSTIC CRITERIA FOR 291.8 ALCOHOL WITHDRAWAL

A.  Cessation of (or reduction in) alcohol use that has been heavy and prolonged.

B.  Two (or more) of the following, developing within several hours to a few days after Criterion A:

(1) autonomic hyperactivity (e.g., sweating or pulse rate greater than 100)

(2) increased hand tremor

(3) insomnia

(4) nausea or vomiting

(5) transient visual, tactile, or auditory hallucinations or illusions

(6) psychomotor agitation

(7) anxiety

(8) grand mal seizures

C.  The symptoms in Criterion B cause clinically significant distress or impairment in social, occupational, or other important areas of functioning.

D.  The symptoms are not due to a general medical condition and are not better accounted for by another mental disorder.

*Specify* if:
**With Perceptual Disturbances**

## ▼ DIAGNOSTIC CRITERIA FOR 292.89 AMPHETAMINE INTOXICATION

A.  Recent use of amphetamine or a related substance (e.g., methylphenidate).

B.  Clinically significant maladaptive behavioral or psychological changes (e.g., euphoria or affective blunting; changes in sociability; hypervigilance; interpersonal sensitivity; anxiety, tension, or anger; stereotyped behaviors; impaired judgment; or impaired social or occupational functioning) that developed during, or shortly after, use of amphetamine or a related substance.

C.  Two (or more) of the following, developing during, or shortly after, use of amphetamine or a related substance:

(1) tachycardia or bradycardia

(2) pupillary dilation

(3) elevated or lowered blood pressure

(4) perspiration or chills

(5) nausea or vomiting

(6) evidence of weight loss

(7) psychomotor agitation or retardation

(8) muscular weakness, respiratory depression, chest pain, or cardiac arrhythmias

(9) confusion, seizures, dyskinesias, dystonias, or coma

D.  The symptoms are not due to a general medical condition and are not better accounted for by another mental disorder.

*Specify* if:
**With Perceptual Disturbances**

## ▼ DIAGNOSTIC CRITERIA FOR 292.0 AMPHETAMINE WITHDRAWAL

A.  Cessation of (or reduction in) amphetamine (or a related substance) use that has been heavy and prolonged.

B.  Dysphoric mood and two (or more) of the following physiological changes, developing within a few hours to several days after Criterion A:

(1) fatigue
(2) vivid, unpleasant dreams
(3) insomnia or hypersomnia
(4) increased appetite
(5) psychomotor retardation or agitation

C. The symptoms in Criterion B cause clinically significant distress or impairment in social, occupational, or other important areas of functioning.

D. The symptoms are not due to a general medical condition and are not better accounted for by another mental disorder.

## ▼ DIAGNOSTIC CRITERIA FOR 305.90 CAFFEINE INTOXICATION

A. Recent consumption of caffeine, usually in excess of 250 mg (e.g., more than 2–3 cups of brewed coffee).

B. Five (or more) of the following signs, developing during, or shortly after, caffeine use:
(1) restlessness
(2) nervousness
(3) excitement
(4) insomnia
(5) flushed face
(6) diuresis
(7) gastrointestinal disturbance
(8) muscle twitching
(9) rambling flow of thought and speech
(10) tachycardia or cardiac arrhythmia
(11) periods of inexhaustibility
(12) psychomotor agitation

C. The symptoms in Criterion B cause clinically significant distress or impairment in social, occupational, or other important areas of functioning.

D. The symptoms are not due to a general medical condition and are not better accounted for by another mental disorder (e.g., an Anxiety Disorder).

## ▼ DIAGNOSTIC CRITERIA FOR 292.89 CANNABIS INTOXICATION

A. Recent use of cannabis.

B. Clinically significant maladaptive behavioral or psychological changes (e.g., impaired motor coordination, euphoria, anxiety, sensation of slowed time, impaired judgment, social withdrawal) that developed during, or shortly after, cannabis use.

C. Two (or more) of the following signs, developing within 2 hours of cannabis use:
(1) conjunctival injection
(2) increased appetite
(3) dry mouth
(4) tachycardia

D. The symptoms are not due to a general medical condition and are not better accounted for by another mental disorder.

*Specify* if:
**With Perceptual Disturbances**

## ▼ DIAGNOSTIC CRITERIA FOR 292.89 COCAINE INTOXICATION

A. Recent use of cocaine.

B. Clinically significant maladaptive behavioral or psychological changes (e.g., euphoria or affective blunting; changes in sociability; hypervigilance; interpersonal sensitivity; anxiety, tension, or anger; stereotyped behaviors; impaired judgment; or impaired social or occupational functioning) that developed during, or shortly after, use of cocaine.

C. Two (or more) of the following, developing during, or shortly after, cocaine use:
(1) tachycardia or bradycardia
(2) pupillary dilation
(3) elevated or lowered blood pressure
(4) perspiration or chills
(5) nausea or vomiting
(6) evidence of weight loss

(7) psychomotor agitation or retardation

(8) muscular weakness, respiratory depression, chest pain, or cardiac arrhythmias

(9) confusion, seizures, dyskinesias, dystonias, or coma

D. The symptoms are not due to a general medical condition and are not better accounted for by another mental disorder.

*Specify* if:
**With Perceptual Disturbances**

## ▼ DIAGNOSTIC CRITERIA FOR 292.0 COCAINE WITHDRAWAL

A. Cessation of (or reduction in) cocaine use that has been heavy and prolonged.

B. Dysphoric mood and two (or more) of the following physiological changes, developing within a few hours to several days after Criterion A:

(1) fatigue
(2) vivid, unpleasant dreams
(3) insomnia or hypersomnia
(4) increased appetite
(5) psychomotor retardation or agitation

C. The symptoms in Criterion B cause clinically significant distress or impairment in social, occupational, or other important areas of functioning.

D. The symptoms are not due to a general medical condition and are not better accounted for by another mental disorder.

## ▼ DIAGNOSTIC CRITERIA FOR 292.89 HALLUCINOGEN INTOXICATION

A. Recent use of a hallucinogen.

B. Clinically significant maladaptive behavioral or psychological changes (e.g., marked anxiety or depression, ideas of reference, fear of losing one's mind, paranoid ideation, impaired judgment, or impaired social or occupational functioning) that developed during, or shortly after, hallucinogen use.

C. Perceptual changes occurring in a state of full wakefulness and alertness (e.g., subjective intensification of perceptions, depersonalization, derealization, illusions, hallucinations, synesthesias) that developed during, or shortly after, hallucinogen use.

D. Two (or more) of the following signs, developing during, or shortly after, hallucinogen use:

(1) pupillary dilation
(2) tachycardia
(3) sweating
(4) palpitations
(5) blurring of vision
(6) tremors
(7) incoordination

E. The symptoms are not due to a general medical condition and are not better accounted for by another mental disorder.

## ▼ DIAGNOSTIC CRITERIA FOR 292.89 HALLUCINOGEN PERSISTING PERCEPTION DISORDER (FLASHBACKS)

A. The reexperiencing, following cessation of use of a hallucinogen, of one or more of the perceptual symptoms that were experienced while intoxicated with the hallucinogen (e.g., geometric hallucinations, false perceptions of movement in the peripheral visual fields, flashes of color, intensified colors, trails of images of moving objects, positive afterimages, halos around objects, macropsia, and micropsia).

B. The symptoms in Criterion A cause clinically significant distress or impairment in social, occupational, or other important areas of functioning.

C. The symptoms are not due to a general medical condition (e.g., anatomical lesions and infections of the brain, visual epilepsies) and are not better accounted for by another mental disorder (e.g., delirium, dementia, Schizophrenia) or hypnopompic hallucinations.

## ▼ DIAGNOSTIC CRITERIA FOR 292.89 INHALANT INTOXICATION

A. Recent intentional use or short-term, high-dose exposure to volatile inhalants (excluding anesthetic gases and short-acting vasodilators).

B. Clinically significant maladaptive behavioral or psychological changes (e.g., belligerence, assaultiveness, apathy, impaired judgment, impaired social or occupational functioning) that developed during, or shortly after, use of or exposure to volatile inhalants.

C. Two (or more) of the following signs, developing during, or shortly after, inhalant use or exposure:

    (1) dizziness
    (2) nystagmus
    (3) incoordination
    (4) slurred speech
    (5) unsteady gait
    (6) lethargy
    (7) depressed reflexes
    (8) psychomotor retardation
    (9) tremor
    (10) generalized muscle weakness
    (11) blurred vision or diplopia
    (12) stupor or coma
    (13) euphoria

D. The symptoms are not due to a general medical condition and are not better accounted for by another mental disorder.

## ▼ DIAGNOSTIC CRITERIA FOR 292.0 NICOTINE WITHDRAWAL

A. Daily use of nicotine for at least several weeks.

B. Abrupt cessation of nicotine use, or reduction in the amount of nicotine used, followed within 24 hours by four (or more) of the following signs:

    (1) dysphoric or depressed mood
    (2) insomnia
    (3) irritability, frustration, or anger
    (4) anxiety
    (5) difficulty concentrating
    (6) restlessness
    (7) decreased heart rate
    (8) increased appetite or weight gain

C. The symptoms in Criterion B cause clinically significant distress or impairment in social, occupational, or other important areas of functioning.

D. The symptoms are not due to a general medical condition and are not better accounted for by another mental disorder.

## ▼ DIAGNOSTIC CRITERIA FOR 292.89 OPIOID INTOXICATION

A. Recent use of an opioid.

B. Clinically significant maladaptive behavioral or psychological changes (e.g., initial euphoria followed by apathy, dysphoria, psychomotor agitation or retardation, impaired judgment, or impaired social or occupational functioning) that developed during, or shortly after, opioid use.

C. Pupillary constriction (or pupillary dilation due to anoxia from severe overdose) and one (or more) of the following signs, developing during, or shortly after, opioid use:

    (1) drowsiness or coma
    (2) slurred speech
    (3) impairment in attention or memory

D. The symptoms are not due to a general medical condition and are not better accounted for by another mental disorder.

*Specify* if:
**With Perceptual Disturbances**

## ▼ DIAGNOSTIC CRITERIA FOR 292.0 OPIOID WITHDRAWAL

A. Either of the following:

(1) cessation of (or reduction in) opioid use that has been heavy and prolonged (several weeks or longer)

(2) administration of an opioid antagonist after a period of opioid use

B. Three (or more) of the following, developing within minutes to several days after Criterion A:

(1) dysphoric mood
(2) nausea or vomiting
(3) muscle aches
(4) lacrimation or rhinorrhea
(5) pupillary dilation, piloerection, or sweating
(6) diarrhea
(7) yawning
(8) fever
(9) insomnia

C. The symptoms in Criterion B cause clinically significant distress or impairment in social, occupational, or other important areas of functioning.

D. The symptoms are not due to a general medical condition and are not better accounted for by another mental disorder.

## ▼ DIAGNOSTIC CRITERIA FOR 292.89 PHENCYCLIDINE INTOXICATION

A. Recent use of phencyclidine (or a related substance).

B. Clinically significant maladaptive behavioral changes (e.g., belligerence, assaultiveness, impulsiveness, unpredictability, psychomotor agitation, impaired judgment, or impaired social or occupational functioning) that developed during, or shortly after, phencyclidine use.

C. Within an hour (less when smoked, "snorted," or used intravenously), two (or more) of the following signs:

(1) vertical or horizontal nystagmus
(2) hypertension or tachycardia
(3) numbness or diminished responsiveness to pain
(4) ataxia
(5) dysarthria
(6) muscle rigidity
(7) seizures or coma
(8) hyperacusis

D. The symptoms are not due to a general medical condition and are not better accounted for by another mental disorder.

*Specify* if:
**With Perceptual Disturbances**

## ▼ DIAGNOSTIC CRITERIA FOR 292.89 SEDATIVE, HYPNOTIC, OR ANXIOLYTIC INTOXICATION

A. Recent use of a sedative, hypnotic, or anxiolytic.

B. Clinically significant maladaptive behavioral or psychological changes (e.g., inappropriate sexual or aggressive behavior, mood lability, impaired judgment, impaired social or occupational functioning) that developed during, or shortly after, sedative, hypnotic, or anxiolytic use.

C. One (or more) of the following signs, developing during, or shortly after, sedative, hypnotic, or anxiolytic use:

(1) slurred speech
(2) incoordination
(3) unsteady gait
(4) nystagmus
(5) impairment in attention or memory
(6) stupor or coma

D. The symptoms are not due to a general medical condition and are not better accounted for by another mental disorder.

## ▼ DIAGNOSTIC CRITERIA FOR 292.0 SEDATIVE, HYPNOTIC, OR ANXIOLYTIC WITHDRAWAL

A. Cessation of (or reduction in) sedative, hypnotic, or anxiolytic use that has been heavy and prolonged.

B. Two (or more) of the following, developing within several hours to a few days after Criterion A:

(1) autonomic hyperactivity (e.g., sweating or pulse rate
greater than 100)
(2) increased hand tremor
(3) insomnia
(4) nausea or vomiting
(5) transient visual, tactile, or auditory hallucinations or illusions
(6) psychomotor agitation
(7) anxiety
(8) grand mal seizures

C. The symptoms in Criterion B cause clinically significant distress or impairment in social, occupational, or other important areas of functioning.

D. The symptoms are not due to a general medical condition and are not better accounted for by another mental disorder.

*Specify* if:
**With Perceptual Disturbances**

## ▼ DIAGNOSTIC CRITERIA FOR SUBSTANCE INTOXICATION DELIRIUM

A. Disturbance of consciousness (i.e., reduced clarity of awareness of the environment) with reduced ability to focus, sustain, or shift attention.

B. A change in cognition (such as memory deficit, disorientation, language disturbance) or the development of a perceptual disturbance that is not better accounted for by a preexisting, established, or evolving dementia.

C. The disturbance develops over a short period of time (usually hours to days) and tends to fluctuate during the course of the day.

D. There is evidence from the history, physical examination, or laboratory findings of either (1) or (2):

(1) the symptoms in Criteria A and B developed during Substance Intoxication
(2) medication use is etiologically related to the disturbance*

**Note:** This diagnosis should be made instead of a diagnosis of Substance Intoxication only when the cognitive symptoms are in excess of those usually associated with the intoxication syndrome and when the symptoms are sufficiently severe to warrant independent clinical attention.

*\***Note:** The diagnosis should be recorded as Substance-Induced Delirium if related to medication use. Refer to Appendix G for E-codes indicating specific medications.

*Code* [Specific Substance] Intoxication Delirium: (291.0 Alcohol; 292.81 Amphetamine [or Amphetamine-Like Substance]; 292.81 Cannabis; 292.81 Cocaine; 292.81 Hallucinogen; 292.81 Inhalant; 292.81 Opioid; 292.81 Phencyclidine [or Phencyclidine-Like Substance]; 292.81 Sedative, Hypnotic, or Anxiolytic; 292.81 Other [or Unknown] Substance [e.g., cimetidine, digitalis, benztropine])

## ▼ DIAGNOSTIC CRITERIA FOR SUBSTANCE WITHDRAWAL DELIRIUM

A. Disturbance of consciousness (i.e., reduced clarity of awareness of the environment) with reduced ability to focus, sustain, or shift attention.

B. A change in cognition (such as memory deficit, disorientation, language disturbance) or the development of a perceptual disturbance that is not better accounted for by a preexisting, established, or evolving dementia.

C.  The disturbance develops over a short period of time (usually hours to days) and tends to fluctuate during the course of the day.

D.  There is evidence from the history, physical examination, or laboratory findings that the symptoms in Criteria A and B developed during, or shortly after, a withdrawal syndrome.

**Note:**  This diagnosis should be made instead of a diagnosis of Substance Withdrawal only when the cognitive symptoms are in excess of those usually associated with the withdrawal syndrome and when the symptoms are sufficiently severe to warrant independent clinical attention.

*Code* [Specific Substance] Withdrawal Delirium:
(291.0 Alcohol; 292.81 Sedative, Hypnotic, or Anxiolytic; 292.81 Other [or Unknown] Substance)

## ▼ DIAGNOSTIC CRITERIA FOR SUBSTANCE–INDUCED PERSISTING DEMENTIA

A.  The development of multiple cognitive deficits manifested by both

(1) memory impairment (impaired ability to learn new information or to recall previously learned information)
(2) one (or more) of the following cognitive disturbances:
   (a) aphasia (language disturbance)
   (b) apraxia (impaired ability to carry out motor activities despite intact motor function)
   (c) agnosia (failure to recognize or identify objects despite intact sensory function)
   (d) disturbance in executive functioning (i.e., planning, organizing, sequencing, abstracting)

B.  The cognitive deficits in Criteria A1 and A2 each cause significant impairment in social or occupational functioning and represent a significant decline from a previous level of functioning.

C.  The deficits do not occur exclusively during the course of a delirium and persist beyond the usual duration of Substance Intoxication or Withdrawal.

D.  There is evidence from the history, physical examination, or laboratory findings that the deficits are etiologically related to the persisting effects of substance use (e.g., a drug of abuse, a medication).

*Code* [Specific Substance]–Induced Persisting Dementia:
(291.2 Alcohol; 292.82 Inhalant; 292.82 Sedative, Hypnotic, or Anxiolytic; 292.82 Other [or Unknown] Substance)

## ▼ DIAGNOSTIC CRITERIA FOR SUBSTANCE–INDUCED PERSISTING AMNESTIC DISORDER

A.  The development of memory impairment as manifested by impairment in the ability to learn new information or the inability to recall previously learned information.

B.  The memory disturbance causes significant impairment in social or occupational functioning and represents a significant decline from a previous level of functioning.

C.  The memory disturbance does not occur exclusively during the course of a delirium or a dementia and persists beyond the usual duration of Substance Intoxication or Withdrawal.

D.  There is evidence from the history, physical examination, or laboratory findings that the memory disturbance is etiologically related to the persisting effects of substance use (e.g., a drug of abuse, a medication).

*Code* [Specific Substance]–Induced Persisting Amnestic Disorder:
(291.1 Alcohol; 292.83 Sedative, Hypnotic, or Anxiolytic; 292.83 Other [or Unknown] Substance)

## ▼ DIAGNOSTIC CRITERIA FOR SUBSTANCE–INDUCED PSYCHOTIC DISORDER

A. Prominent hallucinations or delusions.

**Note:** Do not include hallucinations if the person has insight that they are substance induced.

B. There is evidence from the history, physical examination, or laboratory findings of either (1) or (2):
   (1) the symptoms in Criterion A developed during, or within a month of, Substance Intoxication or Withdrawal
   (2) medication use is etiologically related to the disturbance

C. The disturbance is not better accounted for by a Psychotic Disorder that is not substance induced. Evidence that the symptoms are better accounted for by a Psychotic Disorder that is not substance induced might include the following: the symptoms precede the onset of the substance use (or medication use); the symptoms persist for a substantial period of time (e.g., about a month) after the cessation of acute withdrawal or severe intoxication, or are substantially in excess of what would be expected given the type or amount of the substance used or the duration of use; or there is other evidence that suggests the existence of an independent non-substance-induced Psychotic Disorder (e.g., a history of recurrent non-substance-related episodes).

D. The disturbance does not occur exclusively during the course of a delirium.

**Note:** This diagnosis should be made instead of a diagnosis of Substance Intoxication or Substance Withdrawal only when the symptoms are in excess of those usually associated with the intoxication or withdrawal syndrome and when the symptoms are sufficiently severe to warrant independent clinical attention.

*Code* [Specific Substance]–Induced Psychotic Disorder:

(291.5 Alcohol, With Delusions; 291.3 Alcohol, With Hallucinations; 292.11 Amphetamine [or Amphetamine-Like Substance], With Delusions; 292.12 Amphetamine [or Amphetamine-Like Substance], With Hallucinations; 292.11 Cannabis, With Delusions; 292.12 Cannabis, With Hallucinations; 292.11 Cocaine, With Delusions; 292.12 Cocaine, With Hallucinations; 292.11 Hallucinogen, With Delusions; 292.12 Hallucinogen, With Hallucinations; 292.11 Inhalant, With Delusions; 292.12 Inhalant, With Hallucinations; 292.11 Opioid, With Delusions; 292.12 Opioid, With Hallucinations; 292.11 Phencyclidine [or Phencyclidine-Like Substance], With Delusions; 292.12 Phencyclidine [or Phencyclidine-Like Substance], With Hallucinations; 292.11 Sedative, Hypnotic, or Anxiolytic, With Delusions; 292.12 Sedative, Hypnotic, or Anxiolytic, With Hallucinations; 292.11 Other [or Unknown] Substance, With Delusions; 292.12 Other [or Unknown] Substance, With Hallucinations)

*Specify* if:
**With Onset During Intoxication:** if criteria are met for Intoxication with the substance and the symptoms develop during the intoxication syndrome
**With Onset During Withdrawal:** if criteria are met for Withdrawal from the substance and the symptoms develop during, or shortly after, a withdrawal syndrome

## ▼ DIAGNOSTIC CRITERIA FOR SUBSTANCE–INDUCED MOOD DISORDER

A. A prominent and persistent disturbance in mood predominates in the clinical picture and is characterized by either (or both) of the following:
   (1) depressed mood or markedly diminished interest or pleasure in all, or almost all, activities
   (2) elevated, expansive, or irritable mood

B. There is evidence from the history, physical examination, or laboratory findings of either (1) or (2):

    (1) the symptoms in Criterion A developed during, or within a month of, Substance Intoxication or Withdrawal
    (2) medication use is etiologically related to the disturbance

C.  The disturbance is not better accounted for by a Mood Disorder that is not substance induced. Evidence that the symptoms are better accounted for by a Mood Disorder that is not substance induced might include the following: the symptoms precede the onset of the substance use (or medication use); the symptoms persist for a substantial period of time (e.g., about a month) after the cessation of acute withdrawal or severe intoxication or are substantially in excess of what would be expected given the type or amount of the substance used or the duration of use; or there is other evidence that suggests the existence of an independent non-substance-induced Mood Disorder (e.g., a history of recurrent Major Depressive Episodes).

D.  The disturbance does not occur exclusively during the course of a delirium.

E.  The symptoms cause clinically significant distress or impairment in social, occupational, or other important areas of functioning.

**Note:** This diagnosis should be made instead of a diagnosis of Substance Intoxication or Substance Withdrawal only when the mood symptoms are in excess of those usually associated with the intoxication or withdrawal syndrome and when the symptoms are sufficiently severe to warrant independent clinical attention.

*Code* [Specific Substance]–Induced Mood Disorder: (291.8 Alcohol; 292.84 Amphetamine [or Amphetamine-Like Substance]; 292.84 Cocaine; 292.84 Hallucinogen; 292.84 Inhalant; 292.84 Opioid; 292.84 Phencyclidine [or Phencyclidine-Like Substance]; 292.84 Sedative, Hypnotic, or Anxiolytic; 292.84 Other [or Unknown] Substance)

*Specify* type:
    **With Depressive Features:** if the predominant mood is depressed
    **With Manic Features:** if the predominant mood is elevated, euphoric, or irritable

**With Mixed Features:** if symptoms of both mania and depression are present and neither predominates

*Specify* if:
    **With Onset During Intoxication:** if the criteria are met for Intoxication with the substance and the symptoms develop during the intoxication syndrome
    **With Onset During Withdrawal:** if criteria are met for Withdrawal from the substance and the symptoms develop during, or shortly after, a withdrawal syndrome

# ▼ DIAGNOSTIC CRITERIA FOR SUBSTANCE–INDUCED ANXIETY DISORDER

A.  Prominent anxiety, Panic Attacks, or obsessions or compulsions predominate in the clinical picture.

B.  There is evidence from the history, physical examination, or laboratory findings of either (1) or (2):
    (1) the symptoms in Criterion A developed during, or within 1 month of, Substance Intoxication or Withdrawal
    (2) medication use is etiologically related to the disturbance

C.  The disturbance is not better accounted for by an Anxiety Disorder that is not substance induced. Evidence that the symptoms are better accounted for by an Anxiety Disorder that is not substance induced might include the following: the symptoms precede the onset of the substance use (or medication use); the symptoms persist for a substantial period of time (e.g., about a month) after the cessation of acute withdrawal or severe intoxication or are substantially in excess of what would be expected given the type or amount of the substance used or the duration of use; or there is other evidence suggesting the existence of an independent non-substance-induced Anxiety Disorder (e.g., a history of recurrent non-substance-related episodes).

D. The disturbance does not occur exclusively during the course of a delirium.

E. The disturbance causes clinically significant distress or impairment in social, occupational, or other important areas of functioning.

**Note:** This diagnosis should be made instead of a diagnosis of Substance Intoxication or Substance Withdrawal only when the anxiety symptoms are in excess of those usually associated with the intoxication or withdrawal syndrome and when the anxiety symptoms are sufficiently severe to warrant independent clinical attention.

*Code* [Specific Substance]–Induced Anxiety Disorder (291.8 Alcohol; 292.89 Amphetamine (or Amphetamine-Like Substance); 292.89 Caffeine; 292.89 Cannabis; 292.89 Cocaine; 292.89 Hallucinogen; 292.89 Inhalant; 292.89 Phencyclidine (or Phencyclidine-Like Substance); 292.89 Sedative, Hypnotic, or Anxiolytic; 292.89 Other [or Unknown] Substance)

*Specify* if:
**With Generalized Anxiety:** if excessive anxiety or worry about a number of events or activities predominates in the clinical presentation
**With Panic Attacks:** if Panic Attacks predominate in the clinical presentation
**With Obsessive-Compulsive Symptoms:** if obsessions or compulsions predominate in the clinical presentation
**With Phobic Symptoms:** if phobic symptoms predominate in the clinical presentation

*Specify* if:
**With Onset During Intoxication:** if the criteria are met for Intoxication with the substance and the symptoms develop during the intoxication syndrome
**With Onset During Withdrawal:** if criteria are met for Withdrawal from the substance and the symptoms develop during, or shortly after, a withdrawal syndrome

## ▼ DIAGNOSTIC CRITERIA FOR SUBSTANCE–INDUCED SEXUAL DYSFUNCTION

A. Clinically significant sexual dysfunction that results in marked distress or interpersonal difficulty predominates in the clinical picture.

B. There is evidence from the history, physical examination, or laboratory findings that the sexual dysfunction is fully explained by substance use as manifested by either (1) or (2):
(1) the symptoms in Criterion A developed during, or within a month of, Substance Intoxication
(2) medication use is etiologically related to the disturbance

C. The disturbance is not better accounted for by a Sexual Dysfunction that is not substance induced. Evidence that the symptoms are better accounted for by a Sexual Dysfunction that is not substance induced might include the following: the symptoms precede the onset of the substance use or dependence (or medication use); the symptoms persist for a substantial period of time (e.g., about a month) after the cessation of intoxication, or are substantially in excess of what would be expected given the type or amount of the substance used or the duration of use; or there is other evidence that suggests the existence of an independent non-substance-induced Sexual Dysfunction (e.g., a history of recurrent non-substance-related episodes).

**Note:** This diagnosis should be made instead of a diagnosis of Substance Intoxication only when the sexual dysfunction is in excess of that usually associated with the intoxication syndrome and when the dysfunction is sufficiently severe to warrant independent clinical attention.

*Code* [Specific Substance]–Induced Sexual Dysfunction:
(291.8 Alcohol; 292.89 Amphetamine [or Amphetamine-Like Substance]; 292.89 Cocaine; 292.89 Opioid; 292.89 Sedative, Hypnotic, or Anxiolytic; 292.89 Other [or Unknown] Substance)

*Specify* if:
**With Impaired Desire**
**With Impaired Arousal**
**With Impaired Orgasm**
**With Sexual Pain**

*Specify* if:

**With Onset During Intoxication:** if the criteria are met for Intoxication with the substance and the symptoms develop during the intoxication syndrome

## ▼ DIAGNOSTIC CRITERIA FOR SUBSTANCE–INDUCED SLEEP DISORDER

A. A prominent disturbance in sleep that is sufficiently severe to warrant independent clinical attention.

B. There is evidence from the history, physical examination, or laboratory findings of either (1) or (2):

    (1) the symptoms in Criterion A developed during, or within a month of, Substance Intoxication or Withdrawal

    (2) medication use is etiologically related to the sleep disturbance

C. The disturbance is not better accounted for by a Sleep Disorder that is not substance induced. Evidence that the symptoms are better accounted for by a Sleep Disorder that is not substance induced might include the following: the symptoms precede the onset of the substance use (or medication use); the symptoms persist for a substantial period of time (e.g., about a month) after the cessation of acute withdrawal or severe intoxication, or are substantially in excess of what would be expected given the type or amount of the substance used or the duration of use; or there is other evidence that suggests the existence of an independent non-substance-induced Sleep Disorder (e.g., a history of recurrent non-substance-related episodes).

D. The disturbance does not occur exclusively during the course of a delirium.

E. The sleep disturbance causes clinically significant distress or impairment in social, occupational, or other important areas of functioning.

**Note:** This diagnosis should be made instead of a diagnosis of Substance Intoxication or Substance Withdrawal only when the sleep symptoms are in excess of those usually associated with the intoxication or withdrawal syndrome and when the symptoms are sufficiently severe to warrant independent clinical attention.

*Code* [Specific Substance]–Induced Sleep Disorder: (291.8 Alcohol; 292.89 Amphetamine; 292.89 Caffeine; 292.89 Cocaine; 292.89 Opioid; 292.89 Sedative, Hypnotic, or Anxiolytic; 292.89 Other [or Unknown] Substance)

*Specify* type:

**Insomnia Type:** if the predominant sleep disturbance is insomnia

**Hypersomnia Type:** if the predominant sleep disturbance is hypersomnia

**Parasomnia Type:** if the predominant sleep disturbance is a Parasomnia

**Mixed Type:** if more than one sleep disturbance is present and none predominates

*Specify* if:

**With Onset During Intoxication:** if the criteria are met for Intoxication with the substance and the symptoms develop during the intoxication syndrome

**With Onset During Withdrawal:** if criteria are met for Withdrawal from the substance and the symptoms develop during, or shortly after, a withdrawal syndrome

# Index

Page numbers in **boldface** type refer to tables or figures.

Adolescent substance abuse
(*continued*)
   treatment outcomes for,
        424–426
      attrition rate, 424
      contribution of treatment
           variables, 426
      effects of psychiatric
           symptomatology, 425
      individual outcome, 424
      predictors of productivity at
           discharge, 424–425
   treatment philosophy for, 421
   treatment variations for, 421
   types of adolescents in
        treatment for, 422
α-Adrenergic agonists, 68–69
Affect regression, 255
Affect regulation, 240, 248, 307
Affective disorders, 27, 132, 243
   adolescent substance abuse
        and, 420, 421
   alcohol abuse and, 74, 75
   among persons admitted to
        therapeutic communities,
        396
   primary versus secondary, 75
Affective experience, 240
Affective flooding, 255
Aftercare, 365
   for adolescents, 430–431
   employee assistance programs
        and, 378–379
   therapeutic communities and,
        406, 408
Aggressive feelings, 239, 240
Agoraphobia, 244
Akathisia, 78
Al-Anon, 269, 317, 320, 321,
     333–335, 422, 430
Alateen, 422, 430
Alcohol abuse treatment, 67–86
   behavioral interventions with
        biofeedback measures,
        82–83
   detoxification, 67–71
      mild to moderate alcohol
           withdrawal, 68–69
      severe alcohol withdrawal,
           69–71

individual psychotherapy,
     263–272
outcome research on, 35–42.
     *See also* Treatment
     outcomes
patient-treatment matching
     strategies, 11, 13–14, 19,
     **41,** 41–42
pharmacotherapy during
     abstinence phase, 71–81
   for comorbid disorders,
        74–79
      antidepressants, 73, 75–76
      anxiolytics, 76–78
      neuroleptics, 78–79
      vitamins, 79
   disulfiram, 71–73
   lithium, 73
   naltrexone, 73–74, 233–234
   for organ damage secondary
        to ethanol intake,
        79–81
      Alcohol Amnestic Disorder,
           79
      esophageal variceal
           bleeding, 79–80
      liver disease, 80
   psychologic interventions,
        81–82
   social interventions, 83–86
      educational approaches,
           85–86
      legal approaches, 84–85
Alcohol amnestic disorder (AAD),
     79, 265
Alcohol dementia, 27
Alcohol Dependence Scale, 30
Alcohol dependence syndrome,
     12–13
Alcohol hallucinosis, 27
Alcohol use, 26
   "controlled," 4
   driving under the influence of
        alcohol, 82, 83, 386–387
   eliciting history of, 27–29
   idiosyncratic intoxication, 27
   laboratory examination for, 31
   local ordinances related to, 386
   noradrenergic responses to, 15
   during pregnancy, 431

serotonin function and, 15, 16,
     75–76
signs of intoxication, 29
Alcohol withdrawal, 68–71, 265
   goals of treatment for, 68
   mild to moderate, 68–69
   in patients who also abuse
        barbiturates, 71
   in patients who also abuse
        benzodiazepines, 71
   protracted withdrawal
        syndrome (PWS), 74, 266
   psychiatric symptoms
        demonstrated during, 5
   severe, 69–71
Alcohol withdrawal delirium,
     69–71
   criteria for, 69
   duration of, 69
   hospitalization for, 69
   treatment of, 69–71
Alcohol Withdrawal Scale (AWS),
     67, 68
Alcoholic beverage taxes,
     84–85
Alcoholic system, 318–319
Alcoholics Anonymous (AA), 6,
     11, 46, 56, 125, 242, 247, 254,
     263, 303, 304, 320, 321,
     351–357, 370, 391, 408
   for adolescents, 422, 430
   characteristics of persons likely
        to affiliate with, 352–353
   dropout rate from, 356
   effectiveness of, 36–37, 264,
        354–356, 389
      AA is not always helpful,
           354–356
      treatment is not always
           necessary, 356
   encouraging patients to attend,
        269
   frequency of attendance at,
        353, 354
   growth of, 351
   high profile of, 351
   for persons with borderline
        personality, 266
   for persons with schizophrenia,
        266

psychodynamics applied to, 248–249

rejection of, 253, 353, 356

use in network therapy, 259

variables linked to good outcome of, 353–354

what to encourage patients to do in, 353–354

when to refer to, 351–353

Alcoholism

age at onset of, 15–17

antisocial, 16

anxiety and, 266

borderline personality and, 266

cocaine use and, 277

combined with other drug use, 12, 277

cost to society of, 359

dementia and, 265

depression and, 266–267

developmentally cumulative, 16

developmentally limited, 16

family systems view of, 296–297

family therapy for, 315–327

genetic and environmental predisposition to, 264

inheritance of, 15, 16

intergenerational transmission of, 316–318

marijuana use and, 95

negative-affect, 16

pharmacokinetics in persons with, 75

primary and secondary, 13

psychodynamics of, 264–265

psychopathology and, 13, 31–32, 74–79, 265

schizophrenia and, 266

sociopathy and, 17–18

subtypes of, 11–20. *See also* Typologies of addiction

multidimensional, 14–18

unidimensional, 12–14

Alcoholism-induced subacute organic mental disorders, 74

Alexithymia, 240

Alprazolam, 76, **181,** 182

Amantadine, 130

Amblyopia, alcoholic, 79

γ-Aminobutyric acid (GABA) receptor, 180, 185

Amitriptyline, 76

Amobarbital, **188**

Amotivational syndrome, 101

Amphetamine, 26. *See also* Stimulant use

acute reactions to, 112–114

binges on, 114

depression demonstrated during withdrawal from, 5

epidemiology of use of, 111–112

half-life of, 113

interactions with monoamine oxidase inhibitors, 130

neurochemical actions of, 113, **114**

Amytal. *See* Amobarbital

Angel dust, 150. *See also* Phencyclidine

Anhedonia, poststimulant, 121, 122, **123**

Antabuse. *See* Disulfiram

Antidepressants, 5, 8

for alcoholic persons, 37, 38, 73, 75–76, 267

for insomnia during opioid withdrawal, 200

methadone maintenance and, 212

safe use with naltrexone, 232

with sedative effects, 76

for stimulant-abusing persons, 126–130, **127–128**

who are also on methadone maintenance, 128–129

Antiparkinsonian drugs, 78

Antipsychotic drugs. *See* Neuroleptics

Antisocial personality disorder (ASPD), 5, 9, 420

alcohol abuse and, 13, 17, 74

among persons admitted to therapeutic communities, 395

DSM criteria for, 17

opioid addiction and, 217

types of, 18

Anxiety

cannabis-induced, 97

hallucinogen-induced, 145–146

related to intoxication and withdrawal, 5

stimulant-induced, 115

Anxiety disorders, 276

adolescent substance abuse and, 420, 421

alcoholism and, 13, 74–76, 266

among persons admitted to therapeutic communities, 395

opioid addiction and, 217

prevalence of, 5

Anxiolytics, 26

for adverse reactions to cannabis, 98, 100

signs of intoxication with, 29

use in alcoholic persons, 36, 76–78

Arylcyclohexylamines, 26, 27, 149

Assertive techniques, 339

Assessment of patient, 25–32

adolescents, 427–429, **428**

for comorbid psychiatric disorders, 31–32

dependence syndrome and diagnosis of substance use disorders, 26–27

eliciting patient history, 27–29

factors that interfere with diagnosis, 25

failure to diagnose substance abuse, 25

family systems approach to, 322–323

interviews with significant others for, 30

laboratory examination for, 31

physical and mental status examination, 29–30

primary goal of, 25

screening instruments and structured interviews for, 30

Atenolol, 68

Ativan. *See* Lorazepam

Attention-deficit hyperactivity disorder (ADHD)

adolescent substance abuse and, 420, 421

adult, 77–78, 132, 133

natural history of, 94–95
patterns of abuse, 92–93
potency of cannabis
preparations, 94
preemployment screening for,
96
during pregnancy, 431
prevalence of, 91
psychopathology and, 91
reasons for decline in, 92
recognizing need for no
treatment for, 107
residual effects of, 96
as stepping stone to use of
stronger drugs, 93–94
treating abuse and
dependence, 101–103
abstinence syndrome,
102–103
cessation of use, 101–102
early recovery, 103
initial and extended phases
of, 101
long-term treatment, 103
treating acute psychiatric
reaction, 97–98
adverse reactions, 97–98
cannabis delusional disorder,
98
delirium, 98
flashback syndrome, 98
intoxication, 97
treating chronic psychiatric
disorders associated with,
99–101
cannabis as cause of
psychotic disorders,
100–101
cannabis as self-medication,
99–100
chronic cannabis syndrome,
101
psychosocial correlates, 99
treatment facilities and
procedures for, 103–107
behavioral therapy, 107
family therapy, 105
group therapy, 105–106
inpatient programs, 103–104
outpatient programs, 104

psychotherapy, 104–105
12-step programs, 106–107
Carbamazepine (CBZ)
for alcohol-benzodiazepine
withdrawal syndrome, 71
antikindling effects of, 70
for severe alcohol withdrawal
syndrome, 70
for stimulant-abusing persons,
130
thrombocytopenia induced by,
70
Carbohydrate-deficient
transferrin (CDT), 83
Carbon monoxide, in cigarette
smoke, 158
Cardiac arrhythmias, 152
Cardiomyopathy, alcoholic, 69
Cardiovascular complications, 197
CareUnit programs, 56, 57
Catapres. *See* Clonidine
Center for Therapeutic
Community Research, 406
Centrax. *See* Prazepam
Cerebrospinal fluid findings, in
alcoholic persons, 16, 17
Cheilosis, 197
Chemical Abuse/Addiction
Treatment Outcome Registry,
56
Chemical Dependency
Assessment Scale (CDAS), 426
Chemical dependency (CD)
treatment, 56–57
for benzodiazepine
dependency, 186
compared with therapeutic
communities, 56
components of, 56
definition of, 56
duration of, 56
effectiveness of, 56–57, 61
follow-up after, 56
profile of patients receiving, 56
reasons for varying results of, 57
Chloral hydrate, 68, **188**
Chlordiazepoxide, **181,** 185
for alcohol withdrawal
mild to moderate, 69
severe, 70

high-dose withdrawal from, 182
Chlormethiazole, 71
*m*-Chlorophenylpiperazine, 16
"Chocolate thai," 94
Chronic obstructive pulmonary
disease (COPD), 69, 158, 159
Cigarette burns or scars, 197
Cigarette smoking, 157–174. *See
also* Smoking
Citalopram, 76
Civil Addict Program (CAP),
58–59, **60**
Clinical Institute Withdrawal
Assessment for Alcohol Scale
(CIWA-Ar), 67–70
Clonazepam, **181**
Clonidine
methadone maintenance and,
212
for mild to moderate alcohol
withdrawal, 68, 69
for opioid detoxification, 198,
202–204, **203**
Clonidine-naltrexone withdrawal,
204, **205**
Clorazepate, **181**
Cluster analysis, 18–19
Cocaine, 26, 82. *See also* Stimulant
use
abstinence phases, 119–122,
**120**
crash (acute dysphoria),
119–120
extinction (postwithdrawal
conditioned
dysfunction), 122
withdrawal (poststimulant
mood dysfunction),
120–121, **123**
acute reactions to, 112–114
alcohol use and, 277
binges on, 113–114
controlled low-intensity regular
use of, 117
cost of, 143
delusions due to, 115
depression demonstrated
during discontinuance of,
5
half-life of, 113

prevalence of, 5
primary versus secondary, 75
Designer drugs, 142
Desipramine, 13
  for cocaine-abusing persons, 127, **127–128**
    who are also on methadone maintenance, 128–129
  for phencyclidine withdrawal, 154–155
  use in alcoholic persons, 75, 76
Detoxification
  of adolescents, 430
  from alcohol, 67–71
  clonidine-aided, 202–204, **203**
  clonidine-naltrexone, 204, **205**
  definition of, 192
  family level, 323–325
  inpatient treatment for, 362
  from opioids, 191–207, 333
  of persons admitted to therapeutic communities, 396
  without subsequent treatment, 46
Developmental sequencing model, 15, 16
Diabetes mellitus, 69
*Diagnostic and Statistical Manual of Mental Disorders*
  adolescent substance use in, 417
  antisocial personality disorder in, 17
  benzodiazepine dependency in, 189
  cannabis use in, 96–98
  classes of psychoactive substances in, 26
  cocaine use in, 119
  criteria for psychoactive substance dependence in, 26–27
  definitions of severity of dependence in, 27
  organic mental syndromes associated with substance abuse in, 27
  substance use disorders in, 11, 12

tobacco use in, 157, 158, 172
Diagnostic Interview for Children and Adolescents, 426
Diagnostic Interview Schedule, 395
Diagnostic Interview Schedule for Children-Revised (DISC-R), 426
Diazepam, 180, **181,** 185
  for adverse reactions to cannabis, 98, 100
  for alcohol withdrawal delirium, 69–70
  for alcohol withdrawal seizures, 71
  for anxiety reduction in alcoholic persons, 76–77
  high-dose withdrawal from, 182
  low-dose withdrawal from, 182–183
  for phencyclidine intoxication, 152
Diazepam-binding inhibitor, 17
Dihydrocodinone, 193
Dihydromorphine, 193
Dilaudid, 198, **198**
Dimethoxymethylamphetamine (DOM, "STP"), 141. *See also* Hallucinogens
Dimethyltryptamine (DMT), 141, 143. *See also* Hallucinogens
Diphenhydramine, 200
Disulfiram, 8, 71–73, 270, 320
  compared with naltrexone, 224, 227
  compliance with, 72
  dosage of, 72
  effectiveness of, 37, 38, 71–72
  hepatotoxicity of, 72
  involvement of spouse in program using, 256–257
  safe use with naltrexone, 232
  side effects of, 72
  subcutaneously implanted, 38–39
  use in patients with schizophrenia, 72, 78
L-Dopa/carbidopa, 130
Dopamine-β-hydroxylase activity, 72, 78

Doral. *See* Quazepam
Doriden. *See* Glutethimide
Double Trouble, 266
Doxepin, 76, 77
Drives, 239–240
Driving under the influence of alcohol (DUI), 82, 83, 386–387
Dromoran, **198**
Dropouts
  from Alcoholics Anonymous, 356
  from therapeutic communities, 51–52, 406–407
Drug Abuse Reporting Program (DARP), 51, 52, 54, 218, 424
Drug Abuse Treatment Outcome Study (DATOS), 406
Drug Abuse Warning Network, 92
Drug experimentation, 93–94
Drug Use Screening Inventory (DUSI), 427
"Dry drunk," 266
Dual diagnosis patients, 13, 31–32, 265–267, 276–277, 306, 360, 410. *See also* Psychiatric disorders
Dummy mist, 150. *See also* Phencyclidine
Dust, 150. *See also* Phencyclidine
Dysphoria
  naltrexone-induced, 225
  poststimulant, 115–116, 120–121
Dysthymia, 243, 276
Dystonia, 152

Eating disorders, 303, 420, 421
"Ecstasy," 141. *See also* Hallucinogens
Ego, 239–240, 243, 244, 247–248
Ego psychology, 239, 245, 247–248
Electrical aversion therapies, 36
Electroconvulsive therapy (ECT), 153
Electroencephalogram (EEG)
  during benzodiazepine withdrawal, 182
  hallucinogen effects on, 144
  sleep, 119, 121

Embalming fluid, 150. *See also* Phencyclidine
Emergency room visits
  cannabis-related, 92
  identification of alcoholic persons during, 388
Empathy of therapist, 40
Emphysema, 159
Employed persons, naltrexone treatment for, 227–228
Employee assistance programs (EAPs), 369–382
  attractiveness to employers, 372
  components of, 370
  discovery of employed substance-abusing persons, 369–370
  dynamics of implementation of, 375–379
    diagnosis and use of treatment, 377–378
    policy diffusion and training, 376
    policy statements, 375–376
    posttreatment, 378–379
    referral routes, 371–372, 376–377
    staffing and program design, 379
  efficacy of, 379–381
  history of, 370
  mainstreaming substance abuse treatment and, 370–371
  percentage of work force covered by, 372, 381
  process of, 371–372
  variations in organization of, 370
  workplace functions served by, 372–375
    contribution to health care cost containment, 374
    provision of due process for employees, 373–374
    provision of gatekeeping and channeling in employees' use of health care, 374

reduction of supervisory and management responsibility, 372–373
    retention of employees, 372
    transformation of workplace organizational culture, 375
Enabling behavior, 269
Encephalopathy
  hepatic, 80
  Wernicke's, 68, 70, 79
Endorphins, 225
Epidemiologic Catchment Area survey, 74
Equagesic. *See* Meprobamate
Equanil. *See* Meprobamate
Esophageal variceal bleeding, 80
Estazolam, **181**
Ethchlorvynol, **188**
*N*-Ethyl-1-phencyclohexalamine (PCE), 149
Euphoria, 247
  hallucinogen-induced, 143
  stimulant-induced, 112–115, 118
Euphoric recall, 103
Exercise, 365

Fagerstrom Tolerance Questionnaire (FTQ), 160
Family
  alcoholic, 319
    subtypes of, 323
  with alcoholic member, 319
  assessment of, 322–323
  boundaries within, 341
  detoxification of, 323–324
  development of, 319
  effects of ethnicity of, 343–344
  factors associated with adolescent substance abuse, 420
  functional analysis of, 320, 339, 344–345
  interactional behavior in, 323
  life-cycle phase of, 345–346
  participation in intervention, 334
  readjustment after cessation of substance abuse, 347

regulatory behaviors of, 319
  stress and coping in, 318
Family behavior loop mapping, 323
Family environment, 316, 324
Family of origin technique, 338
Family therapy, 6, 279, 280
  for alcohol problems, 315–327
    advantages of, 316
    Al-Anon groups for, 321
    aspects of alcoholism that impact on, 317–318
    behavioral family models for, 319–320
    confusion about implementation of, 317
    family functioning model for, 320
    family systems model for, 318–319, 322–325
      assessment strategies for, 322–323
      family detoxification in, 323–325
    integration of models for, 321–322
    obstacles to, 327
    overview of treatment models for, 318
    reasons for increasing interest in, 315–316
    research on, 316
    social network therapy for, 320–321
  for cannabis-abusing persons, 105
  compared with network therapy, 258–260
  effectiveness of, 281
    for alcohol problems, 325–327, 332
      treatment outcome literature on, 326–327
    for other drugs, 331–332
  for other drugs, 331–347
    developing system for establishing and maintaining abstinence, 332–336
      achieving abstinence, 333

Phenytoin, 70, 71
Phoenix House, 51, **52,** 57, 304, 336
Physical examination, 29
    for cannabis use, 95
    of opioid-addicted persons, 196–197
    for phencyclidine intoxication, 151
Piloerection, 197
"Pink cloud," 270
1-Piperidinocyclohexane carbonitrile (PCC), 149
Placidyl. *See* Ethchlorvynol
Polydrug-abusing persons, 12, 277–278
Positive addictions, 295–296
Positron emission tomography (PET), 121, 122
Posthallucinogen perception disorder, 27
"Potheads," 93,100. *See also* Cannabis
Powerlessness, 240
Prazepam, **181**
Preemployment drug screening, 96
Preferred provider organizations (PPOs), 374
Pregnancy, 202
    adolescent substance abuse and, 431–433
        epidemiology of, 431
        phenomenology of, 431–432
        prevention intervention for, 432–433
    fetal effects of substance abuse during, 431
    incidence of substance abuse during, 431
    methadone maintenance during, 210–212, 215–216
    naltrexone use in, 232
    testing adolescents for, 428
Prison-based treatment. *See also* Correctional treatment programs
    methadone maintenance, 210

naltrexone for probationers in work-release programs, 228–229
therapeutic communities, 410
Problem Oriented Screening Instrument for Teenagers (POSIT), 427
Prochlorperazine, 70
Propoxyphene, 198
Propranolol
    for akathisia, 78
    for anxiety disorders in alcoholic persons, 77
    for mild to moderate alcohol withdrawal, 68
    use for cocaine overdose, 116
Propylthiouracil, 80
ProSom. *See* Estazolam
Protracted abstinence syndrome, 74
Protracted withdrawal syndrome (PWS), 74, 266
Psilocybin, 141, 142. *See also* Hallucinogens
Psychedelic drugs. *See* Hallucinogens
Psychiatric disorders
    adolescent substance abuse and, 420–422, 426–427
    alcoholism and, 13, 74–79
    cannabis use and, 99–101
    comorbid with substance abuse, 13, 276–277
        assessment for, 31–32
        differential diagnosis and treatment of, 265–267
    demonstrated during intoxication and substance withdrawal, 5
    differentiating from substance abuse, 31–32
    group therapy for patients with DSM Axis II diagnoses, 306
    independent of substance use, 5
    methadone maintenance and, 217
    in persons admitted to therapeutic communities, 395–396, 410

psychodynamic treatment of, 243
stimulant abuse and, 122–123, 132
Psychoanalytic psychotherapy, 239–241, 263, 271
Psychodynamic psychotherapy, 239–250, 263, 280
    acceptance of self in recovery, 247
    for adolescents and young adults, 242
    applied to groups and self-help, 248–249, 303–305, 310–312
    characteristics of patients choosing, 242
    compared with addiction counseling, 385–386
    contraindications to, 244
    determining focus of, 246–247
    ego psychological model of rehabilitation, 247–248
    for family of drug-abusing person, 337–338
        countertransference, 338
        overcoming resistance, 338
        role in interpretation, 338
        working through, 338
    frequency and duration of sessions for, 245
    indications and rationale for, 242–244
    initiation of, 244–245
    myths about, 249
    as part of combined treatment approach, 246
    patient-therapist relationship, 249
    pitfalls to avoid in, 250
    positive prognostic indicators for, 242
    precautions about use of, 245
    setting for, 245
    stages of, 246–247
    for stimulant abuse, 125–126
    technical aspects of, 245
    timing of interpretations in, 245
    treatment parameters for, 246

watching for relapse during, 247

Psychodynamic theory, 239–242
 applied to addictive process, 240–241
 applied to treatment, 241
 early development of, 239–240
 implications for research, 241–242
 recent developments in, 240–241
 usefulness of treatment outcome research, 241

Psychodynamics of alcoholism, 264–265

Psychoeducational approaches
 for alcohol problems, 36, 85–86
 for groups, 304

Psychosis. *See also* Schizophrenia
 acute toxic, 98
 cannabis-induced, 100–101, 144
 hallucinogen-induced, 144–146
 Korsakoff's, 265
 phencyclidine-induced, 144, 150, 152–154
 stimulant-induced, 122–123

Psychotherapy. *See also* Family therapy; Group therapy; specific types of psychotherapy
 for cannabis abuse, 104–105
 combined with other treatment services, 281–282
 compared with addiction counseling, 276–277, 308–309, 385–386
 definition of, 276
 goals of, 276
 for hallucinogen abuse, 147
 individual
  for alcoholism, 81–82, 263–272
  for other drugs, 275–282
 interventionist and directive approach of, 263

Psychotomimetics. *See* Hallucinogens

Public forum, 303–304

Pulmonary complications, 197

Purple, 150. *See also* Phencyclidine

Pyridoxine deficiency, 79

Quazepam, **181**

Rational Recovery, 353, 356
Rationalization, 291
Recreational drug users, 12
Reductionism, 244
Referral
 to employee assistance programs, 371–372, 376–377
 process for substance-abusing adolescents, 427–429, **428**
 to therapeutic communities, 396
 to 12-step programs, 351–353
Regression, 239–241
Relapse, 247, 254–256
 compared with slip (lapse), 173–174, 271, 287, **287–288**
 covert antecedents of, 290–292
 definition of, 287, **287**
 high-risk situations for, 287–290, **289**
  coping successfully with, 289
  inability to cope with, 289–290
  interpersonal conflict, 288
  negative emotional states, 288
  social pressure, 288–289
 network therapy and, 259
 psychodynamic understanding of, 243
 during recovery from cannabis use, 103
 during recovery from stimulant abuse, 123
Relapse prevention (RP), 255, 280, 285–297
 behaviors to which model is applied, 285–286
 cognitive reframing for, 292
 definition of, 285
 effectiveness of, 281
 global life-style strategies for, 292, **295,** 295–296
 goals of, 286
 life-style balancing for, 291–292
 naltrexone for, 230–231

relapse-prevention groups for adolescents, 430
 skills training for, 292
 for smokers, 166, 172–174
 social support in couples and families for, 296–297
 specific intervention strategies for, 292–295, **293**
 for stimulant-abusing persons, 131
 training in therapeutic communities, 408
 as treatment goal, 6, 286
 treatment goals and, 286
 treatment philosophy and, 286
Relapse rehearsal methods, 294
Relaxation training, 170
Renal failure, acute, 152
Reproductive complications, 197
Resistance, 338
Resource allocation, 7
Restoril. *See* Temazepam
Restricted environmental stimulation therapy, 170
Reward dependence, 15
Rhabdomyolysis, 152
Rifampin, 212
Risk-taking behaviors, 242
Ritanserin, 130
Rocket fuel, 150. *See also* Phencyclidine

Safety issues, 7–8
 in group therapy, 310–311
"Say No to Drugs" campaign, 433
Scaffolding therapy, 269–270
Schizophrenia, 5, 132, 217
 adolescent substance abuse and, 420, 421
 alcoholism and, 266
 among persons admitted to therapeutic communities, 396
 cannabis use and, 99–100
 distinguishing from hallucinogen-induced psychosis, 144
 lysergic acid diethylamide as model of, 144
 phencyclidine as model of, 150

Schizophrenia *(continued)*
  treatment in alcoholic persons, 78–79
  use of disulfiram in patients with, 72, 78
School-based prevention programs, 430–431
Sclerotherapy, for esophageal variceal bleeding, 79–80
Screening instruments, 30
  Addiction Severity Index, 13–14, 30, 365
  Adolescent Alcohol Involvement Scale, 426
  for adolescents, 30, 426–427
  Alcohol Dependence Scale, 30
  Alcohol Withdrawal Scale, 67, 68
  Beck Depression Inventory, 30
  CAGE questionnaire, 30, 83
  Chemical Dependency Assessment Scale, 426
  Clinical Institute Withdrawal Assessment for Alcohol Scale, 67–70
  Diagnostic Interview for Children and Adolescents, 426
  Diagnostic Interview Schedule, 395
  Diagnostic Interview Schedule for Children-Revised, 426
  Drug Use Screening Inventory, 427
  Fagerstrom Tolerance Questionnaire, 160
  Hamilton Anxiety Scale, 77
  Hamilton Depression Rating Scale, 77
  Inventory of Using Situations, 430
  Kiddie Schedule for Affective Disorders and Schizophrenia, 426
  Michigan Alcoholism Screening Test, 30, 82, 83, 388
  Minnesota Multiphasic Personality Inventory, 14, 18
  Personal Experience Inventory, 426
  Problem Oriented Screening Instrument for Teenagers, 427
  Situations Confidence Questionnaire, 430
  Stanford Hypnotic Clinical Scale, 170
  Structured Clinical Interview for DSM-III-R, 30
  Symptom Checklist-90, 70, 162
  T-ACE questionnaire, 30
  Teen Addiction Severity Index, 427
  Tellegan Absorption Scale, 170
  Tennessee Self-Concept Scales, 395
Secobarbital (Seconal), 181, 182, **188**
Secular Organizations for Sobriety, 353
Sedapap. *See* Butalbital
Sedative-hypnotics, 26, 179–189. *See also* Benzodiazepines
  benzodiazepine abuse and dependence, 180–181, **181**
  benzodiazepine withdrawal syndromes, 182–189
  intoxication with, 29, 181–182
  marijuana use and, 93
  for mild to moderate alcohol withdrawal, 68
  phenobarbital withdrawal equivalents for, **188**
Seizures
  alcohol withdrawal, 69–71
  bupropion-induced, 78
  during opioid detoxification, 201
  phencyclidine-induced, 152
Selective serotonin uptake inhibitors, 76, 79
Self-care, 240, 242, 248, 305, 307, 310
Self-control training
  for alcohol problems, 39–40
  relapse prevention model as, 286
Self-destructiveness, 240, 242, 264
Self-efficacy, 165, 289–290
Self-efficacy ratings, 294
Self-esteem, 247–248, 305, 307, 419
Self-help programs. *See* Alcoholics Anonymous; Cocaine Anonymous; Narcotics Anonymous; Twelve-step programs
Self-medication, 12, 240, 255, 276, 305
Self-monitoring procedures, 293
Self psychology, 239
Self-talk, 296
Serax. *See* Oxazepam
Serotonin (5-HT), 15, 16, 75–76
Severity of dependence, 12–13
  Addiction Severity Index, 13–14, 30, 365
  DSM definitions of, 27
  Teen Addiction Severity Index, 427
Sexual disorders, 303
Shame, pathological, 240
Sherman, 150. *See also* Phencyclidine
Shock incarceration (SI), 59–60
Situational Competency Test, 293–294
Situations Confidence Questionnaire (SCQ), 430
Skeletal complications, 197
Smoking, 157–174
  diagnosis and assessment of, 162–165, **163**
    assessment of physiologic addiction, 163–164
    psychological assessment, 164–165
      assessment of attitudes and cognitions, 164–165
      behavioral assessment, 164
      emotional meaning of cigarettes, 165
      social assessment, 165
  in DSM, 157, 158, 172
  factors supporting smoking behavior, 160–162
    etiology and stages of smoking, 160
    physiologic factors, 160–161